THE INDIVIDUAL, MARRIAGE, AND THE FAMILY

THE INDIVIDUAL, MARRIAGE, AND THE FAMILY

SIXTH EDITION

LLOYD SAXTON
COLLEGE OF SAN MATEO

WADSWORTH PUBLISHING COMPANY
BELMONT, CALIFORNIA
A DIVISION OF WADSWORTH, INC.

Sociology Editor **Sheryl Fullerton**
Production Editor **Jane Townsend**
Interior Designer **Cynthia Bassett**
Cover Designer **Merle Sanderson**
Print Buyer **Barbara Britton**
Copy Editor **Anne Draus**

Photo Researcher **Lindsay Kefauver**
Scientific Illustrators **Judith Lopez, Darwen Hennings, Vally Hennings**
Technical Illustrator **Joan Carol**
Compositor **Boyer & Brass, Inc.**

Cover Painting: Fernand Léger, *Hommage to Louis David*, 1948–49, Musée National d'Art Modern. Photo: Scala/Art Resource. Copyright SPADEM, Paris/VAGA, New York, 1986. Part opening and chapter opening photos and paintings: p. 1: Mary Cassatt, *The Boating Party* (detail), 1893–4. National Gallery of Art, Washington, D.C., Chester Dale Collection. p. 2: Jim Anderson/Woodfin Camp & Associates. p. 21: Pablo Picasso, *The Lovers* (detail), 1923. National Gallery of Art, Washington, D.C., Chester Dale Collection. p. 22: Albrecht Durer, *Adam and Eve*, 1504. Fogg Art Museum, Harvard University, Cambridge, William Calley Gray Fund. p. 72: Courtesy San Francisco Public Library. p. 109: Barbara Alper/Stock, Boston. p. 167: © Joel Gordon. p. 208: Mary Cassatt, *The Letter* (detail), 1891. National Gallery of Art, Washington, D.C., Rosenwald Collection. p. 233: John Singer Sargent, *Mr. and Mrs. Isaac Newton Phelps Stokes* (detail), 1879. The Metropolitan Museum of Art, New York. Bequest of Edith Minturn Phelps Stokes, 1938. p. 234: Doris Lee, *Country Wedding* (detail), 1942. Albright-Knox Art Gallery, Buffalo, New York, Room of Contemporary Art Fund, 1943. p. 286: Bill Ray, *Life* Magazine. © 1963 Time, Inc. p. 330: George Henry Boughton, *The Waning Honeymoon* (detail), 1878. The Walters Art Gallery, Baltimore, Maryland. p. 363: Gustav Vigeland, *The Family*, 1917. The Vigeland Sculpture Park, Oslo, Norway. p. 364: Hazel Hankin/Stock, Boston. p. 398: Henry Moore, *Rocking Chair #2*, 1950. Hirschhorn Museum and Sculpture Garden, Institution, Washington, D.C. p. 445: Eastman Johnson, *The Hatch Family* (detail), 1871. The Metropolitan Museum of Art, gift of Frederick H. Hatch, 1926. p. 473: Rose Skytta/Jeroboam, Inc.

A study guide has been specially designed to help students master the concepts presented in this textbook. Order from your bookstore.

Printed in the United States of America

4 5 6 7 8 9 10—90 89 88

ISBN 0-534-05682-2

Library of Congress Cataloging-in-Publication Data

Saxton, Lloyd.

The individual, marriage, and the family.

Includes bibliographies and index.
1. Marriage—United States. 2. Family life education. 3. Family—United States. I. Title.
HQ728.S28   1986   306.8'0973   85-17905
ISBN 0-534-05682-2

FOR NANCY

BRIEF CONTENTS

Preface · xiii

Part One   Introduction · 1

1   The Paired Bond and Our Contemporary Society · 2

Part Two   Gender, Love, Sex, and Courtship in Pair Bonding · 21

2   Gender: Maleness and Femaleness · 22

3   Love and Pair Bonding · 72

4   Sexual and Erotic Behavior · 109

5   Courtship: Dating and Marital Choice · 167

6   Singlehood: A Prelude to Marriage · 208

Part Three   The Married Couple · 233

7   The Nature of Marriage · 234

8   Divorce and Remarriage · 286

9   Marital Interaction: Conflict and Communication · 330

Part Four   The Family · 363

10   The Nature of the Family · 364

11   Reproduction: The Biological Basis of the Family · 398

12   The Family with Small Children · 445

13   The Family and Economic Reality · 473

Glossary · 507

Bibliography · 513

Name Index · 541

Subject Index · 547

CONTENTS

Preface · xiii

PART ONE   **Introduction · 1**

1   The Paired Bond and Our Contemporary Society · 2

Pair Bonding · 3
Pair Bonding and Social Patterns · 8
Summary · 17 / Questions · 18 / Suggestions for Further Reading · 19

PART TWO   **Gender, Love, Sex, and Courtship in Pair Bonding · 21**

2   Gender: Maleness and Femaleness · 22

The Fundamentals of Gender · 22
The Emergence of Gender · 26
Gender in Historical Perspective · 52
Summary · 69 / Questions · 70 / Suggestions for Further Reading · 71

3   Love and Pair Bonding · 72

Loving and Liking · 73
Love and Limerence · 75
Love and Attachment · 79
The Traditional Faces of Love · 82
Styles of Loving · 92
Infatuation · 96
Love and Jealousy · 99
Learning to Love · 103
Summary · 106 / Questions · 108 / Suggestions for Further Reading · 108

4 Sexual and Erotic Behavior · 109

The Meaning of Sexuality in Different Cultures · 110
Male Sexuality · 118
Female Sexuality · 129
The Complexity of Sexual Interaction · 139
Sexually Transmissible Diseases (STDs) · 146
Summary · 163 / Questions · 165 / Suggestions for Further Reading · 165

5 Courtship: Dating and Marital Choice · 167

Methods of Mate Selection · 168
Dating in Our Society · 176
The Field of Eligibles · 183
The Mystery of Attraction · 185
Sexuality in Dating: Premarital Copulation · 199
Summary · 205 / Questions · 206 / Suggestions for Further Reading · 207

6 Singlehood: A Prelude to Marriage · 208

The Rising Number of Single Adults · 208
Categories of Singles · 213
Life-styles of Singles · 214
Cohabitation · 223
Summary · 229 / Questions · 230 / Suggestions for Further Reading · 231

PART THREE   The Married Couple · 233

7 The Nature of Marriage · 234

The Meaning of Marriage as an Institution · 235
The Meaning of Marriage for the Individual · 241
Child-free Marriage · 257
Intermarriage · 261
Marriage While in College · 267
The Life Cycle and Marriage · 269
Summary · 282 / Questions · 284 / Suggestions for Further Reading · 284

8   Divorce and Remarriage · 286

The Probability for Divorce · 287
The History of Divorce · 301
Annulment · 305
The Meaning of Divorce for the Individual · 306
The Meaning of Divorce for Children · 314
Remarriage following Divorce · 317
Special Problems in Remarriage · 321
Summary · 327 / Questions · 328 / Suggestions for Further Reading · 329

9   Marital Interaction: Conflict and Communication · 330

The Nature of Conflict · 331
Coping with Conflict Productively · 335
Coping with Conflict Destructively · 342
Common Patterns of Attack and Defense · 347
Maintaining Effective Communication · 349
The Breakdown of Effective Communication · 354
Summary · 360 / Questions · 361 / Suggestions for Further Reading · 361

PART FOUR   The Family · 363

10   The Nature of the Family · 364

The Importance of the Family · 365
The Meaning of Family · 366
The Family in Transition · 372
Family Violence · 387
Summary · 394 / Questions · 396 / Suggestions for Further Reading · 397

11   Reproduction: The Biological Basis of the Family · 398

Pregnancy · 399
Childbirth · 409
Infertility and Its Treatment · 414
Birth Control · 416
Methods of Birth Control · 421
Abortion · 435
Summary · 442 / Questions · 443 / Suggestions for Further Reading · 443

12 The Family with Small Children · 445

The Developmental Sequence · 445

Components of Healthy Development · 450

The Nature of Discipline · 462

A Child's Personality: Its Effect on the Family · 466

Summary · 469 / Questions · 471 / Suggestions for Further Reading · 471

13 The Family and Economic Reality · 473

Money and Marital Conflict · 474

The Meaning of Money Management · 475

Directing Cash Flow · 476

The Meaning of Credit · 483

Getting Your Money's Worth · 489

Paying Taxes · 498

The Importance of Regular Investments · 499

Summary · 503 / Questions · 505 / Suggestions for Further Reading · 506

Glossary · 507

Bibliography · 513

Name Index · 541

Subject Index · 547

PREFACE

The Individual, Marriage, and the Family explores the nature of males and females and the nature of male-female interaction in our society, both before and after marriage. Biological, sociological, and psychological theory and research are brought to bear upon the everyday life experiences of the individual. In addition, our own contemporary patterns of male-female interaction are fitted into a historical context, with present-day methods of relating in dating, courtship, and marriage compared and contrasted with those of other cultures and other peoples, both past and present.

The organizing theme of the text is that of the *paired bond*. What is it? What is its relation to intimacy? How is it formed in our contemporary mass society? How is it expressed in affectional and sexual interaction in dating and marriage? What is its relation to gender, or maleness and femaleness?

Many new topics have been added to the sixth edition. For example, in light of current divorce statistics (one in two marriages now ends in divorce), and with more than one-third of all married people now in their second marriage, new sections have been added on the breakup of marriage, with special reference to the meaning of extramarital behavior for the husband and for the wife; the meaning of divorce for both husband and wife; the meaning of divorce for children; the six stages of divorce; re-entry into the world of singlehood and dating following a divorce; the decision to enter into a second marriage; special problems of a second marriage, especially those

endemic to the role of stepmother or stepfather; and, finally, problems of family violence, including wife battering, husband battering, child battering, and child molesting.

Many topics in the last edition have been greatly expanded, including those of women, work, and childrearing; intimacy, idealism, and romantic love. In addition, every chapter has been updated and revised to reflect recent research, theory, and demographic data. The text contains nearly eight hundred references.

With this edition, the text enters the age of the computer, and many aspects of the revision process were greatly facilitated by the use of a computer. The two chapters on human sexuality from the last edition have been combined into one: Chapter 4, "Sexual and Erotic Behavior." And the three chapters on marriage and divorce have been combined into two new chapters: Chapter 7, "The Nature of Marriage" and Chapter 8, "Divorce and Remarriage." Thus, the total number of chapters is now thirteen, rather than fifteen.

The institutions of marriage and the family have undergone some deep-seated changes in recent years. Cohabitation—virtually unknown just two decades ago—has acquired institutional status; the incidence of singlehood has more than doubled among young adults; the one-person household is rapidly becoming the dominant household form in major cities; and the single-parent family is now the fastest-growing family form. Nevertheless, all but about five percent of our population still marry at some point in their lives, with the expectation that they will live together many years longer than their great-grandparents did, because of increased life expectancy. Moreover, virtually all children are raised within some type of family. Thus, marriage and the family are still among the most significant social institutions and are central to the consciousness of most individuals.

The Individual, Marriage, and the Family is an exploration of dating and courtship, sex and love, and maleness and femaleness in today's world, as well as an exploration of marriage and the family, with all of their stability and strife. Most of us learn from our own experience what it means to be a boy or a girl, a man or a woman—to grow up, date, discover sex, fall in love, marry, have children, and raise a family. This book provides an added dimension to that experience by examining much of the behavior that is central to the human condition and making it more accessible to interested and involved readers. As Plato said, "The unexamined life is not worth living."

I should like to express my appreciation to the following professors of marriage-and-family courses, who have been generous with their time in providing me with advice and suggestions during the preparation of this edition: Linda Ade-Ridder, Miami University, Oxford Campus; Betsy Bergen, Kansas State University; Darla Botkin, University of Kentucky; Jane Cunningham, Youngstown State University; Thomas Holman, University of Wisconsin-Stout; Gregory Kennedy, Central Missouri State University; Carolynne Kieffer; Hart Nelson, Pennsylvania State University; R.S. Schwartz, Winona State University; and Frank Zulke, Chicago Citywide College.

I would like to express my thanks to Thomas E. Lasswell and Marcia Lasswell for their contributions from their book *Marriage and the Family* to Chapter 8 of the first printing of this book.

I must also acknowledge a continuing debt of gratitude to Professor Alfred C. Clarke of Ohio State University and Professor Henry L. Manheim of Arizona State University, who acted as editorial consultants throughout the development of the first edition; to Professor Carl C. Rogers of The La Jolla Institute for the Study of the Person, to whom many of the key concepts in this book may be traced; to my many colleagues and students who provided a rich source of both inspiration and ideas; to Faye Ward, whose expert assistance in entering the material into a computer was invaluable; and finally, to my wife, Nancy, whose contribution was one of active collaboration.

Lloyd Saxton
September 1985

P A R T   O N E

Introduction

C H A P T E R   1

The Paired Bond and Our Contemporary Society

Pair Bonding
Pair Bonding and Social Patterns

The unexamined life is not worth living.

Plato (Apology)

In the following pages we shall trace the passage of the individual from singlehood through the formation of a paired bond, marriage, the establishment of a family, and eventually back to singlehood. In doing so, we shall explore the meaning of gender (maleness and femaleness) in all its biological, social, and psychological manifestations and the meaning of love in its many guises.

We shall trace the development of the individual through dating, exploring the wonder of why one person is attracted to another and how this attraction deepens into a mutual decision to marry. And we shall look at the nature of marital interaction, especially as it involves conflicts and problems of communication.

Despite the importance of male-female interaction in the experience and consciousness of the individual, virtually everyone has great uncertainty about almost all its aspects, and these uncertainties can be agonizing. On the one hand, the language of the sexes is replete with bewildering paradoxes:

He: I walk the streets and see beautiful girls, but I don't know how to meet one.
She: I'd like to meet him, but I don't know how.
He: I'm afraid to ask for a date or even to talk to her. What would I say? Besides, she'd probably say no.
She: How do I know if he likes me?

On the other hand, there is the moment of rapturous fulfillment when eye contact can be a physical shock, and a fleeting touch may transform one's day into a wonder of enchantment.

I was really miserable, dreading the rest of the day, and now I feel fantastic. Everything is suddenly changed. It's incredible that we're talking like this!

Even with such an ecstatic beginning, the interaction between the couple does not always remain so idyllic. Many marriages do not succeed, and the union that begins in excitement may dissolve into disappointment, resentment, and bitterness as the couple struggle to resolve conflicts and reestablish lines of communication.

"Why are you so quiet?"
"Oh, it's nothing. I guess I'm just a little tired."
"That must be the thousandth time you've said that."
"I'm sorry. If you'd only try to understand."

Married persons are no longer free to "hang out" with the old crowd, to prowl favored haunts, or to go bowling or partying whenever the mood strikes. They may be shaken by the realization that the freedom they sought in marriage was a mirage, and that they have simply exchanged one set of constraints for another. They may begin to fear that their youth is behind them, that they have been thrust abruptly into the responsibilities of adulthood. They often feel "stuck" with the reality of their everyday life, dissatisfied but helpless to change (Rubin 1976). A young married woman sums up these feelings:

Life sure doesn't match the dreams, does it? Here I am living in this old, dumpy house and the furniture is a grubby mess. I still have those pictures of the storybook life in my head, but I have a lot more sense now than when I was young. Now I know we are lucky just to keep up with the bills (Rubin 1976, p. 72).

A young husband sums up his feelings:

I spend a lot of time wondering how I got myself into this spot in the first place. I'd look at my old buddies, and they were still having a good time, nobody telling them what to do and how to spend their money, working when they felt like it. I'd look at those guys who weren't married yet and wish I were still there (Rubin 1976, p. 77).

PAIR BONDING

Before we explore this labyrinth of human interactions—probing the meanings of gender, human sexuality, love, conflict, and communication—it is important to understand the basic concept of the paired bond and the fundamental aspects of our society in which the paired bond forms and then either persists or dissolves.

The Meaning of the Paired Bond

A *bond* is anything that ties, binds, or fastens together. A *paired bond* is a very strong reciprocal attraction or attachment between two people. It is an expression of shared communion, intimacy, affection, respect, admiration, emotional dependency, and love. It is the pure, joyous exhilaration created by the mere presence of another human being. (A paired bond may also form between a person and an animal. See the vignette, "Pair Bonding with an Animal.")

The paired bond may form relatively quickly, or gradually build through many shared experiences, interests, and activities. It may be asexual (nonerotic), such as the paired bond between mother and son or mother and daughter; or it may be sexual (erotic), such as the paired bond between lovers or between husband and wife. When pair bonding occurs, each member of the couple feels comfortable, self-assured, and contented when the other is present or felt to be accessible; each may be uneasy in the other's absence—uncomfortable and restless, daydreaming about the other, and feeling an increasing hollowness at the lack of the

Drawing by Koren; © 1975 The New Yorker Magazine, Inc.

"I'm sorry, but it just isn't working out between us, Jeffrey. You're an orange, and I want an apple."

other's presence or accessibility. Once formed, the paired bond can be very enduring.

Pair bonding has been the subject of speculation by poets, philosophers, and theologians since earliest recorded history, and it is now being subjected to the investigative techniques of modern science. Yet the nature of the mysterious force that impels most persons—male and female alike—to seek a paired bond and to feel a sense of loneliness during this seeking process still defies complete explanation. (See the vignette, "Is Pair Bonding Genetically Programmed?")

The Development of the Paired Bond

Pair bonding between mother and child seems to depend upon the initial skin contact and eye-to-eye contact during the first few hours and days following birth (see Chapter 12). With older children and with adults, pair bonding is usually related to shared interests, shared activities, and shared ideas. It often seems, though, to depend initially upon the physical appearance of the other or upon some imponderable psychological factor, such as a *limerent* attraction—that is, a strongly compulsive, overwhelming attraction and bonding to the other (see Chapter 3).

Most people aren't especially attracted to one another. Acquaintances and friendships form only rarely and paired bonding is even rarer—whether it develops gradually during the course of a friendship or occurs suddenly at a first meeting. For example, how many acquaintances, friends, and paired bonds have you formed from the potential thousands that have been available to you from childhood?[1] Once a paired bond has formed, this

---

[1]People who live in small, isolated communities do not have this wide range of choice, of course. Pair bonding often occurs from *propinquity* in these situations, or simply as a result of being thrown together with the other (see Chapter 5).

Pair Bonding with an Animal

Eight out of ten owners feel that their pets are sometimes their closest companions. Ninety-nine percent of owners talk to their pets, and about 40 percent talk to the pets as confidants. More than half of all pets sleep in the same bed with the owner, and an additional one-third sleep in the same room.

People who love animals talk to them, brag about them, groom them, take them to veterinarians and sometimes treat them more humanely than they do their fellow human beings. Why? Because they offer love and affection that is entirely nonjudgmental. Like children, they depend upon us, but unlike children they never grow up, never ask for the car and seldom cry, fuss or say no. Love . . . for animals has occurred . . . since the days of the ancient Egyptians (Meer 1984, p. 60).

One person in four looks upon a pet as a human member of the family, and an additional 58 percent view the animal as an "almost human" member. Only one person in six treats a pet strictly as an animal (Horn and Meer 1984).

Half of all pet owners keep pictures of their pets in a wallet or on display at home or in the office, one-fourth own a drawing or portrait, and another one-fourth celebrate the pet's birthday. Pet-food products take up 240 linear feet of shelf space in the average supermarket, making it the single largest category of supermarket items (Horn and Meer 1984).

When the pet dies, 97 percent of the bereaved owners older than fifty suffer some disruption in their daily lives, such as problems on the job. Pet cemeteries offer funeral services to owners who feel that this might help them cope with their loss (Horn and Meer 1984).

---

usually excludes (or makes much less likely) the formation of other bonds.

Intimacy

One of the characteristics of the couple who has formed a paired bond is intimacy. *Intimacy* is defined as the experiencing of the essence of one's self, in intense physical, intellectual, and emotional communion with another (Kieffer 1977). With some intimates, the physical aspect is most important; with others, the intellectual or emotional factor may be most important.

The need for intimacy is a basic human need (Maslow 1971, Fromm 1970). Maintaining closeness with another human being is the center of one's existence until the very end of life (Angyal 1965). In day-to-day experience, everyone is dependent upon regular and daily interaction with intimates. It is this depend-

able and consistent communion that provides not only a basis for sustaining one's sense of reality, but also the validation of one's identity and place in the world (Kieffer 1977, Berger and Kellner 1970).

Intimacy is first experienced in the pair bonding that occurs with a family member. As noted earlier, most people have experienced a great depth of intimacy in the pair bonding that occurs with the mother, and many have experienced it with the father, with brothers or sisters, or with other family members. Intimacy in pair bonding is then experienced in childhood with someone outside the family—a "best friend." It may be experienced to some degree in adulthood in casual social interactions and with business friends. The intimacy of close friendship usually has greater depth, of course, than intimacy with a business associate. And the intimacy in dating is perhaps the strongest, especially when the

Is Pair Bonding Genetically Programmed?

The question of whether the force that generates pair bonding has genetic origins is an interesting one. Such appears to be the case, since many forms of life above reptiles in the evolutionary hierarchy demonstrate pair bonding. For example, herring gulls usually mate for life and can recognize their mates among dozens of gulls flying at considerable distances (Ardrey 1966). Geese demonstrate virtually all the paired-bond behavior of human beings (Lorenz 1970). Beavers, tigers, wolves, whales, foxes, and porpoises all form paired bonds that often endure for the lifetime of the couple. Although the paired bond is usually heterosexual, sex is not the only force holding the pair together; in fact, sexual loyalty may not even be observed. For example, the Calicebus monkey, which lives in the forest of Bolivia, forms such a devoted paired bond that the couple often sit, and even sleep, with their tails intertwined (Ardrey 1966). When the female comes into estrus, however, the male becomes sexually adventurous and the female becomes receptive to strange males. Yet the Calicebus monkey epitomizes virtually the ultimate in close, paired-bond affiliation.

Although very little is known about how and why paired bonds form, or why one individual may feel such an overwhelming attraction for another, pair bonding obviously has survival value for the species. If the bonding holds a pair together after the female becomes pregnant and after offspring arrive, the young ones have a greater chance for survival than if the mother alone has to look after them.

couple fall in love. The intimacy that usually becomes an integral part of serious dating is every bit as deep as the intimacy first experienced in childhood with the mother, but it is of a different quality. Intimacy in dating usually involves romantic and limerent aspects of love, as well as the companionate, altruistic, and attachment aspects characteristic of the pair bonding of mother and child (see Chapter 3). Intimacy in dating may also involve passionate love, with the added dimension of sex and eroticism (see Chapter 4).

Because of the crucial function that intimacy plays in a person's life, and because of the difficulties that occur in its absence, the importance of establishing and maintaining intimate relations can scarcely be overemphasized (Kieffer 1977, Maslow 1971).

A stranger to our land might well conclude, after being exposed to a fair sampling of our songs and our product advertising, that it is life, liberty, and the *pursuit of intimacy* that propel our political, economic, and social system. The need for intimacy stimulates many individuals to go about attempting to splice intimate episodes of sufficient quantity and quality into their lives so that they may experience excitement, ego-enhancement, and a sense of meaning. For some persons the search ends in fulfillment of an enduring type; for others it goes on forever, with one disappointing episode after another ultimately totaling a lifetime of searching. Others eventually give up the search and resign themselves to living without intimacy (Kieffer 1977, p. 268).

Breadth in Intimacy

The *breadth* of intimacy refers to how many interests the couple share and how many activities they enjoy doing together—conversing, studying, listening to music, playing music, playing games, participating in sports, watching games or sports, going to the theater, going to a concert, shopping, attending political rallies, visiting friends, dancing, and so on. The more activities they share and the more ideas they discuss together, the greater the breadth of their intimacy.

Openness in Intimacy

Openness means self-disclosure. You are open (in this sense) to the extent that you are able and willing to disclose your innermost thoughts and feelings to the other without feeling vulnerable or threatened. Unless your relation with the other is "intimate," you probably tend to be somewhat guarded or cautious about revealing too much about yourself. An open disclosure of yourself can be very threatening, because it leaves you vulnerable to the possibility of disapproval, nonacceptance, or outright rejection.

Openness is more important to intimacy than breadth. A couple may spend a lot of time together, in various activities. But if their relation involves little self-disclosure, they aren't really intimate. Breadth alone, without openness, does not constitute intimacy. Yet it is possible for a couple to be very open with one another even though the breadth of their activities is relatively limited.

Openness is not an all-or-nothing, either-or phenomenon, of course. Rather, openness is on a continuum—from slight to great, it exists in terms of degree.

Approaching someone that you don't know but would like to know, and initiating a conversation, form the beginning of openness because these actions leave you vulnerable to rejection. If the other does not wish to accept this overture of friendship, you might be put down, quashed, flattened by being slighted or ignored. The reason such an experience can be so devastating is that you must lower your guard to some extent to make even a tentative approach. Only a very self-assured person can withstand initial rejection and persevere, seeking to establish the opening moves of a

friendship (first through persistence in starting a simple conversation).

If initial overtures are accepted, they might be expanded into more activities, more time spent together, more dates, more things to do together. If the other does not refuse this expanding breadth, the sheer amount of time and variety of activities may lead to more and more openness. It is not possible to say at what point the relation becomes "intimate." Breadth alone does not make intimacy, as we have seen, and openness is a matter of degree. Every experience of intimacy is unique.

Depth in Intimacy

Depth, the third dimension of intimacy, is a measure of how deeply involved you are, how important the other is to you, and how deeply committed you are. Like breadth and openness, depth also falls on a continuum and may be experienced in all degrees from very slight to very great. While each intimate relation is unique, there is a normal progression of intensity: The depth becomes increasingly greater as the dimensions of breadth and openness become more intense. When intimacy is characterized by great depth, simply being with the other brings feelings of contentment, satisfaction, tranquility, and well-being—a sense of wholeness or completeness. It is essentially within the depths of intimacy, in a sense "uniting" with the other, that the greatest rewards are to be found (Kieffer 1977).

Plato (427–347 B.C.), in his *Symposium*, proposed a mythology to describe this mystical experience of union with another human being. In this classical Greek mythology, early humans had four arms, four legs, two faces, and two sets of genitals. The transformation came when they were dissected:

Now when the work of dissection was complete it left each half with a desperate yearning for the other, and they ran together and flung their arms around each other's necks, and asked for nothing better than to be rolled into one . . . when we are longing for and following after that primeval wholeness, we say we are in love.[2]

From the time of Plato to the present, a vast literature—operas, novels, ballets, drama, and poetry—has explored the subject of depth in intimacy, as do contemporary movies, television programs, and popular song lyrics. This preoccupation of the arts with the meaning of intimacy is a reflection of its importance in the consciousness of men and women in all societies and all cultures—from earliest recorded history to the present.

PAIR BONDING AND SOCIAL PATTERNS

Pair bonding always occurs in ways that are patterned by the society in which the individual is immersed. All male-female interactions are channeled into cultural norms. These societal supports, patterns, regulations, laws, expectations, and opportunities—everything that makes up the social structure within which we live—are so much a part of our lives that we simply take them for granted. Paradoxically, we are so immersed in our social structure that we are not usually aware of it; society is to humankind as water is to a fish.

Position and Role

An important phenomenon characteristic of all known societies is that virtually every interaction one person can have with another is socially defined, and the behavior appropriate for the interaction is rigorously specified. For example, one person relates to another not only as "wife" or "husband" or as "boyfriend" or "girlfriend," but also as "customer," "bus driver," or "passenger." Sociologists call these socially defined relations *positions*, and all positions carry a prescribed *role*—the behavior appropriate for the position. These concepts of position and role are fundamental to an analysis of behavior in a society. For example, if a dating couple beings to have difficulty in relating, the source of the conflict may often be found by looking for problems in role interaction.

If the role behavior appropriate for a position is not performed as expected, the relation, or interaction, that is based on the position *must* break down. This is easy to understand if one examines a relatively simple, straightforward role interaction: If two persons are occupying the position "tennis player," each must be aware of and agree on the role behavior regarded as appropriate for this position—hitting a tennis ball over the net with a racket before it has bounced more than once and observing such conventions as "in" and "out" and the rules of scoring. If one person in the position "tennis player" does not behave in accordance with such role expectations, the couple cannot relate as "tennis players," and the interaction must break down.

To give another example: If you drive across a bridge with a tollgate, you are occupying the position "driver," while the person in the tollbooth is occupying the position "toll collector." As the driver, you hold out the toll; the person in the position "toll collector" accepts it; and you drive through. Any breach of this expected role behavior has repercussions. A toll collector who delays taking the toll would soon have a long line of angry, honking drivers lined up before the booth. A driver who drives through without paying the toll would soon have a highway patrol car pulling up behind with flashing lights.

In a more complex example: If two people

---

[2]Plato, *Symposium*, in the *Dialogues of Plato*, volume I, trans. Jowett (New York: Random House, 1937).

hold the positions "executive" and "secretary," the executive's appropriate behavior includes being relatively courteous and considerate and providing a salary as agreed, while the secretary's role includes appearing promptly in the morning, performing secretarial services, and being relatively good-natured. Any breach of this anticipated role behavior by either may lead to a breakdown in the relation. For example, if the executive is consistently rude or does not provide the salary agreed upon, the secretary may quit. If the secretary is consistently late or insubordinate, does not perform the services agreed upon effectively or efficiently, or is bad-natured, he or she may be fired.

The importance of performing expected role behavior is obvious for the positions "tennis player," "executive," and "secretary," but it is much less obvious in positions where role behavior is not spelled out either by the rules and conventions of a formal situation or by the contractual obligations of a business arrangement. For example, a young man attempting to strike up an acquaintance with a young woman who is walking across campus may not be familiar with the role behavior appropriate to the position "young man attempting to meet young woman." Unless the young woman is unusually perceptive, kind, and understanding, with a good deal of insight into the young man's dilemma, he will flounder and fail because he is not able to perform the expected role behavior—behavior that will, in turn, elicit the appropriate role behavior from the young woman, who is in the position "young woman being approached by young man."

In the positions "husband" and "wife," role behavior is even more complex, with virtually an infinite number of permutations. A husband or wife may not know precisely what behavior to perform or what to expect from the other, since intimate needs and role expectations are often unconscious. In many marriages, either the relation goes well or it

does not, without either person consciously or deliberately fulfilling role expectations. Thus, when the relation does not go well, the couple may be either unaware or unable to verbalize the source or the nature of the difficulty.

In short, a couple who is dating or married often loses sight of the basic principle that underlies virtually all human experience: Any interaction between two people depends on *mutual reciprocity* of *role behavior* that is appropriate to the societal *position* each is occupying at the moment. This principle is just as true for intimate, personal transactions as for formal ones. However, an important difference between an intimate and a formal interaction is that the expected role behavior cannot always be precisely spelled out in an intimate interaction. Rather, fulfilling anticipated role behavior must depend largely on such factors as mutual goodwill, affection, liking, respect, sensitivity of perception, openness to experience, and willingness to drop mutual barriers. These qualities are not contractual, as are the expectations in a formal or business arrangement. This makes an intimate relation at once more valuable and more fragile.

Secondary and Primary Relations

One characteristic of social interaction is that it takes place in terms of position and role. Another characteristic of all social interactions is that they may be characterized as either secondary relations or primary relations, and there are important differences between these two.

We all relate to other people from the time we are born until we die (unless we are one of the rare few who manage to live in isolation as recluses). But most of these interactions are either with people whom we do not know very well or with people whom we do not know at all; the interaction occurs because of the function each person can fulfill for the other. This *function*—the service performed or the goods provided—is the basis of most social interactions in our society, with each person relatively unimportant as a unique individual. This kind of interaction, where the focus is upon the function, is called a *secondary relation.*

A secondary relation is relatively brief, formal, and impersonal. The function each person is fulfilling for the other (the goods or services provided) is clearly specified, and calls for an agreed-upon reciprocity (or equivalent value in goods and services provided and received by each) and for a penalty to be applied if this reciprocity is not forthcoming.

In contrast, if we relate to someone informally, freely, and spontaneously, and if the focus is upon the other person's unique characteristics as an individual (rather than upon the function being fulfilled), this is called a *primary relation.* In a primary relation, the human values of affection, acceptance, compassion, understanding, and respect are not only important, they are essential to the interaction. The primary relation is the opposite of a secondary relation in terms of the human values involved (see Table 1-1).

A primary relation is also different from a secondary relation in that the satisfaction obtained from the interaction is chiefly *intrinsic* (providing its own satisfaction, or being pleasurable in and of itself). For example, when two people on a date are dancing, they are doing so because each is receiving intrinsic satisfaction from the interaction. This is a primary relation. Compare this with the couple dancing together in a Taxi Dance Club of the 1930s. The hostess would dance with a patron to collect a token payment that could be exchanged for 10 cents (the goods provided for her services). There was no intrinsic pleasure on her part. The patron received intrinsic pleasure but paid for it with the token. This was clearly a secondary relation. (The refrain of a popular song of the period was "Ten cents a dance/That's what they pay me.")

Since personal qualities are an essential

TABLE 1-1

Characteristics of primary and secondary relations

Characteristics of Secondary Relations	Characteristics of Primary Relations
Impersonal	Personal
Formal	Informal
Precise	Spontaneous
Deliberate	Intimate
Contractual	Extended *quid pro quo* unspecified
Specific *quid pro quo* specified[a]	
Human qualities of affection, compassion, etc., relatively unimportant	Human qualities of affection, compassion, etc., very important
Personal characteristics relatively unimportant	Personal characteristics of each very important
Emphasis on the function, or service, each is fulfilling	Emphasis on the interaction of the couple
Satisfactions usually symbolic	Satisfactions usually intrinsic

[a]*Quid pro quo* means "something for something."

part of the primary relation, individuals are not interchangeable, as they are in a secondary relation. For example, it matters very little who waits on you in a supermarket (a secondary relation). If the checker who is packing your groceries stops to go on a coffee break and is replaced by another, you hardly notice it. In a secondary relation, the other person is replaceable—the focus is upon the service being performed or the goods received, rather than on the other person. In contrast, if someone you were dating was suddenly replaced by another, you would not only notice it, but it would matter a great deal. In a primary relation, the focus is upon the personal qualities of the other, rather than upon the service being provided or the goods received, and it matters very much who the other person is.

Of course, *secondary relations* and *primary relations* are absolute terms representing the

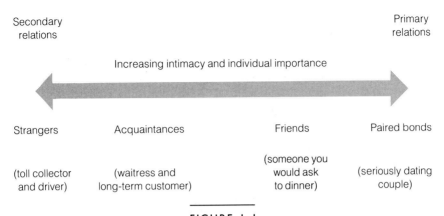

FIGURE 1-1
Primary and secondary relations are on a continuum.

polar ends of a continuum of possible relations. In the real world of human experience, any given interaction falls somewhere *between* these two extremes (see Figure 1-1) Moreover, a relation that starts out as secondary may move, either gradually or quickly, toward the primary end of the continuum. (All relations start out as secondary, of course, except those that are very quickly established—a sort of "love at first sight" phenomenon—or those that form very early in life, such as the bonding between mother and child.) The pattern of progression is usually from stranger to acquaintance to friend and finally, perhaps, to paired bond. For example, suppose you walk into a favorite coffee shop after an absence of several weeks and find that, in the meantime, a new waitress has been hired. Initially, your interaction with this waitress is clearly secondary. Her function is to provide you with the satisfaction of food and service, while you provide her with the satisfaction of paying the check. However, if you become interested in her as a person with unique qualities, the relation might begin to move toward the primary end of the continuum. If she responds and is interested in you as a person (rather than someone who is simply paying for her services), the relation might eventually

progress to the extreme primary end of the continuum by becoming a paired bond.

Interest in the other as a person is not always reciprocated, of course. The interaction may have some of the qualities of a primary relation for one person but be purely a secondary relation for the other. For example, in the Taxi Dance Club situation, the hostess might not be interchangeable as far as the patron is concerned; he might be very attracted to her and refuse to dance with any of the other hostesses. Her personal qualities might be an essential part of the transaction for him, whereas for her, the relation is purely secondary. She receives no intrinsic pleasure at all from dancing with the patron, but does so simply to get the token.

It is also possible for a relation to move in the other direction—away from the primary end and toward the secondary end of the continuum. Thus, a young woman may begin to refuse dates if she "cools off" toward a young man, or a married couple may "fall out of love" and become very formal and impersonal in any necessary interaction (such as meeting in a lawyer's office to discuss a property settlement when they are contemplating divorce).

The closer the relation is to the primary end of the primary-secondary continuum, the

A relation that starts out as secondary may move, either gradually or quickly, toward the primary end of the continuum.

Ellis Herwig/Stock, Boston

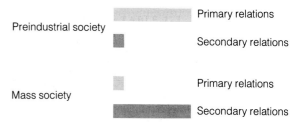

A mass society is characterized by a greater dependence on secondary relations and less dependence on primary relations, whereas the opposite is true of a preindustrial society.

FIGURE 1-2

Primary and secondary relations in preindustrial and mass societies

---

more complex it becomes, the more subtle are the satisfactions received, and the more difficult it becomes to assess the relative value of the satisfactions to each person and to establish a *quid pro quo*. This is because role behavior in a primary relation cannot be specified precisely or made part of a contractual obligation (either expressed or implied) in which every single activity that brings satisfaction to the other is spelled out. Rather, as we have seen, fulfilling anticipated role behavior in a primary relation must depend chiefly on each person wanting to please the other or deriving intrinsic satisfaction from doing so.

If the desire to please (and the satisfaction derived from it) are lacking, reciprocity of role behavior cannot be established simply by contract, as it could be in a secondary relation such as a business arrangement.

Preindustrial Societies and Mass Societies

Different societies have characteristic differences in the ways they utilize secondary and primary relations. In a small preindustrial society there are relatively more primary relations and fewer secondary relations, compared with a mass society. Nearly everyone in a small preindustrial society knows everyone else and matters to nearly everyone else: there is much more intimacy. In a mass society, primary relations are relatively rare, and most interactions are in the form of secondary relations (see Figure 1-2).

Our own society is classified by sociologists as a mass society. A mass society is not simply a large society, but one that is characterized by (1) mass production of commodities; (2) mass manipulation of taste (by advertising, promotion, and "public relations") for the marketing of the mass-produced commodities; (3) an urbanized community structure; and (4) highly specialized functions for the individual members of the society, especially those in the upper social strata—functions that require a long period of preparation and training (Martindale 1966).

Courtesy Sidney Janis Gallery, New York

Depersonalization and loneliness are common experiences
in our contemporary mass society.
George Segal: *Rush Hour*, 1983.

In a mass society the greater reliance on secondary relations after a person has reached young adulthood (and is no longer living within a family) can lead to depersonalization and loneliness. In our society, for example, it is quite possible for a single adult who is not living at home to go through an entire day—day after day—without experiencing a single primary relation. He or she can ride to school or to work on a bus (secondary relation with the bus driver), sit quietly in class or in an office (secondary relation with the teacher or with co-workers), eat lunch in a coffee shop (secondary relation with the waiter or waitress), and go to a movie in the evening (secondary relation with the cashier). The result can be self-devaluation and loneliness, painful and frightening experiences that are linked to boredom, anxiety, isolation, and depression. If an individual relates impersonally for too long, some essential element of that person's humanity erodes away (see Chapter 6).

Emotional security, companionship, and love are so important that their absence may cause sickness and even death. Loneliness is correlated with a high incidence of such diseases as cirrhosis of the liver, tuberculosis, pneumonia, diabetes, rheumatic fever, and cancer. When matched for age, occupation, and other characteristics, nearly twice as many single men die of heart disease as do married men.

The fact is that social isolation, the lack of human companionship . . . and chronic human loneliness are significant contributors to premature death . . . nature uses many weapons to shorten the lives of lonely people (Lynch 1977, pp. 3–4).

The physical and emotional gratification that comes from dating and marriage is increasingly important because it helps counterbalance the formalized, limited, procedural, and impersonal behavior with which we are chiefly involved in our contemporary mass society. In dating and marriage we seek the intimacy and personal fulfillment that are absent in the depersonalized formal world that makes up most of our existence, a world in which we are regarded as exchangeable commodities, with our chief value being the functions we perform or the services we provide. In serious dating or in marriage, each person may become so significant to the other that the experience constitutes a new dimension of awareness. This is essentially what is meant by "being in love," and the desire to experience it is what makes marriage in our mass society both unusually valuable and highly demanding. It may also help explain the high incidence of divorce: Since so much is now expected from marriage, the probability of failure is increased.

Marriage is no guarantee of year-round or round-the-clock intimacy even though [it] provides for a major share of the emotional needs of millions of individuals. It offers security, stability, and convenience in the fulfilling of daily needs and desires. No other living arrangement yet devised has provided so well for so many personal needs and desires of so many individuals, males and females. As newlyweds discover, after marriage, certain problems remain unresolved; certain needs for in-

timacy are yet unfulfilled. Even when one's spouse is physically available, he or she may not be *intimately* available when one needs or desires closeness. She or he may be occupied with work, studies, or children, or may simply need to be alone or psychologically apart for a while (Kieffer 1977, pp. 281–282).

Subsocieties and Subcultures

In addition to the patterns of position and role and the characteristics of secondary and primary relations, all societies are divided into subsocieties, and each of these subsocieties has its own subculture, which may differ in many important ways from the other subcultures in the overall society.

Culture and society are inseparable. While *society* is a group of people, *culture* is the way these people behave, along with everything they use in their behavior—the tools and artifacts, the language, attitudes, customs, and religious observances that distinguish the society. In addition, most societies are not a homogeneous group of people with a single culture. Rather, most societies—certainly our own—are made up of a number of *subsocieties*, each with its own characteristic *subculture*. In our own society, all male-female interactions, including dating, sexual and erotic behavior, and marriage and family interaction differ significantly from one subculture to another. For example, there are significant differences in these regards in the subsocieties made up of different *social classes, religions,* and *race*. It is, therefore, misleading to treat male-female interactions as though we were one large homogamous society. Although this is true in many respects, in other respects it is not.

For this reason, reference is often made throughout the text to statistically measurable differences in behavior among the three major subcultures of class, religion, and race (or ethnic group); and charts and tables will be included that illustrate these differences.

Social Class

All societies are composed of different levels or *strata* that extend from higher to lower.[3] Some members of a society have more status, power, and wealth and obtain more of the wanted goods of the society than other members, who have relatively little power, status, and wealth and obtain fewer of the wanted goods. The individuals in the various levels form subsocieties whose subcultures are measurably different from one another.

Some societies are rigidly stratified in what is called a *caste* system. A society that has a caste system designates precisely where every individual fits into the stratification. Moving from one caste to another is forbidden, as is intermingling of the castes. For example, a person from one caste may not marry a person from another caste.

In our society, we do not designate stratification formally in this way; rather, the layers form in response to such societal forces as amount and source of income, occupation, level of education, and nature and location of residence. A convenient index of a person's position in this stratification system in our society is membership in what sociologists call *social class*.

Social classes are designated as upper, middle, and lower, with each of the classes divided again into upper and lower. So we have an upper-upper and a lower-upper, an upper-middle and a lower-middle, and an upper-lower and a lower-lower class. The upper class includes the truly powerful, wealthy decision makers of the society. Those in the upper-middle class are, in general, professionals, managers, or owners of businesses. Lower-middle class people are, roughly, those who wear a white collar to

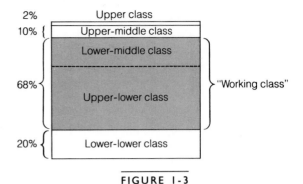

FIGURE 1-3

Stratification into social classes in the United States

work, such as salespeople, bank tellers, and office workers. Upper-lower class people are usually "blue-collar" workers who perform services and create goods. Together, the upper-lower and lower-middle classes form the backbone of the "working class" subsociety. The lower-lower class is composed of unskilled workers, transients, and the unemployed.

The percentages of our population in these social classes vary with one's definition of class, from community to community, and from area to area. In general, however, most sociologists agree that, nationwide, about 2 percent of our society is in the upper class, about 10 percent is in the upper-middle class, about 68 percent is in the working class (lower-middle and upper-lower), and something like 20 percent constitutes the lower-lower class (see Figure 1-3).

There are problems with the concept of social class. Exceptions abound, definitions are difficult to establish and even more difficult to apply, cross-class characteristics occur (high school education but relatively high income or middle class residence), and some people don't seem to fit into the classification system at all (sports stars, celebrities). Moreover, in our society it is possible to move from one class to another—usually through education—so that one might be in a different social

---

[3]The term *strata* comes from *stratification* or *stratified*, which in geology refers to the characteristic rock structure of one layer upon another.

class from one's parents or from one's brothers or sisters. *Family name*, which is a basic determinant of position in a caste system, contributes to one's social class membership only indirectly (in terms of such factors as education, source of income, amount of income, and residence).

The stratification is genuine, however, even though the social class concept is not always an accurate reflection of it. With all its shortcomings, the concept of social class does provide a convenient, if rough, index of one's position in the stratification system of our society.

As noted before, the concept of social class is important in the study of male-female interactions because there are major differences in the attitudes and behaviors (subcultures) of different social classes. For example, lower class wives describe their husbands quite differently from middle class wives. When lower class wives are asked what they value most in their husbands, the three attributes given most readily are:

He's a steady worker.
He doesn't drink.
He doesn't hit me. (Rubin 1976, pp. 93–94)

These attributes are not mentioned at all by middle class wives. Rather, they focus on such traits as the following:

He is very understanding.
He is a very sharing person.
We have a good deal of closeness in communication—a shared intimacy. (Rubin 1976, pp. 93–94)

Religion

Another important subsociety is formed by religious groups, although the importance of religion as a subsociety is not nearly as great in our society as it is in other societies. In Northern Ireland, for example, Catholics and Protestants actively oppose each other, and intermarriage or even cross dating is highly

unlikely. Even in the United States, it was until very recently relatively unusual for a Catholic to marry a Protestant or a Jew to marry a Gentile. Religious lines were crossed in this way by only about one in ten persons. (It is now about four in ten.) Although the incidence of such cross-religion marriages is now increasing, they are still not the norm (see Chapter 7). And some Protestant sects, such as the Amish, are militantly opposed to intermarriage and positively forbid dating or marriage outside the group.[4]

Race

Finally, many important subsocieties in the United States are formed by race. In fact, since our society is a melting pot—a conglomerate of many races from all over the world, each with its own subculture—racial subsocieties form a very important part of our culture. In the 1980s in our society, the major racial groups are Asian-Americans and blacks. However, because there is little demographic information available regarding such factors as dating, marriage, divorce, and marital and family interaction among other racial groups, we shall limit our discussion of racial subcultures to blacks.

Blacks form the largest racial subsociety in the United States, and they have many demographic characteristics that are quite different from whites; these differences will be acknowledged throughout the text wherever they are significant. For example, the divorce rate among blacks is more than twice

---

[4]The Amish church is one of the most conservative sects of the Mennonites. These people have settled mainly in Pennsylvania, Ohio, and the Midwest in the United States. They still use horse and buggy for transportation, wear distinctive clothes (black suits and hats for men and boys and long dresses for women and girls—with no buttons, since buttons are not mentioned in the Bible), and permit no radios or television sets in their communities. The Amish have a very distinct subculture, quite different from other Protestant sects and the rest of America.

Most people, whatever their social class, religion, or race, feel a need to share a sense of belonging with another person.

the divorce rate among whites. The unemployment rate is also much higher for blacks, and family income is a significant variable in many aspects of familial interaction.[5] It will also be

emphasized, of course, that blacks share many of the demographic characteristics of whites and are indistinguishable from whites in terms of many cultural factors.

SUMMARY

One of the basic human needs is the need to relate to other people. Secondary relations are essential because they provide goods and services that a person in a mass society cannot produce alone. However, a secondary relation does not recognize the human qualities or the individual characteristics of each person and is not intrinsically satisfying. In a primary relation, a person is deemed important as an individual and thus receives intrinsic satisfaction. It is probably essential for the average person's well-being to maintain a minimum number of primary relations, as well as at least one of the ultimate of these relations—the paired bond. Most people apparently feel a need to share a sense of belonging with another person, to form a paired bond.

One of the characteristics of a couple who have formed a paired bond is intimacy, which is defined as the experiencing of the essence of one's self in intense physical, intellectual, and emotional communion with another. Three parameters of intimacy are breadth, openness, and depth. Breadth refers to how many interests and activities the couple share. Openness refers to the degree of self-disclosure and is more important than breadth. Depth refers to the degree of commitment or how important each person is to the other.

Pair bonding must take place within the society in which the individuals live. In all societies, interactions may be analyzed in terms of the social position each person occupies. There is always a role behavior (which may be very complex) that is expected of the person in each position. So long as the

---

[5]In 1982 about 29 percent of all black men between the ages of twenty and sixty-four were not employed. Unemployment among teenage blacks was even higher—double this figure in some areas (Cordes 1985). 1982 was a year in which the unemployment rate dropped nationally, production soared, and the New York Stock Exchange began one of the longest bull markets in history, adding nearly 500 points to the Dow Jones Average in a surge of fourteen months.

Lynne Jaeger, Weinstein/Woodfin Camp & Associates

anticipated role behavior occurs, role reciprocation is possible. If role reciprocation does not occur, the interaction must cease. This is obvious in positions that are highly structured (such as "tennis player") or in interactions that are contractual (such as between "executive" and "secretary"). Although the necessity of role reciprocation is not so obvious in personal or intimate relations, it is just as important. This principle is often overlooked. When a personal interaction breaks down, it is helpful to analyze the failure in terms of role reciprocation.

Primary relations are personal and intimate; individual characteristics are a significant aspect of the transaction. Secondary relations are formal and impersonal, focusing on the function of each individual in the transaction.

Secondary relations are relatively more common in a mass society such as ours, compared with preindustrial societies. Because primary relations are relatively scarce in our mass society, the few that remain have assumed special significance for the individual. We expect to receive from the primary relations of dating and marriage the companionship, emotional support, security, affection, and love that are necessary for our confirmation of ourselves as unique and valued persons.

All large societies are composed of a number of subsocieties, each with its own subculture. For example, all large societies are stratified, with some members of the society having higher status and acquiring more of the wanted goods of the society than other members. In our society, this stratification is measured by social class membership, which is usually designated as upper-upper and lower-upper, upper-middle and lower-middle, upper-lower and lower-lower. Together, the lower-middle and upper-lower classes form the working class. Other important subsocieties are formed by religious affiliation and others by racial membership.

QUESTIONS

1. What is meant by the term *paired bond*? Give several examples of paired bonds in our society.

2. What is meant by *intimacy*? Distinguish between *breadth, openness*, and *depth* in intimacy. Give an example of each to illustrate your answer.

3. In sociological terms, what is meant by the concept of *position*? Give several examples.

4. What is meant by the concept of *role*? Give several examples.

5. What is meant by *role reciprocation*? Give several examples.

6. What is meant by the phrase *quid pro quo*? Why is an analysis of quid pro quo important in studying male-female interactions in dating or marriage?

7. Why is role reciprocation sometimes more difficult to maintain in an intimate interaction than in a formal or business transaction?

8. What are the chief characteristics of secondary relations in our society?

9. What are the chief characteristics of primary relations in our society?

10. Explain the statement: Primary and secondary relations are on a continuum.

11. Explain the statement: Our society is characterized by a relative scarcity of primary relations compared with secondary relations.

12. Distinguish between the concepts of *society* and *culture*. What is meant by a *subsociety*? A *subculture*? Give three examples of important subcultures in our society.

13. What are the characteristic occupations of the upper-middle class in our society? Of the lower-middle class? Of the upper-lower class? Of the lower-lower class?

14. About what percentage of our society is in the upper class? The upper-middle class?

The working class (lower-middle and upper-lower classes)? The lower-lower class?

15. Why are the institutions of dating and marriage so important as sources of personal satisfaction in our society?

SUGGESTIONS FOR FURTHER READING

Hendrick, Clyde, and Hendrick, Susan. *Liking, Loving, and Relating.* Monterey, Calif.: Brooks/Cole, 1983.

Hinde, R. A. *Towards Understanding Relationships.* London: Academic Press, 1979.

Kanmeyer, Kenneth C. W. *Confronting the Issues: Marriage, the Family, and Sex Roles.* 2nd ed. Boston: Allyn & Bacon, 1981.

Kelley, H. H. *Close Relationships.* New York: W. H. Freeman, 1983.

Knapp, Mark L. *Interpersonal Communication and Human Relationships.* Boston, Mass.: Allyn & Bacon, 1984.

Lynch, James J. *The Broken Heart: The Medical Consequences of Loneliness.* New York: Basic Books, 1977.

Money, John. *Love and Love Sickness: The Science of Sex, Gender Difference, and Pair Bonding.* Baltimore: Johns Hopkins University Press, 1980.

Rubenstein, Carin, and Shaver, Phillip. *In Search of Intimacy.* New York: Delacorte Press, 1982.

Rubin, Lillian Breslow. *Intimate Strangers: Men and Women Together.* New York: Harper & Row, 1983.

——— . *Worlds of Pain.* New York: Basic Books, 1976.

Weiss, Robert S., ed. *Loneliness: The Experience of Emotional and Social Isolation.* Cambridge, Mass.: MIT Press, 1974.

Zimbardo, Philip G. *Shyness.* Reading, Mass.: Addison-Wesley, 1977.

PART TWO

Gender, Love, Sex, and Courtship in Pair Bonding

CHAPTER 2

Gender: Maleness and Femaleness

The Fundamentals of Gender
The Emergence of Gender
Gender in Historical Perspective

I am a man and you are a woman.
I can't think of a better arrangement.

Groucho Marx

Gender is the concept of maleness or femaleness. It refers to the physical characteristics (anatomical and physiological), the social behavior, the self-image (gender identity), and the psychological and behavioral tendencies and abilities that differentiate men from women and boys from girls.

Gender is basic in all social interactions. Whenever we meet anyone, however briefly or casually, we notice the other's gender. If we remember the person at all, whatever else we may forget, we never forget that person's gender.

Although there is much social interaction in which it is not important, gender is involved in many significant interactions. If the relation is erotic or romantic, gender is a key aspect. When the interaction is related to reproduction, gender differences are essential.

In a paired bond, gender is the basis of erotic interaction, love, dating, courtship, marriage, and the production and nurturance of children. The manifestations of gender underlie virtually every topic in this book.

THE FUNDAMENTALS OF GENDER

The subject of gender characteristics has fascinated generations of poets, novelists, theologians, philosophers, and other observers of the human scene. These characteristics are now actively researched by many scientists—biologists, sociologists, psychologists, anthropologists, and historians. We shall draw from the findings of all of these disciplines as we explore the meaning and manifestations of gender.

Gender characteristics are initially determined by the information encoded in the gene library of each of the human body's 100 trillion cells. This gene library is the basis of our very existence and of all our biological behavior. Information is encoded in the genes in a language of chemistry written in the construction of DNA molecules. The gene library contains everything the body knows how to do without conscious intervention. This ancient information is written in careful, exhaustive, redundant detail—how to breathe, how to digest food, how to maintain blood pressure, how to recognize patterns, and how to reproduce.[1]

How each of us is constructed, then, depends on the information in our gene libraries, and part of each library contains instructions relating to gender. As we shall see, the differentiation into gender is determined by the sex chromosomes, which contain the genes, which contain the DNA molecules upon which our biological construction is based.

Another biological source of gender is hormonal. The sex hormones—androgen (male) and estrogen (female)—direct the development of biological gender characteristics from before birth until death.

These biological factors are only one aspect of gender, however. Interacting with these biological factors is the social aspect of gender—the characteristic differences in the societal behavior of boys and girls, of men and women. This aspect of gender is called *gender-role behavior* and stems from *gender-role socialization*. Individuals with male biological gender characteristics are treated differently from those with female biological gender characteristics. This differential treatment leads to the development of different social behavior of males and females, or gender-role behavior.

You also form a gender identity as part of your self-image, regarding yourself as either male or female. This third factor of gender—*gender identity*—is actually the most powerful determinant of all in directing the behavioral manifestations of maleness or femaleness.

There are, then, three interacting, interrelated aspects of gender: *biological* factors, *social* factors, and *gender identity*. Acting together they have profound effect upon the person you are and the life you lead. For the remainder of the chapter we shall explore these three factors.

Primary Gender Characteristics

The most obvious components of gender are those that are physically related to reproduction. They are called the *primary gender characteristics* and include gestation, menstruation, and lactation (milk production) in the female, and sperm production in the male (see Table 2-1).[2] These primary gender characteristics are biological imperatives. They are not available to the opposite gender and cannot be

---

[1] This encyclopedia of information, which is contained in the nucleus of each of your cells, is astonishingly miniaturized. There are 5 billion bits of information in the genes of each cell of your body. A *bit*—a shorthand expression for *binary digit*—is a single unit of information. To designate one letter in the alphabet would take 5 bits. About 10,000 bits of information are in a virus, which is about the amount of information on this page. A bacterium needs about 10 billion bits of information to construct itself and function, which is about 100 printed pages. A free-swimming, one-celled amoeba needs about 400 million bits in its gene library; it would require about eighty 500-page books to make another amoeba. The 5 billion bits needed by a human being, if written in English, would fill 1,000 volumes. Every one of your 100 trillion cells contains this complete library of instructions on how to make every part of you (Sagan 1980).

[2] *Gestation* refers to the nine-month period of pregnancy during which the female supports her unborn offspring inside her body. *Menstruation* refers to the cycle of ovulation that recurs every twenty-eight days in the average nubile female.

TABLE 2-1
Primary gender characteristics

Women	Men
Gestation	Sperm production
Lactation	
Menstruation	

Primary gender characteristics are biological imperatives and may not be reversed by any known treatment.

made available by any known method. No man can gestate, menstruate, or lactate, and no woman can produce sperm.

These primary physiological characteristics are, of course, related to anatomical differences. Male and female human beings have different internal and external anatomies according to their roles in reproduction. They also have characteristically different neural pathways, or brain functions, as we shall see. As adults they have somewhat different behavioral characteristics based upon their differences in biology.

As fundamental as the primary gender characteristics are, however, they do not necessarily *determine* gender. For example, a man may not produce sperm (he may be sterile) and still be regarded as a male. He may, in fact, be indistinguishable from other males, except that he cannot sire offspring. Similarly, many women do not gestate or lactate, and some do not even menstruate. Ballerinas, for example, usually start menstruating years later than the average girl, yet the ballerina is often regarded as the embodiment of the female ideal.[3] In

short, as important as the basic anatomical and physiological features of gender are, they alone do not constitute gender—it is far more complex.

Secondary Gender Characteristics

Other important characteristics of gender are those that develop when a person enters adolescence and becomes a young adult. At this time, the average man becomes larger, stronger, and fleeter than the average woman, has a thicker skin, a lower voice, and different hair distribution.[4] The average woman has a layer of fat beneath her skin augmenting her different skeletal and muscular development. Thus, the average woman's body is smaller, softer, and more rounded than the average man's.[5] These typical differences between males and females are called the *secondary gender characteristics*. They occur as a result of the action of the sex hormones (androgen and estrogen) that begin to flood the bloodstream at the onset of puberty. Hormones are chemical messengers that direct physiological activity within the body. From puberty on, males have a relatively higher level of *androgen* in their bloodstream, and females have a relatively higher level of *estrogen*.[6]

---

[3]The explanation for this phenomenon apparently lies in the leanness of the ballerina. When the level of fat in the body drops below 22 percent (as opposed to 26–28 percent for the average twenty-five-year-old), menstruation may cease. In the case of adolescents, a body fat level of less than 17 percent delays the onset of puberty (O'Herlihy 1982, p.50).

[4]If a boy is castrated before puberty, he will never develop these secondary gender characteristics; for example, his voice will not deepen. Adult male sopranos were very much in vogue in Europe until the nineteenth century. These castratos continued to sing with the pure soprano tones of a young boy.

Although hair is distributed differently on the bodies and faces of men and women, the pattern of scalp hair is similar in both genders—except for a greater tendency toward baldness in men, which is partially caused by the male sex hormone testosterone (the other cause is genetic). It is interesting to note in this regard that although the sex hormone makes men more subject to baldness than women, it is more acceptable for women to wear wigs in our contemporary society. (In fifteenth- to eighteenth-century Western European societies, wigs were commonly worn by upper and middle class men.)

[5]In addition to giving her a typically rounded contour (in contrast to the more rugged contour of the average male), this layer of fat also makes it easier for a woman to float in water and to learn how to swim.

The secondary gender characteristics that develop at puberty in response to the sex hormones differentiate men and women only in terms of the *norm* (or the *populations* of men and women), of course. There are obviously great individual differences. Some men are smaller, weaker, and have more rounded contours and higher voices than the average woman, while some women are taller, more angular, stronger, and have deeper voices than the average man.

Gender Role

As important as biological gender characteristics are, they are chiefly important only as they are translated into social behavior. As noted earlier, social behavior that is gender related is called gender-role behavior. *Gender-role behavior* is the behavior expected of a person as a function of his or her biological gender. All known societies expect biological males to behave differently from biological females from infancy on.

Gender role is closely related to the physical aspects of gender, the most important of which is the biological imperative that women bear children. This unique capacity of women has led to their being assigned gender-role behavior for nurturing and socializing children. Other gender-role behavior that can be performed without interfering with childbearing and child rearing has also been assigned to women in all known societies.

This division of labor according to gender has been described by sociologists as representing a distinction between expressive roles and instrumental roles. The *expressive* role involves nurturant and emotional needs—main-

taining harmonious interactions within the family, for instance—and has been traditionally linked to the female gender. The *instrumental* role, in contrast, deals with the manipulation of objects, people, or events—such as building, hunting, and using weapons and tools—and has been traditionally linked to the male gender.

Both genders may function in either instrumental or expressive roles, of course, but the instrumental functions of women have traditionally been limited to those that can be done close to home while looking after children, whereas men's instrumental functions have taken them away from the home and are not necessarily related to child care. We shall return to this point later in the chapter.

Gender Identity

The final component of gender is your sense of yourself as a male or female, or your gender identity. *Gender identity* is the core of your self-image, your perception of yourself as a unique individual. Gender identity begins to take definite form at about age three and is well established by age five. From this time on, a person normally regards himself or herself first and foremost as either a male or a female, and other aspects of the self-image follow. There are people known to have established self-images without identifying themselves as male or female, but as partly both. However, they are very rare indeed (Money and Tucker 1975).

Your gender identity is the result of two interacting forces. One is your perception of your own biology or anatomical characteristics. The second is your perception of the way other people treat you. For example, very young boys and girls notice that they have different external anatomies and ask questions about the difference. They are told that one is a "little boy" and the other is a "little girl." From infancy, boys and girls are also treated differently, and different behavior is expected from them. This differential treatment of males

---

[6]Testosterone is a component of the male sex hormone androgen. It stimulates the development of secondary gender characteristics in men and predisposes the male to be more aggressive than the female in infrahuman species. Evidence for this effect of testosterone (or other components of androgen) in humans is controversial.

and females is characteristic of all known societies and is the chief force in the initial development of each person's gender identity.

Gender Identity/Role

Gender identity and gender role together form the single, inseparable entity that is expressed in the formulation *gender identity/role*. Gender identity is the inward experience of gender role; gender role is the outward expression of gender identity.

Gender identity is your sense of yourself as a male or a female. Gender role includes everything you feel, think, do, and say that indicates—to yourself as well as to others—that you *are* a male or a female. Thus, gender role and gender identity are not two separate things, but rather different aspects of the *same* thing. Together, they form a unity in each person's experience, a unity that is the inner and outer expression of gender (Money and Tucker 1975).

The High Social Visibility of Gender

Gender-role socialization, together with gender identity/role, leads to a high *social visibility* of gender. Even in a society in which the biological manifestations of gender are covered by clothes, gender is highly socially visible. This is due to the convention (which occurs in all known societies) that men and women wear different hairstyles, adornments, and cosmetics. These send a clear, unequivocal message identifying a person as male or female. In addition, names are almost always recognized as male or female, so that the gender of a person is apparent even in his or her absence.

Despite the seeming triviality of such gender-related conventions and the occasional use of ambiguous clothes (such as jeans) or names (such as Leslie), these cultural devices are an important aspect of social interaction. A person whose appearance is not in accordance with these conventions is sending conflicting signals, and since a person's gender is one of the first things we note (and never forget), conflicting signals can cause unease. (They may even cause resentment or anger.) Yet, even though a person may be sending conflicting gender signals to some extent, it is very unusual to meet someone whose gender is not immediately apparent.

THE EMERGENCE OF GENDER

As we have seen, gender is a complex phenomenon, involving not just biology, but also the social factors of gender role and the psychological factors of gender identity/role that together form the indivisible unity of gender identification.

Early assumptions suggested two separate pathways to adult gender: one leading to manhood and the other leading to womanhood, both beginning at the sex chromosomes inherited at conception. In fact, there are not two pathways but rather a *single* pathway with a number of forks, where the individual turns in either the male or the female direction. Thus, a person becomes a male or a female by stages—conception, prenatal development (before birth), infancy, childhood, puberty, adolescence, and finally adulthood. Most individuals turn smoothly in the same direction at each fork, toward maleness or femaleness. But wrong turns also occur, leading to the various sexual *anomalies*. (*Anomaly* means a deviation, or something not according to expectation.)

Biological Correlates of Gender

The initial basis of gender is, of course, biological. Males and females have significantly different physical characteristics. (It is equally true, of course, that most of their biologies are identical.) Biological differentiation into male and female begins with the sex chromosomes.

The Sex Chromosomes

Chromosomes are the ribbonlike strands of genetic material.[7] There are forty-six chromosomes within each cell of your body. Two of these are *sex chromosomes.* The sperm or egg cells *in* your body are not really part *of* your body; each has twenty-three chromosomes, one of which is a sex chromosome.

There are two kinds of sex chromosomes: the *Y chromosome* (so-called because it looked like a *Y* under the microscope to the biologist who first identified it) and the *X chromosome* (which contains an extra "arm" and looks like an *X*). The X and Y chromosomes determine all the gender-related characteristics of the developing embryo and fetus. The other chromosomes determine other genetic characteristics. All eggs have an X chromosome, but the sperm may have either an X or a Y (in addition to the twenty-two other chromosomes).

If the sperm that reached and fertilized the egg from which you originated was an X-bearing sperm, you have an XX chromosomal structure (plus forty-four other chromosomes) in every cell of your body, and you are a biological female. If a Y-bearing sperm reached and fertilized the egg from which you originated, you have an XY chromosomal pattern in each cell of your body, and you are a biological male (see Figure 2-1).[8] Since all the 100 trillion cells

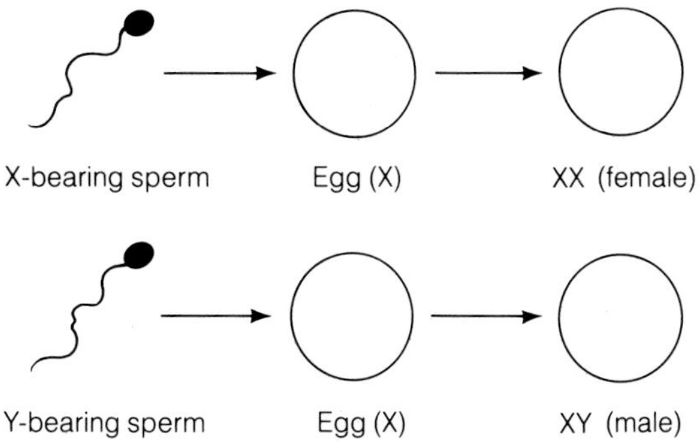

FIGURE 2-1
Gender is determined by the sperm.

in your body have the same chromosomal pattern, you are an XY male or an XX female in every cell of your body, unless a chromosomal anomaly occurred (more on this later).

There are perhaps as many as 140 XY conceptions for every 100 XX conceptions (Money and Tucker 1975). However, the male embryo and fetus have a much higher death rate than the female, so the ratio at birth is about 105 boys to 100 girls.[9] This higher death rate of the male continues after birth, so that by age twenty-five there are about equal numbers of men and women in the population. From this point on, women begin increasingly to outnumber men (see Table 2-2). By age seventy-five, there are nearly twice as many women as men. The average woman's life expectancy is 7.5 years longer than the average man's.[10]

The Sex Hormones: Prenatal Stage

For the first six weeks after conception, the embryo is all-purpose, with *growth buds* that can develop into either male or female organs.

---

[7]They are called chromosomes because they looked like tiny, highly colored ribbons to early biologists peering through the first microscopes (*chromo* means color). The chromosomes are made up of genes, which in turn are constructed of DNA molecules, as noted earlier.

[8]There is a very simple way to determine a person's chromosomal pattern. Since every cell in the body may be expected to have an identical chromosomal pattern, cells obtained by lightly scraping the inside of the cheek may be placed on a microscope slide, stained, and examined for a distinctive spot of color (the Barr body) that indicates an X chromosome. The Y chromosome may be just as readily seen by utilizing another stain that produces a flourescent patch on a Y chromosome.

[9]U.S. Bureau of the Census, "Ratio of Males to Females, by Age Group, 1910 to 1983" (1985).

[10]U.S. National Center for Health Statistics, *Vital Statistics of the United States,* annual (1983), and provisional data (July 8, 1984).

TABLE 2-2

Ratio of males to every 100 females by age group, 1920 – 1983

Age (years)	1920	1940	1960	1980	1983
	Birth rate: approximately 105 males for every 100 females				
Under 14	102.1	103.0	103.4	104.6	104.7
14 – 24	97.3	98.9	98.7	101.7	102.7
25 – 44	105.1	98.5	95.7	97.4	98.1
45 – 64	115.2	105.2	95.7	90.7	90.7
65 and over	101.3	95.5	82.8	67.6	67.1
All ages	104.1	100.7	97.1	94.5	94.6

There are more males than females in the United States until age twenty-five; after that age, there are more females than males. At age sixty-five, there are only sixty-seven males for every one hundred females.

Source: Data from U.S. Bureau of the Census, "Ratio of Males to Females, by Age Group, 1910 to 1983" (1985, p. 30).

For example, there is a pair of *gonads*, which can develop into either testicles or ovaries. There are *wolffian tubes* that are capable of developing into the internal genitalia of the male, and *mullerian tubes* that can develop into the internal genitalia of the female (depending on the sex hormone mix, one will develop and the other will wither away). There is a tiny protruding bud of tissue called a *genital tubercle* that will develop into either a penis or a clitoris (again, depending on the hormone mix). Below this genital tubercle is an opening that either fuses together in the male (forming the scrotal sac that contains the testicles) or stays open in the female (forming the labia).

During the first six weeks following conception, the XX and XY embryos proceed along the same neutral pathway of sex development. But by the end of the sixth week, there is a fork in the road. At that point, the Y chromosomes of a male embryo send a message in some as yet undetermined way to the two gonads, and they respond by becoming testicles. If no Y chromosome is present, another six weeks go by before the primitive, undifferentiated gonads begin to develop into ovaries, packed with enough egg cells to last a lifetime.

When the gonad has differentiated into a testicle, it starts to manufacture sex hormones—*androgen* (the male sex hormone) and *estrogen* (the female sex hormone), but the mix contains much more androgen than estrogen. Influenced by this predominantly androgen hormone mix, the wolffian structures develop while the mullerian structures wither away.

The wolffian structures become the *seminal vesicles*, the *prostate gland*, and the long tubes called the *vas deferens*, while the genital tubercle forms the *scrotum*, which receives the testicles when they descend about seven months after conception. (For further definition and description of these biological structures, see Chapter 4.)

If the prenatal hormone mix is not predominantly androgen, the wolffian structures begin to wither away, while the mullerian structures develop into a *uterus, fallopian tubes*, and upper *vagina*; the genital tubercle becomes a *clitoris*; and the opening below the genital tubercle develops into *labia*. The development of the external genitalia begins during the third or fourth month after conception and is usually complete by the fifth month. In the chronology of prenatal sexual differentiation, the external organs are finished last (see Figure 2-2).

There is one more step in prenatal sex dif-

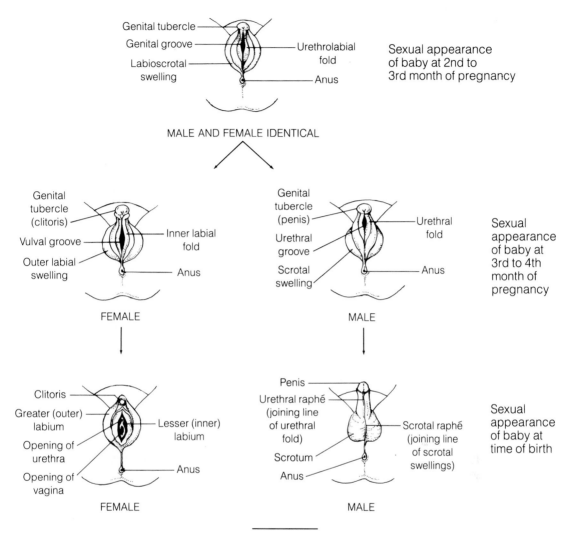

FIGURE 2-2

Differentiation of external genitalia

ferentiation: the influence of prenatal sex hormones on the brain. Obviously, female brains must be constructed to direct such processes as menstruation, whereas male brains must be constructed to direct such processes as erection of the penis. However, there is now evidence that the prenatal sex hormone mix has other more complex effects on the brain, influencing social behavior as well. This is an im-

portant and intriguing topic that will be explored in some detail in the later section, "Biosocial Correlates of Gender."

Sex Hormones: Adolescence and Adulthood

Beginning in the early teens (in most individuals), the sex hormones (androgen and estrogen) again act to bring about profound gender differences. At this time the blood-stream is flooded with sex hormones, released from the testicles in the male and the ovaries in the female, which cause emergence of the secondary gender characteristics described earlier. This phenomenon is called *puberty* and instigates the beginning of adolescence.

In animals other than humans, the behavioral effects of the sex hormones are enormous, especially in the male. For example, a bull is typically aggressive, dominant, and fierce. He must be handled carefully, cannot be kept in an enclosure with other bulls, cannot usually be used for labor, and has meat too tough to be marketed for human consumption. However, if he is castrated (has his testicles cut off) before he reaches puberty—thus effectively removing the chief source of testosterone—he is typically docile and submissive. The castrated male or steer can be kept in an enclosure with other steers, can be used to pull ploughs or carts, and has flesh that is relatively soft and tender. In short, the bull and the steer have significantly different behavioral and physical characteristics caused by the presence (or absence) of testosterone in their bodies.

Among house pets, the unneutered male tomcat is very aggressive and apt to fight with other toms in competition for a female and to protect his territory. If the tom is castrated early enough in his life, the aggressive fighting tendencies either do not emerge at all or are much lessened. (After these aggressive behaviors have been established, however, they may continue after neutering, but to a lesser degree—illustrating the fact that even in some infrahuman animals, factors other than biological forces determine adult gender behavior.)

In the infrahuman female animal, the release of sex hormones into the bloodstream causes the *estrous cycle* to occur, brings about "presenting behavior," and impels the mother to nurture her young.[11]

The behavioral effects of the sex hormones in men and women are controversial. There are typical behavioral differences between males and females, of course, but the current feeling is that while biology predisposes certain behaviors, making them more likely to develop, the social factors are equally important. (This topic will be explored in the later section, "Biosocial Correlates of Gender.")

It *is* commonly accepted, however, that the flood of sex hormones in the bloodstream at puberty is probably responsible for the increasingly urgent and romantic interest that typically occurs at this time, although social factors are also involved, of course. Moreover, the sex hormones that flood the bloodstream at puberty cause the development of the secondary gender characteristics, as noted earlier. These are, in turn, followed by changes in behavior. They have a profound effect on a person's gender identity/role and on other people's responses in all social interactions. The importance of the secondary gender characteristics may be clearly seen in their absence—if they do *not* develop on schedule, the person will probably experience a profound identity crisis that may amount to panic (Money and Tucker 1975).

For a summary of the development of one's adult gender identity/role, see Figure 2-3.

Social Correlates of Gender

The social correlates of gender are inextricably interrelated with the biological factors. Biology dictates much of how others in the society relate to the person from infancy, and this treatment leads to the establishment of

---

[11]The *estrous cycle* is the cyclic release of the ovum, analagous to the menstrual cycle in humans. The position infrahuman female mammals adopt to encourage copulation is called "presenting." The female chimpanzee, for example, will bend forward in a crouching position and elevate her posterior. All male mammals except man always copulate from the rear. (Among human beings, copulation may occur from the rear, but usually takes place in a face-to-face position. See Chapter 4.)

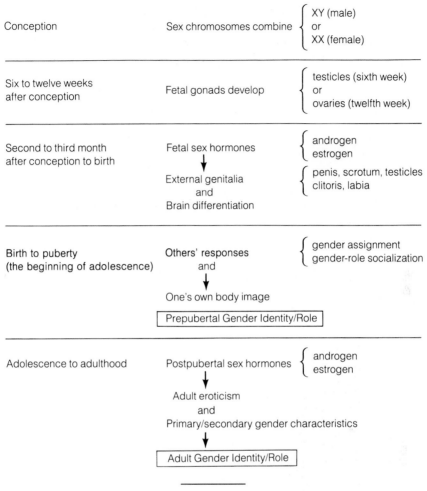

FIGURE 2-3

The development of adult gender identity/role

gender identity/role (along with the person's perception of his or her own anatomy).

Biological development sets the stage for gender-role socialization, which begins at birth. The infant is identified as either a male or a female by the appearance of the external genitalia. Once this *gender assignment* is made, the infant is given a gender-related name and is soon dressed in gender-related clothing and given gender-related toys. All

these social factors influence the development of gender differences in males and females from birth.

Research finds that little boys are encouraged to be more aggressive and more independent than little girls. Both the father and the mother usually encourage the boy to be masculine—to be rougher in play and to act "like a little man"—teasing or ridiculing him for departures from this model. Girls, in contrast, have

The Metropolitan Museum of Art, New York, Harris Brisbane Dick Fund, 1928

Winslow Homer: *Winter—A Skating Scene,* 1868

traditionally been encouraged to be neat and clean, to play quietly, and otherwise to behave in a "feminine" way. The toys that parents buy and give to children usually reflect the gender-role differentiation that is characteristic of our society. By the time a child is five years old and starts school, he or she is likely to be firmly entrenched in a stereotyped gender role. Experiences in school then reinforce this stereotype even further. Teachers expect girls to be quieter and less aggressive in the classroom than boys, and to engage in much less physical activity. Many teachers also encourage boys to dominate girls in the classroom, even though these teachers are usually women (Sadker and Sadker 1985, Baumrind 1972, Howe 1971).

Biosocial Correlates of Gender

As noted earlier, gender identity/role is a function of the interaction of biological and social factors (or "nature" and "nurture"). An intriguing question is: Which is more important—biological or social determinants of behavior? The answer apparently is that biology predisposes or makes more likely a certain behavioral pattern, while social factors then modify or direct this biological predisposition.

For example, male brains are programmed prenatally to direct behavior that is typically more active and more aggressive than female behavior. Whether or not this behavior develops, however, depends upon the social expectation and the gender identity of the person.

In infrahumans, however, prenatal programming of the brain is relatively more important.

"Male" and "Female" Brains in Monkeys

The evidence for the importance of prenatal programming of the brain in monkeys is very clear. When pregnant monkeys are injected with androgen their female offspring play like males rather than females as youngsters—

Winslow Homer: *Raid on a Sand-Swallow Colony—
"How Many Eggs?,"* 1874

National Gallery of Art, Washington, Rosenwald Collection

"Male" and "Female" Brains in Humans

It is very clear that prenatal male and female human brains are programmed, under the direction of the sex hormones, to direct different behaviors in regard to certain biological processes. For example, male brains are programmed to direct such biological functions as erection of the penis and the intricate processes that occur with ejaculation. Similarly, female brains are programmed to direct such biological functions as menstruation and ovulation and the extraordinarily intricate processes that are necessary to support the fertilized egg while it develops into an infant.

However, does this preprogramming of the brain include a predisposition to direct *social* behavior differently in males and females? The answer could be found if a group of pregnant women, with female embryos, were injected with androgen. Although this can be done with monkeys, it cannot be done with human beings; it is not considered ethical to give a pregnant woman androgen injections simply to observe the effect on her female offspring. However, if a group of women could be found whose fetuses had been accidentally exposed to androgen, the effects could be observed.

John Money managed to locate twenty-five women to whom this had happened—women who had been given a drug that accidentally prenatally androgenized their fetuses.[12] The drug contained progestin, a synthetic hormone related in chemical structure to androgen, and it was administered to prevent miscarriage. (At the time this occurred—in the 1950s—it was not known that fetal androgenization would be a side effect; the use of progestin for this purpose has now been discontinued.) This prenatally androgenized group of girls was then compared with a similar (*control*) group whose

acting much more aggressively, boisterously, and roughly than normal female monkeys. As these "prenatally androgenized" monkeys mature, their assertive behavior and their mating behavior become more similar to those of normal male monkeys (Jensen 1973, Goy 1970). The prenatal androgenization of a female brain apparently changes the neural pathways in the brain, so that the monkey's social behavior is characteristically male rather than female.

Although monkeys are the closest animals to us in terms of biology, extrapolating the findings of such studies to human beings is purely speculative and may lead to erroneous conclusions. What is true of a monkey is not necessarily true of a human being.

---

[12]John Money is a director of the Psychohormonal Research Unit at the Johns Hopkins Medical Institution. He is one of the foremost researchers in the field of gender characteristics and related topics.

mothers had not received the drug.[13] The findings were intriguing: In terms of many psychological traits and tendencies, the prenatally androgenized group differed from the control group.

For example, the prenatally androgenized girls proudly described themselves as "tomboys," preferred to play with guns and cowboy gear rather than dolls, and liked to join boys in rough group games, whereas members of the control group preferred to play quietly with other girls. When they reached adolescence, the prenatally androgenized girls were much less interested in romance, dating, and courtship than the girls in the control group, and they lagged far behind their age mates in beginning to date and in venturing into sexual involvement with boyfriends.

Fully one-third of the prenatally androgenized girls said they would prefer not to have children, while the other two-thirds were rather perfunctory and casual about their anticipation of motherhood—lacking the enthusiasm of the girls in the control group, all of whom were sure they wanted to be mothers.

When questioned about their feelings regarding the relative desirability of "career versus marriage," the majority of the prenatally androgenized girls either preferred a career or wanted to be married as well as have a career. Among the girls in the control group, marriage was unanimously favored over career, and for most of them marriage was their most important goal (Money and Ehrhardt 1972).

There was no gender identity/role confusion among the prenatally androgenized girls, however. None wished to be a boy or pretended to be a boy (although many expressed dissatisfaction with being girls). Moreover, nothing in their histories indicated that they were more

likely to become lesbians than any other girls (Money and Tucker 1975).

How can these results be interpreted? Obviously, the prenatal influence on neural pathways in the brain had some effect. However, the behavioral results, while relatively significant, were well within the range of what is regarded as appropriate behavior for females in our society. Many girls who have not been prenatally androgenized are tomboys.

Apparently, prenatal androgenization affects the neural pathways of the brain by lowering the threshold for some types of behavior (making it more likely that they will occur) and raising it for others (making it less likely that they will occur). There is no evidence at this time that prenatal androgenization creates any new brain pathways or eliminates any that would otherwise be there.

The Importance of Gender Identity in Directing Behavior

Gender identity is a psychological factor—it is partially based on biology, but it develops as a result of the interaction of the person with the society. There is evidence that this psychological factor of gender identity is more important than biology in determining gender-role behavior. We shall examine two kinds of research illustrating this principle: (1) studies of matched pairs of *hermaphrodites*, one of whom received the gender assignment of "male" at birth, while the other received the gender assignment of "female,"[14] and (2) studies of identical twins, one of whom received the gen-

---

[13]The control group was matched with the prenatally androgenized group in terms of age, intelligence, race, and social and economic backgrounds.

---

[14]A *hermaphrodite* is a person with both male and female biological characteristics. For example, a chromosomal (XX) female fetus may be exposed to a prenatal overdose of androgen (or synthetic progestin) that does not interfere with the differentiation of internal female reproductive organs but does masculinize the molding of the external genitalia. At birth, the baby may look like a girl or a boy, depending on the strength and timing of the sex hormone exposure. (See the section, "Gender Anomalies," later in this chapter for more on hermaphroditism.)

der-role socialization of a male and the other the gender-role socialization of a female.

First let us look at the evidence for the importance of socialization in studies of matched pairs of hermaphrodites. A matched pair of hermaphrodites is two persons with the same chromosomal gender and essentially the same biology, but with external genitalia whose appearance is ambiguous. If one of this pair is identified as a male at birth and the other is identified as a female, they are a *matched pair* biologically. If one of this matched pair is given the gender assignment "female" at birth, whereas the other is given the gender assignment "male," one will receive the gender-role socialization of a female and the other the gender-role socialization of a male. The importance of socialization may then be compared with the underlying biology.

An example will make this clear. Suppose a baby is a chromosomal (XX) female but has a penislike clitoris and fused labia that resemble a scrotum. If she is (mistakenly) assigned as "male" at birth by the delivering physician, she will be given a boy's name and will be treated as a boy from then on (receiving the gender-role socialization of a male). However, when she reaches puberty, her ovaries will begin to release a hormonal mix that is predominantly estrogen, and she will develop a feminized body.

Researchers have found that, despite the overwhelming evidence that she is a biological female, the person in such a predicament will continue to identify "himself" as a male and regard the developing female characteristics as a deformity. That person will have an adult gender identity/role indistinguishable from that of a normal chromosomal (XY) male even though the person has the XX chromosomes and the biology of a female (Money and Tucker 1975).

What happens to the other half of this matched pair, the one who was correctly identified as a female at birth and raised as a female? What effect does the prenatal androg-

enization have on her life? The answer is, apparently, very slight effect. Her external genitalia can be repaired surgically to approximate that of a normal female. She will grow up behaving as other girls do, except for a tendency toward "tomboyism," and may marry and have children. She will have the gender identity/role behavior of a female as an adult and will be indistinguishable from other women, despite her prenatal androgenization (Money and Tucker 1975).

The same results have been found in other types of hermaphrodites. In each case, apparently, the person will fulfill the gender identity/role consistent with upbringing and socialization, despite the underlying biology. This research provides a clear-cut illustration of the overriding importance of gender identity—even when it opposes biology—in determining adult gender characteristics.

The second type of research that we shall cite comes from studies of identical twins, one of whom is reared as a female and the other as a male. Since identical twins develop from a single fertilized egg, they have identical chromosomal patterns and their biologies are essentially identical.[15] If one member of a pair of identical twins is reared as a female and the other as a male, the effects of prenatal brain development and prenatal gender-role socialization can be compared.

Such an experiment could not be conducted by deliberately misassigning the gender of one twin, of course; this would be highly unethical. However, many studies of identical twins— one of whom has been assigned a different gender from the other—have been done. Since these studies provide important evidence that

---

[15]Even identical twins are not necessarily exposed to the same prenatal hormones, of course, since individual differences may set up different barriers to these hormones. The presumption, however, is that the biologies of identical twins are essentially similar and that any differences in gender-role behavior are a function of social influences.

gender-role socialization is more important than biology in establishing gender identity/ role, we shall cite one such case in detail.

A young couple took their identical twin boys to a physician to be circumcised when the boys were seven months old. The physician used an electric cauterizing needle to remove the foreskin of the first twin who was brought into the operating room. When this baby's foreskin didn't give on the first try, or the second, the physician increased the current. On the third try, the surge of heat literally cooked the baby's penis. Unable to heal, it dried up and in a few days fell off completely like the stub of an umbilical cord. When the baby was about fifteen months old, the decision was made to reassign his gender as a girl. The parents began using a girl's name and dressing and treating "her" as a girl. At the age of twenty-one months, the child was brought to Johns Hopkins for removal of the testicles and feminization of the external genitalia (Money and Tucker 1975).

Although "she" had been the dominant twin in infancy, by early childhood her behavior was quite different from that of her twin brother. She preferred dresses to pants, enjoyed wearing hair ribbons, bracelets, and frilly blouses, and flirted with her father. Quite unlike her brother, she was neat and dainty, experimented happily with styles for her long hair, and often tried to help in the kitchen. Her record offers convincing evidence that gender-role socialization overrides the prenatal effects of sex hormones in determining gender identity/role (Money and Tucker 1975).[16]

In conclusion, it seems evident that although the development of appropriate gender characteristics is extraordinarily complex and is influenced by both biology and social experience, biology is not destiny. Men and women are certainly different in their biolo-

gies, but there are only four biological imperatives (the primary gender characteristics of menstruation, lactation, and gestation in the woman, and sperm production in the man). Beyond this, the overriding determiner of gender characteristics is apparently one's gender identity (see Figure 2-4).

Genetic Differences in Traits and Abilities

Populations of males and females differ in many regards (other than primary and secondary gender characteristics). On the one hand, for example, many studies find that, from infancy on, females have greater verbal facility than males, receive subtle vocal and visual messages more accurately, are less distracted by sight while listening, are more attentive to sounds and their emotional meanings, are more socially empathic, and are more interested in people. They also have better night vision than males, more sensitive taste buds, greater tactile sensitivity in all parts of the body, and better hearing, especially in the higher tones (McGuinness and Pribram 1979).

On the other hand, researchers find that males are usually more active than females and are superior in mathematical skills and visual-spatial skills.[17] Researchers also usually find males to be more aggressive, although some find that girls are just as aggressive as boys but demonstrate aggression differently.[18]

Aggression should not be confused with assertiveness. Aggression is hostile in intent and hurtful in effect. Assertiveness is the ability to make one's interest and desires known to

---

[16]Other studies with identical twins have also reached this conclusion (Money and Ehrhardt 1972).

---

[17]Note, for example, that in the regional play-offs for the U.S. Rubik's Cube championship in 1981, all winners were male, although many females competed. Solving the Rubik's Cube, of course, demands both an interest and a facility in manipulating visual-spatial components.

[18]For example, Feshbeck and Feshbeck (1973) found, in a study of first graders, that girls were more unkind and unfriendly toward a newcomer than boys were. Girls announced directly that the newcomer was not welcome, moved away, ignored the new child, expressed disdain, and rejected all of the newcomer's efforts to play with them. Boys, on the whole, were more willing to admit the newcomer to their group.

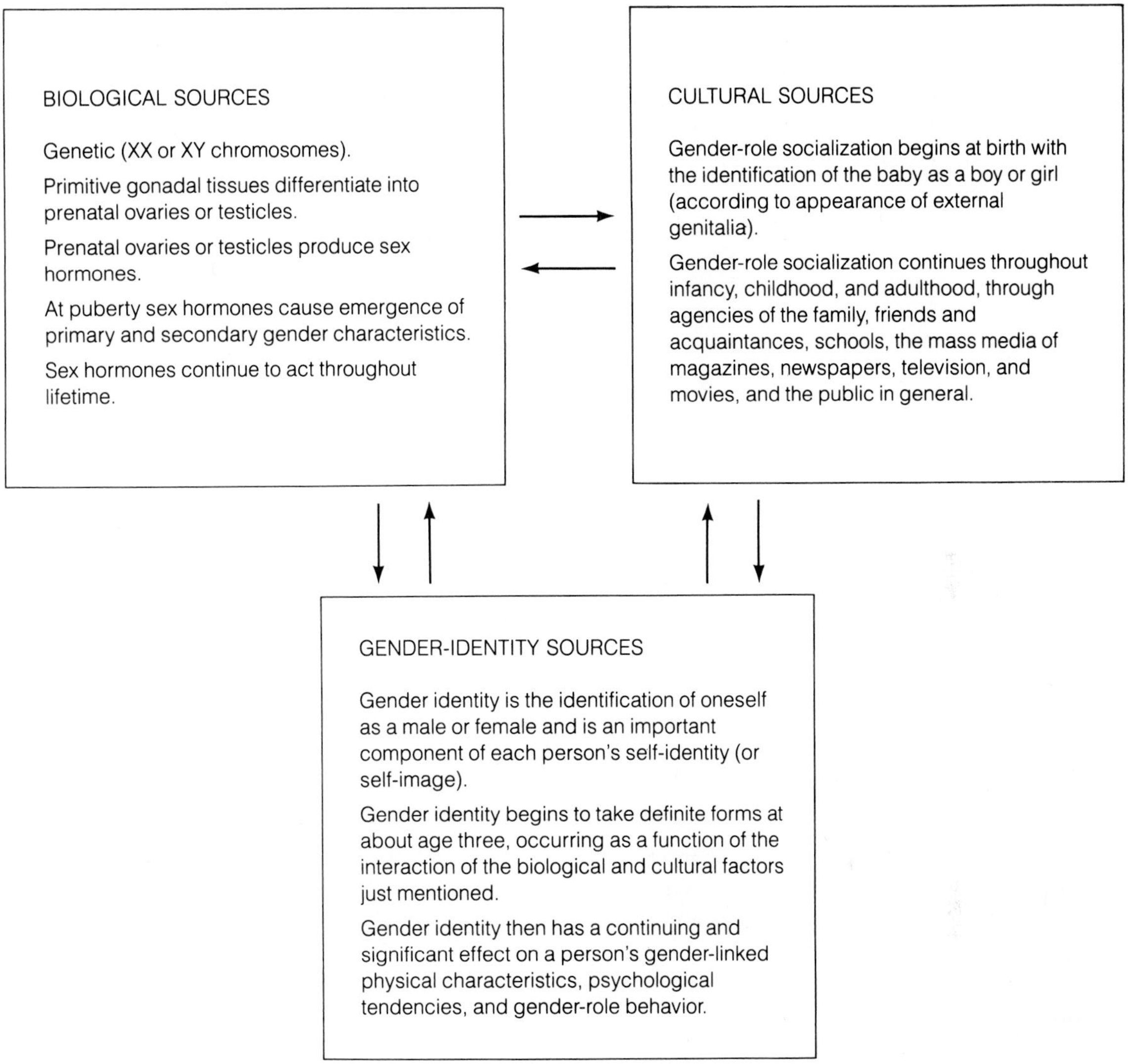

BIOLOGICAL SOURCES

Genetic (XX or XY chromosomes).

Primitive gonadal tissues differentiate into prenatal ovaries or testicles.

Prenatal ovaries or testicles produce sex hormones.

At puberty sex hormones cause emergence of primary and secondary gender characteristics.

Sex hormones continue to act throughout lifetime.

CULTURAL SOURCES

Gender-role socialization begins at birth with the identification of the baby as a boy or girl (according to appearance of external genitalia).

Gender-role socialization continues throughout infancy, childhood, and adulthood, through agencies of the family, friends and acquaintances, schools, the mass media of magazines, newspapers, television, and movies, and the public in general.

GENDER-IDENTITY SOURCES

Gender identity is the identification of oneself as a male or female and is an important component of each person's self-identity (or self-image).

Gender identity begins to take definite forms at about age three, occurring as a function of the interaction of the biological and cultural factors just mentioned.

Gender identity then has a continuing and significant effect on a person's gender-linked physical characteristics, psychological tendencies, and gender-role behavior.

Evidence from matched pairs of hermaphrodites and other sources indicates that, although the bases of gender characteristics are highly complex and interrelated, the overriding factor seems to be one's gender identity.

FIGURE 2-4

Sources of adult gender characteristics

others, and in this regard women are probably no different from men (Argyle et al. 1968).

It should be emphasized that although researchers usually find that females are less aggressive than males, there is no evidence that females (girls or women) are more *submissive*, or that females are more likely to withdraw or yield under an attack. In mixed adult

Mary Lou Retton, who was awarded a perfect 10 for her performance on the horse vault in the 1984 Olympic Games, is only one example of a superb female athlete.

AP/Wide World Photos

Evidence from studies of epileptics indicates that, whereas a man is more likely to have his speech center on the left of his brain and spatial skills on the right, a woman's verbal and spatial abilities are more likely to be duplicated on both sides of the brain (Goleman 1978). This difference between the genders in brain lateralization (having different characteristics in the left and right sides of the brain) may have important implications for activities that combine linguistic and spatial skills. For example, it may be easier for women to perform tasks that combine the two in a single activity, such as understanding what a person is communicating nonverbally as well as verbally. This may give rise to greater social or interactional skills or a greater ability to understand others intuitively.

Contrary to common belief, there is no evidence that males are genetically programmed to be better athletes than females, except in sports where size and strength are important advantages. In sports such as swimming and bicycle racing women are under no genetic handicap, and there is no reason why they can't perform as well as men. Before puberty, there is no difference at all in genetic capacity for sports, except those differences that are the result of cultural factors. (See the vignette, "Are Males Superior to Females in Athletic Ability?")

Even if male-female differences in traits and abilities do exist and are genetically based, what is the practical significance of these differences? If baby boys are genetically programmed to be more active than baby girls (on the average), or females have more verbal facility than males, or males have better visual-spatial perception, what does this signify? First, individual differences in these regards are more important than group norms. Second, the influence of gender-role socialization (that is, its effect on the gender identity/role and upon expectations of the individual) is far more important than the relatively slight differentiation in genetically based abilities.

pairs or in groups, the leadership role tends to be assumed by a man in the early stages, but in later stages women appear to be as dominant as men (Maccoby and Jacklin 1974).

Are Males Superior to Females in Athletic Ability?

Traditionally people have believed that males have greater athletic ability than females. However, although women were virtually barred from sports in U.S. society until the twentieth century, they now play most competitive sports just as well as men except at the top levels, and even there women are now surpassing men in some events. For example, swimmer Diana Nyad, who swam around Manhattan Island in 1976, beat the men's fastest time by about two hours. The gap between the track records of men and women has dwindled significantly, especially for long-distance races. Men and women are well matched in bicycling, since their leg strength relative to body weight is equal. Women are also equalling or even surpassing men in competitive diving, swimming, and tumbling. (Mary Lou Retton, "America's Sweetheart" whose gymnastic performance electrified spectators at the 1984 Olympic Games, is only one example of a superb female athlete.)

It is even becoming apparent that women have the same potential for strength development as do men of comparable size. Although the strength difference between nonathletic men and nonathletic women is quite pronounced, these differences are apparently more a function of life-style than biology. For example, in a brief period of weight training, women increased their strength by 30 percent in ten weeks, whereas men increased theirs by only 26 percent (Douglas and Miller 1977). This study found an even greater relative increase in arm and shoulder strength, with women's strength increasing 26 percent while men's increased only 17 percent. After six months, women were able to press weights of 150 pounds, which is considerably more than the average untrained man can press. Moreover, since athletes probably use no more than 20 percent of their muscle strength, the size of a woman's muscles should not prevent her from approaching the strength of a man. Female athletes have traditionally not trained with weights for fear of developing bulky muscles. However, muscle contour depends on testosterone levels in the bloodstream. In one study, female athletes increased their flexed bicep circumference by only a quarter of an inch after six months of lifting, although their upper-arm strength increased considerably (Douglas and Miller 1977).

The most recent studies find no significant difference in athletic ability between boys and girls under age twelve, except those that can be attributed directly to different experiences. For example, boys can throw a ball farther than girls can when using the preferred arm, but if the inexperienced (non-preferred) arm is used, boys and girls throw a ball the same distance.

It is difficult to compare males and females in factors of athletic ability other than strength and endurance. For example, should skill in balancing be measured by ability to walk on a narrow beam (girls do better) or ability to climb a free-standing ladder (boys do better)? Reaction time is another characteristic in which sometimes males and sometimes females do better, depending on the design of the test. Recent studies find no perceptible difference in psychological factors such as achievement drive between male and female athletes (Douglas and Miller 1977).

In the world of sports, then, in which men have long dominated, it appears that biological characteristics are a relatively negligible factor, while training, experience, expectation, and self-image are far more significant.

For example, whatever inherent handicap men might have in verbal facility and intuitive skills (as compared to women), they have nevertheless dominated such fields as oratory, poetry, and diplomacy. Nor has men's lower inherent ability for fine-muscle movements kept them from becoming violinists, surgeons, and magicians. Nor have their inherently less sensitive taste buds kept them from becoming successful chefs. Certainly any skill improves

Wendy Watriss/Frederick Baldwin/Woodfin Camp & Associates

Gender-role socialization is becoming more relaxed; it is now commonplace for girls to play Little League baseball with boys.

with practice, and the amount of practice a person gets in any field depends upon gender-role socialization, interest, expectations, and opportunity—all of which are social, not biological, factors.

Some jobs such as fire fighting, some aspects of police work, piano moving, oil rigging, and logging may be difficult for most women because of the importance of size and strength (although some women are stronger than the average men who hold these jobs). Certainly, however, for more than 99 percent of all occupations in our contemporary society, there is no reason why members of both genders cannot perform equally well, depending on such individual factors as interest, aptitude, ability, education, training, expectation, opportunity, and self-image.

For a summary of gender-linked differences in abilities and in physical and psychological traits, see Figure 2-5.

Masculinity and Femininity

Individuals who demonstrate what the society regards as predominantly male characteristics are usually called *masculine*, whereas those who demonstrate what the society regards as predominantly female characteristics are usually called *feminine*. However, the cultural ideals of masculinity and femininity differ markedly from one society to another.

In a group that idealizes *macho* qualities in men, aggressive behavior is regarded as masculine and submissive behavior is regarded as feminine. In contrast, in societies where macho qualities are *not* idealized in men, the man who is gentle, courteous, and considerate may be regarded as embodying idealized masculine qualities, while women may be admired for their capabilities and independence.

Masculinity and femininity are not necessarily related to one's social role. For example,

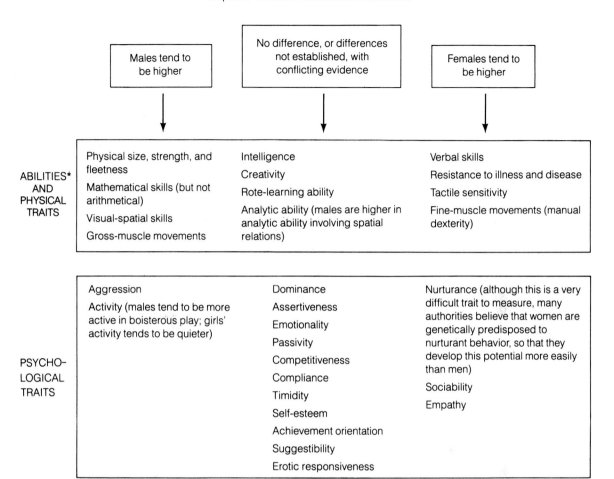

	Males tend to be higher	No difference, or differences not established, with conflicting evidence	Females tend to be higher
ABILITIES* AND PHYSICAL TRAITS	Physical size, strength, and fleetness Mathematical skills (but not arithmetical) Visual-spatial skills Gross-muscle movements	Intelligence Creativity Rote-learning ability Analytic ability (males are higher in analytic ability involving spatial relations)	Verbal skills Resistance to illness and disease Tactile sensitivity Fine-muscle movements (manual dexterity)
PSYCHO-LOGICAL TRAITS	Aggression Activity (males tend to be more active in boisterous play; girls' activity tends to be quieter)	Dominance Assertiveness Emotionality Passivity Competitiveness Compliance Timidity Self-esteem Achievement orientation Suggestibility Erotic responsiveness	Nurturance (although this is a very difficult trait to measure, many authorities believe that women are genetically predisposed to nurturant behavior, so that they develop this potential more easily than men) Sociability Empathy

*Gender-linked abilities not included here are the four biological imperatives (gestation, lactation, and menstruation in the female, and sperm production in the male).

FIGURE 2-5

Gender-linked differences in abilities and in physical and psychological traits

Sources: Data from McGuinness (1979), McGuinness and Pribram (1979), Goleman (1978), Rossi (1978), and Maccoby and Jacklin (1974).

if two lawyers—one man and one woman—are arguing a case before a jury, their social roles are identical, yet this does not necessarily mean that the role is either masculine or feminine. The female lawyer might well be the epitome of femininity as it is defined in our so-ciety, and yet she may present her case as forcefully and successfully as the male lawyer. In other words, the woman does not have to be masculine in appearance, dress, or manner to be an effective, persuasive, and skilled attor-ney. Nor does she have to be feminine. The

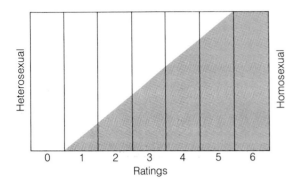

0 exclusively heterosexual with no homosexual experience
1 predominantly heterosexual, only incidental homosexual
   experience
2 predominantly heterosexual, but more than incidental
   homosexual experience
3 equal heterosexual and homosexual experience
4 predominantly homosexual, but more than incidental
   heterosexual experience
5 predominantly homosexual, but incidental heterosexual
   experience
6 exclusively homosexual

FIGURE 2-6

Heterosexual-homosexual rating scale

Source: From *Sexual Behavior in the Human Male* by Alfred C.
Kinsey et al. (1948). Reprinted by permission of the Kinsey
Institute for Research in Sex, Gender, and Reproduction, Inc.

appearance or the manner of masculinity or
femininity has little or no significance in this
situation.

Masculine and feminine social roles are
often different in our society, but the behavior
typically identified as masculine is not necessarily superior. For example, it is always the
male dancer who lifts the ballerina in a *pas de
deux* and the ballerina who permits herself to
be lifted. Yet the male dancer is not regarded as
superior in status to the ballerina. The status
of each depends on individual performance
and is unrelated to gender or to who lifts whom.

Masculinity and femininity have traditionally been regarded in our society as opposite poles on a single continuum. According to
this bipolar view, a person high in masculine
qualities would necessarily be low in feminine

ones, while the person low in feminine qualities would necessarily be high in masculine
ones. In this bipolar concept of masculinity-
femininity a person who possesses both masculine *and* feminine traits would be regarded
as emotionally disturbed, with unresolved
problems of gender identity. This bipolar concept has now been discredited. Research finds
that a person who is high in both masculine and
feminine traits is *more* emotionally healthy
and socially adjusted than one who is high in
one set of traits but low in the other (Spence
and Helmreich 1978).

A person high in both masculine and feminine traits is called *androgynous.* An androgynous person usually has a high level of self-
esteem, is achievement oriented, is socially
competent, and has no confusion of gender
identity (Spence and Helmreich 1978).

Homosexuality: A Variant in Gender Expression

Homosexuality, which is defined as sexual (or
erotic) attraction (or response) to a person of
the same gender, is no longer regarded as
abnormal behavior by either psychologists or
psychiatrists. In 1973 the American Psychiatric Association removed it from their list of
abnormal behaviors, and the American Psychological Association followed suit two years
later, in 1975. It is now formally regarded by
both the psychiatric and the psychological
establishments as simply a *variant* in sexual
expression, and it carries no implication of
abnormality.

Incidence of Homosexuality

A generation ago, the Kinsey report, *Sexual
Behavior in the Human Male* (1948), shocked
our society with its revelations of hitherto unsuspected incidence of homosexuality. Kinsey
found that there were not two separate populations of heterosexuals and homosexuals, but
that heterosexuality and homosexuality occur

on a continuum. To illustrate this principle, Kinsey devised a heterosexual-homosexual rating scale that extended from 0 to 6, indicating seven ratings or degrees of heterosexual-homosexual experience (see Figure 2-6).

Kinsey (1948) found that among the total white male population at age twenty, 69 percent were exclusively heterosexual while 5 percent were exclusively homosexual. At age twenty-five, 79 percent were exclusively heterosexual while 3 percent were exclusively homosexual.[19] However, Kinsey (1948) found that 37 percent of the total male population had at least some homosexual experience to the point of orgasm after adolescence; for those males who remained single until age thirty-five this figure was 50 percent. Moreover, the Kinsey report found that 25 percent of males had "more than incidental" homosexual experience for at least three years after age fifteen, that 13 percent had more homosexual than heterosexual experience, and that 10 percent were exclusively homosexual for at least three years.

How accurate were the Kinsey figures? There has been a great deal of disagreement. For example, Hunt (1974) found that the Kinsey figures are misleadingly high because of the overloading of the sample with interviews from the homosexual community. William Simon, in analyzing the Kinsey data, found the figure for all males who have "something more than incidental" homosexual experience to be closer to 10 percent rather than the 25 percent reported by Kinsey (Karlen 1971)—this agrees with Hunt's (1974) findings.[20] Kinsey estimated that 10 percent of all white males were "more or less exclusively homosexual" for at least three years after age fifteen, whereas Simon put the figure at 2–3 percent in analyzing the same data (Karlen 197).

Part of the problem in trying to ascertain the incidence of homosexuality in our society is this disagreement in analyzing raw data. However, another difficulty is inherent in the complexity of relating the incidence of homosexuality to various demographic categories. For example, homosexuality decreases with age among the total male population (after rising to a peak in adolescence and early adulthood), but increases with age among the unmarried population. Married men of any age have a lower incidence of homosexuality than single men of the same age.

Further complications are introduced by the varying incidence of homosexuality among other demographic groups. Some examples: Homosexual relations occur most often in men who go through high school but not beyond, and least often in those who go to college; the lower the occupational level, the higher is the incidence of homosexuality; the urban male has a higher incidence of homosexuality than the rural male (nearly double for some age cohorts);[21] Protestants have a higher incidence than Catholics (nearly twice as high in some age cohorts); and the differences between religiously devout persons and religiously inactive persons of the same faith are even greater than the differences between two equally devout persons of different faiths.

Despite disagreement in analyzing raw data and despite the complexity of various interacting demographic factors, it does seem clear that a rather large minority—somewhere between 10 and 25 percent—of the young adult male population probably has "more than incidental" homosexual experience (although

---

[19]Kinsey did not include blacks or other minority groups in his study. In other studies (Pietropinto and Simenauer 1977, Hunt 1974) the incidence of homosexuality among blacks was found to be about twice the rate among whites. Incidence among Hispanics, native Americans, and Asian-Americans in our society is unknown. In the study by Kinsey, *Sexual Behavior in the Human Female* (1953)—also limited exclusively to the white population—researchers found the incidence of female homosexuality to be about half that of male homosexuality.

[20]William Simon was for a number of years a research associate in the Kinsey Institute and has since done special work on homosexuality.

---

[21]A *cohort* is a group of individuals that have some statistical factor in common, such as an age group. The term is widely used by demographers.

the incidence varies significantly according to such factors as age at marriage, education, occupation, religious affiliation, religious conviction, rural or urban community, and race). It also seems clear that most homosexual activity takes place between unmarried males, and that the incidence of homosexuality drops markedly after marriage. Finally, it seems clear that the incidence of males who are exclusively homosexual is somewhere between 1 and 4 percent—researchers agree rather closely on this range (see Table 2-3).[22]

Research indicates that the incidence of female homosexuality or *lesbianism* is perhaps from one-third to one-half that of male homosexuality (Tavris and Sadd 1977; Hunt 1974; Kinsey, 1953, 1948).[23]

Episodic and Obligatory Homosexuality

To clarify the various levels or degrees of homosexual experience, Money and Tucker (1975) use the concepts of episodic homosexual and obligative homosexual.

Money defines *episodic homosexual* as a person who is essentially heterosexual but engages in homosexual behavior occasionally or for a limited time. He also places the person

---

TABLE 2-3

Incidence of male homosexuality in this society

	Percentage
Exclusive (obligative) homosexuality	1 – 4
Exclusively homosexual for at least three years	2 – 8
"More or less exclusively" homosexual for at least three years	2 – 10
At least as much homosexual as heterosexual experience for at least three years	4 – 18
"More than incidental" homosexual experience for at least three years	10 – 25
Any overt homosexual contact to orgasm	20 – 37

Figures given are for white males; incidence among black males is about twice that of whites.

The high figures are from Kinsey's (1948) total sample; the low figures are from Pietropinto and Simenauer (1977), Hunt (1974), Karlen (1971), Bieber et al. (1962), and Kinsey's 100 percent samples of men's clubs, schools, classes, and other groups.

The high figures are interesting because they have long been quoted as an accurate representation of our population; the low figures are probably a closer approximation of the demographic reality. (For discussion and more detail, see text.)

The incidence of homosexuality is higher among unmarried males than among married males, among urban groups than rural groups, among the less educated than the more educated, among low-status occupations than high-status occupations, among Protestants than Catholics, among religiously nondevout than devout, and among younger males than older males (except among unmarried males, where the rate increases with age).

Because of these interrelated factors, any statement regarding the overall incidence of homosexuality is of limited value.

---

[22]Some examples: Kinsey (1948) found the figure to be 4 percent; the study by Bieber et al. (1962), perhaps the most ambitious and best-known work of its type, found 1 to 2 percent of adult American males to be exclusively homosexual; Hunt (1974) found 1 percent of males who rated themselves as "mainly or totally" homosexual; Pietropinto and Simenauer (1977) found the figure to be 1.3 percent for adult white males, with about twice this figure for blacks (2.5 percent); and finally, the Mattachine Society, one of the oldest homophile organizations in the United States, estimates that 1 percent of the adult males in the country are exclusively homosexual and belong to the openly homosexual community in their cities, with perhaps another 1 to 2 percent that are exclusively homosexual and avoid the openly homosexual community but are a part of the homosexual "underground."

[23]For example, Kinsey found that 15 percent of single women and 2 to 3 percent of married women had at least one homosexual experience after age nineteen; Hunt's comparable figures were 12 percent and 3 percent. Tavris and Sadd found the same 3 percent; however, their data reveal that, of these, 1.7 percent had done so only once, 0.8 percent had done so occasionally, and only 0.4 percent had homosexual relations often.

who alternates between male and female sex partners—a pattern usually called *bisexual* or *ambisexual*—into the category of episodic homosexuality.

Money defines *obligative homosexual* as a person who is exclusively homosexual throughout his or her lifetime. The obligative homosexual is erotically, aesthetically, and romantically attracted solely to members of his or her own gender, and feels no such attraction to members of the opposite gender (Money and Tucker 1975).

Money finds that episodic homosexuality occurs among young males chiefly because they are inexperienced or shy in relating to girls or are living in a situation where girls are not readily available, such as a boarding school, a military camp, or a detention center. Presumably episodic homosexuality would occur among females for the same reasons, although Money considered only the male homosexual in his discussion.

Money also finds that obligative homosexuals may be divided into those who prefer to assume the masculine role in romantic and erotic advances and those who prefer the feminine role, although there are also those who have no preference in this regard and may take either role. A male homosexual who prefers a masculine role may be almost indistinguishable from a heterosexual male in his social interactions. He differs little from other men except for the focus of his romantic, aesthetic, and erotic interests; he may even occasionally be attracted to women. However, an obligative male homosexual who prefers the feminine role differs from the average heterosexual in ways other than his romantic, aesthetic, and erotic preferences. He may exhibit feminine responses and behavior in many social interactions. Like a woman, he enjoys receiving a man's penis. This is the one type of homosexual who is obviously "different" in that he sends conflicting gender messages. If it were possible to stereotype homosexuals as effeminate in appearance and behavior (it is not), this is the person who would most closely fit. The limp-wristed type of male homosexual (the term used by the homosexual community itself is *queen)* is statistically rare, although the precise incidence is unknown (Money and Tucker 1975).[24]

Rocky Weldon/Jeroboam, Inc.

The incidence of female homosexuality in our society is about one-third to one-half that of male homosexuality.

Similarly, the obligative female homosexual (lesbian) who prefers the male role in romantic and erotic advances and who has a masculine appearance and manner (known as *butch* in the

---

[24]The opposite of the effeminate *queen* is the supermale, macho, "leather-and-chain" homosexual (called *rough trade* by the homosexual community). Another stereotype is the squash-playing, suntanned, athletic, or "executive-type" homosexual. Although the incidence of both these types is probably higher than that of the queen type, most homosexuals do not fall into any category or stereotype at all, but are indistinguishable from heterosexuals in manner, dress, appearance, activities, and interests (except for choice of sexual partner), as well as in self-esteem and emotional stability (Bell and Weinberg 1978).

Depending on various demographic factors such as education, race, and rural or urban community, 10 to 20 percent of young men have some active homosexual experience, although only 1 to 4 percent are obligative homosexuals throughout their lives.

Terry Evans/Magnum Photos Inc.

homosexual community) is also statistically rare. The great majority of female homosexuals are indistinguishable from other women in manner or appearance, although again the incidence of "mannish" lesbians is unknown (Bell and Weinberg 1978).

Attitudes toward Homosexuality

Attitudes toward homosexuality have seesawed through the ages and from culture to culture. The ancient Greeks accepted it simply as an alternative to heterosexual behavior, whereas the ancient Hebrews regarded it as a capital offense: "If a man lies with a man as with a woman, both have committed an abomi-nation; they shall be put to death" (Lev. 20: 13). The Romans were quite relaxed about many kinds of sexual behavior in classical times, but with the spread of Christianity, homosexuality was increasingly condemned. By the sixth century A.D., the Justinian Code doomed homosexuals to torture and mutilation as a prelude to death.

In the United States today, homosexuals have been systematically ostracized by much of the society until very recently. Homosexuality was regarded as an abnormality by the American Psychiatric Association until 1973 and by the American Psychological Association until 1975. Homosexuals were routinely dismissed from military and government serv-

The ancient Greeks accepted homosexuality simply as an
alternative to heterosexual behavior.
Greek vase (detail)

ice until 1978, when the U.S. Court of Appeals
ruled that the Pentagon could not discharge
homosexuals from the military without offering
specific reasons in addition to homosexuality.
According to a nationwide poll by Indiana University's Institute for Sex Research in 1978,
fully two-thirds of the adult population considered homosexuality to be "very obscene and
vulgar," and a third of these thought homosexuals should be jailed or put on probation.

There is some indication, however, that the
U.S. population may be growing more tolerant
of homosexuality. One indication of this, of
course, is the reclassification by both APAs in
the mid-1970s. In some areas, homosexuals
have won political rights and even grudging social approval. There is a Gay Rights Movement, gay student groups have been formed on
many college campuses, and some well-known
and highly publicized figures have openly proclaimed their homosexuality.

Some religious groups still consider homosexual relations as unnatural and sinful, but
others have subscribed to the view that homosexuality is merely an alternate form of natural
sexual expression. An influential statement by
British Quakers in 1963, for example, held that
"homosexual affection can be as selfless as
heterosexual affection" and therefore is not
necessarily "a sin." At a 1967 symposium on
homosexuality sponsored by Manhattan's
Cathedral Church of St. John the Divine,

ninety Episcopal priests agreed that the church should classify homosexual acts between consenting adults as "morally neutral" and such acts should be judged by the results, which may very well be good. The Reverend Walter D. Dennis, then Canon of St. John's, said, "A homosexual relation should be judged by the same criteria as a heterosexual marriage—that is, whether it is intended to foster a . . . relation of love" (Auchincloss 1968, p. 74).

In recent years a number of theologians have challenged the Catholic church's teaching that homosexual activity is morally wrong. They argue that a committed relation between two members of the same sex is better than no marriage at all and certainly better than promiscuity. In addition, many priests advise sexually active homosexuals to take communion and offer special mass for members of Dignity, a nationwide organization of Catholic homosexuals (Sciolino 1984).

Well-Being and Homosexuality

All research from 1957 (Hooker) to the present finds that homosexuals are no more apt to have psychological or social difficulties than heterosexuals. In fact, at least two studies (Reiss and Miller 1974, Wilson and Green 1971) found a higher incidence of emotional disturbance among heterosexual women than among lesbians they studied. Apparently, the only significant discernible difference between homosexuals and heterosexuals is that homosexuals prefer, in varying degrees, to relate affectionately, aesthetically, romantically, and erotically to members of their own gender (Paul 1981, Masters and Johnson 1979, Bell and Weinberg 1978).

A homosexual is, nevertheless, a member of a minority group and may be subject to the pressures and difficulties commonly experienced by minorities. For this reason, most homosexuals prefer to dissemble or remain "in the closet," professing to be heterosexuals in their conversation, attitudes, and life-styles. Although many homosexuals "come out" or openly avow their homosexuality, the Mattachine Society estimates that at least two-thirds of homosexuals attempt to "pass" as heterosexuals, maintaining a low sexual profile and revealing their preference only to other homosexuals in relatively safe situations (Hunt 1974).

Causes of Homosexuality

The causes of homosexuality are very complex, involving physical, social, and self-identity factors. They are not well understood, but then the causes of heterosexuality (or erotic attraction to the *opposite* gender) are not very well understood either.

A major study of homosexual men and women by the Kinsey Institute for Sex Research (Bell et al. 1981) failed to find support for most of the traditional theories about the origins of homosexuality. These theories have emphasized the parent's role, the lack of heterosexual opportunities in adolescence, or traumatic heterosexual experiences in adolescence. Rather, the Kinsey Institute report concludes that a homosexual orientation seems to stem from a deep-seated predisposition, possibly biological, that first appears in childhood. For males in particular, sexual orientation seems to evolve early in life—often before the teenage years. The study found that homosexual feelings almost always preceded homosexual activities by several years.

Support for the biological predisposition toward homosexuality is provided by the first clear laboratory evidence of biological differences between homosexual and heterosexual men—dissimilar responses to certain hormones. In a group of homosexual men the pattern of response to an estrogen injection was found to be between the responses of heterosexual men and heterosexual women (Gladue 1984).

The Kinsey Institute study also found that homosexuals were no more likely than heterosexuals to have been traumatized by an early heterosexual experience, and they did not have fewer heterosexual dating experiences than heterosexuals. The main difference found was that the homosexuals were less likely to have enjoyed their youthful heterosexual encounters.

Although the homosexual men tended as youths to be less involved socially than other boys were, isolation from peers apparently has no independent causal connection to the development of a homosexual orientation. Rather, this relative isolation seemed to reflect the fact that the prehomosexual boys felt and acted "different" from other boys (Bell et al. 1981).

The same study found that boys who grew up with dominant mothers and weak, inadequate fathers were no more likely to become homosexual than those in any other family settings. Other studies have found that children of homosexual parents have no higher incidence of homosexuality than children of heterosexual parents (Green 1978). Finally, there is no evidence that homosexuality is caused by the seductive attentions of a homosexual person (Bell et al. 1981).

In light of present evidence, it seems that the obligative homosexual differs from the heterosexual in terms of some innate biological factor, which remains to be discovered. Episodic homosexuality, however, may stem from any number of interacting factors that are chiefly social or psychological.

It should be emphasized that the attraction of an obligative homosexual to a person of the same gender is not simply sexual; it is fully as affectionate and romantic as heterosexual interaction. The intensity of the emotional involvement, the fear of rejection, the importance of aesthetic details, the romantic fantasies and dreams regarding the other person— all these elements of affectionate and erotic attraction are the same for the homosexual as for the heterosexual. As noted earlier, the only difference is that the object of the homosexual's attention is a person of the same—rather than the opposite—gender. This important point has long been obscured by prejudice, half-truths, fears, and misunderstanding. (See the vignette, "The Personal Experience of Obligative Homosexuality.")

Gender Anomalies

The various aspects of gender are usually *concordant* (in accordance with one another). That is, the chromosomal (XY) male has a hormone mix with a preponderance of male sex hormones, the gender-role socialization of a male, and the gender identity of a male. Similarly, the chromosomal (XX) female has a hormone mix with a preponderance of female sex hormones, the gender-role socialization of a female, and the gender identity of a female.

However, the various aspects of gender may be *discordant* (not in accordance with one another). For example, it is quite possible for a chromosomal (XY) male to have body tissue that does not respond to the masculinizing male hormones so that he has the secondary gender characteristics of a female. Or a chromosomal (XX) female may have a preponderance of female sex hormones and the gender identity of a female but have received the gender-role socialization of a male. In either case, the three aspects of gender—biology, socialization (or culture), and gender identity—are not concordant, and gender confusion results.

Although there are endless possibilities for such confusion, they fall into four general categories: chromosomal anomalies, hermaphroditism, transsexualism, and transvestitism.

Chromosomal Anomalies

Gender anomalies may begin at conception, with the fertilized egg failing to have a normal

The Personal Experience of Obligative Homosexuality

The fears and wistful longings of a young obligative homosexual who wishes to "pass" for a heterosexual and feels that there is something shameful about his sexual orientation are expressed with much sensitivity in an autobiographical novel by John Reid (pseudonym) (1973) that has received great critical acclaim. In the novel, Reid describes how from early childhood he was erotically and romantically attracted to boys and not to girls. Until his early twenties, he took great pains to conceal these feelings, counterfeiting heterosexual responses in order to be regarded as "normal" by his friends. In a very revealing passage he describes his difficulties in doing this.

Noticing attractive girls was not as easy as it sounds. . . . As I was attracted by boys, not girls, I had to use the most mechanical techniques in deciding which girls were "attractive." . . . I would nervously rush through a little check list. I knew girls in laced shoes or combat boots were out. I knew legs were important and had heard someone talk scornfully about girls with "piano legs," so I tried to avoid those. I would ignore any girls whose heads did not at least come up even with parking meters as they walked by, as well as those whose heads brushed the bus stop signs. Frizzy redheads, for some reason, were out. The hardest part, especially under winter coats, was to determine whether a girl was "built" or just fat. There was nothing whatever to be gained by leering and chortling over a dog. One slip like that and my cover would be blown: *You're not really attracted to girls!* YOU'RE FAKING IT! (pp. 41 – 42).

After successfully disguising his interest in boys and his disinterest in girls throughout his high school years, the problem intensified when Reid enrolled as a freshman at Yale.

The first thing I did that year was subscribe to *Playboy.* Like a blind man at a silent movie I would religiously thumb through my monthly *Playboy,* forcing myself to check out, leer, and nudge my roommate Roger. I liked *Playboy* because I didn't have to worry about chortling over a dog by mistake. I would hang the centerfold on the wall over my bed for all to see (p. 47).

When Reid did decide to "come out of the closet" and openly avow his homosexuality, he found an enormous sense of relief.

Anyway I had come to know more about myself that summer, and I had decided quite definitely there was nothing "wrong" with the way I was, nothing to feel guilty about. I was tired of feeling guilty. . . . I began to feel indignity, instead (p. 146).

Nevertheless, the struggle Reid has with himself is revealed in the fact that he uses a pseudonym in writing the book. Although he has revealed his sexual orientation to his friends, he still hesitates to reveal it to the general public—ostensibly to spare his parents the grief and publicity were his homosexuality to become generally known.

XX or XY chromosomal structure. For example, the fertilized egg may have an XO chromosomal pattern, with one X chromosome missing. The adult with this pattern is a female but usually has a deficient reproductive system. Or the fertilized egg may have an extra X chromosome (XXX). The adult with this chromosomal structure is very definitely a female but is often mentally deficient (Money and Tucker 1975).

Males with an extra Y chromosome (XYY) tend to be taller than average, and research indicates that they are also more aggressive and impulsive and slower to develop self-control. Curiously, although the XYY male is "supermasculine" in terms of size and aggression, he is often sterile (Money and Tucker 1975).

The male with an extra X chromosome (XYX) typically has a low level of androgen and underdeveloped primary and secondary gender characteristics, commonly suffers from gender-identity confusion, has a low sex drive, and is often sterile (Money and Tucker 1975).

Hermaphroditism

In biology, the term *hermaphrodite* refers to a plant or animal that normally possesses both male and female reproductive systems on the same individual. Most flowering plants, for example, are hermaphroditic; the flowers contain both male and female sexual parts.

It is extremely rare for a human being to be fertile as both a male and a female; when the word refers to humans *hermaphrodite* is defined more broadly as a person with physical characteristics of both genders. Occasionally, for example, a baby is born with a male (XY) chromosomal pattern, testicles, and a preponderance of male hormones in his hormone mix, but imperfectly formed genitalia—a small, open-ended penis, undescended testicles, and an incompletely fused scrotum. Similarly, a female baby with XX chromosomes, ovaries, and preponderance of female hormones in her hormone mix may be born with an unusually enlarged clitoris and partially fused labia, so that the external genitalia resemble those of a male.

Such infants are often misassigned as the wrong gender at birth—the chromosomal male receiving the gender assignment "female," while the chromosomal female receives the gender assignment "male." This misassignment may not be discovered until the person reaches puberty, when unexpected secondary gender characteristics begin to develop. At this time, the genetic female, who has been raised as a male and has the gender identity of a male, begins to develop breasts and other female secondary gender characteristics. The genetic male, who has been raised as a female and has the gender identity of a female, begins to develop a deeper voice, a beard, and other secondary gender characteristics of a male.

In such cases the person's gender may be re-defined in accordance with his or her newly developing physical characteristics, or the physical characteristics may be altered by administration of synthetic hormones so that they conform to the person's gender identity. As we have seen, gender identity almost invariably overrides biology, so that the usual choice is to alter the physical structure. Cost to the individual in terms of self-doubt, anguish, and social adjustment can be, of course, horrendous.

Transsexualism

Occasionally one's gender identity conflicts with one's anatomy *and* with gender-role socialization. For example, an XY male who has a normal male sex hormone mix, whose body tissue responds normally to these hormones, and who has experienced the gender-role socialization of a male, may nevertheless feel that he really is a woman—trapped in a man's body. Similarly, an XX female with a normal female sex hormone mix and the gender-role socialization of a female, may feel that she really is a man trapped in a woman's body. The person who feels such a discordance between gender identity on the one hand and biological and gender-role aspects of gender on the other is called a *transsexual*.

In short, transsexuals have gender identities that are not in accordance with their biologies or their gender roles. They feel uncomfortable with their bodies and with the social ramifications of their gender-related places in society.

Medical science can now help transsexuals change their bodies to conform to their gender identities. A man can have his penis, scrotum, and testicles surgically removed and replaced with a functioning vagina. With sex hormone therapy, he can then develop the breasts, body contours, and hair distribution of a normal female. Similarly, a woman can undergo treatment to become a man: Her breasts can be surgically removed and male genitalia constructed, and hormone therapy can give her the typical male secondary gender characteristics.

Such operations have their limits, however. The new woman's body cannot become pregnant, and science has not yet found a way to construct an erectile penis for the new man. The basic task can, however, be accomplished. The person can be given a physical body in which he or she can feel comfortable—one that is in accordance with his or her gender identity. Moreover, the courts support the new gender identification of the person who has undergone such a sex change—the person is now legally considered to be the reassigned gender. The male restructured as a female is now identified as a female on her driver's license, may participate in formally organized sports as a female, and may marry as a female. Similarly, the genetic female who is now restructured as a male is considered legally to *be* a male and has all the usual male social and legal prerogatives.

Sex-change surgery is lengthy, painful, and expensive. That so many transsexuals go through the process indicates how strongly gender identity is felt—even when it conflicts with the biological reality and with a lifetime of gender-role socialization.

Transvestitism

A *transvestite* is a person who periodically feels compelled to impersonate and wear the clothes of the opposite gender (to *cross-dress*) and to be accepted in a social situation as a member of the opposite gender (to *pass*). Most transvestites are men. The male transvestite is usually not homosexual and is not necessarily effeminate (as our culture defines the term). On the contrary, he is often very masculine in appearance, manner, and dress and often works in an occupation that is characteristically macho, such as truck driver, stevedore, or construction worker (Money and Tucker 1975).

In the United States today most communities have laws prohibiting transvestitism, although these laws are seldom enforced.

There are no reliable figures on the incidence of transvestitism.

GENDER IN HISTORICAL PERSPECTIVE

Although the specific form of gender-role behavior varies from one society to another, all known societies assign different roles to males and females and socialize them differently from infancy to fulfill these roles.

As we have seen, two basic factors underlie this role differentiation: the biological imperative that women bear children and the social convention that women usually have the chief responsibility for the care of children or seeing that they are cared for. This does not mean that most families throughout history have assigned the mother sole responsibility for caring for her children.[25] On the contrary, in most of the world's societies throughout history, and in our own society until the late nineteenth century, child care was shared by the husband (who also worked in or near the household), older siblings, other relatives, and other nonfamily members of the household (Margolis 1984). However, women have always had the final reponsibility for organizing and providing for child care, especially for infants and very young children, even though mothers are not necessarily the primary or exclusive caretakers of their own children (Gough 1971).[26]

---

[25]It should be noted that the contemporary nuclear family household in the United States, with the mother relatively isolated, is very unusual. The married women's residence in a nuclear family household—made up exclusively of parents and children—is found in only 6.1 percent of the societies listed in the massive *Human Relations Area Files,* the largest systematic compilation of cross-cultural data in the world.

[26]One study of 186 societies around the world found that less than half—46 percent—of the mothers were primary or exclusive caretakers of infants. In another 40 percent of the societies in the sample, primary care of infants was the respon-

Since women have traditionally fulfilled economic roles that are consistent with child-bearing and child care, they have performed work that can be done within or near the home and that does not seriously interfere with their function of bearing and then assuming the responsibility, with older siblings and female relatives, for rearing these children (Gough 1971).[27]

The Movement of Women into the Work World

During the latter part of the nineteenth century and the early part of the twentieth century, more and more families were moving into cities and urban areas where the husband and father could find work in a factory or mill.[28] By the end of the nineteenth century in the United States, the typical family no longer lived on a subsistence farm, where they would produce as well as consume the economic goods necessary for family life. Women were no longer able to provide for an equal or greater share of the family subsistence needs with work done in or near the home, and for the first time in human history most women became dependent on their husbands to provide economic support for themselves and their children.[29] This pattern persisted from the late nineteenth to the mid-twentieth century, with the average middle class wife in U.S. society economically dependent upon her husband (Margolis 1984, Gough 1971).

Not until the 1940s did married women with children begin to enter the world of employment outside the household in significant numbers—coincident with the impact of World War II upon the fabric of U.S. society.[30] Women filled the urgent need for workers in shipbuilding and other war-related industries as men were drafted into the armed services. Women were also quickly initiated into the business world of offices and stores. These trends continued after the war. It should be noted that women were earning only about 60 percent of working men's pay, and that this discrepancy still persists (see Figure 2-7). This issue will be discussed further in a later section, "Gender Inequities."

From 1940 to 1960, the proportion of married women who worked outside the home doubled—from 15 to 30 percent (Harris 1981). The trend continued to accelerate in the decades of the 1960s and 1970s. By 1980, 80 percent of young married women, with husbands but with no small children, were working. (If there was a child between ages six and seventeen in the family, 63 percent of mothers were working; if there was one or more children under age six, 49 percent were working.) All told, more than half of all married women in their prime reproductive years—under age 25—were working full-time outside the home. Most employed mothers (71 percent in March 1984) worked full time—thirty-five hours a week or more.[31] By 1984, as a result of the growing number of employed mothers, the

---

sibility of others, usually siblings (Margolis 1984, Lambert et al. 1979, Weisner and Gallimore 1977).

[27]In societies with an economic system based on hunting and gathering or agriculture, young children typically are cared for by older siblings or by their mother or another female relative while the woman is gathering or gardening (Minge-Klevana 1980, Brown 1970).

[28]In 1800, 90 percent of the population in the United States lived on subsistence farms. This dropped to 19 percent in 1900 and to 2.4 percent in 1982 (U.S. Dept. of Agriculture, Economic Research Service, 1984, p. 649).

[29]For more than 99 percent of human history, during the Hunting and Gathering Period and the Agricultural Period (which began about 5–6,000 years ago with the invention of the plow in the Middle East), women provided more than an equal share of the economic and subsistence goods of the family (Gough 1971). Until the late nineteenth century in the United States, the agrarian economy presented no clear-cut separation between the home and the world of work. Male and female spheres of activity were contiguous and often overlapped, and the demands of the domestic economy ensured that neither gender was excluded from productive labor (Margolis 1984, Beecher 1977, Ariès 1965).

---

[30]In 1940, for example, only about 15 percent of the married women in the United States were working, and most of these were of the lower class (Harris 1981).

[31]U.S. Bureau of Labor Statistics, *Special Labor Force Reports*, Nos. 13, 130, and 134 (1984), and *Monthly Labor Review* (January 1985).

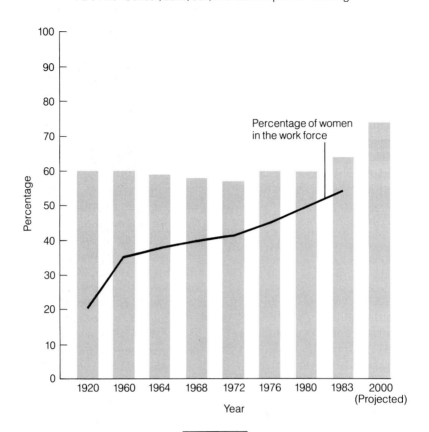

FIGURE 2-7

Women in the work force and their percentage
of men's pay

Sources: U.S. Bureau of Labor Statistics, "Employed Persons
by Selected Characteristics: 1970 to 1983" (1985);
U.S. Bureau of the Census, "Median Income of Families
and Unrelated Individuals, in Current (1982) Dollars:
1955 to 1982" (1985),
and earlier issues; Smith (1985);
Smith and Ward (1984).

traditional nuclear family—consisting of a wage-earning husband, a wife homemaker, and minor children—accounted for less than 5 percent of all American households (see Figure 2-8).[32]

The movement of married women with young children into the world of work outside the home has, of course, caused a problem in child care. Indeed, this conflict between the need to provide nurture for school-age children and the need to work outside the home is one of the gravest concerns of our time. In a survey of working women, 29 percent of the clerical, service, factory, and plant workers cited child

[32]U.S. Bureau of Labor Statistics, *Special Labor Force Report* (October 9, 1984).

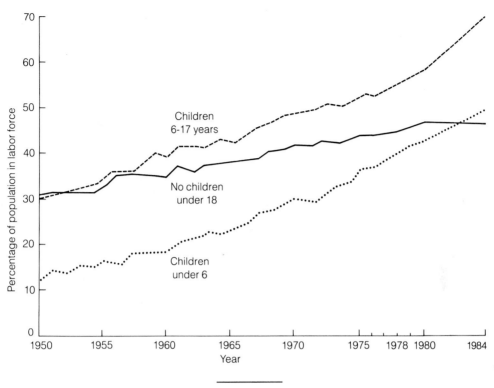

FIGURE 2-8

Work force participation rates of married women, with
husband present, by presence and age of own children,
1950–1984

Source: Data from U.S. Bureau of Labor Statistics, *Special
Labor Force Reports*, Nos. 13, 130, and 134 (1984), and
Monthly Labor Review, (January 1985).

care as one of their major problems. Among
professional, managerial, and technical workers, it was even higher—36 percent (U.S.
Commission on Civil Rights 1981).

How are the essential functions of nurturance and socialization provided for children in
our contemporary society when the mother
leaves the household to work? This dilemma of
working versus child care is being resolved in
various ways. Many mothers place the pre-
school child (or children) in a commercial day
care center; others leave the child with a relative (often a grandmother) who lives nearby (or

shares the household); others use a mothers'
cooperative, where mothers take turns caring
for each other's children.

The older, school-age child may simply be
given a key to the house. Sociologists and
psychologists are concerned about these
"latch-key" children who come home from
school and let themselves into an empty house.
There are at least 2 million latch-key children
in the United States between the ages of seven
and thirteen. Studies find that mothers of
latch-key children often worry about the effect
of their absence on their children's well-being

Sociologists and psychologists are concerned about the plight of "latch-key" children who come home from school and let themselves into an empty house.

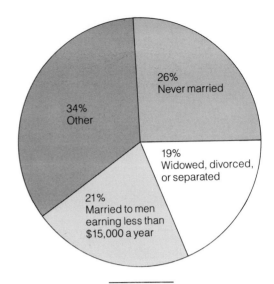

34% Other

26% Never married

19% Widowed, divorced, or separated

21% Married to men earning less than $15,000 a year

FIGURE 2-9

Women in the work force in 1983

Source: Data from U.S. Bureau of Labor Statistics, "Women in the Work Force, 1983" (October 1984).

and often feel guilty about what they uneasily perceive as "neglect" of their parental responsibilities.[33]

Parents will continue to find various solutions to the problem of child care both for preschoolers and for school-age children since no one—psychologist, sociologist, or politician—envisions a return to the agrarian society of the past, with most mothers working in or near the household and with a support network of other women, siblings, and other relatives to manage the nurture and rearing of infants and children.

Unmarried women have also been entering the work force in rising numbers since the era of World War I, and this trend also accelerated

in the 1940s.[34] Twenty-five million new jobs were filled by women (married and unmarried) between 1947 and 1978. By 1983, women were swelling the work force at the rate of almost 2 million every year, and two out of three new jobs were taken by women.[35]

The idea persists that women work for psychological rewards or "pin" money; however, studies find that most women work for

[33]U. S. Commission on Civil Rights, *Child Care and Equal Opportunity for Women* (1981).

[34]Unmarried women, especially those of the lower class, began entering the work world in the eighteenth century in England and in the nineteenth century in the United States, holding menial jobs and working in factories and mills. (There was little other work then available for women.) By the 1920s, women had begun to penetrate the world of business as part of the sweeping cultural changes that occurred in response to World War I (they replaced men who had been sent overseas). During the 1920s and 1930s, unmarried women moved increasingly into white-collar positions as secretaries, telephone operators, and sales clerks in retail stores. Few married women worked, however—whether lower or middle class—unless their husbands had abandoned them, had died, or were seriously ill and incapacitated. As we have seen, by 1940, only about 15 percent of the married women in U.S. society were working, and most of these were of the lower class (Harris 1981).

[35]U.S. Bureau of Labor Statistics, *Special Labor Force Reports*, Nos. 13, 130, and 134 (1984).

precisely the same reason that men work—"to put food on the table." In late 1984, for example, The National Commission on Working Women reported that of the women in the work force in 1983, 26 percent had never married; 19 percent were widowed, divorced, or separated; and 21 percent were married to men earning less than $15,000 a year (see Figure 2-9).

The Change in Women's Childbearing Functions

Married women could not have entered the world of employment outside the household so long as there were housefuls of children to care for. Families were largest in the eighteenth century, but still the average woman had seven children at the beginning of the nineteenth century. In the mid-nineteenth century, one-third of all married women had seven to ten or more children.[36] Even at the beginning of the twentieth century, the average married woman had five children—which means that half of all married women had more than this number—and families of nine or ten children were not uncommon (Westoff and Parke 1972).

Until the twentieth century in the United States, a married woman was expected "to be fruitful and multiply" and was regarded as lazy or selfish if she did not have a large family. Not only were wives expected to bear many children, but they had little choice in the matter. Virtually all married women were woefully ignorant about reliable methods of contraception. In the late nineteenth and early twentieth centuries, when families were moving from subsistence farms to urban areas and children became economic burdens, married women were sometimes in desperate straits trying to care for large families in crowded tenement conditions, and the demand for information re-

garding contraception became urgent. Legislators, who had already enacted bills outlawing abortion, responded to this new threat to public morality with stringent measures controlling the dissemination of birth control information. At the federal level, Congress enacted legislation that prohibited sending information on contraceptives through the mail. (This was the infamous "Comstock Law" of 1873). This law was rigorously enforced; violation was punishable by a heavy fine *and* ten years in prison. Following this federal legislation, a series of state statutes were enacted to limit the availability of contraceptives.[37] Twenty-four states banned the advertising, publication, or distribution of information on contraceptives, and another fourteen states made it illegal for anyone, even a physician, to inform anyone about birth control devices. In these states, physicians were forbidden, by law, to provide their patients with information regarding contraception, and the physician who violated this law was likely to be sentenced to a prison term of ten years at hard labor. The claim that the physician was acting in the best interests of the patient, whose life would be endangered by pregnancy, was not an adequate defense (Gordon 1983, Gray 1979, Wilson 1979, Mohr 1978, Smith 1974).

In 1912 Margaret Sanger, a public health nurse in New York City, began a virtually single-handed campaign to provide help for women who were desperate to avoid further pregnancies. It was largely through this one dedicated woman's efforts that the general

---

[36]U.S. Bureau of the Census, *Historical Statistics of the United States*, Part I (1975, p. 53).

[37]It is interesting to note that contraceptives are still rigorously restricted and regulated in many predominantly Catholic countries. For example, in the Republic of Ireland contraceptives for men and women are now sold by pharmacists only to married couples who have a physician's prescription that specifies that the contraceptives must be used for "bona fide family planning." In 1985, a bill was introduced into Parliament that would make contraceptives available to anyone over the age of eighteen. The Roman Catholic church immediately denounced the move; the Archbishop of Dublin described the proposed change as "an invitation to turn to the path of self-indulgence and engage in premarital sex" (Associated Press, Dublin, February 7, 1985).

In the late nineteenth and early twentieth centuries, married women were often
forced to care for large families in overcrowded tenements.

Millard Sheets: *Tenement Flats,* 1934

National Museum of American Art, Smithsonian Institution, Washington

public attitude toward the use of contraceptives began to change, and the laws prohibiting the dispensing of birth control information and birth control devices were repealed. (See the vignette, "Tell Jake to Sleep on the Roof.")

Scholars are not certain just how women controlled their fertility prior to the twentieth century. Although the use of various contraceptive devices has been traced to the time of the pharaohs, 5,000 years ago, contraceptive techniques were not widely understood or used by most women, and many of the methods that were used were notably ineffective (Finch and Green 1963). Surprisingly enough, modern scholarship finds that infanticide was much more widespread in Western civilization than is generally recognized (Skolnick 1983, Shorter 1975, Trexler 1973, Langer 1972).

In the eighteenth and nineteenth centuries, for example, infanticide was one of the major

Tell Jake to Sleep on the Roof

Margaret Sanger was in New York City in 1912, working for the Visiting Nurses Association—a group of public health nurses dedicated to taking care of poverty-stricken women. These nurses went into the homes of women who lived in the tenements between 14th Street and East Broadway, where half a million people were crowded into an area designed for about one-fifth that many, living seven or eight to a room. The main task of the association was to help the women in this area through the ordeal of childbirth, which for many was a yearly event. These women were poor and malnourished, and many of them were ill. Many died in childbirth or from subsequent complications, and because they could not face still another child to care for, self-induced abortions were commonplace. The method frequently used was to insert a sharp instrument, such as a knitting needle, through the cervix to puncture the amniotic sac.

Something happened one hot summer afternoon in 1912 that was to change Margaret Sanger's life and, in time, have an enormous effect on the consciousness of our entire country. She was summoned to the room of a woman named Sadie Sachs, who was twenty-seven years old, had six children, and, in desperation, had tried to abort her current pregnancy. She was hemorrhaging so badly that Mrs. Sanger was unable to stop the bleeding. She ran for a doctor who was able to bring the hemorrhage under control but warned Mrs. Sachs that another such attempt might well be fatal. Mrs. Sachs, who was barely conscious at the time, whispered to the doctor, "Tell me the secret, please! How can I prevent it?" The doctor, who was leaving the room, turned briefly and said, "Oh, you want to have your cake and eat it, too, do you? I'll tell you the secret. Tell Jake to sleep on the roof" (Gray 1979, p. 54).

The attitude of the time was that "conjugal relations" were a husband's privilege and a wife's duty; if she became pregnant, that was God's will. Condoms were available, but it was an unusual husband who

could be persuaded to use one. Withdrawal before ejaculation was also possible, but it was even more difficult to persuade a husband to do that.

Jake chose not to sleep on the roof, use a condom, or withdraw, and Sadie Sachs was pregnant again a few months later. This time, when she tried to abort the fetus, the hemorrhaging was fatal. Margaret Sanger arrived just a few minutes before Sadie Sachs died.

The callous attitude of the doctor and the medical establishment, which was actively opposed to disseminating any information about birth control or contraceptive techniques whatever the situation, outraged Margaret Sanger. She was deeply moved by the plight of thousands of women who would risk death rather than another pregnancy. The hopelessness of these women's attempts at birth control, their high mortality rate, the naked and hungry babies wrapped in newspapers to keep them from the cold, the young children with pinched, pale, wrinkled faces dressed in rags—these conditions troubled Mrs. Sanger so deeply that she became increasingly involved in a movement to provide women with birth control information. By 1916 she was dedicating herself completely to this cause (Sanger 1937).

Margaret Sanger was arrested time after time and thrown in jail, but she persevered in fighting, almost single-handedly, the American Medical Association and the U.S. government. By sheer determination and stubborn persistence, she finally succeeded in having local, state, and federal laws prohibiting birth control repealed, and in 1923 she established the first legal birth control clinic in New York City—eleven years after Sadie Sach's death. The law against sending contraceptive information through the mail was modified in the mid-1930s. During the 1940s and 1950s many states modifed or repealed their laws prohibiting contraception, and finally in 1965, the U.S. Supreme Court struck down all remaining state laws prohibiting the use of contraceptives. Margaret Sanger died a year later in 1966.

methods of population control in Europe, and public attitudes were remarkably lenient. One London coroner said he had never known a woman to be punished for killing her baby, "no matter how flagrant the circumstances." Moreover, it was difficult to draw a line between infanticide and putting an infant in a foundling home, since the mortality rates in the latter were as high as 80–90 percent in England and France during the eighteenth and nineteenth centuries. The mortality rates led one writer to suggest that the homes put up signs saying, "Children killed at government expense." In France where under the Napoleonic Code children could be left in foundling homes anonymously, it is estimated that perhaps one-third of the foundlings were *legitimate* children left in the homes by their parents (Langer 1972, p. 98.)

There is no evidence that infanticide was ever widely practiced in the United States. However, prior to the nineteenth century, there were no laws prohibiting abortion during the first few months of pregnancy, and it was undoubtedly quite commonplace. The first laws banning abortion at all stages of fetal development were passed between 1821 and 1841, and by the time of the Civil War nearly every state had such laws. Abortion was, nevertheless, quite common in the late nineteenth century, with an estimated rate of one abortion for every five or six live births. Most contemporary physicians agreed that the primary motive for abortion was control of family size. They cited as evidence the fact that by far the largest group practicing abortion were married women. Both illegal and self-induced, abortion was quite dangerous, of course, and the mortality rate was frightfully high (Margolis 1984, Gordon 1983, Gray 1979, Mohr 1978). (For a discussion of contemporary methods of contraception and the controversy regarding legalized abortion, see Chapter 11.)

With the laws against providing information regarding contraception repealed, information on contraceptive techniques became increasingly available, and public attitudes regarding contraception began to change. In consequence, the birth rate, which had been falling since the colonial period, continued to drop—interrupted by the "baby boom," which peaked in the 1950s—and by 1984 the average married woman had fewer than two (1.8) children (see Figure 2-10).[38]

Demographers predict that the trend toward smaller families will not only continue but will be augmented by increasing numbers of married women who voluntarily remain childless. If these predictions are fulfilled, fully one-third of married women (who were age twenty to twenty-four in 1981) will have no children.[39] (See the vignette, "Fertility Rates, Race, Income, and Education.")

The key to understanding the changing role of women in our society is the change in attitude toward the desirability of having children. The entry of married women into the world of outside employment could not take place without a drop in the birth rate, which could not have happened without a radical change in our society's attitude toward contraception. There are undoubtedly many complex and interrelated reasons for the falling birth rate and for the radical change in our society's attitude toward the use of contraception, but one of the most significant is *economic determinism*, the doctrine that many important cultural patterns stem from economic forces.[40] As children became economic burdens, it became economically expedient for women to bear fewer children (Margolis 1984). Coincident with the change in the economic meaning of children was a change in our society's atti-

---

[38]U.S. Bureau of the Census, "Households, Families, Subfamilies, Married Couples, and Unrelated Individuals: 1950 – 1982" (1984); U.S. National Center for Health Statistics, *Vital Statistics of the United States*, annual (1985).

[39]U.S. Bureau of the Census. "Population Profile of the United States: 1981" (1982).

[40]Economic determinism is also called *cultural materialism*. Cultural materialism is the theoretical perspective that views changes in cultural patterns of behavior as stemming from the society's material pursuits.

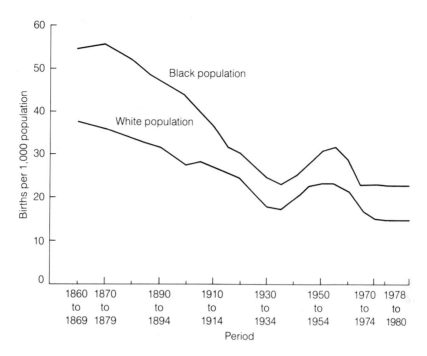

The birth rate has been dropping for both blacks and whites, except for the "baby boom" that peaked in the 1950s.

FIGURE 2-10

Birth rates of blacks and whites, 1860–1980

Sources: Data from U.S. Bureau of the Census, "Birth Rates, by Race, 1860 – 1975" (1978, p. 3); U.S. National Center for Health Statistics, *Vital Statistics of the United States,* annual (1984).

tude toward the advisability of contraception. Much of this sweeping attitudinal change can be traced to the dedicated efforts of Margaret Sanger, of course. But if the climate of opinion had not been favorable (because of economic determinism), would her efforts have been successful? It is an interesting question.

A second factor underlying the entry of women into the world of work outside the household is, of course, the change in the economy from agriculture to industry. This change reduced women's economic productivity within the household to virtual insignificance compared with their productivity in preindustrial times.[41]

In short, from the point of view of economic determinism, twin forces—(1) the reversal of the economic worth of children and (2) the relative lack of women's economic productivity within the household—led to a change in attitude toward the advisability of large families and relaxation of the condemnation of birth control. A lower birth rate ensued, making possible the massive movement of married

---

[41]It is ironic that while social forces and technological changes were eroding the wife's economic productivity within the home, leaving childbearing and child-rearing functions as her chief contribution, these same forces were making children economic liabilities (rather than assets).

Fertility Rates, Race, Income, and Education

Although it is true that the fertility rates in the United States as a whole have dropped steadily for the past two centuries to reach an average of 1.8 children per married woman in the early 1980s, this overall average obscures significant differences in the fertility rates of different ethnic groups. For example, in 1981, the rate of live births for Hispanic women was 50 percent higher than the rate for non-Hispanic women.

Moreover, teenage childbearing is relatively more frequent among the Hispanic population; in 1981 an estimated 19 percent of mothers of Mexican origin and 23 percent of mothers of Puerto Rican origin were under age twenty, compared with 12 percent of white non-Hispanics. The fertility rate for teenage blacks was even higher—26 percent of black mothers were under age twenty. Demographers find a correlation between teenage mothers and low income.

Teen-age pregnancy is a symptom of poverty; teen-age pregnancy rates are highest where income is lowest. Young girls who have low self-esteem and no hopes for the future are the ones most likely to become young mothers (Dunkle 1984).

The rate of births to unmarried mothers also varies significantly with race. Among blacks 57 percent of births were to unmarried mothers in 1981, as were 46 percent among those of Puerto Rican descent, and 25 percent among all those of Hispanic origin. Among non-Hispanic whites about 10 percent of births were to unwed mothers. Thus, compared with non-Hispanic whites, out-of-wedlock births were nearly six times as high among blacks, nearly five times as high among Puerto Ricans, and two and one-half times as high among all Hispanic mothers.

The trend toward women marrying later, having their first child later, having low fertility, achieving higher levels of education, and moving into higher-level jobs is characteristic only of the mainstream of American society. Another trend (especially among Hispanics and blacks) is still toward early pregnancies, large families, low levels of education, low-status jobs (or unemployment), and low levels of income (see Figure 2-11).

Sources: Data from U.S. National Center for Health Statistics, *Vital Statistics of the United States*, annual (1984); Margaret Dunkle, codirector of The Equality Center in Washington, D.C. (1984).

---

women into the world of work outside the household—a movement that began in the 1940s, accelerated in the 1960s, and continued into the 1970s and 1980s (Margolis 1984, Harris 1981, Gray 1979).[42]

---

[42]There have always been exceptional women, of course, who have managed both successful careers and marriage with children. A notable example is Marie Curie (1867 – 1934) who not only earned a living as a professional chemist and physicist in France during the late nineteenth and early twentieth centuries, but won two Nobel Prizes—one in 1903 in physics (which she shared with her husband, Pierre) and another in 1911 in chemistry (after her husband's death). (See the section on double-income families in Chapter 10.) Also in the nineteenth century, Queen Victoria (1819 – 1901) certainly put

Gender Inequities

Despite the fact that men and women are equally capable of performing most activities in our society, they are far from equal in their professional, business, social, and political opportunities. Most positions of authority, sta-

---

the stamp of her personality upon an entire era. Under her reign (she succeeded to the throne at age eighteen) England, acting from the base of a tiny island, amassed a huge empire and achieved worldwide economic and political dominance (as well as notable achievements in the arts and sciences). Victoria had nine children; of course, she also had a good deal of professional help to nurture and rear them.

TABLE 2-4
Political power of women in America, 1973 and 1983

Office	1973	1983
U.S. Senators[a]	2	2
U.S. House of Representatives	16	22
Governors[b]	0	0
Top state office holders	28	16
Lieutenant Governors	0	4
Secretaries of State	9	15
State Treasurers	7	9
State House Representatives	363	816
State Senators	62	173
Mayors[c]	12	72

[a]In January 1985, Jo-Anne Coe became Secretary of the Senate, the first woman to hold the position since it was created in 1789.

[b]In 1984, Martha Layne Collins became Governor of Kentucky.

[c]In cities with over 30,000 population, figures are for 1972 and 1982.

Sources: Data from Women's Center of the Democratic National Committee, press release (September 2, 1984); Center for the American Woman in Politics, Institute of Politics, Rutgers University, New Brunswick, New Jersey, informational releases (1984).

TABLE 2-5
Percentages of males and females who are managers and administrators, 1970–1982

	1970	1975	1982
Male	14.2%	14.0%	14.7%
Female	4.5%	5.2%	7.4%

Source: Data from U.S. Bureau of Labor Statistics, *Special Labor Force Bulletin* 2096 (1984, p. 417).

tus, and prestige are held by men, and this has been true for virtually all societies throughout most periods of history.[43] No society has ever been discovered in which females have had a dominant share of the power. Legends of Amazon tribes where women ruled over men are simply myths, with no basis in historical fact (Schlegel 1977, Aronoff and Krano 1975, Hammond and Jablow 1975).

In our own contemporary society women in general have very little political power. Although women are a majority in the population, they are only a tiny minority in terms of political offices they hold (see Table 2-4). A survey by *Fortune* magazine (June 1978) found that in the business world less than 0.2 percent of the directors of the country's major companies were women, and businesses owned by women accounted for only 2 percent of the nation's business receipts in 1977.[44] In 1984, only one company on *Fortune*'s list of the 500 largest industrial corporations had a woman chief executive. That woman, Katherine Graham of the *Washington Post Company*, readily admits that she got the job because her family owns a controlling share of the corporation (Fraker 1984). In 1984, women had only four of the 154 spots in the Harvard Business Schools Advanced Management Program, a prestigious thirteen-week conclave to which companies send executives they are grooming for the corridors of power (Fraker 1984).

Although there are, as yet, few women in top executive positions, women are gaining ground in midmanagement (managerial and administrative positions), with the percentage nearly doubling in recent years. For example, the number of women in these positions jumped from 4.5 percent in 1970 to 7.4 percent in 1982, while the percentage of men in these positions remained essentially unchanged (see Table 2-5).[45]

[43]Women have occasionally held positions of great power, of course. Queen Elizabeth gave her name to an age during the lusty period of the Renaissance, as Queen Victoria did during the nineteenth century in England. In more recent times, Golda Meir in Israel, Indira Gandhi in India, and Margaret Thatcher in Great Britain have provided vigorous leadership.

[44]U.S. Bureau of Labor Statistics, "Labor Force Participation Rates of Married Women" (1979).

[45]U.S. Bureau of Labor Statistics, *Special Labor Force Bulletin* 2096 (1984, p. 417).

However, among women who do enter executive positions, many have sacrificed marriage and children for their careers. Studies of executive women find that 52 percent had never married, were divorced, or were widowed, and 61 percent had no children. A similar study of male executives found that only 5 percent of these men had never married or were divorced, and even fewer—3 percent—had no children (Fraker 1984).

Although women are now a major part of the work force in the United States (52.7 percent in 1982), on a national average they still earn far less than men.[46] For example, white women nationally working the full year receive about 61 cents for every dollar paid to a man.[47]

Women are paid less not only for unskilled and semiskilled labor, but also for work that requires special training or an academic background. For example, the median income for women in professional and technical jobs was only 64 percent of the salary of men with similar jobs in 1981.[48]

In upper level jobs, a study of MBA women students at the Stanford Business School, polled shortly before their graduation in 1974, found that the top salary they expected to earn during their careers was only 60 percent of that expected by men in the class. Four years later, in 1978, the ratio had fallen to 40 percent (Fraker 1984). For a summary of the median full-time wages and salaries of men and women over age sixteen by race, see Figure 2-11.

Since retirement benefits are based on wages earned, the average lower pay for women extends into their retirement years. The average benefit for a woman retiring in 1983 was about 40 percent of the average benefit for a retiring man.[49]

The lower average pay for women stems from two factors: (1) The occupations that are traditionally held by women are paid less than the occupations traditionally held by men, and (2) women are often paid less for equivalent work. The practice of paying women less than men has been justified on three major grounds. First, it is alleged that a woman is working only to support herself, whereas a man is responsible for the entire family. This justification is used less frequently today than it was in the past. Second, it is alleged that women are less reliable—they frequently get sick and miss many more days of work. Finally, it is alleged that since women don't really need jobs, they quit after employers have invested time and money in training them.

Research studies find that, contrary to the last two assumptions, women (compared with men) miss only slightly more days of work (averaging 5.3 missed days per year as compared with men's 4.6),[50] and (when occupational level and income are held constant so that a direct comparison may be made) women do not differ significantly from men in terms of quitting their jobs. (See the vignette, "Women's Economic Roles: Myths and Realities.")

Two current trends may ultimately redress the disparities between women's and men's pay. One is the likelihood that following the Supreme Court decision in 1981, increasing numbers of women will demand equal pay for equivalent work.[51] Second is the growing trend

---

[46]U.S. Bureau of Labor Statistics, "Employed Persons, by Sex, Race, and Occupation: 1972 to 1982" (1984, pp. 419–20).

[47]Using the same comparison, black women made 56 cents and Hispanics 53 cents (U.S. Bureau of Labor Statistics, *Special Labor Force Bulletin* 2096 (1984).

[48]U.S. Bureau of the Census, "Number of Workers with Earnings and Median Earnings, by Occupation of Longest Job Held and Sex, 1981" (1984, p. 434).

---

[49]U.S. Bureau of the Census, "Retirement Benefits Based on Wages Earned" (1983 and 1984).

[50]U.S. National Center for Health Statistics, *Vital and Health Statistics*, Series 10 (1984).

[51]Recognizing this disparity, the U.S. Supreme Court established the principle in 1981 that women must be paid the same as men for equivalent work, and it defined *equivalent* as "work that fulfills essentially the same function, or requires the same amount of training or education." It does not have to be precisely the *same* work.

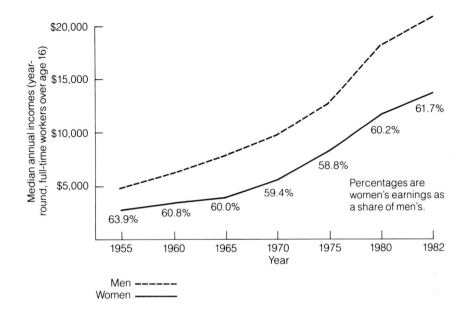

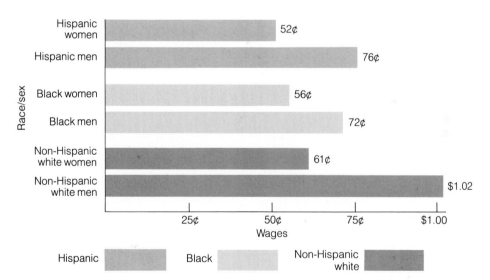

Mean earnings of year-round, full-time workers by sex and race expressed as a comparison to earnings of all men. For example, black women earn 56 cents for each $1 earned by all men (1982 figures).

FIGURE 2-11

The earnings gap between men and women, black, Hispanic, and non-Hispanic white, 1955 – 1982

Source: Data from U.S. Bureau of Labor Statistics, *Special Labor Force Bulletin* 2096 (1984).

Women's Economic Roles: Myths and Realities

There are many widely held misconceptions regarding women's economic roles in our society.

Myth: The wealth of our nation is mainly in the hands of women. Only one-third of the population regarded as "wealthy" are women. Moreover, the financial holdings of many of the younger women in this group are in the form of assets assigned to them in name only for tax purposes, while a father or husband retains the actual control (Amundsen 1971).

Myth: Women are not worth hiring where any training or investment is involved, since they just get married or become pregnant or quit. Women do indeed quit jobs more often than men, and frequently they give family-related reasons. However, women are more frequently hired for more menial, more routine, duller jobs than men are (or jobs for which they are overqualified, such as the clerk-typist position filled by a college-educated woman), and turnover rates among these jobs are very high. For example, auto assembly—a dull, routine job—has the highest job turnover rate of all, even though it is overwhelmingly male. When occupational level and income are held constant, men and women do not differ significantly in turnover rates (U.S. National Commission for UNESCO 1977).

Myth: Women lack the physical strength for many highly skilled and well-paid manual jobs, especially in the crafts. Given current machinery, most such jobs rarely entail more physical exertion than that involved in carrying a sixty-pound child or transporting a desk typewriter from one office to another, both tasks done frequently by women. Moreover, it is clear that some men are physically weaker than most women, whereas some women are stronger than most men.

Myth: Women are much better off today, in terms of job opportunities and pay, than they were a generation ago. Employed women are still concentrated in relatively few occupations, and although the numbers and proportions of women in higher-paying professional and technical jobs have increased significantly, their earnings continue to average about 60 percent of men's. (The Supreme Court decision of 1981 providing that women must be paid the same as men for equivalent jobs may have far-reaching social repercussions in this regard.)

Sources: Data from U.S. Internal Revenue Service, *Statistics of Income*, 1962 and 1972 (Summer 1983); U.S. Bureau of the Census, Special Demographic Analyses, CDS-80-8, *American Women: Three Decades of Change* (1983, p. 1).

---

of women entering college, thus qualifying for better-paying occupations. In 1984 more than half of all college and university students were women, up from 40 percent in 1970. Moreover, women were earning 30 percent of all law degrees (from 5 percent in 1970) and 23 percent of all medical degrees (up from 8 percent in 1970) in 1984 (Linden 1984). These two trends—more women demanding equal pay for equivalent work, and more women qualifying for higher-level jobs through education—may lead in the closing decade of the twentieth century to widespread societal changes regarding job status and job pay social discrimination against women.

Reasons for Male Dominance

What has led to the historical dominance of men over women?[52] The historical dominance of men over women seems to rest upon two factors. One is that women are the gender that bears children; this is a biological imperative.

---

[52]Men are, on the average, larger and stronger than women, but this probably has little to do with why men have dominated women in terms of political, social, and economic power. After all, if size and strength were of any great significance, the biggest people—men or women—would occupy most positions of power, status, and wealth, and this is obviously not the case. Certainly in our contemporary society, the superior size and strength of the average man compared with the average woman

The second is that in all societies, women have been assigned the ultimate responsibility for care of the children or seeing that they are cared for. Reiss (1980) sums this up as follows:

Two features of gender roles in all cultures are: (1) female ties to child rearing and (2) male ties to economic and political power. While it is true that in many cultures males do a large share of the child rearing and, conversely, women do a large share of the economic work, this does not alter the basic gender-role priorities for the two genders. The basic root cause of this crucial division of labor in gender roles is the tie of the female to the child, which historically gives males the reins of power (p. 62).

The child-care function that has been universally assigned to women has greatly reduced the likelihood of women's gaining power and dominance in the society. Men, in contrast, have typically been assigned full-time work outside the home as their chief priority (although they have also shared in child care), and they have accordingly controlled the economic and political power structures (Reiss 1980, Gough 1971).

Now that the birth rate has dropped significantly, women in our society are moving increasingly into the world of work outside the household. In consequence, they have been moving slowly toward greater social, economic, and political equality. Cultural changes that will give women greater responsibility, economic returns, and political power in the world outside the family are moving slowly, however. There are several reasons for this. First, such changes reverse a great historical trend, altering gender roles that have endured since the dawn of human history. Moreover, the suspicion (if not conviction) that women

are destined to function chiefly in a gender role that emphasizes nurturant characteristics is by no means dispelled. Then, there are many women who prefer the child-care role and do not wish to participate in the economic and political power roles of our society to any greater extent. This has been demonstrated in the debates on the Equal Rights Amendment (ERA). Researchers also find that women are more easily satisfied than men with low-paid and low-status work (Smith and Ward 1984, Galenson 1973).

Other women are quite ambivalent about child care versus employment, feeling guilty about the possible neglect of their children and yet feeling that they must contribute to the economic well-being of the family—which usually means working outside the home. Many women are thus caught on the horns of dilemma: If they stay home and care for children, they can't produce economic goods; if they leave home to produce economic goods, they can't take care of the children.

Finally, how can men be persuaded to move from their powerful economic and political positions to the child-care role? Few groups voluntarily give up power. Some men have moved in this direction, but child care is still chiefly a female activity (Komarovsky 1976, Petros 1975).[53]

Gender-Role Stereotypes

It is just a short step from assigning women role behavior that is consistent with pregnancy and with the nurture and socialization of infants and children, to the assumption that women have inborn characteristics that are different from men in areas *not* related to child care, such as those necessary for success in

---

are virtually meaningless. In fact, it is questionable whether superior size and strength have ever been a factor, even in the dawn of human history. Perhaps the cunning use of traps and snares and tracking skills were more important even then. The advances of human beings in understanding nature and controlling the environment have depended not on size and strength (there are many larger and stronger animals) but on the manipulation of tools and ideas.

---

[53]Other contemporary societies have been at least moderately successful in moving men into child-care roles by legislative and union action. In Sweden, for example, men and women are regarded as equivalent in this regard, as well as in economic, social, and political potential. (For details, see "Sweden: The Western Model," in Reiss 1980.)

politics, science, the arts, or finance. It was also assumed until the twentieth century that women were less intelligent than men and less rational.[54] So long as virtually all women identified with their roles as housewives and mothers, the stereotypes that women were unable to compete effectively with men in business, science, the arts, politics, and sports simply reflected the cultural norm.[55]

However, a growing number of women in our society no longer identify themselves solely in terms of looking after a household and family, and the gender-role stereotypes limiting women's life-styles are becoming anachronistic. They are, nonetheless, very persistent, and are often held unconsciously. For example, does the following seem like a truly egalitarian statement, acknowledging the wife to have the same freedom of expression and freedom of life-style as the husband?

Both my wife and I earned Ph.D. degrees in our respective disciplines. I turned down a superior academic post in Oregon and accepted a slightly less desirable position in New York where my wife could obtain a part-time teaching job and do research at one of the several other colleges in the area. Although I would have preferred to live in a suburb, we purchased a home near my wife's college so that she could have an office at home where she would be when the children returned from school. Because my wife earns a good salary, she can easily afford to pay a maid to do her major household chores. My wife and I share all other tasks around the house equally. For example, she cooks the meals, but I do the laundry for her and help her with many of her other household tasks (Bem and Bem 1970, pp. 97–98).

To test whether all the hidden assumptions about the woman's "natural" role have been eliminated and the traditional gender-role stereotyping repudiated, we can reverse the gender in the statement. If the marriage is egalitarian, then its description should retain the same flavor and tone.

Both my husband and I earned Ph.D. degrees in our respective disciplines. I turned down a superior academic post in Oregon and accepted a slightly less desirable position in New York where my husband could obtain a part-time teaching job and do research at one of the several other colleges in the area. Although I would have preferred to live in a suburb, we purchased a home near my husband's college so that he could have an office at home where he would be when the children returned from school. Because my husband earns a good salary, he can easily afford to pay a maid to do his major household chores. My husband and I share all other tasks around the house equally. For example, he cooks the meals, but I do the laundry for him and help him with many of his other household tasks (Bem and Bem 1970, p. 98).

When the genders are reversed in this way, it becomes apparent to most readers that the first statement was not egalitarian but rather an unconscious perseveration of traditional gender-role stereotyping.

It seems archaic to us today to read that many school boards rigorously imposed the following rules for women as recently as 1920:

Do not get married; do not leave town at any time without permission of the school board; do not keep company with men; be home between the hours of 8 P.M. and 6 A.M.; do not loiter downtown in ice-cream stores; do not smoke; do not get into a carriage with any man except your father or brother; do not dress in bright colors; do not dye your hair (Zerfoss 1974).

---

[54]For example, women were not allowed to vote until 1920 in the United States because it was felt that they could not understand the issues. The nineteenth Amendment to the Constitution of the United States extended the right to vote to women in 1920.

[55]There have always been exceptions to such stereotypes, of course. In this regard, the name of George Sand comes to mind. George Sand (1804–1876) was the pseudonym of the French novelist who defied all the conventions of her age, wrote some eighty novels that were widely popular, and supported herself and her two children chiefly by her writing after obtaining a divorce from her husband, a country squire. She demanded for women the freedom in living that was a matter of course for the men of her day, and she had scandalous affairs with many of the leading figures of the period, including the composer Chopin. Her early novels were romantic, but her later ones often expressed her serious concern with social reform.

Perhaps by the turn of the century, the current discrimination imposed on women will seem just as outmoded.

SUMMARY

Gender is the concept of maleness or femaleness and has three bases: biological, cultural, and gender identity.

The initial manifestations of gender are physical and may be traced to the XX or XY chromosomes. XX chromosomes direct the development of prenatal gonadal tissue into ovaries; XY chromosomes direct the development of prenatal gonadal tissue into testicles, about six weeks after conception. These embryonic ovaries or testicles then produce sex hormones (estrogen and androgen) that direct the development of the other internal and external sex organs.

Each person's gender identity is a function of his or her biological structure and appearance and the gender-role socialization that imposes expectations for "masculine" or "feminine" behavior. Thus a person comes to view himself or herself as a male or a female, with related expectations for social interaction. This identity as a male or a female is a very important part of one's self-image and forms as early as three years of age.

For most persons, gender identity is consistent with the physical aspects of gender and the perceived role. Anomalies do occur, however. For example, the appearance of the external genitalia may be indeterminate at birth, causing the person to be assigned the wrong gender (hermaphroditism). A chromosomal (XY) male may have the gender identity of a female, feeling himself to be a woman trapped in a male body, or a chromosomal (XX) female may feel herself to be a man trapped in a female body (transsexualism).

Homosexuality is no longer considered an anomaly or abnormal but rather a *variant* in sexual expression. Homosexuality may be either episodic or obligative. Episodic homosexuals (which may include 10 – 25 percent of the male population at some period of their lives) eventually become heterosexual. The 1 – 4 percent of the male population who are obligative homosexuals remain so throughout their lifetimes. The source of homosexuality is unknown, although it is conjectured that the source of episodic homosexuality may be environmental or opportunistic, while the source of obligative homosexuality may be rooted in the individual. The incidence of female homosexuality is about half that of male homosexuality.

Although researchers are discovering some behavioral differences between males and females that are apparently innate or biologically based, the only characteristics that are gender specific are the four biological imperatives (gestation, menstruation, lactation, and sperm production). Nevertheless, our society expects males to behave differently from females and treats them somewhat differently from infancy on. This difference in treatment is called gender-role socialization and is based historically on the biological imperative that women bear children. Since the chief responsibility for rearing children has also fallen to women, a gender-role division of labor emerged in all societies, assigning to women the work that was compatible with child care. Nevertheless, in early societies, women's food-producing activities were indispensable to the subsistence of the family, while men always played a significant role in the socialization of children. This relative equality of productivity and child rearing began to change with the shift in economy from agriculture to industry, when men left subsistence farms to earn money away from home. This had two effects: Men were less often available for socializing children, and other institutions began to provide the economic goods formerly produced by women at home. Thus, women, for the first time in history, were not as economically productive as men.

As women's nurturing function grew more important, ironically the average number of children in the family became progressively smaller—children had become economic liabilities rather than assets. Public opinion regarding birth control began to change, and, largely through the efforts of Margaret Sanger, laws prohibiting the dissemination of information regarding birth control and the use of contraceptive devices were repealed. As public opinion changed and birth control information and techniques became available, the birth rate steadily dropped.

As a result of these two factors—fewer children and relative lack of economic productivity in the household—more and more women began to leave their homes in search of outside employment. As the United States entered the 1980s, most married women were working outside the home. Women's pay, however, averages only about 60 percent of men's, and women are underrepresented in the top-level jobs. This may be expected to change in light of the U.S. Supreme Court's decision regarding equal pay for equal work regardless of gender, and the growing insistence of women's groups, labor unions, and other organizations that women be granted equivalent pay as well as equivalent status to that of men. This movement toward egalitarianism as yet chiefly involves middle class, white women, however. Hispanic and black women still tend to have large families and work in low-paying, low-status jobs.

QUESTIONS

1. What are the biological bases of gender?
2. What are the cultural bases of gender?
3. How is gender-role socialization accomplished in our society?
4. Discuss the statement: By the time boys and girls are five years old, each is firmly entrenched in a stereotyped gender role.
5. Discuss the importance of self-identity as a basis of gender.
6. What is meant by *gender identity/role*?
7. What is meant by the statement: Gender is highly socially visible.
8. The various aspects of gender are usually consistent; if they are not, gender anomalies occur. What forms do such anomalies take?
9. What is the incidence of homosexuality in our society?
10. What is the difference between episodic homosexuality and obligative homosexuality?
11. Discuss why both APAs removed homosexuality from the category of abnormal behavior.
12. Discuss our society's current attitudes toward homosexuality.
13. What was the significance of the study of prenatally androgenized females?
14. In Money and Ehrhardt's study (1972), in what behavioral ways did fetally androgenized females differ from their matched counterparts?
15. What is meant by a *matched pair*?
16. What is the significance of studies of matched pairs of hermaphrodites?
17. What is the significance of studies of matched pairs of twins?
18. Discuss the relative importance of biological and social factors in determining adult gender characteristics.
19. Why was work divided into men's work and women's work in hunting and gathering societies?
20. What role (if any) did the subsistence farmer have in socializing the children? How does his role then compare with the father's role now?
21. As the shift from agriculture to industry occurred, what social forces motivated couples to have smaller families?

22. What happened during the shift from agriculture to industry to change the function of the family in our society?

23. Discuss the importance of the woman's contribution to the family's economic well-being in hunting and gathering and agricultural societies.

24. What sociological and demographic factors have led women to work outside the home in our postindustrial society?

25. Trace the change in attitudes and laws regarding the dissemination of information on birth control in our society from the nineteenth century to the present.

26. Discuss the relation between family planning (contraception) and the entry of women into the work world.

27. Do you believe that men and women should perform the same nurturing functions in society, or should women be chiefly responsible for the care and rearing of children?

28. Granted that child care and rearing are essential functions in any society, how would you suggest that these tasks be accomplished?

29. Give an example of a gender-role assumption that is unconscious.

30. Discuss the extent of gender-role inequities in our contemporary society.

31. What are some widely held myths regarding women's economic role in our society?

32. Discuss the importance of gender to behavior in our society.

SUGGESTIONS FOR FURTHER READING

Albin, Mel, and Cavallo, Dominic, eds. *Family Life in America, 1620 – 2000*. St. James, N.Y.: Revisionary Press, 1981.

Badinter, Elizabeth. *Mother Love, Myth and Reality: Motherhood in Modern History*. New York: Macmillan, 1981.

Cable, Mary. *The Little Darlings: A History of Child Rearing in America*. New York: Scribner's, 1975.

Ehrenreich, B. *The Hearts of Men: American Dreams and the Flight from Commitment*. New York: Anchor Press, 1983.

Gordon, Michael. *The American Family in Social-Historical Perspective*, 3rd ed. New York: St. Matthews, 1983.

Gray, Madeline. *Margaret Sanger*. New York: Marek, 1979.

Haller, John S., and Haller, Robin M. *The Physician and Sexuality in Victorian America*. New York: Norton, 1974.

Hyde, Janet Shibley. *Half the Human Experience: The Psychology of Women*, 3rd ed. Lexington, Mass.: Heath, 1985.

Margolis, Maxine. *Mothers and Such: Views of American Women and Why They Changed*. Berkeley: University of California Press, 1984.

Money, John, and Tucker, Patricia. *Sexual Signatures: On Being a Man or a Woman*. Boston: Little, Brown, 1975.

Schaffer, Kay F. *Sex Roles and Human Behavior*. Cambridge, Mass.: Winthrop, 1981.

Seward, Rudy R. *The American Family: A Demographic History*. Beverley Hills, Calif.: Sage, 1978.

Skolnick, Arlene, and Skolnick, Jerome H., eds. *Family in Transition*, 4th ed. Boston: Little, Brown, 1983.

Stockard, Jean, and Johnson, Miriam M. *Sex Roles: Sex Inequality and Sex Role Development*. Englewood Cliffs, N.J.: Prentice-Hall, 1980.

Stratton, Joanna L. *Pioneer Women: Voices from the Kansas Frontier*. New York: Simon & Schuster, 1982.

C H A P T E R   3

Love and Pair Bonding

Loving and Liking
Love and Limerence
Love and Attachment
The Traditional Faces of Love
Styles of Loving
Love and Infatuation
Love and Jealousy
Learning to Love

There is no greater nor keener pleasure than that of bodily love—and none which is more irrational.

Plato (Apology)

One of the key aspects of pair bonding, of course, is love.

Love is one of the most important things in life. People have been known to lie, cheat, steal and kill for it. Even in the most materialistic of societies, it remains one of the few things that cannot be bought. And it has puzzled poets, philosophers, writers, psychologists and practically everyone else who has tried to understand it (Sternberg 1985, p. 60).

One reason a precise definition of love slips through the semanticist's net is that it is so multifaceted, with so many subtle and often contradictory manifestations. Another reason is that the meaning of love can differ widely from one individual to another—with an even wider range of meaning than the concept of sexuality.

The reality of love is inescapable, however. Its importance is experiential, not verbal or rational. The inability to capture its characteristics in a precise definition does not imply that it is unimportant. Many aspects of reality—some of the most important—are experiential in this way and defy rigorous definition or interpretation. One can use language to point to such an experience, but a definition in words cannot capture the reality of the phenomenon. This paradox regarding the difficulty of expressing a profound and concrete reality in verbal terms is summed up beautifully by the Zen aphorism:

The finger pointing at the moon
Is not the moon.

What is the meaning of love in the consciousness and experience of the individual? (See the vignette, "The Individual's Experience of Love.") Can *true love* have more than one meaning? Does *loving* differ from *being in love*? What is the relation between love and sex? These are questions that will be explored in this chapter.

LOVING AND LIKING

Surprisingly enough, research on the nature of love finds that it is not simply the ultimate of *like*. Rather, loving and liking, while sharing many characteristics, are quite different in others. For example, it is not uncommon to hear a person say that he or she loves someone, such as a father, but does not like him: "I have never really been able to understand my father, and we've never been able to get along, but of course I love him."

Zick Rubin (1973), in his pioneering work on the distinction between loving and liking, pointed out that liking is usually associated with either affection or respect, or both. Love, in contrast, is characterized by feelings of comfort, ease, warmth, and security when the other is present or felt to be accessible—replacing feelings of desolation, loneliness, and isolation when the other is either absent or felt to be inaccessible.

Rubin found a good deal of correlation between liking and loving, but his analysis discovered the correlation to be only "moderate." Specifically, the coefficient of correlation be-

tween feelings of loving and feelings of liking (directed toward the same person) for his men subjects was .56, and the coefficient of correlation between feelings of loving and feelings of liking (directed toward the same person) for his women subjects was .36.[1] Thus, with men, the overlap between their feelings of loving and liking is moderate; but with women, the overlap is almost insignificant. Apparently women can like a person without loving the person, or love someone without liking. Another interpretation is that the women in Rubin's study were able to distinguish between their feelings of liking and loving more accurately than were the men. Rubin (1973) sums this up as follows:

It is possible that this difference is a consequence of the distinctive specializations of the two sexes. In most societies, men tend to be the task specialists, while women tend to be the social-emotional specialists. By virtue of their specialization in matters involving interpersonal feelings, women may develop a more finely tuned and more discriminating set of interpersonal sentiments than men do. Whereas men may often blur such fine distinctions as the one between liking and loving, women may be more likely to experience and express the two sentiments as being distinct from one another (p. 220).

More recent research (Davis 1985) confirms that love and friendship have many different qualities while sharing many others. Both friendship and love share the following characteristics:

— *Mutual enjoyment* of each other's company most of the time (although there may be temporary states of anger, disappointment, or mutual annoyance)

— *Mutual acceptance* of one another as he or she is, without trying to change or make the other over into a better person

---

[1]The *coefficient of correlation* is a statistical concept that measures the degree of relatedness between two events. A score of 1.00 is a perfect correlation, with the two events coinciding perfectly. A score of 0 indicates no correlation at all. A score of .70 or higher is usually considered to be quite significant, and a score of .30 is insignificant. Scores between .30 and .70 are considered moderate.

The Individual's Experience of Love

The following are students' replies to the question, What is love?

Love is the feeling that your special person is the most important thing in the world to you. It means wanting to be with that person all the time whether in person or in spirit. It means feeling like you have something so powerful inside you that you are going to explode. Love is a very special closeness and caring. For me love also means that when I'm being held by the one I love that nothing can hurt me, that I am safe and secure.

Love is caring for another person as much or even more than you care for yourself. Security. Warmth. Sharing everything. Looked upon as eternal. Self-enhancing. Life has more meaning and fulfillment. Love causes all the good qualities to come out in people.

When you feel an emptiness when the other person is gone, then you are experiencing love. When you're with each other, you feel fulfilled and complete. It can make you feel secure within yourself knowing someone loves you. When someone is "in love" you feel better when you are with the other person. The other person makes you feel whole.

Love is sharing, caring, living for, helping of another person or persons with whom you enjoy—it is the ultimate in life—it's what you live each day for. Love—a kind of fondness for a person. Emotional feelings and respect for someone. Being able to give a little of yourself and not expect anything back. A brightening of the senses when you are together. It's the security of knowing that someone cares. Needing someone emotionally.

Love is when you feel like you're part of your loved one. It's when you feel like your world will break if your lover leaves you. Love is when you think of someone you love and you feel warm or you tingle in your spine.

Love is a warmth you feel when you see and touch that special person. That person is your best friend, sexual partner, or just someone you would be willing to do anything, including starving, for. Love is giving of your mind and body totally to that special person.

Love is a very important requirement for wholeness. Without love I feel incomplete as a person.

— *Mutual trust*, in the sense that each assumes that the other will act in accordance with one's best interest

— *Mutual respect*, in the sense of each assuming that the other exercises good judgment in making important decisions and choices and will usually do "what's right"

— *Mutual assistance*, with each inclined to support the other—that is, being able to count on the other in times of need, trouble, or personal distress

— *Mutual understanding*, with each having a sense of what is important to the other, of why the other does what he or she does

— *Mutual spontaneity*, with each feeling free to act naturally and spontaneously, without restraint, in the company of the other—to abandon all attempts at pretense or attempts to impress the other or play a role

— *Mutual confiding*, sharing experiences and feelings with the other, however intimate or remote, with no dissembling or caution

In addition to these characteristics of friendship, love includes another category that Davis (1985) calls the passion cluster. The *passion cluster* consists of the three factors of fascination, exclusiveness, and sexual desire (see Figure 3-1):

— *Fascination:* Lovers tend to be fascinated with each other and pay attention to or think of each other, even when they should be involved in other activities.

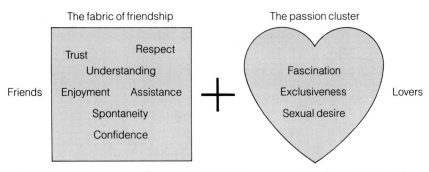

Lovers share the characteristics of friendship but also possess the characteristics of the passion cluster: sexual desire (which they may or may not act upon), exclusiveness, and fascination.

FIGURE 3-1

Lovers and friends

Source: Data from Davis (1985).

They are preoccupied with the other person and tend to think about, look at, want to talk to, or merely be with the other ("I would go to bed thinking about what we would do together, dream about it, and wake up ready to be with him again." "I have trouble concentrating; she just seems to be in my head no matter what I am doing.") (Davis 1985, p. 24).

—— *Exclusiveness:* Lovers tend to exclude all others from their special relationship with each other.

Their paired bond is so essential in their consciousness that it is given priority over all other friendships that each may have, and no one else is admitted to their special, shared intimacy. . . . ("What we have is different than I've ever had with anyone else.") (Davis 1985, p. 24).

—— *Sexual desire:* Lovers want, need, and expect physical intimacy with each other. They want to touch, fondle, caress. This need for physical intimacy has sexual overtones and will include sexual intimacy if possible—although this need may be overridden by moral, religious, or practical considerations.

Although the feelings of lovers are deeper and more intense than the feelings of friends, the love affair may also be less stable and more volatile than friendships (Davis 1985).

It is interesting to note that, although the majority of "best friends" were of the same gender, 27 percent of subjects in the study listed a member of the opposite sex as a best friend. Moreover, 56 percent of the men and 44 percent of the women named a member of the opposite sex as a close friend. These friendships were explicitly categorized as "nonromantic" (Davis 1985).

LOVE AND LIMERENCE

The aspect of love that really sets it apart from liking is the phenomenon of limerence. *Limerence* is defined as an inexplicable, overwhelming attraction and bonding to another—a phenomenon that defies scientific explanation but has long been recognized by literature. It is often to the limerent aspect of love that one refers with the term *love*, especially when referring to love in a paired bond.

The theme of limerence has been explored by major writers from biblical times to the present. (A notable example is William Styron's *Sophie's Choice* [1979]). It is the subject of operas, ballets, short stories, and countless song lyrics—whether Broadway show tunes, jazz, country-western, or rock. It has changed the course of history in real life. A relatively recent example is the abdication of King Edward VIII of Great Britain to marry Wallis Simpson ("the woman I love"). Another familiar example from history is the extraordinary limerent attraction of Nicholas II (the last Czar of all the Russias) to Alexandra (a young German princess), which had a profound effect on Western civilization. Nicholas II was an extraordinarily powerful figure, with absolute autocratic domination over one-sixth of the world. His limerent attraction to Alexandra is seen by some historians as leading to the fall of Czarist Russia and the rise of communism (Massie 1967). An entry in Nicholas II's diary expresses his depth of feeling:

I dreamed that I was loved, I woke and found it to be true and thanked God on my knees for it. True love is the gift which God has given, daily, stronger, deeper, fuller, purer (Massie 1967, p. 38)

Despite its recognition by artists and its importance in real life, not only to individuals but also to the rise and fall of dynasties, limerence has been largely ignored by psychologists, sociologists, and social historians until the publication of Tennov's *Love and Limerence* (1979) following fourteen years of research.

Tennov's research found that limerence is a serious phenomenon that has a profound effect on the limerent person, who experiences it as a compulsive, overwhelming, tumultuous, absorbing attraction. She also found that many individuals are nonlimerent, and these persons have difficulty in accepting the validity of the limerent experience.

The Initial Awareness
of Limerence

A limerent attraction may begin suddenly, as exemplifed in the film *The Godfather*, when young Corleone (hiding in Sicily after killing a New York police captain) sees a group of schoolgirls on a mountain trail and is utterly transfixed by one of them. His bodyguards explain that he has been struck by "the thunderbolt."[2]

Limerence can also occur gradually, over a period of time, with the person not aware of when it first begins to grow.

Limerence enters your life pleasantly. Someone takes on a special meaning. It may be an old friend unexpectedly seen in a new way (Tennov 1979, p. 17).

Or, as Money (1980) put it:

Like the charismatic religious experience of being saved or born again, falling in love may be sudden and dramatic—love at first sight—or it may be a slow and gradual realization (p. 64).

The Phenomenon
of Crystallization

Stendahl, in his nineteenth-century classic *Love* (1975), used the term *crystallization* to describe the limerent attraction.[3] If a branch of a tree, he said, is tossed into a salt mine and allowed to remain there for several months, it undergoes a metamorphosis. It remains a branch, but the salt crystals transform it into an object of shimmering beauty. In an analagous manner, although more quickly, the traits of the *limerent object* (the person who is the focus of the limerent attraction) are crystallized by mental events in which the attractive characteristics are exaggerated and the unattractive characteristics are given little or no attention. According to Stendahl, then, limerent people interpret the object of their attraction in the most favorable light. Lim-

---

[2]The French phrase *coupe de foudre* refers to a sudden, compulsive attraction to another person; it literally means a "thunderbolt."

[3]Stendahl is the pen name of Marie Henri Beyle (1783 – 1842).

A couple experiencing mutual limerence are totally involved with one another.
Charles Dana Gibson: *The Weaker Sex VII—The Story of a Susceptible Bachelor,* 1903

erent people do not exactly misperceive; rather, they focus on the positive aspects and seem unconcerned about what appear to be defects to others. Popular tradition has attributed this process to blindness ("love is blind"), but it is really a matter of emphasis. However the limerent object may appear to others, the limerent bias brings forth the positive and plays down the unfavorable. Moreover, neutral aspects of the person are perceived as charming and delightful.

"Anything that belonged to her acquired a certain magic. *Her* handbag, *her* notebook, *her* pencil. I abhor the sight of toothmarks on a pencil; they disgust me, but not *her* toothmarks. Hers were sacred; her wonderful mouth had been there." (Tennov 1979, p. 31)

The emphasis on desirable qualities in the other has often been referred to by writers as *idealization*. But idealization differs from crystallization in its implication that the other is molded to fit a preformed, romantic conception. In crystallization the actual and existing features of the limerent object are merely enhanced. Idealization implies that unattractive features are overlooked. In limerence these features are usually seen but emotionally ignored. In Tennov's study of 2,000 couples, two-thirds of the men and three-fourths of the women were able to indicate their partner's character defects, physical defects, and bad habits. But perception of these defects did not impede the development of limerence.

Obsession and Fantasy in Limerence

One characteristic of limerence is the person's obsessive preoccupation not only with the other but also with shared experiences or events. "There was the park bench we sat on" or "That was the song we danced to last year." These connections need not be logical or even close. It is not that the event or the recollection reminds the limerent person of the other, but rather that the perceptual presence of the other in the limerent person's consciousness defines all other experiences in relation to it (Tennov 1979).

If an experience has no connection with the limerent object, the limerent person makes one. Limerent people wonder or imagine what the other would think of the book in their hands, the scene they are witnessing, the fortune or misfortune that is befalling them. They visualize how they will tell about it, how the other will respond, what will be said between them, and what actions will (or might) take place in relation to it. As they engage in their ordinary daily activities, they invent intricate scenarios for possible upcoming events. Endlessly, they plan the next encounter, going over every detail of what they will do to improve their image in the other's eyes. They hope and anticipate. They recall with vividness what the other said and did. They search out alternate meanings of those behaviors. It is as if each word and gesture are permanently available for review, especially those that can be interpreted as evidence of "return of feeling." Daydreams dominate the limerent consciousness and are clearly directed toward a meeting or conversation that might take place, eventually culminating in a moment of mutuality when limerent feelings are returned. This is the goal of the limerent person, and its achievement brings almost indescribable delight (Tennov 1979).

Positive and Negative Limerence

The experience of limerence can be a very positive one, bringing joy, happiness, contentment, and delight if the limerence is returned. If it is not returned, the experience can be agonizing, plunging the limerent person into the depths of anguish and despair. The pain and agony of unrequited love (when the limerent object does not return the emotion) has been the subject of poetry, ballet, opera, and novels, as well as contemporary song lyrics ("I can't get you out of my mind").

Money (1980) describes this negative aspect of limerence as being "love-sick" or "love-lorn" and "heartbroken" if the limerence is not returned.

The love-sick mind becomes distracted by its other duties and commitments and is preoccupied instead with a hypertrophia of desire and longing for the beloved.[4] There is not a sense of well-being except in the presence of the lover, who thus holds extraordinary responsibility and wields inordinate power over the life of the other. Once you have become a part of the mental furnishings of your lover's mind, there you stay forever trapped and unable to engineer your own escape. The consequences can be very profound, either for joy or suffering. The suffering becomes intense when love becomes so one-sided that one of the partners leaves and rejects the love-sick call for reunion. Then love-sickness becomes a broken heart. Love-lorn suffering is intense. It is like the grief of bereavement. Such melancholy may become laced with rage that escapes in retaliation dreams or nightmares of homocidal and suicidal jealousy. Sometimes the dreams become real-life dramas (p. xiii).

The Course of Limerence

At the first crystallization (the initial focusing on the other's admirable qualities), perhaps 30 percent of the limerent person's waking thoughts revolve around the other. At the height of limerence, or the second crystallization, the person spends virtually 100 percent of time not spent performing essential tasks, thinking about the other person. This preoccupation may remain at that level for days or weeks with only small and temporary respite; it may begin to undergo a final decline; or, most

---

[4]*Hypertrophia* is the condition of growing abnormally large.

typically, it may drop and then rise again one or more times before the decline that almost always follows sooner or later. Limerence at 100 percent may be ecstasy or it may be despair, and limerence may change from positive to negative at any level of intensity. The pleasantness or unpleasantness of the limerent state seemed almost unrelated to either the intensity of the reaction or its duration (Tennov 1979).

The Duration of Limerence

Tennov found the duration of limerence (ranging from mild to strong) to be anywhere from a few days, weeks, months, or years to the lifetime of the couple. The average duration, however, was about two years. Other writers have pointed out that a strong paired bond of this duration (two years) has significant survival value for the species, since it allows time for a woman to become pregnant, bear a child, and begin a new family. Limerence that lasts longer than two years also has survival value, since it tends to keep both parents together, cooperating with each other in protecting, caring for, and socializing the young. Since human offspring require an extended period of nurture and socialization if they are to survive and become members of the group, it is to the advantage of the species that parents form a relatively enduring paired bond. The longer the bond lasts, the better it is for the species (Morris 1973, Money and Ehrhardt 1972, Goode 1959). (See the vignette, "The Major Characteristics of Limerence.")

LOVE AND ATTACHMENT

Closely related to limerence is the phenomenon of attachment. *Attachment* is defined as a sort of bonding, which brings feelings of warmth, comfort, and security when the other is present or felt to be accessible. When the other is not present or felt to be accessible, *separation distress* occurs, which is defined as feelings of devastation, insecurity, and loneliness.

The Persistence of Attachment

One of the strangest and least explicable aspects of attachment is its curious persistence.[5] It is usually the last aspect of love to remain—long after other components such as idealization, trust, and caring have withered away, along with such "liking" correlates of love as affection, admiration, and respect. It is not unusual for attachment to be so tenacious that a couple may reconcile and remarry even after a divorce fraught with bitterness and resentment. Weiss (1975) describes the extraordinary persistence of attachment:

Idealization is apt to fade under the constant exposure of daily life. Trust may be eroded by small and large disappointments and betrayals. Feelings of identification may give way to a view of the other as critic and antagonist. Instead of feeling reassured and augmented by their relation, the partners may feel oppressed and diminished by it.

Yet with love seemingly ended, the husband and wife may continue to feel uncomfortable, edgy, or restless when the other is inaccessible. Contrary to what they believe they want, they may be drawn to one another. Attachment gives rise to a sense that home is where the other is. It persists even in bad marriages, even when the ultimate result of going home is that things start up again (p. 39).

---

[5]A demonstration of the extraordinary persistence of attachment was the case of an Oregon couple in 1978. In the first case of its kind, a wife charged her husband with rape while they were still living together. This was no ordinary lover's spat; if convicted, the husband faced a prison sentence of several years, and the wife's attorney did everything possible to bring this about. However, a few days after the jury found for the defendant and all charges were dismissed, the couple reconciled, the wife dropped the divorce proceedings, and the husband moved back into the house. (A few months later, they again separated, divorce proceedings were reinstituted, and this time it became final.)

The Major Characteristics of Limerence

Limerence is commonly experienced by many people in our society. There are others who do not experience it as an aspect of love and cannot imagine experiencing it. The relative numbers of limerent and nonlimerent persons have yet to be determined, but preliminary research indicates that limerence is far more common than nonlimerence—most people experience it at least once. Limerence is basically defined as compulsive thinking of, dreaming of, and emotional involvement with another person (or "limerent object"), a general intensity of feeling that leaves other concerns in the background. It may be experienced either as intense joy, pleasure, or ecstasy, or as extreme pain, suffering, or great depression. It is thus the source of the greatest happiness or the greatest despair but may be experienced on a scale ranging from low to high. It occurs in two stages: (1) first crystallization, when the person is excessively preoccupied with thoughts of the other for about 30 percent of the waking time not devoted to essential tasks, and (2) second crystallization, when preoccupation with thoughts of the other occupies virtually 100 percent of the time. The major characteristics of limerence are:

An emotional reliance on the other's actions; characteristic mood swings from ecstatic highs (when reciprocation is evident) to despondent lows (when it is not).

Acute longing for reciprocation of affection, attention, love, and limerence from the other.

Fleeting and transient release from the agonies of limerence through vivid fantasies of the limerent attraction being returned.

Acute sensitivity to any reaction or response from the other that could be interpreted favorably.

Buoyancy, a feeling of "walking on air," when reciprocation seems evident.

Emphasis on the admirable qualities of the other while avoiding dwelling on the negative qualities.

Confusion, fear of rejection, and incapacitating shyness in the limerent object's presence during the initial stages of limerence.

Intensification of limerence through adversity (up to a point).

An aching in the center of the chest, just below the sternum.

Inability to react limerently to more than one person at a time.

In the early stages of limerence, physical correlates often include a pounding heart, trembling, pallor, flushing, awkwardness, and stammering.

Persons who are in the grip of a limerent attraction that is not returned are characteristically nervous, anxious, fearful, apprehensive, and terribly concerned that their actions will bring about loss of the limerent object, which is perceived as ultimate disaster.

Duration of limerence varies; it may be very short—a few hours or days—or it may last a lifetime. The average duration is about two years.

Attachment Does Not Need Encouragement

A second unique characteristic of attachment is that it may occur with no encouragement from the other, and even in the face of outright abuse. This is seen most clearly in children but is by no means limited to them. Children are often attached to one or both parents whatever the parents' characteristics, so long as the parents are felt to be accessible. The parents need not be affectionate or considerate of the children's health or well-being. This feeling of attachment may persist even when the children do not especially like or admire the parents and do not feel friendly toward them.

Children who are battered and bruised by parents will continue to feel attachment to them. Attachment, like walking or talking, is an intrinsic capacity that developed under appropriate circumstances; it is not willed into being after a calculation of its advantages (Weiss 1975, p. 44).

It is not unusual for strong feelings of attachment to occur in adults despite discouragement (Tennov 1979). Indeed, a recurring theme of popular song lyrics is the persistence of attachment in the face of rebuff ("Just when I thought I was over you/Those memories come crashing through").

Separation Distress

As we have seen, separation distress occurs when the attachment figure is felt to be inaccessible. This can be seen very clearly in children, who have not yet learned to disguise their emotions as adults often do. For example, two-year-olds usually play happily only as long as their mothers remain in sight. A child of this age continually checks for the presence of the mother, interrupting play activities to see if she is in sight. An older child plays happily out of sight of the mother only if she is known to be accessible (Weiss 1975).

Although adults may endure short periods of being away from the attachment figure without feeling separation distress, loss of the other person causes distress in acute and devastating forms. Thus, rejection in a love affair may lead to extreme despondency and even suicide. When the attachment figure is lost through death, 95 percent of the survivors suffer intense grief; this loss is one of the leading causes of premature death (Lynch 1977, Glick et al. 1974). Apparently a "broken heart" is not just a poetic image but a stark reality for the person experiencing separation distress.

Loneliness

Weiss (1975) defines *loneliness* as a diffuse feeling of separation distress without a specific attachment figure. Beginning in adolescence (and perhaps before), it is quite possible for there to be no figure in a person's life whose accessibility provides the comfort and security associated with attachment. Parents usually fulfill this role throughout childhood.[6]

One characteristic of adolescence or young adulthood is that the person usually begins to search for an attachment figure other than a parent. In the absence of such a figure, a person may experience all the symptoms of separation distress without directing these feelings toward a specific person. Instead, the feelings of desolation or emptiness are related to the world in general.

The symptoms of loneliness are like those of separation distress, except that instead of pining for a particular figure the individual pines for anyone who could love and be loved, and instead of angrily or tearfully demanding the return of a particular figure, the individual will lament the barrenness of the world (Weiss 1975, p. 42).

The search for an attachment figure is also a search for intimacy, of course. The attachment figure and the intimate share many characteristics. *Intimacy*—the experiencing of the essence of one's self in intense emotional, physical, and intellectual communion with another—also brings a sense of fulfillment when the other is either present or felt to be accessible, and a sense of desolation (separation distress) when the other is absent or inaccessible, as we have seen (Chapter 1).

---

[6]This is not to say that attachment to a parent ceases with adolescence, of course. Attachment to a parent often remains well into adulthood, with the parent remaining an attachment figure even after one has a child of one's own. Thus, the death of the parent, and the ultimate and irrevocable breaking of the attachment, may cause a period of deep mourning, melancholy, or grief, even in the adult.

THE TRADITIONAL FACES OF LOVE

Since love is manifested in many different forms, and the experience of love is multifaceted and sometimes paradoxical (with negative limerence bringing anguish, for example), it is a highly complex concept to define. The problem is exemplified by the fact that there was no word in classical Greece for our word *love*. In its place the Socratic Greek had three words: *philos,* meaning an attraction that was characterized by a deep, enduring friendship; *agape*, meaning the self-sacrificing, nondemanding, "spiritual" satisfaction that a person feels when providing for another; and *eros*, meaning a passionate, sexual attraction.

Since about the twelfth century in Western civilization, love has been manifested in four facets: (1) the shared interests and concerns and intimacy of friendly or *companionate* love, (2) the self-sacrificing concern for the other's well-being of *altruistic* love, (3) the intensity and erotic preoccupation of *passionate* love, and (4) the idyllic beauty and idealism of *romantic* love. These four faces of love have been thought of as merging to form the idealization of love in marriage in our contemporary society.

Companionate Love

Companionate love may begin with limerence and then continue after limerence has faded away, or a couple may be simply drawn together without experiencing any limerent attraction at all—that is, their interaction is companionate from the beginning. Companionate love is sensible, calm, relaxed, and has strong overtones of liking, admiration, and respect. Companionate love seems to be based on conversation, friendship, shared activities, and emotional closeness or intimacy.

Companionate love provides a sense of satisfaction in simply being with the other. Each person in a companionate love relation can depend upon the other for emotional security, for caring, affection, emotional support, and—perhaps most important of all—intimacy. These are precious commodities of inestimable value in our contemporary mass society, and their absence may be experienced as physically and emotionally devastating, as we have seen (Chapter 1).

Married couples spend much more of their time together at the comfortable and rewarding levels of companionate love than at the exalted heights of romantic or passionate attraction; it is undoubtedly the most commonly experienced aspect of love in marriage.

Don't walk in front of me
I might not follow
Don't walk behind me
I might not lead the way
Walk beside me
And be my friend

                Camus

Altruistic Love

Altruistic love is close to the Greek concept of *agape*. It is defined as the emotional satisfaction one receives from providing nurture for another instead of for oneself. Altruism, or altruistic love, is probably a necessary ingredient to any combination of love in a paired bond. It may even predominate in the relation, as it did in Sidney Carton's relation with Lucie in Dickens's *A Tale of Two Cities*. Carton sacrifices his life so that Lucie might be happy, even though this happiness takes the form of her loving another. (Lucie is unaware of Carton's devotion.) In this example of altruistic love at its ultimate, there are also strong romantic elements—Carton idealizes Lucie—but no sexual elements. There are also, of course, strong limerent elements; thoughts of Lucie overwhelm most of Carton's waking hours.

In infrahuman animals, the manifestation of caring for offspring even at the jeopardy of one's own life is reflexive-instinctive, so that the mother is impelled to nurture, care, and protect as a function of hormonal activity.

In the laboratory, maternal behavior can be induced in the female simply by hormonal injections—and it can be terminated in the same manner (Kephart 1977, p. 42).

In primates, and especially in human beings, the need to provide nurture for another is less reflexive and more diffuse. The evidence from Harlow's studies (1962) with the rhesus monkey, for example, indicates that nurturing in the primate is a learned phenomenon, occurring chiefly as a result of having received nurturant care in infancy.

Whatever its source, this aspect of behavior—caring for another taking precedence over caring for oneself—is essential to the continuation of life. Sorokin (1973) suggests that the basis of altruistic love is a need for living organisms to be helpful to one another. Life could not occur at all, or could occur only at the unicellular level, if this behavior were not characteristic of all life forms. Interaction and *symbiosis* occur from the unicellular level on up and are manifested in "innumerable reactions of cooperation and aid, at least as frequent and common as the actions-reactions of the struggle for existence" (p. 641).

Among all organisms, altruistic tendencies and egoistic tendencies occur in a relatively close balance: The need to interact in an integrative, unifying, harmonious way is counterbalanced by the need to demonstrate aggression, antagonism, destruction, and self-interest. Species compete with species for available space, oxygen, water, and food, and individuals compete with other individuals in most environments for the basic goods of life. In human societies, then, "brotherhood tempered by rivalry" is the foundation of most social behavior (Wynne-Edwards 1964).

The term *passionate love* describes a deep, compelling love, often with a strong erotic or sexual element.

Passionate Love

The term *passionate love* has often been used to describe love that has a strong limerent component. It usually is used to mean a deep, compelling love, often with a strong erotic or sexual element. When love and sexual desire—each a very powerful emotion in its own right—occur together directed toward the same person, each emotion reinforces the other. If the experience is mutual, with both persons passionately in love with each other, each may be virtually transported into another dimension of experience. Many elements of passionate love are those of limerence, of course.

Passionate Love at a Distance

Passionate love does not always include erotic fulfillment. A couple may be passionately in love with no erotic contact beyond holding hands or even simply looking at one another, which might be electrifying. For example, the love affair of Elizabeth Barrett and Robert Browning was deeply passionate, yet their only physical contact with one another was during occasional visits when they were under the very close surveillance of Elizabeth's family. (Elizabeth was virtually a bedridden invalid at the time and was carefully guarded by a tyrannical Victorian father.) They nevertheless managed courtship—chiefly through letters—and were married in 1846.

Elizabeth Barrett Browning's sonnet celebrating the experience of a deeply passionate, idealized love is regarded as one of the most notable in our language.

How do I love thee? Let me count the ways.
I love thee to the depth and breadth and height
My soul can reach, when feeling out of sight
For the ends of Being and ideal Grace.
I love thee to the level of every day's
Most quiet need, by sun and candlelight.
I love thee freely, as men strive for Right;
I love thee purely, as they turn from Praise.
I love thee with the passion put to use
In my old griefs, and with my childhood's faith.
I love thee with a love I seemed to lose
With my lost saints,—I love thee with the breath,
Smiles, Tears, of all my life!—and, if God choose,
I shall but love thee better after death.

Sonnets from the Portuguese, XLIII

It is possible for passionate love to occur without contact, with the lovers unable, for various reasons, to express their love physically. A famous example of this is the love affair of Robert Browning (the illustrious English romantic poet) and Elizabeth Barrett. (See the vignette, "Passionate Love at a Distance.")

Romantic Love

Contemporary romantic love is visionary, idyllic, imaginative, and adventurous. It is the idealization of beauty, grace, and charm in the woman and strength, courage, and sacrifice in the man. Like passionate love, romantic love also has a high component of limerence. It may also be combined with sexual or erotic attraction and fulfillment. But this was not always the case.

Our modern concept of romantic love originated in the twelfth century as *courtly love*, which was embodied in the devotion of a knight errant who swore eternal fealty to his lady.

However, courtly love was always asexual. Sex was presumed to be ignoble, degrading, and animalistic; proper chivalric conduct demanded an absence of overt sexual relations between a courtly lover and his lady.[7] The knight's love was expected to personify the Platonic ideal of selfless courage and sacrifice on his lady's account, with no physical contact and often no communication.[8] If the courtly lovers did communicate, it was usually very brief—a few lines (perhaps of verse) might be exchanged, as the knight swore eternal fidelity. Sometimes a token, such as a flower, would be granted the knight from his lady. Their relation might never be acknowledged publicly, and there was no possibility of the courtly lov-

---

[7]Hunt (1959) suggests that "evidently there were . . . forces at work . . . implicit in early Christianity, which established the diametrical opposition between sexuality and love." (p. 149)

[8]Platonic love transcends physical desire to emphasize the purely spiritual or ideal relation between a man and a woman—a relation in which all yearning and aspiration for sexual fulfillment have been either suppressed or sublimated.

ers ever expressing their relation sexually. In the prototype of romantic love, Launcelot was enamored of Guinevere, who was King Arthur's queen and forever unobtainable to Launcelot.

Many observers of the human scene have suggested that the asexual aspect is essential to the experience of romantic love—in other words, the emotion of romantic love occurs as a result of blocking the drive for sexual expression. For example, Young (1943) stated:

In romantic love the lovers are at once aroused and inhibited sexually. This state of conflict evokes the disturbing emotion known as "being in love." The more strongly an individual is excited by sexual stimulation and the more completely this biological urge is frustrated, the greater will be his emotional disturbance.

Allport (1924) felt that when

. . . the sexual drive of the wooer is not released, every detail of the beloved from head to toe is . . . a stimulus which helps to augment the tonus already present in the pelvic viscera. This is the condition of being blindly in love.

As the popular belief of the nineteenth and early twentieth centuries stated, "After he's had you, he won't want you"—implying that if you don't let him "have" you, he'll be sexually frustrated and fall in love with you.

Critics of this hypothesis have found it much too ingenuous, however, and point out that romantic attraction can occur as an end in itself, independent of sexual needs, whether these needs are frustrated or satisfied. Malinowsky (1929), for example, found that strongly individualized, passionate, and enduring romantic attractions occur among the Trobriand Islanders, whose society openly accepts sexual activity and among whom no individual may therefore be presumed to be sexually frustrated or deprived.[9]

Whether the involvement in contemporary romantic love is erotic or not, the principal role that each person plays is to fulfill the other's romantic expectations.

Olive R. Pierce/Stock, Boston

The prevailing view in our contemporary society is that romantic love is an emotion that may occur either in the absence of *or* in the presence of sexual fulfillment. This view accepts two separate and distinct needs, sexual and romantic, but hypothesizes that these two needs are closely related and may ultimately be interdependent in a love affair or a marriage. If both needs are satisfied by the same person—who is then a sex object *and* a romantic love object—the gratification resulting from fulfilling erotic needs reinforces feelings of romantic love. This kind of sexual and romantic interaction may produce an intense intimacy and immediacy of communication that will strengthen the couple's mutual commitment.

Historical Origins of Romantic Love

Since the modern concept of romantic love is so important in dating and courtship, and since it has undergone some curious transformations

---

[9]See also Ellis (1949), Sears (1943), Moll (1925), and Bell (1902).

since its inception (in ancient Rome), we shall trace its development in some detail.

Ironically enough, the concept of what we now call romantic love is based on a medieval misinterpretation of the classical love poetry, particularly that of Ovid.[10] To the classical poets, romantic love was an etiquette or game that was cynically designed to promote successful seduction and certainly did not idealize either the admired person or the interaction.

This literary conceit all but disappeared in Europe with the fall of Rome and the emergence of the Christian era. It persevered, however, in North Africa (which was heir to much of the classical tradition of Greek and Roman erudition). The tongue-in-cheek, hyperbolic classical love poetry of Ovid and his contemporaries found fertile ground in the delicate Saracen taste for beauty and sensuality, and the classical concept of romantic love (as an exercise in seduction) became an integral part of the Saracen culture.

In the late eleventh century the classical concept of romantic love crossed the Mediterranean and was adopted by the Moorish culture of Spain. By the twelfth century, it had been carried across the border into neighboring France by wandering minstrels—the troubadours—and so made its way back to European culture after an absence of some twelve hundred years.

However, in the treatment by the troubadours the classical concept of romantic love underwent a curious and ironic transformation. Based upon a misunderstanding of Ovid's verses, romantic love was interpreted to mean the idealization of the unattainable woman, who was chastely adored by a self-sacrificing man devoted to her service. The twelfth-century French troubadours sang of this ideal as the embodiment of the highest form of man-woman relations. It came to be called "courtly love."

This idealized concept of romantic love was celebrated in vast numbers of extraordinarily popular ballads. Troubadours wandered through the French countryside singing endless variations of the dashing knight on a white charger, who had taken vows of eternal fealty to his lady, an unattainable ideal of feminine beauty. (Ovid would have been astonished.) By about the middle of the twelfth century, the concept of chivalric devotion to a lady representing the feminine ideal had crossed the Channel to become a central theme of the English troubadours.

European writers were captivated by the concept, and the theme of service to an unattainable ideal love began to appear in the literature (as well as the ballads) of both England and France. A familiar prototypical example was the long prose tale *Launcelot and Guinevere*, a romantic narrative embodying the chivalric concept of self-abnegation and the idealization of women. It has survived, virtually unchanged, to the present day.[11] The virtue, beauty, and divinity of women came to be considered the chief opportunity for a man to enoble himself by denying all carnal attraction and dedicating himself to his virtuous lady's service.

On the surface, it would be hard to conceive of a more unlikely time for a philosophy of selfless devotion to women to have emerged. Prior to the twelfth century women had been thought of chiefly as a source of sin. They were denounced from the pulpit as "temptresses" to lust, whose function was to tempt men from the path of virtue, while civil authorities regarded women as little more than *chattel*.[12] Wives could be beaten by their husbands with no

---

[10]See Ovid's *The Art of Love*, a poetic description of frivolous love affairs and the art of seduction.

[11]*Camelot*, the Broadway musical (later a motion picture), is a retelling of the Launcelot legend.

[12]*Chattel* is defined as all tangible property, movable or immovable, except real estate.

penalty in law "provided death does not ensue." Women's testimony was legally inadmissable in court, and they could not represent themselves in legal actions (Hunt 1959).

Despite vows of fealty and vassalage, petty nobles were still constantly warring upon one another without pretext other than the bold hope of gain . . . fighting and hunting remained the basic interests of the noblemen. They accepted tourneys in place of actual combat, but even these long continued to be bloody and ferocious affairs. Such men would hardly seem candidates for gentle emotions and silent suffering (Hunt 1959, p. 145).

Why courtly love—which considered woman as divinely chaste and the source of man's highest inspiration and ideals—should have spread so rapidly and become a way of life and social philosophy for the nobility of the Middle Ages is by no means entirely clear, and, as in all social developments, there were many complex factors involved. Among the forces at work, according to historians, were (1) the increasing deification of the Virgin Mary,[13] (2) the changing socioeconomic conditions caused by the feudal system,[14] (3) the Crusades,[15] and finally (4) to the newly founded order, wealth, and leisure of the society, which provided the young sons of the aristocracy with the time and inclination for a consideration of the finely wrought philosophies of the classical and Eastern cultures (Tuchman 1978).

Apparently the concept and practice of courtly love met a need to "find duties which would refine and tame men's manners" in a feudal order that was emerging from barbarism (Hunt 1959, p. 150). Nevertheless, it is ironic that the concept of courtly love, which was to revolutionize the sociosexual philosophy of Western civilization, was based upon a misinterpretation and misunderstanding of a literary conceit detailing a philosophy of deceit and seduction.[16]

Beginning in the twelfth century, the ideal of courtly love began to spread very gradually from the nobility and the aristocracy through ever lower levels of the society, until a bourgeois version of romantic love was reached, four hundred years later, in the early sixteenth century. Like the aristocratic version, it idealized woman and chivalric devotion to her service, but it was not limited to knights and nobility. By the mid-sixteenth century this concept of romantic love had pervaded the rising middle class of merchants, shopkeepers, officials, and professionals.

Another three hundred years were to pass before romantic love and marriage were blended, however. Marriage was a frankly sexual relation, and romantic love and sex were still thought to be irreconcilable. Marriage had to do with practical affairs; it consisted of the "joining of lands, the cementing of loyalties, and the production of heirs and future defenders. But . . . love for an ideal woman—what

---

[13]A contradiction existed throughout all medieval thought between the exalted image of the Virgin Mary, through whom salvation was sent to humanity, and the image of Eve (and all earthly females), through whom man was led to destruction. The rise in the idealization of women by no means occurred overnight; during this period of increasing acceptance of the female as an embodiment of virtue, tens of thousands of women were burned at the stake as the embodiment of evil (Tuchman 1978, Hunt 1959, Biegel 1951).

[14]For example, the cloistered living habits of the few women in the feudal castle encouraged the many soldiers—the knights—of the castle to idealize the nearly unattainable noblewomen of the environment. The fealty to the women of the castle was also an extension of the feudal system, in which men swore their allegiance and protection to a sovereign lord and his lands, in return for which the knights received status and lifelong support and the grace and blessings of the Church, which was feudal itself and chiefly responsible for the social order.

[15]The religious wars against the Moors gave the knights a firsthand taste of the Saracen culture and, as all wars do, encouraged the idealization of the women at home for whom they were fighting. (The identification of the war effort with the will of the Virgin must also have had some role in this idealization of the female.)

[16]Three hundred years or more may not be summed up so briefly without much oversimplification, of course. The interested student will find fascinating and detailed accounts of the complex subject of the development of courtly love in Goode (1959), Hunt (1959), Durant (1957, 1953, 1950), DeRougemont (1956), Biegel (1951), Coulton (1930), and Howard (1904).

had that to do with details of crops, and cattle, fleas and fireplaces, serfs and swamp drainage?" (Hunt 1959, p. 137).

Marriage and sex relations were contained within an official relation, whereas romantic love . . . remained outside of marriage on an individual basis. Marriage was the public and responsible one. Marriage was permanent and stable, a means of conserving property and rearing children . . . romantic love lasted only so long as the personal preference for each other was fervid (Cavan 1969, p. 407).

Romantic love was finally blended with marriage in the Victorian era of the nineteenth century. (Victoria was crowned queen in 1837.) In fact, the Victorian era not only combined romantic love with marriage, but a woman's love was thought to be proper *only* if she was (or was soon to be) one's wife. The romantic concept of the nineteenth century changed the ideal of courtly love to meet the needs of a business-oriented society.

The theme of romanticism became prominent in such mass media as advertising, song lyrics, newspapers, comic strips, short stories, and novels. Beginning in the nursery children were conditioned in the romantic roles expected of them as teenagers and adults, and by the early twentieth century romance became the most vital aspect of dating, courtship, and marriage.

The nineteenth century did not blend romantic love and sex, however. Romantic love, most emphatically, did not include sexual or erotic elements for the Victorians. Sex was thought of as crude and vulgar, having nothing to do with romance.[17] The female ideal was a sweet, tender, girl-mother, in whom sexual desire was considered pathological. "The model

for the bond between the sexes was the complex of feelings so graciously depicted in medieval romances" (Biegel 1951, p. 327). The typical "romantic" of the period prided himself on his ability to fall passionately in love with a woman, devote himself to her service, yet remain sexually restrained.

Victorian copulation was hasty, ashamed, and uncommunicative; the husband "took his pleasure," or "had his way." He was acknowledged to have an "animal" nature, and his wife's duty was to accept that fact. Copulation took place only at night (under cover of darkness) and night clothes were not removed during its performance. Petting was taboo. Ideally, the virtuous but tolerant wife submitted while her husband performed "the sex act" as quickly and circumspectly as possible. Queen Victoria advised wives to "close your eyes, and think of England!"[18]

The romantic ideal of the period forbade women to be sexually seductive in any way. A wife was considered the source of ethical values; her function included raising the "cultural tone" of the family and leading her husband's mind to dwell on "higher things."

Until the Victorian era sex had often been condemned but had always been treated frankly. Victorians, however, introduced prudery into the mainstream of English (and American) life. Pregnancy became "in a family way," legs became "limbs," pants became "nether garments," and copulation became "the sex act."[19]

---

[17]Sexual love had always been condemned by some splinter groups, of course (for example, Calvinists and Puritans), but never by the majority of a society except perhaps during early medieval times. Even then, the condemnation was frank, with no linguistic prudery; sex was sinful, not obscene. The concept of obscenity apparently owes its origin to the Victorians.

[18]As with any generalization, there were widespread exceptions to this professed Victorian ideology. Some marriages were characterized by enjoyment of sex, there were some passionate love affairs, and many women defied the sociosexual norms of the period and admitted to frank eroticism (privately if not publicly). In addition, there was a vast underground of sexuality in Victorian England that was not normally visible or admitted. There were an estimated eighty thousand prostitutes in London alone, and it was common practice for young country girls to go to London to enter "the sporting life" (see Gaylin 1976, Marcus 1966, *My Secret Life* [anonymous] 1894).

[19]The use of euphemisms by no means ended with the Victorians, nor with the Edwardians, nor with the contemporary era. Although "in a family way" now sounds anachronistic, we often

Adolescent boys of the nineteenth and early twentieth centuries were taught to regard "pure women" as sexless. Hence, when he married and copulated with his wife the man was degrading her—sex was destroying the romantic ideal.

The hero of popular stories was invariably sentimental and sexless, relatively free from the ignoble demands of eroticism, idealizing his emotional attachment to the heroine as "pure" love. In the words of an editor of the *Saturday Evening Post*, one of the most popular publications in the United States until World War II, both the hero and the heroine were to be portrayed as "solid from the waist down."

However, sweeping changes of women's position in society were occurring during the late nineteenth and early twentieth centuries. By the twentieth century, women had been granted legal equality with men in most Western nations; they could own property, make contracts, bring suit, and, in general, function as legal "persons." They won the rights to vote and to run for political office in the United States in 1920. As the century progressed, more and more occupations opened to women, and by 1950 women had moved (to some extent) into the sciences, professions, and arts. In 1890, fewer than one wife in ten worked; by 1950, one in five worked (see Chapter 2).

As the second half of the twentieth century began, American women had gained an economic independence unique in the history of Western civilization, and the stage was set for the emergence of the next interpretation of romantic love.[20] By 1960 new societal attitudes toward sex and romantic love were signaled in the mass media by the frank acceptance of sexuality in popular song lyrics, by the open depiction of sexuality and eroticism in Broadway musicals and plays and in motion pictures, and by the emergence of a new type of folk hero who—as well as being romantic in the classical medieval tradition—was openly erotic.

Like his predecessors—from Launcelot to Tarzan of the Apes[21]—this new romantic hero was full of derring-do, self-sacrificing to the point of death for a noble cause, skilled in the martial arts, and devoted to a struggle against overwhelming odds to rescue a woman in distress.[22] However, the young woman he rescued by dint of almost superhuman effort was also a sexual prize. The romantic ideal was now combined with a frank recognition of the pleasurable aspect of erotic interaction.[23]

---

hear "passed away" to mean dead. The curious term *sex act* is commonly seen in textbooks, and it is not unusual to find the phrase "going all the way" in newspapers—especially in syndicated columns that advise readers on matters of the heart—although the term *copulation* is now becoming admissible in the daily press to some extent. This makes possible the curious coinage *oral copulation*—a strange, hybrid euphemism that manages to avoid the explicit *fellatio* while still conveying the intended meaning. This spares the sensibilities of readers in the best Victorian tradition. (In 1981, newspapers and syndicates covering a widely reported trial in California involving a member of the California state legislature constantly used the term *oral copulation*.)

[20]Prior to the 1960s, the self-administered code of the motion picture industry prohibited the showing of couples together in the same bed, even though they were married. For example, in the well-known *Thin Man* films (with William Powell and Myrna Loy), Nick and Nora Charles were always portrayed as occupying twin beds. This extended well into the 1960s as exemplified by Dick Van Dyke and Mary Tyler Moore in the classic television series, "The Dick Van Dyke Show."

[21]It is interesting to note that the 1981 motion picture *Tarzan, the Ape Man*, with Bo Derek as Jane, does portray Tarzan sexually. This caused some concern to the administrators of the literary estate, which obtained a court action directing that some of the nude scenes in the film be removed on the grounds that they were not in accordance with the tradition of the original publication.

[22]A good example of this cultural change is the very popular fictional hero of the 1960s, James Bond (007)—a creation of Ian Fleming, a British writer whose books became very popular in the United States during the 1960s.

[23]It should be noted that, although the concept of a union of romantic love and eroticism did not find general acceptance until the second half of the twentieth century, the first indication that such a blend was to develop can be traced to the court societies of Austria, Spain, France, and the Netherlands as early as the sixteenth and seventeenth centuries. At that time, while the bourgeoisie was adopting and promulgating the earlier sociosexual culture of the court, the court itself began to accept sexual and erotic behavior as consistent with the ideals of romantic love, and "began to award the gallant's service to his beloved with sexual favors"—blending for the first time courtly love and sexual fruition (Biegel 1951, p. 327).

"I fell in love with you the first time I heard your message on the answering machine."

Contemporary Romantic Love

Is contemporary romantic love consistent with erotic attraction and fulfillment? The answer must be yes. That is, romantic love *may* be combined with eroticism. It may also be asexual or unerotic, of course, especially in young lovers. It is quite possible for the intensity of a limerent and romantic attraction to remain on the same idealized level as that depicted by the medieval romances, and this is often the case. Romantic love can be quite intense with no overtones of sexuality.

Whether the involvement in contemporary romantic love is erotic or not, the principal role that each person plays in relating to the other is to fulfill the other's romantic expectations— so that, as a pair, they conform to the romantic pattern drawn from countless role models in books, comic strips, television shows, and motion pictures to which they have both been exposed from infancy. They label the emotions they feel as "romantic," and they then feel and behave in accordance with "romantic" expectations. Not only does each person idealize the other, but each also tries to fulfill the ideal of the other.

Contemporary romantic love is characterized by an all-encompassing one-to-one relation. A couple wishes to be alone with each other because "privacy and secrecy make identification easy, and the two build up a feeling of their own, furnished with their shared memories" (Cavan 1969, p. 386).

Are women more romantic than men? Do women dream more about romantic fulfillment than men? Do young women spend more of their time immersed in fantasies about meeting a daring, dashing, handsome, and ardent admirer (the knight on the white charger) than young men spend daydreaming about their feminine ideal (the princess in the tower)? Research is inconclusive. It is women who buy and read the romantic novels of such writers as Barbara Cartland[24] and such magazines as *True Romance*, whereas men tend to read *Field and Stream*, *Car and Driver*, and *Infoworld*. Men are traditionally expected to talk about sports, cars, and business, whereas women are supposed to be more interested in discussing affairs of the heart. Yet virtually all love songs are written by men, as are virtually all ballets, operas, and ballads.

In country-western songs it is the woman who is usually portrayed as sacrificing everything for the man she loves, whereas men's feelings are often represented as less urgent, more muted. Men are often portrayed as drifters (wandering knights?), usually brushing aside passionate or tender emotions ("Baby, baby, don't get hooked on me").

However, research finds that men are much more vulnerable to falling romantically in love than are women, and they fall in love much more quickly than do women. For example, in one study in which men and women were asked how early in the affair they had become aware that they were in love, 20 percent of the men said they had fallen in love before the fourth date, as compared with 15 percent of the women. At the other extreme, 45 percent of the women were still not sure whether they were in love by the twentieth date, as compared with only 30 percent of the men (Kanin et al. 1970).

Since women have much more to gain or lose from a serious love affair, they are perhaps genetically programmed to be much more cautious—for it is a biological imperative that women are the ones that become pregnant with all the responsibilities that this implies. It is therefore conceivable that women have been conditioned during millions of years of genetic heritage to be more cautious than men about becoming deeply involved without the formal commitment that secures protection, support, and partnership in the eventuality of childbirth and the ensuing responsibility for rearing the child.

Not only do men fall romantically in love more quickly than women, but they also cling more tenaciously to a dying love affair than do women, and they are more depressed, lonelier, and less able to function effectively when the relation ends. Men find it harder to accept the fact that they are no longer loved—that the affair is over and there is nothing they can do about it. Women are more philosophical and more practical in taking steps to meet new people and make new friends (Hill et al. 1976). It is interesting to note in this regard that three times as many men as women commit suicide after a disastrous love affair (Walster and Walster 1978).

Can contemporary romantic love be combined with marriage? Again, the answer must be yes. In fact, romantic love has now become the major reason for marrying. The couple are expected to fall romantically in love, then marry because they *are* in love. The modern concept of romantic love has assumed enormous importance in dating, courtship, and marriage. Contemporary American society not only makes romantic love a primary basis for marriage, but, once married, a person is expected to derive all romantic satisfaction within the framework of marriage. If extramarital romantic involvement does occur, our cultural expectation is that it must either be discontinued or be institutionalized by divorce and remarriage.

Can romantic love continue in marriage? The contemporary feeling is yes, it can. However, it does not always do so. About half

---

[24] The English author Barbara Cartland has produced an extraordinarily successful series of romantic novels, with a very avid following of readers—virtually all of whom are women. Her books have sold in the millions.

of all marriages end in divorce, as we shall see (Chapter 8). Of those that do not end in divorce, many are chronically unhappy with the couple held together by various practical concerns. As we have seen, attachment is the last component of love to remain, persisting long after all romantic feelings have withered away.

Even though the ideal in our society now combines romantic love with marriage, many observers have pointed out that the values of romantic love contradict those of marriage. The emphasis in romance is upon freedom; the emphasis in marriage is upon responsibility. Values in romantic love are personal; in marriage they are familial. Romance is private, tumultuous, idiosyncratic, and characterized by an intensity of experience and heightened awareness; marriage is public, stabilized, routine, and often mundane.

The social setting of Europe in which the modern concept of romantic love developed, clearly separated the institution of romance from that of marriage, as we have seen. Marriage was arranged by the families involved and was based upon practical considerations unrelated to whatever personal attraction the man and the woman might or might not feel toward each other. Marriage was not an institution to provide for the fulfillment of personal desires, but rather a sober relation that provided for societal and economic needs and for the establishment and maintenance of a family.

However, despite many contradictory characteristics between romance and marriage, romantic love is not necessarily opposed to married love. Romantic love not only may continue after marriage but conceivably may even be enhanced by it. If a person identifies her husband or his wife as a real person rather than as a projection of idealized needs, then marital interaction can deepen the romantic love of dating and courtship. Of course, if the identification is not founded upon reality, disillusion will inevitably result from the close, constant everyday contact that is characteristic of

marriage, which forces an acknowledgment of the reality of the person, rather than the idealized vision.

Variations of Love

In any serious paired bond there is usually an interplay of limerent, romantic, passionate, companionate, and altruistic elements of love. The relative importance of each component varies from one couple to another, as well as for the same couple from one time to another. Thus, limerence, passion, and romance may be more prominent in some marriages and in some serious paired bonds than in others.

In the early stages of any paired bond, the limerent, passionate, and romantic components are probably more prominent than in the later stages. In a good relation, each partner fulfills the current emotional need of the other much of the time—whether romantic, companionate, or limerent—even if this need is not always mutual. In fact, such need fulfillment in marriage is often alternate rather than simultaneous. Alternate provision of emotional need satisfaction is characteristic of maturity and of a paired bond that is enduring. (For an elaboration of this point see the section "Learning to Love" later in this chapter.)

STYLES OF LOVING

Since love is such a complex emotion involving many components, it is not surprising that there are different styles of loving that vary widely from one another. Despite the wide range of possibilities, a Canadian psychologist, John Alan Lee, found that there are only three major styles of loving. Other variations are compounds or mixtures. Lee (1973) analyzed some four thousand published accounts of love—from classical Greece to the present—and compared them with empirical studies of contemporary love experiences. The three major styles of loving that emerged are eros, ludus, and storge. *Eros* is a passionate, all-developing love; *ludus* (pronounced "loo-doos") is a playful, flirtatious love; and *storge* (pronounced "store-gay") is a calm, companionate love. These major categories of love do not usually occur in their pure forms, but rather in combinations. For example, *mania*, a common form of love that will be described later, is a blend of eros and ludus. Every individual tends to express love in one of these forms; that is, a storge person is unlikely to fall in love the same way an eros person does.

Lee's discovery helps explain the difficulty of understanding the paired bond of another couple ("What does she see in him?"), as well as the pain and puzzlement that occur when a person characterized by one style of loving attempts to relate to a person characterized by a different type. One important contribution of Lee's research is the recognition that, although each person defines true love in terms of personal experience and personal style of loving, this experience can be completely different from another person's. Thus, Lee concludes that each type of love is equally valid and that no one type is necessarily "truer" than another. "True love" is what it means to the individual, even though this may be as different as storge from eros.

Eros Lovers

Lee describes eros as characterized by an immediate, powerful limerent attraction at first meeting, accompanied by such physiological reactions as increased pulse rate, shortness of breath, and trembling and such sensations as a tight band across the chest or a fluttering in the stomach. Looking into the other's eyes can cause a sensation approaching shock, so that sustained eye contact becomes virtually impossible. MacDonald (1971) gives an intriguing description of this phenomenon:

Something moved somehow behind her eyes, maybe like a pair of eyes behind them, suddenly opening to look out at me. It is something happening, like the world turning over and stopping at an angle you didn't know about. . . like being trapped there, like our eyes got caught somehow, and I couldn't move away (p. 17).

In addition, it is not unusual for an eros person to be literally struck dumb when first encountering an ideal other, to be unable to make any sensible conversation. The eros lover is, then, very susceptible to a limerent experience. In fact, limerence is a very important aspect of the eros person's consciousness.

The type of beauty that each eros person holds as a vision or the embodiment of an ideal is so specific that he or she can sort through a number of photographs very quickly and select the ones that portray this idealized concept of beauty. (Other types of lovers cannot do this.) It is, thus, not surprising that an eros person experiences intense feelings of excitement, anticipation, and hope at the first sight of someone who represents the physical embodiment of an ideal—especially since the specifications are so precise that they are fulfilled only by a very few.

This "love at first sight" phenomenon does not mean, however, that the eros person is interested only in physical beauty. "Love at first sight" is merely a shorthand expression for saying "the kind of love that begins with a powerful physical attraction." The couple establish a sustained paired bond only if this visual attraction is followed by emotional, sexual, and intellectual rapport (Lee 1975).

More than any other kind of love, eros is characterized by an active and imaginative interest in sexual fulfillment. Eros people typically press for an early sexual relation and usually become lovers shortly after meeting. Nothing is more deadly to eros than lack of sexual enthusiasm or a puritanical approach to sex. If the eros person is attracted to someone who is not freely erotic, his or her joy is short-lived and the relation is likely to disintegrate.

Although the possibilities for sustained eros in a paired bond are rather remote, Lee did find

Abigail Heyman/Archive Pictures, Inc.

For ludus lovers, love is a game to be played for amusement, pleasure, and excitement.

coyness, coquetry, and gallantry are all part of the ludus strategy and add spice and pleasurable tension to the couple's interaction. Unlike eros lovers, ludus lovers are quite content with their detachment from the intense feelings of love and are not jealous or possessive.

The ludus person does not have a specific vision of ideal beauty as does the eros person but has a wide range of physical tastes, and anyone who falls within that range is considered a desirable partner. This is exemplified by the lyrics in *Finnian's Rainbow*: "When I'm not near the girl I love, I love the girl I'm near."

When a ludus lover has the misfortune to select an eros lover for a ludus adventure. attempts to keep the relation pleasantly casual are usually not successful because of the eros lover's limerent attachment. The breakup can thus be quite painful for the eros person. However, when the game of ludus love is played by two people who understand the rules and the expectations, the relation can be ended quite gracefully, especially since each has at least one other partner at the same time and neither has expected to obtain lasting satisfaction but only an interlude of adventure, excitement, and (often) sexual satisfaction.

that the ideal of eros is sometimes fulfilled in real life. Cuber and Harroff (1965) estimate that such relations occur in perhaps 10 percent of marriages (see Chapter 7).

Ludus Lovers

In contrast to eros lovers, ludus lovers experience a love affair as essentially a game to be played for amusement, pleasure, and excitement, with no lasting commitments. Ludus is most easily played with several partners at once, and not telling each partner about the other is completely acceptable. A ludus lover engages in sex for fun, not emotional rapport, and is much more willing to delay sexual satisfaction than is the eros lover, for whom sex is an integral part of the fascination. Flattery,

Storge Lovers

Storge is an unexciting, uneventful, and unpassionate love, quite different from either eros or ludus. It is a companionate form of love, a love of quiet affection based on practical considerations with goals of marriage, children, and an established place in the community.

Whereas eros lovers study each other's faces, talk endlessly about each other's past lives and current feelings, and are intensely aware of the fact of being in love, storge lovers treat each other simply as old friends. In fact, storge has such a low profile, compared with Lee's other typologies of love, that it may be difficult to distinguish from ordinary friendship. Certainly, to the eros or ludus person, storge is not really love at all. To the storge person, however, the playfulness of ludus is a mockery of serious love and the ecstasy of eros is an illusion. A storge person is definitely non-limerent and cannot imagine the intensity of feeling and impulsive involvement character-istic of a limerent attraction.

Storge people do not have any ideals of physical beauty, and there is no dramatic be-ginning in storge. Storge people either drift into marriage with someone who enjoys the same interests and activities, or they deliber-ately plan to marry a compatible person. The storge person would be puzzled and confused by an eros or ludus partner who expects a more dramatic experience. Once married, storge people are relatively undemanding and non-possessive. They are not upset, for example, by a partner's lengthy physical absence.

Classic examples of storge occur among people who grow up together as neighbors or meet as schoolmates, but storge can also de-velop between people who meet as adults—especially if they have similar backgrounds and *might* have grown up together.

Sexual intimacy comes late in the slow de-velopment of storge, not because the storge person necessarily takes a puritanical attitude toward sexual pleasures, but because rapid progress toward sexual intimacy is considered inappropriate. Sex does not become a factor in storge until after an intellectual and emotional understanding has been achieved, and even then the storge person does not anticipate emotional intensity. The concept of ecstasy is, of course, completely beyond the range of ex-pectations. It is therefore not surprising that sexual disappointment is far less likely to break up the storge pair than it is an eros or ludus pair.

Although storge is rarely hectic or urgent, it is not without its disagreements and conflicts, and storge partnerships do not always survive. If a breakup does occur, however, the storge lovers are very likely to remain good friends. It would be inconceivable to a storge person that two people who had truly loved each other at one time could hate each other simply because they had ceased to be lovers.

Manic Lovers

Manic love is a combination of eros and ludus. A manic lover is characteristically limerent, with the second crystallization of limerence occurring rather quickly. Usually the limer-ence is negative; the manic lover is racked by yearning and moodiness, alternating between momentary highs of irrational joy and lows of anxiety and depression. The slightest lack of response from the other causes pain and re-sentment, whereas any sign of warmth brings enormous relief. The manic lover's pleasure is always short-lived, however, since needs for attention and affection are virtually insatiable. Manic lovers seem almost possessed by some strange demon, gripped by a sort of madness that seizes them and produces a torment of un-satisfied desire and humiliation.

Mania is the theme of innumerable romantic novels with the familiar characteristics of ex-treme jealousy, helpless obsession, and a trag-ic ending. The literature of love portrays the manic lover as a person whose feelings are beyond rational control and who is tossed about by self-doubt and the winds of fortune.

Manic lovers see difficulties and crises as challenges to their devotion. If there are no dif-ficulties, they invent them, seeing rivals every-where and distrusting the other's sincerity. From the manic lover's point of view, extreme jealousy is perfectly reasonable, since it is a proof of love.

Sexual intimacy only brings new problems to the manic lover. Uncertain of his or her attractiveness and lacking a genuine rapport with the other, the manic lover is unable to participate in a mutually compatible sexual relation.

It is theoretically possible for a manic attachment to develop into a lasting love, but Lee found only rare instances of this. For the relation to endure, the other person must have the patience and ego strength to ride out the possessiveness, the recriminations, and the stormy emotions. Only an eros person is likely to do this. A ludus person would never tolerate the manic lover's extremes, and while a storge person may try to be kind, he or she would be unable to reciprocate the manic lover's intensity.

Mania rarely ends happily, and most manic lovers remain troubled by the experience for months and even years. A period of hatred of the former partner is almost essential if the manic lover is finally to achieve an attitude of indifference. During the recovery period, the manic lover is often in a condition popularly known as "on the rebound." This period can be very dangerous for any new partner, since the unrequited manic lover is likely to take a quite luduslike role. Once a successful relation has been achieved, he or she will very probably drop the new partner, thus evening the score for the prior disappointment. If the new partner is a ludus person, there is no problem, of course; but if he or she is manic, the cycle of broken heart and heartbreaker begins another round.

Most of the manic lovers in Lee's sample believed that the experience of falling in love had been profitable despite the pain, since the extremes of manic emotion had enabled them to realize how much they could care for another person.

The Infinite Varieties of Love

There are endless possible combinations of the major types of love, so the experience of love may be infinitely varied. Moreover, a person's typology of love is not necessarily fixed, even for the duration of a specific love affair. In addition, a person may experience love with one person quite differently from love with another. However, most people usually have rather narrow range of concepts, experiences, and ideals of love (such as essentially eros with some elements of ludus).

Given the bewildering varieties of love that may occur with a blend of the three major categories of eros, ludus, and storge, it is not surprising that disappointments in love frequently occur. A person who regards his or her own definition of love as the only "true" or valid one is puzzled or impatient when encountering examples that do not fit those preconceptions. Also, a person may become devastated by the failure to relate successfully to someone whose expectations for love are completely different from his or her own. In contrast, a person who is aware of the many forms that true love may take is likely to be much more flexible and thus has an enormous advantage in successfully transversing the maze of an intimate relation. If you are interested in seeing what type of lover you are, according to Lee's formulation, answer the questions in Table 3-1.

LOVE AND INFATUATION

Infatuation is chiefly a point of view. What is regarded as love—especially a limerent attraction—by the person involved is often referred to as simply "infatuation" by a person not involved. Thus, a person who feels a limerent attraction would probably define it as romantic or passionate love. A disinterested observer might say that the person is "simply infatuated" and "not experiencing real love." Infatuation is thus very difficult to define, except in the eyes of the observer. Moreover, as noted earlier, real love varies according to the experience of the participant and according to the style of loving. A storge person would certainly regard a limerent attraction as an infatuation, as might a ludus person.

Psychologists try to define infatuation in more objective terms and point to characteristic differences between infatuation and love. For example, infatuation tends to focus on a

---

TABLE 3-1

The love chart

To find out what type of lover you are, answer each question as it applies to a current boyfriend or girlfriend, lover or spouse.

A = almost always, U = usually, R = rarely,
N = never (or almost never)

1. You have a clearly defined image of your desired partner.
2. You felt a strong emotional reaction to him or her on the first encounter.
3. You are preoccupied with thoughts about him or her.
4. You are eager to see him or her every day.
5. You discuss future plans and a wide range of interests and experiences.
6. Tactile, sensual contact is important to the relation.
7. Sexual intimacy was achieved early in the relation.
8. You feel that success in love is more important than success in other areas of your life.
9. You want to be in love or have love as security.
10. You try to force him or her to show more feeling and commitment.
11. You declared your love first.
12. You are willing to suffer neglect and abuse from him or her.
13. You deliberately restrain frequency of contact with him or her.
14. You restrict discussion and display of your feelings with him or her.
15. If a breakup is coming, you feel it is better to drop the other person before being dropped.
16. You play the field and have several persons who could love you.
17. You are more interested in pleasure than in emotional attachment.
18. You feel the need to love someone you have grown accustomed to.
19. You believe that the test of time is the only sure way to find real love.
20. You don't believe that true love happens suddenly or dramatically.

If you answered A or U to 1 – 8 you are probably an eros lover. If you answered A or U to 3 – 4 and 8 – 12, your love style tends to be manic. If you answered A or U to 13 – 17 and R or N to the other questions, you are probably a ludus lover. If you answered A or U to 17 – 20, together with R or N for the other statements, your love style tends to be storge. (Remember, there are many intermediate styles of love, and a person's love style may shift from time to time or from partner to partner.)

Source: Adapted from Lee (1974, p. 45).

single aspect of the other, whereas love focuses on the whole person. An infatuated person tends to relate to the other as an object to be manipulated, controlled, or used, whereas a person in love tends to identify with the other. Furthermore, this identification tends to be persistent and enduring in love, while infatuation tends to be relatively short-lived. Infatuation is self-centered, whereas love is other-centered. That is, infatuation tends to be characterized by preoccupation with oneself and with one's own feelings. Love is oriented toward the well-being of the other and tends to be less self-conscious or concerned with feelings of difficulty or inadequacy, with the person in love feeling more self-assured, secure, and adequate than the infatuated person feels. A person in love is active and open to sensory experience and feels healthy and keenly alive, delighting in all aspects of the environment—food, friends, sights, and sounds. A person in love is moved to put dreams into action.

In other words, what is generally regarded as love involves a limerent attraction that is reciprocated, and the relation is characterized by a good deal of altruistic love. By contrast, the person is usually called "infatuated" who feels awkward, constrained, self-conscious, unfulfilled, fragmented, and insecure—withdrawing from sensory experience and contact with others, becoming less and less aware of incoming stimuli, daydreaming, staying away from friends, being unable to eat. These are characteristics of a person who is experiencing a limerent attraction that is *not* reciprocated. Often, then, we regard a person as infatuated if the limerence is not returned and feelings are negative, and as being in love when the limerence is reciprocated and feelings are positive.

From this point of view, then, infatuation *binds* energy, while love *releases* energy. The person in love (experiencing positive reciprocated limerence) functions more efficiently with greater drive, increased awareness, and an eagerness for achievement, whereas an infatuated person (experiencing negative limerence not reciprocated) is relatively incapacitated and less able to function effectively.

Because of our society's emphasis on the importance of romantic love (or reciprocal limerent attraction), the young eros person often dreams of the fulfillment of love long before he or she even encounters a possible candidate. Flaubert expressed this hauntingly in his autobiographical novel, *November*:

The puberty of the heart precedes that of the body: I had more need of loving than of enjoying, more desire for love than for pleasure. Today I cannot even imagine the love of first adolescence, when the senses are nothing and the infinite alone holds sway. Coming between childhood and youth, it is the transition between them and passes so quickly that it is forgotten.

I had read the word "love" so much in the poets and had repeated it to myself so often to charm myself with its sweetness that to every star that shone in a blue sky on a gentle night, to every murmur of the stream against its banks, to every ray of sun on the dewdrops I would say "I am in love! Oh, I am in love!" And I was happy, I was proud, I was ready for the finest acts of devotion, and above all, when a woman brushed me in passing or looked into my face, I wished I might love her a thousand times more, be even more at her mercy than I was; I wished my heart would throb so violently as to burst my breast asunder.

There is an age, as you will remember, when you

smile vaguely as there were kisses in the air. Your heart swells in fragrant breeze, your blood beats warm in your veins. You wake up happier, richer than the night before, more lively, more excited. . . . As you walk in the evening and breathe the scent of cut hay and listen to the cuckoo in the wood and watch the racing stars, is not your heart purer, more bathed in air, in light, in blue than the peaceful horizon when the earth meets the sky in a tranquil kiss? Oh, the fragrance of women's hair! The softness of the skin of their hands, the penetration of their gaze![25]

A young eros person dreaming of the fulfillment of idyllic love sometimes focuses on a temporary limerent object chiefly in response to a culturally conditioned need for a romantic or limerent love experience. These early affairs of the heart are often called *infatuations, crushes,* or even *puppy love.* If the limerence is in the second crystallization stage and is negative, however, the pain, agony, and disappointments are experienced deeply by the person involved. Often such early experiences are regarded by psychologists and by novelists, poets, and lyricists as a sort of "beautiful training ground" that enables the youthful eros person to become immersed in powerful emotions and resolve the inevitable problems, disappointments, and nonfulfillments of relating to another person who also has needs and makes demands.

Mature love involves a paired bond characterized by reciprocal interaction with a perceived equivalence of function, as we have seen. The other person (or limerent object) in a serious love relation of this type is an individual with unique characteristics and needs.

What is also usually defined by our society as infatuation is the relatively short-lived limerent involvement of a youthful couple as perceived by their elders. Thus, what is called infatuation often precedes what our society defines as mature love. From this point of view, a

---

[25](New York: Serendipity Press, 1966), pp. 32 – 34. Reprinted by permission.

person in a negative, nonreciprocated limerent attraction may shift from the energy-binding, self-centered, withdrawn, unrealistic, and manipulative characteristics of this situation—commonly called infatuation—to the energy-releasing, other-centered, outgoing, unselfconscious, and altruistic characteristics of what is regarded as mature love.

LOVE AND JEALOUSY

Love and jealousy are very closely related, since jealousy is often felt as an aspect of love. Both are very strong emotions that can push almost everything else out of awareness.

Unlike love, however, jealousy is often an "underground" emotion, not readily acknowledged. We are frequently ashamed of feeling jealous, regarding it as a reflection of self-concern rather than concern for the other. Jealousy is often regarded as an immature, self-indulgent emotion—childish and selfish. We have been taught in childhood that jealousy is unseemly. ("Aren't you ashamed—jealous of your little brother!")

What Is Jealousy?

Jealousy occurs in response to a perceived loss—either real or imagined—that takes place when a satisfaction that one has been receiving is withdrawn and then redirected.[26] It can be extremely painful.

I didn't know that anybody could hurt so much and live. I suppose it's jealousy. I didn't know it was like this. I thought jealousy was an idea. It isn't. It's a pain. But I don't feel as they do in Broadway melodramas. I don't want to kill anybody. I just want to die (Dell 1926, p. 231).

Even minor problems can be a source of jealousy if they threaten a person with a loss of intimate attention that the person regards as rightfully his or hers.

Jealousy isn't reserved for those cataclysmic moments when a husband packs his electric toothbrush and runs off with the lady next door. It is ready to spring at far, far less provocation—a lingering glance at a bell-bottomed bottom, an extended conversation with that long-haired 19-year-old or even an undue enthusiasm for the lady-next-door's views on water pollution. In fact, we can become jealous of our husand's family, his business partner, his best friend, his psychiatrist or his entire bowling team if we feel he is seeking or finding in them something that he isn't getting from us (Viorst 1970, p. 92).

Sexual jealousy is simply a special form of the emotion that occurs with the withdrawal and redirection of the provision of sexual satisfaction. It is often the most insidious form of jealousy because potentially powerful feelings and needs are at stake and because sexual fidelity is often used as an index of caring in our society and is therefore closely associated with feelings of self-worth.

Jealousy usually has less to do with fear of sexual betrayal, however, than it does with a fear of loss of intimacy. In a good marriage partners share intimate experiences and find satisfactions with each other; either spouse may well feel threatened if the other seems to be sharing experiences and finding important intimate satisfactions elsewhere. For example, it is quite possible for a person to be jealous of a child. (See the vignette, "Jealousy of One's Own Child.")

Although jealousy is often thought of as an emotion that occurs when attention, affection, intimacy, or love is withdrawn and then directed toward another *person*, it is quite possible to be jealous of an *activity* or *physical*

---

[26]Jealousy and envy are closely related and often occur together, but they stem from different sources. *Envy* is concerned with the desire to have something that is possessed by another, whereas *jealousy* is concerned with the maintenance of something we already have in the face of an apparent challenge.

Jealousy and grief are also closely related, but we experience *grief* when we have lost something and do not expect to get it back; jealousy is concerned with having something (that we regard as rightfully ours) taken away and given to another or redirected toward an activity that we do not share.

Jealousy of One's Own Child

Jealousy can be particularly distressing to a married couple when it involves their own child. This type of jealousy can sometimes be handled and diverted if it is understood and accepted. It is understandable, for example, for a man to be jealous of a baby who he feels displaces him as the main object of his wife's affection and concern, invading the intimacy and privacy of their marriage and making enormous demands on her time and energy.

The new arrival, after all, requires more time and energy from the mother than would a lover. The father may feel that he is deprived not only of sex and affection, but also of innumerable services previously performed by his wife—in-

cluding things as simple as her availability for small talk . . . and he feels guilty about this jealousy. One jealous father asked disgustedly: "What kind of monster am I to be jealous of my own baby?" (Clanton and Smith 1977, p. 50).

It is always a shock to recognize and admit this feeling. This kind of jealousy can be handled constructively and creatively, however, once it is acknowledged and accepted. For example, if a father begins to see a child as a person who needs him, rather than as a rival, he might join his wife in providing nurture for the child, thus restoring the emotional balance of the marriage and redirecting jealousy and a sense of loss into emotional growth.

---

object. Thus, one might be jealous of the other's work, the other's hobbies or sports, or whatever takes attention away from oneself. Abigail Van Buren, in her nationally syndicated advice column, reflects this commonly accepted feeling that a married couple owe virtually all their time to each other and to no one or nothing else.

Dear Abby:

Fred and I have been married 14 years—if you can call this a marriage. Fred says that a marriage is a job, like any other job, and since everybody gets at least one day a week off from his job, a man should get a day a week off from his marriage. So, Fred works at our marriage six days a week, but takes Sundays off.

He leaves the house Saturday night, and I don't see him again until early Monday morning. He puts about 350 miles on his car and I don't have the slightest idea where he's been.

I never heard of any other couple with this kind of arrangement, have you? But the way Fred explains it, it makes sense.

Is he crazy, or am I?

Fred's Wife

Dear Wife:

Marriage is a seven-day-a-week job, and there's no time off for good (or bad) behavior. Fred is far from crazy, but I'm not so sure about you, if you're buying it (1978, p. 53).

Some writers maintain that all jealousy is outmoded and unfashionable and should not be a problem between "emotionally mature" adults (McCary and McCary 1982, O'Neill and O'Neill 1972, Smith and Smith 1970). This persuasion overlooks the fact that love and jealousy are closely interrelated, however. To love is to risk losing that love. And any loss or threat of loss can arouse fear and anxiety, which may in turn activate feelings of insecurity and self-doubt and the fear of losing a valued intimacy—in a word, jealousy.

Everyone is insecure to some extent in the face of a threat of a significant loss. Everyone values important possessions (including love of another), and nobody is free from occasional bouts of self-doubt (Coleman 1984). Perhaps mature, free-spirited, generous, loving people should not feel jealous, but the fact is that, if the threat is real and significant, they probably do.

Anthropologists have found no society in which jealousy is completely absent. For example, sexual jealousy occurs in both highly sexist societies and relatively nonsexist societies, and in both sexually restrictive societies and sexually permissive societies. Even in societies with the least amount of jealousy, such as the Arctic Eskimo, there are individual examples of jealousy that can be quite intense—even though they run counter to the cultural norm and social expectations (Stephens 1982).

In an ideal paired bond, jealousy is minimized by mutual caring. Each partner has the power to hurt the other but rarely uses it, and although the potential for jealousy is present, it rarely or never occurs.

Love creates need and power; that's why loving is dangerous, why some people don't do it at all. I need my lover if I'm to be entirely happy; it is only he who knows me, finally. I have the power to hurt him as he does me, by seeming to love him less, by leaving him. One doesn't seek this power. It's a gift, growing out of the intensity of one lover's feelings for the other. I understand that at some point he chose to make himself vulnerable to me, as I've chosen to make myself vulnerable to him. If there is trust in love instead of terror, it comes from the understanding that neither lover will take advantage of the power the other has granted (Durbin 1977, p. 44).

Although there has been little research on jealousy and research samples have been small, available evidence indicates that men are more likely to deny feelings of jealousy and women are more likely to acknowledge them. However, men are more likely to express jealous feelings through rage or violence, although such outbursts are often followed by feelings of depression, gloom, and despondency. Men are more likely to blame the other, the third party, or the circumstances, whereas women are more likely to blame themselves. Jealous men are more likely to focus on the *sexual* activity of the other, whereas women are more likely to focus on the *emotional* involvement between the man and the third party (Corzine 1974, Reik 1949, Gottschalk 1936).

Pathologically Destructive Jealousy

Jealousy can make a normally calm, sensible, intelligent person act in a totally unreasonable way—seething with anger, resentment, and rage and erupting into violence.[27] Jealousy may even be seen as legitimizing such actions, giving the jealous person the right to be cruel. This anger may extend from relatively mild manifestations of resentment to murder or even extended torture.[28] Jealousy is responsible for a large number of what the police call "crimes of passion," in which husbands beat, stab, or shoot wives (or lovers), and wives beat, stab, or shoot husbands (or lovers). The "love me or I'll kill you" syndrome is quite common to the human condition.

A graphic and dramatic example of the "love me or I'll kill you" syndrome is that of the thirty-three-year-old graduate student at the University of California in Berkeley, who was convicted of first-degree murder and sentenced to imprisonment of twenty-five years to life in January 1984 for killing his fiancee. He

---

[27]See Mowat (1966) for an interesting account of persons who have committed murder under the influence of jealousy.

[28]An example of the latter is the infamous deKaplany case, which occurred in a suburb of San Francisco in 1962. Geza de-Kaplany, an anesthesiologist at a local hospital, was jealous of his beautiful young bride of five weeks (she was not only beautiful, but talented and the sole support of her mother). Feeling slighted by her alleged unfaithfulness (which she denied), he lashed her to the bed, drew on surgical gloves, and tortured her by applying acid to her face, eyes, and body with gauze. (Her lungs were seriously burned by the acid fumes that she inhaled, and she would have been an invalid and blind, as well as horribly disfigured, had she lived.) Her screams of agony were sufficiently disguised by the sound of a radio played at high volume that neighbors did not call the police for nearly an hour. She died after two months of intensive care, mutilated beyond help. DeKaplany, after a vigorous and extraordinarily competent defense, was sentenced to a relatively short term and was released from prison in 1976.

accosted her as she was leaving the school where she was teaching, stabbed her several times, and then stabbed himself twice. He told the court that he killed his fiancee and then tried to take his own life because he was despondent over the fact that she had moved out of their apartment after an argument (*San Francisco Chronicle*, January 10, 1984).

Jealousy is usually expressed much less violently, of course—through verbal cruelty, recriminations, and charges of unfairness ("How can you do this to me after all we've meant to each other?"); threats of getting even ("What's sauce for the goose is sauce for the gander"); or an appeal to duty or marital vows.

Jealousy may also be expressed by long sieges of silence—the jealous one remains aloof and uncommunicative, and the air is filled with unstated charges of grieved innocence and wounded trust. The stony silence pattern may succeed in punishing the other without being overtly aggressive, resting the jealous person's case upon the guilt feelings the other is presumed to have.

Such periods of silence, as well as the verbal attacks, are usually accompanied by alternating demands and pleas that the withdrawn attention, intimacy, or love be returned. If this combination of pressures is successful, the one who has withdrawn love may try to put the relation back on its former footing by asking for understanding and forgiveness ("It's you I really love"). This occurs, however, only if the one who has withdrawn love really *wants* to return the relation to its former intimacy and trust.

Even if the pattern of silence, attacks, pleas, and demands does succeed in persuading the other to restore love and intimacy, the seeds of resentment may have been sown (both in the jealous person and in the controlled or manipulated partner) so that the relation may never regain its former closeness.

Love is not a commodity that can be bargained for; it is not subject to contractual obligations. An intimate interaction must rest upon goodwill and mutual affection and re-

spect, with the manifestations of love freely granted. "Love cannot be a duty, because it is not subject to the will" (Russell 1967, p. 574).

Jealousy may not be expressed outwardly at all, but may be turned inward upon oneself. That is, instead of aggression (whether overt or covert) being directed against another, a person may display a pattern of self-degradation, self-accusation, and self-blame.[29] This can lead to feelings of inferiority and even tendencies toward self-destruction (whether slowly through alcohol or drugs or swiftly through suicide).

The jealous person who directs the feeling of loss inward and becomes morose, dejected, and self-destructive often derives satisfactions that are called *secondary gains*. For example, one secondary gain is the feeling of *self-righteousness* a person might generate by condemning the other's behavior as "cheating" or betraying the person's love and trust. Paradoxically, this feeling of self-righteousness can exist side by side with feelings of betrayal and dejection. Another secondary gain is the *solicitous attention* that might be secured from others. A person who is tortured by self-pity over a lover's infidelity (real or imagined) often receives sympathy, comfort, and nurture from friends and relatives. Both this emotional support and the feeling of self-righteousness can operate very effectively as secondary gains and reinforce the "sufferer's" jealousy.

Handling Jealousy Constructively

How may jealousy be dealt with constructively? In general, jealousy may be handled constructively (1) if its dynamics are understood and accepted, (2) if one values the well-being of the other as well as one's own well-

---

[29]In its extreme form, deriving satisfaction from self-degradation is called *masochism*, and the masochist may regress to a state of helplessness or complete submission, displaying self-denial and misery (Coleman 1984).

being, and (3) if one is able to see the situation in perspective.

For example, suppose a husband is at a party where his wife (who enjoys flirting) is spending a good deal of time in animated conversation with another, good-looking man. The husband finds himself becoming more and more agitated and uncomfortable and begins to feel undeniable twinges of jealousy. He might handle the situation constructively as follows:

I asked myself some questions. For example, why is she animated? Obviously, she is having a good talk. Perhaps I don't discuss things that interest her much—maybe I should work a bit harder, be less conversationally predictable. Do I love her? Yes. (If I didn't, why would it matter *how* animatedly she talked to someone else?) Since I do love her, why shouldn't I be pleased that she is enjoying herself? Don't I want her to have a good time at the party? Or do I think because she is enjoying a good conversation she is arranging a tryst with a Good-looking Fellow? Obviously not.

Once I realized that my wife's conversation with someone else took nothing away from me—in fact, it pointed to a way I could improve our relation—I also realized there was no reason for jealousy (Lobsenz 1977, pp. 30–31).

This is not to say, of course, that one can always deal with the problem of jealousy solely by self-examination. Since jealousy involves an interaction between oneself and others, dealing with it constructively usually means acknowledging the feelings of the other person (as well as one's own feelings). Jealousy can rarely be treated in isolation.

Your jealousy is not your problem alone. It is also a problem for your partner and for the person whose interest in your partner sparks your jealousy . . . typically, three or more persons are involved in the production of jealous feelings and behaviors. Ideally, all three should take on part of the responsibility for minimizing its negative consequences (Clanton and Smith 1977, p. 163).

Is it constructive to simply repress feelings of jealousy, or to shut them out of awareness by counteracting jealousy with an "I don't care" attitude? These courses of action are possible, of course, but they do not eliminate the jealousy. Rather, they drive it underground where it will continue its corrosive influence, manifesting itself in such forms as vague aggressiveness, irritability, indifference, submission, or false friendliness toward the rival who has usurped one's love.

Moreover, driving it underground makes the jealousy unavailable to conscious awareness, where it might be dealt with constructively. The jealous person is far wiser to recognize the jealousy, acknowledge it, and try to deal with it constructively either by self-examination or by talking it out frankly with the other person. (See Chapter 9 for a discussion of problems of communication, psychological game playing, and ways of maximizing the probability that intimacy will be restored.)

LEARNING TO LOVE

The ability to experience love, to give and receive this most mysterious though most basic of all emotions, is apparently a learned characteristic that is acquired in developmental stages from infancy to adulthood. Although the need to experience demonstrations of love is innate and is essential to survival in infancy and to well-being in adulthood, the ability to feel and express love is apparently learned through cultural conditioning.

The emotion of love is first experienced in infancy as a result of receiving nurture, usually from one's mother. Infants who are held and fondled come to identify the resultant satisfaction with themselves and to perceive themselves as objects of worth—objects that are associated with the experience of deep and positive need satisfaction. It may be said that they come to love themselves. Apparently an infant must have this experience of himself or herself as a love object before he or she can experience love in a relation with another.

Persons who lack this initial experience of love will, as they mature, try to compensate for their lack of self-love by demonstrating a greedy self-interest—by perceiving others chiefly in terms of their usefulness and by manipulating them for personal gain. This is called *selfishness*, which is the antithesis (or opposite) of self-love.

Close observation shows that while the selfish person is always concerned with himself, he is never satisfied, is always restless, always driven by a fear of not getting enough, of missing something, of being deprived of something. He is filled with burning envy of anyone who might have more. If we observe (him) still closer . . . we find that this person is basically not fond of himself, but deeply dislikes himself (Fromm 1970, p. 115).

By contrast, a person operating from a firm base of self-love extends this sense of self-acceptance and self-regard to the acceptance and regard of others, especially significant others.

The infant's first significant other or love object (other than the self) is usually the mother, who is, of course, the figure from whom an infant most often receives nurture. Other members of the immediate family and other persons who actively provide nurture also become love objects as an infant grows into childhood and his or her experience broadens. In addition, inanimate objects (stuffed animals and dolls) and pets may receive the child's early feelings of loyalty, devotion, concern, and love and be sources of intense satisfaction.[30]

Infants are characteristically dependent in relating to others—taking everything and supplying nothing. In an adult-infant nurturant pattern, the infant derives satisfaction in receiving nurture, while the adult derives satisfaction in providing nurture (see Figure 3-2).

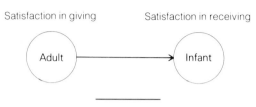

FIGURE 3-2
Nurture pattern of adult and infant

By ages three to five, children characteristically begin to demonstrate increasing independence, insisting on being allowed to tie their own shoes, button their own clothes, and do other tasks. Dependency needs remain, of course, but they decrease in relative importance from then on (see Chapter 12).

By adulthood, the focus shifts to the need for interdependence, with a person providing as well as receiving both physical and emotional support or love—thus beginning the cycle again. In adulthood, we are expected to *provide* our offspring with the love we ourselves *received* as children.

One characteristic of adult-adult love is that, instead of simply providing emotional support and nurture for the other, each expects to receive love and affection as well as provide it. This is not to say that children do not provide love to the parents, but rather that the emphasis shifts—from total provision of love in infancy, to a reciprocal interaction of receiving equivalent demonstrations of love in adulthood.[31]

The pattern of adult-adult nurture provision and love may be either *simultaneous*, with each person providing for the other at the same time he or she is receiving from the other, or *alternate*, with one person providing at one time and receiving at another time (see Figure 3-3).

---

[30]Animal experiments have demonstrated that the infant rhesus monkey will not survive when reared alone unless he has a soft cloth he may cling to and fondle. Even when the cloth is removed only briefly for laundering, the monkey becomes very disturbed (Harlow 1959). Parallel behavior may be observed in human infants and children (see Chapter 12).

[31]There are, of course, great individual differences to this generalization—"the course of true love never runs smooth"—for in some families the children provide more love to the parents than they receive from them (the classic example is chronic child abuse), and in some families there is little love exchanged (or provided) by either the parents *or* the child.

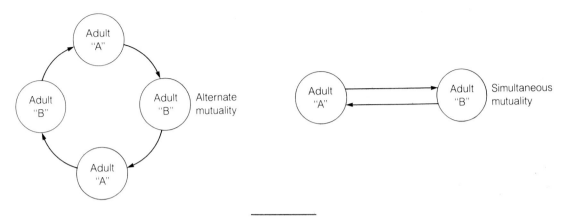

FIGURE 3-3

Nurture pattern of adults

Simultaneous mutuality of nurture-need provision is characteristic of dating and courtship. If this mutuality did not occur, the relation would stop with the first date. If the couple continues to see each other, it is because each is receiving satisfaction, pleasure, contentment, or excitement as well as providing for it.

In marriage, however, this simultaneous mutuality of satisfaction does not always occur, and each must be emotionally mature enough to delay gratification.[32] Of course, in a stable paired bond, the satisfaction each provides for the other is balanced over time. If the provision of nurture and demonstrations of love and affection always go in one direction, the relation will disintegrate.

Thus, all three needs—dependence, independence, and interdependence—are present in a person from early childhood on, but the emphasis in these needs shifts from dependence to independence to interdependence as the person proceeds through the developmental stages from infancy to adolescence to maturity. "Infantile love follows the principle:

'I love you because I need you.' Mature love says: 'I need you because I love you'" (Fromm 1970, p. 34).

In Freud's psychosexual theory of personality development, the earliest stage of development, which chiefly entails self-love, is known as the *narcissistic* period, after the Greek myth of Narcissus, who fell in love with his own reflection in the still waters of a pool. Unable to possess the image (the act of trying to grasp it would cause it to shatter into ripples) he pined away and was turned into a flower by the gods.

In the second stage, which Freud called the *Oedipal* period after the Greek myth of Oedipus, love is focused chiefly on the mother, and the father is seen as a rival.[33]

The stage when close emotional attachments are characteristically formed with members of the same gender is known as the *homosexual* period and extends from about age eight to about age twelve. This is followed by the *heterosexual* period, which extends

---

[32]One characteristic of emotional maturity is the ability to postpone or delay gratification or need satisfaction.

---

[33]In the classical Greek play *Oedipus Rex* by Sophocles, the son murders his father and marries his mother. For a fuller account of Freudian terms and their meanings, see Mullahy (1955), Thompson (1951), English and Pearson (1945), and Freud (1938). For an excellent brief discussion, see Crawley et al. (1973, pp. 105 – 109).

through adolescence into maturity and is characterized by the shifting of emotional attachments from friends of the same gender to friends of the opposite gender. The *adult* period, which is characterized by mature love, emphasizes giving or providing nurture rather than receiving it. This completes the cycle, with the adult providing nurture, emotional support, and love to others.

In Freudian terms, a person may be *fixated* at any of these psychosexual stages and remain oriented chiefly to the characteristics of that stage. For example, an adult—though fully developed physically, socially, and economically—may still be narcissistic or incapable of any but self-love.[34] The severely disturbed adult may not be capable of even that and may remain fixated at a prenarcissistic level.

A person fixated at the homosexual stage may never proceed to a heterosexual stage. Similarly, a fixation at the heterosexual stage may limit the capacity of a person for mature love. (This is not to imply that mature love is the exclusive province of the heterosexual; both the homosexual and the heterosexual are capable of proceeding to mature love, if mature love is defined as an emphasis on giving rather than receiving.)

It must not be assumed that a person proceeds from stage to stage in discrete jumps. Each stage blends into another. Moreover, as the person proceeds through the psychosexual developmental stages, it is the *emphasis* that changes; elements of all preceding stages remain. Thus the adult characterized by mature love retains the elements of narcissistic love, for example, as a base on which other elements are established—love of mother, family, friends, husband or wife, and, finally, children.

---

[34]When the person is fixated at the narcissistic stage in this way it is called "secondary narcissus"; it indicates that the *libido* (sexual energy) is directed exclusively toward oneself, and that the person is therefore incapable of emotional relations with others.

SUMMARY

Love is such a subtle and complex emotion that it defies a simple or precise analysis. It is like an onion, which reveals more and more of itself as layer after layer is peeled away, yet it remains tantalizing beyond scientific categorization.

Love shares many of the aspects of liking, such as affection, respect, and admiration, but other aspects of love are different from liking. In fact, the correlation between loving and liking is only moderate.

A unique characteristic of love is limerence, which is a strong, compulsive attraction to another that goes through two stages: (1) first crystallization, when about 30 percent of the limerent person's waking time not occupied by essential pursuits is spent with thoughts of the other, and (2) second crystallization, when virtually 100 percent of waking thoughts are spent in this way. When limerence is returned, it causes virtually indescribable joy, happiness, and contentment (often called ecstasy); when it is not, the limerent person suffers acute distress, agony, and pain. Limerence can occur and persist despite lack of encouragement and even abuse, so long as the limerent person feels there is some hope of reciprocation.

Another unique characteristic of love is the attachment or bonding to the other that creates a very strong feeling of comfort or satisfaction when the other is present or felt to be accessible, and acute feelings of longing or depression (separation distress) when the other is neither present nor felt to be accessible. A diffuse separation distress, with no attachment figure, is experienced as loneliness. Attachment is the last characteristic of love to fade away, long after such aspects as liking, respect, and trust have vanished. Curiously enough, bonding or attachment sometimes occurs even in the face of discouragement or outright abuse.

The four faces of love, long recognized in our society, are companionate, passionate, romantic, and altruistic. Companionate love is sensible, calm, relaxed, and has strong overtones of liking, admiration, and respect. Simply being with the other provides a sense of satisfaction. Married couples spend more of their time together at the comfortable and rewarding levels of companionate love than at the exalted heights of romantic or passionate attraction.

Passionate love has a strong limerent aspect and a strong erotic component. It is characterized by an intensity of involvement, with little notice paid to mundane or everyday affairs. It is a sharp contrast to companionate love.

The aspect of love in which the other person is viewed in a highly idealized fashion is called romantic love. Romantic love was initially asexual, with the romantic lovers married, not to one another, but to others. By the nineteenth century, romantic love was acceptable between married couples but was still asexual. The model Victorian wife submitted to sexual activity as a duty necessary for procreation. By the second half of the twentieth century, sex was no longer referred to as "rearing its ugly head" but began to be increasingly regarded as a normal and acceptable aspect of romantic attraction and involvement.

Altruistic love is similar to the concept of *agape* of classical Greece. It is the emotion experienced when providing nurture for another person brings more satisfaction than providing for oneself. Altruistic love is probably a component of any serious paired bond, but it becomes more important with maturity. The experience of love varies from one couple to another and from time to time for the same couple.

Lee (1973), a Canadian researcher, found that there are three major styles of loving: eros, ludus, and storge. Manic love is a combination of eros and ludus. Eros lovers are erotic, romantic, and limerent. Ludus lovers are playful, flirtatious, and joyous. It is quite possible for a ludus lover to be in love with more than one person at the same time, and he or she does not have an ideal of love, as does the eros lover. The storge lover is sensible, calm, and practical. Storge love is based on shared interests and experiences and on mutual contentment and satisfaction. Manic lovers illustrate a combination of eros and ludus qualities, are highly limerent, but experience the agony and pain of nonreciprocated limerence. They have wide mood swings, with periods of intense joy when they regard their attraction as being returned. Each person regards his or her own experience of love as "true" or "real."

Infatuation is essentially a value judgment. The person experiencing the emotion considers it love. Another who is observing the experience may regard it as infatuation. In general, infatuation is not regarded as true love but as a short-lived, immature, selfish, and self-centered emotion—binding energy rather than releasing it.

Jealousy is an emotion very closely related to love. It is felt when a person perceives a threat that he or she will lose the other. Destructive patterns of jealousy can erupt into extreme violence, potentially harmful to oneself, to the other, or to a third party who is regarded as stealing the other's affection. Jealousy is universal in human societies, although it is more commonly experienced in some societies than in others. Jealousy can be dealt with constructively if it is frankly acknowledged and understood.

Although love may be defined in various ways, every definition agrees that love is important and necessary for infant survival and adult well-being. We develop the innate capacity to love as the result of receiving nurture and altruistic love in infancy. Experiencing ourselves as loved, we perceive ourselves as lovable and significant others as loving. In other words, it is only after we have learned to love ourselves that we can love others.

According to current theories of personality development, we love first ourselves, then our mothers (or mother surrogates), then like-gender friends, and then other-gender friends. Finally, we experience mature love, in which we derive greater satisfaction from providing nurture than from receiving it. We reach such maturity by incorporating each new developmental stage of love into our personalities.

QUESTIONS

1. How would you define the concept of *love*?
2. What were the three terms used in classical Greece to define the various aspects of love? What did each of these terms mean?
3. What is *limerent* love?
4. What is the phenomenon of *crystallization* in limerent love?
5. How important is limerence as an aspect of love?
6. What is meant by *attachment* in a paired bond?
7. How persistent is attachment in a paired bond?
8. What are the four traditional aspects of love in a paired bond?
9. In a contemporary typology the three types love are eros, ludus, and storge. What are the major characteristics of each of these?
10. Describe manic love, which is a compound of eros and ludus.
11. How would you define *infatuation*? What is its relation to love in a paired bond?
12. How would you define *jealousy*? Give an example of jealousy.
13. What is the relation of jealousy to love?
14. How can jealousy be handled constructively?
15. What is meant by the adult-infant nurture pattern? Give an example of this pattern.
16. There are two nurture patterns characteristic of adults: alternate mutuality and simultaneous mutuality. Give an example of each that clarifies how they differ.
17. Fromm (1970) makes an interesting distinction between infantile love and mature love. How does he define each of these types of love?

SUGGESTIONS FOR FURTHER READING

Brecher, Edward M. *Love, Sex, and Aging: A Consumer's Union Report*. Boston: Little, Brown, 1984.

Clanton, Gordon, and Smith, Lynn G., eds. *Jealousy*. Englewood Cliffs, N J.: Prentice-Hall, 1977.

Coutts, Robert L. *Love and Intimacy: A Psychological Approach*. San Ramon, Calif.: Consensus, 1973.

Fromm, Erich. *The Art of Loving*. New York: Bantam, 1970.

Lee, John Alan. *The Colours of Love*. Toronto, Canada: New Press, 1973.

Marcus, Steven. *The Other Victorians*. New York: Basic Books, 1966.

Marshall, Megan. *The Cost of Loving: Women and the New Fear of Intimacy*. New York: Putnam, 1984.

Money, John. *Love and Love Sickness*. Baltimore: Johns Hopkins University Press, 1980.

Murstein, Bernard I. *Love, Sex, and Marriage through the Ages*. New York: Springer, 1974.

Rubin, Zick. *Liking and Loving*. New York: Holt, Rinehart & Winston, 1973.

Stendahl. *Love*. Translated by Gilbert and Suzanne Sale. New York: Penguin Classics, 1975.

Tennov, Dorothy. *Love and Limerence*. New York: Stein & Day, 1979.

Walster, Elaine, and Walster, G. William. *A New Look at Love*. Reading, Mass.: Addison-Wesley, 1978.

C H A P T E R   4

Sexual and Erotic Behavior

The Meaning of Sexuality in Different Cultures

Male Sexuality

Female Sexuality

The Complexity of Sexual Interaction

Sexually Transmissible Diseases (STDs)

Everyone is an expert on sex—especially those who know least about it.

Yiddish saying

The most obvious manifestation of gender is sexual behavior. *Sexual behavior* is any behavior that is based on gender; it may vary from mild flirtation to the all-consuming passion of Romeo and Juliet. The emotion that results when sexual behavior is fused with love may reach an intensity that is nothing short of astonishing; it has been explored by countless poets, dramatists, and lyricists, as well as by philosophers, theologians, psychologists, sociologists, and sexologists.

Marriage is in part a sexual relation between two persons each of whom has real and demanding erotic needs. Anyone who lacks the anatomical, physiological, and psychological knowledge about the basic elements of human sexuality is greatly handicapped in establishing a satisfactory marriage. A person who not only lacks such information but entertains harmful misinformation is in a virtually hopeless predicament. It has been estimated that fully half of American marriages are characterized by sexual discord, disharmony, and misunderstanding, often to the point of desperation (Masters and Johnson 1966).

In this chapter we shall examine the basic elements of sexuality. These elements form a significant cornerstone of mutually harmonious and rewarding marital interactions.

THE MEANING OF SEXUALITY IN DIFFERENT CULTURES

All societies make some provision for acceptable reproductive behavior—if one did not, the society would soon cease to exist. However, all societies also seek to control the pleasurable (erotic) aspects of sexuality as well as the reproductive aspect. Societies vary enormously in both the extent to and the rigor with which they exercise control over sexual behavior—ranging from an *antisexual* position that looks upon sex as degrading and even immoral, to a *prosexual* position that regards eroticism as an opportunity for pleasure, recreation, and intimacy.

Antisexual Societies

The Manu of New Guinea regard sex as a necessary evil, an unpleasant chore that men and women must perform, but only to fulfill the necessity for reproduction (Frumkin 1973). There are no romantic stories in the Manu culture and no romantic songs or dances.[1] "Kissing is unknown, and breast stimulation and similar forms of love play. . . are generally lacking. . . . To the Manus sex is a sin" (p. 447).

In other societies, erotic pleasure is acceptable for men, but not for women. For example, Saudi Arabian girls are required to undergo a ritualized *clitoridectomy* (surgical amputation of the clitoris) when they are about eight years old. This effectively removes the capability for

erotic (pleasurable) response, while leaving the reproductive abilities intact. (The dangers of childbirth are greatly increased, of course, because the scar tissue that forms after the operation is relatively inflexible.) The operation is often done without an anesthetic and is excruciatingly painful; the pain persists for days, sometimes for the remainder of the woman's life. In some countries (for instance, in Somalia and Mali) clitoridectomies are performed in hospitals, but in others the procedure is usually done in the home by an older woman who has become recognized as a specialist. It is not unknown, however, for a father to simply seize his daughter and cut out her clitoris. Because so many clitoridectomies are performed under unsanitary conditions chronic infections are common; these infections may lead to infertility and sometimes to incontinence (inability to control urination and defecation). In some cases, uncontrolled bleeding and shock can bring about immediate death (Davies 1984). Clitoridectomy is still performed in more than half of African states (Hosken 1979).

The World Health Organization (WHO) in 1977 found that at least thirty countries go beyond simple clitoridectomy to practice pharaonic circumcision on girls or young women.[2] *Pharaonic circumcision* consists of excising (cutting off) the clitoris, the labia minora, and most of the labia majora. The sides of the vulva are then almost completely stitched together. Pharaonic circumcision has a permanently adverse effect on the health of the young woman and does control her erotic activity by lowering the likelihood that she will receive pleasure from sex. The custom occurs mainly in Africa and the Middle East but also in Australia and some South American countries ("Pharaonic Circumcision" 1977).

Other societies (for example, Brazil, Spain, Sicily, and Mexico) do not surgically mutilate

---

[1]It is interesting to note that there is no word for *love* in the Manu language (Frumkin 1973).

[2]The procedure is known as *pharaonic circumcision* because it has been practiced in Upper Egypt and was known to the ancient Egyptians (Davies 1984).

females but control their opportunities for pre-marital sexuality by rigorously *chaperoning* them until they are married. The young woman is never left alone with the young man but is always accompanied by a chaperone—an adult of unimpeachable reputation who supervises her activities.

In other countries, such as Morocco, and in rural areas of Greece, Sicily, Italy, and Eastern Europe, the bride is traditionally required to fly a bloodstained sheet from the window the morning after the wedding to provide proof of her virginity at marriage—that she had been deflowered (her hymen ruptured) by her bridegroom on the wedding night. (This also proves the virility of the husband and that the marriage has been consummated. In Marrakesh, the husband is then borne along the streets on the shoulders of jubilant friends.)

Prosexual Societies

Prosexual societies, cultures that accept the erotic aspect of sexuality for both men and women, are at the opposite end of the prosexual-antisexual continuum. The most openly prosexual and uninhibited peoples are probably those that inhabit the various tropical islands. For example, among the Trobriand Islanders of the South Pacific children become acquainted with sex at a very early age by observing their parents *copulating.*[3] They imitate this behavior with erotic games of their

own, which gradually develop into the passionate liaisons and partnerships of adolescence and adulthood (Frumkin 1973).

Polynesians encourage free sexual experimentation and play among their children, who observe nude dancing and demonstrations in techniques of copulation. Masturbation is either ignored or encouraged (Danielsson 1973). As soon as boys have reached physical maturity and undergone the circumcision rite (at about age fourteen), they are instructed sexually by an older woman. "He is taught to perform cunnilingus, to kiss and suck her breasts, and to bring his partner to climax several times before he reaches orgasm" (Marshall 1971, p. 44). Girls are expected to develop an appetite for sex at about the same age, when they start to menstruate.

Among the Marquesans, also of the South Pacific, "regular coitus is begun before puberty. . . and sexual play is a favorite form of activity. Exclusive sexual possession is socially disapproved. Sexual jealousy is considered in poor taste" (Frumkin 1973, p. 448).

Until the present century, when American attitudes infiltrated the cultures of many Pacific island peoples, there was no word in the Tahitian language for *immoral* and no word corresponding to *illegitimate*. The word for *fun* was the same as that for *copulation*. Young adults were permitted full sexual freedom when their sex drives were at their peak. Pregnancies were welcomed. Babies were absorbed into the households of the grandparents, who were happy to accept the responsibility for their care and nurture (Frumkin 1973).

Our Society

Until this century our own society was closer to the antisexual than the prosexual end of the continuum. However, elements of prosexuality, which had always been present, became increasingly evident during the third quarter of this century. As we continue through the

---

[3]*Copulation,* which is defined as inserting the penis into the vagina, is the only formally acceptable term in our language that is precise, explicit, and grammatically flexible (*copulating, copulated, would have copulated, will copulate,* and so on.) The term *coitus* is also precise and explicit, but it can be used only as a noun. Other terms that are often seen in textbooks are imprecise (there are many *sex acts*), vague (*intercourse* can have many meanings), euphemistic (*making love*), or misleading (*sleeping together*). The Middle-English term *fuck* is precise, explicit, and grammatically flexible, but is usually regarded as vulgar (although it is now being seen more often in literary usage). Since *copulation* is the only term for penile-vaginal insertion that is precise, explicit, grammatically flexible, and socially acceptable, it will be the term used throughout this text.

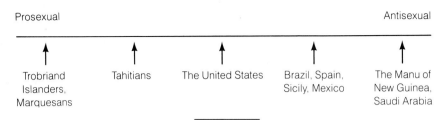

Prosexual   Antisexual

| Trobriand Islanders, Marquesans | Tahitians | The United States | Brazil, Spain, Sicily, Mexico | The Manu of New Guinea, Saudi Arabia |

FIGURE 4-1

The prosexual-antisexual continuum

final quarter, the two forces are vying with about equal effect (see Figure 4-1).

Our Traditional Heritage

Our sexual heritage stems from the traditional antisexuality of the medieval church, when such writers as St. Augustine (A.D. 354–430) stated categorically, "The act of generation is sin itself—a sin transmitted *ipso facto* . . . to the new creation."[4] This doctrine of the sinfulness of sex, even when limited to reproduction, has been remarkably persistent in Western civilization. In the United States, for example, as recently as the nineteenth century eminent gynecologists regarded sexual desire in young women as "pathological." The Attorney General officially proclaimed that "nine-tenths of the time a decent woman does not feel the slightest pleasure in intercourse" (Hunt 1967, p. 319).

Until the second quarter of the twentieth century, eroticism was not generally acceptable in women, and only grudgingly accepted in men. The purpose of sex was reproduction. Contraception was forbidden by law, as was providing information about contraceptive techniques. For a physician to provide information regarding conception—even to a married woman with several children—was a felony, punishable by imprisonment and hard labor, as we have seen (Chapter 2).

As we near the end of this century, the traditional approach to sexuality that has endured since medieval times is being increasingly challenged by a "naturalistic-acceptance" view of sex that regards both the reproductive *and* the pleasure-giving, erotic aspects of sex as normal, natural, healthful, and good—in any case, of no concern to society as long as the two persons involved are mature enough to accept the responsibility for their actions. Not only are contraceptive information and devices readily available, but abortion is now legal.[5] And cohabitation (living together without being married), which was totally unacceptable to the white middle class until the late 1960s, is now approaching institutional status (see Chapter 6).

From the naturalistic-acceptance point of view, sexual behavior is considered primarily as a method of *relating* and can have many meanings and consequences. On one hand, if people relate to each other sexually in ways that are selfish, exploitive, ruthless, or callous, such a relation is wrong or "bad," just as a similar type of asexual (nonsexual) relation is bad. On the other hand, sexual or asexual relations that are warm, friendly, and understanding and that deepen intimacy and communications are regarded as "good" so long as the couple are

---

[4]St. Augustine, *Confessions* (c. 400).

---

[5]Abortion has been legal in the United States since 1973, following the U.S. Supreme Court decision that a woman has the right to abortion if she wishes it during the first trimester; medical restrictions apply during the second and third trimester (see Chapter 11).

"Today, class, we are going to see a movie. You may not understand what the actors are saying, for they will be speaking Swedish."

able and willing to be responsible for their actions.

This naturalistic-acceptance view of sexual activity is now widely held as legitimate after marriage even by such staunch traditionalists as the Catholic church, within which the doctrine of St. Augustine originated. For example, in 1951 Pope Pius XII affirmed that "the husband and wife shall find pleasure and happiness of mind and body." However, the official position held by all organized religions and by schools and the judiciary still emphasizes the traditional view of sexuality before marriage as probably undesirable—although the incidence of premarital copulation and cohabitation began increasing in the late 1960s (see Chapters 5 and 6).

As a society, we still tend to fall close to the antisexual end of the prosexual-antisexual continuum in many regards. For example, many segments of our society and many individuals tend to regard sexuality as "dirty"; consider masturbation sinful, degrading, or injurious to one's health; and subscribe to the doctrine that sexual energy may be conserved or saved and then diverted into nonsexual activities—that is, sublimated.

Sexuality as "Dirty"

In our society, sexual matters, whether anatomical or behavioral, are commonly associated with the concept of "dirt." One reason sexuality or erotic behavior is considered to be "dirty" by so many people may simply be "dirt by association" (Dundes 1966, p. 103). The male urinates through the penis, and urine and urination are generally regarded as "dirty"—hence the penis and, by extension, erotic behavior are also "dirty." The female does not urinate through the vagina, but the opening to the urethra is just above the entrance to the vagina, and so urination is often associated with the vulva.

By a further extension, if sex or eroticism is "dirty," a sex joke is a "dirty" joke, a story about sex is a "dirty" story, and a photograph or drawing portraying nudity is a "dirty" picture. Most striking in this regard is our identification of words *themselves* as "dirty." So rigorous is this taboo that it is not unusual for a textbook, expressing detailed precise information on sexuality, to use such euphemisms as *the sex act* and *intercourse*, rather than a specific and unambiguous term such as *copulation*. For these writers, apparently the word *copulation* is "dirty" or too blunt or too precise—even though the subject matter is specifically sexual.[6]

Masturbation

A society's attitude toward masturbation is perhaps the most significant index to its position on the prosexual-antisexual continuum,

---

[6]It is interesting to note that *no* textbook has yet been published that uses explicit Anglo-Saxon terms for sexual anatomy and activity, even though these terms can now be found in standard dictionaries, are increasingly heard on the legitimate stage and in motion pictures, and are seen in both popular and literary publications. For example, such words as *fuck, screw, cunt,* and *prick* appear frequently in the third volume of John Updike's *Rabbit* trilogy, *Rabbit Is Rich* (which won the Pulitzer Prize for literature in 1982). The first volume of the trilogy, *Rabbit, Run,* published in 1960, did not use these words, which are commonly regarded as "dirty."

Drawing by Dedini; © 1966 The New Yorker Magazine, Inc.

"I __know__ sex is no longer a taboo subject. I just don't feel like discussing it all the time, that's all."

inasmuch as masturbating has no reproductive function.

Prosexual societies are not only permissive toward masturbation but encourage it on the grounds that it provides important training for copulation. Antisexual societies, in contrast, find it an obvious target and condemn masturbation as repulsive, degenerate, immoral, and perverted "self-abuse."

The notion that masturbation is harmful began in the eighteenth century with Tissot, a French physician, who, with no evidence whatsoever, wrote a book in which he ascribed most of the known physical ills of the time to masturbation (Tissot 1764, pp. 57–67). The medical establishment of the period not only accepted Tissot's doctrine of the evils of masturbation, but added some of their own—including *insanity*. By the mid-nineteenth century this doctrine of the evils of masturbation was held to be *medical fact*—with not a smidgen of evidence (Dearborn 1973).

Representative of this extraordinary state of affairs within the medical community was *Dr. Kellogg's Plain Facts for Young and Old,* published in 1879. Kellogg's book was enormously popular—it sold over a million copies (a huge number for this period) and was both quoted and imitated widely.

Of all the vices to which human beings are so addicted, no other so rapidly undermines the constitution and so certainly makes a complete wreck of an individual. . . . It wastes the most precious part of the blood, uses up the vital forces, and finally leaves the poor victim a most utterly ruined and loathsome object (Kellogg 1879).

Kellogg cites the case of one "poor victim addicted to the loathsome vice" whose father, driven to distraction and with his son's best interest in mind, cut off the boy's testicles to stop him from masturbating. In Kellogg's view, the father's action was not only understandable, but commendable, since it saved the boy from the "inevitable consequences of a practice he was powerless to stop." Dr. Kellogg was not unique in his time; he reflected the general attitude of the medical establishment (Levine and Bell 1956).

Female masturbation was considered to be even worse; it was regarded with nothing short of horror. Until the late nineteenth century, medical literature advocated amputation of the clitoris (which is analogous to cutting off the penis), cautery (burning) of the clitoris, and suturing (sewing closed) the labia as measures against female masturbation (Levine and Bell 1956).

Handcuffing was widely advised for both boys and girls who were powerless to stop themselves from "the evil practice." The handcuffs, which were fastened to the head of the bed, would be removed in the morning, when the diligent parents could presumably keep an eye on the troubled youngster. Ministers advocated prayer and earnest supplication to God for both the parents and the youngsters, and everyone urged the beneficial effects of chopping wood (presumably to exhaustion) and cold baths (Levine and Bell 1956).

It is interesting to note that although this doctrine has no scientific evidence whatsoever to support it, medical opinion did not begin to change until the 1920s. Even then, change was gradual, and Tissot's doctrine was not generally discredited by the medical establishment until the 1960s. Some physicians, many religious leaders, and a large percentage of the general population (especially in the lower class), still maintain the beliefs advocated by Tissot, although sexologists now advocate masturbation as not only normal, but desirable and beneficial (Rosen and Hall 1984, Dearborn 1973).

Conservation of Sexual Energy

Another implicitly antisexual concept is that a person has a finite (limited) amount of sexual energy, and therefore "excessive" orgasm—whether from masturbation, petting, or copulation—is a reckless squandering of "vital fluids" that will leave one a nervous wreck and result in impotence in the male. This notion that "wastage of the vital fluids" will cause debility was widespread in U.S. society until the early thirties (Hall 1909, Dickerson 1930).

The concept that sexual energy may be conserved (or wasted) is not a product of our own culture, however; it can be traced as far back as the early Greek period, when it was supported by such eminent philosophers as Empedocles, Diocles, and Plato. These classical Greek philosophers believed that semen originated in the brain, and that "excessive" ejaculation would therefore drain intellectual energy. This belief was based upon a sketchy (and inaccurate) knowledge of anatomy and physiology and is difficult to sustain today.

When research began to illuminate the murky area of this doctrine of the conservation of sexual energy, the evidence not only failed to support it, but contradicted it. One of the most interesting discoveries of the Kinsey (1948) research was that boys who have a higher-than-average frequency of ejaculation during adolescence continued to have a higher-than-average frequency throughout middle and old age. Then, in 1966, Masters and Johnson's trailblazing research supported Kinsey's findings. Apparently, the more sexually active a boy is in adolescence, the more active he will be throughout his lifetime. The doctrine of conservation of sexual energy seemed to be replaced by the doctrine of "use it or lose it."

The Sex Researchers

Until Alfred Kinsey and his associates published their monumental work *Sexual Behavior in the Human Male* in 1948, little valid information was available about what people do sexually. *Sexual Behavior in the Human Female* followed five years later, in 1953.

The classic Kinsey interview asked each subject 350 questions, covering every conceivable aspect of erotic activity. Kinsey interviewers went everywhere—into manufacturing plants, colleges, churches, and prisons. More than seventeen thousand interviews were conducted, and the statistical theory, from which conclusions were drawn, was exhaustively checked and reviewed. A system of cross-checks was devised. For example, histories of both husband and wife were taken (and their statements compared), and there were follow-ups after two years and after four years.

However, Kinsey and his group did not observe sexual behavior directly. They simply catalogued it. Kinsey was a taxonomist, and taxonomy is the branch of science that names, describes, and classifies. This is all that Kinsey and his associates did—they named, described, and classified the type, the extent, and the frequency of various sexual activities in our society. It was not until a decade later that attempts were made to understand human sexual behavior by observing it directly.

In 1966, William Masters and Virginia Johnson ventured the unthinkable when they published their trailblazing *Human Sexual Response*, a report of systematic and painstaking research on copulating couples observed in the laboratory. This was a daring achievement and would not have been acceptable at the time of Kinsey.

Masters and Johnson attempted to penetrate (if not remove) the shroud of ignorance that had covered human sexual behavior since Eve tempted Adam in the Garden of Eden. Masters and Johnson managed to reveal, in scrupulous detail, how the human body reacts to sexual stimulation—tracing the physiological responses from the first stirrings of erotic desire through orgasm and subsequent relaxation. They not only observed human sexual behavior directly, but recorded their observations with specially devised equipment. They were successful in developing a camera that could be housed (together with necessary illumination) in a plastic penis, so that the interior of the vagina could be photographed during simulated copulation. Changes in such major physiological systems as blood pressure, heart rate, involuntary muscle contractions, breathing depth and rate, and skin response (flushing) were measured by electronic instruments. Hundreds of subjects participated, engaging in masturbation, petting, oral-genital stimulation, and copulation; their ages ranged from eighteen to eighty-nine years.

Masters and Johnson have been criticized for ignoring the role of love (and other emotions) in erotic response. They do not deny the importance of emotion (whether love, affection, and admiration, or fear, dread, and dislike), but in their initial research they chose to focus on the physiological correlates of erotic arousal—leaving the study of the psychological and social factors of sexuality and erotic experience to later studies.

Female sexuality is far more complex than the male's, as we shall see, and to date there is no research evidence regarding the validity of the conservation of sexual energy in the female (see the vignette, "The Sex Researchers").

Sublimation

Closely related to the doctrine of conservation of sexual energy is the idea that any use of sexual energy must be compensated for by a lessening of nonsexual energy; that is, a person who is active sexually has less energy for other activities such as athletics, work, or creative expression. This doctrine was formalized as a psychoanalytic concept by Sigmund Freud (1938), who used the term *sublimation* to describe it.[7] Countless athletes, writers, opera singers, and ballet dancers have remained celibate during strenuous physical, artistic, or creative efforts because of the assumption that they would thereby have more energy to use in nonsexual activities.

During various periods of history, warriors have abstained from copulation on the eve of battle to conserve and then divert their energy to combat. Athletes have been urged to abstain from copulation before competition (and from masturbation at all times) to conserve and then divert energy into athletic prowess.

Research has found no evidence to support this doctrine of sublimation, however, and some evidence that contradicts it. For example, Kinsey (1948) found that men who had a high frequency of ejaculation (throughout their lives) were also more active in nonsexual activities—more creative, more productive, and more successful. However, the men in the sample who had a relatively low incidence of ejaculation were also less active in other areas of their lives—relatively less creative, less productive, and less successful than the "high-incidence" men. If sublimation had occurred, the opposite would have been true. (Again, there are no available data for women in this regard.)

It is conceivable, of course, that a person who sincerely believes in the doctrine of sublimation may experience a redirection of sexual energy, although this may be so rare that it did not show up in the Kinsey data. For example, do Catholic priests (who take vows of chastity) redirect or sublimate their sexual energy? Or are they, in general, "low-incidence" men? What is the incidence of broken vows (masturbation and copulation) in this group? Do faith and religious conviction have such a strong psychological effect that they override aspects of sexuality? Very little concrete research has been done in these areas.

In the absence of evidence, the doctrine of sublimation must be regarded with skepticism, however. Masters and Johnson (1966) found that athletes should be able to perform at maximum ability after copulation if they are allowed a sufficiently long recuperation period—one to five minutes. In the 1976 Olympics, athletes were quartered with their wives (and girlfriends) for the first time in the history of the Games, and their performances did not seem to be impaired. And in 1982, the coach of the Forty-Niners football team shattered the cherished tradition that sexual activity drains an athlete's strength when he allowed the players to "sleep with" their wives before the Super Bowl. (They won the game.)

The Meaning of Perversion

A *perversion* is an abnormal sexual act. Although a few activities are considered perversions in all societies, the definition of what is regarded as abnormal usually differs from one society to another—and even within sub-societies of each society. The acts that are considered abnormal, or perversions, in all societies, however, are *necrophilia* (sexually molesting a corpse); *coprophilia* (sexual arousal at the sight, smell, or taste of feces); *urophilia* (becoming sexually aroused at the sight, smell, or taste of urine); *zoophilia* (dependence upon an animal for sexual arousal and orgasm); *pedophilia* (sexually molesting a child); forcible, injurious *rape*; extreme *sadism* (with injury to the victim); extreme *masochism* (with injury

---

[7]The concept of sublimation extends far back into Christian, Hebrew, Greek, and even more ancient asceticism, however.

to oneself); and *incest* (copulating with a relative).[8]

With these exceptions, whether a specific sexual activity is considered a perversion depends upon the attitude of the society or subsociety in which the behavior takes place. For example, homosexuality was regarded as both a sin *and* a crime by the Jews of the Old Testament but was exalted as the highest form of love in classical Greece. In our society, masturbation is often considered a perversion by the lower class but is commonly regarded as desirable by the middle class (and by all sexologists). Displaying the genitalia is frequently considered to be a perversion by the lower class (and by some religious groups), whereas middle class couples may display the genitalia quite casually in the privacy of their own homes and may prefer a lighted room for copulation.

Most lists of perversions bear little relation to the way most people behave, to accepted behavior in other societies or subsocieties, or to biological normalcy. Almost any activity one could imagine has made someone's list. From a sexologist's point of view, any activity that is pleasurable to each of the couple and is not injurious to either is "normal."

Christian missionaries in the nineteenth and twentieth centuries preached that any copulative position except the woman-supine – man-prone arrangement was a perversion, although this position is relatively rare in world societies, and the most common position is crouching, face to face (Ford and Beach 1970).

Cunnilingus (oral stimulation of the female genitalia) and *fellatio* (oral stimulation of the male genitalia) are legally defined as perversions and carry substantial criminal sanctions in some states, whereas they are regarded as normal in other states (and as desirable by sexologists).

A correspondent to *Playboy* (May 1985) describes her experience with fellatio as follows:

I like going down on him because my mouth is more sensitive than my vagina. I can simply feel more of what is happening . . . as he becomes more and more aroused. . . . I become very excited knowing that he is having such a good time. . . . The greatest part . . . is when he ejaculates. . . . I get the full pleasure of every muscle contraction (p. 51).

MALE SEXUALITY

Sexuality is based upon gender—maleness and femaleness—and gender is an extraordinarily complex blend of physical, social, and psychological factors, as we have seen (Chapter 2). The fundamental basis of sexuality is, of course, physical—anatomy and physiology. The psychological and social aspects of sexuality must rest upon this physical basis.

In tracing the characteristics of sexuality, we shall first review the anatomy and physiology of the male and of the female, and then explore the very important complex of psychological and sociological factors that contribute to the reality of erotic experience.

Male Sexual Anatomy

In the male, the *gonads* that produce the *sperm* (the male sex cells or *gametes*— see Figure 4-2) are ovoid-shaped organs called *testicles*, of which the normal male has two. The testicles vary in size but are generally about two inches

[8]Incest is prohibited in all societies, but the definition of what constitutes incest varies from one society to another. For example, some societies have approved a marriage of brother and sister (Middle-Kingdom Egypt), and some societies assign the father the right to penetrate his daughter's hymen, to copulate with her on her wedding night as part of the nuptial ceremony (Tannahill 1980). In our society, sexual relations between father and daughter, mother and son, brother and sister are defined as incestuous by all states, as are sexual relations between grandparents and grandchildren. However, sexual relations between uncle and niece, between aunt and nephew, and between cousins are regarded as incestuous in some states, but not in others.

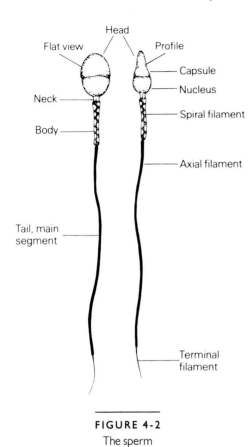

FIGURE 4-2

The sperm

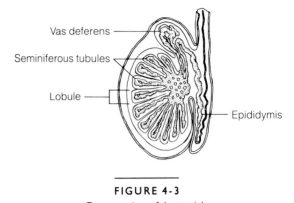

FIGURE 4-3

Cross section of the testicle

long and an inch and a half in diameter. Because sperm cells are sensitive to even a small rise in temperature and must be maintained at a temperature lower than the interior of the body, the testicles (which produce and store the sperm) are enclosed in a sac called the *scrotum*, which hangs outside the body, between the legs, at the base of the abdomen.

Within the testicles are several *lobules*, small divided areas that contain many winding and tightly coiled *seminiferous tubules* in which the sperm are produced (see Figure 4-3). Each testicle has 300 to 600 of these tightly coiled tubules. If a tubule were to be uncoiled and stretched out, it would be between one and two feet long. If all the tubules in a man's testicle were laid end to end, they would reach for an astonishing half a mile.

Sperm are produced in truly fantastic quantities in the *germinal tissue* that lines the walls of the tubules. Sperm production (*spermatogenesis*) is continuous, with the average man producing the astronomical number of 4–5 billion sperm cells each month. Each of these cells is a separate organism, with its own life cycle, from birth to death. Since sperm cells have only twenty-three chromosomes each (the *soma* or body cells have forty-six), they are regarded as foreign organisms by the body and are subject to attack by the man's defense system. They must be protected from this attack by *guard* or *nurse cells*, each of which has about ten to twenty sperm cells under its care.

Each single sperm cell, as tiny as it is, carries one-half the genetic material necessary to create an entire adult human being. This material is encoded in DNA molecules in the sperm's head. When a single sperm, out of the enormous multitudes produced, unites with an egg cell in the woman's fallopian tube, a new individual comes into being—the fertilized egg, which is about the size of the period at the end of this sentence. This very tiny, single-celled organism, now containing the forty-six chromosomes characteristic of the human body cells, will divide and divide again, until it reaches the 100 trillion cells characteristic of the adult human being, with highly specialized organs—including the brain, which provides the person with a sense of self and the curiosity and the ability to question his or her own origin. (For a further discussion of the remarkable events relating to human reproduction, see Chapter 11.)

The organ that carries the sperm into the body of the woman (so that reproduction can take place) is the *penis*. The penis is located at the base of the abdomen and in its *flaccid* (soft) state lies upon the scrotum. The loose skin of the penis is a continuation of the skin of the scrotum. The penis consists chiefly of spongy tissue surrounding the sperm- and urine-carrying tube, the *urethra*. The opening to the urethra at the tip of the penis is called the *meatus*. The main body of the penis is called the *shaft*; it extends about three-fourths of the length of the penis. The smooth, cone-shaped head at the end of the shaft is called the *glans*. It is covered with a very thin, sensitive tissue and a heavier, retractable *foreskin*, which is an extension of the loose skin covering the shaft.[9] (See Figure 4-4 for more details of the male urogenital system.)

The glans of the penis is by far the most erotically sensitive part of the average man's body.[10] The surface tissue, which is very similar to the skin covering the lips, contains an ex-

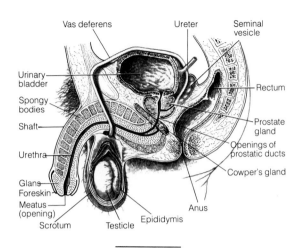

FIGURE 4-4

Male urogenital system

traordinarily high concentration of nerve endings, especially at the *corona*, the crownlike ridge at the back of the glans. The most sensitive area of the corona is the *frenum*, on the lower surface of the glans where the foreskin is attached (see Figure 4-5).

The average length of the adult penis when flaccid is three to four inches with a diameter of slightly less than one inch. When the penis responds to erotic stimulation, whether psychological or tactile (touch), blood flows into its spongy tissue faster than it flows out. As the penis becomes engorged with blood, it gradually erects (the erection may take anywhere from a few seconds to several minutes). As it erects it increases in size and becomes stiff and hard, projecting out from the body and pulling the now taut scrotum upward. The erect penis is called an *erection*. Almost all erections are about six inches long and about an inch and a half in diameter (Katchadourian and Lunde 1980).[11] (See Figure 4-6.)

---

[9]*Circumcision* consists of trimming away the foreskin to expose the glans of the penis and is commonly practiced in many societies. In some societies, especially in Africa and among the aborigines of Australia, it is performed at puberty as an initiation rite to manhood and a test of courage. Among Jews it is an ancient ritual performed by a *Mohel* (qualified performer of ritual circumcision) on the eighth day after birth, in a ceremony called the *Bris Milah*, as a religious covenant. Until the late 1970s it was routinely performed on more than 80 percent of male babies in our society, ostensibly for hygienic purposes. Its incidence is now decreasing, however, since current medical opinion is that circumcision not only serves no purpose but also carries a significant complication rate and in rare cases has caused the baby's death (Paige 1978).

[10]An erotic sensation has to do with sexual excitement, arousal, tension, or pleasure. An erotic sensation can occur either with stimulus of one or more of the senses (such as touch, vision, scent) or through mental imagery or fantasy.

---

[11]In regard to penile size, a correspondent to *Playboy*, who worked for several years in a massage parlor, measured 1,681 erections and found that 97 percent were about six inches. Only seven (0.04 percent) were as long as eight inches.

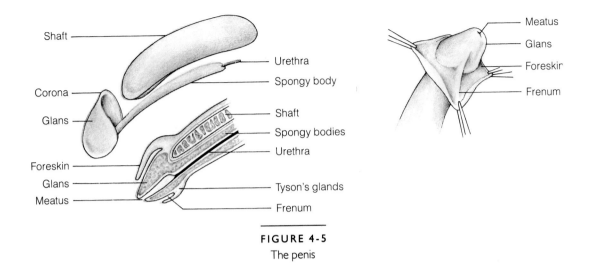

FIGURE 4-5

The penis

The Two Types of Erection

There are two types of penile erections with extremely important differences: the cerebral erection and the reflex erection.[12] The *cerebral erection* is caused by psychological stimuli. The male can neither cause this erection to happen nor stop it from happening; it is beyond deliberate control. It may occur very quickly (within a few seconds) at a very inopportune time (such as in class or on a bus), or it may fail to occur when it is most desired (when the opportunity for copulation is available). It may last for just a few minutes or for an hour or more.

The cerebral erection is a very common occurrence in young males, but it occurs less and less often beginning in the late teens or early twenties. When this happens, the male may begin to worry that he is becoming *impotent* (unable to achieve erection). If the cerebral erection does not occur when he is attempting copulation, the failure can be dis-

astrous—devaluating and embarrassing. Fear of failure can itself stop the cerebral erection, causing more fear, which further impedes the erection—a cycle that can have tragic results. Masters and Johnson (1966) estimate that fully 20 percent of men, terrified at what they view as the advent of impotence, attempt suicide before they reach age thirty-five.

When the cerebral erection does not occur during an attempted copulation, the female may also feel devalued. She may feel rejected, sexually unattractive, or undesirable. Feelings of rejection or devaluation often lead to anger—blaming the other person for one's own feelings of self-doubt or frustration.

Fortunately, there is a second type of erection, which not only can be brought about at will, but also continues to occur reliably even when the cerebral erection occurs less and less frequently. This second type of erection is called a *reflex erection* and is caused not by psychological, but by tactile stimuli of an erogenous zone (an *erogenous zone* is an area of the body that responds to tactile stimulation, causing a sense of erotic excitement or pleasure).

The entire penis (the shaft and the glans) is a primary erogenous zone in most men, but the

---

[12]The *morning erection* is apparently a third type of erection. Although it has been traditionally ascribed to the pressure of a full bladder, the cause of the morning erection is simply unknown (Hastings 1963).

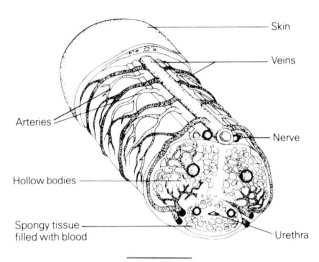

FIGURE 4-6
Cross section of the erect penis

corona, the meatus, and the frenum are especially sensitive. The nipple is another primary erogenous zone for about half of all men; they respond to tactile stimulation of the nipple with penile erection and even orgasm. For many men, the *perineum* (the area between the base of the scrotum and the anus) is a primary erogenous zone, containing a rich supply of nerve endings. These men respond with rapid erection to pressure on the perineum. The anus is also richly supplied with nerve endings and is a primary erogenous zone for about half of all men (Kinsey et al. 1953, 1948).

The tactile erection continues to occur throughout the lifetime of the average man (Starr and Weiner 1981, Kelly 1973). In a young man (under age thirty-five) the reflex erection usually occurs within a few seconds to a few minutes of tactile stimulation of the penis or other primary erogenous zones; with and older man it may take somewhat longer.[13]

The Erotic Response Cycle in the Male

One of the important findings of Masters and Johnson (1966) was that everyone goes through the same cycle of erotic response when responding to tactile stimulation. Males and females alike proceed through four phases of erotic response: excitement, plateau, orgasm, and resolution.

The Excitement and Plateau Phases in the Male

When the male enters the *excitement* phase, the most obvious sign is penile erection. Other significant physiological changes that characteristically occur during this phase are an increase in blood pressure and pulse rate, con-

[13]The reflex erection does not inevitably occur, of course, since it may be impeded by such physiological factors as fatigue, alcohol, or drugs, and such psychological factors as guilt,

shame, fear, or apprehension. Moreover, following orgasm, the penis will usually return to its flaccid state and will not become erect again, whatever the stimulation, until a recovery period has passed—the refractory period. (See the text for a discussion of this male characteristic.) The sexual dysfunction of persistent impotence does sometimes occur, of course, but is relatively rare (Kinsey et al. 1948).

traction of involuntary muscles, and nipple erection (Masters and Johnson 1966).

With continued tactile stimulation, the male enters the second phase of erotic response: the *plateau* phase. During this phase all physiological characteristics of the excitement phase continue, but in addition the coronal ridge of the glans enlarges further and the color deepens. Beginning a year or two before puberty a few drops of a clear, slippery substance, called the *preejaculatory fluid*, may appear at the meatus during the plateau phase.[14]

The Orgasm Phase in the Male

With continued tactile stimulation,[15] the male enters the third phase of erotic response, the *orgasm* phase, which is characterized by a series of profound physiological changes. A sensation of "suspension" signals the onset of orgasm. This sensation is then immediately followed by involuntary muscular contractions that may involve the whole body, while the facial expression typically becomes "tortured" (Masters and Johnson 1966). During orgasm, which lasts three to four seconds, the heartbeat may more than double from its norm of 70–80 beats per minute to 180 beats per minute, similar to that of an athlete at the peak of effort; blood pressure may double; and the breathing pattern becomes deeper and faster. (In most individuals orgasm is accompanied by increasing *anoxia*—shortage of oxygen— which causes the person to gasp and gulp for air.) The senses of smell, taste, hearing, sight, and touch are all temporarily diminished, with the degree of loss paralleling the intensity and duration of the orgasm. Brain-wave patterns

change, representing an altered state of consciousness. As with all human experience, there are great individual differences in the experience of orgasm, however, and physiological changes vary from very extreme to mild.

The subjective experience of orgasm—how it feels to the individual—also varies from one person to another. Orgasm may be experienced as compulsively pleasurable by one person and as only a mild "tickling" sensation by another. Also, the same person may experience orgasm differently at different times, depending upon the physical, psychological, and social factors involved.[16] Orgasm is usually an intensely pleasurable experience, however, and is normally followed by a profound sensation of well-being and contentment. This feeling often persists for some time—even a day or longer (Rosen and Hall 1984, Proctor et al. 1974, Masters and Johnson 1966, Kinsey et al. 1953, 1948).

One reason for the subjective feelings of well-being and contentment may be the increased level of testosterone in the bloodstream that occurs with erotic stimulation and orgasm. (See the vignette, "Testosterone Level and Well-Being.")

Most males (80 percent) in our society experience their first orgasm long before puberty. The cerebral erection occurs in the male from infancy on, and long before their teens most males have learned that rubbing the penis produces a sensation of pleasure. Some learn this through their own experiments, and others learn it from their peers. The prepubertal boy goes through the same phases of erotic response—excitement, plateau, orgasm, and resolution—with tactile stimulation

---

[14]It is assumed (but not definitely known) that this preejaculatory fluid is produced in *Cowper's glands*—two small bodies, each about the size of a pea, situated just above the perineum (see Figure 4-4).

[15]Tactile stimulation will bring about an erotic response only if the male is psychologically prepared to make this response, of course. It is not simply mechanical.

[16]Hunger, fatigue, and drugs change the characteristics of the physical response, as does the interval of time that has occurred since the last orgasm. Psychological and social factors may be extraordinarily complex, but obviously the other person who is involved in the orgasm, and the situation under which it takes place, are going to have a significant effect upon how the orgasm is experienced.

Testosterone Level and Well-Being

A high level of testosterone, the male sex hormone, in the bloodstream is related to good health: to the building of new proteins, tissues, and cells (including red and white blood cells); to increased bodily defenses against infection; and to a generalized feeling of well-being. In contrast, a low testosterone level in the bloodstream is related to a generalized loss of a feeling of well-being, the breakdown of proteins, the wasting away of tissues, the loss of calcium from the bones, the death of cells (including red and white blood cells), and a lowering of bodily defenses against infection.

The testosterone level in the bloodstream increases with erotic stimulation. For example, testosterone levels increase markedly with copulation or with extensive petting and remain high for several hours before gradually returning to a lower level.

It has recently been determined that visual erotic stimulation also increases the testosterone level significantly and that the level remains relatively high for several hours following this stimulation. This was discovered in a study in which men viewed a color film of people petting and copulating. The penis of each observer was fitted with a *plethysmograph,* which measures the duration and intensity of erection. Catheters were also inserted into the forearm vein of each viewer, and blood samples were drawn every fifteen minutes (beginning forty-five minutes before the film was viewed and continuing for two hours after the viewing). Meanwhile, a matched control group of men watched a film with no erotic content.

The plethysmograph records showed that all the men who watched the pornographic film experienced full erections, while the blood samples showed that their testosterone levels rose an average of 35 percent. The control subjects showed no significant variation in testosterone level (Brecher and Brecher 1976).

---

of the penis hundreds of times before he reaches puberty, and he is physiologically capable of ejaculation (Kinsey et al. 1948).

Ejaculation

After puberty (which usually occurs between ages eleven and fourteen) male orgasm is accompanied by the ejaculation of about a teaspoonful of fluid (which is called *semen* or *ejaculate*). This fluid contains the sperm cells. At puberty, then, the male is considered biologically mature—in the sense that he is now capable of reproduction.

As with all physiological responses (including orgasm) the characteristics of the ejaculation differ markedly from one person to another, and from one time to another with the same person. Semen is usually viscous (thick) and milky, but it may vary from gelatinous at one extreme to thin and watery at the other. It may either seep from the meatus or spurt forcibly; it may consist of one or several spurts, and the amount may vary from a few drops to a teaspoonful. These differences are related to various factors, some of which are apparently inborn characteristics while others are transient, depending upon the circumstances. For example, if a man ejaculates more than once during a relatively short time, both the amount of semen and the force with which it is ejaculated diminish. Ejaculatory force and the amount of sperm also gradually diminish with the age of the man (after age twenty-five to thirty).

The ejaculate (or semen) normally contains 200 to 500 million sperm cells and may contain as many as a billion (see Figure 4-2). Once ejaculated, the sperm die almost immediately unless they are able to make their way to the

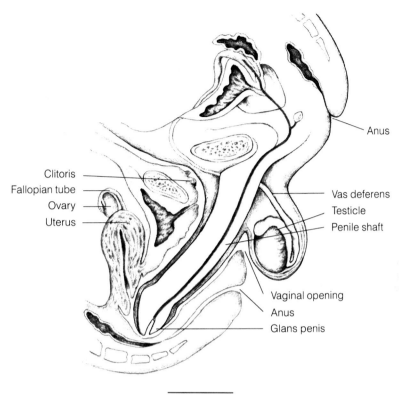

Clitoris

Fallopian tube

Ovary

Uterus

Anus

Vas deferens

Testicle

Penile shaft

Vaginal opening

Anus

Glans penis

FIGURE 4-7

Cross section of the penis in the vagina

woman's fallopian tubes, where they may survive for two or three (or possibly as long as five) days (see Figure 4-7).[17]

Semen is produced chiefly in the *seminal vesicles* and in the *prostate*, both glands near the surface of the rectal wall. (As we have seen, sperm are produced in the testicles.) Before the sperm reach the urethra, they pass through the *epididymis* (a maturation chamber over the back and upper part of each testicle) and through the *vas deferens*, a small tube about eighteen inches long (see Figure 4-8). By an intricate set of interacting physiological processes, the semen is precisely timed to be released into the urethra simultaneously with the release of sperm. The timing is a miracle of coordinated physiological events that rivals the countdown procedures of a missile launch.

The Resolution Phase in the Male

Following orgasm, the person returns to normal physiological functioning during the fourth phase of erotic response, the *resolution* phase. During this phase all physiological systems—such as muscle tension, pulse rate,

---

[17]It is quite possible that sperm may live long enough to reach the vagina if the man ejaculates near it (on the thighs or abdomen), even if the woman is clothed (or partially clothed). Pregnancy may then occur, without vaginal penetration by the penis; the woman may still be technically a virgin, with an intact hymen that has not been ruptured. It is a myth, however, that it is possible for a woman to become pregnant in a swimming pool or hot tub if a man ejaculates in the water.

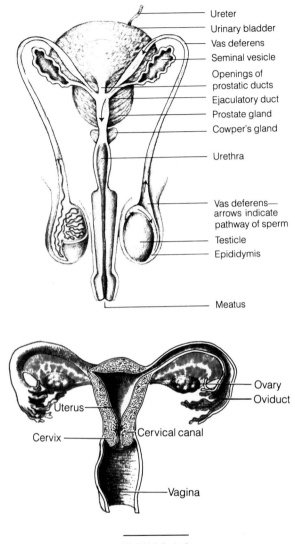

- Ureter
- Urinary bladder
- Vas deferens
- Seminal vesicle
- Openings of prostatic ducts
- Ejaculatory duct
- Prostate gland
- Cowper's gland
- Urethra
- Vas deferens— arrows indicate pathway of sperm
- Testicle
- Epididymis
- Meatus
- Ovary
- Oviduct
- Uterus
- Cervical canal
- Cervix
- Vagina

FIGURE 4-8

Cross section of male genitalia (showing movement of sperm) and female genitalia

blood pressure, and breathing—return to their pre-excitement norms, and the penis subsides to its flaccid state.

As part of this resolution phase, the male must go through a *refractory period* before he is physiologically capable of entering the excitement phase again. During this refractory period, tactile stimulation of the penis may be uncomfortable, annoying, or even painful. The refractory period may last for only a few minutes in the young male, who is often capable of two or three (or more) orgasms with only brief refractory periods. Beginning in the mid-twenties, however, the refractory period often lasts for several minutes to an hour or more; it may last for several hours or even days (Masters and Johnson 1966).

This physiological characteristic of the male translates into very important behavioral consequences for sexual interaction. If the man ejaculates before the woman has experienced orgasm, his erection will subside as he returns to the resolution phase. He must then remain in the resolution phase until the refractory period has run its course; he will be unable to reenter the excitement phase until this has occurred, and he will be relatively uninterested in erotic activity. This physical imperative cannot be changed. Therefore, if sexual harmony in the relation is to be achieved, it is important that the man delay ejaculation until the woman has proceeded through the excitement and plateau phases and has experienced orgasm. Indeed, for many women three to four orgasms are the norm before erotic satiation occurs. (See the section, "Female Sexuality," later in this chapter.)

Simply stated, the goal then for the male is to delay ejaculation, while for the female the goal is to reach orgasm. Fortunately, these goals may be reached—although *premature ejaculation* (ejaculating too quickly) is the most common sexual dysfunction in young men (Masters and Johnson 1966).

Sexologists find that the average male can train himself to delay ejaculation indefinitely. This requires a training period in which the male learns to experience during masturbation a series of "miniorgasms" without ejaculation. With the technique so learned, the plateau phase can be extended for an hour or more. To achieve this ejaculatory control, sexologists advise that the male use the "stop, start" method. Instead of the persistent, rapid up-and-down stroking of the erection with one hand until ejaculation occurs (in from one to four minutes), the male is advised to use an intermittent stroking technique, stopping the stroking just before ejaculation occurs (perhaps experiencing a miniorgasm) and then

resuming stroking when the urge to ejaculate has subsided. When the male is able to maintain erection without ejaculation for at least fifteen minutes, he may go on to half an hour. When he has sustained arousal for half an hour without ejaculating, he will be able to do so indefinitely (Brauer and Brauer 1984, Petersen 1977, Masters and Johnson 1966).

Sexologists also advise that prolonged erection may be achieved by using varying techniques along with the basic up-and-down stroking with one hand: turning the hand so that it is thumb down rather than thumb up; making a ring of the thumb and forefinger; rolling the penis between two hands; using both hands to stroke from mid-shaft outward in both directions at once, toward the glans and toward the base; twisting the shaft one way and the glans the other with a back and forth twisting motion; holding the penis in one hand and rubbing the glans against the palm of the other hand; stroking the glans, the meatus, the frenum, or the corona, instead of the shaft; and lightly stroking the glans with a fingernail (Brauer and Brauer 1984).

Finally, imminent ejaculation may be interrupted if the glans is gripped firmly where it joins the shaft, with the forefinger at the frenum and the thumb at the top of the corona (Masters and Johnson 1966).

The problem of the female achieving orgasm will be examined in the section, "Female Sexuality," later in this chapter.

The Male Schedule of Orgasm

Although the average male experiences erection and orgasm from early childhood, his pattern (or incidence) of orgasm is irregular until his first ejaculation, with the advent of puberty. Beginning with puberty, more than 90 percent of men begin a regular schedule of ejaculation (with orgasm), and this pattern or schedule remains relatively unchanged for the remainder of the man's lifetime, with only a

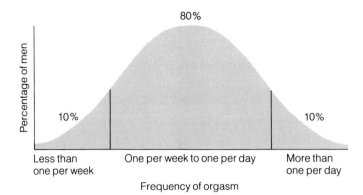

Most young adult males in our society experience about 3.5 orgasms per week, or one about every seventy-two hours. Eight in ten males fall within a range of one per day to one per week. One in ten experience fewer than one per week, or more than one per day, although some may go as long as five years without an orgasm, and some experience twenty-five to thirty per week. All of these characteristic experiences of orgasmic frequency are within the normal range.

FIGURE 4-9

Incidence of orgasm in the postpubertal male, as reported by Kinsey et al. (1948)

gradual decline in incidence (Starr and Weiner 1981).

The average man ejaculates about three and a half times per week, or just about once every other day. Eight men in ten fall within the average range, which extends from about one orgasm (with ejaculation) per day to one per week (see Figure 4-9).

Of the one in ten men who fall outside this range in the high-frequency group, some will ejaculate four to five times per day. Of the one in ten in the low-frequency group, some will ejaculate only once or twice per year, and about one man in a hundred goes for as long as five years without ejaculation (Kinsey et al. 1948).

Aging and Sexuality in the Male

Men experience aging as a very gradual psychoendocrine and psychosexual process,

with great individual differences in both its onset and its progress.[18] These changes in the aging male (typically beginning about age fifty to sixty) include lessened frequency of erection and ejaculation, longer time required to achieve full erection, greater likelihood of incomplete erection, earlier loss of complete erection, longer refractory period, greater likelihood of ejaculatory delay, and greater likelihood of nonejaculatory masturbation or copulation. However, the aging male can usually copulate longer than the young male without ejaculating; that is, premature ejaculation is not a problem. There is no evidence of a male *climacteric* ("change of life") comparable to the female climacteric, which denotes

---

[18]*Psychoendocrine* refers to the effect of hormones from the endocrine glands upon physiological responses, emotions, and behavior.

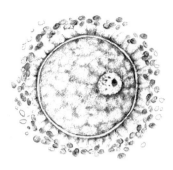

FIGURE 4-10
The ovum

the end of regular ovulation (Starr and Weiner 1981, Money 1980, Kelly 1973).

Psychoendocrine aging in the male is a product of many events, one of which is a decrease in the testosterone level in the bloodstream.[19] The youngest age at which such a process may begin is generally fifty. However, a good proportion of men ages seventy to eighty still have not manifested this psychoendocrine change, and some men in their nineties have the same hormonal levels as those under age fifty (Money 1980).

Aging does not usually bring a change in the average man's interests, appreciation, or enjoyment of erotic activity. Gerontological studies of sexuality find that, on the contrary, the prime determinant of an older man's sex life is simply the availability of a willing and cooperative partner (see Chapter 7). With such a partner, men usually show only a gradual decrease in the frequency of copulation, although there is great individual variation. In general, the earlier and more vigorous the sexuality of youth, the later and more vigorous the sexuality of aging, as we have seen (Starr and Weiner 1981, Money 1980, Kinsey et al. 1953, 1948).

FEMALE SEXUALITY

Female Sexual Anatomy

The female *gonads* that produce the human egg cell (*female gamete* or *ovum*) are the *ovaries*, the homologue (counterpart) of the male testicles.[20] Just as a man has two testicles, a woman has two ovaries. However, unlike the testicles, the ovaries are situated deep inside the body, in the pelvis, below and to each side of the navel. The ovary, like the testicle, is ovoid and about an inch and a half in diameter. It is made up of glandular tissue and *egg sacs (follicles)*. At birth a female has all the egg sacs she will ever have—about fifty-thousand in each ovary—but only 250 ever become active and produce an egg, or ovum (see Figure 4-10).

Unlike a man, who continuously produces sperm cells and may ejaculate as many as 5–10 billion per month, a woman produces only one ripe egg per month—from about her fourteenth to her forty-fifth to fiftieth year. Beginning with puberty, about every twenty-eight days a follicle in one of the ovaries erupts, releasing an egg, which is gradually swept into that ovary's *fallopian tube*.[21] One end of this tube opens to partially enclose each ovary and leads from that ovary to the *uterus* (also called the *womb*), a thick-walled expandable organ within which the fertilized egg will develop during the *gestation* period or *pregnancy*. The rupture of the egg sac and release of the egg are called *ovulation* (see Figure 4-11). (For further discussion of pregnancy and reproduction see Chapter 11.)

---

[19]As noted in Chapter 2, testosterone is a behaviorally significant component of the male sex hormone androgen.

[20]As noted in Chapter 2, *homologue* means developed from the same prenatal tissue. That is, the same tissue will develop into ovaries or testicles, labia or scrotum, penis or clitoris, depending upon the prenatal hormone mix present, which in turn depends upon the presence (or absence) of sex chromosomes (XX in the female, XY in the male).

[21]The egg is swept into the fallopian tube through the action of cilia—tiny hairlike structures—and the slow movement of fluid. The egg itself, unlike the sperm, is incapable of independent motion.

As with the male, the external genitalia (collectively called the *vulva*) are at the base of the abdomen between the legs. They consist of *labia majora* (outer lips) and *labia minora* (inner lips), which close the entrance to the *vagina*. The labia are the homologue of the male scrotum. The *clitoris*, which is the female homologue of the penis, is situated just below the point where the labia join near the top of the vulva (see Figure 4-12).

The vagina extends from the labia minora to the *cervix*, the opening between the vagina and the uterus. As we have seen, during copulation the erect penis is inserted into the vagina to ejaculate against the cervix (see Figure 4-7).

Although it plays no role in reproduction (as does the penis) the clitoris is extremely important in the sexual consciousness of most women, since clitoral stimulation is their chief source of erotic arousal and orgasm (Hite 1976, Masters and Johnson 1966). Like the penis, the clitoris consists of a shaft as well as a glans but, unlike the penis, the shaft does not hang free and only the glans may be felt. The glans of the clitoris is usually about the size of a pea.[22] Like the glans of the penis, the glans of the clitoris has an abundance of nerve endings. When erotically aroused (usually by tactile stimulation), the shaft of the clitoris extends in length but does not erect away from the body. The glans grows harder and harder and does extend from the clitoral prepuce (the *prepuce* is the homologue of the foreskin). As it does, it becomes extremely erotically responsive and sensitive to tactile stimulation.

Inside the entrance to the vagina is a membrane called the *hymen* (the maidenhead). The

FIGURE 4-11
Ovulation

hymen partially closes the entrance to the vagina in some individuals, and is absent or nearly absent in others.[23] It has no role in either reproduction or sexual pleasure. If the hymen does partially close the vaginal entrance, it may act as a barrier to the initial copulation. This type of hymen must tear when the erect penis is thrust into the vagina the first time, causing bleeding, discomfort, and even pain.[24] (See Figure 4-13 for more details of the female urogenital system.)

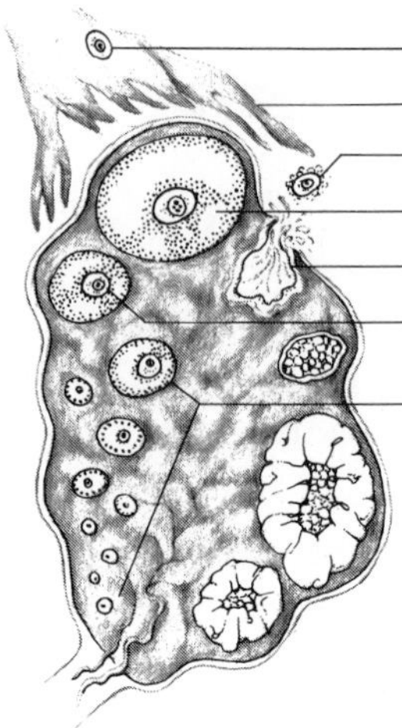

The Erotic Response Cycle in the Female

In common with the male, the female reacts to appropriate stimuli by a progression through

---

[22]It is interesting to note that in our society the size of the clitoral glans is usually compared to a pea, whereas in Asian literature it is said to be about the size of a pearl and is often called the "pink pearl" or the "jewel without price." Moreover, the clitoral glans is often mentioned in Asian literature as an object of great beauty. Poets extoll its velvety texture, delicate fragrance, and exquisite sensitivity. Cunnilingus is called "licking a lotus blossom" (see Kronhausen and Kronhausen 1969).

---

[23]The unruptured hymen is considered very important in some societies, but it is quite possible for a girl to be a virgin and still have little or no hymen. The hymen may be absent from birth, or it may be ruptured by insertion of tampons or by active participation in sports.

[24]An unusually thick hymen with a very small perforation can inhibit initial copulation but can be opened easily by a simple and painless procedure in a physician's office.

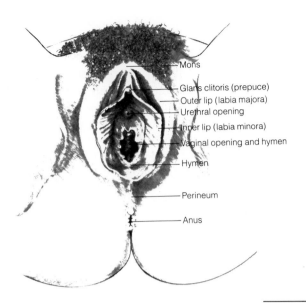
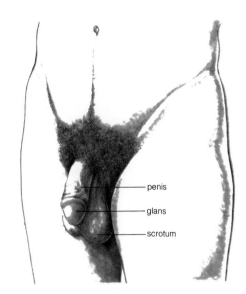

FIGURE 4-12

External genitalia of the female and the male

The Excitement and Plateau Phases in the Female

four phases of erotic response: excitement, plateau, orgasm, and resolution. However, she does not go through the refractory period during resolution.

The Excitement and Plateau Phases in the Female

A primary erogenous zone in most females is the clitoris (which is the homologue of the penis). However, the *mons* (the fleshy mound just above the vulva)[25] and the vulva (especially the labia minora) are also important erogenous zones. The *G spot* may also be an important erogenous zone in many women, although the existence of the G spot has not yet been confirmed anatomically. (See the vinette, "The G Spot."). The nipple is a primary erogenous zone for about half of all women, as it is for men. Many women react very strongly to nipple stimulation with erotic response and

even orgasm. The entire breast may be an erogenous zone for the woman, whereas response in the man is usually limited to the nipple and the *areola* (the pigmented area surrounding the nipple). The *perineum* (the area between the anus and the vulva) contains a rich supply of nerve endings and is an erogenous zone in many women, as it is for men. The anus is also richly supplied with nerve endings and is a primary erogenous zone for about half of all women, as it is for men. In addition, almost any area of the body surface— ear, thigh, nape of the neck, throat, feet, fingers, toes, and even eyebrows—may be a source of erotic arousal, with great individual differences in this regard (Kinsey et al. 1953).[26]

---

[25]The full name of the mons is the *mons veneris*, which is a Latin term meaning the "mountain of Venus."

---

[26]It is interesting to note that the Japanese kimono is designed to display the nape of the neck, which is considered highly erotic in traditional Japanese culture; the breast, however, is considered an antierotic feature by the Japanese, who admire small, flat breasts. Incidentally, admired breast shapes vary widely in different societies—from high and conical to small and upright to long and pendulous (Ford and Beach 1970).

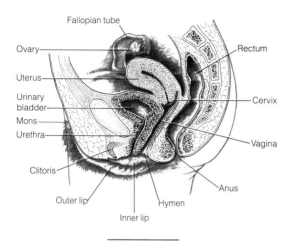

FIGURE 4-13
Female urogenital system

When a woman responds to tactile stimulation of an erogenous zone by entering the excitement phase, this is signaled by vaginal lubrication. Vaginal lubrication is the female counterpart of penile erection in the male. Within ten to thirty seconds of erotic stimulation a lubricating substance is exuded from the walls of the vagina (Masters and Johnson 1966).

The physiological reality that vaginal lubrication is the counterpart of penile erection translates into very important behavioral differences between men and women: A man cannot copulate without an erection—that is, he must be in the excitement phase. However, a woman *can* copulate without vaginal lubrication—that is, when she is *not* in the excitement phase. This basic behavioral difference between men and women is extremely important in understanding male-female relations: Copulation is *automatically* pleasurable for a man because of his physiological characteristics, but it is *not* necessarily pleasurable for a woman because of hers. On the contrary, although she is physically capable of copulating, the woman who does so without being in the excitement phase will probably find the

experience boring, uncomfortable, annoying, and perhaps even painful.

The cardinal rule to be derived from this physiological reality is very simple: The man should delay penetration (copulation) until the woman is in the excitement phase of erotic response (Masters and Johnson 1966). Fortunately, the stimulation the woman requires need not be with the penis (which may not always remain erect). Digital (or labial) stimulation of the clitoris (or other primary erogenous zones) is just as effective and may even be preferred.

As many women have already indicated, genital sex is better with digital sex. The tender touch, the passionate caress, the genital rub, the titillating probe, and all those other infinite maneuvers that humans are best equipped to do, can be much more satisfying to women than simply a longer time span between intromission and ejaculation (Hong 1984, p. 51).

As noted earlier, the man's goal is to delay orgasm; the woman's goal is to reach orgasm. This difference in men's and women's erotic natures stems from a fundamental difference in their erotic physiologies. If this difference in male and female characteristics is not understood, the couple's prospect for a satisfactory sex life is almost nonexistent. Their interaction will be characterized by frustration, resentment, and bitterness instead of mutual pleasure, deepening communication, and shared intimacy.

In addition to vaginal lubrication, the inner two-thirds of the vagina expand (balloon) during the excitement phase, and both the inner and outer lips (labia) of the vulva swell and protrude, becoming very sensitive to erotic stimulation. Other physiological changes include significant increases in pulse rate and blood pressure, nipple erection, contraction of involuntary muscles, and flushing of the skin. The labia minora, especially, change from pink to red (Masters and Johnson 1966).

As do males, many females first experience erotic arousal through masturbation. However, they are more likely to be strongly inhib-

The G Spot

Some researchers have found, in about 50 percent of women they have examined, a primary erogenous zone called the G spot (or Grafenberg spot) located on the frontal vaginal wall about halfway into the vagina, with the precise spot (and its size) varying from one woman to another. When stimulated, it swells until it covers an area an inch or more across. In some women, it is fully as erotically sensitive as the clitoris, and continued stimulation of the G spot will produce orgasm. Some women say that when orgasm follows stimulation of the G spot, they release fluid as if they were ejaculating (Ladas et al. 1982, Zilbergeld 1982). One subject reported:

I have always had orgasms, but I have never had much stimulation when the penis was completely inside my vagina. In fact, sometimes my excitement and arousal would end abruptly when the penis entered me completely. I have always been most excitable when the penis was only one-half or one-third its way into my vagina. Now I know why—at that point it hit my "magic spot" (Ladas et al. 1982, p. 40).

An anatomical structure that would explain the phenomenon of the G spot has not yet been discovered.

---

ited about masturbating than are males, and if they do masturbate, females begin, on the average, a good deal later than males—many females do not begin masturbating until they reach their dating or even their early married years (Hunt 1974).[27]

Physiologically a woman is equally as erotically responsive as a man, reacting just as quickly to adequate stimulation. Women, like men, usually masturbate to orgasm rather quickly (the median figure is just under four minutes). Those women (and men) who do take more time do so deliberately to prolong erotic arousal and pleasure (Masters and Johnson 1966).

However, unlike the male, female masturbatory methods include great individual differences. In fact, no two women were observed to masturbate in identical fashion in the Masters and Johnson (1966) study. Most masturbate by lightly and rapidly stroking the clitoris, but the rhythm of stroking (fast or slow), type of stroking (vertical, circular), intensity of stroking (light, heavy), and the area stroked (shaft, glans, adjacent areas) are different for each woman. Moreover, unlike the male, who can masturbate to orgasm in any position, many women must have not only the body in a special position (supine, prone, side) but also the legs (flexed, straight). Concurrent vaginal entry (by finger or dildo),[28] breast (nipple) stimulation, and fantasy also vary for each woman.

It must be emphasized that these differences are often *necessary* for a woman to experience orgasm, and even a slight variation from the pattern may be found antierotic or

---

[27]A study of middle class women found that a significant number felt that masturbation had a positive effect on their sex lives (DeMartino 1974). Another study of middle class married women found that the frequency of masturbation was highest for women who described themselves as persons who enjoy novelty and stimulation rather than routine—a characteristic of women with both high intelligence and high self-esteem (Fisher 1973). Another study found that women who masturbate frequently have significantly higher sex drives than other women (Abramson 1973). Hite (1976) found that many women achieve orgasm more successfully through masturbation than through copulation.

[28]A dildo is an object that is inserted into the vagina to cause erotic pleasure. It may be a common household object (such as a candle) or an item especially designed for the purpose.

Requirements for Female Erotic Response

The female may not respond erotically to tactile stimulation as predictably as the male, whose erotic response is virtually automatic. A few moments of rapid up-and-down stroking of the penis (simulating the thrusting of copulation) will almost invariably elicit orgasm in the male. When he varies this technique it is usually only for variety or to prolong the plateau phase and deliberately delay (or avoid) orgasm. In contrast, the female may be unable to reach orgasm without a specific combination of stimuli that she has discovered is effective for her, forming a technique that is tailored to her individual erotic nature. A stimulus that will quickly bring one female to orgasm may have no effect on another, or may even be annoying. In addition, the female may respond only in a specific body position; or with her legs just so; or with accompanying nipple stroking, squeezing, or rolling between thumb and finger; or when she is immersed in a particular, vivid fantasy; and so on. The range of combinations of these (and other) factors is virtually unlimited. Hite (1976), for example, found not only that females used six basically different types of masturbatory techniques, but that within these types there is great individual variation. The six basic types are: (1) stroking the clitoris (in various ways) while lying on her back; (2) lying on her stomach and stroking her entire vulval-clitoral area; (3) pressing and thrusting her vulval-clitoral area against an object; (4) rhythmically pressing her thighs together and then releasing them, often by swinging, twisting, or shaking her foot; (5) directing a steady or pulsating stream of water against her clitoris; and (6) thrusting one or more fingers or a smooth, round, long object (such as a candle) into her vagina. The range of combinations of various techniques that are effective in eliciting orgasm in the individual female is illustrated in the following examples from Hite's (1976) report:

I lie down and begin . . . my favorite fantasy. . . . After about five minutes of this I'm ready, very lubricated. I lift one knee slightly and move my leg to one side, put my middle finger on or around the clitoris and gently massage in a circular motion. . . . After the first orgasm I do not fantasize any longer, but concentrate entirely on the delicious feeling in my vagina and surrounding areas, continuing the same movement of my finger, but slightly faster and in about one minute, I have another orgasm (p. 26).

I stimulate my clitoris with the third finger of my right hand (I find it very difficult to do with any other finger) until I begin to feel excited. Then I use my left hand to stimulate my nipples at the same time. I have hardly ever come without simultaneous nipple stimulation (p. 30).

If I go into the bathroom and straddle the corner of the sink, and rock back and forth I can have wonderful orgasms! I have tried to stimulate myself while I'm in bed, but it's futile. . . . I can be stimulated but not to orgasm. . . . Throughout my teen-age years (I am now twenty) I used to hop on the back of my desk chair and put a book in front of me on the desk and have orgasms for as long as I wanted! (p. 46).

In my teens I branched out into public masturbation in boring classes and during a sermon when I was a member of the choir. All I did was cross my legs and squeeze the thigh muscles together repeatedly for two or three minutes. But even with the utmost control it was impossible to avoid a slight convulsion at the moment of orgasm, which I would disguise by a coughing fit or having to lean over to scratch my leg (p. 49).

I remove the head from my shower to allow a steady stream of water to come out. And I open the vaginal lips, exposing my clitoris. The water can be slightly hot for more stimulation, and hips can be moved slightly to tantalize and prolong the enjoyment. I usually do it standing up. Lying down is more beautiful, but you get your hands and face wet. This orgasm tops them all for me, and can be multiple (p. 50).

---

even annoying (Hite 1976). (See the vignette, "Requirements for Female Erotic Response.")

The discovery that the type and rhythm of stroking, the body position, and other factors necessary for orgasm are unique for each woman is extremely important for sexual harmony in the relation. If a woman is not aware of her individual requirements for erotic arousal and orgasm (or if she fails to acquaint her partner with her erotic individuality), she will probably become increasingly indifferent to her sexual life. This slackening of erotic interest and lack of erotic response may then be significant factors in the couple's joint dissatisfaction with their relation.

When a woman enters the plateau phase of erotic response vaginal lubrication increases, the labia minora change to a deeper red, the outer third of the vagina continues to contract, while the inner two-thirds balloon further, and the glans of the clitoris grows even larger and harder (Masters and Johnson 1966).

The Orgasm Phase in the Female

As with the male, the third phase of female erotic response is orgasm. Physiologically, the experience of orgasm is virtually identical for females as for males except that the female does not ejaculate. Heart rate and blood pressure double; muscles rhythmically tense and relax; breath comes in gasps; various surface areas of the skin flush; the senses of smell, hearing, sight, and touch are temporarily diminished, with the degree of loss paralleling the intensity and duration of the orgasm; and facial expression typically becomes tortured. As with males, the average female orgasm lasts three to four seconds, but some women experience much longer orgasms—as long as twenty to sixty seconds (Masters and Johnson 1966).

Although the female does not ejaculate, the subjective experience of orgasm is the same as it is for males. This was illustrated very clearly in a study in which men and women were asked to write descriptions of what the experience of orgasm meant to them—"how it felt." Any words that revealed the gender of the person were then changed to neutral words (for example, *clitoris* or *penis* to *genitals*). These descriptions were then given to a panel of evaluators.[29]

---

[29]The panel of evaluators included male and female gynecologists, clinical psychologists, and medical students.

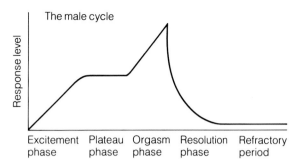

The male cycle

Response level

Excitement phase | Plateau phase | Orgasm phase | Resolution phase | Refractory period

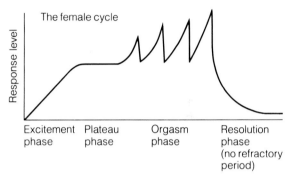

The female cycle

Response level

Excitement phase | Plateau phase | Orgasm phase | Resolution phase (no refractory period)

A man typically has a single orgasm and then must go through a refractory period before he is physiologically capable of entering the excitement phase and experiencing a second orgasm. A woman does not experience the refractory period and may have several orgasms before returning to the resolution stage.

FIGURE 4-14

Typical male and female sexual response cycles
Source: Data from Masters and Johnson (1966).

The members of this panel were unable to tell whether the description of orgasm had been written by a man or a woman; their success rate was no better than chance (Proctor et al. 1974). (See the vignette, "The Similarity of Male and Female Orgasms.")

One significant difference between males and females in erotic response, however, is that the female does *not* undergo a refractory period. She may experience several orgasms, one after the other, before proceeding to the resolution phase. In fact, the average woman in our society is not satiated (satisfied and content) *without* several orgasms. Merely

The Similarity of Male and Female Orgasms

Which of the following descriptions of orgasm were written by males and which by females? (Correct answers are at the bottom of the box.) (From Proctor et al. 1974.)

M_____ 1. Just before I reach orgasm, I feel warmth in
F_____ my genital area. The warmth turns into a heat which spreads up my back and all the way into my fingers and toes. Although I am usually fairly quiet during most of lovemaking, at orgasm I often moan quite loudly.

M_____ 2. Basically, I feel a glow that starts in my genit-
F_____ als, and then spreads through my whole body. Sometimes one orgasm is enough, and other times, it is not completely satisfying.

M_____ 3. For me, orgasm feels like a building wave of
F_____ emotion. First I notice a pulsing sensation that is quite localized, then it spreads through my whole body. Afterwards, I feel tired but also superrelaxed.

M_____ 4. I concentrate all my attention on the sensa-
F_____ tions in the genitals, and when I come, I completely lose contact with everything around me. My body feels incredibly alive and seems to vibrate. Afterwards, I just want to hold my lover and be very still.

M_____ 5. Sexual orgasm just seems to happen to me. I
F_____ can't explain how or why, but I suddenly experience an intense rush of feeling, and then it's gone, just as suddenly. Often, I want to experience it more than once.

M_____ 6. Just before orgasm, I am mostly aware of the
F_____ muscle contractions. When the orgasm comes, I feel my whole body sort of explode, and then slip into a deep relaxation, so that I feel I can hardly move.

M_____ 7. My anxiety about sex definitely inhibits my
F_____ orgasm. There are times that I feel some intense sensations, but usually I am too inhibited to let myself go. If I am not very comfortable with my partner, it is very difficult to come. I have orgasms most easily when I masturbate.

M_____ 8. I think orgasm is overrated. I sometimes
F_____ spend over an hour getting turned on, and then the orgasm takes only a few seconds. I'd like to learn how to make the feeling or orgasm last longer.

Answers: F, F, M, M, F, F, M, M

---

experiencing a single orgasm can leave her feeling frustrated, unfulfilled, and dissatisfied—still in a state of sexual arousal, in the excitement or plateau phase (see Figure 4-14 on the previous page). Moreover, each successive orgasm is more intense and more extensive (Masters and Johnson 1966). (See the vignette, "Summary of Male-Female Differences in Erotic Response.")

The Resolution Phase in the Female

In the fourth phase of erotic response—the *resolution* phase—the female returns to her nor-

mal physiological functioning. Pulse rate, blood pressure, breathing, and muscle tension all revert to their preexcitement levels. The labia, clitoris, vagina, and uterus return to their unstimulated size and position as vasocongestion (congestion of vacular tissue such as blood vessels) subsides.

The Uniqueness of Female Sexuality

Unlike the man, who begins a regular pattern or schedule of orgasm (with ejaculation) at puberty, the sexual nature of each woman is

Summary of Male-Female Differences in Erotic Response

The female is capable of copulation without being in the excitement phase, but such a copulation will probably cause feelings of displeasure, annoyance, disgust, or even pain. The male, however, is not capable of copulation unless he is in the excitement phase; copulation is, therefore, automatically pleasurable for the male.

The female does not go through a refractory period; she is physiologically capable of reentering the excitement phase at once following orgasm. The male *must* go through a refractory period before he is physiologically capable of reentering the excitement phase following orgasm.

The female may characteristically experience two or more orgasms before she is erotically satiated. The male is usually satiated with one orgasm, after which he must go through a refractory period.

When the female does experience more than one orgasm in succession, each one is more intense. When the male experiences more than one orgasm in a single sexual episode (with a brief refractory period following each orgasm) each successive orgasm is less intense.

The orgasm usually lasts for about three to four seconds for both males and females. However, the female orgasm may last for as long as twenty to thirty seconds.

The female does not ejaculate with orgasm, whereas the postpubertal male does.

---

unique, following no regular pattern. Kinsey (1953) regarded this as his most important discovery regarding women.

As noted earlier, most men have a schedule of orgasm that may be stated as a statistical norm, as can the probability of variation from this norm. There is no such pattern for women; erotic responsiveness and frequency of orgasm do not follow a statistical norm. Moreover, while a man remains in about the same incidence group from puberty through old age, a woman may change her characteristics of erotic response and her frequency of orgasm from time to time and from situation to situation. Indeed, the variations in erotic behavior are so great among women that one woman may be incapable of understanding the meaning of sexuality for another woman (Kinsey et al. 1953).

As compared with 80 percent of men, only about 25 percent of women have experienced orgasm by puberty, and for those who have, it may have been only a single occurrence. Thus, most (75 percent) of adolescent females have no understanding of the meaning of eroticism and sexuality from their own experience (Kinsey et al 1953).

The Female Reproductive System

During copulation the vagina receives the erect penis, which ejaculates against the cervix. The sperm then make their way through the cervix, through the uterus, and into the fallopian tubes by lashing their tails in a swimming motion, traveling about an inch a minute (see Figure 4-7).

Fertilization (conception) normally takes place in a fallopian tube when a sperm cell fuses with the egg to form a fertilized egg (a *zygote*). (For further details of the processes of

1. Ovum ripens within the follicle. Uterus lining is smooth and gradually thickening.

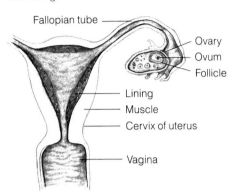

Fallopian tube

Ovary
Ovum
Follicle

Lining
Muscle
Cervix of uterus

Vagina

2. Ovulation: The ovum is released from the follicle. Uterus lining thickens, preparing for possible implantation.

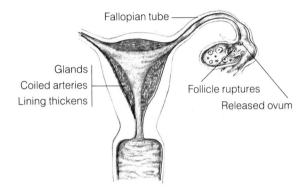

Fallopian tube

Glands
Coiled arteries
Lining thickens

Follicle ruptures
Released ovum

3. Ovum travels through tube. Lining thickens with more fluid in glands and more blood in coiled arteries.

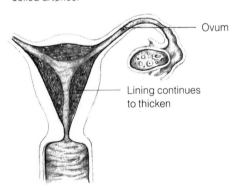

Ovum

Lining continues to thicken

4. Unfertilized egg disintegrates. Lining sloughs off and leaves the body.

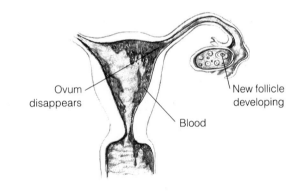

Ovum disappears

New follicle developing

Blood

FIGURE 4-15
The menstrual cycle

conception, pregnancy, and childbirth, see Chapter 11.)

If no sperm are present in the fallopian tube, conception cannot occur and the egg disintegrates. Blood and other material in the thickened uterine walls are then sloughed off through the vagina in a process called *menstruation*, which usually lasts about four days. The cycle of ovulation, engorgement of the uterine wall with blood, menstruation, and subsequent ovulation is called the *menstrual cycle* (see Figure 4-15). This cycle normally repeats itself every twenty-eight days in the average woman, although in some women it is longer or shorter than twenty-eight days, and the cycle may be irregular. Moreover, the cycle may be interrupted or delayed by such factors as emotional stress, fatigue, hormonal condition, and diet. Conception always interrupts the cycle; ovulation and menstruation cease with pregnancy.

The beginning of menstruation in a girl's life is called the *menarche* and signifies that she has entered puberty and adolescence. She is now usually thought of as *nubile* (capable of reproduction). However, she may menstruate for two or three years before she is truly fertile— either because her eggs are not yet capable of producing a *viable* (capable of life) zygote or because she does not yet have the delicately tuned hormonal regulation necessary for implantation to occur in the uterine wall. This phenomenon is called *adolescent sterility*.

In our society, most girls experience the menarche at age twelve to fourteen. The average age at which puberty begins for American girls is dropping about six months every decade, however, and one-third of the girls in our society now reach puberty at or before age eleven. One hundred years ago, the average American girl reached puberty between the ages of fifteen and seventeen (Planned Parenthood 1978). In other societies, the menarche may occur earlier (age nine or ten) or later (age fifteen or sixteen), depending on such factors as prenatal care, diet, climate, and altitude.

Aging and Sexuality in the Female

The menopause (ending the process of ovulation), occurs in the average woman in our society between ages forty-five and fifty, and the menstrual cycle stops. This period in a woman's life begins the *climacteric* ("change of life"). The climacteric is not a sudden event but extends for about fifteen years, from the menopause to approximately age sixty to sixty-five, and entails gradual changes in all body tissues.

Earlier beliefs that the menopause is an extremely traumatic period in a woman's life are not borne out by research. Most women do not experience the menopause as a critical event but instead feel an increased sense of serenity and well-being and report fewer complaints after the menopause than before (Brock 1979).

Although the menopause marks the end of ovulation in women, it does not halt their erotic response. In fact, many are even more erotically responsive after the menopause than they were before (Brock 1979).

THE COMPLEXITY OF SEXUAL INTERACTION

The physical aspects of erotic response and sexuality are extraordinarily complex. The psychological and social aspects augment this complexity immeasurably. Sexual interaction can be spontaneous, pleasurable, and satisfying if the couple are well-matched sexually,[30] but if the couple are poorly matched, they may experience disappointment, despair, anger, and rage. Unfortunately, the latter is often the case (Masters and Johnson 1966).

People are incorrigibly themselves. They are shy, cheerful, dissatisfied. They like one another, and are mysteries to one another . . . and the seesaw of their erotic interests rarely balances (Updike 1979, p. 10).[31]

Erotophiles and Erotophobes

It is obvious that individuals differ enormously from one to the other in terms of erotic interest and responsiveness, and that the range of individual differences is huge. Copulation, to the individual, may be compulsively pleasurable, mildly pleasurable, mildly uncomfortable, disgusting, or even painful.

---

[30]The pleasure and satisfaction that each can derive from the other may then be highly intense, especially if they are also in love.

[31]John Updike's *Too Far to Go* (1979) is a collection of short stories that traces the decline and fall of a marriage.

"No wonder it didn't work. You were doing page 26 and I was doing page 43."

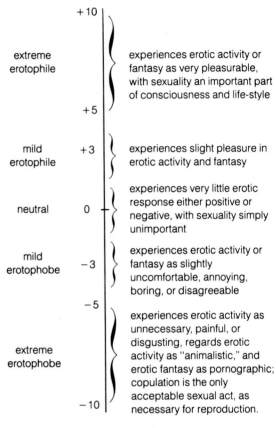

Human behavior is enormously diverse from one individual to another and does not fit precisely into any scheme or categorization. Moreover, a person may move from one characteristic to another from time to time, depending upon many factors. In general, however, our population may be represented upon a continuum that extends from very positive erotic characteristics through neutral to very negative. There is probably no other important human potential with such a wide range of response.

FIGURE 4-16

The erotophile-erotophobe continuum

A person who finds sex pleasurable is called an *erotophile*, while a person who does not is called an *erotophobe*. Erotophiles experience sexuality as an extremely significant part of their consciousness and life-styles. They often are preoccupied with sexual themes, enjoy pornography, have rich fantasy lives relating to erotic activity, and are interested in exploring variations of sexual behavior (Byrne 1977).

Erotophobes, in contrast, feel that sexual behavior is relatively unimportant (except for reproduction), feel uncomfortable about sexual matters, are very conservative regarding variations of sexual behavior, and find pornography distasteful or boring (Byrne 1977). Of course, most people are neither extreme erotophobes nor extreme erotophiles, but rather are somewhere in between (see Figure 4–16).

The range of sexual interest is illustrated by an interesting study in which married couples were given a list of ninety-six leisure activities. They were then asked to pick the five acti-

vities they enjoyed most, rating them from those *most enjoyed* to those *least enjoyed*.

"Reading books" was selected by more than a third (37 percent) of the wives as their most pleasurable activity, while "sexual/affectional activities" was chosen by a little less than one-

Simply viewing an attractive young woman may cause a man to enter the excitement phase of erotic response.

fourth (23 percent), 1 percentage point ahead of "sewing for pleasure" (Mancini and Orthner 1978).

"Sexual/affectional activities" was the first choice for nearly half (45 percent) of the husbands. (Note that more than half—55 percent—did *not* pick sex as their favorite activity.) "Attending athletic events" was the second most popular activity for men, and "reading books" was the third (Mancini and Orthner 1978). Although the husbands were significantly higher than the wives in their preference for erotic activities, *most* husbands in the study would rather do something else—watch an athletic event or read a book.

Other research (Flax 1984) finds that although relatively more men are rated higher in eroticism than women (68 percent versus 44 percent), about 45 percent of our population—men and women alike—are "sexually conservative" or "nonsexual" (about a fourth of these are high in sensuality but low in eroticism).

Male-Female Differences in Erotic Experience

Coupled with the spread of erotic interest and with the wide range of individual differences in eroticism, there are enormous differences between men and women in our society in terms of their erotic characteristics—their responsiveness and its importance in their lives. Much of this difference in erotic interest and responsiveness stems from their different physiological characteristics, as we have seen. Since the average man almost automatically proceeds through the excitement and plateau phases to orgasm (while the woman may not even reach the excitement phase), and since he

Erotic Matching and Mismatching in Marriage

What will a couple's marriage be like if they are both at the erotophobe end of the scale? If they are both at the erotophile end of the scale? If they are both about halfway between these two extremes?

What will the marriage be like if the wife is near the erotophile end and the husband is near the eroto-phobe end of the scale? If the wife is near the erotophobe end and the husband is near the erotophile end?

It is not difficult to predict the scenarios in these different types of marriages.

---

almost invariably experiences orgasm with copulation (whereas she may not), and since the woman may be urged to copulate when she is not in the excitement phase of erotic response, it does not take much imagination to predict the scenario of the average marital copulation. He is likely to go to sleep following orgasm whereas she probably remains wide awake—stimulated just enough to be restless. If their sexual interaction usually follows this pattern, it would be surprising if she does not become increasingly irritated, resentful, and angry as the initial romantic and erotic ideals with which she entered marriage change into feelings of disillusion and frustration, and finally bitterness and resentment. Moreover, it could be predicted that she will become increasingly antierotic (erotophobic). In this scenario, the average husband may expect to become increasingly deprived, disappointed, and frustrated, and increasingly irritated, resentful, and angry. These characteristics describe the sexual interactions of fully 50 percent of married couples in our society (Masters and Johnson 1966). (See the vignette, "Erotic Matching and Mismatching in Marriage.")

Studies find that nearly two-thirds of both middle class and working class women experience problems with erotic arousal and orgasm. About 15 percent of all wives rarely or never experience orgasm, and those that do, do so only about half the time (Frank et al. 1978, Hunt 1974).

Middle class women state that they characteristically experience such sexual difficulties as "too little erotic stimulation," "inability to relax," "partner choosing inconvenient time," and "disinterest." Following the typical American pattern, these women's husbands underestimate their wives' erotic problems—assuming that so long as the wife neither complains nor refuses to copulate, all is well. Interestingly enough, despite such sexual disharmony, the middle class couples in this study characterized their marriages as "essentially satisfactory," indicating that their marital problems were "no worse than might be expected" (Frank et al. 1978).

The Special Plight of Working Class Wives

It is, of course, possible to increase the possibility for mutual sexual satisfaction in marriage simply by applying even a rudimentary knowledge of the basic imperatives regarding the physiology of erotic arousal in the male and in the female. Ironically, however, studies find that with working class wives, a husband's solicitous interest regarding the wife's sexual potential may actually have an adverse effect. Many of these economically pressured and overworked women found their husbands' concern that they reach orgasm oppressive—one more burden in an already harried life. One of the subjects put it this way:

It's not enough if I just let him have it, because if I don't have a climax, he's not happy. . . . It's really important for him that I reach a climax, and I try to every time . . . but it's hard enough to do it once! What will happen if he finds out about those women who have lots of climaxes? (Rubin 1976, pp. 151–53).

It is important, however, to emphasize that although the stereotype of the reluctant wife being pursued by the ardent husband characterizes many marriages, this pattern is reversed in a sizable minority. Rubin (1976) found that in one in five lower class marriages the wife was more interested in erotic behavior than was her husband, and the wife claimed that her husband even deliberately withheld sexual satisfaction from her:

Now I can hardly ever get him to do it any more no matter how much I try or beg him. He says he's too tired, or he doesn't feel well, or else he just falls asleep and I can't wake him up (Rubin 1976, p. 150).

Rubin also found that, although the husband was initially the sexual aggressor in many marriages, this pattern might be reversed after several years. For example, one couple in the research had copulated four or five times a week for six months before the wedding and for ten years of marriage, without the woman once experiencing orgasm. The wife then began to read about women's sexuality, studying literature on the subject, and also began to read some pornography. One night, as she tells it:

The earth shook. I couldn't believe anything could be so great. I kept wondering how I lived so long without knowing about it. I kept asking Fred why he had never made me understand before (Rubin 1976, p. 150).

At this point, her husband abruptly lost interest in sex, and the couple then fell into the 20 percent of marriages in which the woman is more ardent than the man, who is "too tired," disinterested, and erotically unresponsive—a puzzling and ironic comment on the vast complexity of sexual interaction.

Cultural Influences on Women's Sexuality

In the light of these findings it is not surprising that many studies have found that, on the average, women tend to be less erotically interested and responsive than men in our society.[32] Early theories suggested that this relative lack of erotic interest or responsiveness in the average woman compared to the average man was biologically based (see Kinsey et al. 1953). This point of view has been discounted by subsequent research, however. Current theory finds that each woman's sexuality, in addition to her own unique characteristics, is largely a function of cultural factors. After all, the physiological capacity for erotic response is greater in the female than in the male, as we have seen. Therefore, it would seem that the physical disinclination theory does not fit the facts.

One source of evidence for the importance of culture in women's eroticism comes from studies of other societies. For example, a study of the people of Mangaia—an island of the Polynesian group—finds that Mangaian women are fully as erotically oriented as men. In this culture, women not only invariably experience orgasm while copulating, but each of the couple expects that the woman will experience at least three orgasms before the man ejaculates. There is no word for *frigidity* in the Man-

---

[32]See, for example, Mancini and Orthner (1978), Frank (1978), Rubin (1976), Hunt (1974), Masters and Johnson (1966), Kinsey (1953).

gaian language—the concept is unknown (Marshall 1971).[33]

In Western civilization, a study at the University of Hamburg found that women students were no different from men in their responses to viewing erotic material. Subjects were shown slides and movies depicting masturbation, fellatio, cunnilingus, and copulation. The subjects were then rated in terms of (1) their physiological reactions during the experiment and (2) their sexual behavior during the twenty-four hours following the experiment. Not only did the research find no significant differences in erotic response between men and women in both these regards, but it also found that a large percentage of the women (about 40 percent) experienced a slightly *more* intense erotic arousal than did the average man (Schmidt and Sigusch 1970).

Cross-cultural comparison of these studies indicates that if a woman does not experience erotic arousal, either during copulation or in response to visual stimuli, this unresponsiveness is a function of the characteristics of the culture and is not biologically based. (If it were biologically based, there would be no difference in this regard from one culture to another.)

Heiman (1975) wondered whether women in our society might not *be* just as erotically responsive as the Hamburg women, but not be *aware* of their arousal. To test this hypothesis, instead of asking for a verbal report of a man's or a woman's subjective reaction to explicitly erotic material, Heiman managed to measure physiological arousal *directly*. To do this, she devised a method of recording the degree of vasocongestion in the vagina and in the penis.[34] Remember that vasocongestion in these organs is directly related, physiologically, to erotic arousal (Masters and Johnson 1966).

Heiman found that when men and women college students listened to descriptions of sexual behavior on a tape recorder, the degree of vaginal vasocongestion in the women was the same as the degree of penile vasocongestion in the men. Moreover, vaginal vasocongestion was greatest when the women were listening to descriptions of explicitly graphic sexual behavior. This seemed to bear out Heiman's hypothesis that women are just as erotically responsive as men, but they unconsciously deny it because they are culturally conditioned to do so (Heiman 1975).

It is interesting to note that *most* women in the study denied any erotic sensation or emotion *at all*, and many of the women who were the *most* aroused stated that they found pornography boring and were "turned off" by it. Nearly half (42 percent) of the women who showed the *greatest* physiological response insisted that they felt *no* response. Moreover, self-appraisal in this regard did not improve significantly over time, with a large percentage remaining unaware of extreme changes in their own physiologies (Heiman 1975).

These and other studies would indicate that there is no inherent difference between men and women in capacity for sexual arousal, but that women in our society have been, for the most part, conditioned to deny their sexuality from early childhood.

---

[33]The term *frigid* means antierotic or sexually unresponsive; it has been largely replaced by the term *preorgasmic*, following Masters and Johnson's (1966) finding that women formerly regarded as frigid will respond by proceeding through the four phases of erotic response with adequate preparation and appropriate stimulation.

[34]Erotic response in the man was measured by means of a ring fitted around the base of the penile shaft, while erotic response in the woman was measured by a device placed just inside the entrance of the vagina to measure changes in the vaginal pressure, pulse, and blood volume. Validation studies indicate that this device (a photoplethysmograph) does measure physiological response in women reliably.

Even though women have often been conditioned from early childhood to deny their sexuality, there is no inherent difference between women and men in their capacity for sexual arousal.

Constance S. Lewis/Woodfin Camp & Associates

However, other theorists point out that copulation (and erotic arousal associated with it) has a far different meaning for the woman than for the man because it is the woman who becomes pregnant. Thus, a woman invests far more in copulation than a man, and she is genetically programmed—after millions of years of evolutionary selection—to be more reserved and more cautious in her erotic response than a man. For a woman, copulation may not be taken lightly but must always be regarded as leading to possible pregnancy. Therefore, she is reluctant to respond unless the man is bound by emotional ties, so that he will be likely to support and protect the child. The man, in contrast, may be genetically programmed to respond erotically and copulate with as many women as possible, since this maximizes the probability that his genes will endure and proliferate (Symons 1979).

From this point of view, theorists suggest that love, romance, affection, liking, and respect, and the male's status (as a possible protector and provider) are inextricably bound up with erotic interest and erotic response in the female—at a deeply unconscious, genetically programmed level (Symons 1979).

Perhaps both points of view are correct—the cultural inhibition theory and the genetic programming theory. Women do invest far more than men in copulation and perhaps are genetically programmed to choose their partners carefully; in addition, cultural factors undoubtedly have significant influence.

SEXUALLY TRANSMISSIBLE DISEASES (STDS)

Inherent in any type of sexual interaction is the possibility of acquiring a sexually transmissible disease (STD)[35]—unless the interaction is always with the same partner who does not have such a disease. The incidence of sexually transmissible diseases has now passed the epidemic stage to reach pandemic proportions. For this reason, we shall explore the problem in some detail.

The STD Pandemic

The United States is currently experiencing a rising tide of STDs. The statistics are startling. Twenty-seven thousand new cases of STD are contracted every day. If this incidence continues, one out of every four persons between the ages of fifteen and fifty-five will acquire an STD (see Figure 4-17).

Unlike syphilis and gonorrhea, which usually respond to antibiotics, some of the rapidly accelerating STDs have confounded modern medicine. They cannot always be cured, and may sometimes result in chronic pain, sterility, abnormal pregnancies, brain-damaged children, and cancer. In the case of AIDS the outcome is almost certainly death. Of the twenty-five or so diseases now known to be spread through sexual contact, it is estimated that genital herpes has infected half a million new victims annually for the past several years, gonorrhea struck some 2 million Americans in 1984, and syphilis 90,000. The fastest-growing STD, chlamydia, infects 3–4 million women each year in the United States causing sterility in 20 percent of cases; half of those

who have the disease can spread it to others without knowing it (Washington et al. 1985).

The most serious sexually transmissible diseases are syphilis, gonorrhea, chlamydia, genital herpes, and AIDS. The incidence of AIDS is still relatively low (although rising rapidly), but it is by far the deadliest of STDs, since there is no cure or treatment, and 80 percent of its victims die within three years of being diagnosed (Perlman 1984). Syphilis is also dangerous but can be successfully treated—although the consequences of delaying treatment can be frightful. Although gonorrhea is usually self-limiting, it can lead to sterility or a serious debilitating or crippling disease. Chlamydia may be successfully treated in its early stages. Herpes, which causes a painful outbreak of blisters and ulcerated sores in the genital area is painful and annoying but not fatal, although it does have a striking association with cancer of the cervix and can cause death in a baby born to an infected mother. As with AIDS, there is as yet no effective treatment or cure for genital herpes (Straus et al. 1984, Gotwald and Golden 1981, Kaufman et al. 1981).

Factors Contributing to the Rising Incidence of STD

As prevalent as STDs are in our society, most persons are unfamiliar with the basic facts regarding acquisition and prevention of these diseases. Researchers find that most young people are not aware of the need to protect themselves from STDs and that they usually do not go to a clinic (or other source) for information until they begin to experience painful symptoms. Young people are unaware that gonorrhea generally has no symptoms in women, and that syphilis usually has no symptoms in either men or women. A person may have such a disease and not know it. Yet a person who does have a disease with no symptoms

---

[35]The term *venereal disease* (VD) is being replaced by the more accurate term *sexually transmissible disease* (STD), although both terms are still commonly seen and heard.

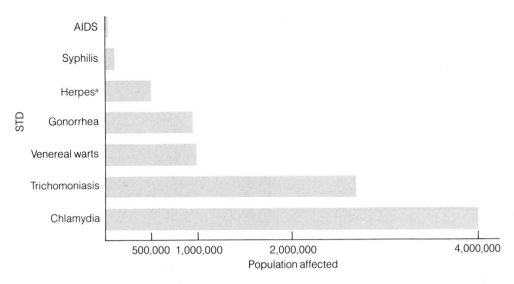

^aSince there is no cure for herpes the yearly incidence is cumulative, and the Centers for Disease Control estimate the number of persons with herpes may be as high as 20 million.

If the current rate of incidence continues, one out of every four persons in the United States will acquire an STD; there are 27,000 new cases every day.

FIGURE 4-17

New cases of STDs in the United States, 1984
Source: Data from U.S. National Center for Health
Statistics, *Special Report on Common Infectious
Diseases—Including STDs* (1984); U.S. Public Health
Service, "AIDS Update" (January and February 1985), and
STD Fact Sheet (March 1985).

may nevertheless transmit it to another with whom he or she has sexual contact (Seaman 1980).

Preventing STD

The surest way to prevent STD is to be monogamous, since if neither partner has an STD to begin with there is no possibility of contracting such a disease. Another way to lower the likelihood of contracting an STD is to use *prophylaxis*, precautionary measures taken before, during, and shortly after possible exposure to infection.

At least five methods of effective prophylaxis are currently recognized. Although none is 100 percent effective, each method provides a certain amount of protection—some more than others.

Precoital Inspection of the Genitalia

Quite often gonorrhea can be detected in a man by a "short-arm inspection," including a "milking" of the urethra (Brecher 1977). Many prostitutes are as skilled in making a short-arm inspection as are physicians, and this no doubt explains the relatively low rate of infection in well-trained prostitutes as compared with untrained nonprofessionals (Stein 1974, Brecher 1973). The technique of the short-arm inspection can easily be learned (Brecher 1977). Inspection of the vulva (for obvious discharge) is not as effective, since gonorrhea is usually asymptomatic (with no detectable symptoms) in women.

Precoital Disinfection of the Genitalia

Washing the penis and the vulva with soap and water before copulation reduces the danger of infection. It is especially effective if the water is hot. In some Western European countries the *bidet* is commonly used for this purpose. (American dwellings rarely have bidets, so women in our society must wash the labia and vagina in a shower or bathtub).[36] The use of the bidet has been credited in France with the remarkably low gonorrheal rate in that country (Brecher 1977, 1973; Stein 1974). (A precoital douche is *not* usually recommended by physicians since it disturbs the acid-alkaline balance of the vagina, and vaginal irritation may result.)

Postcoital Disinfection of the Genitalia

Simply washing the penis, labia, vagina, and surrounding areas thoroughly with hot soapy water as soon as possible *after* copulation also lessens the likelihood of infection. Promptness is probably as important as thoroughness in this technique (Brecher 1977, 1973; Stein 1974). In countries where the bidet is available, authorities attribute the remarkably low gonorrheal rate of *post*coital use of the bidet as well as *pre*coital use.

A medicated douche for use after copulation is an effective prophylactic,[37] but many physicians do not recommend medicated douches (Singh et al. 1972).

Urination immediately following copulation has a prophylactic effect since the acidity of the urine provides a hostile environment for *gonococci* (the infectious agent in gonorrhea); in addition, both they and other pathogens may be flushed away (Brecher 1977).

The Condom

Although condoms have had a very bad press—receiving little favorable mention in magazines or newspapers, and none on television—they are a very cheap and effective method of preventing STDs.[38] If condoms were more popular and more readily obtainable (there are still legal restrictions on the availability of condoms in many states), increased use of condoms might very well turn the tide of STD in the United States, as it has done in Sweden (Kolata 1976). With the rapidly rising incidence of genital herpes and AIDS, the use of condoms has been increasing, however. Sales quadrupled from 1980 to 1984; 59 percent of the buyers were women (Liberatore 1984).

It should be noted that Japan has developed condoms that are less than one-third the thickness of American ones, and these have been used for some time with great effectiveness in reducing the incidence of STD in Japan (Seaman 1980). They are not yet available in the United States since they have not been approved by the Food and Drug Administration. If they are marketed in the United States and prove more acceptable than current mod-

---

[36]In view of the remarkable effectiveness in lowering the incidence of STD as well as its advantage of providing the aesthetic rewards of clean genitalia, the absence of the bidet as a part of the American culture is a curious comment on our essentially antisexual heritage. The bidet is apparently unacceptable to our society because it is a frank admission that something sexual is going on in the house.

---

[37]Developed in the Venereal Disease Research Laboratory of the U.S. Public Health Service.

[38]A properly used condom prevents the transmission of gonorrhea more than 90 percent of the time (Secondi 1975). It also offers protection against herpes (Conant et al. 1984). It will also prevent most other STDs unless the source of the infection is on a nongenital area, such as the inner thigh (Rosen and Hall 1984).

els, they may contribute to a downward trend in the incidence of STD in our society (Seaman 1980).

Vaginal Prophylaxis during Copulation

Many common contraceptive creams and jellies are effective prophylactic agents against STDs. The recent switching of many millions of women from vaginal creams and jellies to the contraceptive pill and to the intrauterine device (IUD) is probably one factor in the rising incidence of STD in the United States (Seaman 1980).

The Importance of Regular Checkups

Anyone who is not monogamous is exposed to the possibility of STD and should have regular medical checkups. It is quite possible to have an STD with no symptoms whatsoever and to pass the disease along to a sexual partner.

The Chief Characteristics of Seven STDs

Since the incidence of STD is so high—especially among young people—and ignorance and misinformation are so widespread regarding the characteristics of these diseases, we shall close this section with brief descriptions of genital herpes, chlamydia, trichomoniasis, gonorrhea, venereal warts, syphilis, and AIDS.

Genital Herpes

Since physicians are not required to report cases of genital herpes to federal authorities, no one knows for sure just how widespread the disease is, but the Centers for Disease Control estimate that it may be as high as 20 million, with 500,000 new cases contracted annually— making genital herpes the most ubiquitous of all STDs (see Figure 4-17).

Ever since the Roman emperor Tiberius tried to halt an epidemic nearly 2,000 years ago by prohibiting kissing at public ceremonies, people have attempted unsuccessfully to control the infection known as herpes. Although there are many types of herpes infections caused by this versatile family of viruses, two types are especially widespread. Type I (which was the concern of Tiberius) has inflicted cold sores on an estimated 90 percent of the U.S. population. Type II is characterized by painful blisters that closely resemble cold sores but form on the tip of the penis or on the scrotum of men, and on the inside of the vagina or on the cervix of women. It is also possible for Type I to lodge in the genitalia and for Type II to cause cold sores on the lips or mouth. Both Types I and II are known as the "viruses of love" because they are spread through intimate person-to-person contact.

Type II (genital herpes) has been spreading rapidly (see Figure 4-18). Herpes II is now distributed throughout the world and is the most common form of STD in Great Britain as well as in the United States, which has an estimated 5–20 million victims, with at least 300,000 new cases each year (see Figure 4-17).

The initial invasion of the herpes virus often goes unnoticed. It may be introduced into the system without causing any clear symptoms, or the first blister may form where it is undetected—at the back of the mouth or inside the vagina. Thousands of the viruses formed from the original invader are then carried by the bloodstream to other parts of the body to penetrate nerve cells. Instead of attacking the host cell, however, the herpes virus merely waits there, lying dormant—sometimes for years (Gerson et al. 1984).

Any of several events that lower the person's resistance to infection can trigger the virus's release: physical or emotional stress, hormonal changes coincident with menstruation, the biochemical upheaval of puberty, or other infections. When the virus leaves the nerve cell nucleus where it has been lodged, it

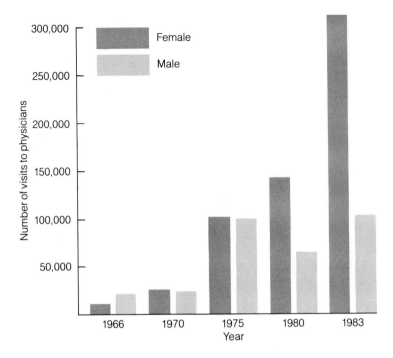

The number of visits to physicians for treatment of genital herpes infections has risen dramatically over the past eighteen years.

FIGURE 4-18

Herpes—the new epidemic

Source: Data from U.S. Public Health Service, "Genital Herpes Infection—United States, 1966–1979" (March 1982), *National Disease and Therapeutic Review* (January 1985).

enters the skin or a mucous membrane of the host, where it produces a tingling, burning sensation, and, a day or two later, a blister (the familiar cold sore).

The fluid-filled blisters that characterize the first stage of herpes usually break down within twenty-four hours, leaving painful shallow ulcers that may take several days to heal. During this time fresh blisters may appear, so the disease may perpetuate itself for from one to four weeks before clearing up without treatment. Recurrences are common.

If the victim of genital herpes is pregnant, the baby may be infected during birth, with serious, even fatal, results. Many obstetricians now prefer to perform a cesarean section rather than risk a normal delivery if there is a possibility of herpes infection (Knox et al. 1982, Hamilton 1980, Yeager 1979).

Finally, research indicates that genital herpes may be linked to cervical cancer. Studies consistently find that women who have genital herpes have a higher incidence of cervical cancer than other women (Hamilton 1980, Shapiro 1977).

Tiberius's ban on kissing was only the first of many attempts to stop herpes. The blisters have been burned by exposure to electric current, anesthetized through frequent applications of ether, painted with red dye while ex-

Courtesy San Francisco City Clinic

Courtesy San Francisco City Clinic

healthy people; however, the data suggest that there is no long-term benefit of this treatment and that although these measures are sometimes helpful for some people, as yet there is no known cure (Straus et al. 1984). The Food and Drug Administration approved oral Acyclovir in 1985 but suggested the drug not be used for longer than six months at a time until more is known about it (*Science News*, February 2, 1985, p. 71).

Chlamydia

Perhaps the fastest growing and most commonly sexually transmitted disease is chlamydia, a bacterial infection that was simply included with other NGUs (nongonococcal urethritis) until 1983 because its diagnosis was so cumbersome, time consuming, and expensive that it was seldom made. With the development of a simpler, cheaper test (that does

posed to fluorescent light, and treated with Acyclovir, an antiviral drug used in injection and ointment form and designed to prevent the fantastic replication of herpes (*Harvard Medical School Letter,* October 1981). New research has found that oral Acyclovir can suppress the disease for long periods in otherwise

not require the culture of suspected chlamydia cells in a laboratory) the diagnosis of chlamydia became more common and its rapidly rising incidence was revealed. As with general herpes, physicians are not required to report cases to the federal authorities, so no one really knows the true extent of chlamydia.

One reason for the rapid rise in the incidence of chlamydia is that a physician may diagnose the symptoms as gonorrhea and prescribe penicillin—which does not clear up the infection, so the person continues to be a carrier.

Chlamydia has a longer incubation time than gonorrhea. The first symptoms in men are an early-morning watery discharge accompanied by a hot or itchy feeling inside the penis. Difficult or painful urination occurs later, with the intensity of the symptoms varying from individual to individual. For many men the only consequence of chlamydia is mild discomfort. But many others develop an inflamed prostate, and if the infection goes deeper, it can affect the male's sperm ducts and cause sterility (Rosen and Hall 1984).

One of the most striking characteristics of chlamydia is that its most severe consequences are visited upon women and babies. An infected woman may have symptoms similar to those of a man, or she may be symptom-free. But untreated, chlamydia in the woman frequently moves to the uterine lining and fallopian tubes, causing pelvic inflammatory disease (PID). PID is usually accompanied by pain and fever and can cause blockage of the fallopian tubes with a buildup of scar tissue (Washington et al. 1985). According to the Centers for Disease Control, one in seven women of reproductive age has been treated for PID, and more than 1 million cases are diagnosed every year. This condition (which may also be caused by gonorrhea) affects an estimated 20 percent of all women who seek treatment for infertility. Of those women whose infertility is caused by tubal blockage, more than one-half have had chlamydial infections.

Although some studies in the past have indicated that birth control pills might be useful in protecting against PID caused by both chlamydia and gonorrhea, recent research has found that chlamydial infection appears two to three times more frequently in women taking oral contraceptives (Washington et al. 1985).

PID is also associated with premature delivery and life-threatening ectopic pregnancies, in which the fertilized egg is implanted in the fallopian tube (rather than in the uterus). If a woman has had a PID, she is eight times more likely than an uninfected woman to have an ectopic pregnancy (Wertheimer 1985).

Chlamydia may remain dormant in the woman's cervix for years without her knowing it. A baby born to the woman during this time may contract the disease during the process of birth. It is estimated that at least 5 percent of newborns are exposed to chlamydia (or some other form of NGU); 40 percent of these contract it and develop serious lung or eye infection (Yeager 1979). In 1984, there were more children affected by STD than there were children affected by polio during the entire polio epidemic of the 1950s (Wertheimer 1985).

Although chlamydia does not respond to penicillin, it may be treated successfully in the early stages with tetracycline or erythromycin, which must be administered for ten to fourteen days because the organism is so persistent.

Trichomoniasis

Trichomoniasis is the third most common sexually transmissible disease in the United States. Men usually have no symptoms, but women almost always experience a heavy yellowish-green vaginal discharge. Both sex partners must be treated to prevent reinfection. Trichomoniasis is often regarded as harmless, but various complications may occur if it is untreated (Harris 1977). Trichomoniasis now is effectively treated with a single dose of *metronidazole* (Rein 1981).

Gonorrhea

Gonorrhea is one of the most widespread of all human diseases, but it is one of the few such diseases that does not infect laboratory animals, so medical research is very limited. It has occurred throughout the history of Western civilization, and its origin is unknown. It may not be detected by a blood test. Gonorrhea is caused by a bacteria (*gonococcus*) and is limited mainly to the mucous membrane in the urethral or rectal tissue.[39]

Although often self-limiting, clearing up without treatment in about three weeks, the gonorrheal infection may go deeper into the tissue of the prostate, the epididymis, or the testicles of the male, causing pain and swelling of the scrotum, or into the fallopian tubes of the female, causing pain and swelling in the lower abdomen.[40]

Between fifty thousand and eighty thousand young women in the United States become sterile each year as a result of gonorrhea. Gonorrhea also causes infertility in men, but to a much lesser extent (Weismer 1978).

The incidence of gonorrhea increased rapidly in the United States in the late 1960s. In the last few years the increase has slowed and remained relatively steady. However, gonorrhea is more than twice as prevalent today as it was ten years ago, and more than three times as prevalent as it was in 1950 (see Figure 4-19). Persons under twenty-five run the greatest risk of contracting gonorrhea; 38 percent of all cases occur among twenty- to twenty-four-year-olds and another 25 percent among teenagers between fifteen and nineteen years old. The highest age risk for males is twenty to twenty-nine years of age, and for females, fifteen to twenty-four years of age.[41]

Gonococcal invasion of the blood may occur in both the male and the female, with the disease spreading throughout the body to cause infection of the extragenital tissue. Joints are the most frequent sites of such infection, and painful arthritis may occur within one to three weeks after the initial contact. Other infections may be inflammation of a tendon and its sheath (*tenosynovitis*), skin lesions, or inflammation of the membrane of the spinal cord and brain (*meningitis*).

Gonorrhea is almost always contracted through genital, anal, or oral sexual activity.[42] Infection through contaminated articles (towels, drinking glasses, toilet seats, doorknobs, and so on) is theoretically possible but highly unlikely, since *gonococci* usually live for only a few minutes outside the host's tissue.

Women who are taking birth control pills have a much higher chance of contracting gonorrhea than other women. If a woman who uses no method of birth control copulates with a man who has infectious gonorrhea she is thought to have a 30 percent chance of contracting the disease; if she is taking the pill, the chance increases to more than 90 percent (Seaman 1980). This higher incidence of infection is apparently due to the changes the pill causes in the acid-alkaline balance of the vagina, making it more susceptible to the gonorrheal gonococci, as well as to other annoying infections such as a yeast infection (Shapiro 1977).

In men, gonorrheal infection of the urethra is unmistakable in about 80 percent of cases; the mucous membrane lining of the urethra be-

---

[39]A person may also acquire a form of gonorrheal infection of the eye (gonorrheal ophthalmia) if the eye comes in direct contact with an infectious gonorrheal discharge. Newborn babies are especially subject to this form of the disease because they may acquire it in their passage through the cervix of the gonorrhea-infected mother. Until about 1950, more blindness (10 percent) in the United States was caused by congenital gonorrheal ophthalmia than any other single cause. Now, because of this danger, the eyes of newborn infants are routinely treated with erythromycin, tetracycline, or silver nitrate solution—a precaution that has virtually eliminated this form of the disease (U.S. Public Health Service, *Morbidity and Mortality Weekly Reports*, annual supplement, December 1984).

[40]U.S. Public Health Service, *STD Fact Sheet* (March 1980).

[41]U.S. Public Health Service, "STDs" (1984).

[42]Ibid.

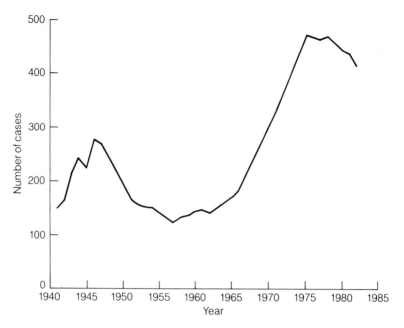

1941–1946 fiscal years (twelve-month period ending June 30 of the years specified)
1947–1982 calendar years

It is estimated that as many as 600,000 to 1 million cases went unreported.

FIGURE 4-19

Gonorrhea: reported cases per 100,000 population,
United States, 1941–1982

Source: Data from U.S. Public Health Service, "STDs"
(1984, pp. 29–32).

---

comes inflamed and swollen within two to eight days after the man acquires the disease. Urination is accompanied by a sharp burning pain and a yellowish discharge of pus, which is highly contagious. Twenty percent of men infected with gonorrhea never develop any symptoms, however. They are, nevertheless, highly contagious carriers and may infect sex partners.[43]

In women, as noted earlier, fully 80 percent of gonorrheal infections are free of symptoms. There is no pain or burning sensation; any dis-

charge may be so slight that it may pass unnoticed or be attributed to other sources of vaginal irritation (such as a yeast infection),[44] to nervousness or fatigue, or to ovulation (with its increased mucous flow). Spot checks of all women, seen by physicians for any purpose, find that 7–25 percent of women are carriers of gonorrhea, although routine tests do not reveal these carriers. The gonococcus can be found only if the physician takes a smear and culture sample from the cervix and, in suspicious

---

[43]Ibid.

[44]Vaginal yeast infections (which are quite common among women who are taking contraceptive pills or certain antibiotics) often mask gonorrheal infection.

cases, from the anus and the throat as well.[45] As with men, symptom-free women are highly contagious and may infect sex partners. The complex folds of the lining of the vagina may harbor the gonoccoci for months. Rectal gonorrheal infections in both men and women may also be symptom-free, although some discomfort and mucous discharge may develop if the infection persists.

Because a blood test for gonorrhea has not yet been developed, diagnosis must rely on a microscopic examination of a penile, vaginal, endocervical, or rectal smear for the presence of gonococci, or on a culture growth from these areas. For the male, these tests are quite reliable, and in 90 percent of cases the smear test alone, which takes just two or three minutes, is sufficient for diagnosis. In the female, however, fully 60 percent of tests for gonorrhea are inconclusive, because the gonococci quickly migrate into the fallopian tubes (Burns et al. 1983).[46]

No case of gonorrhea in a woman should be considered cured until three successive normal smears from the cervix are obtained, at least two of which should be examined immediately after a menstrual period (Kaye 1979, Thomas 1977). Even then the patient must be regarded with suspicion. One of the greatest problems of gonorrhea is that it often remains undetected (usually in women but sometimes in men) while the carrier continues to spread the disease.

If treatment is prompt, gonorrhea can be cured. Depending on the physician's judgment, an oral medication or an intramuscular injection may be used—or a combination of both (Cohen et al. 1984, Brown et al. 1982).[47]

A person who contracts gonorrhea may have been exposed to syphilis at the same time. Because the clinical signs and symptoms of gonorrhea develop several weeks prior to those of syphilis, the patient may be treated for gonorrhea, and the effects of the treatment may mask or delay the signs of syphilis. When this occurs, syphilis will develop and may be unnoticed. It is therefore of vital importance either to treat each case of gonorrhea as if syphilis has also been contracted or to test the patient for serologic evidence of syphilis each month for at least four months following treatment of gonorrhea (Kaye 1979, Thomas 1977).

Venereal Warts

Another type of STD that is on the rise is venereal warts, the incidence of which is double that of genital herpes—with an estimated 1 million new cases diagnosed in 1984 (see Figure 4-17). Caused by the papilloma virus, the warts are transmitted through the secretions exchanged during copulation.

Venereal warts have been increasingly linked with malignancies and premalignant conditions affecting the cervix, vagina, vulva, penis, and anus. A pregnant woman with venereal warts can also transmit them to her baby during delivery; in infants the warts can lodge in the larynx, trachea, and lungs, causing serious damage.[48]

---

[45]U.S. Public Health Service, "STDs" (1984).

[46](Data also from U.S. Public Health Service, *Criteria and Techniques for the Diagnosis of Gonorrhea,* 1979.) One new test for gonorrhea—called the *Gonozyme*—is an enzyme test that detects gonorrheal antigens in cervical and urethral specimens. The predictive values of a positive *Gonozyme* in this study were 90.5 percent for cervical specimens, and 97 percent for urethral specimens from men with urethritis (Burns et al. 1983). In 1985 researchers at Stanford Medical Center reported the development of a potential vaccine that may enable the body's immune system to defend itself against infection by the gonococcus (Schoolnik 1985).

---

[47]The U.S. Public Health Service now recommends four different treatments: (1) a single intramuscular dose of procaine penicillin plus probenecid, (2) a single oral dose of ampicillin or amoxicillin plus probenecid, (3) a five-day course of tetracycline or erythromycin, or (4) a single oral dose of a quinolone derivative called rosoxacin. A strain of gonorrhea resistant to all forms of penicillin (abbreviated PPNG—penicillinase-producing *Neisseria gonorrhea*) has been successfully treated with the antibiotic spectinomycin (U.S. Public Health Service, "STDs" 1984; Berg and Harrison 1981).

[48]U.S. Public Health Service, *STD Fact Sheet* (1985).

Phase	Symptoms	Infectious	Detection	Duration
Incubation period	No signs or symptoms	Not infectious	Cannot be detected by blood test	10–60 days (usually 4–6 weeks)
Primary stage	Fifty percent chance of infectious lesion at site of infection	Highly infectious if chancre (infectious lesion) is present	Can be detected by blood test	2–6 months
Secondary stage	Infectious lesions may occur on any area of body but are usually on mucous membranes or on warm, damp skin	Highly infectious if lesions are present	Can be detected by blood test	Usually 4–6 weeks (may recur as long as 2 years)
Latent period	No signs or symptoms	Not infectious since lesions are not present	Can be detected by blood test	Usually 10–30 years (may extend for 50 years)
Tertiary stage	Many illnesses that may be quite serious, debilitating, or crippling, causing blindness, heart trouble, insanity, and even death	Not infectious since lesions are not present	Blood test is not applicable since the disease is obvious	Chronic illness may last for years until death

FIGURE 4-20

The five phases of syphilis

Since warts, like herpes, are caused by a virus, they cannot be cured by antibiotics. Treatment is local. One common form of treatment is an application of podophyllin (from the mandrake plant) in benzoin ointment, washed off after four hours. This "burns" off the warts, with repeated applications, although they may recur. If this treatment is ineffective, the warts may respond to freezing with liquid nitrogen. In some cases they may be treated by curettage, x-ray, or surgery (Petersdorf 1983).

Syphilis

This most serious STD first appeared in the Western world in Spain among sailors who had returned from the New World in 1493. From there it spread rapidly throughout Europe, known as the "Neapolitan disease" and the "French pox." Through the Middle Ages, the Renaissance, the Reformation, and the advent of industrialization syphilis crippled, blinded, and killed unknown numbers of victims.

Syphilis is a very complex disease that goes through five phases (see Figure 4-20). Its symptoms mimic many other diseases, so it is often misdiagnosed. It can lie dormant and unsuspected for years and may have no recognized symptoms at all during the two phases when it is highly infectious, the primary and secondary stages. It may not be revealed by any symptoms at all until it reaches its final phase—the tertiary stage, years after contraction—when it may suddenly explode into serious and crippling forms.

Syphilis is contracted when the *spirochetes* from the serum of an infectious lesion (a sore containing spirochetes) invade the bloodstream of a new host. This invasion usually occurs through a mucous membrane but may occur through broken skin on any part of the body (even a tiny nick or scratch).[49] Since the infectious lesion is most often on the genitalia, syphilis is usually acquired through sexual contact.

An incubation period follows the invasion of the bloodstream of the new host; during this period there are no signs or symptoms of the disease, and it is not infectious. Nor can it be detected by a blood test during the incubation period. The incubation period usually lasts from four to six weeks, but may be as short as ten days or as long as sixty days.

The primary stage follows the incubation period and may last from two to six months. In about half of all cases, the primary stage is signaled by the appearance of an infectious lesion (chancre). The site of this lesion is the point where the spirochetes entered the body of the new host. It has no typical appearance—it may resemble acne, a cold sore, a blister, or a simple abrasion. Moreover, the lesion often occurs inside the vagina or the rectum, where it may easily escape detection even during a medical examination. It usually clears up within a few weeks with no treatment.

In the 50 percent of cases in which the lesion does not occur, the primary stage of syphilis is not infectious, since all other physiological secretions—saliva, seminal fluid, vaginal fluids—are not infectious.

Syphilis can be contracted only from the serum of an infectious lesion, from the blood (or blood plasma) of an infected person (during a blood transfusion, for example), or by a fetus directly from the bloodstream of a pregnant woman.[50]

Because the spirochetes are fragile and can live for only a short time outside the host's body, it is highly unlikely for syphilis to be transmitted through such secondary sources as drinking glasses, soiled towels, doorknobs, toilet seats, or bathtubs, although this is theoretically possible.[51]

During the secondary stage of syphilis, highly infectious lesions may occur intermittently on almost any area of the body (especially where the skin is warm and moist), although they usually appear on a mucous membrane. These lesions may take almost any form—a crack on the corner of the mouth or nostril, a small pimple or ulcer, acnelike abrasions, or cold sores. These lesions are painless, do not itch, and may easily go unnoticed or unrecognized. They usually clear up without treatment in four to six weeks but may recur for as long as two years.

In slightly less than half the cases, the secondary stage of syphilis is also signaled by the appearance of a rash almost anywhere on the body. This rash (when it occurs) may appear on the palms of the hands or soles of the feet, the genital areas, the face, abdomen, or legs, or inside the mouth, vagina, or rectum. Since it is neither itchy nor painful it may easily be mistaken for a heat or drug rash, and usually clears up quickly without treatment. Also, in slightly less than half the cases, the secondary stage of syphilis may be accompanied by such symptoms as a slight feeling of illness, a slight fever, a headache, a sore throat,

---

[49]The mucous membranes of the penile glans and the vagina are the most frequent sites of infection, but other mucous membranes such as those of the labia, rectum, tongue, or interior of the mouth may also provide entrance for the spirochetes.

[50]Congenital syphilis is acquired by a fetus directly from the bloodstream of the mother when the spirochetes penetrate the

placental defenses. This invasion of the placental defenses occurs only after the fourth month of pregnancy (Reeder and Mastroianni 1983). Since congenital syphilis may be prevented if the syphilitic mother is diagnosed and cured before this time. prenatal blood tests are required in forty-five of the fifty American states. Since initiation in the 1940s of efforts to control syphilis, reported cases of congenital syphilis dropped from 17,600 in 1941 to 259 in 1982, a decline of 98 percent (U.S. Public Health Service, "STDs" 1984).

[51]Survival of the spirochetes outside the host's body is usually limited to a few minutes and never exceeds an hour or two, even under ideal conditions (warmth and dampness).

Sex Myths: A Summary

1. Sexual energy can be conserved. (Not true. Masters and Johnson found, as did Kinsey, that regular sexual activity in youth and middle age is the single most predictive factor of sexual activity in old age.)

2. Sexual energy not only can be conserved, but can then be diverted (sublimated) to other activities. (There is no evidence to support this well-established doctrine, and there is evidence to the contrary. Kinsey, for example, found that subjects in the low-incidence group (in terms of sexual performance) had a low energy level and were characteristically apathetic and disinterested in nonsexual areas of their lives. In contrast, the high-incidence group had a high energy level and were characteristically creative and productive in nonsexual areas of their lives. If sublimation occurred, the opposite would be true.)

3. Sexual energy may be temporarily diverted. (The question of temporary sublimation must still be left open; however, there is no direct evidence to support it and some direct evidence to contradict it. Masters and Johnson, for example, found no evidence that even continued and persistent ejaculation in the male is followed by any subsequent physiological debilitation.)

4. Masturbation is physically harmful. (Not true. There is no evidence to support this contention.)

5. Excessive masturbation is physically harmful. (In the opinion of Masters and Johnson, among others, this notion is no longer tenable. In women multiple orgasms are normal, and in men the ability to ejaculate is self-limiting.)

6. Size of the penis indicates virility. (Not true. Masters and Johnson found no relation between penile size and virility.)

7. A large penis is more satisfying to the woman. (Not necessarily true. Although some women are more erotically responsive to a large penis, Masters and Johnson found that with most women there is no relation between penile size and erotic satisfaction.)

8. The pubic bone of the woman may seize the penis. (Not true. This notion is probably based on the phenomenon of "locking" that occurs in dogs, which is the consequence of the shape of the canine penis with its bulbular end in erection. "Locking" does not occur in human beings. The rather rare occurrence of a vaginal sphincter muscle spasm gives support to this myth.)

9. People are either homosexual or heterosexual. (Not true. Kinsey found that homosexuality and heterosexuality are on a continuum, with a few exclusively homosexual people and a few exclusively heterosexual people at either end of this continuum, and most people in between these two extremes. Money found that homosexuals were either "obligative" or "episodic"; the episodic homosexual is not exclusively homosexual and might change from being predominantly homosexual to being predominantly (or even exclusively) heterosexual as the circumstances of his

---

swelling of the lymph glands, or hair falling out in patches.

The latent period follows the secondary stage of syphilis. There are no signs or symptoms during the latent period; the person has no indication that he or she has the disease and is not infectious. During this period, the spirochetes tend to leave the bloodstream and lodge in the various tissues of the host—the nervous system, blood vessels, and all major organs. The latent period may last from two to fifty years, although the usual duration is ten to thirty years.

The fifth and final phase of syphilis is the tertiary stage, which starts when the disease suddenly breaks into the open after lying dormant and unsuspected for years during the latent period. It explodes in any number of forms and seriously incapacitates one out of three victims through insanity (*paresis*), blindness, paralysis, heart trouble, severe crippling of the joints, or other illness. One in ten dies of the effects of the disease during this stage (Sparling 1979).

The U.S. Public Health Service has reported an increase in the incidence of syphilis

or her life change. Most people are, of course, predominantly heterosexual for most of their adult lives.)

10. A ruptured or absent hymen means that the girl is not a virgin. (Not true. The hymen may be ruptured by nonsexual activity. Moreover, it is not uncommon for a girl to be born without a hymen.)

11. Women are slower than men in responding to erotic stimuli. (Not necessarily true. Erotic response may occur in a woman within ten to twenty seconds after appropriate erotic stimulation begins. An unmistakable physiological indication of this is the lubrication of the vagina, which results from the "sweating" of the vaginal walls during the first phase of erotic response. Whether this happens depends upon many psychological and social factors, of course.)

12. A woman ejaculates with orgasm. (Not true.)

13. A woman's subjective experience of orgasm is different from a man's. (Not true. It is true that there are great individual differences in the subjective experience of orgasm. However, there are no greater differences in this regard *between* men and women than there are *among* men and women. These individual differences are based on biological, psychological, and social factors; they are *not* based on whether the person is a man or a woman.)

14. Multiple orgasms in the woman are a myth. (Not true. Masters and Johnson found that the typical woman in our society may not be erotically satiated until she *has* experienced three or four orgasms in succession, and some are capable of experiencing as many as thirty or forty.)

15. It is important that copulating couples who are in love experience simultaneous orgasm. (Not true. While simultaneous orgasm can be very gratifying, being compulsive about trying to achieve it can be disastrous, with each failure inducing feelings of guilt and disappointment. Taking turns is much more practical and much more conducive to a harmonious interaction—with the occasional simultaneous orgasm occurring spontaneously.)

16. A person is usually sad, tired, or depressed after orgasm. (Not true. This is perhaps the most curious myth of all. Profound tranquility, contentment, and elation are the most typical feelings following an orgasm, unless the person feels guilty or ashamed.)

17. Gonorrhea is no more dangerous than the common cold. (Not true. Gonorrhea can have serious, debilitating, and crippling consequences.)

18. A woman who has gonorrhea has a urethral discharge, the same as a man. (Not necessarily true. There is usually no urethral discharge. Since other tests are often inconclusive as well, it may be very hard to detect gonorrhea in a woman. She may, nevertheless, be highly infectious to a sex partner.)

19. A person who contracts a sexually transmissible disease is then immune to this disease and can't contract it again. (Not true. A person can be infected again and again by the same STD without building up a resistance to the disease.)

20. You can tell if you have syphilis because a rash breaks out. (Not true. In more than half the cases of syphilis there are no symptoms at all—no rash, no chancre.)

Sources: Money (1980), Masters and Johnson (1966), Kinsey (1953, 1948).

---

in the last few years. From 1978 to 1982, rates increased 44.9 percent for men and 50 percent for women. Persons age twenty to twenty-four have the highest rate of reported cases of syphilis (41.7 percent), followed by those age twenty-five to twenty-nine (36.8 percent) and those age fifteen to nineteen (20.7 percent).[52]

Prompt treatment is now available for this most insidious of diseases that has plagued humanity for so long. The disease may be halted by adequate doses of penicillin (or other antibiotics such as tetracycline), and the infection usually clears up within eight to ten days. A cure cannot definitely be accepted, however, until the reaction to a blood test, such as the *Wasserman*, if consistently normal for several years (Rein 1981). Syphilis that is treated before it reaches the tertiary stage can be cured with little or no permanent damage. In cases that have reached the tertiary stage, damage cannot be reversed, but any further damage can be prevented (Rosen and Hall 1984). (See the vignette, "Sex Myths: A Summary.")

---

[52]U.S. Public Health Service, "STDs" (1984).

AIDS (Acquired Immune Deficiency Syndrome)

AIDS is a new disease in the United States, first recognized in 1979.[53] It involves a breakdown of the body's immune system—hence the name Acquired Immune Deficiency Syndrome, usually abbreviated to its acronym AIDS.[54] With the body's immune system attacked, the victim of AIDS is subject to a host of serious infections and diseases. The first signs of AIDS, which may not appear for five years after the victim has been infected, may include such symptoms as unexplained weight loss, slight fever, flulike symptoms, generalized lymphadenopathy (disease of the lymph nodes), and Kaposi's sarcoma (a rare malignant skin disease) (Jaffe et al. 1983).[55] After these initial symptoms, the victim may acquire any number of serious and incapacitating infections as the body's immune system grows increasingly helpless. Autopsies reveal that regardless of the cause of immediate death, devastation from AIDS infections strikes virtually every major organ system of the body. The deterioration of the body is so great that the death rate exceeds 80 percent for patients who have been diagnosed as having AIDS for more than three years (Perlman 1984).

Researchers believe the AIDS virus is carried by semen and blood (Gravell et al. 1984, Francis et al. 1983).[56] There has been no evidence of transmission by saliva or of airborne spread.[57] The virus that causes AIDS can attack brain cells as well as the immune system, leading to premature senility (Gallo 1985).

Starting with a single case in 1979, there were 800 cases of AIDS in the United States in three years, from 1979 to 1982. In 1983, the incidence rose to 2,237 new cases, and in 1984, to 3,830 new cases (see Figure 4-21). In early 1985 a total of 9,405 victims of AIDS had been reported, of whom 4,533 had died.[58] The associate director of the Centers for Disease Control AIDS Task Force estimated "conservatively" that at least 16,000 Americans will have developed AIDS by the end of 1985—an increase of 1,000 new cases a month (Jaffe 1985). It is estimated that as many as 1 million Americans had been infected with AIDS by 1985; these people are able to transmit the infection to their sexual contacts, even if they show no symptoms of the disease themselves. Those who are infected with the AIDS virus but do not develop AIDS may fall victim in the future to an array of diseases, including cancer, because of their compromised immune systems (Curran 1985).

Patients have also contracted AIDS from receiving blood transfusions (see Table 4-1). The spread of AIDS closely resembles that of hepatitis B virus infection, herpes virus infections, and other virus infections (Hsia et al. 1984).

The incubation period of AIDS is estimated

---

[53]Although the first known case of AIDS in the United States was diagnosed in San Francisco in 1979 and was regarded as a new disease, one of the most tantalizing mysteries of medical research is where did it come from? Some scientists feel that the virus originated in Central Africa, especially in Zaire (formerly called the Belgian Congo), where Kaposi's sarcoma (a rare form of cancer of the skin), which is a common complication of AIDS, has been endemic for years. The number of AIDS cases in Zaire is now estimated to be 7,000, with as many as twenty new cases occurring every day. Unlike American AIDS patients, most Zairian victims are neither homosexual nor drug abusers, and many are women. Scientists believe that the AIDS virus (or a close relative) has existed in Africa for generations in remote rural areas. Then, in the mid-1970s the migration of rural residents to crowded urban areas created ideal circumstances for the virus to multiply. Haitians went to Zaire in the 1960s to help run the new nation's government, and they brought the virus with them when they returned home; it turned up in Haiti in the mid-1970s. Vacationing American homosexuals brought it from that island to the United States. It seems likely that AIDS also spread from Africa to Western Europe, since most of the French and Belgian victims formerly lived in or near Zaire (Seligmann et al. 1984).

[54]An *acronym* is made up of the first letters of each word in a title.

[55]Data also from U.S. Public Health Service, "Update on AIDS—United States" (1982).

---

[56]Ibid.

[57]However, in the absence of precise knowledge regarding the transmission of AIDS, the Centers for Disease Control has published guidelines for medical personnel who work on AIDS patients, recommending that caution be exercised in handling all body secretions (U.S. Public Health Service, "AIDS: Precautions for Clinical and Laboratory Staffs," 1982).

[58]U.S. Public Health Service, "AIDS Update" (April 10, 1985).

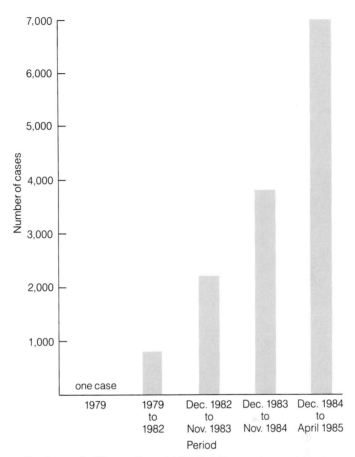

The Centers for Disease Control AIDS Task Force estimates that at least 16,000 Americans will have developed AIDS by the end of 1985 (Jaffe 1985).

FIGURE 4-21

AIDS cases in the United States, 1979–1985

Source: Data from U.S. Public Health Service, "Aids Update" (November 30, 1984, January 28, 1985, and May 10, 1985).

to vary from two to fourteen years, with a mean incubation period of 5.5 years. This estimate is based on studies of people who contracted AIDS through blood transfusions, which represent the best opportunity for charting incubation periods since the actual date of infection is known. Long incubation periods may be concealing the heterosexual cases that are quietly incubating across the nation, just as the AIDS virus was widespread in the gay community long before AIDS was discovered. Because heterosexuals tend to have fewer sexual partners than gay men, it is anticipated that AIDS will spread less rapidly among heterosexuals than among gays. However, some scientists feel that eventually the proportion of heterosexuals contracting AIDS will exceed that of homosexuals, and that AIDS will

TABLE 4-1

Adult AIDS patients by group, in the United States,
December 1983–November 1984

Patient group	Number of cases	Percentage of cases
Homosexual/bisexual	2,802	73.2
I/V drug user	668	17.4
Haitian	111	2.9
Blood transfusion recipients	50	1.3
Hemophilia patient	28	0.7
Heterosexual contacts	27	0.7
Noncharacteristic	144	3.8

Source: Data from U.S. Public Health Service, "Aids Update"
(November 30, 1984).

emerge as a standard STD among American heterosexuals (Curran 1985).

It is not known at present why homosexual males are the chief victims of AIDS in the United States. (As noted earlier, women and heterosexuals are also contracting the disease in rising numbers in Zaire.) It is possible that hormonal or other unknown differences will prove to be the explanation; or that some other unknown infectious agent, more common among homosexuals, may act in tandem with the AIDS virus; or that the use of amyl nitrate (much more common among homosexuals) may act in some unknown way to make the person more susceptible.[59] It is very likely, however, that the answer lies simply in two major factors. First, anal copulation is much more common among homosexuals than among heterosexuals. Anal copulation is by far the riskiest sexual behavior for contracting AIDS, apparently because the activity permits the AIDS virus to be injected from the active partner's semen directly into the receptor's blood through abrasions in the rectal tissues. Second, there is a far greater incidence of contact—with attendant exposure to risk—among male homosexuals compared with heterosexuals. A 1984 study of AIDS victims, for example, found that the median number of sex partners that each homosexual male had related to with physical intimacy was 1,100, with a few of the men reporting as many as 20,000.[60] The median number of different partners for a matched control group of homosexual men was 550 (Meredith 1984). In an earlier study, 15 percent of homosexual men reported having between 500 and 1,000 sex partners, and more than 25 percent reported having more than 1,000 (Bell and Weinberg 1978). These frequencies far exceed the number of different sexual partners characteristic of heterosexual men (Brecher 1984, Lews and Schwartz 1977, Gordon 1976, Hunt 1974).[61]

It is interesting to note that cases of AIDS are concentrated mainly in California and New York, and many states have none or one case.[62] This is presumably because patterns of sociosexual activity are quite different in these states, and the population of homosexuals is higher in California and New York (see Figure 4-22).

Fear of AIDS may have a significant effect in changing the sociosexual behavior of our society, especially among the male homosexual population. For example, a San Francisco

---

[59]Amyl nitrate is a nonprescription drug that may be enclosed in a glass capsule or "popper." The capsule is then broken ("popped") and the fumes inhaled at the moment of orgasm to increase the sensation.

---

[60]The *median* is a measure of average, with one-half the population above it and one-half below it.

[61]Hunt (1974) concludes, for example, in his systematic survey of sex and single people, that singles usually become sexually involved only in an atmosphere of emotional closeness, and that "easy sex" is relatively unusual in this group (see Chapter 6). Other surveys of premarital dating behavior find that the extent of promiscuity among heterosexuals is far below that of homosexuals (Robinson and Jedlicka 1982). Although there are exceptions, the highly promiscuous heterosexual "swinging single" is a statistical rarity (see Chapter 6).

[62]AIDS has become the leading cause of death among young men in San Francisco and in the borough of Manhattan. AIDS deaths among San Francisco single men who are thirty-five years old—the median age of AIDS victims—"exceed cancer, heart disease or accidents, and the mortality of all other disease causes of death combined" (Jaffe 1985).

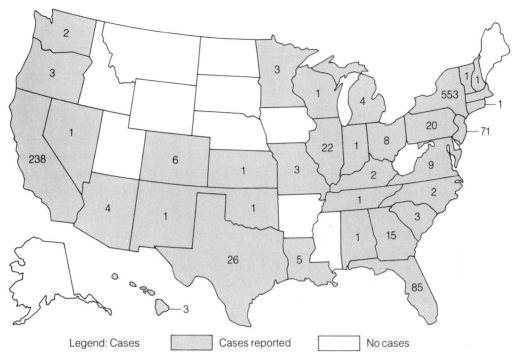

Legend: Cases ▢ Cases reported ▢ No cases

New York City reported 45 percent of the cases of AIDS by 1982; California reported 21 percent.

FIGURE 4-22

Distribution of AIDS by states, 1979–1982

Source: Data from U.S. Public Health Service, "Update on AIDS—United States" (December 1982).

study that questioned homosexual men about their sex practices in 1982 and again in 1984 found a 50 percent reduction in the number of sexual partners during this time. When asked about the reason for the lessened activity, the subjects cited fear of contracting AIDS (Winokur 1984).

As we enter the last half of the decade of the 1980s, researchers are making every effort to find a vaccine that will prove an effective treatment or cure for AIDS. If they are successful, AIDS will join the other diseases—once potential disasters—that have been brought under control. If they are not, and the disease continues to spread, it may take an enormous toll—with its average five-year incubation period during which the infected person may transmit it to others, and its swift progress to a host of deadly diseases after diagnosis.

SUMMARY

Societies range widely in their attitudes toward sexuality, from the prosexual to the antisexual, with our own society falling about halfway between these two extremes. We still tend to identify sex with dirt or filth, although the view of sexuality as a source of pleasure and an important aspect of communication is gradually gaining ground, as is the understanding of women's erotic potential. One indication of a society's place on the prosexual-antisexual continuum is its attitude toward masturbation. It is interesting to note that masturbation was regarded not only as immoral but also as the cause of many serious medical and physical ailments until halfway through the present century, when attitudes began to change.

Until recently in our society, it was popular to maintain that sexual energy could be conserved. The Kinsey studies, however, found the opposite to be true: The more sexually active a boy is in adolescence, the more active he will be in middle and old age. (Data regarding women in this regard are ambiguous.) Another doctrine that found no support in the Kinsey research was that of sublimation, which maintains that not only can sexual energy be conserved, but it can then be redirected into nonsexual channels such as sports and artistic or professional efforts. This doctrine of sublimation is now increasingly regarded with scepticism.

All individuals, men and women alike, go through the same four phases of erotic response: excitement, plateau, orgasm, and resolution. Men, however, must go through a refractory period during the resolution phase before they are again physiologically capable of responding to erotic stimuli. There is no refractory period for women, who may have several orgasms in each erotic episode.

Women in our society are quite different from men in terms of erotic interest, however, and usually respond to fewer psychological stimuli. Research has found that this relative lack of interest and response in women is apparently a result of cultural factors rather than biology.

One reason why women may be less erotically responsive than men in our society may be traced to physiological differences, however. A man must be in the excitement phase of erotic response before he can copulate (since penile erection is a characteristic of this phase in the male), whereas a woman is physically capable of copulation without being in the excitement phase. However, since vaginal lubrication is one of the characteristics of this phase in the female, copulation before reaching the excitement phase may be uncomfortable and is hardly likely to be pleasurable. If copulation is delayed until *both* are in the excitement phase, it is more likely that both will experience orgasm.

Another physiological distinction is that most women will enter the excitement phase only with clitoral stimulation; the clitoris—not the vagina—is the homologue of the penis.

The meaning of copulation to the individual and the individual's reaction, for men and women alike, extend over a very wide range—from compulsive ecstatic pleasure, through disinterest and boredom, to pain and disgust. There is no other important human activity that is characterized by such a wide range of meaning. Those in the positive range in this continuum are called *erotophiles*, while those in the negative range are called *erotophobes*. If both of the couple are in roughly the same place on the erotophobe-erotophile continuum, their erotic interaction will be far different than if they are widely separated on the scale.

Some sexologists have estimated that fully 50 percent of American marriages are characterized by sexual incompatibility. The acknowledgement of women's erotic needs has brought about an improvement in this regard, but changes are taking place slowly. Both middle class and working class wives have expressed dissatisfaction with their erotic lives.

The mature male ejaculates with orgasm (the prepubertal male does not). The ejaculate (semen) contains the sperm cells (the male gametes) that, during copulation, are deposited by the penis into the vagina of the woman. If the woman ovulates within about twenty-four hours of the time of copulation, a sperm cell from the ejaculate may unite with the ovum or egg (the female gamete) of the woman in the fallopian tube to create a new single-celled organism, the fertilized egg—which may then divide and multiply into the 100 trillion cells that make up a human being.

Sexually transmissible diseases (STDs) are rampant in our society, having passed the epidemic stage to become pandemic. Since many STDs can cause serious, irreparable damage, the importance of prompt diagnosis and treatment cannot be overemphasized. A person who has possibly been exposed to an STD should have a medical checkup that specifically looks for the diseases. Gonorrhea is asymptomatic in fully 80 percent of women, though they can infect sexual partners. Syphilis can lie dormant for years, unsuspected, before finally erupting into an irreversible and incapacitating form that may include blindness, severe heart trouble, insanity, or death.

QUESTIONS

1. What is meant by the term *prosexual-antisexual continuum*? Give an example of a prosexual society. What are its characteristics? Give an example of an antisexual society. What are its characteristics?

2. Where would you put our society on the prosexual-antisexual continuum? Discuss your answer.

3. What is meant by the doctrine of conservation of sexual energy? Discuss the present societal attitude toward this doctrine.

4. What is meant by the doctrine of sublimation? Discuss the present societal attitude toward this doctrine.

5. What is meant by sexual perversion? What are the three categories of perversion? What activities are considered perversions by all societies?

6. What are the two types of penile erection? Discuss their important differences in terms of male-female erotic interaction.

7. What are the four phases of erotic response? Describe the characteristics of each phase in the male and in the female.

8. What is the refractory period? Discuss its

significance in terms of the couple's erotic interaction and mutual erotic satisfaction.

9. Discuss the relation between psychological factors and physiological factors in erotic arousal.

10. What is meant by the term *biological imperative*? Discuss its importance in terms of male-female erotic interaction.

11. What does the term *homologue* mean? What is the female homologue of the penis? Discuss the importance of this fact in terms of erotic interaction and response.

12. What is the female physiological correlate of penile erection? Discuss the significance of this correlate in terms of male-female erotic interaction.

13. Discuss the statement that women are physiologically more capable of erotic response than men are.

14. Women are, in general, less erotically responsive than men in our society. Discuss the evidence that this is culturally, not biologically, based.

15. Describe the erotophile-erotophobe continuum and discuss its significance for marital harmony.

16. What is the menarche? The menopause? The climacteric? How does the climacteric affect a woman's sense of well-being? Her erotic interest and response?

17. What is meant by STD? Describe the seven STDs discussed in this chapter.

18. Discuss the importance of early detection and treatment of some STDs.

19. Why is it naive to try to understand human sexuality only in terms of its reproductive function?

SUGGESTIONS FOR FURTHER READING

Beach, Frank A., ed. *Human Sexuality in Four Perspectives*. Baltimore: Johns Hopkins University Press, 1977.

Feldman, Harold, and Parrot, Andrea, eds. *Sexuality: Contemporary Controversies*. Beverly Hills, Calif.: Sage, 1984.

Gotwald, William H., and Golden, Gale Holtz. *Sexuality: The Human Experience*. New York: Macmillan, 1981.

Greenwood, Sadja. *Menopause Naturally*. San Francisco: Volcano Press, 1984.

Grumbach, Doris. *The Ladies*. New York: Dutton, 1984.

Hyde, Janet Shibley. *Understanding Human Sexuality*. New York: McGraw-Hill, 1982.

Masters, William H., and Johnson, Virginia E. *The Pleasure Bond: A New Look at Sexuality and Commitment*. Bantam, 1976.

Nass, Gilbert O.; Libby, Roger W.; and Fisher, Mary Pat. *Sexual Choices: An Introduction to Human Sexuality*. Belmont, Calif.: Wadsworth, 1981.

Ostrow, David G., and Sandholzer, Terry A. *AIDS: Questions and Answers about Acquired Immune Deficiency Syndrome*. New York: Irvington, 1984.

Ostrow, David G.; Sandholzer, Terry Alan; and Felman, Yehudi M., eds. *Sexually Transmitted Diseases in Homosexual Men: Diagnosis, Treatment, and Research*. New York: Plenum Medical Books, 1983.

Rosen, Raymond, and Hall, Elizabeth. *Sexuality*. New York: Random House, 1984.

Symons, Donald. *The Evolution of Human Sexuality*. New York: Oxford University Press, 1979.

Tannahill, Reay. *Sex in History*. New York: Stein & Day, 1980.

Victor, Jeffrey S. *Human Sexuality: A Social Psychological Approach*. Englewood Cliffs, N.J.: Prentice-Hall, 1980.

C H A P T E R   5

Courtship: Dating and Marital Choice

Methods of Mate Selection
Dating in Our Society
The Field of Eligibles
The Mystery of Attraction
Sexuality in Dating: Premarital Copulation

To be loved, be lovable.

Ovid (The Art of Love II)

Courtship is a universal function in the animal kingdom. In order for sexual reproduction to take place, it is necessary for the male and the female to cooperate; the sperm must reach the egg so that the egg will be fertilized and the genetic components of each parent will be combined.

Among land animals, courtship is designed, when it is successful, to lead to copulation—which accomplishes the fertilization of the female egg and the beginning of a new generation.[1] Courtship is not simply a hit-or-miss procedure. From insects to humans, all animals have evolved complex courtship procedures. The male must approach the female in a highly ritualized pattern of behavior if he is not to be rejected. In some species, courtship can be very dangerous. For example, the male

---

[1]Among aquatic animals, fertilization usually takes place outside the body. Nevertheless, courtship rituals are often quite complex. The male stickleback fish demonstrates a vivid display of colors to the female and attacks and drives away competitors. He hovers very close to her while she deposits her eggs in a prepared hollow in the streambed, and then he covers them with his melt (sperm cells).

black widow spider is only a fraction of the size of the female, and if he does not approach her carefully, he will be killed and eaten. He must first pluck the web in a certain rhythm before moving next to her. He then strokes her abdomen before depositing the sperm. His departure must then be precipitous or he will still be seized and consumed. If she is disturbed by any deviation from the courtship ritual the penalty is death and dismemberment.

Among wild horses, the male conducts his courtship by fighting and defeating other stallions before mounting and copulating with the mare, who has watched the encounters. She becomes the mate of the strongest, most dominant stallion in a courtship procedure that is highly formalized. The stallion collects as many mares as he can in this way. He must then guard both his territory and his harem of mares, keeping vigilant watch over each and driving away any challenger.

In human societies, courtship procedures vary enormously from one culture to another. In some societies courtship is solely the responsibility of the parents, who approach one another in a series of carefully orchestrated moves designed to acquire the best possible match for their son or daughter. The young people themselves have very little choice, and personal characteristics are not considered important. In other societies, it is the responsibility of the young adults to find their mates, and personal considerations are *very* important. The courtship consists of a process in which one tentatively approaches another who is regarded as attractive and, if the attraction is mutual, the two form a paired bond and gradually extend and deepen the encounter.

Whatever the form, courtship is universal in human experience, with institutional status in all societies. It forms the first stage of the family system—the interlocking institutions of *courtship, marriage,* and the *family*—which ensures the production and the nurture of the children that constitute the next generation and perpetuate the society.

METHODS OF MATE SELECTION

The essential element of courtship—whatever species is involved and whatever form it may take—is mate selection. In human societies, the methods of mate selection range from an extreme in which the parents make the choice and the young people have no say in the matter (*mate selection by parental arrangement*) to an extreme in which the young people themselves choose one another and the parents have no veto power (*mate selection by mutual choice*). Although most societies fall somewhere between these two extremes, most societies are also closer to the *parental arrangement* end of the continuum.

Traditional Patterns of Parental Arrangement

In most of the world's societies, the responsibility for marital choice rests with the parents. Even some of the large industrial nations still follow the traditional pattern of mate selection by parental arrangement. For example, it is estimated that 40–50 percent of all Japanese marriages are arranged in this way.

In marriage by parental arrangement, marriage is seen as a means of providing for the continuity of the family and ensuring its economic growth. Title to property is usually held by the family, and marriage contracts are often made in the names of the two families, with the signatures of the bride and the groom sometimes not even required (Mace and Mace 1974).

A go-between is used to approach the family of a prospective bride or bridegroom, to exchange information and photographs, and to check into the family's background. Those seeking to arrange a marriage have three basic requirements: the potential bridegroom should have "prospects," the potential bride should be beautiful or intelligent, and each should have money.

In societies where marriage occurs by parental arrangement, it is viewed as a means of providing for the continuity of the family and ensuring its economic growth.

David Austen/Stock, Boston

Each family is thus looking for a union that will be economically advantageous and with someone who has a respected family name, is healthy and well educated, and has a good genetic line. Personal considerations of mutual attraction are often disregarded, and love is presumed to follow marriage, not precede it.

The institution of *dowry* is used in societies where the woman is considered an economic liability, supported by her family until marriage and then by her husband. A dowry can be money or property (such as stocks and bonds, a goat, or cattle) given by the parents of a bride to her bridegroom, either to become solely his or to be shared by him through belonging legally to his wife.

In many societies, the dowry is indispensable. In contemporary Greece, for example, it is all but impossible for a girl to marry without

sufficient dowry; the father and brothers together assume the responsibility of providing one. It is a cardinal rule in these families that no brother may marry until every sister has been provided with a husband. Moreover, family honor demands a lavish wedding feast. If the bridegroom comes from out of town, the cost of boarding him and his family and guests must be borne by the bride's family. In countries where dowries are the custom, a father with several daughters faces financial ruin unless he is relatively wealthy.

The institution of *bride price* is the opposite of the dowry and is used in societies in which the woman is considered an economic asset, contributing to the family's income through her skills and labor. In these societies, instead of being offered a dowry, the groom's family is asked to pay a bride price. In Africa, elaborate techniques and precise property evaluation (usually involving livestock) have long been used in many communities to determine bride price. In Japan, a contemporary bridegroom usually must provide a bride price of about $2,000, chiefly as a status symbol (about half this money finds its way back to him as a cash present from the bride's parents; the other half is recycled into household goods to equip the new home). In Taiwan, where the average earnings per family were about $10,000 per year in 1978, the bride price ranged from $1,300 to $2,600, and very rich families would hand over the equivalent of $10,000 for a suitable match. The money is regarded as a sign of status and good intentions. After the marriage, most is returned to the bridegroom and goes into household furnishings, as in the Japanese system.

In many societies in which marriages are arranged, parents often use the services of a marriage broker, so that the maneuvering takes place between two professionals. The marriage broker's information, skills, and resources are usually regarded as indispensable; a family that does not use a broker is often at a serious disadvantage and may even be deluded by misrepresentations. When two professionals negotiate, both families are protected. If the marriage broker makes a mistake, his or her reputation suffers and future clients will be scarce.

A marriage broker seeks out the parents of a marriageable son or daughter who might be acceptable to the client and tentatively approaches them. The broker vouches for the client's age, health, education, skills, training, social status, and appearance. If the client is a man, the marriage broker negotiates for the dowry (the bride price is usually fixed). If the parents are interested, very cautious formal exchanges begin, with no commitment implied. If both families wish to pursue the negotiations after these initial exchanges, conferences are arranged, which lead to a formal engagement.

In selecting an appropriate bride, the groom's family considers such assets as the woman's genetic characteristics (good health, intelligence), her family name, the value of her dowry or the cost of the bride price, the effect of the alliance on merging lands or properties or loyalties, and, finally, her own skills. Above all, she must be a member of the community; she must definitely be a member of the same social class. Romantic considerations, or personal compatibility of the couple, are usually given a minimum of attention.

Young people in these societies do not seem to resent arranged marriages but rather approve of them. For example, Mace and Mace (1974) found that girls in contemporary India are delighted to be relieved of the pressures and responsibilities of selecting a mate and entering a marriage.

We girls don't have to worry at all. We know we'll get married. When we are old enough our parents will find a suitable boy, and everything will be arranged. We don't have to go into competition with each other. . . . Besides, how would we be able to judge the character of a boy? . . . We are young and inexperienced. Our parents are older and wiser, and they aren't deceived as easily as we would be. I'd far rather have my parents choose for me. It's so important that the man I marry should be the right one. I could easily make a mistake if I had to find him for myself (p. 151).

After a marriage has been arranged, the engaged couple is regarded as unalterably committed to each other, so that engagements are as binding as marriage itself. In contemporary Spain and Sicily, for example, if the woman's fiance attempts to break the engagement, it is not only culturally acceptable but almost mandatory that he be hunted down, and even murdered, by her father or brothers. Engagements, in fact, are so important that the celebrations accompanying them are far more elaborate than the wedding celebration is in our society. Ryan (1958) describes one such ceremony in Sri Lanka:

The prospective bridegroom accompanied by all his male relatives, all dressed up in the best clothes they possess or can borrow, walks in procession to the house of the girl, where her relatives, also decked in finery, receive them formally. Tea, rice, and curries are served. Then the agreement, in involved legal language, is read out, and the astrologer announces in detail the propitious times for the various stages of preparation, and for the wedding itself. Now the prospective bride and groom solemnly exchange rings, flowery speeches are made by the representatives of families, and half of the promised dowry is handed over (p. 75).

In most such societies, the couple are at least consulted about the arrangement; their own inclinations are, to some extent, respected—that is, they may exercise some veto power if their parents' choice is totally unacceptable to them. In addition, a young man sometimes may be allowed to court a woman of his choice after both families have approved.

There are very little data on the success or failure of parentally arranged marriages, mainly because "failure" (that is, termination of the marriage) is seldom considered a possibility. Nor is personal happiness a factor in "successful" marriages; marriage is meant primarily to fulfill social and economic needs. Each spouse has certain minimum standards of role performance (income provision, protection, homemaking, and childbearing), and as long as these standards are maintained, the marriage is considered successful.

Because the standards are so strongly culturally conditioned, only a social renegade would violate them. When, on rare occasions, these standards are violated—for example, when a husband deserts his wife or fails to provide a minimum income, or, in some societies, when a wife cannot bear children—the only recourse for the injured spouse generally is the family, who will assess the problem and decide whether the marriage contract has been breached. If personal unhappiness is a cause of marital problems, usually the two persons must simply adjust to unhappiness. (In India,

an unhappy wife often must make a serious suicide attempt before her family is moved to intervene on her behalf.) In all such cases, the marriage can be terminated, but only with great shame to both families, particularly to the family of the irresponsible, inadequate, or unhappy spouse.

Cultural Variations of Parental Control

The various methods of marital choice that have been used in societies throughout the world are all designed to handle the problem of finding satisfactory marriage partners for young women. Since the woman is the one who may become pregnant, all societies are far more concerned with regulating her sexual behavior than with regulating the sexual behavior of the man.

Although marital choice by parental agreement is the method most often used, there is a wide range of variants. For example, in many societies young women are expected to marry as soon as they become nubile (capable of reproduction) or even earlier. In India, it was the custom until very recently, for even a high-caste girl to be betrothed at birth, or when she was an infant or young child, and to marry when she was ten or eleven years old (or even younger). She would then go to live in the household of her bridegroom, supervised by her mother-in-law, although the marriage was not consummated until the child bride reached puberty (at which point there was usually another ceremony).

A second method that is commonly used in various societies is to rigorously control and supervise the social activities of young women. These young women are never left alone in the company of a young man without the presence of a *chaperone* (an adult of unimpeachable reputation), who can be trusted to maintain strict vigilance over the activities of the young couple. This chaperone system is still commonly practiced in many societies, such as Spain, Sicily, Greece, and some areas of Mexico and South America.

A third method, widely used in many societies, is to devise psychological barriers and restraints, conditioning young people to be so shy of one another that they are unlikely to relate sexually until their late teens or early twenties, when a suitable marriage is expected to take place. For example, in rural areas of Ireland intermingling of young men and women rarely occurs, and a wall of reserve exists between them well into their twenties and even thirties.

A fourth method allows young people some freedom to associate with one another with relatively little parental supervision and institutionalized shyness, but with the understanding that the couple are expected to marry if the woman becomes pregnant.[2] For example, in rural Norway a suitor may visit his future wife in a special room set aside for this purpose, and sexual intimacies are condoned. In some areas of Holland the couple cannot be married unless the woman is pregnant. (See the vignette, "The Bride Must Be Pregnant.")

A fifth method allows young people some freedom to associate with one another with relatively little parental supervision, and the society does *not* necessarily expect that pregnancy will lead to marriage. If the woman becomes pregnant, the child is looked after by the mother's relatives and is absorbed into her family. For example, Samoan adolescents are permitted relatively free access to one another, and the mother's family welcomes the birth of a child (Mead 1959).

Finally, a method that defies categorization, and was apparently never practiced very widely but by a small splinter group in the United States, was known as *bundling*. Bundling was a courtship custom that was practiced in New England in the eighteenth and early nineteenth centuries. It originated in Holland and Great Britain as part of the European peasant custom of a long, slow courtship. After the rest of the household had retired, the courting couple would lie together on a bed, either fully or partially dressed, "bundled" in blankets. Sexual intimacies were not permitted, however; the couple were often separated by a board, and sometimes the girl's legs were tied together. The custom of bundling was supported by such practical considerations as the cold New England winters and the scarcity of expensive fuel. It was expedient for a man who called upon a young woman to remain "bundled" with her overnight, allowing the fire to die down, rather than to travel the long distance back to his own residence along icy winter roads.

In U.S. society, all of these various methods were used to some extent by various groups, but parental supervision was very strict in virtually all groups until the twentieth century—not only in the middle and upper classes, but in the lower classes as well. It was virtually impossible for a young woman to meet a young man unless she was introduced by a member of her family; if he was interested, he asked permission to "call" upon her.[3]

The American Heritage

Contemporary patterns of courtship and marital choice in the United States stem from three basic cultural heritages: the Mediterranean legacy, the Nordic legacy, and the Amerafrican legacy. Although ours is a vast and complex society with many individual variations,

---

[2]It is interesting to note in this regard, that in 1982, 48 percent of white women with a premaritally conceived first birth, married before the birth of the child; the corresponding figure for black women was 10 percent (U. S. Bureau of the Census, "Percentage of Women with a Premaritally Conceived First Birth who Married before the Birth, by Age and Race: 1982," (1985).

[3]In the eighteenth century, when a young man even asked for permission to call on a girl, he was in effect asking for permission to marry her; in the nineteenth century, convention had relaxed somewhat, but the first call was still considered a public indication of interest and marriage.

these three cultural legacies have been chiefly responsible for forging the dominant patterns of contemporary sociosexual interaction on which pair bonding is based.

The Mediterranean Legacy

The Mediterranean legacy is often referred to as the Judeo-Christian heritage, but its origins are much older than the Bible, and its geographic representation went far beyond the biblical realm of Judea, through India to China and Japan. It is the tradition of the virgin bride coupled with the double standard of inequality of the sexes. The Mediterranean legacy presumably originated in the development of urbanization in the Middle East.

In the Mediterranean legacy, marital selection was strictly under parental control. The bride was expected to remain a virgin until marriage, and she became the sexual property of her husband after marriage. Copulation before marriage was punishable by death for the woman, as was a wife's copulation with anyone but her husband after marriage. Sex had two meanings, procreational and recreational, but sex within marriage was to be procreational only; recreational sex was acceptable outside of marriage only for the man.

Women were regarded as either madonnas or whores. Madonnas were bound by rules of chastity and fidelity, bore children for their husbands, and provided their families with nurture, grace, and the gentler qualities of the spirit. Whores provided sexual pleasure, were essentially evil or wicked, and tempted men from the paths of righteousness. Madonnas were personified by the Virgin Mary, while whores were personified as witches and were burned by the thousands in medieval Europe (Tuchman 1978).

The Mediterranean legacy is characterized by the *double standard*—using one standard to judge male behavior and another standard to judge female behavior. For example, premarital copulation is much more acceptable for males than for females. Extramarital copulation is frowned upon, but more severely for females than for males. Control of property and wealth is chiefly vested in males, who are permitted more economic, social, and political freedom than females. The woman's place is thought to be in the home, bearing, rearing, and nurturing children, and elevating the moral tone of the family.

Although the Mediterranean legacy is one of the chief bases of sociosexual ideals and patterns of behavior in our society, its influence has been gradually lessening over the centuries. Especially rapid and significant changes have occurred in the past two decades in our society.

The Nordic Legacy

Today's adolescents and young adults who violate the doctrine of the Mediterranean legacy of the virgin bride and the double standard are, whether they know it or not, adopting a contemporary counterpart of another ancient tradition—one that covered a region more vast than the term *Nordic* (Scandinavian) implies. This is the tradition of the betrothal system, and it emphasizes relative egalitarianism in sexual interaction. It is usually regarded as centering chiefly in Scandinavia, where there was resistance to the incursion of the Mediterranean legacy, which spread into northern Europe as an adjunct of Christianity. In the seventeenth century, the Nordic legacy crossed the Atlantic, from northern Britain and Scotland to New England. Although Scandinavia was patriarchal and dominated by men in its political and military institutions, the society was characterized by relative equality of the sexes in social and erotic interaction (Money 1980).

In the Nordic legacy, betrothal, not marriage, was the institution that marked the beginning of an established paired bond between two young people and legitimized their sociosexual interaction. Their betrothal was

The Bride Must Be Pregnant

In the village of Staphorst, about 120 miles northeast of Amsterdam, in Holland, some ten thousand people follow a sociosexual convention that has endured from Holland's tribal laws.

In Staphorst, a woman cannot be married in the Reformed Association Church unless she is pregnant. Thus, Friday evenings are set aside for premarital copulation by young couples. The father of a marriageable girl erects a heart-shaped copper plate on the front door of the family's home, announcing that his daughter is receiving suitors. The girl then leaves her bedroom window open for young men to climb through. The custom has endured since A.D. 1000, when fishermen left the north ports of the Zuider Zee and settled in virtual isolation at what is now Staphorst to become farmers.

Except for the methods of courtship, the villagers have very harsh regulations regarding sexual behavior, guiding their lives according to the mandates of strict Calvinism. For example, anyone (man or woman) who commits adultery is humiliated and degraded by being paraded through town bound hand and foot in a manure cart, pelted with dung by people who line the street. The person is then exiled from the community for life.

Source: Data from Groenman (1978).

---

expected to be followed by marriage when the young woman became pregnant.

As recorded in nineteenth-century Finland, the season for betrothal was early spring, when the snows began to melt and the days began to lengthen. Young unmarried women slept in a loft and either unlatched the trap door or hung a rope outside their upstairs window to admit visitors—young men who banded together to serenade them. It was the young women, not their parents, who decided whether to invite the young men in and whether to ask them to return. When a young woman and a young man became romatically interested in one another, their friends were expected to allow them to meet together alone, and the young couple then followed a prescribed ritual. The young man would stay all night but remain fully clothed and above the covers. Then, visit by visit, he would proceed to greater intimacy— first getting under the covers with his clothes on, then under the covers with his clothes off. At this point, the couple would announce their intention to become betrothed.

Formal betrothal, which was a very significant event, soon followed and was marked by celebration and ceremony. Betrothal was followed by marriage, but only if the young woman became pregnant.

The Nordic legacy was ready-made for the age of birth control—an age in which adolescents and young adults can live together in an erotic-sexual relation and yet postpone parenthood until they are ready to assume its responsibilities.

This time-honored betrothal system has been receiving increasing emphasis in our society during the last two decades—in the move away from the Mediterranean legacy of "bad girls do and good girls don't," in a decreasing emphasis on the importance of the virgin bride, in a decline of the double standard, and in a gradual emergence of economic and social egalitarianism for women. Critics of the trend toward greater freedom in erotic matters feel that this represents a loss of moral standards. Other observers feel that the growing economic, political, and social independence of women in our society is a long-overdue positive force, and that the trend away from the Mediterranean legacy toward the betrothal system of the Nordic legacy is simply one aspect of this shift.

The Amerafrican Legacy

The moral positions of both the Nordic legacy and the Mediterranean legacy rest upon the assumption of a presumably permanent liaison between the young couple—a liaison ultimately to be legitimized by marriage.

The tradition of black African slaves in this country was different from either of these two legacies, however. Slaves had the legal status of animals and were regarded as the property of their owners. Lovers had no legal right to marry or even to remain together. If the woman became pregnant, she did not have the right to keep her child. To remain together as lovers, to marry, and to establish a family unit with the birth of a child were not legal rights of slaves. Whether the master chose to bestow these privileges upon them depended upon his attitude toward human rights and his own philosophy of slavery. (See William Styron's *Confessions of Nat Turner* for an illuminating description of life under slavery in the South.) There was certainly no guarantee that the master would regard a liaison involving slaves as an important human condition. Rather, slaves were often bred as animals; such owners not only had little regard for slaves as human beings, but often even refused to recognize them as human. Other owners were, of course, more humane and allowed their slaves to marry and made every effort to keep families together.[4]

A young slave mother was sent to her assigned work while her baby stayed in the yard in the care of yard slaves—the elderly and the infirm. Regardless of their genealogical relation, these older people constituted the grandparental generation. Thus the cultural pattern of slavery was that infants and juveniles were looked after by the aged (or grandparent surrogates) while the young parental generation did the daily work of the plantation. The plantation manager decided what was supplied to the children for food, shelter, and clothing.

The plantation manager's place has been taken today by the governmental department of welfare. A culture of poverty has been perpetuated in which young mothers are obliged to live on welfare, supplemented by inadequate wages, while their young children are left by day in the care of someone else—typically a grandmother. Some 40 percent of black families are single-parent families headed by women, and more than half of black children are reared in such single-parent families (see Chapter 10).

Most of these children are born to unmarried mothers, and the young fathers may or may not contribute to their support.[5] The father usually remains in close contact with the family, however, even if he does not feel obligated to do so; he does not repudiate his paternity but is instead rather proud of it. Urban ghetto children usually know who their fathers are, even if their mothers are unmarried. Nevertheless, the paired bond in this system is relatively loose and impermanent, since

[4]There are little historical data regarding how often slave families were allowed to remain together or how often they were sold and permanently separated, since statistics were not usually kept by slave owners, whose own morality was officially Judeo-Christian. It is known, however, that there were slave-breeding customs analogous to animal husbandry, and that it was common for slave-owning males, their sons, and their male relatives and friends to exercise their sexual rights of ownership with female slaves. (If a white woman did the same and was discovered, she was regarded as having been raped by the slave, who usually paid the penalty with his life.)

[5]As Reiss (1980) notes, illegitimacy is even more prevalent in Jamaican society, where about two-thirds of all children born to lower class black mothers are illegitimate. Many of the Jamaican men feel inadequate in fulfilling the role of husband in terms of providing housing, income, and job permanency, and thus they avoid this role. A good proportion of these consensual unions are later legalized by marriage, but many end with the male leaving.

Although in the United States dating is the primary way in which young people get to know one another, in most of the world's societies dating as we know it is virtually unknown.

Steve Malone/Jeroboam, Inc.

cannot provide economically for their own offspring, and they remain so impoverished that, as grandparents, they still do not have an adequate budget for the care of grandchildren. . . . As a byproduct of such a system, women are given an excess of independence and responsibility in comparison with men, but not the necessary economic support and authority with which to exercise their responsibility (pp. 60–61).

It is also true, of course, that most blacks in our contemporary society do not follow the Amerafrican legacy. Sixty percent of black families consist of a husband and a wife, who rear nearly half of all black children. Christianity became a major force in black life in the South in the eighteenth and nineteenth centuries, and many blacks became devout Christians, usually Protestant. Fundamental Christian ideals regarding erotic-sexual contact were emphasized, and family structure was very close. This heritage is still apparent today.

In the black community today, the Mediterranean legacy is extremely important in many groups, as is the Nordic legacy to others. Nevertheless, the Amerafrican legacy is still current in other groups, and it may be traced to its origin in the eighteenth century.

DATING IN OUR SOCIETY

Although courtship in our society stems from many cultural legacies, they all converge in the pattern of mate selection by mutual choice known as *dating*. Dating is a relatively recent development that has achieved institutional status only in the present century in our society; it is still very rare in most of the world. It is virtually unknown in China (with one-fourth of the world's population); it is almost unknown in India (with one-sixth of the world's population); it is still relatively rare in most areas of Africa, South America, Mexico, and around the Mediterranean in Greece, Sicily, Spain,

it is not formally legitimized by either betrothal or marriage. Offspring are provided for partially by welfare and partially by the young mother (sometimes with the young father's help), while they are physically looked after by the grandparental generation. As Money (1980) points out:

There is much that is positive in the Amerafrican system of paired bonding and erotic/sexual relations—the system of grandparent responsibility and of rotating the care of children across three generations. Its great defect is . . . that there is no effective, institutionalized economic support for the rotational system of child care . . . thus, young parents

and Portugal; it is usually prohibited in Egypt, Saudi Arabia, Iran, Iraq, Libya, Abyssinia, and other countries. The Soviet Union is so diverse a society that it is hard to typify. Most areas of Western Europe now accept dating but not to the extent that it is accepted in the United States, Great Britain, Canada, Australia, New Zealand, and in the islands of the Oceanian group, such as Polynesia and Melanesia.

In the United States, dating has emerged as the virtually universal method by which young people get to know one another, develop the ability to relate to one another sociosexually, and ultimately marry.[6]

The Emergence of Dating

Dating, which allows young people relatively unsupervised freedom to meet and socialize, began to emerge in our society as a method of courtship in the late nineteenth century, but it was not firmly established until the 1920s (Mead 1959). Before this time, casual meetings at unsupervised social affairs were highly unlikely and "pickups" were virtually unknown. The danger of a girl meeting an unsuitable prospect was minimized by careful parental supervision. She was, most emphatically, never left alone to meet boys casually and indiscriminately.

Even after a couple had been formally introduced, and their courtship had proceeded to the engagement stage, they were not supposed to be alone together; they attended social affairs only in the company of friends or relatives. Some lovemaking in the form of mutual caressing and petting undoubtedly occurred, but because of the difficulty of being alone, it was much less frequent than it became after dating was instituted.

The traditional pattern of carefully supervised sociosexual interaction between young people began to change in the late nineteenth and early twentieth centuries because of the influence of two factors: (1) new economic conditions and (2) changing women's roles. As we saw in Chapter 2, the movement of working class women to occupations outside the home began as methods of mass production (adapted from eighteenth-century England) were developed during the latter part of the nineteenth century in the United States. This brought women into casual contact with men without the formality of introductions. It also weakened the patriarchal authority of the father, who no longer provided the sole source of occupation on family subsistence farms.

The first women to move into the world of work outside the home were lower class women, who were employed in factories and mills. However, beginning about 1915 they began increasingly to move into the business world of offices and stores, and this opened the world of outside employment to young middle class women, who prior to this time had been chiefly limited to such occupations as teacher, governess, or "lady's companion."

This increasing emancipation of women in business and education was paralleled by a new freedom for women to engage in physical activity, including active sports, and to wear less restrictive clothing. Before the early twentieth century women were hampered by the whalebone corsets they wore, which squeezed their waists (and internal organs) into a twelve- to fourteen-inch circumference.[7] It was also considered unsuitable for women to engage in strenuous sports. (Women were admitted as participants for the first time in the Olympic Games of 1920.)

---

[6]All but about 5 percent of our population ultimately marry (see Chapter 6).

---

[7]The whalebone corset was gradually discarded about the turn of the century, and by the 1920s it had been replaced by the "girdle," which was commonly worn until well into the 1960s, when "pantyhose" became the fashion.

Dating allows relatively unsupervised freedom for young people to meet and socialize.

A major movement of women into the work world occurred during World War I, when the mass shifting of men from civilian employment into the armed forces led to a sudden surge in jobs for women as secretaries, clerks, and sales personnel—positions that had been occupied solely by men. Use of the typewriter and the telephone, both of which were invented near the close of the nineteenth century, expanded rapidly, and scores of young women became typists and telephone operators as business firms grew and multiplied.[8] The increasing number of young women in the business world was accompanied by an in-

creasing growth of coeducation as young women were admitted to high schools and colleges in ever-growing numbers. Although young women were by no means completely free from supervision, these changes in the work world and in the educational world did make it possible for women to associate with men on an increasingly casual basis.

Another significant development in this regard that occurred in the early twentieth century was the invention of the automobile. Its rapidly expanding use in the 1920s made greatly increased mobility possible. (See the vignette, "The Impact of the Automobile on American Society.") The automobile provided transportation to the roadhouses and nightclubs that were beginning to spring up, and it also served as a small, intimate, mobile parlor where couples could easily obtain privacy.

---

[8]The telephone was invented by Alexander Graham Bell and patented by him in 1876 and 1877. The modern typewriter that prints both upper- and lowercase letters appeared in 1878.

The Impact of the Automobile on American Society

Probably no single technological development has had a greater impact on the average person's daily life than the automobile. This rapid technological change took place in just a few years—in the decade from 1910 to 1920.

In 1900 there were actually less than 150 miles of paved roads in the United States, and personal transportation was by horse and buggy. Fewer than eight thousand cars were registered, and they were used chiefly as playthings for the wealthy. The first cross-country trip by automobile was completed in 1903 and took fifty-two days.

Then, in 1908 Henry Ford, a self-taught engineer without a high school education, designed the Model T (affectionately known as the *flivver* or the *Tin Lizzie*). Just five years later, in 1913, he introduced the production technique of the moving assembly line, which was quickly adopted by other manufacturers. By 1918 there were nearly 5 million cars in America; production has been rising rapidly ever since. Other widespread changes have also made an enormous impact on our way of life—the electric light, the telephone, the radio, the motion picture, television—but none has had the impact of the automobile.

Meanwhile, the newly invented telephone provided a means of close personal communication that reached right inside the home. A young man could now communicate directly with a woman without going through the formality of being welcomed by her family. The cinema (or motion picture) was another invention of the period that provided young couples with a dark and relatively secluded place to go, as well as with matinee idols whose romantic behavior they could emulate. Newspapers, magazines, and the newly invented radio further publicized the romantic ideal, so that young couples were provided with role models on every hand.

The "old-fashioned girl" was soon regarded as a "flat tire." The idealized version of femininity in the "roaring twenties" was the *flapper*, a thoroughly urbanized and industrialized transformation of the *Gibson Girl* of the late nineteenth century. In keeping with her emancipated place in society, the flapper wore skirts above the knee (they had been ankle length for centuries); shingled, bobbed, and marcelled her hair (which had once reached her waist); and replaced the whalebone corset with brief panties. With her new freedom she "went out" with young men outside her family circle whom she met at parties or at work. Within one generation, age-old rituals of courtship began to seem old-fashioned and even quaint. The new patterns of relating came to be called "dating" (Mead 1959).

Dating differed from prior sociosexual interaction between young people in several important ways. First, an introduction of the young man to the young woman by a member of the family was not considered necessary. Rather, it became perfectly appropriate for a young couple to meet casually without introductions on a beach, at a party or a dance, on a tennis court, at school, at the place of employment, or in any one of a number of places. Second, there was no commitment, either public or private, on the part of either the man or the woman, to continue the relation beyond the actual time of the date itself. Third, the date was planned by the couple rather than arranged by parents or others. Fourth, physical intimacies were not explicitly prohibited.

Finally, there was little supervision; the young couple were left on their own in relative freedom.

Since the time of this gradual emergence of dating as the chief method of marital choice in our society, it has won virtually universal acceptance, reflecting widespread changes in our patterns of social behavior.[9] By the 1930s and 1940s, young people of all social classes would have been surprised to learn that dating had not always been accepted, and they were very impatient with parents who regarded casual meetings as "pickups"—a stigma associated with the lower class. By the 1950s and 1960s, the young people of the 1930s and 1940s were themselves parents, and misgivings regarding the practice of dating were limited to the grandparents' generation, who were thought to be long out of touch with the modern scene. By the 1970s and 1980s, dating was so taken for granted that the time-honored method of careful supervision and mate selection by parental arrangement seemed archaic, quaint, and buried in the mists of history.

In addition to its widespread acceptance, dating has undergone many changes since its inception. It was initially rather formal—the couple were carefully and sometimes elaborately dressed, and the young man was expected to request a date well in advance. It was not thought proper for the woman to initiate the date except under very unusual circumstances. By the 1960s, dating had become increasingly casual and spontaneous—dress codes were relaxed, and it was becoming increasingly acceptable for the woman to initiate the date. Meanwhile, emphasis was shifting more and more toward the importance of the personal interaction of the young couple.

By the late 1960s, polls were beginning to reflect significant changes in sexual behavior

in dating, and authorities on college campuses were beginning to abandon the effort to act *in loco parentis* (in the absence of parents) in supervising students' social lives. By the 1970s, many large cosmopolitan universities had established coeducational dorms. Although initially visitation between men's and women's rooms in these dorms was regulated or at least frowned upon, these attitudes soon relaxed and men visitors in women's rooms and women visitors in men's rooms became commonplace. By the mid-1970s, our society had moved into still another stage of sociosexual freedom—the practice of living together without being married—and by the late 1970s, this had become a common practice in many universities and colleges. Parents who had shocked their own parents by dating were now shocked in turn.

The Experience of Dating

Like so many terms that are widely used and understood, the term *date* is very difficult to define. What precisely is a date? If the occasion is an appointment, a business transaction, an accidental meeting, or an invitation to share a table or to have lunch or dinner with no overtones of shared personal interest implied, it is not a date. For example, in an episode of the well-known "Mary Tyler Moore Show," which is still seen in syndication, Mary protests that having dinner with an importunate admirer (Ted Baxter) does not constitute a date: "Oh, no! This is not a date! Whatever it is, it's not that! It's not a date!"

Although the institution of dating is specifically an instrument that introduces the adolescent to heterosexual social behavior and serves as the culturally accepted method for mate selection, it is by no means limited to these functions. A date also provides fun, recreation, adventure, romance, and an opportunity for the young person to gain experience in relating to someone of the opposite gender. In the close intimacy of dating, a person often explores his or her innermost feelings, ideals,

---

[9]There are some groups in the United States in which people do not date, in the contemporary sense; marital choice is still characterized by rigorous control and parental approval. One such group is the Amish of Pennsylvania.

and convictions, finding new depths in old emotions and experiencing new emotions.

Nor is dating limited to adolescents and young adults. People of all ages may date—those who have never married, those who have been divorced or widowed, even those who *are* married. It is still called a date even if there is no possibility for courtship or marriage. The date may be between a single person and a married person, or between two people who are married to others, although both situations are usually considered illicit in our society. Finally, the date may be homosexual, with all the social and emotional concomitants and overtones of a heterosexual relation.

A date is a unique event in that it always implies some special intimacy between the couple, although this may vary, of course, from very slight to very extensive. No matter how casual the date, however, this implication of a special caring or choosing is always implied. If one or the other does not feel comfortable with this implication on a first date, further dates are usually refused.

Thus, a request for a date, as well as its acceptance or refusal, usually involves heightened awareness of the other person. The couple is established (to some extent) in a relation or interaction that is different from a casual encounter or a business appointment. For the duration of the date, each assumes a special significance for the other and is consciously aware of this significance.

The adolescent usually enters the dating world gradually, first relating to the opposite gender in casual groupings that may occur almost anyplace—school playgrounds, churches, one another's homes, coffee shops, bowling alleys, skating rinks, tennis courts, or beaches. This type of grouping gradually develops into true dating, as the young people begin to pair off, getting to know each other on a one-to-one basis. Since arranged marriages are no longer the norm in our society, if young people did not follow this process, they would never marry.

Initial dating often includes two couples (double dating)—a custom that provides mutual security and the sharing of an unfamiliar (and often scary) situation. When one person (usually the boy) takes the plunge and risks rejection by asking the other for a date, a significant event has taken place, marking a change in sociosexual development. Even for a person who has grown up in a family with brothers and sisters in residence, relating on a one-to-one basis with a nonfamily member of the opposite gender can be uncomfortable, even agonizing, at first. However, most people make the adjustment, despite occasionally painful difficulties. Moreover, since initial dating usually involves a wide variety of partners (playing the field), if an embarrassing or awkward mistake *is* made, it is not necessarily a catastrophe (although the memory of a disaster may haunt a person for years). Often mistakes are even helpful, since they provide concrete experience about how *not* to relate sociosexually. Thus, a mistake in attempting to interact on a date may be rectified on the next date, so that the person gradually gains increasing skill and ease.

Random, casual dating usually develops into dating one person more or less exclusively—a practice often known as "going steady," although the term is not always used. Such exclusive dating is often a prelude to courtship, or it may *be* courtship. The decision of whether each wishes to marry the other usually occurs during this final stage of serious, intimate dating.

Going steady appeared to be more common in the late 1970s and in earlier years, and to occur at younger ages. In 1958, for example, 68 percent of young college women said they had gone steady, as compared with 77 percent in 1968, and 85 percent in 1978. The average age at first going steady was 17 in 1958, 16.7 in 1968, and 15.9 in 1978 (Bell and Coughey 1980).

An individual does not usually marry the first person he or she dates seriously and steadily (Landis and Landis 1977). As dating becomes serious, with the marital choice aspect of dating gaining emphasis, one or the other usually breaks off the relation—although men are more reluctant to break off than women, and they suffer more and longer after a breakup (as noted in Chapter 3). After a period of recovery following this breakup, the individual usually starts dating again, with casual, random dating leading once more to exclusively dating one person. After a series of involvements in this way, all but 5 percent of the population finally establish a paired bond that is strong enough and persistent enough to survive an engagement (formal or informal), and the couple marry.

As part of this final phase of serious, intensive commitment, the couple may decide to live together. Since about 95 percent of our population eventually marry, although they do so about a year later than they did a decade ago, unmarried cohabitation is apparently an extension of the dating and courtship phase of marital choice, rather than a replacement for marriage (see Chapter 6). Until the 1970s, living together without being married occurred only rarely and was usually limited to the lower class. It is now approaching institutional status, however, and is very common in all classes of our society.

Class Differences in Dating

Although dating is now the universally accepted method for courtship in the United States, there are significant differences in the dating behavior of the upper, the middle, and the lower classes.

Upper Class

The upper class exercises far more control, supervision, and regulation of dating activities than the middle or lower class, both directly and indirectly. Supervised dances and parties are the norm in the upper class, going steady is unusual (a wide variety of partners brings more status), and there is more control over necking and petting. Dates are drawn from school acquaintances, and most upper class children go to private schools where they meet children from other upper class families. Chance meetings with someone from the middle or lower class are relatively rare. This cultural isolation is characteristic until college, where there are opportunities to meet and date people from the middle and lower classes. Even then, however, cultural patterns tend to persist, and family influence remains very great.

At age eighteen, the upper class girl is formally presented to society, enters the adult world of committees and clubs, and begins a round of social activities during which she is introduced to a wide range of eligible men of acceptable social level. When the couple become engaged, the engagement is formally announced, and when they marry, the wedding is also formal.

For members of the upper class marriage usually occurs about four years later than the national median—mid-twenties for upper class women and the late twenties for upper class men (Carter and Glick 1976).

Middle Class

The children of middle class parents are not so rigorously supervised and controlled as those of the upper class. There is, however, a good deal of supervision in many school, church, and family functions. Instead of the wide variety of dates that brings status in the upper class, going steady with one person at a time is more characteristic of the middle class, although going steady does not necessarily imply a permanent alliance. However, for the duration of the going-steady status, each of the couple is expected to be exclusively available to the other (if one reneges on this implicit agreement, the going-steady status is seriously risked).

Since rejection can be very painful, initial

approach in asking for a date is usually very cautious and tentative, with the grounds for retreat fully prepared ("I don't really like her"). A best friend might be approached first and asked, "What does she think of me?" Or an intermediary might be sought out, "See if you can can fix me up." Some prior assurance of success is sought, if it is at all possible, before a person ventures to ask for the first date. Casual "hanging around" in one another's homes is very common in the middle class. Initial interaction may occur during this "hanging around" without the couple specifically being "on a date." Risk of rejection is thus minimized.

Much dating is sports oriented—swimming, roller skating, ice skating, playing tennis, playing volleyball, or simply "hanging around" at a beach, a lake, a river, a ski run, or a bowling alley. Attendance at commercial establishments—coffee shops, "creameries," drive-ins, and so on—is also very common in middle class dating.

Petting is virtually universal among middle class dating couples. It may be very protracted and intimate, serving to some extent as a substitute for copulation. Engagement of members of the middle class is often announced in the press; there is usually a formal, though not elaborate, wedding. Marriage usually occurs in the early twenties for the middle class woman and in the mid-twenties for the man (Carter and Glick 1976).

Lower Class

Lower class dating is less supervised and less controlled by the family than either upper or middle class dating. The family dwelling is too small and crowded and the parents are usually too tired and preoccupied with money problems to provide entertainment for teenage children and their friends. Therefore, lower class dates usually take place in commercial establishments, rather than in the home. As with middle class (and upper class) dating, much lower class dating is sports oriented. Serious,

unsupervised, steady dating usually begins in the mid-teens, and copulation during these dates is casually expected, especially by the male. Copulation usually occurs without a prelude of petting (extended petting may even be considered a perversion). When a girl becomes pregnant, marriage is expected to take place (Rubin 1976; Kinsey et al. 1953, 1948).

Although lower class boys rarely date outside their social class, a girl may date "up," especially if she is physically attractive. She must have other qualities as well, however, if such dates are to be more than casual and random; she must acquire middle class language, manner, dress, and attitude.

Engagements are not usually announced in the lower class, and weddings are often informal, although lower class weddings may also be very elaborate, with the male members of the wedding party appearing in rented tuxedos and the women in special gowns. A hall may be rented for the reception, food is often catered, and musicians play for dancing. The usual age at marriage is the mid-teens for the lower class young woman and the early twenties for the young man (Carter and Glick 1976).

THE FIELD OF ELIGIBLES

Although we use the system of mate selection by mutual choice in our society, the belief that the choice is completely free is an illusion. While a young person might appear to be free to choose anyone he or she pleases, to court and perhaps to marry that person, in actuality this apparent freedom of choice is hedged by many cultural restrictions, both conscious and unconscious.

In choosing a mate, everyone is bound inexorably by two opposing forces that create what sociologists call the *field of eligibles*—the population within which marital choice may be made (see Figure 5-1). These opposing forces are *exogamy* (the pressure to marry outside a group) and *endogamy* (the pressure to marry within a group).

Exogamy

Exogamy is the pressure to marry outside the family, although the definition of what constitutes a "family" varies from one society to another. For example, it was prohibited for a person to marry anyone with the same surname, even if there was no blood relation, during the T'ang Dynasty in medieval China (A.D. 618–907)—an extreme example of exogamy.

All societies forbid marriage of mother to son, father to daughter, grandparent to grandchild, uncle to niece, or aunt to nephew, and virtually all societies forbid marriage of brother to sister or half-brother to half-sister.[10]

In our society, exogamy prohibitions vary from state to state, with the exceptions just noted, which are universal. For example, it is illegal for first cousins to marry in some states, yet perfectly legal in others.

Endogamy and Homogamy

Endogamy, which opposes exogamy and is the pressure to marry *within* a group, is based upon the human characteristic to fear, distrust, or hate an outsider. This characteristic is found, to some extent, among all people in varying degrees. Some individuals, some groups within a society, and some societies are far more distrustful than others of an outsider.

In our society, an important aspect of endogamy is homogamy. *Homogamy* is the force that impels a person to date, and ultimately, marry someone of about the same race, religion, ethnic group, age, educational level, intelligence, social class, and family background. For example, interracial marriages occur rarely in our society[11] although a U.S. Supreme Court decision invalidated all state miscegenation (intermarriage) laws in 1967.

Interfaith marriages now account for about 40 percent of all marriages in the United States, so that religion is not as strong a homogamous force as race. Ethnic group membership may act as a force for homogamy, with the couple sharing many of the same traditions and interests, but its influence is hard to measure. Similarly, it is very difficult to measure the influence of social class as a homogamous factor. Certainly, social class is related to such factors as residence, school, church, as well as the person's speech patterns, vocational level, income, and many other factors, and so it is obviously a homogamous force. A marriage that "mixes" two people from different races, religions, ethnic groups, or social classes is called an *intermarriage* (see Chapter 7).

Other homogamous factors, such as educational level, intelligence, and age, are not usually regarded as factors in an intermarriage by sociologists, but nevertheless they are important homogamous forces. People with a high school education tend to associate with and marry one another, as do those with a college education or a graduate level education. Most couples who date seriously and get along very well with one another probably have about the same level of intelligence—although, again, intelligence as a force for homogamy is difficult to measure.

Finally, age is a very significant force for homogamy. A person usually dates and marries someone of about the same age.[12] The highly publicized marriages between men in their sixties or seventies and women in their teens and twenties are statistically insignif-

---

[10]There have been exceptions to this prohibition; for example, in the Middle Kingdom of ancient Egypt brother-sister marriages were not only permitted, but were preferred. Such marriages also took place in the royal family of early Hawaiian rulers.

[11]About 1.4 percent of marriages in our society are interracial (see Chapter 7).

[12]U.S. Bureau of the Census, "Marital Status and Living Arrangements" (1984).

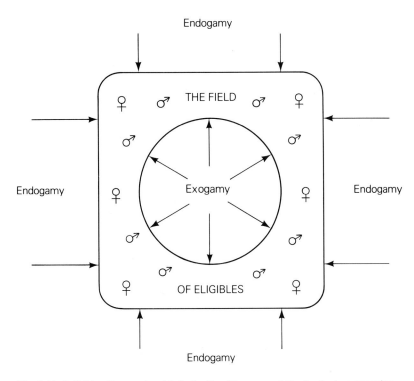

The field of eligibles (for marriage) is limited in all known societies by the two opposing forces of *endogamy* (fear and mistrust of outsiders) and *exogamy* (prohibition against marrying a close relative).

FIGURE 5-1
The field of eligibles

icant, and marriages between older women and younger men are even rarer. Such marriages are usually noted in the press because the older person often has an exceptionally high status in our society (wealth, power, reputation).

Parameters in which opposite—rather than similar—characteristics are found to be attractive are termed *heterogamous* forces. It seems reasonable, for example, that opposites attract in terms of such traits as dominance-submission, nurturance-dependence, masochism-sadism, or vicariousness-achievement. However, although such heterogamous attractions undoubtedly exist, they are very difficult to measure.[13]

THE MYSTERY OF ATTRACTION

Within the field of eligibles (which is formed by the opposing forces of endogamy and exogamy) young people in our society may exercise freedom of choice in choosing whom to court and whom to marry. Why does the person choose the one that he or she does? Why are we each

[13]The theory of heterogamy in dating and mate selection is intriguing but has not been substantiated by research. Although some complementary characteristics are probably present in mutual attraction, they apparently occur in a complex blending with homogamous factors and are difficult to tease out. (See Heiss and Gordon 1964; Murstein 1961; Schellenberg and Bee 1960; and Winch 1958.)

It is quite possible to be attracted to two people at the same
time and find a final choice very difficult to make.
Charles Dana Gibson, *The Weaker Sex I—The Story of a
Susceptible Bachelor*, 1903

© 1903 by Collier's Weekly

attracted to one person, and not another? Why are we not always liked in return? There is much that remains unknown about this mystery of attraction (and its opposite face, rejection). For example, it is not as yet possible to explain the overwhelming, compulsive attraction of limerence. However, much attraction seems to be based upon such factors as propinquity (closeness in time and space), the circumstances under which the meeting takes place, the relative status of each of the couple, and whether the attraction is mutual—that is, reciprocated.

The first impression is important, because if it is not favorable the person usually does not make any effort to know the other better, and first impressions are usually based upon physical appearance. Studies find that physically attractive people are assumed to have other valued qualities as well; they are regarded by most of us as being more interesting, poised, social, outgoing, sensitive, and nurturant than the average person. They are assumed

to be more dependable, trustworthy, and moral (Cash and Janda 1984, Dion et al. 1972).

Ask most people to list what makes them like someone on first meeting and they'll tell you personality, intelligence, sense of humor. But they are probably deceiving themselves. The characteristic that impresses people the most, when meeting anyone from a job applicant to a blind date, is appearance. As unfair and unenlightened as it may seem, attractive people are frequently preferred over their less attractive peers. Research begun in the early 1970s has shown that not only do good looks influence such things as choice of friends, lovers and mates, but that they can also affect school grades, selection for jobs, and even the outcome of a trial. Attractive people are viewed as being happier, more sensitive, more interesting, warmer, more poised, more sociable, and as having better character than their less attractive counterparts (Cash and Janda 1984, p. 47).

The first impression is sometimes based on something other than physical appearance, of course, such as social skills (friendliness), abilities (in dancing, singing, sports), possessions (wealth, sports car), status (entertainer, sports star, professional), and reputation (we are often prepared to like a person before the meeting).

There are also individual differences in what is regarded as attractive. Some women are attracted to tall men and others to short men, although research finds that most women like men of about medium height (Graziano et al. 1978). Some men like plump girls, and other men like slim girls; the popular ideal is slim in our society, but most societies prefer plump women (Ford and Beach 1970). Some people give very high marks to qualities that others consider relatively unimportant. This is fortunate, otherwise the only people dating and marrying would be the "beautiful people" or those of very high status. That virtually everyone is attractive to someone is shown by the fact that more than 95 percent of all men and women in the United States ultimately marry (see Chapter 6).

Propinquity

Although first impressions are often very important and physical appearance is often the basis of the first impression, it is surprising how often simple *propinquity* determines whom one dates and marries. Most people marry someone they have met in the neighborhood or someone who has attended the same school or church, or played tennis on the same courts, or worked in the same office.

Sheer exposure to one another usually causes two people to like each other better, despite any negative first impression that each has made on the other. Research finds that people tend to like others whom they encounter often, just because of this frequent encountering. This growing appreciation of the other's good qualities apparently occurs because, in common with all species, we tend to evaluate someone we have not seen before or do not know well as potentially dangerous, whereas repeated exposure causes the person to become familiar, and familiarity breeds liking. The aphorism that "familiarity breeds contempt" is not usually accurate (Zajonc 1968).

A research study that dramatically illustrates the importance of propinquity examined the interaction of residents in a housing unit in which the apartments were arranged around U-shaped grassy courts with two end units in each court facing the street. The study found that the likelihood of two people becoming friends correlated to how far apart their apartments were. Friendships sprung up most frequently between next-door neighbors, less frequently between people whose apartments were separated by two units, and still less frequently as the distance between apartments grew to three units. As the distance between apartments increased, the number of friendships dropped so rapidly that it was rare to find a friendship between people who lived in apartments more than four or five units apart. The architects had unwittingly shaped the social lives of the residents (Festinger 1951).

The same study also found that any architectural feature that caused a resident to encounter others frequently, tended to increase that person's popularity. For example, a person whose apartment was near the entrance or the exit of a stairwell, or near a mailbox, had significantly more friends than other residents. In contrast, any architectural feature that took a resident out of the traffic mainstream had a chilling effect on that person's popularity. For example, people who lived in the two end apartments of each unit, which faced the street rather than the court, had less than half as many friends as anyone else in the unit (Festinger 1951).

It is interesting to note that even celebrities, who ostensibly have an enormous range of prospects, usually marry someone they have met on a day-to-day basis. For example, comedienne Joan Rivers came to know Edgar when they worked together on a television

When people respond to one another favorably, they tend to look at one another, lean toward one another as they talk, and have an open stance.

script; Julia Child, the "French Chef," met her husband, Paul, at work; Susan Ford married a secret service agent assigned to guard the family after her father left office; and Patty Hearst, heiress to a vast newspaper empire, married her bodyguard.

The practical implications of such research as the apartment complex study seem to be that if you arrange your life so that you increase the opportunities to associate with a variety of potential acquaintances, companions, or friends, you will maximize the probability of finding someone whom you will be especially attracted to and who will be attracted to you.

Body Language

When two people meet they communicate non-verbally as well as verbally, and the nonverbal aspect of their interaction may be more impor-tant. Feelings of friendliness as well as feel-ings of indifference or hostility are clearly revealed by the unconscious manifestations of posture and stance. In some situations, fully 90 percent or more of feelings and attitudes are communicated nonverbally (Hall 1976, 1973, Mehrabian 1971).

When people are responding to one another favorably, they tend to look at one another, lean toward one another as they talk, and have an *open* stance (arms hanging loosely or spread apart). Conversely, people who do not like one another (or are angry at the moment) tend *not* to look at one another, lean apart or away from one another, and have a *closed* stance (arms folded, legs crossed, body turned away or face averted). This nonverbal communication is received (usually unconsciously) and re-sponded to. For example, if a person is relating to someone who leans away with face averted, he or she senses the rejection or hostility even though the verbal content of the communication may be friendly (Hall 1976, 1973, Mehrabian 1971).

Another important aspect of body language is eye contact. We tend to maintain more eye contact with a person whom we like than we do with casual acquaintances or strangers—or people we don't like. Strangers or casual acquaintances spend only about a third of the time in eye contact when they are talking together—glancing away most of the time and then glancing back again. People who like one another tend to spend most of the time looking into one another's eyes (Rubin 1973, Argyle 1967).

A more subtle aspect of "the language of the eyes" is the *pupillary response*. Everyone understands that the pupils of our eyes change size in response to light intensity, growing larger in a dim light (to admit more illumination) and smaller in a bright light. (This is why, when we go into a darkened theater on a Saturday afternoon, we are blinded for a time until our pupils can adjust by enlarging to admit more illumination.) It is not usually understood, however, that our pupils also enlarge when we look at something we perceive as attractive, and contract when we view something we perceive as unattractive.

Thus, if you look at someone you like, the pupils of your eyes become larger. If you look at someone you don't like, the pupils of your eyes become smaller. Conversely, when someone looks at *you* and likes you, the pupils of the person's eyes become larger; if the person doesn't like you, the pupils become smaller. If the dislike is intense, the pupils may shrink to virtual pinpoints.

This pupillary response occurs unconsciously. It cannot be deliberately controlled. An individual's true feelings, or the true feelings of the person he or she is relating to, are revealed by the pupillary response, and there is nothing either one can do to control this response. Any dissembling, masking, or camou-

flaging of true feelings must be done verbally or by nonverbal body language that is under conscious control. The aphorism that "the eyes are the windows of the soul" appears to be borne out by this research.[14]

Studies have found that when we relate to another we unconsciously check out the size of the person's pupils. If they are large, we unconsciously interpret this to mean that the person likes us. If the pupils shrink, we interpret this to mean that the person dislikes us. Since we like to be liked, we react more favorably to a person who regards us with large pupils than we do to one who regards us with small pupils. This nonverbal communication of pupillary size is a significant factor in whether one person responds to another with attraction or aversion. (See the vignette, "Attractiveness and Pupil Size.")

In addition to manifesting our feelings through body language, we each maintain a private "space bubble" around ourselves—and we let only a few people penetrate this bubble. The size of the bubble depends on how well we know the other person and whether we like the person or not. For example, in our society a preferred distance for someone we do not know or do not like, or for a casual acquaintance, is between four and seven feet. If the person comes closer than this, we grow uncomfortable and uneasy. If the person moves within a three-foot space we move away, retreating or backing off. If it is not possible to back off—for example, if we are in a corner of the room at a cocktail party—we may begin to feel

---

[14]Experienced poker players have long been aware of this pupillary response. They hide their eyes behind a lowered eyeshade or dark glasses or use some other means to prevent their pupils from being read by the other players in the game. The pupillary response to filling a full house, for example, or matching a hole card would be an immediate tipoff. The phenomenon was certainly known as early as the T'ang Dynasty to Chinese jade dealers. The proprietor of a shop would carefully watch a prospective buyer's eyes as he handled a piece of jade; the pupillary response would reveal his true feelings, putting the proprietor in a very advantageous position in subsequent bargaining.

Attractiveness and Pupil Size

An interesting illustration of the importance of pupillary size to the degree of attraction was obtained from a study in which the copy of a photograph of an attractive girl was retouched to enlarge her pupils. Thus there were two photographs of the same girl, identical in every respect except that in one photograph she had large pupils and in the other she had small pupils. When a large group of subjects were asked in which photo the woman seemed to be more sympathetic, warmer, happier, or more attractive, they picked the one with the large pupils. Moreover, the subjects' own pupils grew wider when they looked at the photo with the large pupils, and smaller when they looked at the other (Hess 1975).

Another experiment examined the effects of using one drug to dilate pupils for one encounter, and then a different drug to make the same pupils smaller for another encounter. When the groups of subjects encountered the person whose pupils had been artificially dilated, they described her in such terms as *soft*, *gentle*, and *open*. In contrast, when subjects encountered the same woman whose pupils were artificially small, they described her as *harsh*, *brassy*, and *cold* (Hess 1975). Apparently, then, the pupillary size not only reflects emotional states, but also serves as a clue that all of us use in assessing how other people feel and how we feel about them. We seem to be aware, unconsciously, that large pupils indicate interest and therefore warmth and acceptance.

This phenomenon has been used for some time to enhance the attractiveness of young women in some societies. For example, in southern Italy and in the antebellum South of our own country, young women used belladonna to dilate their pupils as part of their standard cosmetic equipment. They believed that putting drops of belladonna in their eyes before a ball or other social occasion would make them more attractive. (The word *belladonna* means "beautiful lady.")

---

threatened, responding with hostility and aggression, or we may become tense, depressed, and withdrawn (Cromie 1978, Hall 1976).

The zone from about three or four feet to about eighteen inches is limited to people we know and like. These people are freely permitted to come within this zone (Cromie 1978, Hall 1976).

However, we permit only intimates within an eighteen-inch zone. If a stranger moves within this eighteen-inch space bubble, we react swiftly with alarm, becoming either angry or defensive.[15]

An interesting research study that was designed to illustrate the importance of this eighteen-inch zone took place in a library. A woman experimenter would enter the library and take a seat next to a woman who was sitting alone at a library table. The experimenter would then move within this eighteen-inch zone of the other woman. Researchers found that the subject would react by drawing in her body, turning away, or marking off her bubble territory with books, a purse, or articles of clothing (Cromie 1978).

In another study, graduate students played the role of police officers. When the "police officer" would move within the eighteen-inch

---

[15]An exception to this reaction, of course, occurs in such situations as a crowded elevator, bus, or two adjoining stools at a counter in a coffee shop. In such situations we accept the intrusion with stiffness and a ritualized procedure. For example, in the elevator we usually stand with our arms pressed against our sides, looking straight ahead. In the coffee shop, strangers sitting on adjacent stools generally ignore one another.

zone of a student he was questioning, the student's speech became unsteady and jerky, and he would glance away frequently, fidget, and give other obvious signs of being uncomfortable and either defensive or hostile (Cromie 1978).

The appropriate course of action indicated by these studies regarding the importance of the eighteen-inch zone is to be very aware of the other person's responses when you penetrate this space bubble in trying to establish a friendly or affectionate relation. If the response is relaxed, warm, friendly, and encouraging, you are being admitted as an intimate. If you do not get such positive feedback, it might be well to back off, re-enter the zone briefly (testing the reaction), and wait for the subtle signs (body language cues) that the barriers are down.

There are great individual differences, in this regard, of course. Generally, however, when two people penetrate one another's eighteen-inch zone with mutual acceptance, this signals a readiness for intimacy.

There are social situations when the zone is expected to be relaxed and convention permits closeness and even touching—for example, in dancing or body contact sports.

The size of the personal space bubble is characteristically different from one culture to another. For example, in Latin America and the Middle East, strangers comfortably converse at a distance that we reserve for personal friends in our society. When an American steps back in such a situation, an Arab concludes that the American is cold and unfriendly. In the Mediterranean countries, business people do not place a desk between themselves and a visitor but prefer close, even physical, contact (Hall 1976).

Associated Circumstances

One of the key aspects of attraction is often the circumstances in which the meeting or the interaction takes place. These *associated circumstances* can have surprising force.

Apparently, we are attracted to those with whom we associate in pleasant surroundings or events. Conversely, we tend to dislike those with whom we associate in unpleasant situations. (Kings and other rulers used to cut off the heads of the messengers who bore ill tidings.)

Psychologists have gathered considerable evidence for this principle that liking someone and enjoying being with the person is related to the situation in which the interaction takes place. In a study that illustrates this principle, half the subjects (men and women) met in a comfortable, pleasant room; the other half met in an uncomfortable, unpleasant room. They were subsequently given a questionnaire designed to ascertain how much they liked one another. Those who had met in the comfortable surroundings liked one another significantly more than those who had met in the unpleasant room (Griffitt 1970).

In another study, subjects were asked to give their impressions of photographs of men and women. The photographs were judged by two groups of evaluators. One group viewed the photographs in a very pleasant room with beautiful draperies, elegant paintings, comfortable chairs, and soft lighting. The other group judged the same photographs in a shabbily furnished room with dirty walls, uncomfortable chairs, and a harsh overhead light. Both men and women viewers in the pleasant room rated the photographs as relatively more attractive than did viewers in the unpleasant room (Maslow and Mintz 1956).

The practical implications of these findings are quite intriguing. Apparently, it is important to manage your life so that the time you spend with intimates is spent as much as possible in pleasant surroundings and circumstances—if you wish to maximize the probability that your mutual affection and regard will continue (Murstein 1971).

Relative Status

We usually like and wish to know better those who are about our status. Research studies find that the average person does not expect a "perfect" dating partner, but rather hopes to have a partner whose relative desirability is about the same as his or her own.

Although we prefer partners who are more desirable than ourselves, our actual choices are influenced by matching considerations. We all tend to end up with partners of approximately our own social value. Thus, our selection of a mate appears to be a delicate compromise between our desire to capture an ideal partner and our realization that we must eventually settle for what we deserve (Walster and Walster 1978, p. 141).

This inclination of a person to be attracted to someone of about the same status is seen most clearly in terms of physical appearance. In an interesting research study that illustrates this principle, dating couples were observed in various places (theater lobbies, parties, and so on), and their physical appearances were rated on a scale from 1 to 5 in half-point intervals. The study found that 60 percent of the young couples were separated by only half a point on the scale, 86 percent were separated by one point or less, and no couple was separated by more than two and one-half points (Silverman 1971).

The study also found that the more similar two people were in physical appearance, the more they would touch (allowing the other within the eighteen-inch zone). For example, 60 percent of the "highly similar" couples touched, as compared with 46 percent of the "moderately similar" couples, and only 22 percent of the "dissimilar couples" (Silverman 1971).

Another example of this tendency to be attracted to someone of about the same status as oneself is found in evidence that couples are often matched in terms of psychological charac-

teristics—such as degree of emotional maturity. Research finds that "emotionally mature" people find one another attractive and that "emotionally immature" people do so as well. When a person who is relatively mature emotionally is attracted to and marries someone who is emotionally immature, the tendency is for the emotionally mature person to experience personality decompensation, so that he or she comes to match more closely the characteristics of the emotionally immature person, rather than the opposite (Coleman 1984).

An interesting question that arises, then, is: What happens when a person beats the odds? That is, what happens when a person ends up with a date (or a marriage) with someone who is clearly superior (or inferior) to his or her own status in terms of important physical, psychological, or social qualities?

Research finds that if the imbalance is very pronounced, there are three possibilities. First, the superior person will change to more closely approximate the other person, so that a match is obtained. Second, the relation will be characterized by disharmony and unhappiness, with the higher-status person feeling angry, cheated, and resentful, while the one who has the lower status feels uneasy and guilty.

What happens when the Prince marries Cinderella? It's obvious, of course, why the Prince might be dissatisfied: he can never really forget that he *could* have married a Princess. But, Cinderella . . . might have cause for unhappiness too . . . on the one hand, she is eager to keep the Prince's love. After all, what are her chances of attracting so desirable a partner a second time? On the other hand, she is painfully aware that the Prince has little reason to stay with her. Thus, both the "superior" and the "inferior" partner in an inequitable relation might feel uneasy (Walster and Walster 1978, p. 142).

Or third, the relation is doomed to failure, and it will end (Coleman 1984, Walster and Walster 1978). In dating, the end is simply a refusal to continue dating; if the couple marry before the disharmony reaches this point, the end is desertion or divorce.

Trade-offs:
Attractive Compromises

Although it seems clear that men and women tend to pair off with others who have about the same status in various important physical, psychological, and social qualities, it is also clear that this matching does not usually occur with *every* quality. Generally a person must compromise—that is, accept someone who is high in a wanted quality, though low in another. This lower-ranked trait is *traded off* for the higher.[16]

For example, a woman may find a man attractive if he has an important position in society or is wealthy, even though she may not be attracted by his physical appearance. This facet of male-female interaction is captured beautifully by P. D. James in her novel, *Unnatural Causes* (1967):

Without being the least attracted to him physically she was beginning to find him interesting, even a little intriguing. It was surprising what the possession of two hundred thousand pounds could do for a man. Already she could detect the subtle patina of success, the assurance and complacency that the possession of power or money invariably gives (p. 114).

Or suppose a man is attracted to the physical appearance of a woman but feels that she has a relatively low level of intelligence. He may accept the compromise, trading off the intelligence for the beauty. These two examples are, of course, the two most common cliches of seemingly disparate matches.

A handsome man may use his physical assets to capture a beautiful woman—*or* he may pursue a woman who is far plainer than himself, but is warmer and more dependable than he is. An aging politician who proposes marriage to a young, attractive woman may be trading his prestige and power for her beauty and youth. There is compelling evidence that men and women do engage in such complicated balancing and counterbalancing in selecting mates (Walster and Walster 1978, p. 139).

There is a low-water mark or a point below which one will not go, or course, in accepting a relatively low level in a specific trait if this trait is regarded as important. That is, no matter what other attractive qualities another might have, if a person considers that other too low in an important quality, then he or she will not find the other desirable.

As noted earlier, such trade-offs are often unconscious. A person does not usually deliberately add up the points but simply feels an emotional response based upon the combination of qualities (wanted and unwanted) that the other has.

An interesting illustration of this phenomenon of trading off one trait for another was found in the results of a research study that asked:

Who is the best-looking—you or your partner? Describe your partner's physical attractiveness by checking one of the following five choices:
1. Much more physically attractive than I
2. Slightly more physically attractive than I
3. As attractive as I
4. Slightly less attractive than I
5. Much less attractive than I

The men and women who thought that they were "more physically attractive" than their partners stated that their partners' other assets balanced things out. For example, their partners were especially loving, self-sacrificing, or wealthy. Similarly, those who regarded themselves as "less attractive" physically than their partners, felt that they themselves pos-

---

[16]Such trade-offs are not necessarily done deliberately; they may very likely be unconscious.

sessed compensating traits (Berscheid et al. 1972).

In another, quite different study, which illustrates the same trade-off theme, fifth and sixth grade preadolescent girls were rated on their physical attraction in terms of facial beauty, figure, grooming, and "sex appeal." Years later they were tracked down to find out what kind of marriage each had made. The girls who had been rated "high" in physical attraction had married men whose social positions far exceeded their own. The presumption made was that these girls had traded off physical attraction in exchange for social position (Elder 1969).

Reciprocal Interaction

In an initial attraction, the other person is not necessarily even aware of the effect he or she is having. It is obvious, however, that a relation cannot develop without *reciprocal* (mutual) interaction; that is, a man may find watching a beautiful actress night after night very rewarding, but unless they meet and relate to one another, the relation simply cannot develop.

Initial attraction can occur under either of two different circumstances: an open field or a closed field. In a *closed field* (for example, small classes or seminars, offices, or church groups) physical proximity forces the couple to interact to some extent. In an *open field*, however, the person who finds the other attractive must take the initiative, quickly making an approach (or "move") since the opportunity is temporary. The other may leave at any time or may be approached by someone else who seizes the opportunity first.

When one person approaches the other and the reciprocal interaction begins, it can take many forms—forms that have emerged from our culture as ways to develop potential paired bonds. Pairing off and bantering at a party, on a tennis court, or between classes often follow a prescribed ritual, with each person trying to probe and discover important aspects of the other, while trying to appear as attractive as possible. (In the roaring twenties, when dating was in its infancy in our society, the initial tentative probing and interaction became known as a "line.")

This is not to imply that this procedure, however stylized, is necessarily deliberate; if it is, it should not *seem* to be. In fact, the most severe test in this "ballet of love" (a series of relatively ritualized, prescribed steps) is *not* to put oneself forward too obviously, and yet to make major points that may be perceived as attractive. Often this is done with throwaway lines—"When I was hitchhiking in Greece this summer . . ."—the point of which is not the anecdote that follows, but the fact that one was in Greece at all.

Some people are very adept at this initial interaction—confident, unself-conscious, mildly self-deprecating, amusing—and these people may be observed to have attracted a large number of acquaintances, companions, and friends. Most people, however, often find relating to an attractive stranger uncomfortable, confusing, and painful, and they stumble through their initial encounters as best they can. They make some points willy-nilly but throw away just as many or more, and then anguish over what might have been said (but wasn't) or what was said (but shouldn't have been). One way or another, however, most people make it through this initial period of reciprocal interaction (although one might be haunted for years by lost opportunities and visions of what might have been if only that especially attractive person, glimpsed briefly, could have been approached).

Sometimes mutual attraction is immediate, with each person spontaneously drawn to the other. This "love at first sight" syndrome (the eros type of love discussed in Chapter 3) is exemplified by many famous passages in literature, such as that described by Shakespeare in

Romeo and Juliet. Romeo catches sight of Juliet across a crowded dance floor and is immediately smitten. He speaks to her and, even though their families are sworn enemies and Romeo has crashed the party uninvited (it is a masked ball), Juliet immediately responds, and reciprocal attraction is established (Act I, Scene V).

In other instances, the attraction is initially one-sided, and the one who is most attracted must diligently court the other, trying to provide rewards that are sufficiently attractive to bring the relation into balance. In fact, ideal reciprocity is probably rare, and most relations are somewhat unbalanced, with one person loving more and the other permitting himself or herself to be loved.

The one being "pursued" may see as a complication the presumed motivation of the pursuer. For example, if an heiress believes that she is liked "for herself" (that is, for her own personal qualities), she may respond differently than if she suspects that her pursuer's engaging behavior is designed to get his hands on her money. In other words, the very same behavior may be perceived as either charming or offensive, depending upon the suspected motivation for the behavior.

One interesting question young people often discuss is whether it is better to play "hard to get" or to frankly admit that one likes the other person. A study designed to test this question found that it makes no difference. In this study the attractive female experimenter played "hard to get" for half the male subjects, either refusing a date or accepting very reluctantly, and for the other half she accepted the date eagerly. In a series of five experiments, the same results were obtained. The men (who were subjects in the experiment) liked the "easy-to-get" woman and the "hard-to-get" woman equally well. The best answer, then, to the question, How should we behave in order to maximize the probability of attracting someone that we feel attracted to? seems to be simply to act naturally. There is apparently nothing to be gained by playing "hard to get" (Walster et al. 1973).

Anticipating the Other's Response

The degree of attraction we feel for another is modified by our anticipation that he or she will respond favorably. Thus, we might perceive someone as highly attractive, but if the person is regarded as beyond our reach, we will modify our feelings ("worshiping from afar").

For example, suppose a young woman is invited to a party and finds, when she enters the room, that she knows virtually no one there. Suppose she looks around the room and sees a very attractive young man. On a scale of 1 to 10, he clearly rates a *10* in her value system. Does she immediately move toward him, engage him in conversation, and try to win his interest? Not necessarily. For on the heels of her initial attraction comes a swift appraisal of her own chances. Suppose she regards the probability of his reciprocating as very low—perhaps 4 on a scale of 10. The *attraction quotient* is the product of two factors: the degree of attraction one feels (10 in this example) multiplied by the perceived possibility for success in beginning a relation (4). In this example, the attraction quotient would be 10 times 4, or 40. Not very high on a scale of 100. She will probably not make the approach.

The young woman looks around the room and spots another guest quietly standing by himself. He is relatively attractive—perhaps an 8. Unconsciously, she evaluates her perceived chance for reciprocation as relatively high—perhaps a 9. The attraction quotient in this case would be 8 times 9, or 72, which is relatively high on a scale of 100 and certainly higher than the attraction quotient of 40 for the first person. It could be predicted then, with relative certainty, that the woman would move toward the second man.

The Problem of Shyness

According to Zimbardo (1977) shyness is one of the most prevalent psychic syndromes in the United States. In a random survey of more than five thousand persons, Zimbardo and his colleagues found that 40 percent had been shy for most of their lives and 60 percent of these considered it a serious personal handicap. There were men and women who lived in virtual isolation, without friends, any sex life, or even the ability to look into a mirror.

Shy people are very concerned about being negatively evaluated; they regard other people as their "judges." They therefore have an excessive fear of taking social risks or venturing an approach that has an uncertain outcome. They have an excessive concern for security in relating to others. Zimbardo classifies most shy people as "dispositionally" shy—they are convinced that they suffer from some defect that makes them inferior. Others are classified as "situationally" shy—they blame their misery on outside influences.

Shyness can be conquered if one takes deliberate steps to do so. Many people who were shy as children stop being shy at some point in adulthood. The fact that shyness can be overcome is demonstrated quite graphically by the number of very successful people with high self-esteem who have had problems with shyness. For example, Barbara Walters, Carol Burnett, Lawrence Welk, and Rosey Grier have all admitted to having struggled with shyness as a serious problem in their lives.

Zimbardo found that the simple exercise of greeting everyone that you pass in your normal environment (neighborhood, school, office, and so on) brings immediate and gratifying results.* Most people being greeted in this way wish to make contact with another person, but they are themselves too shy to open up and make the initial overture.

Make an agreement with yourself to speak at least once in every class session or group that you are in, and your shyness will be gradually overcome. Very shy people can start by doing some "scary" things, such as saying hello to three strangers, and build from there, controlling their anxieties by imagining desired consequences rather than fearful ones. They can make a deliberate attempt to overcome shyness through *active listening*—assuming an attentive posture, smiling, nodding occasional approval, and looking interested. This moves one's focus of attention from oneself to the other person, and as the focus of attention shifts, shyness is lessened. Moreover, it is very flattering to be listened to in this way, and the speaker usually becomes very receptive to further acquaintance; in contrast, a person who is *not* being listened to experiences a feeling of rejection and a disinclination toward further acquaintance.

*For a further discussion of these methods, see *Shyness* by Philip G. Zimbardo (1977) of Stanford University, who has done extensive research on the subject.

If the perceived satisfaction of the initial attraction is high enough, or the limerence is strong enough, the woman may approach the first man, of course, and continue the pursuit despite little hope for success. This pattern is depicted in a novel by John Fowles, *The Collector* (also a motion picture), in which a young man, driven to desperation by unrequited love, "collected" the girl as he would a butterfly and imprisoned her in a basement room, hoping to force her to love him. Love, of course, cannot be forced, so his hopes were doomed to tragic failure.

The opposite result may occur when a person regards someone as beyond reach who is not. Pierre, for example, in Tolstoy's *War and Peace*, says (in effect) to Natasha that although he cannot imagine her accepting him, he must try since he could not bear to lose so important a prize without an attempt, however, futile. To his great delight Natasha does accept him—a long shot that paid off. (This aspect of attraction is, of course, reflected in such folk sayings as "Nothing ventured, nothing gained" and "Faint heart ne'er won fair lady.")

One's expectation for success in winning another's approval or affection is related to the problem of shyness. *Shyness* means shrinking from human contact. A person who suffers from shyness anticipates rejection and so is unable to make the initial approach.

Shy people are less likely to communicate effectively with others, since they do not present themselves in the best possible light. Shyness prevents a person from speaking up, expressing an opinion, or asking questions. Shy people lose out by not experimenting with life and by letting other people and situations control their reactions. Extreme shyness can result in loneliness, anxiety, and depression. A shy person is prevented from realizing his or her full potential and from enjoying the company of other people. (See the vignette, "The Problem of Shyness.")

Self-Esteem

The opposite of shyness is, of course, high self-esteem, but there are other differences between people with high self-esteem and those with low self-esteem. For example, the person with low self-esteem is forever alert to criticism, which he or she immediately accepts and long remembers, but feels uncomfortable with praise.

A person with high self-esteem is quick to recognize and respond to another's expression of affection, whereas a person with relatively low self-esteem regards an expression of affection with skepticism and requires continual assurance. The person with low self-esteem may even argue the point after assurances of affection and love are made:

You: "Do you love me?"

Mate: "Yes, of course I love you."

You: "Do you *really* love me?"

Mate: "Yes, I really love you."

You: "You are *sure* you love me—you are absolutely sure?

Mate: "Yes, I'm absolutely sure."

You: "Do you know the meaning of the word *love*?"

Mate: "I don't know."

You: "Then how can you be sure you love me?"

Mate: "I don't know. Perhaps I can't."

You: "You can't, eh? I see. Well, since you can't even be sure you love me, I can't really see much point in our remaining together. Can you?"

Mate: "I don't know. Perhaps not."

You: "You've been leading up to this for a pretty long time, haven't you?"

(Greenberg and Jacobs 1966)

One solution to the problem of low self-esteem is to simply role-play the behavior of a person with high self-esteem. A person who *acts* self-assured often comes to *feel* self-assured, generating such feelings by a sort of self-fulfilling prophecy. Moreover, a person who is role-playing self-assurance receives the immediate reward of getting responses from others that are normally received by people with high self-esteem (Coleman 1984).

The Dating Differential

The *dating differential* is the principle that men tend to date (and marry) "down," whereas women tend to date (and marry) "up" in regard to certain key factors such as age, height, intelligence, educational level, and social class (Landis and Landis 1977, Carter and Glick 1976).

Thus, although age is one of the homogamous factors influencing dating, courtship, and marital choice, and although most married couples are about the same age, in most dating

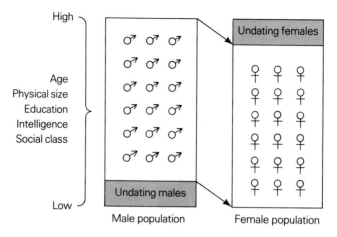

Males tend to date "down" and females to date "up" in terms of such factors as age, size, education, intelligence, and social class. This leaves a residue of undating women of relatively high status, whereas the undating men are of relatively low status. It also means that from about age twenty-five on, women have far fewer eligible men who are available for dating or marrying, whereas men who are twenty-five or older are not handicapped in this regard.

FIGURE 5-2
The dating differential

couples the woman is somewhat younger than the man, and in most marriages the wife is somewhat younger than the husband. This means that when a woman is twenty-five or over, her prospects for dating (and marrying) dwindle, because she is looking for dates in the thirty-and-over age group—a group that contains relatively few available men. In consequence of the principle of the dating differential, a woman finds that, beginning about her mid-twenties, she meets fewer eligible men each year. Moreover, most of the men she meets who *are* eligible are divorced (often with financial obligations, such as child support). As an unmarried woman reaches her early to late thirties, the dating differential makes it even less likely that she will meet an eligible prospect.

Men, however, are in a completely different position because of the demographic realities. In general, a man in his mid-twenties dates

women in their late teens or early twenties—an age range that contains a large pool of unmarried women. When a man reaches his thirties, he may still date women who are in their teens or early twenties as well as women in their late twenties—in all, a large population of eligible women.

In terms of dating possibilities, then, age has completely different meanings for women and men—a difference that has significant and far-reaching implications. For example, if a young unmarried couple decide to live together, do so for several years, and then separate, the woman is in a completely different position from the man in terms of her dating (and marrying) potential.

This phenomenon of the dating differential also helps explain why unmarried women often have relatively higher status than unmarried men of the same age. Since there are about equal numbers of young men and young women

Physical intimacies in dating are permissible in our society but not in most other societies.

Mark Antman/The Image Works

dating sexual intimacies are not strictly forbidden. In the first half of the twentieth century this usually meant simple petting. However, the 1960s saw sweeping changes in our culture. Women entered the work force in increasing numbers, college campus demonstrations erupted over the conflict in Vietman, the pill was developed, and general sexual attitudes began to change. For the first time since the Kinsey reports, researchers began to find an increase in the incidence of premarital copulation.

Changes in Sexual Behavior

The term *premarital copulation* does not necessarily mean copulation with a person whom one subsequently marries; it simply means copulation that occurs before the person is married.

Kinsey (1948) found that for men the incidence of premarital copulation was correlated with their educational level. For example, 98 percent of men with a grade school education experienced premarital copulation; among men with a high school education, the incidence was 84 percent; among men with a college education, the incidence was 42 percent.

Among women of the same generation, the incidence of premarital copulation was the same for all educational levels, but the age at which it occurred differed. About half of these women—at all educational levels—copulated before they married (each usually with only one man, her future husband). However, about one in three high school-educated women experienced premarital copulation by age twenty; among college women only one in five had experienced premarital copulation by age twenty (Kinsey et al. 1953).

By 1965, the incidence of premarital copulation among male college students had risen to 65 percent (from 42 percent in the Kinsey era) and by 1980 to 77 percent. Meanwhile, the incidence of premarital copulation among women college students under age twenty rose

in any age group, there is a residue of undating and unmarrying women from the higher-status population (in these regards) and men from the lower-status population. This paradoxical and puzzling phenomenon seems unfair, but it is based upon sound demographic principles (see Figure 5-2).

SEXUALITY IN DATING: PREMARITAL COPULATION

As we have seen, one of the major differences between dating and earlier methods of courtship and marital choice in our society is that in

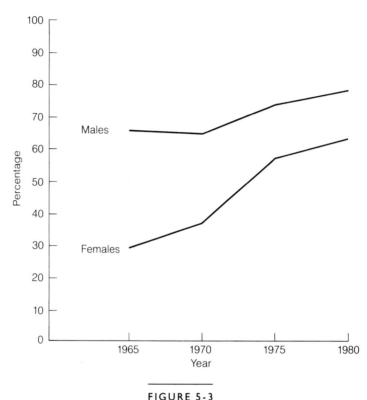

FIGURE 5-3

Incidence of premarital copulation among college
students, 1965–1980

Source: Data from Robinson and Jedlicka (1982, p. 239).

from about 19 percent (one in five) in the Kinsey era to 29 percent in 1967, and by 1980 it had reached 64 percent (Robinson and Jedlicka 1982). (See Figure 5-3). The incidence of premarital copulation among college women age twenty or older rose from Kinsey's 50 percent to 69 percent for those under age twenty-two and to 83 percent for those twenty-two years old or older in 1978 (see Figure 5-4).

College women of all age groups experienced a higher incidence of copulation while engaged than they did while going steady, and a higher incidence while going steady than in casual dating. However, the incidence of premarital copulation rose significantly in all three of these categories during the 1960s and 1970s. For example, in 1958 only 10 percent of

college women experienced premarital copulation on a casual date, as compared with 50 percent in 1978. Among women going steady, the incidence rose from 15 percent to 67 percent, and among those engaged, the incidence rose from 31 percent to 76 percent (see Figure 5-5).

Young college women were also becoming more liberal in their petting techniques during these two decades. For example, in a study in 1980 that asked whether they had participated in oral-genital activities (cunnilingus or fellatio) 74 percent said they had done so while engaged, 63 percent while going steady, and 42 percent in casual dating (Bell and Coughey 1980). (See the vignette, "Changes in Sexual Norms Since the Mid-1960s.")

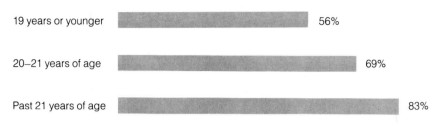

*A *cohort* is a demographic term meaning an age group that does the same thing at the same time, such as being born, dying, getting married, getting divorced, or experiencing premarital copulation.

FIGURE 5-4

Incidence of premarital copulation among college women by age cohorts, 1978

Source: Data from Bell and Coughey (1980, p. 356).

Changes in Sexual Attitudes in the 1980s

Although all studies find that the incidence of premarital copulation increased during the 1960s and 1970s among both male and female college students, sexual attitudes were becoming more conservative as the 1980s began. For example, the incidence of college women who regarded premarital copulation as immoral dropped from 70 percent in 1965 to 21 percent in 1975, but rose to 25 percent in 1980 (Robinson and Jedlicka 1982).

Although there was no corresponding rise among the number of men students regarding premarital sexual copulation as immoral, both men and women in 1980 expressed more conservative attitudes regarding the number of different partners than they had in the mid-1970s. For example, in 1965, 91 percent of women college students felt that a woman who had copulated with a great number of partners was immoral. This figure dropped to 41 percent in 1975 but rose to 50 percent in 1980 (Robinson and Jedlicka 1982). Meanwhile, the incidence of men agreeing with the statement that a woman who had copulated with a great number of partners was immoral was 42 percent in 1965, dropped to 28 percent in

1975, and rose to 42 percent in 1980—the same percentage who thought this was immoral in 1965 (see Figure 5-6).

It will be interesting to see whether future studies find this conservatism a continuing trend and whether this will then be accompanied by a drop or a leveling off in the incidence of premarital copulation (Robinson and Jedlicka 1982).

Meanwhile, in the late 1970s, a study of women of every educational level (not just college students) asked married women of different age groups whether they had experienced copulation before their marriage. Ninety-six percent of those under age twenty said that they had. Of those age twenty-two to twenty-four, 91 percent said that they had (Tavris and Sadd 1977). This incidence is almost double Kinsey's figure of 50 percent for all women a generation earlier, in the 1950s.

Premarital Copulation before Age Sixteen

One of the most interesting findings of the Tavris and Sadd (1977) study was that age *sixteen* seemed to be a magic number in terms of premarital copulation. Girls who had copulated

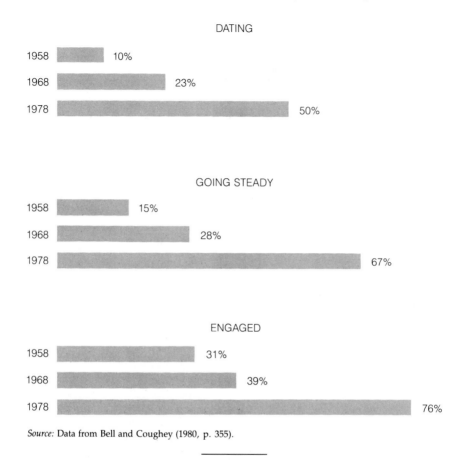

FIGURE 5-5

Incidence of premarital copulation
among college women by dating category,
1958, 1968, and 1978
Source: Data from Bell and Coughey (1980, p. 355).

before that age were significantly different in their subsequent sexual experiences than other girls. For example, 32 percent of girls who copulated before age sixteen did so with more than six different men before marriage, compared with 8 percent of women who did not experience premarital copulation until age sixteen or later.

There was no such difference in the sexual histories of women who experienced premarital copulation for the first time at age sixteen versus age eighteen, twenty, or twenty-five.

The girls who experienced premarital copulation before age sixteen seemed to fall into a different category. They were much more likely to have extramarital affairs and be unhappier in their marriages—with a higher divorce rate (Tavris and Sadd 1977).

Premarital Copulation and Marriage

Do girls who experience premarital copulation have happier marriages, or unhappier marriages, than girls who do not? Does sexual ex-

Changes in Sexual Norms Since the Mid-1960s

The changes that have taken place in sexual attitudes and behavior in our society since the mid-1960s are related to many social and psychological factors. For example, the women's movement during this period was rebelling not only against social, political, and economic discrimination against women, but also against the double standard of sexual behavior.

Abortion was illegal, expensive, and usually a serious medical risk during the 1960s. In 1973 it became legal nationwide (following a U. S. Supreme Court decision) and virtually risk-free medically. Prior to this time, young women often resorted to suicide rather than face an abortion or an unwanted pregnancy.

In the early 1960s women students in colleges and universities were under the strict control of campus authorities. Women were required to live in campus housing facilities, where they were subject to a strict curfew. This practice was gradually relaxed and by the 1980s college women had obtained virtually complete freedom from such supervision and control.

Birth control devices (especially the contraceptive pill, vasectomy, and salpingectomy) became both accessible and culturally acceptable during the 1960s and 1970s. Certainly the social changes regarding premarital copulation and cohabitation could not have taken place without these technological developments (and their cultural acceptance) that, for the first time in human history, separated the reproductive aspect of sexual intimacy from its pleasurable and recreational aspects. The phenomenon of a young couple living together without being married was virtually unknown before the 1960s but became increasingly acceptable in the 1970s and commonplace by the 1980s.

The social and psychological changes in expectation, attitude, and behavior regarding sexual interaction were reflected increasingly in entertainment media. Song lyrics prior to the 1960s were highly romantic, celebrating such experiences as "Moonlight and Roses" and "Tea for Two." Reference to copulation was nonexistent. By the late 1960s this had changed, and song lyrics, Broadway plays and musicals, and motion pictures became frankly sexual. By the mid-1970s, films such as *Behind the Green Door* and *Deep Throat*, which graphically portrayed all manner of sexual activity (fellatio, cunnilingus, various copulative positions, with close-up shots of the penis ejaculating), were shown in first-run theaters and reviewed seriously in national publications. Nightclub performers changed from "pasties" that covered the nipples and a G-string in the early 1960s to nudity above the waist in the mid-1970s. (In some cities the copulation in the nightclub act was not simulated but was genuine, and in other cities it included audience participation.) These changes in the various entertainment media clearly reflected changing social patterns and a new consciousness.

---

perience before marriage help resolve the problems beforehand or create new problems? Do the girls who copulate before marriage have a different personality structure than the other girls, and does this different personality structure translate into either a better or a worse sex life after marriage, and a happier or an unhappier marriage? The answers to these questions, according to the Tavris and Sadd (1977) study, is that premarital copulation has *no* effect, either way, on a subsequent marriage (with the exception of the girls who copulate before age sixteen).

This means that for every woman who feels benefited by copulating before marriage another does not. It means that of all the many factors that go into a good marriage and a good sex life, premarital sex is not one of them. It means that some women have perfectly happy marriages although they were virgins on their wedding day, and that others are perfectly happy to have experimented to their heart's and body's content (pp. 53–54).

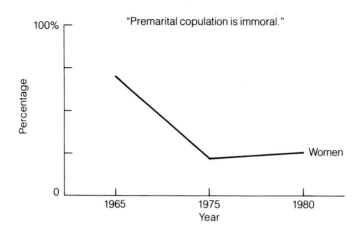

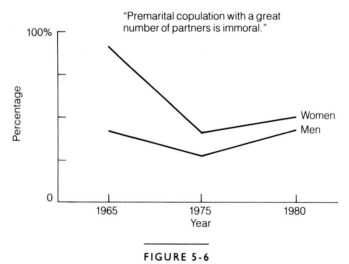

FIGURE 5-6

A growing conservatism among college students

Source: Data from Robinson and Jedlicka (1982).

Premarital Copulation, Love, and Affection

Another finding of the Tavris and Sadd (1977) study was that women are more likely to experience orgasm when copulating with those whom they love; women who copulated more casually were the least likely to reach orgasm. For example, among women who had many encounters with many different men, only 33 percent usually reached orgasm, whereas 87 percent of the women who each had only one lover reached orgasm most of the time.

Another significant finding of the study was that only a relatively small number (7 percent) of women had experienced casual premarital copulation with several men ("one-night stands"). Apparently, despite the dramatic rise in the incidence of premarital copulation, for most American women sexual intimacy is still associated with trust, affection, and love (Tavris and Sadd 1977).

Deterrents to Premarital Copulation

A generation ago, Kinsey (1953) found that the strength of religious conviction was the single most important deterrent to premarital copulation among women. A more recent study (Tavris and Sadd 1977) found that this still held true—89 percent of "nonreligious wives" had experienced premarital copulation as compared with 61 percent of "strongly religious wives." By 1977, however, the "most religious" women in the study were just as likely to have experienced premarital copulation as were the Kinsey study's "least religious" women of the prior generation.

A generation ago, Kinsey (1953) also found that level of education was the second most important deterrent to premarital copulation, and more recent studies find that this is still the case. For example, a 1977 study found that 98 percent of married women with only a grade school education had copulated before marriage, as compared with 75 percent of married women who had postgraduate degrees (Tavris and Sadd 1977).

SUMMARY

Marital choice is based on either parental arrangement or mutual attraction. In either method, husband or wife is selected from a field of eligibles that is defined by the opposing cultural forces of endogamy and exogamy.

Marital choice by parental arrangement, which usually occurs in societies with strong family structure, relies on reason rather than emotion. Economic factors, health, education, personal habits, and family name are the governing factors, rather than the couple's romantic attraction. The marriage results from negotiations between the family of the bride and the family of the groom.

Contemporary patterns of courtship and marital choice in the United States stem from three basic cultural heritages: the Mediterranean legacy, the Nordic legacy, and the Amerafrican legacy. The Mediterranean legacy emphasizes a double standard of inequality of the sexes and places great importance upon the virgin bride. The Nordic legacy emphasizes betrothal, which marks the beginning of an established paired bond between two young people and legitimizes their sociosexual interaction. Betrothal is expected to be followed by marriage if the young woman becomes pregnant. The Amerafrican legacy stems from the slave culture in the eighteenth and nineteenth centuries, when slaves had no legal right to marry. If the female slave became pregnant, she did not have the right to keep her child, although the master could bestow these privileges if he wished. The young slave mother was sent to her assigned work while her baby was cared for chiefly by the infirm and the elderly of the grandparental generation. Some 40 percent of contemporary black families are single-parent families headed by women, and more than half of black children are reared in such single-parent families.

Our society is characterized by marital choice by mutual attraction, rather than by parental arrangement. Since the 1920s, dating has been the accepted method of courtship and choosing marital partners. Dating fulfills several very important functions: (1) It provides entry into the adult pattern of sociosexual relations; (2) it provides experience in adult sociosexual role interaction and the development of social skills; (3) it serves other needs for personality development; and (4) it provides a succession of other-gender partners from which a marital choice may be made. The ritualized pattern of dating behavior is precise and specific, although it varies markedly from class to class.

Even though romantic elements are very important in dating, attraction usually occurs between people who are similar in terms of social class, intelligence, and age, and are members of the same race and the same religion. An individual is also usually attracted to someone who provides rewards or significant satisfactions, who is warm, responsive, affectionate, respectful, and noncritical. Much of this language of attraction is nonverbal and is communicated by such factors as the stance and attitude of the body, the frequency and duration of eye contact, and pupillary size. (If someone likes us, his or her pupils are relatively large, and we unconsciously interpret this as being liked, and we like the person in return.) A person who likes another will permit that other to enter the private space bubble; otherwise, the zone from about eighteen inches to four feet cannot usually be penetrated without arousing apprehension or hostility. Attempting to penetrate the eighteen-inch bubble too soon can cause alarm, resentment, or uneasiness and drive the person away.

People generally like others of about equivalent status but will accept a low-status characteristic if it is balanced by a relatively high-status factor. Whether a person likes another person or not is also influenced by the associated circumstances; if the surroundings are pleasant, the couple are more likely to like one another. People with relatively high self-esteem are quicker to recognize and respond to others' expressions of affection, whereas those with relatively low self-esteem respond more slowly.

Dating differs from all prior sociosexual behavior between adolescents and young adults in that the couple are not necessarily formally introduced, there is no chaperone, there is no commitment on the part of the couple to continue the relation, the event of the date is planned by the young couple themselves, and physical intimacies are not necessarily forbidden (the degree of intimacy varies widely, of course, from the most casual gestures of friendship to copulation). The incidence of premarital copulation remained relatively constant from the 1920s through the 1950s but then rose dramatically during the 1960s and 1970s to level off in the 1980s, when a growing conservatism was detected among college students in regard to premarital copulation. There is apparently no correlation between premarital copulation and marital satisfaction, except for girls who copulate before age sixteen—this group appears to have more sexual partners and a higher divorce rate than girls who wait even a year longer.

QUESTIONS

1. Most societies throughout history have emphasized the importance of parental arrangement in marital choice. What led to the emergence of dating in our society as a method of making marital choice?

2. What is meant by the Mediterranean legacy as a pattern of pair bonding? By the Nordic legacy? By the Amerafrican legacy?

3. How does dating differ from earlier methods of marital choice?

4. How would you define a *date*?

5. What are the social class differences in dating? Discuss the characteristics of dating in the upper class, the middle class, and the lower class.

6. What is the field of eligibles? Define *exogamy*, *endogamy*, *homogamy*.

7. What are the main homogamous factors in determining the field of eligibles in our society?

8. What is meant by propinquity? Give an example of the surprising effect of propinquity on the formation of friendships.

9. What is meant by body language? Give several examples. How are the pupils of the eyes involved in body language?

10. Discuss the effect of associated circumstances on the attraction one person feels for another.

11. What is meant by trade-offs in the attraction one person feels for another?

12. How does one's expectation for success in winning the other influence the degree of attraction felt for that person?

13. What is the dating differential? What is the significance of the dating differential in the actual experience of young women in our society?

14. How important is the problem of shyness in relating to another person? What can be done to help control shyness?

15. Discuss the reasons for the rise in the incidence of premarital copulation during the 1960s and 1970s.

SUGGESTIONS FOR FURTHER READING

Hendrick, Clyde, and Hendrick, Susan. *Liking, Loving, and Relating.* Monterey, Calif.: Brooks/Cole, 1983.

Kammeyer, Kenneth C. W. *Confronting the Issues: Marriage, the Family, and Sex Roles,* 2nd ed. Boston: Allyn & Bacon, 1981.

Kelley, Harold H., et al. *Close Relationships.* New York: W. H. Freeman, 1983.

Kett, Joseph F. *Rites of Passage: Adolescence in America—1790 to the Present.* New York: Basic Books, 1977.

Millar, Dan P., and Millar, Frank E. *Messages and Myths: Understanding Personal Communications.* Port Washington, N. Y.: Alfred A. Knopf, 1976.

Modell, John. "Dating Becomes the Way of American Youth." In *Essays on the Family and Historical Change,* ed. Leslie Page Moch and Gary D. Stark. College Station, Tex.: Texas A & M University Press, 1983.

Murstein, Bernard I. *Theories of Attraction and Love.* New York: Springer, 1971.

Rubin, Lillian B. *Intimate Strangers: Men and Women Together.* New York: Harper & Row, 1983.

Rubin, Zick. *Liking and Loving.* New York: Holt, Rinehart & Winston, 1973.

Ryan, Mary P. *Womanhood in America from Colonial Times to the Present,* 2nd ed. New York: New Viewpoints, 1979.

Zimbardo, Philip. *Shyness: What It Is, What to Do about It.* Reading, Mass.: Addison-Wesley, 1977.

C H A P T E R   6

Singlehood: A Prelude to Marriage

The Rising Number of Single Adults
Categories of Singles
Life-styles of Singles
Cohabitation

Come live with me and be my Love . . .

Marlowe (The Passionate Shepherd
to His Love)

We all start adult life as singles. It is during this stage of singlehood that we learn the meaning of romantic attraction, love, and (for many of us) limerence. Most of us date, court, and select a person to marry. Many cling to singlehood by living with a person for a time without marrying. Many return to singlehood after marriage (about one-half of all current marriages seem to be ending in divorce).[1] Finally, half of those who do remain married throughout their lives return to singlehood upon the other's death and thus end adult life

as they began it. In this chapter we shall explore the various ramifications of singlehood and its meaning for the person.

THE RISING NUMBER
OF SINGLE ADULTS

Singles make up a surprisingly large, and growing, segment of our population. In all age

---

[1] The ratio of divorces to marriages is now about one to two. Demographers disagree about how to interpret this ratio, however, since those divorcing in any one year are not the same people as those marrying. For a discussion of the various ways of estimating the ratio of current marriages ending in divorce, see Chapter 8.

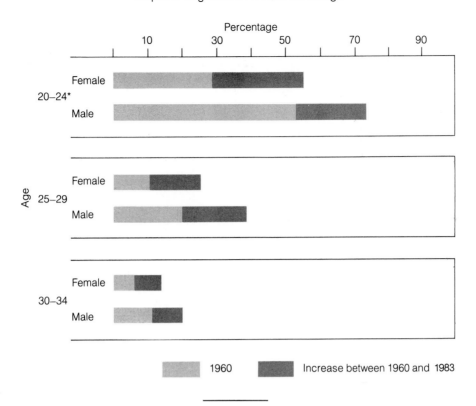

FIGURE 6-1

Increase in the incidence of never-married singles, by
age and sex, 1960–1983

Sources: Data from U.S. Bureau of the Census, "Marital Status
and Living Arrangements, 1977–1980" and "Households and
Families by Type, March 1978" (1980), "Percent Married and
Divorced of the Population, 18 Years and Over:
1960–1983" (1985).

groups, at any given time, more than one-third of all adults in our society are single.[2] Between the ages of twenty and twenty-four, this incidence of singlehood is more than twice that of the married population: In this age group, more than half (57 percent) of young women and more than two-thirds (73 percent) of young men are single (see Table 6-1).

The number of singles in our society has been rising sharply during the past two decades, chiefly because of the rapid growth in the incidence of never-married singles. This rising incidence of never-married singles has been one of the most significant recent changes in life-styles in our society. For example, the proportion of never-married singles among young women age twenty to twenty-four doubled in the two decades from 1960 to 1982, rising from 28 percent to 57 percent. Meanwhile, the proportion of never-married men in this age group rose from 53 percent to 73 percent (see Figure 6-1).[3]

[2]Thirty-three percent of men and 38 percent of women were single in 1982 (see Table 6-1).

[3]U.S. Bureau of the Census, "Marital Status and Living Arrangements" (1984).

TABLE 6-1

Marital status of the U.S. population, age eighteen and over, by sex and age, 1982

MEN

Marital status	Total population (18 & over)	Percentage of total population	18–19	20–24	25–29	30–34	35–39	40–44	45–54	55–64	65 & over
Married	52,543,000	67.2	5.0	26.7	57.9	73.4		81.5	84.9	86.5	77.5
Single	25,590,000	32.8	95.0	73.3	42.1	26.6		18.5	15.1	13.5	22.5
Never married	19,125,000	24.5	94.9	72.0	36.1	17.3	10.0	7.4	5.4	4.6	4.4
Separated[a]											
Divorced	4,605,000	5.9	0.1	1.3	6.0	9.2		9.4	8.2	5.4	3.0
Widowed	1,860,000	2.4	0.0	0.0	0.0	0.1		0.3	1.5	3.5	15.1

[a]In 1982, 3% of men 25–54 years of age were separated.

WOMEN

Marital status	Total population (18 & over)	Percentage of total population	18–19	20–24	25–29	30–34	35–44	45–54	55–64	65 & over
Married	53,625,000	61.9	14.4	42.9	67.4	75.6	79.4	78.5	70.8	37.5
Single	32,952,000	38.1	85.6	57.1	32.6	24.4	20.6	21.5	29.2	62.5
Never married	15,262,000	17.6	84.9	53.4	23.4	11.6	5.6	4.1	4.2	5.7
Separated[b]										
Divorced	6,895,000	8.0	0.7	3.6	8.7	12.1	12.6	10.6	7.7	3.4
Widowed	10,795,000	12.5	0.0	0.1	0.5	0.7	2.4	6.8	17.3	53.4

[b]In 1982, 4.9% of women 25–54 years of age were separated.

Source: Data from U.S. Bureau of the Census, "Marital Status and Living Arrangements" (1984).

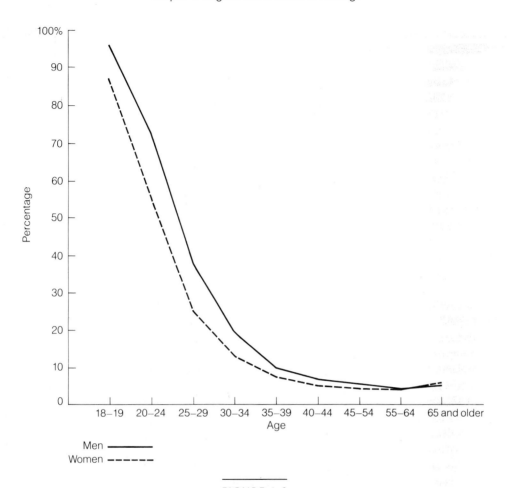

FIGURE 6-2

Incidence of never-married singles in the adult population,
by age and sex, 1983

Source: Data from U.S. Bureau of the Census, "Percent
Married and Divorced of the Population, 18 Years and Over:
1960–1983" (1985).

It is important to note, however, that the rising number of never-married singles does not mean that fewer people are marrying. What is happening is that increasing numbers of young adults are *delaying* their first marriage—usually until their late twenties or early thirties. All but 13 percent of women and 20 percent of men were married by their early thirties, for example, in 1983. Among those who have not yet married by their mid-thirties, two-thirds of the men and about one-half of the women will ultimately marry. Only about 5 percent of our population remain never-married singles throughout their lives (see Figure 6-2).

Growing numbers of young women are delaying their first marriage for various reasons, but the most significant is probably their changing status. With significant numbers of young unmarried women entering the work world, many options for a single life-style are open to them that were not available to prior generations. These young women form a new social class heretofore unknown in human experience—a class of women with the freedom and the opportunities previously reserved solely for *male* unmarried persons, or bachelors.

This phenomenon of young unmarried women experiencing economic and social independence has developed so recently and so swiftly that our language has not yet caught up with the social reality, and we have no word to describe them.[4] *Bachelorette* has sexist overtones (a minibachelor?), and *female bachelor* is a contradiction in terms.[5] The term *spinster* (which originated in the twelfth century and then meant a woman who was earning her living using a spinning wheel) is archaic, as is *old maid*; both terms also usually refer to older women and are not appropriate for young, unmarried women.

Accompanying this rapid increase in the number of economically and socially independent young women has been a change in the general attitude toward marriage. For example, in 1969 only about 3 percent of first-year college women did not expect to marry; three years later, for the women as seniors, this figure had nearly tripled to 8 percent, and fully 40 percent thought it quite possible that they would not marry (Stein 1976). In a national survey conducted in 1971, 32 percent of women college students said they were not sure they wanted the life-style of marriage and were not looking forward to being married (Yankelovich 1972).

In addition, an increasing number of women are enrolling in college. Indeed, for the first time, the percentage of women enrolled in four-year colleges is virtually identical to the percentage of men. Meanwhile, the proportion of women enrolled in traditionally male vocational courses increased dramatically in 1982, when more women than men were enrolled in agriculture and forestry, and an equal number were enrolled in business and commerce.[6]

When women go to college, they marry later for two reasons. First, they tend to delay marriage while they are still in school. Second, they tend to delay marriage after graduation because their education has equipped them to compete for well-paying, interesting jobs. Women in such jobs usually delay marriage longer and have a lower marriage rate than other women. Studies find, for example, that about one in five women with some graduate school education is not married, compared with only one in twenty of the same age group with no college education (Carter and Glick 1976).

Researchers find that, in addition to these changes in the life-styles, attitudes, and educational opportunities of young women, many young adults—men and women alike—are postponing marriage because they think this will increase the likelihood that they may fulfill more of their potential for individual development. As singles, they are not confined by the responsibilities of marriage, nor must they limit their experiences of close companionship and sexual intimacy to one person (Gagnon and Greenblat 1978, Duberman 1977, Glick 1975, Stein 1975).

Finally, demographers point to the effect of the "baby boom" that reached its peak in the mid-1950s. Because women tend to marry men

---

[4]The emergence of socially and economically independent young women did not happen overnight, of course. For a fascinating study of this development see "Blessed or Not? The New Spinster in England and the United States in the Late Nineteenth and Early Twentieth Century" by Ruth Freeman and Patricia Klaus (1984).

By definition, a *bachelor* is an unmarried man. (In feudal times, the term meant a young knight in the service of another knight.)

---

[6]U.S. Bureau of the Census, "College Enrollment of Persons 18–24 Years Old, and Percent of High School Graduates Enrolled in College by Sex and Race: 1960–1982" (1984).

who are two, three, or more years older, women born during the baby boom years reached their average age for marriage a few years before men born at the same time. Thus, in the 1970s, these women were looking for marriage partners among fewer men (those born before the baby boom years). Another reason for the growing number of singles, then, is simply the demographic reality of the excess of young women of marriageable age compared with men. (This phenomenon has been termed the "marriage squeeze" by demographers.)

In addition to rising numbers in the category of never-married singles, the number of singles in other categories is also rising—that is, singles who are divorced and singles who are widowed. The incidence of divorce has been increasing since 1960 and has more than doubled from 1970 to 1980; the interval between divorce and remarriage has been lengthening; and the incidence of divorced people who do not remarry has been increasing. All these factors have contributed to the increase in the number of divorced singles.[7]

The reason for the rise in the number of singles who are widows may be traced to the increasing life expectancy of women, who now outlive men by about seven years.[8] Thus the average wife in the United States (who is about four years younger than her husband) can (demographically) expect to spend her last eleven years as a widow.[9]

For a summary of the number of singles in the United States by sex and by category (never-married, separated, divorced, and widowed) see Table 6-1.

[7]U.S. National Center for Health Statistics. *Vital Statistics of the United States*, (1980, 1983, and 1984), "Marriages and Divorces: 1950 to 1980" (1984).
[8]In 1982, females in the United States could expect to live an average of 78.2 years, compared with 70.9 years for men (U.S. National Center for Health Statistics, U.S. Life Tables and Actuarial Tables, 1985).
[9]U.S. National Center for Health Statistics, U.S. Life Tables and Actuarial Tables (1985).

TABLE 6-2

Categories of singlehood

	Voluntary	*Involuntary*
Temporary	Never-marrieds and formerly marrieds who are not actively seeking spouses but who are not opposed to the idea of marriage.	Never-marrieds and formerly marrieds who are actively dating and seeking spouses but have not yet found one.
Stable	Never-marrieds and formerly marrieds who are choosing to remain single. They may oppose the idea of marriage, or they may have taken vows with a religious order.	Never-marrieds and formerly marrieds who wish to marry but have given up on the possibility and accepted singlehood as a probable life state.

Source: From *Single Life: Unmarried Adults in a Social Context* by Peter Stein. Copyright © 1981 by St. Martin's Press and used by permission of the publisher.

CATEGORIES OF SINGLES

A person may be single for a variety of reasons. He or she may be voluntarily single, either temporarily or permanently, or involuntarily single, either temporarily or permanently. These four categories of singlehood are summarized in Table 6-2.

Voluntary Temporary Singles

Among the *voluntary temporary* singles are those who are postponing marriage or remarriage because other activities such as education, career, or politics have a higher priority. This category of voluntary temporary singles also includes people who are cohabiting—living together without being married—but who expect eventually to marry either one another or someone else.

Voluntary Stable Singles

The *voluntary stable* singles include those who have never married and are satisfied with the state of singlehood; those who have been married but do not intend to remarry; cohabitors who do not intend to marry; and single parents, both never married and formerly married, who are not seeking spouses but who are raising their children alone or with the help of relatives or friends. Finally, the voluntary stable group also includes those for whom religious orders preclude the possibility of marriage, such as nuns, priests, and monks. (Even lay members of religious groups are often urged to take vows of chastity and remain unmarried.)

Involuntary Temporary Singles

The *involuntary temporary* singles would like to be married and expect to marry within a relatively short time. They include younger never-marrieds who do not want to be single much longer and are each actively dating in search of a spouse. The category also includes older men and women who have postponed the idea of marriage for some time but are now actively engaged in dating and searching for suitable marriage prospects.

The group of involuntary temporary singles also includes the widowed and the divorced who are seeking remarriage. It also includes single parents (either never married, divorced, or widowed) who are actively seeking suitable marriage prospects.

In short, all the men and women who are involuntary temporary singles approve of the concept of marriage and would like to be married. This is an important difference between those who are voluntarily single and those who are involuntarily single.

Involuntary Stable Singles

Involuntary stable singles consist primarily of older never-married people who wish to marry but probably never will, and of older divorced or widowed people who have come to accept singlehood as a situation that probably will not change. However, some of the involuntary stable singles are those who are unsuccessful in their pursuit of a husband or wife because of physical, psychological, or social characteristics that make them either unmarriageable or only marginally marriageable.

LIFE-STYLES OF SINGLES

Within these four categories of singles there are as many diverse life-styles as among those who are married. There is certainly no one life-style or personality type that is characteristic of singles. Many factors contribute to the diversity of life-styles among all categories of singles: amount of education, amount of income, source of income, interests, abilities, skills, religious conviction, philosophy of life, geographic area, and age.

There are, however, certain aspects of singlehood that are characteristic of most singles. Singles tend to drift from small towns to large cities; they tend to spend more of their time searching for companionship and intimacy than the married person does; and they tend, more than married persons, to be subjected to certain psychological and physical pressures.

Drifting of Singles into Cities

Most never-married singles, and many who are separated or divorced and live alone (rather than with relatives), tend to move from small towns to medium-sized cities, and from there to large cities and even certain areas of these cities. Their apartments are usually furnished with thrift-store castoffs, and expenses are often shared with roommates (Carter and Glick 1976). A current trend is for singles to move out of their apartments and join the ranks

Frank Siteman/Stock, Boston

There are as many diverse life-styles among singles as there are among those who are married. No one life-style or personality type characterizes singles.

of homeowners; it is estimated that in the late 1970s, in some areas, more than one-fourth of home buyers were single (Wirth 1979).

Singles move from small towns to large metropolitan areas for several reasons. The most obvious is that they want to be near others who are like themselves in interests and life-styles, so that the possibility of meeting congenial companions, making friends, and falling in love is maximized. Socializing in small towns usually takes place in private homes, dominated by married couples. Moreover, there are more things to do and more intellectual stimulation in a city—more social activities, music, drama, ballet, night classes, and so on—than in a small town, where softball games and bowling might be the hub of leisure activities (Jacoby 1975, Starr and Carns 1972).

Finding Companionship

One of the greatest problems for singles, especially those living alone, is to develop and maintain significant friendships. One's self-concept depends largely on the responses of friends, and people who have only secondary relations with others may feel anonymous and fragmented, as we have seen in Chapter 1. Social supports, then, or friendship networks, are a major source of emotional support and satisfaction for singles. Close, caring friendships with people of both genders can provide social continuity and the basic satisfactions of sharing. For some single people friendships may mean emotional survival—not only during difficult times but during trouble-free times as well (Stein 1981).

A recent survey of single men and women in thirty-six states found that the best aspect of being single was freedom, and the worst aspect was loneliness. Only one-third of the single men in the study and one-fifth of the single women liked or desired the single life. The rest regarded it as a waiting period—a special, limited time to do things they'd never done, or a time to look for a husband or wife (Simenauer and Carroll 1982).

Finding Sexual Satisfaction

Although some singles choose celibacy (as a flight from intimacy, as a moral conviction, or as a religious requirement), other singles prefer casual sexuality (thought few may be successful in exemplifying the image of "swinging singles"). However, most singles are more likely to regard copulation as an aspect of caring, an experience that includes affection and love as well as physical pleasure (Tavris and Sadd 1977, Hunt 1974).

Although there has been a dramatic increase in the incidence of premarital copulation since the late 1960s, this does not mean that recreational sex is widespread among singles (Lews and Schwartz 1977; Gordon 1976; Hunt 1974). Hunt concludes, for example, in his systematic survey of sex and single people, that, contrary to the stereotype, "easy sex" is usually not available and that most singles become sexually involved only in an atmosphere of emotional closeness, trust, and caring. He concludes:

The new sexual freedom operates largely within the framework of our long-held cherished cultural values of intimacy and love. Even while it asserts its freedom from marriage, it is an apprenticeship for marriage, and is considered successful by its participants when it grows, deepens, and leads to ever-stronger commitment, and unsuccessful and wasted effort when it does not (Hunt 1974, p. 154).

Many singles believe that it is not possible to truly love more than one person at a time. They

One of the greatest problems for singles is finding companionship.

Erika Stone/Peter Arnold, Inc.

regard sexual intimacy as a means to further communication and as an expression of love, affection, and emotional closeness.

Those singles who adhere to the Judeo-Christian precept of monogamy may move gradually into marriage through the intermediate stop of cohabitation, which implies permanence. For these singles, cohabitation is more than simply a convenient living arrangement; it provides affection, emotional support, and sexual satisfaction. There are, however, different categories of *cohabitors*, as we shall see later in this chapter.

Des Moines Art Center, James D. Edmundson Fund, 1958

Edward Hopper, *Automat*, 1927

Singlehood and Loneliness

Loneliness has been described as a driving force great enough to cause even extremely shy people who suffer severe anxiety to seek social activity. This means that "loneliness is itself more terrible than anxiety" (Sullivan 1953, p. 262). Fromm-Reichmann (1959) noted that loneliness is "such a painful frightening experience that people will do practically anything to avoid it" (p. 1). The lonely person is "tense, restless, unable to concentrate, and driven" (Weiss 1981, p. 153).

The dominant symptom of loneliness is a feeling of boredom or aimlessness. Boredom seems to develop as the tasks that make up one's daily routine lose their meaning and begin to be simply busy work. The day's duties then seem to be a burdensome ritual that one can hardly persuade oneself to perform. There is restlessness and difficulty in concentrating, which prevent the person from becoming absorbed in such distractions as reading, listening to music, or watching television. The lonely person may feel compelled to leave the house and move among people, into the vicinity of sociable warmth or activities (Stein 1981).

Once loneliness is past, the person tends to block it from memory. Having repressed the personal experiences of loneliness, the individual finds it easy to be critical of loneliness in others. Surely (one might argue) it is simple enough to avoid loneliness. All that is necessary is to be pleasant, outgoing, and interested in others rather than oneself. Lonely people, so the argument goes, must therefore find a perverse gratification in loneliness.

Perhaps loneliness, despite its pain, permits (the lonely) to continue a self-protective isolation or provides them with an emotional handicap that forces handouts of pity from those with whom they interact. . . . The lonely are people who move against others or away from others and of course they then feel bad because they are alone. Along these lines, advice for the lonely would seem obvious; be pleasant, outgoing, interested in others, meet people; become part of things (Stein 1981, 154).

For those who are suffering from loneliness, however, advice of this sort seems to miss the point. No matter how much those who are lonely would like to shake it off, no matter how they may berate themselves for permitting it to overcome them, they find themselves possessed by the loneliness, with a sense of desolation remaining as an affliction to the spirit.

One reason for this melancholy persistence of loneliness is that it will not yield to just any sort of interaction with others. Only those who are not lonely suppose that loneliness can be cured merely by ending *aloneness*. Loneliness is not caused simply by a lack of company, any company; rather, it may be dispelled only by a very specific form of social interaction—intimacy. In fact, random socialization may actually increase loneliness; it is quite possible for a person's excruciating loneliness to become even more poignant in the midst of others.

When loneliness does end, however, it ends abruptly—suddenly vanishing without a trace, as though it never existed. There is no gradual recovery, no getting over it bit by bit (Stein 1981).

Studies have found that loneliness is quite prevalent in the United States. In a telephone survey of a national sample, respondents were asked whether during the past week they had ever felt "very lonely" or "remote from other people." Among singles, 27 percent of the women and 23 percent of the men said that they had; among the married, 10 percent of the women and 6 percent of the men had (Maisel 1969). In another study, 28 percent of singles reported loneliness to be the leading problem of their lives (Lopata 1979).

One might expect loneliness to be espe-

cially prevalent among widowed and divorced people, and this was found to be the case. Over 50 percent of the widowed men in the telephone survey reported severe loneliness during the preceding week, as did 29 percent of the widowed women (Maisel 1969).

Hunt (1974), in his widespread review of the literature, found that newly separated singles were especially prone to the agonies of loneliness.

Of all the negative feelings of the newly separated, none is more common or more important than loneliness. Only a minority fail to suffer from it, and even those who most keenly desired the end of the marriage often find the initial loneliness excruciating (p. 125).

The telephone survey also found that those who were poor were especially likely to be lonely (Maisel 1969). The reason for this can only be surmised, but perhaps with low income there is a tendency toward social withdrawal. In addition, there are different life-styles at different income levels, and the life-styles of the poor may be more prone to social failure, and consequent loneliness.

Women on their own sometimes suppose that loneliness is a woman's affliction. They envy what they perceive as the ability of men to go out of the house to theaters or bars or sporting events without having to arrange for an escort or at least an accompanying friend. Research has found, however, that the percentage of single women who are severely lonely is not appreciably higher than the percentage of single men (Weiss 1981).

Apparently women exaggerate the importance of the traditional male prerogative to make the first move. Finding a companion, friend, or lover is no easier for men than for women. In fact, our cultural patterns make it easier after early adulthood for women to establish casual, like-gender friendships than for men to do so. It is also easier for a woman to keep casually in touch with an extended network of not-so-close friends—by telephone,

TABLE 6-3

Marital status and depression

Level of depression	Married	Never married	Divorced	Separated	Widowed
High 1	12%	20%	27%	32%	22%
2	14	18	14	25	22
3	18	23	16	23	15
4	29	24	22	10	21
Low 5	27	16	21	10	20

Source: Pearlin and Johnson (1981, p. 168). Reprinted by permission.

with lunches, or during informal get-togethers—than it is for men (Weiss 1981).

Singlehood and Depression

One of the major problems of loneliness, of course, is that it is likely to be accompanied by depression. A number of studies have found that singles, as compared with married people, are more likely to have various psychological problems such as anxiety, low self-esteem, and a chronic or pervasive lack of joy (Pearlin and Johnson 1981, Bachrach 1975, Lee 1974, Udrey 1974). Table 6-3 illustrates that single people who were formerly married have the highest level of depression, followed by never-married singles, with married people the most free of depression. Among the groups of formerly married singles, those who are sepa-

rated but not divorced are the most susceptible to depression.

As may be seen in Table 6-4 economic problems are much more likely to cause depression in single people, compared with married people. This is not surprising, since, when faced with adversity, married persons have the advantage of being able to draw emotional support as well as concrete help from their spouses. Although supportive and helping relations between people are not limited to marriage, married people are more likely to have an advantage in this regard than singles are.

Research has also found that depression is related to social isolation (see Table 6-5). The unmarried are more likely than the married to be socially isolated and to experience more depression from social isolation. Thus, the unmarried are in double jeopardy in this

TABLE 6-4

Economic strains, marital status, and depression

Level of depression	Severe economic strain		Moderate economic strain		No economic strain	
	Married	Unmarried	Married	Unmarried	Married	Unmarried
High 1	26%	50%	19%	29%	9%	15%
2	17	15	22	21	12	18
3	8	12	16	27	19	17
4	26	16	27	13	30	26
Low 5	23	7	16	10	30	24

Source: Pearlin and Johnson (1981, pp. 165–78). Reprinted by permission.

TABLE 6-5

Social isolation, marital status, and depression

Level of depression	Very isolated		Fairly isolated		Not isolated	
	Married	Unmarried	Married	Unmarried	Married	Unmarried
High 1	13%	28%	11%	24%	11%	21%
2	15	19	13	15	14	16
3	18	19	18	20	19	22
4	28	21	30	21	29	20
Low 5	26	13	28	20	27	21

Source: Pearlin and Johnson (1981, p. 172). Reprinted by permission.

regard. First, a larger proportion live in considerable isolation, and second, they are more likely to be depressed by equivalent conditions of isolation.

Among single parents, there is an especially high correlation between depression and the number of children. It can be seen clearly in Table 6-6 that as the number of children in the household increases, there is a corresponding increase in the proportion of single parents who are highly depressed. By contrast, there is a tendency in precisely the opposite direction among the married, who have a lower incidence of depression as the number of children increases. The net result of these two opposing tendencies is that the difference in depression between the single parent and the married is substantial with three or more children and still significant with one or two.

Depression is also related to physical problems (Coleman 1984). It is not surprising, then, to find that single people are not as healthy, in general, as married people. For example, divorced men, compared with married men, have almost twice as high a death rate for coronary heart disease and cancer. Moreover, compared with married men, divorced men have ten times the rate of tuberculosis; seven times the rate of cirrhosis of the liver, pneumonia, and homicide; nearly five times the rate of suicide; four times the rate of car accidents; three times the rate of hypertension; and twice the rate of lung cancer and strokes (Lynch 1977).

TABLE 6-6

Number of children at home, marital status, and depression

Level of depression	Three or more		One or two		None	
	Married	Unmarried	Married	Unmarried	Married	Unmarried
High 1	12%	34%	12%	26%	11%	20%
2	12	18	14	20	17	19
3	16	17	19	24	20	19
4	31	16	28	18	27	23
Low 5	29	15	27	12	25	19

Source: Pearlin and Johnson (1981, pp. 174). Reprinted by permission.

Finding "Purpose" or Meaning

One characteristic of singles in their late twenties or early thirties is the quest for "purpose" or meaning in their lives. Men and women alike seem to find this age a transition period and often become critical of their social networks, occupations, and living situations. They begin to reevaluate their life-styles—recognizing the possibility that they are dissatisfied, and that unless they take an active hand in bringing about significant changes, these changes will never happen (Starr and Carns 1972).

During this stage, singles often reexamine earlier vocational decisions and weigh possibilities of starting or returning to graduate or professional school. Studies have found that this shift in occupational direction is even more characteristic of women than of men. Many women have no career goals when they graduate from college, and a substantial number in their late twenties consider their occupations to be temporary, unsatisfactory, or "noninvolving." Frequently they see their living arrangements, including cohabitation, in the same critical light during this period. Often a resolution is made—and actively implemented—to start new activities, look for a new occupation, develop new interests, and meet new companions (Schwartz 1976, Starr and Carns 1972).

In the late twenties and early thirties, singlehood appears to have an ambivalent status for many people. On the one hand, it offers an appealing opportunity for freedom and lack of family responsibilities; yet, on the other hand, the cities in which most singles congregate do not encourage easy sociability. Moreover, most work settings seem to provide fewer opportunities for friendship than did the high school or college campus. Singles often look back nostalgically to their school days as a time of easy friendships and exciting future possibilities (Stein 1981).

Singlehood often prompts individuals to expand their interests, test their capabilities, and develop their independence.

© Joel Gordon

The period between ages twenty-eight and thirty-two does not always involve self-questioning and reevaluation of career goals, friendships, and living arrangements, of course. Although for many singles this time is characterized by considerable confusion, turmoil, uncertainty, and struggle with social pressures and one's family, for others the transition to the thirties is simply a time of quiet evaluation of goals and values, coupled with an intensification of effort to achieve them—with no special difficulties or conflicts (Adams 1976).

Singlehood can be a time of re-evaluation of goals and values, coupled with an intensification of effort to achieve them.

© 1981 Ellis Herwig/The Picture Cube

Discrimination against Singles

Discrimination against singles occurs in both hiring and promoting in many businesses. Married applicants and employees with similar qualifications may receive preferential treatment over divorced men and women, while the divorced often receive preference over the never-married. Discrimination of this sort is subtle and is never a stated policy (which would be illegal). However, a survey of fifty major corporations found that only 2 percent of the executives (including junior management) were single—much lower than the percentage of singles in the general population. Fully one-fourth of those with responsibility for hiring personnel stated that they believed singles are "less stable" than married people and are more likely to move to another job after having been trained, or even to leave the area, since they are not held by social networks or family ties. Loan officers in banks often regard singles as worse credit risks than married people, perhaps for much the same reasons (Jacoby 1975).

The popular stereotype that singles are deviant and irresponsible (especially after their early thirties) is often accompanied by a good deal of pressure from parents and friends to marry. Although parents generally do not want their children to marry *too* soon, once the son's or daughter's mid-twenties are past, parental pressure to marry often begins. Parents and friends may imply that the single person is unable to relate to others effectively in the social interactions that lead to courtship and marriage, or is too selfish or irresponsible for marriage, or is perhaps homosexual, impotent, or frigid. Such attitudes can, not surprisingly, create persistent pressure toward matrimony. Moreover, singles are likely to feel more and more estranged from their friends who are married. These are major themes of the popular "Mary Tyler Moore Show," in which Rhoda and Mary represent two career women in their thirties who live in neighboring apartments, are good friends, and feel a continuing pressure to justify their single status to their parents, their landlady, men they date, and just about everyone else.

Stereotypes of Singles

Married people often have distorted views of the life-styles of singles, who themselves often have distorted views of the lives of *other* singles (except those who are their close friends). Singles are often stereotyped as "swingers" who spend their days lounging about the pools in singles-only apartment complexes, their nights dancing in discotheques, their weekends skiing or surfing or ice skating, and their vacations traveling to exotic places. According to this stereotype, they have many interesting encounters with other fascinating singles, both male and female, and lead exciting social and sexual lives with a wide variety of beautiful and intriguing partners. They are often perceived as driving sports cars (instead of station wagons or family sedans), buying expensive clothing in the latest styles (instead of children's outfits), frequenting seaside resorts and tennis ranches, and, in general, experiencing a glamorous, sexy, fun-filled life-style in sharp contrast to the mundane, harried, routine, responsibility-ridden lives of the married. Although there are undoubtedly some singles who do fit this image and fulfill this stereotype, research has found that they are a very small minority. "Swinging singleness" is a life-style experienced by only a few; most people who begin an evening alone in a singles' bar (or in an encounter group) end up going home without a companion for the night.

In the opposite of the "swinging singles" stereotype, singles are often viewed as chronic losers, dining alone in unkempt (or overly tidy) apartments or in embarrassment at a table for two in a restaurant, where they immerse themselves in a paperback book while they eat— lonely, shut out, and depressed. This stereotype is equally unfounded. Although singles do have special problems of loneliness, as we have seen, they certainly have no monopoly in this regard. Moreover, studies have found that singles are just as successful as married people in all occupations, although they are often discriminated against because of the stereotypes.

COHABITATION

The Rapid Rise in Cohabitation

Our society has witnessed an astonishingly rapid change in the social acceptance of young couples simply moving in together and cohabiting. This is a very recent development. A little less than two decades ago, in 1968, a Barnard College sophomore named Lydia LeClair received nationwide attention when she was discovered living off campus with a male Columbia University student. Her battle with school authorities made the front pages of major newspapers from Maine to California, and *Time* magazine did a feature story on her.

By 1972—only four years later—an estimated 10–30 percent of unmarried college students were cohabiting, and by 1984 1,988,000 couples were cohabiting in the United States—most of whom were under 34 years of age (see Figure 6-3).

The percentage of cohabitation in each college varies in relation to such factors as whether the institution is a "commuter" college or has many resident students, the male-female student ratio, the housing regulations and supervision, the definition of *cohabitation*,[10] and research sampling methods (Macklin 1978). Some researchers have found that about half the college students who have not cohabited would like to (see Figure 6-4). That would leave only about 25 percent who have not cohabited and would not want to if they had the opportunity (Macklin 1978).

The shift toward acceptance of cohabitation must be seen as part of a slow evolution in sexual values and behavior patterns that began in the early part of the century with growing urbanization and its increasing opportunities for privacy and anonymity, and with the changing attitudes regarding freedom for women. One can trace from the early 1920s the gradually increasing non-virginity rates for women and the simultaneously increasing acceptance of sexual involvement in a love relation. By the end of the

---

[10]For example, defining *cohabitation* as "having shared a bed for four or more nights a weeks, for three or more consecutive months, with someone of the opposite sex to whom one was not married," Macklin (1974) found that 31 percent of the Cornell sample had cohabited at some time. If "sleeping together overnight or weekends had been included, the percentage would obviously have been much higher."

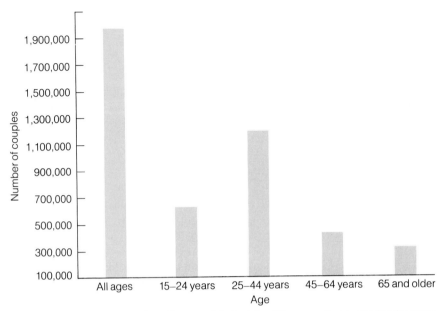

A cohabiting couple consists of two unrelated adults of the opposite sex sharing the same household.

_____

FIGURE 6-3

Number and ages of cohabiting couples in the
United States, 1984

Source: Data from U. S. Bureau of the Census, "Unmarried
Couples, by Selected Characteristics, 1970 to 1984" (1985).

1960s, sexual intercourse among college students who were going steady was a commonly approved practice. . . . One could argue that a natural extension of this was openly to accept spending the night together, and predict that couples who enjoyed being together would come to increase their numbers of nights together (Macklin 1978, p. 4).

Looking into the future, a report from Family Service America (a think tank for managers of business, government, and higher education and nonprofit groups) predicts that there will be more cohabitation, single-person households, unwed-single-parent families, and homosexual couples—that the number of single-person households will continue to rise, pushed up by young people living alone, people

separated or divorced, and spouses surviving the death of husband or wife. Just thirty years ago, 10 percent of households were classified as single-person; today, this classification applies to 25 percent (Darrow 1984).

It is interesting to note that about 28 percent of all cohabiting couples have one or more children present in the household, and, as with married couples, most cohabiting adults live with someone of the same race (Spanier 1983).

Causes for the Increase in Cohabitation

The causes for this rapidly changing social pattern in the 1970s of couples living together

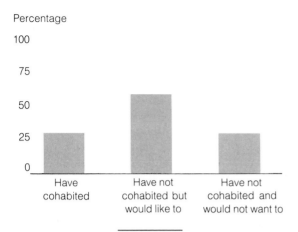

Percentage

FIGURE 6-4

Cohabitation among college students:
incidence and attitudes

Source: Data from Clayton and Voss (1977), Bower and
Christopherson (1977), Henze and Hudson (1974).

ety, received widespread medical endorsement, was hailed enthusiastically in the press, and won immediate popular acceptance.[11]

This technology made it possible for unmarried persons to participate in relations that provided security, warmth, and sexual intimacy that was formerly available primarily through marriage, and to do so without simultaneously undertaking the obligations of parenthood (Makepeace 1975, p. 28).

By the mid-1970s, cohabitation was approaching institutional status, and celebrities such as actress Catherine Deneuve ("the world's most beautiful woman") were frankly discussing their experiences as live-in cohabitors on nationally televised talk shows. As the climate of opinion regarding cohabitation gradually changed, colleges and universities began abandoning their age-old responsibility of supervising *in loco parentis* (in the place of parents) the activities of young unmarried students by enforcing lockout rules and banning men from women's rooms. By the late 1970s, virtually all such regulations had been discontinued in American colleges and universities. Indeed, student health centers were providing contraceptive pills and making available birth control information; after the U.S. Supreme Court decision in 1973 that legalized abortion, many student health services began providing abortions as well.

Campus authorities are increasingly committed to the idea that how students conduct their private lives is their own concern, and that it is not the responsibility of the college officials to serve as substitute parents in supervising the moral behavior of students. The removal of such restrictions has been accompanied by the common availability of birth

without being married are many and complex. The women's movement, which had been relatively inactive for many decades, demanded that women be granted the same rights and privileges as men, with the result that housing regulations for female students became increasingly relaxed, making it possible for large numbers of students to live off campus or to reside in dormitories without a curfew. This change in dormitory regulations made it feasible for students to cohabit, especially those who were living some distance from home. Concurrent changes in the social attitudes increased the likelihood that many would take advantage of this opportunity. These attitudinal changes included an increased acceptance of sexuality outside of marriage and of sexual activity as an expression of affection and intimacy not necessarily related to reproduction. Moreover, for the first time in human history, an effective contraceptive technique (the pill) became widely and even routinely used (see Chapter 11). The contraceptive pill, which became available in the early 1960s in our soci-

[11]The condom, which has been available since the eighteenth century, has never won popular acceptance to the extent of the pill and has usually received a rather bad press. This is ironic since the condom not only is an extremely effective contraceptive if properly used but also acts as a prophylactic, preventing venereal disease (see Chapter 4).

control information and devices, including relatively unrestricted dispensation of contraceptives by student health services (Makepeace 1975, p. 28).

Some women prefer being single—either fitting lovers into their lives without living with them and settling down together, or living with no romantic attachments at all. They may want to make a major commitment to work, or they may simply find that being single can be positive, creative, and peaceful (Doress and Wegman 1984).

The Various Meanings of Cohabitation

Living together without being married can have many meanings, of course, and at least five types of cohabitation may be specified:

1. A temporary casual convenience, with a couple sharing the same living quarters because of simple expediency
2. An affectionate relation based on mutual enjoyment that will continue so long as both prefer it
3. A "trial marriage," with a couple consciously testing the relation before making a permanent commitment
4. A temporary alternative to marriage, with each committed to a permanent relation, while they are waiting until it is more convenient to marry
5. A permanent alternative to marriage, with the couple living together in a long-term committed relation similar to marriage but without the traditional religious or legal commitments

Not unexpectedly, there are important differences among these types, so that regarding cohabitors as one homogenous group can be misleading.

It is not known as yet what proportion of cohabiting couples fall into each of the above five categories. It seems apparent, however, that the longer they remain together, the more likely the couple are to move from the least-involvement category toward forming a perma-

nent and committed relation—a type of trial marriage, a temporary alternative to marriage, or a permanent alternative to marriage.

To live together without marrying is apparently seldom a deliberately considered decision but usually results from a progressive growth of physical and emotional involvement—the couple gradually drift into a pattern of sleeping together more and more frequently and gradually accumulate possessions at one residence. When the decision to live together is deliberately made, it often occurs as a result of some change in circumstances, such as graduation, a change of job, a need for housing, reduced income, or the end of the school year (Macklin 1978).

When college students who were cohabiting were asked to identify the nature of their commitment at the time they started living together, the majority regarded themselves as having been in a strong, affectionate, "monogamous" relation. This caused many researchers to observe that cohabitation among the college age group is essentially a change in the courtship process (Bower and Christopherson 1977, Danzinger 1976, Macklin 1976).

The cohabiting couple share deep emotional involvement but have not yet agreed upon a permanent commitment. Consistent with this is the finding that most cohabiting college couples initially maintain two separate residences and do not spend every night together. Moreover, a two-year follow-up study found that these cohabiting couples were just as likely to break up as dating couples (Rubin 1975).

Are People Who Cohabit Different?

There are both similarities and differences between those who have cohabited and those who have not, but there seem to be more similarities than differences. In comparing cohabitors and noncohabitors on college campuses,

"This is my new friend—Michael. We cook together."

for example, Macklin (1978) found that the cohabiting students were representative of the undergraduate population in general, and that the cohabitation was more a consequence of *opportunity* than the result of any personality characteristics.

Other researchers have found that cohabiting women are more likely to describe themselves as "competitive," "aggressive," "independent," and "managerial" than are noncohabiting women. Cohabiting men are likely to describe themselves as "less managerial and competitive," "warmer" and "more emotionally supportive" than are noncohabiting men (Guittar and Lewis 1974, Arafat and Yorburg 1973). Both male and female cohabitors are likely to hold more liberal attitudes than noncohabitors, are more likely to major in the arts and the social sciences than in the physical sciences and engineering, tend to perceive themselves as more androgynous than noncohabitors, and tend to perceive themselves as more liberated

from traditional gender-role characteristics than noncohabitors. They are not more likely to have come from unhappy or divorced homes, are not significantly less likely to want to marry eventually, and do not have lower academic averages (McCauley 1977, Mackline 1976, Henze and Hudson 1974).

Cohabiting couples tend to mirror the society around them in regard to gender-role stereotyped behavior. They are no more egalitarian than married couples in regard to traditional role behavior such as housework, marketing, and cooking (Stafford et al. 1977; Bower and Christopherson 1977; Makepeace 1975).

Does Cohabitation Lead to Success in Marriage?

The assumption is often made that cohabitation leads to a more successful marriage with a lower incidence of divorce, since the couple have had the opportunity and time to live together in a quasi-marriage before making the plunge into a formalized, legal commitment. It certainly seems plausible that a couple who marry after cohabiting should have discovered some of the areas of conflict and be in a better position to make a realistic decision regarding their compatibility before marriage; and if they *do* decide to marry, their chances for success should be higher compared with those of couples who have not cohabited before marriage. However, studies to date have found no significant differences between married couples who cohabited before marriage and other couples. There is no evidence that couples who lived together before marriage have either better or worse marriages (Macklin 1978).

Despite these findings, it is interesting to note that the vast majority of couples give high positive marks to their experience while they are cohabiting—feeling that it has enhanced their personal growth and maturity—and state that they would not wish to marry without having lived with the other person first (Bower and Christopherson 1977, Macklin 1976).

Legal Problems of Cohabitation

The legal implications of cohabiting vary widely from state to state. As of 1976, for an unmarried couple to live together as though they were husband and wife was a crime in twenty states, and fornication (copulation between an unmarried couple) was a crime in sixteen states. Although rarely enforced, many states set a maximum penalty of a $500 fine and a six-month jail sentence for persons convicted of these crimes. New laws and interpretations can appear at any time, however, so a couple contemplating cohabitation should seek legal information regarding its status in their own state.

Another complication is that a child born to an unmarried couple is considered illegitimate and is subject to many legal and social difficulties. The U.S. Supreme Court did rule in 1977 that a state may not totally bar an illegitimate child's inheritance if the father dies *intestate* (without leaving a will). However, this ruling does *not* mean that illegitimate children must be given the same rights of inheritance as legitimate children.

Even if the cohabiting couple do not have children, they deny themselves protections provided by law, although the legal ramifications have not all been worked out by the courts. For example, an owner may choose not to sell or a landlord not to rent to an unmarried couple. Living together can be grounds for eviction in states where cohabitation or fornication is illegal. Depending on the locale and the attitude of an employer, a person may be refused a promotion or even lose a job. (Firing on the grounds of cohabitation is theoretically unconstitutional, but a precedent for this ruling has not yet been established by the courts.) Because membership in professional associations and licensing may be conditional on the demonstration of moral fitness, it is conceivable that these privileges may be denied to a cohabiting person. Finally, in some states, if the couple break up, one may sue the other for an equal share of all property acquired during the cohabitation (*Marvin* v. *Marvin*, 18 Cal. 3rd. 684, 1976).

Contract Cohabitation

One type of cohabitation that falls into a special category is *contract cohabitation,* an arrangement that seeks to provide the affection and companionship of marriage without the exclusivity, the long-term commitment, and the legal entanglements of marriage; or the benefits of cohabitation without the preceding extensive dating and courtship procedures that are usually necessary.

In contract cohabitation, the employer—who may be a man or a woman—simply pays the employee to cohabit during specified hours for a negotiated sum.[12] For example, an employer might pay an agreed-upon sum of money each month to an employee to prepare breakfast and dinner, provide companionship in the evening, share a bedroom, shop, and do light housekeeping. Hours might be specified as from five o'clock at night to nine o'clock in the morning, with one evening a week off and a week of paid vacation each year. The employer receives a cohabiting companion; the employee gets room and board and a substantial sum of cash each month, while remaining completely free during the daytime to study, attend classes, engage in artistic endeavors such as writing or painting, or even have a second job. Both persons sign a contract specifying and limiting the obligations of each.[13] Van Deusen (1975, p. 152) gives the following as an example of a job description of contract cohabitation:

Specific tasks—Light housekeeping
           Meal preparation
           Household shopping
Estimated time per day: 2 hours
Companionship—Weekdays: 6:00 to 8:00 P.M.
           Saturday: 3:00 P.M. on
           Sunday: All day
           Bedtime: Normally 11:00 P.M.
           Night off: Wednesday
           Vacation time: One week with pay per year

Contract cohabitation is a barter of material and emotional benefits. It combines the *quid pro quo* of a social arrangement with that of a business contract. Each person knows precisely what he or she is expected to provide, and what he or she expects to receive. If the expectation of either person is not fulfilled, the arrangement may be terminated and a new one tried. Of course, contract cohabitation may be an alternative to marriage only for an employer who can afford it. Therefore, most employers are probably middle-aged and either widowed or divorced.

The one revolutionary element in contract cohabitation is the idea that emotional intangibles can be deliberately negotiated for. We tend to think that such intangibles should be provided for "freely"; that they must be "given" and cannot be "bought." Contract cohabitation postulates that money can be exchanged for emotional values.

We are willing to put a dollars-and-cents value on muscular and mental energy, but not on such intangibles as touching and feeling. . . . We accept money as a materialistic symbol, but find it almost "sinful" to think of money as an emotional instrument (Van Deusen 1975, p. 116).

Although contract cohabitation seems to be a very impersonal approach to the most intimate possible relation, it has apparently worked very well for those who have tried it. To what extent contract cohabitation is practiced in the United States, however, is impossible to say.

---

[12]Sexual performance cannot be included specifically in the cohabitation contract, of course, since this would violate the law, but it would be tacitly understood by both parties. Since either party may cancel the contract at any time without giving a reason, if the sexual relation is not satisfactory, the contract would certainly be cancelled.

[13]The specific form the contract must take in order to be legal varies from state to state. Edmond Van Deusen's book, *Contract Cohabitation: An Alternative to Marriage* (1975), includes a sample cohabitation contract. It also describes Van Deusen's own experience as a contract cohabitor and offers complete step-by-step advice on all the practical questions the contract cohabitor is likely to encounter.

SUMMARY

In all age groups, at any given time, more than one-third of all adults in our society are single. Between the ages of twenty and twenty-four, more than two-thirds of young men and more than half of young women are single. The incidence of never-married singles has been rising especially rapidly in the United States during the past few years. The proportion of never-married women age twenty to twenty-four doubled in the two decades from 1960 to 1982 (from 28 percent to 57 percent), while the proportion of never-married men in this age group rose from 53 percent to 73 percent.

This rising incidence of never-married people has been one of the most significant changes in life-styles in our society. There are many reasons for this rise in the number of never-married singles. Chief among them is the increasing number of young women who are living alone in economic independence.

This trend toward singlehood does not mean that the incidence of marriage is dropping, however. By ages thirty to thirty-four, only about 9 percent of women and 15 percent of men are unmarried, and ultimately only about 5 percent never marry.

Some people are voluntarily single, while others are involuntarily single, and both these conditions may be temporary or stable. Within these four categories of singles there are as many diverse life-styles as among those who are married.

Singles tend to drift from small towns into cities, where there is more opportunity for finding companionship and finding sexual satisfaction. Research has found, however, that, contrary to the stereotype, recreational sex is usually not easily available, and most singles become sexually involved only in an atmosphere of emotional closeness, trust, and caring.

One of the chief problems with singlehood is loneliness, often accompanied by feelings of boredom or aimlessness. Loneliness is just as prevalent among men as among women and is often accompanied by depression. A number of studies have found that singles, compared with married people, are more likely to have various psychological problems associated with depression, such as anxiety, low self-esteem, and a chronic or pervasive lack of joy. Singles also have a higher incidence of physical ailments and a higher death rate.

Cohabitation, living together while remaining single, is reaching institutional acceptance in the United States, with nearly 2 million people of all ages cohabiting in 1984 (more than half were between ages twenty-five and forty-four). Twenty-five percent of college students cohabit, and 50 percent of those who have not cohabited say they would like to. Cohabitation varies from a temporary casual convenience, to a permanent alternative to marriage. There is no difference between the incidence of divorce among couples who cohabit before marriage and the incidence of those who do not, although the vast majority of couples give high positive marks to their experience while they are cohabiting. Cohabiting is illegal in some states; a child born to an unmarried couple is considered illegitimate; and if the couple separate, there may be a problem in dividing the property acquired during the cohabitation.

Contract cohabitation seeks to provide the benefits of cohabitation without the extensive dating and courtship procedures that usually precede it. The employer simply pays the employee to cohabit during specified hours for a negotiated sum, combining the *quid pro quo* of a social arrangement with that of a business contract—assuming that emotional intangibles can be deliberately negotiated for, and that money can be exchanged for emotional values.

QUESTIONS

1. Discuss the rising incidence of singlehood in the United States.

2. Discuss the reasons why the incidence of never-married singles has been increasing so rapidly during the past decade.

3. Discuss the four categories of singlehood: voluntary temporary singles, voluntary stable singles, involuntary temporary singles, and involuntary stable singles.

4. What are some of the common stereotypes

regarding singles? Have these stereotypes been substantiated by research?

5. Discuss the problems some singles have faced regarding discrimination.

6. What are some of the stresses of singlehood? What are the psychological and physical manifestations of these stresses?

7. What are some of the benefits and problems of cohabitation?

8. What is meant by contract cohabitation?

SUGGESTIONS FOR FURTHER READING

Bell, Robert R. *Worlds of Friendship.* Beverly Hills, Calif.: Sage Publications, 1981.

Cargan, Leonard, and Melko, Matthew. *Singles.* Beverly Hills, Calif.: Sage Publications, 1982.

Gordon, Suzanne. *Lonely in America.* New York: Touchstone, 1976.

Knapp, Mark L. *Interpersonal Communication and Human Relationships.* Newton, Mass.: Allyn & Bacon, 1984.

Libby, Roger W., and Whitehurst, Robert N., eds. *Marriage and Alternatives: Exploring Intimate Relationships.* Glenview, Ill.: Scott, Foresman, 1977.

Macklin, Eleanor D., and Rubin, Roger H., eds. *Contemporary Families and Alternative Lifestyles.* Beverly Hills, Calif.: Sage Publications, 1983.

Murstein, Bernard I., ed. *Exploring Intimate Life Styles.* New York: Springer, 1978.

Rogers, Carl. *Becoming Partners: Marriage and Its Alternatives.* New York: Delacorte, 1972.

Rubin, Lillian Breslow. *Intimate Strangers: Men and Women Together.* New York: Harper & Row, 1983.

Simenauer, Jacqueline, and Carroll, David. *Singles and Sex: A New Study.* New York: Simon & Schuster, 1984.

Stein, Peter J., ed. *Single Life: Unmarried Adults in Social Context.* New York: St. Martin's Press, 1981.

Weiss, Robert S. *Loneliness: The Experience of Emotional and Social Isolation.* Cambridge, Mass.: MIT Press, 1973.

Warner, Ralph. *Living Together Kit.* Occidental, Calif.: Nolo Press, 1984.

Zimbardo, Philip Z. *Shyness: What It Is and What to Do about It.* Reading, Mass.: Addison-Wesley, 1978.

PART THREE

The Married Couple

CHAPTER 7

The Nature of Marriage

The Meaning of Marriage as an Institution
The Meaning of Marriage for the Individual
Child-free Marriage
Intermarriage
Marriage While in College
The Life Cycle and Marriage

Therefore shall a man leave his father,
and his mother, and shall cleave unto his wife;
and they shall be one flesh.

Genesis 2:24

Marriage is very popular in our society. Indeed, as we have seen in Chapter 6, more than 95 percent of our population ultimately marry at some point during their lives. These people enter marriage with the highest expectations, and for some, their expectations are more than fulfilled; for others—about half of those who marry—the bright promises that marriage held are not fulfilled, and the couple part with sadness, disillusionment, bitterness, and ultimately divorce (see Chapter 8).

In this chapter we shall examine the nature of marriage as an institution and the meaning of marriage for the individual. We shall look at the special categories of marriage: child-free marriage, intermarriage, and marriage while in college. We shall put the potential problem of extramarital sexual behavior into perspective. We shall trace the life cycle of the married individual through the childbearing and childrearing years, through middle age and old age, to finally—for those who do not return to singlehood through divorce, separation, or desertion—the return to singlehood when the spouse dies.

THE MEANING OF MARRIAGE AS AN INSTITUTION

A *social institution* is a collective solution to a social need. It may be as large as the U.S. Army or as small as two people legally bound in marriage. As the army exists as an institution for the protection of the society, so marriage exists as an institution for the perpetuation of the society.

It is conceivable that a society could perpetuate itself from one generation to another without the institution of marriage, but anthropologists have yet to discover a single one that has done so. Marriage apparently serves an essential function for the survival of the group.

Marriage as Part of the Family System

Virtually all children are produced and nurtured within a family,[1] and marriage forms the basis of the family. Thus, the key function of marriage—in all known societies—is the legitimization of children. Together, the three social institutions of *courtship, marriage,* and the *family* form the *family system* in all known human societies on our planet (Reiss 1980). (See Figure 7-1.)

This is not to say that children are never produced by couples who are not married, or that married couples always remain together and cooperate in nurturing their children. Obviously, many children are born out of wedlock, and many married couples divorce while

The family system—consisting of the three factors of courtship, marriage, and the family—is universal. Marriage stands midway between courtship (which precedes it) and the establishment of a family (which follows it) as an interlocking system in all known societies.

FIGURE 7-1
The family system
Source: Data from Reiss (1980).

their children are still quite young. What the family system does in all societies is make institutional provision for a *preferred* method of producing and nurturing children (Reiss 1980).

It should be noted that this universal function of marriage is *not* the legitimization of copulation, nor the legitimization of cohabitation (although these may be important functions in some societies). Virtually all societies accept copulation before marriage, and some societies *prefer* that the woman become pregnant before she is married, as we have seen (in Chapter 5).

The Forms of Marriage

Although marriage is a universal institution, it takes different forms in different societies, varying enormously from one to another. These various forms of marriage fall into one of two basic categories: (1) *monogamy* (one wife with one husband) and (2) *polygamy*. There are three forms of polygamy: *polygyny* (two or more wives with one husband), *polyandry* (two or more husbands with one wife), and *group marriage* (two or more couples living together in one marriage).

Of these basic types of marriages, polygyny is preferred by about 75 percent of the world's societies, about 25 percent prefer monogamy, and less than 1 percent prefer polyandry. Group marriage has occurred rarely, but no-

---

[1]Although it is theoretically possible that children might be produced and nurtured by means other than the family, this is the preferred institution for child production and care in all known societies (see Chapter 10).

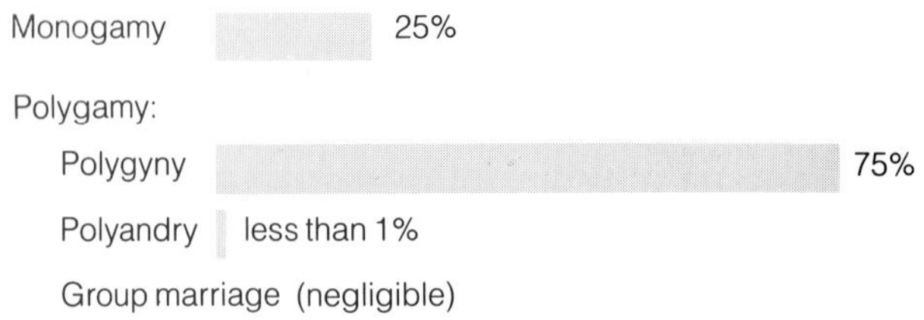

Monogamy		25%
Polygamy:		
Polygyny		75%
Polyandry	less than 1%	
Group marriage (negligible)		

FIGURE 7-2

The forms of marriage preferred by the world's societies, as reported by Murdock (1957)

Source: Data from Murdock (1957).

where as a social norm (Murdock 1957). (See Figure 7-2.)

Our own society is monogamous, not only by custom but by law. Although marriage laws are based upon state rather than federal legislation and vary significantly from one state to another, all states have been required to forbid *bigamy* (the legal term for polygamy) since 1878, the year the U. S. Supreme Court ruled that a plurality of wives violated criminal law and was not defensible as an exercise of religious liberty.[2]

The Marriage Contract

In addition to its universal function of the legitimization of children, marriage performs other functions for the society, and the expectations that these functions will be fulfilled is spelled out by a *marriage contract*. In preliterate societies, the marriage contract is verbal and takes the form of strongly enforced tradition. In our society, except for common-law marriage,[3] the contract is written and must be signed by each of the couple, by two witnesses, and by the public official who performs the ceremony. This contract is a public declaration that (1) establishes the union as one of expected permanence, (2) formalizes and specifies reciprocal rights and obligations that each of the couple is to provide for the other, (3) provides for protection of the legal rights of any children the couple may have, and (4) establishes kinship relations with members of each of the couple's families (Stephens 1982).

Establishing the Expectation for Permanence

In all societies, marriage is regarded as a relatively permanent bond, and in some societies as irrevocable. For example, in most countries in which the major religion is Roman Catholicism (such as Northern Ireland, Italy, and Brazil) divorce is virtually impossible to obtain.[4]

In our own society most wedding ceremonies have a tone of irrevocability about them. This expectation is often expressed in the vows taken during the ceremony—for example, "To have and to hold from this day forward, for better or for worse, for richer, for

---

[2]Before 1878, polygyny (a form of polygamy) was the preferred form of marriage for some religious groups, such as the Mormons.

[3]See the vignette later in this section, "Marriage with No Contract: Common-Law Marriage."

---

[4]Termination of the marriage was virtually impossible in Western civilization until the eighteenth century. Before this it was possible only to have a marriage annulled, and this required a papal decree. Civil divorce began to be granted by legislative action in the eighteenth century; it then came under the jurisdiction of the courts in the nineteenth century. Divorce was still relatively uncommon, however, until our society was well into the twentieth century (see Chapter 8).

Every couple enters marriage with the expectation of permanence.

poorer, in sickness and in health, to love and to cherish, till death do us part."

Most marriage ceremonies in our society take place under the auspices of a minister, priest, or rabbi.[5] And in religious terms marriage is regarded as a *sacrament* (an outward and visible sign of inward and spiritual grace). From this viewpoint, marriage is seen as an institution of divine significance, sanctioned by God and contracted between the spouses and God's earthly representative, the church or synagogue. This doctrine of marriage emphasizes the sacred tie between the couple and

God, with the marriage regarded as "Holy Matrimony" the "Holy Estate," or "God's Ordinance." Once established, marriage is under the jurisdiction of God and presumed to be permanent.

The Roman Catholic church is so emphatic in defining marriage as a divine institution that is not to be tampered with by humans that it does not recognize civil divorce. However, the church may declare a marriage voided by *annulment*, which means that it is formally regarded never to have existed in the first place (see Chapter 8).

Protestants and Jews also regard marriage as a sacrament, with expectation for permanence, but take the position that marital vows for lifelong fidelity are expressions of solemn *intent*, made with all sincerity at the time of the wedding. Although marriages should not fail, they sometimes do—and the persons involved should not be punished for their fallibility. Thus, Protestants and Jews do—reluctantly—accept divorce as valid in ending the marriage and opening the way for a remarriage that will be santified by the church or synagogue.

Most societies throughout the world, and most religions, similarly make provision for divorce, while expecting that most marriages will be permanent and emphasizing the anticipation for permanence at the wedding ceremony. Although the causes for divorce vary, the most common are failure to provide the necessities of life, mistreatment, adultery, and sterility. In all societies, a dowry (if one has been given) or a bride price (if one has been received) usually must be returned when the marriage is terminated.

In societies (usually preindustrial) where the courtship system emphasizes parental selection, and where the marriage means extensive and important social, economic, political, or religious ties, the incidence of divorce is much lower than it is in societies where the courtship system emphasizes mutual choice and the personal values of each of the couple, and where marriage is seen chiefly as a means

---

[5]About three-fourths of wedding ceremonies in the United States are performed within a religious institution, while about one-fourth are civil ceremonies and are performed by an official (such as a Justice of the Peace) who is not a member of the clergy (Landis and Landis 1977).

Drawing by Booth; © 1985 *The New Yorker* Magazine, Inc.

"We are gathered here to join together this man and this woman in matrimony—a very serious step, with far-reaching and unpredictable consequences."

of personal fulfillment. (For further discussion of divorce—its historical background and its present ramifications in our society—see Chapter 8.)

Formalizing the Couple's Rights and Obligations

The marriage contract formalizes and specifies the reciprocal rights and obligations of the married couple, especially in regard to the control and ownership of property. For example, in many Middle Eastern societies, a husband may have four wives at one time and may divorce one of them at any time simply by saying, "I divorce you," in the presence of witnesses, but the divorced wife is not simply abandoned—she retains significant property rights.[6]

In our society, the rights of married couples not only are very complicated but vary from

---

[6]The husband may change his mind and accept the woman back into his household as his wife. However, he may only do this twice—the third divorce is irrevocable. If he wishes to make the divorce final (and irrevocable) at once, he simply says, "I divorce you," three times in the presence of witnesses.

Writing Your Own Marriage Contract

A couple may write their own marriage contract to personal specifications so long as it does not contradict state law. Such a personal contract may be a private matter, or it may be made public as part of the marriage ceremony. Frequently such a contract covers a set period of time, after which it can be renegotiated.

The goal of a personal marriage contract is to help each of the couple define his or her expectations for the marriage. The couple might begin by separately writing down expectations. Then they can compare and negotiate any differences. Areas that are often covered in such a contract are those regarding sexual satisfactions; responsibility for marketing, cooking, and household chores; and financial arrangements.

Attitudes toward the usefulness of such contracts vary widely. In general, a contract is used to specify rights and obligations in an interaction that is formal and limited and may be precisely defined. Thus, the closer a relation is to the secondary end of the primary-secondary continuum, the more important a contract becomes. In a formal, impersonal interaction, such as a business agreement, a contract is usually regarded as essential.

The closer the relation moves to the primary end of the continuum, the more difficult it becomes to spell out the precise satisfactions that are expected. No contract can possibly cover every contingency, and even a formal, business contract must rely extensively on the goodwill of the participants. In such an intimate interaction as marriage, the many psychological satisfactions that each provides for the other cannot possibly be spelled out in contractual terms but must depend on the sensitivity and willingness of each person to bring pleasure to the other.

Nevertheless, negotiating a contract may have the advantage of causing each person to think through important areas of expected marital satisfaction and agree on a mutual view. Any substantial discrepancy can be discovered, and perhaps negotiated, before the marriage.

The most significant aspect of a harmonious and mutually satisfying marital interaction is good communication, and anything that leads to this has a positive effect on the marriage. Moreover, if an important need is not fulfilled after marriage (for one or both of the couple), the contract may provide an important starting point for pinpointing the difficulty and arriving at a mutually acceptable procedure that will provide a solution.

---

state to state, and property may be held in joint tenancy, in community property, or owned by either the husband or the wife alone. However, even if a husband or a wife owns a property outright, he or she may not dispose of it without regard to the other's rights, if this action is contested. Once the marriage contract is signed, each achieves significant rights with regard to the property and actions of the other.[7]

Some couples in our society attempt to formalize the rights and obligations that each owes to the other by writing their own marriage contract. This is perfectly legal, so long as any stipulations in the contract do not violate or contradict state law regarding marriage rights and obligations. (See the vignette, "Writing Your Own Marriage Contract.")

---

[7] It is possible for one of the couple to waive certain specified property rights by signing a quit-claim agreement before the

marriage. For example, a young woman marrying a very wealthy man may be asked to sign such a document, limiting the amount of his estate to which she is entitled in case of death or divorce.

Marriage with No Contract: Common-Law Marriage

In a common-law marriage, the couple are legally recognized as being married, even though they have never obtained a marriage license or gone through a legally constituted marriage ceremony, and they have never signed and recorded a marriage contract. Common-law marriage was more important in our society during the early, pioneer period, when many communities had neither a judge nor a clergyman authorized to perform marriage. The convention developed that if a couple declared themselves to be married before the community and lived together as husband and wife, they were married by common-law. Sometimes, a couple who had such a common-law marriage would go through a formal ceremony when a clergyman or judge was available (the so-called circuit-rider clergyman or judge). Other couples would postpone a formal ceremony until after they had children, sometimes even until the children were grown.

Whether a common-law marriage is legal depends on the state. Common-law marriages are recognized in thirteen states, and some states that prohibit common-law marriage recognize one that is valid in the state where it was contracted (Carter and Glick 1976). Most often, the question of legality arises with reference to inheritance rights and the legitimacy of offspring. With the growing popularity of cohabitation (unmarried couples living together), the legal ramifications of common-law marriage have become complex.

In some states a couple may be recognized as legally married even though they have not gone through a formal ceremony or signed a marriage contract. In these states, the couple are married according to the provisions of *common law*, and in states in which common-law marriages are recognized, they are just as legally binding as marriages that are formalized by a signed contract. (See the vignette, "Marriage with No Contract: Common-Law Marriage.")

Providing for Children's Rights

The marriage contract formalizes the expectation that the couple will provide physical care and emotional support and nurture for any children they may have. It also specifies other rights (property and otherwise) that the children may have. By law, the couple are responsible for the children's physical, psychological, and social well-being. In our society, for example, a child must be provided with adequate food, shelter, clothing, and medical attention, may not be physically abused, and must be educated to certain minimum standards.

Establishing Kinship Relations

When a couple are formally married and the marriage contract is signed and recorded, kinship relations are automatically established. Thus, a marriage joins not only two individuals but also two families, and the precise relation between the in-laws is specified by both tradition and law. In many societies, these in-law relations are significant in everyday interaction. In our society, they have two important legal functions: They establish incest prohibitions, and they set up stable lines of inheritance in the absence of a will.[8]

---

[8]It should also be noted that the family's kinship structure is not necessarily one of blood, and that adopting a child has the

Qualifying for Marriage in Our Society

Before a person may legally marry in our society a marriage license must be obtained from the appropriate government agency. If one or both of the couple cannot take out a marriage license because of their religious beliefs, the *banns* must be published.[9] (An exception, of course, is common-law marriage in states where this is recognized.)

In addition to a marriage license (or published banns), a blood test (to detect evidence of syphilis) is required in most states in our society. Most states also require a delay (usually three days) between the time of the blood test and the issuance of the marriage license. This "cooling-off" period is designed to provide the couple with an opportunity to change their minds before the final signing of the marriage contract. (Many couples do just this: The number of couples who are granted marriage licenses is greater than the number of couples who return to marry.)[10]

A person cannot enter into a marriage contract in the United States without being older than a certain minimum age, which varies from state to state. In most states, the age of eligibility is eighteen for the male and sixteen for the female with parental consent, and twenty-one for the male and eighteen for the female with parental consent. In some states, parental consent is not required of a minor if he or she was previously married; other states allow a female minor to marry if she is pregnant or is already a mother.

All states have incest laws prohibiting marriage between blood relations although the degree of relatedness that prohibits marriage varies to some extent from state to state. All states forbid the marriage of father and daughter, mother and son, brother and sister, uncle and niece, aunt and nephew, and grandparent and grandchild. Most states do not allow marriage between half-brother and half-sister or between first cousins, and some states extend the prohibition to include second cousins. Other states prohibit the marriage of in-laws even where there is *no* blood relation, such as brother-in-law or sister-in-law.

To be married, a couple must appear with a valid marriage license before an official or cleric who is legally permitted by the state to perform marriages. The wedding ceremony that follows must be witnessed by two persons of legal age, and certain portions of the ceremony are prescribed by law. After the ceremony, the couple, the witnesses, and the officiator must sign the license, which must then be sent to the government agency where it is recorded and filed.

THE MEANING OF MARRIAGE FOR THE INDIVIDUAL

Some of the meaning of marriage for the individual is the same as the social meaning. For example, marriage as a legitimization of parenthood has both personal and social meanings. However, much of the significance of marriage for the individual may be unrelated to the social meaning. The individual usually regards marriage chiefly as a source of personal satisfaction.

Why a Person Chooses to Marry

Why should a person choose to marry, when it is quite possible, in today's climate of opinion, for two people to simply live together without

---

same kinship force as giving birth to the child. It is the social definition—not biological ties—that determines who is kin (Reiss 1980).

[9]The *banns* are a public announcement of a couple's intention to marry, providing an opportunity for anyone to object. In preindustrial times, they often took the place of a marriage license or were used in addition to a marriage license.

[10]You may be interested in checking this out in your own community. Simply note the number of marriage licenses applied for (they are listed in the daily newspaper) and compare it with the number of marriages over a period of several weeks.

being married? As we have seen, although a sizable proportion of our population do choose to live together without marrying, all but one person in twenty ultimately marry at some point in their lifetimes (see Chapter 6).

The reasons for marrying are many, complex, and interrelated. In our society, people are expected to marry for love. The attraction between the persons is often limerent and romantic, with each wishing to fulfill the ideals of love and romance within the conventions established by society and without defying the expectations of their families and friends—which means, ultimately, marrying.

Sexual attraction is also a reason for marrying. Research finds that sexual fulfillment usually occurs only in an atmosphere of affection, trust, intimacy, and love (see Chapter 6). Sexual love may also be fulfilled by living together without marrying, of course, but marriage adds a measure of emotional security. It is a proud proclamation, publicly made, that each person chooses, and is chosen by, the other. The need for emotional security, trust, and acceptance, which is symbolized and formalized by a wedding ceremony—a public proclamation of each person's free choice of the other—is certainly a significant force for marriage.

Economic reasons were very important for marrying during the agricultural period when it was difficult to survive without the economic partnership of another, and economics are still undoubtedly involved as a reason for marriage. However, economic reasons for marrying are not nearly so important in this postindustrial age—especially for women. As women begin to gain increasing economic and social equality with men, they are economically and socially free to pursue their own independent careers—without necessarily relying on men for economic subsistence and support.

Many marry to have children, and this coincides with the social reason for the institution of marriage—to legitimize children.

Many marry because of parental pressure, others because of peer pressure.

For many, religious proscriptions or ethical considerations are extremely important, and marriage is regarded as a sacrament, of divine significance. For these people, it is philosophically and ethically unacceptable to live together without being married. Cohabitation is considered not only immoral, but a violation of their own deeply felt ethical and religious principles.

Many of these reasons may be regarded as "pushes"—outside forces or pressures that urge a person toward marriage. Other reasons for marrying might be regarded as "pulls"—forces that originate inside the person, causing a desire or yearning for marriage. Other forces act as "pushes" and "pulls" toward singlehood. The pushes and pulls for marriage and those for singlehood work differently for different people. If the complex of pushes and pulls urging a person toward marriage are, in sum, greater than the complex of pushes and pulls that urge the person toward singlehood, then he or she may move into marriage (see Figure 7-3).

The decision to marry is not a decision in the usual sense of a rational or logical outcome of weighing alternatives, although this is certainly an important part of what is involved. Rather, the decision is a complex of emotional, psychological, social, and rational factors, many of which may be unconscious. However it is arrived at, the decision to marry is certainly one of the most important a person will ever make. It is a *choice point* in life that is irrevocable.[11] The person's life will move in a differ-

---

[11]A *choice point* is a situation that occurs when a person *must* move in one direction or another, and the direction chosen affects all of his or her future. For example, you either marry or you do not marry; there is no third alternative (this is called a "forced choice"). Major choice points in our society, in addition to marrying, are choosing between work and going to college, choosing which college to attend, choosing a career, deciding to have a child or to adopt a child, and so on.

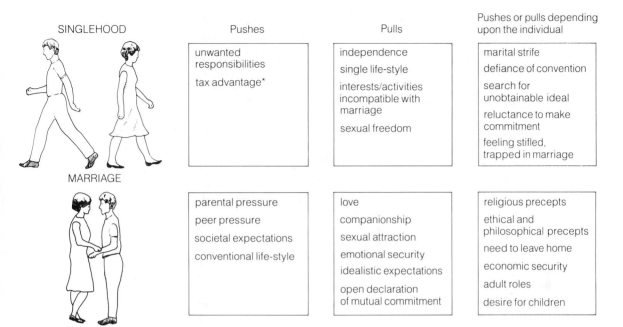

SINGLEHOOD	Pushes	Pulls	Pushes or pulls depending upon the individual
	unwanted responsibilities	independence	marital strife
	tax advantage*	single life-style	defiance of convention
		interests/activities incompatible with marriage	search for unobtainable ideal
		sexual freedom	reluctance to make commitment
MARRIAGE			feeling stifled, trapped in marriage
	parental pressure	love	religious precepts
	peer pressure	companionship	ethical and philosophical precepts
	societal expectations	sexual attraction	need to leave home
	conventional life-style	emotional security	economic security
		idealistic expectations	adult roles
		open declaration of mutual commitment	desire for children

*A married couple, each of whom work, will pay more income tax than if they live together without being married and file separate income tax returns (see Chapter 13).

FIGURE 7-3

Pushes and pulls toward marriage or singlehood
Adapted from: Stein, Peter. *Single.*
Englewood Cliffs, N.J.: Prentice-Hall.

ent direction from that point. Although the marriage may be dissolved through divorce, many significant social and psychological ties remain.

The Changing Meaning of Marriage

Until the present century, in Western society marriage was viewed chiefly as an institution of divine significance, sanctioned by God and contracted between the spouses and God's earthly representative, the church or synagogue. This is still regarded as the essential meaning of marriage by much of the population today, both laity and clergy. However, the emphasis on marriage as a sacred institution is not nearly so great in contemporary times as it was during the medieval period. The emphasis on marriage as a sacred institution shifted initially during the nineteenth century, toward an emphasis on marriage as a civil institution. The emphasis has shifted again during the present century—the personal satisfaction and qualities of the individual are replacing the sacred and the civil as the most important aspect of marriage (see Figure 7-4).

Contributing to this shift in the meaning of marriage is the depersonalization of our contemporary mass society, which makes the few remaining primary relations uniquely important. This growing importance of individual

Prior to the nineteenth century the sacred aspect of marriage was emphasized

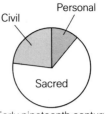

Early nineteenth century

The nineteenth century ushered in an emphasis on the civil aspect of marriage

Late nineteenth century

The twentieth century ushered in an emphasis on the personal satisfactions in marriage

Twentieth century

FIGURE 7-4

Changes in the meaning of marriage in historical perspective

satisfaction in marriage has been augmented by the development of dating, the increased significance of romantic love, the emergence of divorce as a socially acceptable alternative to a failed marriage, and the increasing independence of women.

The Three Fundamentals of Successful Marriage

As complex as marital interaction is, it may be conceptualized in terms of three fundamental components: (1) *congruence of role perception*, (2) *reciprocity of role performance*, and (3) *equivalence of role function*. If these three fac-

tors are present, the marriage will be successful and a source of satisfaction for both. However, if one or more of these factors are absent, the marriage will be a source of dissatisfaction and despair.

Understanding the nature and the importance of these three components of marriage provides a very powerful tool for teasing out the variables of a complex marital interaction when conflicts and difficulties arise.

Congruence of Role Perception

Congruence is a term borrowed from geometry; it means that two events are equivalent. For example, if one triangle can be placed on top of another with the edges coinciding, the triangles are said to be congruent. *Congruence of role perception* simply means that each person perceives his or her own role and the other's role (in a given situation) about the same as the other person does. If we call the two persons Jack and Jill, then congruence of perception rests upon four factors: Jill's perception of her own role, Jill's perception of Jack's role, Jack's perception of his own role, and Jack's perception of Jill's role. Jill's and Jack's perceptions must coincide for each role. If there is a discrepancy in *any* of these four factors, there is no congruence of role perception. In other words, successful marital interaction is impossible unless the wife perceives her role (in any given situation) about the same as her husband perceives it, and he perceives his role about the same as she does. That is, the role expectations of each (in terms of their interaction) must coincide.

Let's look at an obvious example of this principle. If the couple are going to play volleyball, the wife must perceive her role as hitting the ball over the net and into the court and her husband's role as reaching it before it touches the floor inside the court and hitting it back. The husband must perceive his role as reaching the ball before it touches the floor inside the court and hitting it in such a way that it goes back over the net and into the court. The expected action and reaction, which depend on a congruence of role perception, are clear in this relatively simple situation in which each of the couple plays the role of volleyball player.

The technical term used by sociologists for a socially recognizable situation of this sort is *position*. Thus, each person occupies a position (volleyball player, husband, wife, and so on) at any given time, and each position is exemplified by appropriate (accepted and expected) role behavior.

Congruence of perception is obviously essential in an interaction such as playing volleyball. It is equally essential in all the facets of the complex interactions of marriage. In fact, unless there is congruence of perception, there is even *less* possibility for success in the complex interactions of marriage than there is in playing volleyball. The essential element— the congruence of perception—is obvious and crystal clear in the relatively simple expectations of the volleyball game. But role perceptions are often blurred and out of focus—or ignored or forgotten—in the complex interactions that make up the fabric of a marriage. If there is no congruence of perception in playing volleyball, the game will obviously have to be discontinued. If there is no congruence of perception in too many important areas of a marriage, the marriage will disintegrate.

One reason why it is often so difficult to achieve congruence of perception is that the individual frequently regards his or her own attitudes and expectations as *right* and stoutly maintains them, rather than trying to see and understand the attitude and expectation of the other person. When each takes a firm (and stubborn) stand in this way, the difficulty in seeing, acknowledging, and accepting the other's point of view becomes greater and greater, with each person retreating to a firmly entrenched ground of wounded innocence and outraged sensibilities.

Reciprocity of Role Performance

Not only must each person perceive his or her role about the same as the other does (in any specific situation), but the person must then act to implement or *perform* the expected role behavior. For example, if a wife expects her husband to listen attentively and sympathetically to her account of her day's work, it is not enough that he acknowledge this expectation (congruence of perception). He must also *do* just that: listen attentively and sympathetically (*reciprocity of role performance*).

Lack of reciprocity in role performance may be persistent and perplexing unless the couple can first achieve congruence of perception.

That is, one spouse may not perform the expected role behavior because he or she does not perceive that such behavior is expected. Trying to muddle through the difficulty by simply playing the roles has virtually no chance for success. Again, the analogy of playing volleyball illustrates this point. No matter how good each person's strokes may be, the players would simply be working at cross purposes unless their perceptions of what each was doing in relation to the other clearly coincided.

When the couple are still dating, congruence of role perception usually occurs and is followed by reciprocity of role performance. If this harmony fails, each of the couple usually acts to reestablish it, or the couple stop dating because one or both are dissatisfied, puzzled, frustrated, and unhappy with each other. They certainly do not proceed from the courtship phase into marriage.

Many of the interactions that are characteristic of marriage are quite different from those of dating, however. In fact, very little of the dating behavior carries over into marriage. In dating, the couple's interaction is chiefly oriented to recreation, relaxation, companionship, and mutual exploration of the delicious discoveries of their intimacy. There is little or no practice or rehearsal for the interactions that are characteristic of the practical concerns of marriage—with its necessities, economic pressures, and focus upon daily activities that are often disinteresting or routine (as opposed to the exciting, heightened interest and expectations of dating).

This is not to say, of course, that there is no excitement in marriage, or that there is no interest—quite the contrary. But the majority of activities in marriage are different from the majority of activities in dating. It is quite likely that a couple who were very compatible in dating could become less so in the different interactions of marriage. Misunderstandings might occur and escalate and multiply as the couple increasingly fail to perceive and then to provide what each expects from the other.

Equivalence of Role Function

The third ingredient for successful marriage—*equivalence of role function*—refers to the principle that the degree of satisfaction each person receives *from* the other must be about the same as the satisfaction he or she provides *for* the other. Equivalence of role performance is not sufficient for a successful marriage. Each person must receive a measure of satisfaction that is perceived to be relatively equivalent to, or as valuable as, what he or she is providing if the marriage is to be mutually satisfactory.

Again, the analogy with the interaction in the relatively simple process of playing volleyball makes this principle clear. Even though each person might be in agreement regarding the expectation of what each should do, and each performs to the best of his or her ability in accordance with these expectations, the game cannot continue satisfactorily if one player consistently hits much stronger shots than the other. The exchange would be too uneven. There must be an equivalence of function for the interaction to continue.

Of course, this equivalence of function might occur if there is a trade-off of one quality for another. For example, a person might play volleyball with a much weaker player if she is receiving satisfaction in an area other than that relating to the game. For example, she might feel a sense of satisfaction in teaching the other, or perhaps the companionship received is worth the traded off weak hits. Equivalence of perceived satisfaction can be very complex.

In the traditional marriage of the nineteenth century, for example, the husband might provide security, status, and economic support in exchange for the wife providing sexual satisfaction, producing children, and caring for the household. Or a young woman might exchange her youth, beauty, and sexual allure for the man's money, power, and social position. In actual practice, of course, the *quid pro quo* (or mutuality of perceived satisfaction) in a marriage is far more subtle and complex and probably never conforms to the stereotype.[12]

Because of this complexity of trade-offs and differences in perceived values, failure to achieve equivalence of function can be very difficult to recognize or, if it is recognized, to acknowledge. It is even more difficult to correct. It helps enormously to understand, however, that equivalence of function (in the perception of each) must rest upon the foundation of the two prior principles: congruence of perception, followed by reciprocity of performance.

This doesn't mean, of course, that an exact balance need be obtained, nor should it be striven for. The attitude that marriage is a 50–50 proposition can be damaging. In a successful marriage, each partner must be willing to give 60–70 percent of the time, to put in more than he or she takes out. In the long run, however, the giving and taking should balance out.

If either partner enters a marriage determined that all transactions should be equal, the marriage will suffer. As one husband put it, "Sometimes I give far more than I receive, and sometimes I receive far more than I give. But my wife does the same. If we weren't willing to do that, we would have broken up long ago" (Lauer and Lauer 1985, p. 26).

Categories of Need Fulfillment in Marriage

Because of the complexity of interaction in marriage, it is helpful to analyze it in terms of three categories: (1) *material* (biological) needs, (2) *sexual* needs, and (3) *psychological* needs. There is great overlap between these three categories of course; they may be sepa-

---

[12]*Quid pro quo* is a Latin term that means "something for something." It is often used in business transactions to mean that the contractual balance of what each party is providing for the other, and receiving from the other, is equivalent and satisfactory to each.

rated only analytically; in the reality of experience they are an inseparable blend.

Satisfying Material Needs

The fulfillment of a material need brings physical satisfaction (and psychological satisfaction). The physical or biological satisfactions that each person provides for the other in marriage are perhaps the most obvious of all— food, shelter, an orderly household, and money. When one of the couple provides (earns) the money, the other usually provides the food (cooks) and maintains an orderly household (cleans). When they both work to provide the income, housekeeping functions are usually shared, although the wife most often does more than an equal share (see Chapter 10).

In the traditional American society of the nineteenth and early twentieth centuries, the *quid pro quo* with regard to material needs called for the husband to provide the income while the wife fulfilled the necessary housekeeping functions. In our contemporary society, this is unusual, as we have seen (Chapter 2). Most couples now work out for themselves a satisfactory division of labor within marriage.

Nevertheless, however the labor is divided, each person receives, within the marriage, more material or physical satisfactions than he or she could probably receive as a single person. Ideally, marriage provides physical comfort and security in ways that are not available commercially except at great price in the best hotels. Together the married couple provide physical comforts far more effectively than a person could do alone, with no shared participation from another.

People do live alone as singles, of course, and many do so by choice, as we have seen (Chapter 6). When they do, however, they are trading off increased comfort and security for greater freedom. (For a discussion of the pressures and the rewards of single life see Chapter 6.)

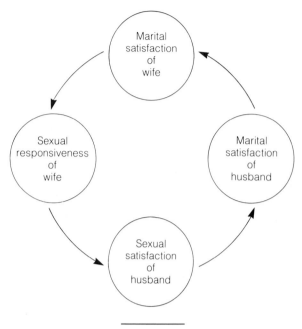

FIGURE 7-5

The complex interaction between marital satisfaction,
sexual responsiveness, and sexual satisfaction
Source: Data from Udry (1968).

Satisfying Sexual Needs

The sexual needs that each person fulfills for
the other are sometimes even more obvious
than the material needs, but the lack of sexual
satisfaction is not always recognized or acknowledged. The couple may not even agree on
the nature of sexual satisfaction for one or
both, or on how a failure might be defined
(whereas they usually agree on the nature of
material satisfactions). Moreover, since most
couples are often reluctant to frankly discuss
sexual expectations and sexual difficulties,
communication often breaks down (whereas
they usually will discuss a disparity of satisfaction in regard to material needs). Thus, a couple may be unable to arrive at even the first
step of marital harmony—a congruence of
perception—in regard to sexual behavior.

A satisfactory sexual interaction (or an
acceptable trade-off) can be the keystone of a
rewarding marriage. Yet there is probably no
area in which failure in all three fundamentals
of a successful marriage—congruence of role
perception, reciprocity of role performance,
and equivalence of role function—is more
likely to occur. Nevertheless, sex can be a very
powerful force for satisfaction and happiness
in the marriage—a significant trade-off for dissatisfaction in other areas, as we have seen
(Chapter 4).

Because of the different physical and
psychological characteristics of men and
women (see Chapter 4), there is a complex interaction between marital satisfaction and
sexual satisfaction in the average husband and
wife. The wife will be sexually responsive if
her marital satisfaction level is high. If she is
sexually responsive, the husband will be sexually satisfied, and if he is sexually satisfied,

The Most Valued Psychological Satisfactions in Marriage

Several hundred couples were interviewed in research designed to find out what characteristics each valued most in the other person. Most of the couples agreed that the following psychological satisfactions were critically important (Walster and Walster 1978, pp. 130–133):

—— Being sociable, friendly, and relaxed

—— Being an intelligent, informed person

—— Being physically attractive and having some concern for physical appearance in regard to such things as clothing, cleanliness, etc.

—— Being warm and affectionate and showing this to the other

—— Responding to the other's personal concerns and emotional needs

—— Openly showing appreciation of the other person

—— Being openly affectionate—touching, hugging, and kissing

—— Participating actively and fully in sexual interactions

—— Respecting the other's need to be a free and independent person

—— Being easy to live with on a day-to-day basis—having a sense of humor—not being too moody

—— Being a good companion, suggesting interesting activities as well as going along with the other's ideas of what might be fun

—— Telling the other about your day's events and what you are thinking about and being interested in hearing about the other's concerns and daily activities

—— Being compatible with the other's friends and relatives, liking them and trying to make them like you

—— Being thoughtful about sentimental things such as remembering birthdays and anniversaries.

---

his marital satisfaction level will be high—making it likely that *her* marital satisfaction level will be high (see Figure 7-5).

Satisfying Psychological Needs

The psychological needs that each person fulfills for the other in marriage are, of course, inextricably interrelated to and interbound with material and sexual needs. Certainly, having a comfortable home stocked with material amenities and enjoying a mutually pleasurable and harmonious sex life will bring psychological satisfaction. However, there are other needs that are principally psychological—rather than material or sexual—that are also important to marital success: the needs for companionship, emotional security, mutual understanding, acceptance, respect, and approval (see the vignette, "The Most Valued Psychological Satisfactions in Marriage"). These needs relate to love, affection, and humor—all of which are manifestations of the human *spirit*. Love, affection, and humor are, perhaps, the most valuable assets in marriage, and lack of psychological satisfaction of these needs can be devastating—even in the presence of material success and sexual compatibility.

Unless there is a significant trade-off, satisfaction must occur in all three areas—material, sexual, and psychological—or the marriage will probably not be experienced as successful by one or both of the couple. Each of these elements of role performance in marriage may be viewed as a link in a chain—a chain that represents the marriage. Since no chain can be stronger than its weakest link, fulfilling only one or two of these elements will cause the marriage to break down. All three

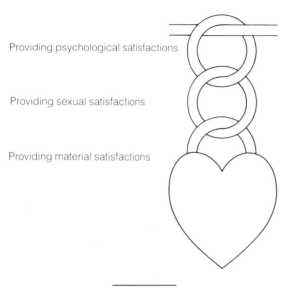

Providing psychological satisfactions

Providing sexual satisfactions

Providing material satisfactions

FIGURE 7-6
The links of a successful marriage

must be at least adequate if the marriage is to be satisfactory (see Figure 7-6).

Types of Marital Interaction

There are as many types of marital interaction as there are marriages, since each marriage and the individuals involved are unique. However, it is possible to categorize marital interactions to some extent. One of the most successful attempts to do this found that marriages could be divided into two types: the *utilitarian* marriage and the *intrinsic* marriage (Cuber and Harroff 1965). Although the research was limited to influential, socially active, economically successful, respected, policy-forming, "significant" Americans, the categories apply to all classes. The subjects of the study described their marriages as happy and stated that they had never considered a divorce or a separation, nor had they ever consulted a marriage counselor. Five distinct lifestyles showed up repeatedly in the way the couples lived together, reared their children,

made their way in the outside world, and found sexual expression. These five life-styles break down into categories of utilitarian and intrinsic marriages, with utilitarian being by far the more common.

Utilitarian Marriage

The *utilitarian marriage* is often characterized by such avoidance responses as working far from home; accepting travel assignments; using one's leisure to engage in club or civic work, church activities, or hobbies; and sleeping in separate bedrooms. It is not an expression of deep personal feelings. People who are in a utilitarian marriage consider it a satisfying, workable, and rational arrangement. It is maintained "for purposes other than to express an intimate, highly important, *personal* relation between a man and a woman" (Cuber and Harroff 1965, p. 106). Instead, such a marriage provides a "fitting constellation for adult living, child rearing, and discharging civic responsibility" (p. 130).

Most utilitarian marriages are either *passive-congenial* or *devitalized*. "Utilitarian marriages, since they most perfectly encompass the passive-congenial and the devitalized elation within the requirements of the monolithic code, probably express the world of men and women for the clear majority of middle-aged couples" (Cuber and Harroff 1965, p. 196). The difference between the two is that the passive-congenial relation never includes any depth of emotional interaction, even during dating or early marriage, whereas the devitalized relation begins as a vital relation with important interpersonal satisfactions. In the passive-congenial marriage, neither partner *ever* intends the marital relation to include deep emotional and physical comfort; each one's energies are channeled into careers, community activities, and finally, rearing children. The couple in a devitalized marriage gradually cease to share interests and activities in a deep and meaningful way. Sexual relations become far less satisfying than they once were; most of their time together is occupied with the children, guests, or community activities. Although there is little overt tension or conflict, role interaction is, for the most part, apathetic or lifeless. Many couples interviewed felt that their devitalized marriages were the most appropriate relation for the middle years and that the vital personal interactions of youth should eventually give way to "other things in life" that are "more worthy" of sustained effort.

A few utilitarian marriages are conflict-habituated. The dominant mode of role interaction in such a marriage is well-controlled tension, with an acknowledgement that incompatibility is inevitable and pervasive. "The overt and manifest fact of habituated attention to handling tension, keeping it chained and concealing it, is clearly seen as the dominant life force" (Cuber and Harroff 1965, p. 46).

Intrinsic Marriage

In contrast to the utilitarian marriage, the *intrinsic marriage* is characterized by the intensity of the feelings each has for the other. Each person believes that the other is indispensable to his or her own satisfaction in any activity, and as many activities as possible are closely shared. In short, each depends on the physical and psychological presence of the other.

From this fountainhead flow positive influences for physical and mental health, as well as creativity. A substantial professional literature in psychiatry confirms the testimony of those in the intrinsic marriages that the vitality of their kind of relation radiates far beyond the elemental ecstasy of the pairing (Cuber and Harroff 1965, p. 141).

This does not mean that the couple whose marriage is intrinsic have lost their separate identities or that they may not on occasion be competitive. However, serious disagreements arise only about important matters and tend moreover to be settled rather quickly and to the satisfaction of each. These disagreements may sometimes be settled by compromise,

sometimes by one or the other yielding, "but these outcomes were of secondary importance because the primary consideration was not who was right or who was wrong, but how the problem could be resolved without tarnishing the relation" (Cuber and Harroff 1965, p. 58).

Sexual difficulties are almost nonexistent in the intrinsic marriage. Sex is usually very important for the couple, often prevading their whole relation.

Some couples . . . just seem to click. They love one another. They find fulfillment in their sexual relations, (as well as) mutual delight in (experiencing) no conflict between their sexual activities and their other human enjoyments . . . indeed, they make no sharp distinction between them. . . . Let us call them, as does Professor Abraham Maslow, "the happy ones" (Brecher and Brecher 1966, p. xii).

Despite its vitality, the intrinsic marriage may change, either becoming a utilitarian marriage or ending in divorce.

People who live in this way place enormous stress on the personal relation—strains that are not present in the utilitarian marriage because of its avoidance devices and its modest expectations about feelings and mutuality (Cuber and Harroff 1965, p. 142).

A personal merging so intimate and so encompassing as the intrinsic relation does not come about by drift or default, and it cannot be sustained by listless attention to a mate.

You either have the whole splendid edifice or the damn thing tumbles down on you. There's just nothing halfway about this kind of life (Cuber and Harroff 1965, p. 145).

Within the intrinsic marriage exist two kinds of relations: the *vital* and the *total*. The difference between them is essentially a matter of degree. The total relation is marked by more areas of interaction than are present in the vital marriage, and almost all activities in the total marriage are shared. Fewer total than vital marriages exist, of course; and those that do exist seem rather like the superb love matches described in paperback romances.

Our society considers total and vital relations to be more appropriate to dating and the early years of marriage than to mature adult behavior. Most couples interviewed by Cuber and Harroff doubted that intrinsic relations could or should exist after husband and wife enter their thirties. Those couples whose marriages were intrinsic recognized that they were in the minority and said that they had always taken pains to conceal the depth of the marital relation from their friends, in order not to be considered odd or deceitful. The norm, then, for the well-adjusted marriage in our society is apparently utilitarian rather than intrinsic.

Extramarital Sexual Behavior

Taboos against extramarital involvement are widespread throughout the world. For example, Murdock (1949) found in his sample of 148 societies that taboo against adultery appeared in 81 percent of them. It was freely allowed in only 5 percent of the societies, although it was conditionally permitted in 13 percent.

Americans, in common with people in many other societies, oppose adultery on several grounds. It is seen as a source of distrust and conflict between the married couple, leading to personal disillusionment, unhappiness, and a broken marriage. It is believed to be a threat to the institutions of marriage and the family. Adultery is also considered deviant and immoral by many traditionally oriented people.

Adultery is a sin in all three major religions in our society—Catholicism, Protestantism, and Judaism. Until the 1960s, adultery was also a criminal offense in all states, and it still remains a criminal offense in most states (although the adultery laws are rarely enforced).[13] Adultery is a ground for divorce in all states that have not abolished all grounds for divorce and substituted "no-fault" divorce procedures. In several states, adultery was for many years the principle ground for divorce. In addition, husbands and wives known to be engaged in adultery have been subjected to widespread social condemnation. Some employers have fired or refused to promote adulterous employees. Given the strong taboo against extramarital copulation, those who practice it usually do so with deceit and in secrecy (Brecher 1984).

A generation ago, Kinsey (1953) found that "strength of religious commitment" was the strongest force inhibiting extramarital copulation for wives, and this apparently still holds true. For example, more recent studies have found that only about 15 percent of "very religious" women experience extramarital copulation, compared with about 36 percent of "nonreligious" women (Tavris and Sadd 1977). Being happily married also appears to be a strong deterrent to adultery among wives. Among husbands, being happily married is the most powerful deterrent, with religion somewhat less important than it is among wives. Lack of opportunity may be another important factor for many (Brecher 1984).

In his study of married couples who are over age fifty, Brecher (1984) notes the following:

The reasons given by our respondents for not engaging in adultery range from love and honor to timidity and lack of opportunity. While there may be subtle differences in detail and emphasis, the fidelity of wives and of husbands appears to have much in common (p. 110).

However, despite religious, legal, social, and economic proscriptions, adultery is widespread in our society. Lifelong marital monogamy is a standard that many people apparently find difficult to maintain over the years.

Extramarital sexual behavior may be very brief and occasional, or it may be serious and

---

[13]In the states now lacking laws against adultery, the state legislatures have not overtly repealed the old laws; instead, in the course of a general revision of their criminal codes, they have incidentally and quietly left out of the new codes criminal penalties for adultery.

Although religious commitment is still a strong inhibiting
force for many couples, it is not the powerful deterrent to
adultery that it was for earlier generations.

Joseph H. Davis, James and Sarah Tuttle, 1836

extended. It is usually more characteristic of husbands than of wives, although in some groups, at some ages, the incidence is higher among wives, as we shall see.

Sociologists recognize two categories of extramarital sexual behavior. Both consist of copulation with someone other than one's spouse, but there are important psychological and societal (if not legal) differences. One category is termed *extramarital copulation* or simply *adultery*,[14] which is usually covert and secret (thus the commonly used expression of "cheating"). The other category is termed *comarital copulation* or *consensual adultery*, which is defined as sexual interaction with someone other than one's spouse, with the understanding that each of the couple shall be free to engage in extramarital sexual activity if

he or she wishes—with the knowledge, consent, and approval of the other (thus the term *consensual*).

Since the first category involves some 25–70 percent of the married population (depending upon such variables as gender, age, employment, and group studied), and the second at least 5 percent, we shall examine both types of extramarital behavior in some detail.

Extramarital Copulation: Adultery

From the turn of the century to the early 1970s at least one husband in two experienced extramarital copulation.[15] The incidence of extramarital copulation among wives was about one-half that of the husbands during this time,

---

[14]The term *adultery* has an interesting heritage. It comes from the verb *to adulterate*, meaning to contaminate or weaken or make impure with the addition of an inferior substance—for example, replacing valuable with less valuable ingredients in a product in order to cheat the buyer. Thus, adultery originally applied only to the woman. If she copulated with a man other

than her husband and became pregnant, and if the husband believed the child was not his own, his blood line would be adulterated—and the woman was said to be guilty of adultery. The penalty in biblical times was death by stoning.

[15]There is no systematic research available regarding the incidence of extramarital copulation before 1900.

with about one in four having an extramarital affair (Hunt 1974, Kinsey et al. 1948).

However, the current generation of wives now engage in extramarital copulation at a younger age than wives did in the preceding generation. So the incidence among *young* (under age twenty-five) wives is now about equal to that of the same age group of husbands (one in two). Furthermore, working wives of all age groups have an incidence of extramarital copulation that is twice as high as that of housewives, equaling that of husbands (Tavris and Sadd 1977, Hunt 1974). Apparently the greater freedom of employed women is reflected in this statistic.

Recent research has found the incidence of extramarital copulation to be higher for some populations. For example, among readers of *Playboy*, young wives (in their twenties) were significantly more likely to have an affair than were the men. Among readers who were over age fifty, 70 percent of the men and just over 30 percent of the women said that they had experienced at least one extramarital affair during their lifetimes (Petersen et al. 1983). After age fifty, the incidence of extramarital copulation falls for both husbands and wives, with 23 percent of husbands and 8 percent of wives reporting that they have had an affair *after* reaching this age. About three-fourths of these adulterous husbands and wives, who were over age fifty at the time of the affair, rated their marriages as "happy" (Brecher 1984).

The meaning of an extramarital affair is often different for a man than it is for a woman. A husband tends to view his straying from the fold as a relatively casual event. A wife, in contrast, tends to view her extramarital activity as significant, serious, and even momentous. A wife tends to see adultery in the context of her marriage and of her overall life pattern. A husband tends to experience an extramarital affair more as an isolated adventure. A woman characteristically describes her extramarital affair in emotional terms, whereas a man tends to describe his in sexual terms (Brecher 1984).

Women's extramarital affairs tend to last longer and are associated with a progressive decrease in marital satisfaction. Men are more likely to associate their extramarital affairs with an increase in marital satisfaction and a decrease in tension and boredom within the marriage. Among older women, the extramarital affair is likely to be a sign of marital discontent; among younger women, the wife is much more likely to be looking for wider experiences—with a motivation similar to that of the husband (Petersen et al. 1983, Glass and Wright 1977). Only about half of all adulterous wives report being emotionally involved when they first meet the men they will have the affair with. The other half first see the men simply as friends or persons they like (Atwater 1979).

Extramarital copulation frequently implies a conscious planning, and this fits the pattern of greater sexual aggressiveness in women. It seems clear that a significant number of young working wives (as well as husbands) deliberately seek sexual experiences outside marriage. Extramarital sex cannot be attributed in all cases to a chance circumstance (Bell 1983). For example, a striking finding in the Tavris and Sadd (1977) study was that extramarital sex as a single event was not the pattern for women. Rather, it usually involved an average of at least six liaisons with each extramarital partner, with a third of adulterous wives having more than ten such liaisons. This seems to imply a willingness to maintain a series of experiences with the same person.

The reasons for engaging in extramarital sexual behavior are many and varied. They stem from a number of different motivations and a complex set of circumstances that cannot be summarized simply. Moreover, a significant difference exists between extramarital copulation that is casual and perfunctory, and an affair that is an intense emotional involvement; there is no one single kind of extramarital affair (Brecher 1984).

Generally speaking, in a happy marriage it is less likely that a partner will seek an outside sexual relation, but each marriage has its own cycles. There are periods of intense satisfaction and closeness, periods marked by neutral feelings, and other periods characterized by unhappiness, emptiness, or conflict. Stresses and dissatisfactions at different points in the marriage cycle influence the occurrence of extramarital relations. Thus, the extramarital affair may reflect not only an individual's needs but the state of the marriage as well (Reiss et al. 1980).

One of the shortcomings of the marriage might be that the wife wants to "make love" while the husband may only want to "have sex." She may turn to an extramarital affair for this reason. Of course, some husbands also want to "make love"—and turn to a romantic affair outside the marriage when the wife refuses to engage in anything except a quick, perfunctory genital encounter in the conventional manner. Brecher (1984) cites, as an example, a sixty-eight-year-old husband who has been married for thirty-nine years to a wife who wants only perfunctory sex.

She is unwilling to engage in sexual variations or extended foreplay, and is often reluctant to have sex at all. Consequently, I seek variety from two widows of about 50 years old—and from young prostitutes . . . the widows are anxious for sex, want variety, no inhibitions. The young prostitutes give me the variety of youth, beautiful bodies—but the experienced widows give me much better sex (Brecher 1984, p. 122).

Reasons for extramarital sexual behavior may include the following:

— *Variation of sexual experience:* The idea of a new partner may suggest a different, new, and exciting experience.

— *Search for emotional satisfaction:* The person may feel that his emotional needs are not being met within marriage and may seek emotional satisfaction outside the marriage.

— *Yearning for romance:* The person may feel that his or her life is passing by, that it is empty of romance. A love affair outside the marriage may seem to hold the promise of an antidote to these feelings of worthlessness and futility.

— *Curiosity:* The person may just want to see what it would be like with someone else.

— *Development from friendship:* Romantic and sexual intimacy may develop until the sexual involvement "just happens." That is, the sexual aspect may not be deliberate or planned; it may simply emerge as a function of increased interest and emotional compatibility.

— *Hedonism:* The person may have extramarital sexual affairs simply because they are pleasurable.

— *Rebellion:* The person may feel that the monogamous expectations of marriage place an undesired restriction on freedom of action, and he or she may engage in extramarital copulation as a gesture of independence. The rebellion may be directed at the marriage partner or may be against social codes in general. The motivating factor is not the extramarital sex partner, but a demonstration of unconventionality and independence to the other or to society in general.

— *Retaliation:* If one person in the marriage discovers that the other has had (or is having) an extramarital affair, the reaction may be a need for revenge. The motivation is not, then, one of sexual desire for another partner, but simply to get even. The motive may be one of revenge, to show the other that "if he (or she) can do it, so can I."

— *Spouse encouragement:* One spouse may encourage the other to engage in extramarital activity in an honest attempt to give the person the opportunity for additional sexual satisfaction. This may occur if one person is much less sexually oriented than the other or if the person is ill or incapacitated. The other aspects of the marriage may be relatively satisfactory.

Gagnon (1977) finds that the extramarital affair often provides stimulation and excitement, especially in the early stages. Each of the couple is very aroused, and they usually have only a brief time to be together. Each is on his or her best behavior, has made a special attempt to look attractive, and feels both expectation and desire—tinged with guilt. All the minutes that the couple have together are special; the combination of guilt and excitement has a heightening effect.

Some people can have extramarital affairs with total discretion and never be discovered. Others leave clues behind—an unusual long-distance phone bill, a credit card receipt from a motel, a matchstick folder, theater ticket stubs—which may be hidden messages that say to the other, "I am having an affair."

These clues may be left behind for a number of reasons. Some want to expiate their guilt by being forced to confess their infidelities. Others leave clues around because they feel hostile toward their mates. Infidelity may be a way to hurt a partner, to gain revenge for some misdeed. Still others allow their affairs to be discovered in order to end a marriage (Strong et al. 1983).

Comarital Copulation: Consensual Adultery

As noted earlier, comarital copulation or consensual adultery differs from extramarital copulation in that each grants the other freedom to copulate outside the marriage. This relaxes the commitment for sexual exclusivity and removes the necessity for deception.

There are two types of comarital copulation: *open marriage* and *swinging*. Swinging differs from open marriage in that husband and wife participate in sexually intimate behavior with another couple (or individual) together, at the same time and place. Involvement with other swinging couples (or with willing individuals) may be instigated through classified advertisements,[16] special bars or clubs, or (less frequently) previous friendships. In an open marriage each person pursues his or her sexual liaisons outside the marriage independently, and each may or may not reveal all details to the other.

Studies have found that at least 5 percent of young married couples (under age thirty) have practiced one or both of these forms of comarital copulation (Johnson 1974, Athanasiou et al. 1970, Smith and Smith 1970). Among young married couples with histories of extramarital copulation, nearly 10 percent have practiced one or both forms of comarital copulation. Among young married couples who have not practiced comarital copulation, one-third say that they probably would if the opportunity arose (Athanasiou et al. 1970). Many studies of comarital copulation have found that it is usually the husband who instigates the practice—about twice as many husbands as wives are interested in "swapping."[17]

Virtually all studies of couples involved in comarital copulation have found the majority to be relatively well-educated, relatively affluent, middle class persons, many of whom are in professional and semiprofessional occupations. They have no special political convictions but range from ultraconservative to radical. They belong to all major religious groups in about the same proportion as the total population, but their religious commitment tends to be relatively low (Smith and Smith 1970). In short, except for their practice of comarital copulation, they are indistinguishable from the rest of the middle class population (Twitchell 1974).

Proponents of comarital copulation point out that some people need variety in sexual expression even though their primary loyalty is to their marriages. For these people, the commitment to sexual fidelity reduces love and sex to duty and obligation; they must either adopt a

---

[16]There are publications that specialize in printing such items.

[17]For example, see Varni (1972), Athanasiou et al. (1970), Bartell (1970), Bell and Silvan (1970), Schupp (1970), and Smith and Smith (1970).

pattern of cheating and deception, or accept the cultural norm of limiting sexual activity to one person—which they regard as a serious infringement on their rights to enrichment and experience. The rationale for comarital sexuality is that it resolves this dilemma by openly allowing each partner to experience a variety of sexual encounters within the fabric of monogamy with the knowledge and consent of the other (Smith and Smith 1970). In a comarital relation, the couple can allow each other the freedom to relate to others sexually (as well as socially), viewing the extramarital experiences as a commitment to personal growth and enrichment (O'Neill and O'Neill 1972).

Proponents of comarital sexuality suggest that no one is always the preferred person in all situations, even though each spouse has chosen the other as the one with whom he or she is most comfortable and contented most of the time; that this primary preference does not change when one partner looks elsewhere to satisfy particular needs such as for excitement or sexual variety; and that the benefits of such a marriage (with freedom as its foundation) are increased zest for living and greater self-awareness. To date, there are virtually no research data to indicate the measure of success in translating this concept into reality.

Opponents to comarital copulation point out that the concept violates the Judeo-Christian religious precept that has forbidden sexual congruence with anyone other than one's spouse since biblical times and that emphasizes the sanctity of marriage and the importance of sexual fidelity. Our culture is based upon this precept, which is absorbed from early childhood and is very deeply embedded in the consciousness of most people.

Opponents to comarital copulation suggest that, cultural prohibitions aside, maintaining a good marriage is far more important than any pleasure that might be obtained by exploring a variety of sexual partners. Such pleasure simply may not be worth the risk of inflicting irre-

parable damage to the delicate fabric of the marriage.

Finally, the possibility of contracting an STD is always present. Fear of exposure to a venereal disease certainly has a cautionary and restraining effect on any casual sexual activity—even if it is consensual.

It is interesting to note that Nena O'Neill who, with her husband, wrote *Open Marriage* (1972)—a book that is often considered the strongest statement in support of comarital sexuality—later concludes that the most stable marriages are, in fact, based on fidelity.

Sexual fidelity is not just a vow in marriage, or a moral or religious belief, but a need associated with our deepest emotions and our quest for emotional security. Infidelity is an extremely threatening situation (O'Neill 1977, p. 199).

CHILD-FREE MARRIAGE

Although the one universal function of marriage is the legitimization of children, child-free marriage is now one of the most rapidly growing forms of marriage in our society.

Incidence of Child-free Marriage

Demographers predict that nearly one-third (30 percent) of ever-married white women age twenty-four in 1978 will have no children, as will 20 percent of nonwhite women.[18] This is quite a change. Until the mid-1970s, only about 10 percent of marriages were child-free, and this was largely due to infertility problems, not because the couple were childless by choice (Mosher 1982). If demographers are correct in their prediction, then the incidence

---

[18]U.S. Bureau of the Census, "Report on Childbearing Trends" (1979) and provisional data (February and May 1981).

Margaret Thompson/The Picture Cube

Although the only universal function of marriage is the legitimization of children, child-free marriage is one of the fastest growing forms of marriage in the United States.

of child-free marriages will increase threefold, and the incidence of those who are child-free by choice will increase at least fivefold.

This 500 percent increase in child-free marriages is occurring because of many interrelated factors. Few couples plan at the beginning of the marriage to remain child-free. The decision to remain child-free is usually reached gradually, in a series of postponements that follow four stages:

1. Initially, childbearing is put off until a definite objective is achieved, such as being out of debt.
2. Subsequently, the couple still intend to have a baby but are increasingly vague about when this event is to occur.
3. The couple begin to debate the pros and cons of parenthood.
4. Finally, the couple make the definite decision to remain child-free (Cutright and Polanto 1977, Lindenmayer et al. 1977, Veevers 1973).

Reasons for the Rise in Incidence of Child-free Marriages

Voluntary childlessness is an extraordinary modification in personal life-style, and the reasons for it are complex. Obviously, one of the chief reasons that the incidence of voluntary childlessness is increasing is the development and availability of an effective technology of contraception, which began with the advent of the contraceptive pill in the 1960s. Until effective contraceptive techniques were both available and socially acceptable, voluntary childlessness was simply not an option for most couples.

Second in importance are the economic factors relating to bearing and raising children, as we have seen (Chapter 2). Not only have children been transformed from economic assets to economic liabilities, but the choice to have a child may also be the most costly decision a couple may make. In 1980, the cost of raising a child to age eighteen was estimated to be at least $254,000 (see Chapter 13).

There are, however, other factors involved in the decision to remain childless. Demographers point to the rapidly rising incidence of cohabitation in the 1970s and the later average age upon first marriage. Some observers feel that increasing drug and disciplinary problems among children—well publicized in television programs, motion pictures, and the daily press—are contributing to the reluctance of people to become parents. These and a host of other subtle, complex, psychological, philosophical, and sociological developments have undoubtedly contributed to the trend toward child-free marriage in ways that may only be conjectured at this time.[19]

Related Demographic Aspects

Demographic factors that correlate with the incidence of child-free marriage are: (1) the wife's age at marriage, (2) how long the couple have remained child-free, (3) the degree of religious commitment, (4) the educational level of the couple, (5) the geographic area in which the couple live, (6) whether the marriage is a first marriage for the wife, and (7) whether the wife is employed.

If a woman has been married for five years and has not had a child, it is very likely that her childlessness will be permanent; 90 percent of all births occur within the first five years of marriage (Baldwin and Nord 1984). After age thirty, the odds for permanent childlessness increase further. Among child-free wives age thirty to thirty-four, it has been estimated that more than 93 percent will not have a child

(Baldwin and Nord 1984). It should be noted, however, that some demographers suggest that this figure might well be invalid in predicting future trends, pointing to the "miniboom" in births that was reported by the U.S. Bureau of the Census in the early 1980s.

Women who do not belong to a church or who do not have strong traditional religious beliefs have a much higher incidence of childlessness than those who are church members or who do have strong traditional religious beliefs (Veevers 1979).

The more education a woman has, the more likely she is to remain childless, especially if she has had four or more years of college.[20] The educational level of the husband apparently has no effect in this regard (Feldman 1981).

Women who live in urban areas are much more likely to be childless than those who live in rural farming areas; the incidence in rural nonfarming areas is about halfway between.[21] Urban areas may be more conducive to voluntary childlessness because they offer young wives a wider variety of acceptable social roles, because they are less traditionally oriented, and because of selective migration of childless couples from rural areas (Veevers 1979).

Among women who marry more than once, rates of childlessness are substantially higher—especially among remarried divorcees—than they are for women who marry only once and currently live with their husbands (Veevers 1979).

Finally, wives who are employed have substantially higher rates of childlessness than do housewives, although it is not clear whether career involvement is the cause or the consequence of the childlessness (Baldwin and Nord 1984).

---

[19]U.S. National Center for Health Statistics, "Marriages and Divorces: 1950 to 1980." *Monthly Vital Statistics Report,* 1984.

[20]U.S. National Center for Educational Statistics. *Digest of Educational Statistics,* annual (1984).

[21]U.S. National Center for Health Statistics. *Vital and Health Statistics,* Series 10, December 1984.

In short, although it is not possible to describe a "typical" child-free couple, it is possible to compile a composite portrait. Available demographic studies suggest that voluntary child-free couples have been married for at least five years without having children, tend to be relatively nonreligious, tend to be college educated, and tend to live in large urban areas. The wives either have married at a relatively late age or are in second marriages. Both husbands and wives are employed in relatively high-income positions.

Often the initial reasons for postponing childbearing might be quite different from later reasons. For example, if the young woman has experienced satisfaction from career success, she may be reluctant to give it up for motherhood. Thus she may postpone, from year to year, having a child, until she finally decides to remain permanently childless or is no longer able to conceive.[22] For example, as noted in Chapter 2, 61 percent of women in executive positions have no children.

Relative Happiness of Child-free Couples

Research data suggest that there is a positive correlation between childlessness and marital satisfaction, and that child-free couples are more likely to report being "happily married" than are couples with children (Baldwin and Nord 1984, Renne 1976). Perhaps one reason for this is that the childless couple characteristically communicate more closely—each person *attends* to the other with a greater intensity than is characteristic of couples with children (Humphrey 1977, Van Keep and Schmidt-Elmendorff 1975, Rosenblatt 1974, Blake 1973). That parents have a lower-intensity in-teraction than child-free couples is not surprising, since, once a child is born, all parents—except the very indifferent, the very rich, or the very innovative—must modify their preferences, desires, interests, and concerns to accommodate the demands and needs of child care. After the birth of a child, the life-style of most couples essentially revolves around the interests and needs of the infant or growing child. The life-style becomes child-centered in many respects, rather than adult-centered. It is involved much of the time with children's interests rather than with adult interests. In short, the social, intellectual, and economic freedom that is attained by reaching adult status is immediately and sharply curtailed by the demands of child care.

Other studies have found that child-free couples are more egalitarian than parents in their interactions with each other; the marriage is less likely to be characterized by authoritarian patterns of dominance. Thus, they work out disagreements more easily and democratically, and their gender roles are relatively interchangeable or androgynous. Again, these findings are not surprising, since the arrival of a child tends to accentuate biological gender differences and reinforce traditional gender roles (at least for the first years of childhood). In consequence, even couples who profess a liberal ideology in regard to gender role typically find that the gender-related division of labor is part of their daily lives (Bram 1978, Cooper et al. 1978, Veevers 1975).

It is impossible, however, to answer the question Is a child-free marriage characterized by more satisfaction and a more rewarding life-style than other marriages? There are simply too many variables. A couple who chooses childlessness will avoid the difficulties but will have to sacrifice the satisfactions of parenthood. Children may bring joys and delights as well as problems. The couple who opts for parenthood must sacrifice many of the advantages of remaining child-free. There is

---

[22]Women who could have conceived in their twenties may become less fertile or even sterile by their thirties. This is especially true for those who have been using the pill (see Chapter 11).

always a trade-off. Undoubtedly, many couples who initially begin by postponing having children do regret their decision when their childlessness becomes irrevocable. (It is possible to solve this problem by adopting a child, of course.) Yet also undoubtedly, other couples do not regret their decision, even though they realize they have sacrificed the satisfactions of parenthood.

Future Incidence of Child-free Marriage

As we have seen, some demographers predict that in the late 1980s there will be a surge in the birth rate among women in their thirties who have been postponing pregnancy. This may have begun in 1982, when the birth rate increased to 17 per 1,000 population, from a low of 15 per 1,000 in the late 1960s. Much of this increase could be traced to the rising birth rate among career women in their thirties who decided to have children. However, the birth rate dropped again in 1983, to 15.9 per 1,000, as the proportion of women still childless at ages twenty-five to thirty-four increased.[23] If this trend continues, it will signal a significant rise in the incidence of child-free marriages. This is not unlikely, given the current trends toward freedom and individualization in lifestyles, equality in gender roles, dual-income marriages, and the rising cost of bearing and raising children (Baldwin and Nord 1984, DeJong and Sell 1977, Poston and Gotard 1977).[24]

Whether we will return to the norms of the past with 90 percent of married couples having children or find that the current incidence of child-free marriage will persist or even increase, only the future will tell.

INTERMARRIAGE

Most marriages are homogamous. That is, as we have seen, although people marry for love, one usually manages to fall in love with another who is of the same religion, race, ethnic group, and social class as oneself. When a person marries someone of a different religion, race, ethnic group, or social class, the marriage is called an *intermarriage* or a *mixed marriage*.[25]

A substantial minority of our population do intermarry, and these mixed marriages often have personal and social characteristics different from homogamous marriages. In this section we shall explore the attitude of our society toward these marriages, the motivation to enter such a marriage, and the success rates of intermarriages (compared with homogamous marriages).

Interfaith Marriage

As noted before, an interfaith marriage is a marriage contracted by two persons of different religions. In the United States, the term *interfaith* usually refers to a marriage that "mixes" a Protestant, a Catholic, or a Jew (the three principal religions of the country), although marriage of a Mormon to an Episcopalian or of an Orthodox Jew to a Reform Jew may also be considered an intermarriage by their families.[26]

Before the separation of church and state in Western societies in the eighteenth and

---

[23]U.S. Bureau of the Census, "Childless Women and Children Ever Born, By Age of Women: 1950 to 1983." *Current Population Reports,* Series P-20, No. 397, 1984.

[24]Ibid.

[25]The concept of intermarriage or mixed marriage is sometimes interpreted more broadly. A marriage is sometimes considered "mixed," for instance, if the bride and the groom belong to two different Protestant sects, or if one is "nonreligious" and the other is "religious," or if they belong to different age groups, or if they have marked differences of intelligence or education (Landis and Landis 1977).

[26]Whether such a marriage is considered "interfaith" depends on the degree of conviction in the particular religious faiths, of course; this may be exceedingly important to some individuals or families.

nineteenth centuries, interfaith marriages were forbidden by law. In a country such as Northern Ireland, marriage between Catholic and Protestant would be impossible even today. Interfaith marriages are now legal in our society but are still rigorously opposed by all three major religions of the United States (Protestantism, Catholicism, and Judaism). This opposition is apparently largely based on two fears: (1) that the family life of the couple may be disrupted if husband and wife do not belong to the same faith, and (2) that religious affiliation may weaken or dissolve as a result of interfaith marriage.

Incidence of Interfaith Marriage

Until the 1970s, interfaith marriage in the United States was extremely rare. In 1957, for example, 88 percent of Protestants married other Protestants, 77 percent of Catholics married other Catholics, and 92 percent of Jews married other Jews.[27]

During the late 1960s and early 1970s an extraordinary surge in interfaith marriages took place (Massarik and Chenkin 1973). By the late 1970s, about one-third of all marriages being performed were interfaith (Barlow 1977). This is nearly a threefold increase in the incidence of interfaith marriage over a very short period of time.

Several reasons may be suggested for the increasing rate of interfaith marriage in our society. Religious differences appear to be less important now than they were in past decades;[28]

the trend of cultural assimilation of many minority groups has given impetus to interfaith marriages; the development of cultural similarities and values (particularly those of the middle class) has tended to diminish religious differences; and institutional controls that forbid interfaith marriages are weakening (Barlow 1977).

Institutional Attitudes toward Interfaith Marriage

Despite the recent rise in the incidence of interfaith marriages, they are still discouraged, and in some cases forbidden, by official religious doctrines of all three major faiths in our society. Protestant denominations all oppose mixed marriage, although some Protestant denominations oppose it much more than others. For example, Jehovah's Witnesses are vehement in their opposition, whereas the Unitarians are much more liberal. Since there are more than 250 varieties of organized Protestantism in America, a wide range of attitudes exists.

Catholicism is much more militant than Protestantism in its opposition to interfaith marriage, requiring that its members be married in the church if the marriage is to be sanctioned and if the person wishes to remain in a state of grace and be able to receive communion.

Catholic participation in a marriage before a civil official or non-Catholic clergy is expressly forbidden, and such a marriage, although legal in the view of non-Catholic clergy and civil authorities, is invalid in the view of the Catholic church. A Catholic who wishes to marry a non-Catholic and remain in a state of grace must first receive dispensation from his or her priest and must make a "sincere promise" to remain steadfast in the Catholic faith and to do "all in his or her power" to have all the children baptized and brought up in the Catholic church. The non-Catholic party must be informed of the promises that the Catholic party makes,

---

[27]The only available data from a nationwide sample dealing with religious affiliation and marriage were collected in the U.S. Bureau of the Census, Department of Commerce, *Current Population Survey*, March 1957, Washington, D.C.

[28]For example, an analysis using data compiled by the National Opinion Research Center found a rather substantial decline in the strength of influences for religious endogamy in the United States. "The influence of norms and social controls may well have been so weak for young Protestants and Catholics that most of the influences for endogamy for them were from geographic separation" (Glenn 1984, p. 726).

and both parties are to be "clearly instructed on the ends and essential properties" of marriage, as they are perceived by the church (Pope Paul VI 1970). Since 1970, a mass may be included as part of the marriage ceremony, subject to the local priest's consent.

The most militant of all in its opposition to a mixed marriage is Judaism, which has regarded interfaith marriage as a sin from its earliest history. Both the Talmud and the Rabbinical Codes declare that intermarriage is punishable by banning, the Judaic equivalent of excommunication.

Judaism does not recognize the legitimacy of civil marriage for its members, and a Jew is properly married only when a rabbi has officiated. Almost no Orthodox and very few Conservative rabbis will agree to officiate at a mixed marriage. Some Reform rabbis are more lenient, however, and many perform the wedding without insisting on the conversion of the non-Jewish partner, if that partner agrees to respect the other's faith and to raise the children as Jews. However, any person who sincerely undertakes to study the history and theology of Judaism may become a Jew and may then be accepted as a proper mate for the Jew whom he or she wishes to marry. The person who converts to Judaism to marry a member of the Jewish faith must promise to raise the children as Jews.

In two out of three Jewish-Gentile marriages, the husband is Jewish and has married outside his religion. (Among Catholics the woman is most likely to marry outside her religion.) About 25 percent of the Gentile wives in a mixed marriage convert to Judaism, and many more identify as Jewish even though they do not officially convert. Two-thirds of the children in these mixed marriages are raised as Jews if the husband is Jewish, and if the wife is Jewish, children are almost always raised as Jewish. Thus, the fears of religious leaders that membership of the group will decrease through intermarriage may be less well found-

ed than they think (Reiss 1980, Massarik and Chenkin 1973).

Motivation for Interfaith Marriage

As in any other kind of marriage, interfaith marriage may take place between two people simply because they fall in love and have complementary needs and interests. Given the widespread opposition to interfaith marriage, however, other factors may help explain why two people choose each other rather than someone of the same faith.

One reason for such a choice may simply be the small number of prospects within a person's own religion as compared with members of other religions. Or it is quite possible that two people of different faiths may marry because they do not consider their religious differences to be important. Moreover, a marriage that is formally classified as an interfaith marriage may, in reality, be no such thing; the couple may be agnostic or have little commitment to either religion and simply accept a nominal identification as "Protestant" or "Catholic" as the easiest way to fill out the marriage application form.

Success of Interfaith Marriage

No one really knows, or perhaps ever can know, whether a difference in the husband's and wife's religions is more or less significant than other differences, such as in physiology, metabolism (energy level), level of sexuality, or membership in social classes. Religious leaders and counselors issue dire warnings about the risks of interfaith marriages, but these opinions represent an unavoidable bias.

Objective research on interfaith marriage is quite limited. Studies that are available have found that, although the figures vary somewhat with the faiths involved, an interfaith marriage seems to have about a 10 percent higher failure rate than a homogamous marriage. There is no

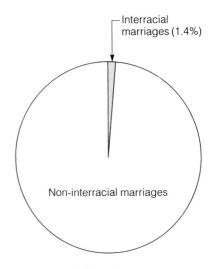

Interracial
marriages (1.4%)

Non-interracial marriages

FIGURE 7-7

Incidence of interracial marriage in the United States, 1983

Source: Data from U.S. Bureau of the Census, "Interracial
Married Couples: 1970 to 1983" (1985).

Susan Ylvisaker/Jeroboam, Inc.

Although black-white marriages are highly socially visible,
they comprise only 3.2 per thousand marriages
in the United States. Of these, the wife is usually white
and the husband black.

doctrination into the other's religion, or the particular religious practices that may interfere with the daily routine of their marriage. And, of course, it is quite possible that differences in religious doctrine may cause problems without the couple being consciously aware of the religious basis of their conflicts.

Interracial Marriage

Although the incidence of interracial marriage has doubled since the 1967 U.S. Supreme Court ruling that invalidated laws against such unions,[29] the incidence of interracial marriage is statistically negligible in the United States.

evidence that Protestant interdenominational marriages (Baptist-Methodist, for example) have a lower stability rate than intradenominational marriages (Baptist-Baptist or Methodist-Methodist) (Heaton 1984, Glenn 1982, Bumpass and Sweet 1972).

It is conceivable that although an interfaith couple do not openly disagree over their separate faiths or engage in discussions about comparative theology or the significance of different religious rituals, one or both of the couple may feel resentment or uneasiness over such factors as birth control, the children's in-

---

[29]Until 1967 many states prohibited interracial marriage by law. In that year the U.S. Supreme Court handed down a decision that all such discriminatory statutes were unconstitutional, and interracial marriage became legal throughout the United States. Before that time, a couple who had been legally married in one state might find that their marriage was declared illegal and void in another state, and that all children were regarded as illegitimate.

In 1983, only 1.4 percent of all existing marriages in 1983 were interracial (see Figure 7-7).[30]

Although it is generally assumed that black-white marriages are more common than they are (probably because they are highly socially visible), black-white marriages account for less than one in four (23 percent) of marriages classified as interracial. In other words, only .32 percent of marriages in the United States are black-white. In about three-fourths of these (72 percent), the wife is white and the husband is black.[31]

Social Attitudes toward Interracial Marriage

The interracial couple in our society is often a target for bigotry and a cause of illogical fear. This is especially true for black-white intermarriages, where both the husband and the wife may be openly or tacitly rejected by most members of white and nonwhite communities alike, and any child born to the couple may be publicly and sometimes legally classified as nonwhite.

The degree of difficulty that an interracial couple faces varies, of course, with their socioeconomic level, place of residence, and races. For example, a mixed marriage in which one person is black provokes more discrimination from the white majority than does a marriage in which one of the couple is Japanese.

Mixed marriages in the lower class sometimes meet with actual physical attack from in-laws, friends, neighbors, and even strangers. A white student on an Ohio or California college campus who marries interracially is likely to be treated with respect, but a white student on a Mississippi college campus might find it very nearly impossible to marry (or even date) interracially.

Few nations have been as determinedly opposed to interracial marriage as the United States. With the exception of the Republic of South Africa and possibly Great Britain, interracial marriages are usually accepted both legally and socially, with little or no disapproval, in almost every other large and racially mixed society in the world.

Motivation for Interracial Marriage

Most interracial marriages occur for the same reasons that homogamous marriages do—mutual heterosexual interests based on romantic or limerant attraction, propinquity, mutual interests, and personality compatibility, as discussed in Chapter 5. In most interracial marriages, the couple probably marry for precisely the same reasons as a racially homogamous couple. However, since a person entering an interracial marriage must be aware of the unusual problems involved, other factors may operate.

A white person may marry interracially for idealistic reasons—that is, to defy the prevalent cultural prejudice of our society. Such a marriage may demonstrate that the person refuses to identify with racial bigotry.

Interracial marriage may occur as a rebellion against parental authority. This presumes, of course, that the parents are racially prejudiced—a presumption that is all too often true.

The lure of the exotic may induce a person to be attracted to someone from another race. Attractions based on such differences are

---

[30]Fifteen groups were recognized as different races in the 1980 U.S. Bureau of the Census Survey: White, Black, American Indian, Eskimo, Aleut, Chinese, Filipino, Japanese, Asian Indian, Korean, Vietnamese, Hawaiian, Samoan, Guamanian, and other. Although persons of Spanish-Hispanic origin are not classified as a separate race, in the 1980 Census the U.S. Census Bureau collected data on Spanish-origin population of the United States with respondents classifying themselves in one of the specific Spanish origin categories listed on the questionnaire—Mexican, Puerto Rican, Cuban, and others. The concept of race as used by the Census Bureau does not denote any clear-cut scientific definition of biological stock (*Statistical Abstract of the United States*, 1985, p. 3).

[31]U.S. Bureau of the Census, "Interracial Married Couples: 1970 to 1983" (1985).

described in the literature of many societies, both ancient and modern.

It should be emphasized, however, that most interracial marriages probably occur for the same reasons that homogamous marriages do, as noted before.

It is conceivable that the motivational factors for interracial marriage may, in many cases, counterbalance the social pressures against the marriage. The very fact that an interracial couple go through with the marriage, despite the difficulties of which they must be aware, indicates their high motivation for marrying. This motivational factor may be so unusually high that the marriage may succeed despite its social context.

Success Rate of Interracial Marriage

Since interracial marriages constitute only about 14 per 1,000 American marriages, it is difficult to assess their outcomes. No national figures are available, and most of the available data do not indicate the exact racial composition of the marriage. Moreover, no major marital adjustment study has yet been made on interracial marriages. Many sociologists indicate that interracial marriages are more hazardous than homogamous marriages, but there is very little statistical evidence to either support or refute this belief (Reiss 1980).

Although black-white marriages have an incidence of divorce that is one to four times higher than that of white-white marriages (depending on various factors such as which spouse is black, age upon marriage, education, and income), an Iowa study found that black-white marriages are actually more stable than black-black marriages (Monahan 1970).[32] Furthermore, the study found that marriages

in which the husband was black and the wife white had a divorce rate that was lower than that of white-white homogamous marriages. Another study found, however, that marriages in which the husband was white and the wife black had a higher divorce rate than homogamous marriages (Heer 1974). These data are puzzling and difficult to interpret but certainly seem to rule out the premise that black-white marriages are necessarily less stable than homogamous marriages in the United States.

Because of their concern about the effect of interracial marriage on their children, wives in black-white marriages are more likely to be childless than those in homogamous marriages (Heer 1974). Sociologists have found, however, no evidence that there is any special discrimination against children of such mixed marriages. The children are simply considered to be blacks by both the white and the black communities, and they are neither more nor less acceptable to either racial community than other black children. The problems of adjustment connected with discrimination against children, then, are concerned only with the disappointment of the white person in the marriage, who might hope for a different response from the white community (Reiss 1980).

Interethnic Marriage

There are no figures available on the incidence of interethnic marriage in the United States. It is usually assumed that it is undoubtedly far more common than interracial marriage, and perhaps even more common than interfaith marriage. However, in the absence of statistical data such assumptions are purely speculative.

Since marriage license applications do not usually request ethnic information, there are also no data available about the divorce rates of interethnic marriage as compared with homogamous marriage.

---

[32]The study was based on data from only one state, Iowa, and so may be atypical, but until other studies are done that contradict this one, the implications are both significant and intriguing.

The structure of our society is such that the immigrant family usually absorbs our language and cultural patterns by the second generation. The children of these families often reject the ethnic identification of their parents in order to enter the mainstream of American life. Ethnic groups seldom persist beyond the first generation in the United States as identifiable or socially visible groups. The ethnic factors that operate in the United States are probably more closely related to the attitudes of the individuals and their relatives and friends, than they are to any generalized discriminatory characteristic of our society.

Interclass Marriage

As we have seen (in Chapter 5) most marriages are homogamous with regard to social class. However, interclass marriages do occur. Since marriage license applications do not require the person to indicate class membership, there are no data regarding the incidence of interclass marriage in the United States.

Interclass marriages do have a somewhat higher divorce rate than middle class homogamous marriages, when the men have married "up" and the women have married "down"[33] (Carter and Glick 1976, Cutright 1971). Apparently this is not because the marriage crosses social class lines, however, but because marital instability is related to income (which, in turn, is related to social class). Low-income families have a higher rate of divorce for many reasons (see Chapter 8).

Conversely, interclass marriages in which the wives marry "up" and the men marry "down" may be expected to have a *lower* incidence of divorce than marriages in which both members are lower class, since such a "mixed" marriage would have a higher income than a homogamous lower class marriage.

MARRIAGE WHILE IN COLLEGE

Incidence of Campus Marriage

Campus marriages are a rather recent phenomenon in our society. Before World War II, many colleges and universities actually expelled students who married while in school. In the late 1940s, however, with the enrollment of thousands of veterans in schools all over the country, the married student ceased to be a statistical rarity. In 1982 about 10 percent of men and 14 percent of women were married and living with their spouses while in college.[34] In addition, 10 to 30 percent of students (depending on the college) were living with someone of the opposite sex without being married (see Chapter 6).

Motivation for Campus Marriage

Perhaps the central reason for the large percentage of student marriages (as well as the growing percentage of cohabitation) is the increasing stresses associated with the contemporary American mass society. Among the present generation of young people, the need to belong—the need for emotional support and security, for companionship, for love, in short, for a permanent paired bond—has become more pressing and significant in the context of our relatively impersonal society. Marriage, or a close paired bond without being married, is expected to fulfill these needs.

---

[33]Demographic studies are published on the relation between income and divorce, and income is usually related to social class.

[34]U.S. Bureau of the Census, "Households, Families, Subfamilies, Married Couples, and Unrelated Individuals: 1950 – 1982" (1984).

Consequences of Campus Marriage

Possibility of Pregnancy

Even with the recent developments in contraceptive techniques, a surprising number of unwanted pregnancies still occur among young married couples. (See the discussion on birth control and unwanted pregnancies in Chapter 11.) A substantial number of campus couples have to deal with the expenses and complications of children who are neither expected nor wanted.

A Stanford University study of the reasons for unwanted pregnancies among college women found that the most frequent reason (for 35 percent) was that the women thought they had copulated during the "safe period." The second most common reason (for 33 percent) was that a contraceptive method has been used but it failed.[35] The third most common reason (for 29 percent) was fear of the side effects of certain contraceptives. Twenty-seven percent thought, "It couldn't happen to me"; 21 percent "put the possibility of pregnancy out of mind"; and 9 percent said, "I half-wanted to get pregnant" (Miller 1975).[36]

Obviously, an unwanted (or even wanted) pregnancy brings problems of crowding, increased expenses, and the logistics of child care. One of the live issues on many campuses today is child care. If women are to have equality of opportunity for educational pursuits, as well as fulfill their biological and social role of producing and raising children, some means must be found to provide for child care without necessitating the mother's full-time responsibility for this function. (For further discussion of this point, see Chapter 2.)

Potential Loss of Parental Subsidy

One problem faced by students who marry while in college is finding enough money to continue school, even in the absence of pregnancy. One source of income is, of course, parental subsidy. Yet, although many parents continue to provide financial support for their children after marriage, others do not.[37] On one hand, parents who withdraw support feel that marriage is a statement of economic independence: "When you marry, don't expect any more help from us." On the other hand, many parents feel that financial assistance is even more vital after marriage than it was before to ensure that their children's education will be completed.

Economic Pressures

If parental subsidy is fully or partially withdrawn following the marriage, the couple, of course, are subject to sustained economic pressure. A much larger percentage of married students, as compared with single students, work part-time and go to school part-time.[38] A common problem for a person who tries to work and go to school at the same time is the threat of low grades because there is not enough time to study. The penalty for a poor performance may be substantial—a substandard income and an unwanted occupation for the remainder of that person's working life.

To give one member of the married couple the freedom to study, the other (usually the wife) may drop out of college and work full-time. This solves the problem for the person who is able to remain in college but curtails the other's intellectual growth and limits his or her capacity for entering a profession or well-paying job. Also, the couple's intellectual and

---

[35]When the respondents were asked what contraceptives they had used, the replies were nothing (54 percent), rhythm (14 percent), contraceptive foam (9 percent), withdrawal (5 percent), diaphragm (5 percent), IUD (3 percent), condom (3 percent), and other methods (2 percent).

[36]The percentages total more than 100 because many respondents gave more than one answer.

[37]U.S. National Center for Education Statistics, *Digest of Education Statistics,* annual, and *Financial Statistics of Institutions of Higher Education* (1984).

[38]U.S. Bureau of Labor Statistics, *Special Labor Force Bulletin* 191, 83-160 (1984).

social development may be unequal, so that the person who remains in college in a sense "outgrows" the other.

Loss of Freedom for Intellectual Inquiry

Perhaps the greatest danger of an early marriage for each of the couple is that intellectual inquiry may be stifled and educational goals may become solely achievement of job qualification rather than inquiry for knowledge and self-development.

Intellectual life demands some kind of postponement of his early domesticity . . . which has always been characteristic of most savages, of most peasants and of the urban poor. . . . In European history it has been the young men of the elite class who have been permitted to postpone responsibility while they have a chance in some reasonably protected environment to think, and to make friends . . . and discuss things, and develop and change their minds and explore. This is the thing we're cutting out in this country.

Early student marriage is domesticating boys so early they don't have a chance for a full intellectual development. They don't have a chance to give their entire time to experiment, to think, to sit up all night in bull sessions, to develop as individuals . . . . There is a tendency to substitute easy domesticity for a period of stretching one's intellectual and ethical muscles before one settles down (Mead 1960).

Effect on Grades

Research on the effect of college marriage on grades is inconclusive. Some studies have shown grades to be improved, whereas others have shown that grades decline (Busselen and Busselen 1975). Moreover, there is no study available on the number of married students who drop out of college, as compared with single students, and without this information, it is difficult to assess grade point averages. Thus, in the light of available research, it is simply not possible to say whether marriage raises or lowers grades for students in general.

Finally, the effect of marriage may be quite different from one individual to another. Students vary in emotional maturity; intellectual maturity; self-knowledge; academic, professional, or career motivation; vocational preparedness; and ability to earn money to subsidize their studies—as well as in ability to resolve the conflicts of marriage. For these reasons, one student may find that his or her grade point average drops substantially following a marriage, while another may actually get higher grades.

THE LIFE CYCLE AND MARRIAGE

Everyone goes through a life cycle that begins with conception and ends with death. The rhythms and cycles that govern our lives are fundamental, and their importance has long been recognized. (See the vignette, "Rhythms and Cycles.")

We each begin life as a single-celled organism (the fertilized egg) and proceed through the prenatal stages to birth—making the enormous transition to become air-breathing creatures. At what point we become "human" during this period is still a subject of controversy (see Chapter 11 for a discussion of this issue in regard to abortion). The first year (infancy) gives way to early, middle, and then late childhood. At puberty we enter adolescence, and then proceed to adulthood. The demographic expectation is that we will enter middle age and then old age, although this was not the expectation until the present century. The fact that people are living longer today means that a greater percentage of the population will experience middle age and old age. In prior generations, relatively few lived to middle age, and even fewer to old age (see Table 7-1).

At some point during the adult stage of the life cycle, all but 5 percent of us marry, and the stages of life from then on are very closely tied to the marriage cycle. The stages of the marriage cycle can be divided into the *prechild*

Rhythms and Cycles

All our lives are governed by rhythms or cycles in a very fundamental way. One day follows another as the sun rises and sets, as the earth spins around. Winter is followed by spring, summer, and fall in endless cycles as the earth circles the sun. The tides sweep in and out as the moon circles the earth. All life is cyclic, with one generation following another in an endless sequence. We all proceed from infancy to old age (unless death intervenes) with the events of our lives marking the passage of time. The importance of these rhythms and cycles has long been recognized. The following excerpt is from Shakespeare, *Julius Caesar*, Act IV, Scene III.

There is a tide in the affairs of men,
Which, taken at the flood, leads on to fortune;
Omitted, all the voyage of their life
Is bound in shallows and in miseries.
On such a full sea are we now afloat;
And we must take the current when it serves
Or lose our ventures.

An even more resonant acknowledgment of the importance of harmony and rhythm comes from the Old Testament (Ecclesiastes 3:1–7):

To everything there is a season, and a time to
  every purpose under the heaven;
A time to be born, and a time to die; a time to
  plant, and to pluck up that which is planted.
A time to kill, and a time to heal; a time to
  break down, and a time to build up.
A time to weep, and a time to laugh, a time to
  mourn, and a time to dance;
A time to cast away stones, a time to gather
  stones together; a time to embrace, and a
  time to refrain from embracing;
A time to rend, and a time to sew; a time to
  keep silence, and a time to speak;
A time to love, and a time to hate; a time of
  war, and a time of peace.

TABLE 7-1

Life expectancy in the Western world

Year of birth	Years of life
B.C.	18
A.D. 1	22
1200	33
1600	33.5
1800	35
1850	40.9
1900	49.2
1946	66.7
1960	70
1975	72.6
1980	73.6
1983	74.5

Sources: Data from Wallechinsky et al. (1981); U.S. Bureau of the Census, *Report on Population Projections* (1984).

years, the *child-rearing* years, the *launch years* (middle age), and the *retirement years* (old age). (For a description of one person's experience with the shifting meaning of marriage through the early and middle years, see the vignette, "What I Was and What I Am Now.")

There has been very little research on the stages of child-free marriage. Undoubtedly these marriages go through a cyclic pattern from the early years through middle age to old age, but little investigation has been done, as yet, regarding these characteristics.

Prechild Years

In terms of satisfaction in the marriage, researchers find that, for most couples, the prechild years are the happiest of all stages in the marriage cycle. Apparently, the best of all

What I Was and What I Am Now

In 1968, a few weeks before we were going to be married, my husband-to-be looked at me and earnestly asked me to make three promises. "Promise me we'll never be bourgeois; promise me we'll never be bogged down by possessions; promise me you'll never grow up."

Just as earnestly, I answered him: "I promise." I was twenty-two; he was twenty-five.

For four years, we lived in our attic apartment surrounded by books, listening to music by candlelight, the air laced with incense. We drank copious amounts of wine, got stoned, ate Italian food. Our furniture was made up of castoffs. Our funds were limited. I wore my hair long and wild. My earrings hung down to my shoulders. On Sundays we went to museums.

We were politically motivated and never missed a peace march. I worked hard for Eugene McCarthy and other peace candidates. After the massacre at Kent State, my husband, in protest, refused to take his finals for his master's degree in history. We talked of living in Europe, away from the America that killed its children.

But in the end we stayed. We had our own children. Our first was born in 1972, our second in 1974. We needed more room. We needed a washing machine, a dryer.

Instead of the Beatles and Beethoven, we listened to Sesame Street records. Reading became impossible. There just wasn't time.

Money became important to us. There were doctor bills, and anyone with children knows what baby shoes cost. Our Sundays were spent at the playground. We gave up pot, afraid we would not be able to handle emergencies.

But through all the changes in our lives, we still clung to a certain vision of ourselves. We were different from our parents. Our children would be brought up in a different atmosphere: more open, with two parents who cared for them equally. They would see their parents openly show affection to each other, be stimulated by their conversation, grow up concerned with the well-being of their fellow human beings.

We moved from our attic to a five-room flat, and then to our own house in a New Jersey suburb. We made new friends. We bought a dining-room set, we did our kitchen. We needed a lawnmower, then lawn furniture.

My hair thinned after childbearing, and I had to cut it short. Dungarees gave way to designer jeans, and the number of gold chains worn by both men and women became a subject of discussion.

Gradually, I became caught up in the consumer society. Furniture, fashion and jewelry were becoming important to me. I polished my nails.

Because of our economic situation, it became necessary for both of us to work, and we spent less and less time with our children.

However, while we felt settled, there seemed to be a constant feeling of uneasiness. Our friends, all good people, seemed to have lived through a different time, with different experiences: As far as I can see, as long as they had no personal involvement in the way, they had no thoughts about it, one way or the other.

I sometimes feel that if I told them of my continuing despair over Cambodia, most of them would not know what I was talking about. These people never wanted anything more than to be replicas of their parents, living comfortable, middle-class lives, passing along these same values to their children.

I am now thirty-four years old. My husband is thirty-seven. We are slaves to our possessions. We live a bourgeois middle-class life and were forced to grow up with the births of our children and the death of my mother.

Aside from my silent melancholy and secret feeling of guilt about my life-style, I am very sorry that without realizing it we have become like our parents just as our friends have come to resemble theirs.

In 1968, when we were married, we believed that our generation would have a lasting influence on the conscience and soul of America. Perhaps we were naive. I now believe more and more that people like us were an aberration, that for every activist, every person with a lasting commitment to the betterment of American society, there were fifty who never considered the war as good or evil, and like their parents

(continued)

before them, consider minorities only in the context of their effect on property values.

As for those of us who care passionately about the war, civil rights, and the quality of life for all humanity, we have become trapped in the labyrinth of our consumer-oriented society. We have forgotten our idealism and given up our dreams.

I am terribly frustrated by this lack of commitment. I am furious with myself for losing sight of my three promises given so earnestly and honestly twelve years ago.

Source: Mirium Picket, *New York Times,* November 15, 1980. © 1980 by The New York Times Company. Reprinted by permission.

---

possible worlds is to be newly married and not have children. Karen Renne (1970) summarizes her study of almost seven thousand parents as follows:

Contrary to popular belief, child-free marriages are more satisfactory than others; parents, especially those currently raising children, were definitely less apt to be satisfied with their marriages (p. 66).

The finding that the prechild years of marriage are usually the happiest for most couples is not new. A generation ago, Blood and Wolfe (1960) conducted extensive interviews with wives in urban, suburban, and farming communities. They concluded:

The first few years of marriage are a honeymoon, which continues the romance of the courtship. With the birth of the first baby, satisfaction with the standard of living and companionship decline. In subsequent years, love and understanding lag. . . . These trends do not involve all couples, but affect a very large proportion of the total. In the first two years of marriage, 52 percent of the wives are very satisfied with their marriages, and none notably dissatisfied. Twenty years later, only 6 percent are still very satisfied, while 21 percent are conspicuously dissatisfied (pp. 87–88).

The concept that children will save a troubled marriage is certainly erroneous; if the marriage is in trouble to begin with, children will only intensify the problems.

Most marriages never return to the happiness level of the prechild stage. However, many research studies agree that the years after the children have left are almost as happy as the prechild years, so the curve of marital satisfaction has a U shape (see Figure 7-8).[39]

This does not mean, of course, that all marriages follow this curve, since there are great differences from one marriage to another, and the degree of marital satisfaction depends more on such factors as quality of communication and degree of commitment than on the stage of the marriage. The studies cited are reports of averages and group data, and there are great individual differences in the effect children have on a marriage. Many couples experience considerable rewards from parenthood, and their degree of satisfaction rises with successive stages in the marriage cycle. These couples take great pride in their children's accomplishments. They manage the child-rearing years with a minimum of conflict and increased satisfaction, despite the added difficulties and complications that children bring to the marriage. When children are wanted and planned for, especially when there are no great economic pressures, they can bring great joy, satisfaction, and a sense of fulfillment.

Child-rearing Years

The prechild stage of marriage is usually relatively brief. Among women married since 1965, nearly one in four had already given birth or become pregnant at the time of her marriage, and 73 percent had given birth to at least

---

[39]Although there is a certain amount of controversy over the details of the curve and the problem of subjectivity defining "marital satisfaction," the research of Rollins and Feldman (1970) that established the U-shaped curve of marital satisfaction over the marriage cycle has been supported by other studies, which are summarized in Spanier et al. (1975).

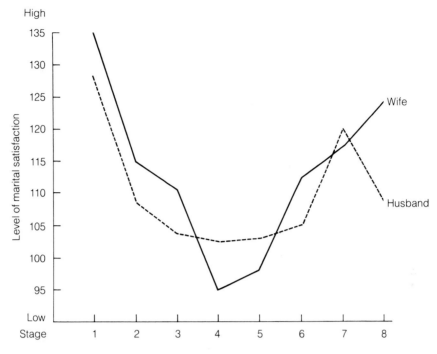

STAGE
1 Prechild years
2 Oldest child under three
3 Oldest child three to six
4 Oldest child six to thirteen
5 Oldest child thirteen to twenty-one
6 First child gone to last child gone—the "launching" years
7 Postchild years to retirement (middle-aged marriage)
8 Retirement to death of husband or wife (progression into old age)

FIGURE 7-8

Satisfaction over the marriage cycle

Source: Spanier et al. (1975, pp. 270–71). Copyright 1975 by
the National Council on Family Relations.
Reprinted by permission.

one child by the first wedding anniversary.[40] Although many couples are now postponing the birth of their first child, as we have seen, 73 percent of women married in the early 1970s had given birth to at least one child by the fifth

wedding anniversary (Baldwin and Nord 1984).

With the transition to parenthood, many changes occur. The couple's income drops sharply at precisely the time when their expenditures increase, since a mother usually stops working (at least for a time) so she can care for the child. When the mother does return to work (as most do), she continues to have the chief responsibility for child care and

---

[40]U.S. Bureau of the Census, "Percentage of Women with a Premaritally Conceived First Birth Who Married Before the Birth by Age and Race: 1982" (1985).

housekeeping. It is not surprising, then, that working mothers often feel harassed, over-worked, and "tied down" (Cowan et al. 1978, Rubin 1976, Campbell 1975).

The demands and difficulties of parenthood, and the problems involved in balancing do-mestic and work commitments, can cause considerable stress and decrease marital satisfaction. Although most couples usually re-port an emotional "high" and a sense of fulfill-ment following a baby's birth, these are often followed by significantly lower feelings of self-esteem (Cowan et al. 1978).

The extensive research in the literature re-garding the impact of children on a marriage has been summed up as follows (Campbell 1975):

Almost as soon as a couple has kids, their happy bub-ble bursts. For both men and women, reports of happiness and satisfaction drop to average, not to rise again significantly until their children are grown and about to leave the nest (age eighteen). Couples with young children also report feeling more stress and pressure than any other group. The mothers, most of whom are between the ages of twenty-five and thirty-four, carry the burden of child-rearing, and the pressures are most acute for them. They are the most likely group to describe themselves as feeling tied down, to express doubts about their marriages, and to wish occasionally to be free of the responsibilities of parenthood (p. 41).

The precipitous drop in the satisfaction of the marriage begins to slow down and level off for the husband when the oldest child reaches age three, but it continues to drop for the wife until the oldest child reaches adolescence, at which time it rises sharply (see Figure 7-8). Apparently teenagers do not require the amount of time and attention that younger chil-dren do, and they also bring increasing grat-ification to their parents. (The reverse may also occur, for example, in a family where teen-agers are the source of grief and despair, especially if they become involved with illicit pursuits such as drug abuse.)

In terms of the marriage cycle, middle age begins when the last child has left home. At this stage couples experience the highest level of satisfaction since the early, prechild years of marriage.

Michael Heron/Woodfin Camp & Associates

Lower class parents do not experience such a high level of reported satisfaction as middle class parents during the teenage stage because they often feel a severe financial pinch. Lower class adolescents are frequently pressured to move out of the home and earn their own living, to establish economic and social inde-pendence.

Middle class parents usually experience ris-ing incomes during the teenage stage, and the children are not generally expected to be eco-nomically independent. Rather, they are often sent to college while the parents continue to be financially responsible for them.[41]

The reported satisfaction level of parents continues to rise during the "launching" stage, which begins when the oldest child leaves home to become financially independent (and

---

[41]U.S. Bureau of Labor Statistics, *Special Labor Force Bul-letin* 191, 83–160 (1984).

The Midlife Crisis: A Nonevent?

Although the mid-forties are often regarded as a time of soul-searching and preoccupation with one's diminishing biological abilities, there is little or no research evidence to support the concept of a midlife crisis.

For women, middle age does bring about the menopause, but, as noted in Chapter 4, the difficulties of the menopause are largely a cultural myth. Most women regard it as a period of increasing tranquility, contentment, and (often) increased sexuality.

For men, there is not even the sudden ending of a biological process, but only a progression of gradual biological changes—certainly nothing that could be called a crisis, except in certain individual cases when the crisis could be psychological.

Skolnick (1978) conducted extensive research on the marriage cycles of eighty-four couples. She summarizes her conclusions regarding the alleged midlife crisis as follows:

In recent years there has been much talk of a "midlife crisis." ... It has been compared to adolescence, in that it involves a questioning of one's basic identity and a concern with sexuality. Only 2 of the 84 marriages studied seemed to be affected by anything like the midlife crisis as it has been described. In one, a seemingly contented marriage of seventeen years broke down when the husband became convinced he was a homosexual; after some experimentation, he decided he wasn't, but the relation with his wife was seriously impaired. Another man reported he was vaguely dissatisfied with his marriage, although he couldn't figure out why, and thought about finding a "cute young mistress" (p. 265).

---

usually to get married) and ends when the youngest child has gone.

Postchild Years: Middle-Age Marriage

In terms of the marriage cycle, middle age is defined as beginning when the last child has left home. It is characterized by the highest satisfaction level since the early years of marriage.

Midlife often announces itself with a surge of new energy . . . or with a growing recognition that we are coming to the end of familiar roles and ways of living. We often take stock of our lives, desiring to use our time and our abilities in new and different ways. . . . We may experience a change in our perspective—a heightened awareness of the passage of time and the value of the time we have left (Doress et al. 1984, p. 439).

As a result of two trends—a longer life expectancy and a shorter childbearing period—a contemporary couple spend about half their married lives in middle and old age, in contrast to earlier generations when few people lived past middle age (Norton 1983).

Although some studies have reported that women entering middle age experience many difficulties of role transition (Lowenthal et al. 1975), recent research has been unable to verify the existence of an "empty nest syndrome"—that is, depression and a sense of uselessness. On the contrary, mothers typically respond to the departure of their children with a sense of relief (Glenn 1975, Rubin 1976).[42]

It is interesting to note that the so-called midlife crisis apparently does not exist. Although changes gradually occur to everyone

---

[42]For an excellent discussion regarding parents' feelings when their children leave home, see *Ourselves and Our Children: A Book by and for Women*, by the Boston Women's Health Book Collective (1978).

Drawing by Claude: © 1974 The New Yorker Magazine, Inc.

"Well, now that the children have all grown up, I guess I'll pull up a chair."

during the life cycle—biologically, socially, emotionally, and intellectually—most people do not experience anything that could be regarded as a crisis. (See the vignette, "The Mid-life Crisis: A Nonevent?" on p. 275.)

Most American parents continue their relation with their adult children after the children have left home, providing reciprocal services, living near them, and visiting regularly. When they live too far apart for regular visiting, they maintain contact by telephone and by letter and often get together for extended visits (Troll et al. 1979).

Retirement Years: Progression into Old Age

There is a good deal of misinformation and misunderstanding about the characteristics of the retirement years and old age. It is widely believed, for example, that elderly people are usually in poor health and have little interest in sex. On the contrary, relatively few elderly people are in poor health, and their interest in sexual activity does not decrease significantly compared with middle age.

When Does Old Age Begin?

Old people themselves often place the beginning of old age at eighty (Starr and Weiner 1981). Most people regard old age as beginning somewhere between age sixty and age eighty (very few people in their fifties are regarded as elderly, whereas very few in their eighties are not). The U.S. Bureau of the Census arbitrarily fixes old age as beginning at age sixty-five, although with the 1978 legislation advancing mandatory retirement age to seventy, *this* may soon be regarded as the "official" beginning of old age.

The average man who survives to age sixty-five can look forward to approximately another fourteen years of life (to age seventy-nine), and

Continuing Achievement after Age Sixty-five

Money, health, and independence are certainly important factors influencing satisfaction during old age, but attitude and expectation are also of great importance. Some people near or over age sixty-five start new hobbies; others begin actively pursuing some long-suppressed artistic or creative interest such as music, writing, or painting; others start new businesses or accomplish a great feat or achieve a position of power and influence. For example:

—— Francis Chichester sailed alone around the world in a fifty-three foot yacht at age sixty-four.

—— Winston Churchill became the British Prime Minister for the first time and started an epic struggle against Hitler at age sixty-five.

—— Colonel Sanders started his Kentucky Fried Chicken franchise chain after age sixty-five.

—— Golda Meir became the Prime Minister of Israel at age seventy-one.

—— Cardinal Angelo Roncalli became Pope John XXIII and inaugurated major changes over five years to start a new era in Roman Catholicism, at age seventy-six.

—— Grandma Moses, (Anna Mary Robertson), who started painting in her late seventies, had her first one-woman exhibit at age eighty, and was still actively working at age one hundred.

—— Konrad Adenauer assumed the leadership of postwar West Germany at age seventy-three, a position he maintained until age eighty-seven.

—— Benjamin Franklin made possible the adoption of the U.S. Constitution by skillful mediation among disagreeing convention delegates, at age eighty-one.

—— Winston Churchill, having resigned from a second term as the Prime Minister of Great Britain at age eighty, returned to the House of Commons as an ordinary Member of Parliament and won another Parliamentary election at age eighty-four.

—— Pablo Casals, cellist and composer, was still giving concerts at age eighty-eight, eight years before his death at age ninety-six.

—— Eubie Blake, ragtime pianist and composer, was still actively working as a musician at age ninety-nine, and in 1982 (a year before his death) he had feature roles in several television specials—a medium that had not been invented when he was in his fifties!

---

the average woman can anticipate another eighteen years (to age eighty-three).[43] In 1983, persons sixty-five or older comprised more than 26.9 million people (nearly 12 percent of the population), with women over sixty-five the fastest growing segment of the American population. (Between 1960 and 1970, the number of women over age sixty-five increased twice as fast as the number of men over this age.) If this trend continues, people over age sixty-five will be 25 percent of the population by the year 2020. Another of the fastest growing groups is those over age eighty-five. In 1983, some 2.5 million Americans were eighty-five or older.[44]

Retirement and Old Age

Retirement and old age are not necessarily synonymous, of course. Many people retire well before old age, and others are still actively working in their seventies, eighties, or even older. (See the vignette, "Continuing Achievement after Age Sixty-Five.")

From the perspective of the marriage cycle, retirement brings many changes. For example, the retired person has more hours to spend

---

[43]U.S. National Center for Health Statistics, U.S. Life Tables and Actuarial Tables, 1949-1951; 1959-1961; 1974-1984 (1985).

[44]Ibid.

Except for the prechild years, the retirement years are the happiest period of the average couple's life.

TABLE 7-2

Ratings of their marriages by couples over age sixty-five

Marital Feature	Percentage
Marital happiness:	
very happy	45
happy	49
unhappy	3
undecided	3
Marriage improved or worsened over time:	
better	53
worse	4
about the same	41
undecided	2
Happiest period in marriage:	
present time	55
middle years	27
young adult years	18

Source: Adapted from Stinnet et al. (1972, p. 667).

with his or her spouse in travel or at home in leisure pastimes, sports, or hobbies, but there is usually less money for such recreational activities.

Satisfaction in Old Age

Satisfaction with one's life is higher during old age than at any other stage of marriage except the prechild years. This forms the second leg of the U-shaped curve of reported marital satisfaction. For husbands, but not for wives, the satisfaction level drops off somewhat at retirement (see Figure 7-8). When couples over age sixty-five were asked to rate their marital happiness, 94 percent were either "happy" or "very happy"; more than half felt that their marriages had improved over time and thought the present time was the happiest in their marriages (see Table 7-2).

Not surprisingly, studies have found that reported satisfaction is greater for higher-income couples than for working class couples (Darnley 1975). If the retirees can continue to live in comfortable surroundings, eat well, indulge their hobbies, and perhaps travel, their satisfaction level is obviously going to be higher than if they cannot do these things. Professional or managerial couples who have received higher salaries during their working lives and more generous pensions for retirement can retire with a better financial position than working class couples for whom retirement often brings a radically reduced standard of living (Darnley 1975). Nearly one out of seven elderly persons experience severe economic depression, existing at a marginal level below the officially designated "poverty line."

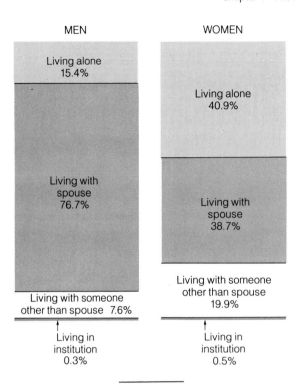

MEN

WOMEN

Living alone
15.4%

Living with
spouse
76.7%

Living with someone
other than spouse 7.6%

Living in
institution
0.3%

Living alone
40.9%

Living with
spouse
38.7%

Living with someone
other than spouse
19.9%

Living in
institution
0.5%

FIGURE 7-9

Living arrangements of men and women after
age sixty-five, 1983

Source: Data from U.S. Bureau of the Census, "Persons 65
Years Old and Over—Characteristics, by Sex:
1960 to 1983" (1985).

The poverty rate for women over age sixty-five is more than double that of men. The majority of the elderly poor are widows, only 5 percent of whom collect deceased spouses' benefits.[45]

The retiree not only must have earned and saved enough to be financially secure during the initial years of retirement, but must also be prepared for the later years, since inflation causes a fixed income to fall further and further with each passing year. Because of the shrinking value of the dollar, a person who is financially secure at retirement may be poverty stricken a few years later.

Old age usually brings with it the role of grandparent. About two-thirds of grandparents enjoy the role; about one-third do not. Some discomfort and disappointment arise from conflict with the adult children over how to rear grandchildren. When this happens, the adult children often try to keep the grandparents at a distance, causing them to feel unappreciated and unwelcome (Wood and Robertson 1976, 1978).

Health in Old Age

Health is a major influence on a person's satisfaction throughout the life cycle, but it is especially important in old age because of the inevitability of declining biological functioning with increasing years.[46] However, contrary to popular belief, the overwhelming majority of the elderly are healthy. In one recent study of older Americans (ages sixty to ninety), 72 percent described their health as "excellent" or "good," while 25 percent rated their health as "fair"; only 3 percent said "poor" (Starr and Weiner 1981; Table 56). The same study found that 29 percent of the respondents were still working (Table 59).

Independence in Old Age

Not only are most older people healthy, but many live independently. Less than 1 percent of those over age sixty-five live in institutions such as nursing homes (see Figure 7-9). Nearly 77 percent of men over age sixty-five live with their wives, and more than 15 percent live in their own homes in essential independence. Less than 8 percent live with someone other than their spouses. About 41 percent of women live alone in their own homes; more than 38 percent live with their husbands; nearly 20

[45]U.S. Bureau of the Census, "Report on Poverty in the United States" (1984).

[46]On the average, those over sixty-five visit physicians 50 percent more often than, and have health care and medical costs nearly four times those of, younger persons (Starr and Weiner 1981).

percent live with someone other than their husbands.[47]

Sexuality after Age Sixty

It is commonly believed that most people have little or no sexual life after age sixty, that they live in some kind of sexual wasteland, with declining interest, responsiveness, and performance. Although Kinsey (1948, 1953) included older people in their sample (the subjects ranged to age ninety), the emphasis was on sixteen- to fifty-five-year-olds. In the Kinsey report *older people* usually refers to those between fifty and sixty.

Long overdue, data about the sexuality of older people are now available in the work of Starr and Weiner (1981). This study specifically addressed the nature of sexuality between ages sixty and ninety-one.

Starr and Weiner found that the sexual responses of women change very little after age sixty. Older women who were sexually active experienced as much (or more) satisfaction in sexual interaction as they did in their younger days—usually achieving orgasm. Three out of eleven of these older women produced vaginal lubrications similar to that of women in their twenties.[48]

Moreover, Starr and Weiner found that there was no age limit to female sexuality. Typical of their respondents' comments is the following from a woman in her eighties:

I want you to know that I am eighty-three years old. He was eighty-five. We had sex right up until the end. We loved it and it was wonderful (p. 52).

Among sexually inactive respondents (20 percent of the total), 96 percent said they desired sexual relations but had no opportunity.

Fifty-seven percent of the sexually inactive said they would desire sexual relations more than once a week, 18 percent would opt for twice a week, and 12 percent for three times a week or more. Only 13 percent would opt for less than once a week.

More women than men lacked the opportunity for sexual relations simply because there are more widows than widowers. Eight out of ten older men are married, as opposed to six out of ten older women. More than 6 million women age sixty-five and older lived alone in the United States in 1982.[49] Starr and Weiner found that since three out of four wives eventually become widows, many women over age sixty are simply without sex partners. The report concludes that the most crucial reason for lack of sexuality in older women was the nonavailability of men.

Starr and Weiner found that 80 percent of men over sixty are sexually active. Among these, more than 50 percent report copulating once or twice a week—a figure comparable to Kinsey et al.'s forty-year-olds; 13 percent reported twice-a-week copulation; 12 percent reported copulating three or more times a week; 18 percent reported copulating five or more times a week; and 9 percent reported copulating daily.

In addition, Starr and Weiner's data refute the assumption that frequency of sexual interaction decline sharply with each decade after age sixty. They found that the average frequency for men in their sixties was 1.5 times per week; for those in their seventies it was 1.4 times per week; and for those in their eighties it was 1.2 times per week—certainly not a precipitous decline.

Starr and Weiner did find differences in the older man's sexuality, compared with the middle-aged man. The erection does not last as long as it does for a younger man, the ejaculate

---

[47]U.S. Bureau of the Census, "Marital Status and Living Arrangements" (1984).

[48]These were women who each had an active sexual episode once or twice a week throughout their mature years.

[49]U.S. Bureau of the Census, "Report on Poverty in the United States" (1984).

is not as forceful and has less volume, and the refractory period may last longer. However, the older man can usually copulate much longer than the younger man without ejaculating.

There is apparently a broader sensate focus in the older man, in contrast to the younger man's focus on penile response and ejaculation. Whereas the younger man feels a compulsion to ejaculate, for the older man the importance of ejaculating is greatly decreased. The older man can derive immense satisfaction from a sexual episode without ejaculating.

Failure to achieve an erection can occur at any age, and after age forty this may occur more frequently. However, a reflex erection is an almost invariable response to tactile stimulation in the sexually interested man, whatever his age (see Chapter 4).

Apparently the fact that copulation occurs less frequently at age seventy-five than it does at age twenty-five does not mean that the sexual experience is less meaningful or satisfying. The quality of the orgasm is far more important than its frequency, and for two-thirds of the sexually active older men the experience of orgasm was often stronger than when they were younger (Starr and Weiner 1981).

The conclusion that must be drawn from these data is that frequency of orgasm is not an accurate measure of a satisfactory sexual life.

Return to Singlehood: Widows and Widowers

All marriages that do not end in divorce must end with a return to singlehood for one of the couple when the other dies. Common emotions evoked by bereavement are regret and guilt ("If only I had . . ."); anger ("It's not fair!"); and denial, or inability to accept the reality of the loss (Kalish 1981). These feelings are accompanied by so much stress that the death of a spouse is assigned the maximum number of "stress units"—100. Other traumatic experiences are scaled down from that. For example, a jail term is assigned sixty-three stress units, being fired

is assigned forty-seven, and sex problems are assigned thirty-nine (Kagan and Haveman 1980; p. 415).

High stress levels not only cause such emotional problems as depression, but also result in lowered resistance to physical ailments. Stress affects the body's immune system, so that the person is less resistant to a wide variety of illnesses and consequently is subject to a higher mortality rate (Soiffer 1982, Hales 1981, Lynch 1977).

Since the average woman's life expectancy is about eight years longer than the average man's, and since the average wife (in a first marriage) is about two to three years younger than her husband, she can expect to spend her last eleven years in singlehood—unless she remarries, of course. But the probability for remarriage for an elderly widow is relatively low.[50] The remarriage rate for widowed women over age sixty-five is one-seventh that for men.[51] That is, for every seven elderly widowers who remarry, one widow remarries. As a result of these three factors (women's longer life span, the relatively low remarriage rate of widows after age sixty-five, and the age differential between husband and wife) only 40 percent of older women are married as compared with 80 percent of older men.[52] (See Figure 7-10.)

In 1983, there were more than 7.6 million widows over age sixty-five in the United States (with a median age of sixty-eight), as compared with about 1.4 million widowers (with a median age of seventy-one).[53] This difference in

---

[50]There is an even greater age discrepancy for wives in second marriages and for wives who have married after the median age for a first marriage; these women can expect to be widows for a longer time than the eleven-year average cited for the "average" widow.

[51]U.S. National Center for Health Statistics, "Marriages and Divorces: 1960 to 1981" (1985).

[52]U.S. Bureau of the Census, "Marital Status and Living Arrangements" (1984).

[53]U.S. Bureau of the Census, "Percent Married and Divorced of the Population, 18 Years and Over: 1960 to 1983" (1985).

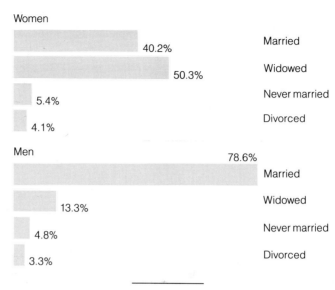

Women

Married 40.2%

Widowed 50.3%

Never married 5.4%

Divorced 4.1%

Men

Married 78.6%

Widowed 13.3%

Never married 4.8%

Divorced 3.3%

FIGURE 7-10

Marital status of persons over age sixty-five
in the United States, 1983

Source: Data from U.S. Bureau of the Census, "Percent Married
and Divorced of the Population, 18 Years and Over:
1960 to 1983" (1985).

marital status is reflected in the living arrangements of older Americans. About 41 percent of women over age sixty-five live alone, as compared with about 15 percent of men, as we have seen.

SUMMARY

Marriage stands midway between courtship and the establishment of a family in an interlocking system. It is an essential part of the culture of almost every known society.

The marriage contract formalizes the couple's rights and obligations toward each other and toward any children they might have. It establishes kinship relations with relatives on each side. Although most people enter into marriage with an expectation of permanence, virtually all societies provide for the possibility of divorce.

Until the present century in Western society, marriage was viewed chiefly as an institution of divine significance, but during the nineteenth century the emphasis shifted toward marriage as a civil institution. In the twentieth century, the meaning of marriage has again shifted, with an emphasis on personal satisfaction. However, all three views of marriage are still important, and most marriages in our society are performed before the clergy and are contracted according to civil law.

A successful marital interaction depends on three fundamental factors: congruence of role perception, reciprocity of role performance, and equivalence of role function, that is, the couple must basically agree about their mutual expectations. They must also interact in a way that fulfills each other's important expectations. And the satisfaction provided by each, for the other, must be of relative equivalence. This role performance occurs in three basic areas: psychological, sexual, and material. Obviously, there are great differences from one person to another and from one couple to another in terms of these expectations, role interaction, and fulfillment. In utilitarian marriages, for example, the focus is mainly on practical matters; in the intrinsic marriage, the focus is on the quality of the interaction between the couple.

Extramarital sexual behavior (adultery) is seen as a source of distrust and conflict, and is considered a sin, in all three major religions in our society. Nevertheless, adultery is widespread, with at least one in two husbands and one in four wives having an extramarital affair. Working wives have an incidence of extramarital copulation that is twice as high as that of housewives (equalling that of husbands), and some surveys find that young wives (in their twenties) may be more likely to have an extramarital affair than the husband. The meaning of an extramarital affair is often different for a man than it is for a woman. Men tend to experience an extramarital affair as an isolated sexual adventure, whereas women characteristically describe it in emotional terms, although the meaning of the affair may vary significantly from one person to another.

Child-free marriages increased markedly during the 1970s and 1980s, and demographers predict that nearly 30 percent of marriages will be child-free in the future. Fully 90 percent of all first births occur within the first five years of marriage; if a woman has been married for this long and has not had a child, it is likely that her childlessness will be permanent. Among childless wives age thirty to thirty-four, it is estimated that more than 93 percent will not have a child.

Interfaith marriages have been increasing in our society since the late 1960s, and it is estimated that about one-third of all marriages are now interfaith, mixing Jews, Protestants, and Catholics. Interfaith marriages have about a 10 percent higher rate of divorce than do religiously homogamous marriages.

Interracial marriages are rare in our society, with an incidence of only 1.4 percent of all marriages. (The U.S. Bureau of the Census recognizes fifteen categories of race.) Very little is known about the success of interracial marriage.

Little is known, also, about the incidence of interethnic marriage in the United States, since marriage applications do not usually ask for ethnic information. Even less is known about interclass marriages, except that the relation of social class to income results in a higher incidence of marriage failure if the husband is the lower class member.

Campus marriages were relatively rare in the United States until the 1940s, with many colleges actually expelling students who married. They are now quite common, however (as is the incidence of couples living together without being married). Whether a campus marriage proves beneficial or not depends on many factors, chiefly economic. A chief danger, of course, is that the freedom of inquiry is limited or curtailed by domestic responsibilities.

Most marriages go through a cycle that begins with the prechild years, moves to the child-rearing years of the parental marriage, the postchild years of the middle-age marriage, and finally into the retirement years and progression into old age. Researchers have found that the satisfaction level follows a U-shaped curve that is highest in the early and later years and lowest during the child-rearing years. However, there are great individual differences in this regard, and the satisfaction and pleasure that children bring to a marriage may outweigh the added difficulties, pressure, and economic hardship.

Most married couples remain in good health after age sixty-five and continue to have an active sex life until the marriage ends with the death of one of the couple. The husband usually dies first, and the wife returns to a period of singlehood that may last for a decade or more. During this time, interaction with other family members, particularly children and grandchildren, becomes especially important.

QUESTIONS

1. What is the one universal function of marriage in all societies?

2. What are the three basic forms of marriage? What is the most preferred form? The least preferred form? Which form occurs in most societies? Discuss the shift in the meaning of marriage from medieval to contemporary times.

3. Discuss the three fundamentals of a successful marriage.

4. Discuss the characteristics of the utilitarian marriage.

5. Discuss the characteristics of the intrinsic marriage.

6. Discuss the difference between extramarital copulation and comarital copulation. What is the incidence of each in our society?

7. Describe the various reasons why a person might engage in extramarital sexual behavior.

8. How did the incidence of child-free marriage change during the 1970s? Describe the possible reasons for this change. What do you think the future trend will be with regard to child-free marriages?

9. What are the possible meanings of the term *intermarriage*?

10. What is the incidence of interfaith marriage in the United States? What has happened to the incidence of interfaith marriages in the United States in the last two decades? Why do you think this change has occurred? Discuss the Protestant attitude, the Catholic attitude, and the Jewish attitude toward interfaith marriage.

11. What is the incidence of interracial marriage in the United States? Discuss our society's attitude toward interracial marriage.

12. What are some of the problems and rewards of marriage while in college? What are some of the difficulties a campus marriage might encounter? What effect does marrying while in college have on the person's grades?

13. Describe the life cycle of a marriage.

14. The curve of satisfaction over the marriage cycle is U-shaped. Discuss the implications of this curve.

15. What is meant by the statement: "The midlife crisis is a nonevent"?

16. Recent research has shattered many stereotypes regarding sexuality after age sixty. Discuss the nature of this research and the chief findings.

17. A significantly greater number of wives are returning to singlehood than are husbands following the other's death. Give three reasons for this.

SUGGESTIONS FOR FURTHER READING

Beer, W. *Househusbands: Men and Housework in American Families.* New York: Praeger, 1983.

Blumstein, Philip, and Schwartz, Pepper. *American Couples: Money, Work, and Sex.* New York: William Morrow, 1983.

Brubaker, Timothy H. *Later Life Families.* Beverly Hills, Calif.: Sage Publications, 1985.

Burgwyn, Diana. *Marriage Without Children.* New York: Harper & Row, 1981.

Carter, L. A., and Scott, A. F., eds. *Women and Men: Changing Roles, Relationships, and Perceptions.* New York: Aspen Institute, 1976.

Markson, E. W. *Older Women*. Lexington, Mass.: Lexington Books of D. C. Heath, 1983.

Rubin, Lillian Breslow. *Women of a Certain Age: The Midlife Search for Self*. New York: Harper & Row, 1979.

———. *Worlds of Pain*. New York: Basic Books, 1976.

Starr, Bernard D., and Weiner, Marcella Bakur. *Sex and Sexuality in the Mature Years*. New York: Stein & Day, 1981.

Steinberg, Lawrence D., ed. *The Life Cycle: Readings in Human Development*. New York: Columbia University Press, 1981.

Stuart, I. R., and Edwin, L. *Interracial Marriage: Expectations and Realities*. New York: Grossman, 1973.

Wells, J. Gipson. *Current Issues in Marriage and the Family*. New York: Macmillan, 1979.

C H A P T E R   8

Divorce and Remarriage

The Probability for Divorce
The History of Divorce
Annulment
The Meaning of Divorce for the Individual
The Meaning of Divorce for Children
Remarriage following Divorce
Special Problems in Remarriage

*There are two ways to catch any knife
that fate may throw at you—
by the blade or by the handle.*

Sicilian proverb

In the preceding chapter we examined the characteristics and the life cycle of a marriage in which the couple remain married. However, many marriages end in divorce. (Divorce fig-

ures usually include annulments, legal separations, and, presumably, desertions.)[1]

---

[1] Annulments and legal separations combined amount to about 7 percent of the divorce figures (U.S. National Center for Health Statistics, *Vital Statistics of the United States*, annual, 1984). Desertion figures are difficult to estimate, since desertions are usually not a matter of formal record, but most desertion figures may be presumed to be ultimately included in the divorce figures, since most lead to divorce.

THE PROBABILITY
FOR DIVORCE

The probability that a given marriage will end in divorce depends upon many different factors. Some of these are simply actuarial—the mathematical probability that of any number of marriages, a percentage of them will reach the divorce courts. These actuarial factors are very complex, however, and there are several different ways to estimate the divorce rate.

In addition to the actuarial factors, there are many individual factors that influence the probability for divorce in any marriage—for example, the age of each of the couple at marriage; their educational levels, occupations, and income; their races; the geographic area of the marriage; the family background of each of the couple; the influence of children; and the emotional maturity of each of the couple.

In this chapter we shall examine each of these variables, and trace the origin of divorce in Western civilization and its increasing incidence in our society. (The one fact that has remained unchanged during the last century in the United States is that the divorce rate has been steadily rising.) We shall also examine the characteristics of the remarriage, as most of those who divorce soon remarry.

Computing the Divorce Rate

Demographers use many methods to estimate the divorce rate from the raw data available to them. We shall cite three of those most commonly used.

Ratio of Divorces to Marriages

One method of arriving at the probability for divorce is simply to compare the divorce rate with the marriage rate. For example, in 1983, the divorce rate was 5.0 per 1,000 population and the marriage rate was 10.5 per 1,000.[2] In that year, the divorce rate was about half the marriage rate (see Figure 8-1). Presumably, then, if this ratio were to continue, about half of all marriages would end in divorce.

One problem with this method of arriving at the prospect of divorce is that the persons who get divorced in any one year are not those who get married. Is it then statistically sound to treat these numbers as though they are of the same group? Moreover, the divorce rate fluctuates from year to year, as does the marriage rate. A method that avoids these objections is to use the refined divorce rate.

The Refined Divorce Rate

The refined divorce rate is defined as the number of divorces each year per 1,000 existing marriages. If this rate is averaged over a twenty-year period, the fluctuation in the divorce rate is taken into account. For example, the average refined divorce rate from 1950 to 1970 was about 10. (The refined divorce rate is stated as a part per 1,000.) This means that during this twenty-year period, 10 per 1,000, or 1 percent of all marriages, ended in divorce each year. Since the average marriage lasted about 31.5 years during this twenty-year period,[3] the total number of marriages ending in divorce was about 31.5 percent (1 percent per year for 31.5 years). This is the figure commonly accepted as the divorce rate from 1950 to 1970.

Ratio of Divorces to Deaths

A third method of computing the incidence of divorce is to compare the percentage of marital dissolutions caused by divorce each year (or other period of time) with those caused by

---

[2]U.S. Bureau of the Census, "Marital Status and Living Arrangements" (1984).

[3]U.S. Bureau of the Census, *Statistical Abstract of the United States* (1971).

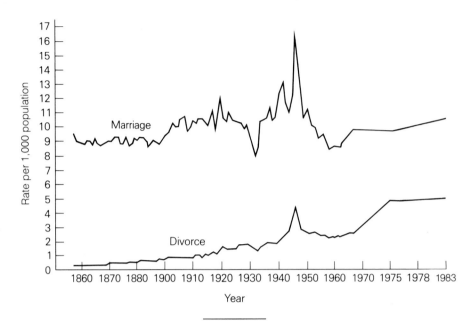

FIGURE 8-1

Marriage and divorce rates per 1,000 population
in the United States, 1860—1983

Source: Data from U.S. Bureau of the Census, "Percent
Married and Divorced of the Population, 18 Years and Over:
1960 to 1983" (1985).

death during the same period. Since all marriages must eventually end in either divorce or
death, many demographers feel that comparing the divorce rate with the death rate gives
the most useful figure—the percentage of marriages that end, not in the death of one of the
couple, but in divorce (Davis 1972).

Using this measure, the final column in
Table 8-1 shows that divorce as a percentage of
total marital dissolutions was very low in
1860; only 3.5 percent of marriages ended in
divorce (rather than death) that year. By 1970,
the number of marriages ending in divorce
(rather than death) had reached 44 percent. By
1983, the last year for which this figure is currently available, 50 percent of marriages were
ending in divorce (rather than death).[4] This
figure corresponds closely to the ratio of divorces to marriages.

In summary, according to the ratio of the
number of divorces to the number of marriages, the estimate of the probability of marriage ending in divorce is currently about 50
percent. According to the refined divorce rate
method, the probability of a marriage ending in
divorce averaged 31.5 percent during the
twenty-year period from 1950 to 1970. According to the ratio of marriages ending in divorce
rather than death, the probability of a marriage
ending in divorce is currently about 50
percent.

Average Time before Divorce

How long, on the average, do unsuccessful
marriages last? During what year of married

[4]U.S. Bureau of the Census, "Marital Status and Living
Arrangements" (1984).

TABLE 8-1

Annual marital dissolutions by death and legal divorce and rates per 1,000 existing marriages, 1860–1970

Year	Dissolutions per year		Per 1,000 existing marriages[a]			Divorces as percentage of total dissolutions
	Deaths[b]	Divorces[c]	Deaths	Divorces	Combined	
1860–64	197,200	7,170	32.1	1.2	33.2	3.5
1865–69	207,000	10,529	31.1	1.6	32.7	4.8
1870–74	226,400	12,417	30.3	1.7	32.0	5.2
1875–79	238,600	15,574	28.7	1.9	30.6	6.1
1880–84	285,400	21,746	30.6	2.3	33.0	7.1
1885–89	290,400	27,466	27.6	2.6	30.2	8.6
1890–94	334,800	36,123	28.3	3.1	31.3	9.7
1895–99	328,800	45,462	24.9	3.4	28.4	12.1
1900–04	390,800	61,868	26.5	4.2	30.6	13.7
1905–09	427,400	74,626	25.4	4.4	29.8	14.9
1910–14	453,600	91,695	23.7	4.8	28.5	16.8
1915–19	551,000	119,529	26.0	5.6	31.6	17.8
1920–24	504,200	164,917	21.9	7.2	29.0	24.6
1925–29	573,200	193,218	22.6	7.6	30.3	25.2
1930–34	590,800	183,441	21.9	6.8	28.7	23.7
1935–39	634,600	239,600	21.9	8.3	30.2	27.4
1940–44	656,400	330,557	20.4	10.3	30.7	33.5
1945–49	681,200	485,641	19.2	13.7	32.8	41.6
1950–54	692,400	385,429	18.2	10.0	28.3	35.9
1955–59	733,600[d]	385,385	18.3	9.2	27.8	34.2
1960–64	n.a.	419,600	n.a.	9.6	n.a.	n.a.
1965–69	n.a.	544,800	n.a.	11.7	n.a.	n.a.
1960	790,400	393,000	18.9	9.4	28.3	33.2
1961	789,200	414,000	18.7	9.8	28.6	34.4
1965	820,800	479,000	18.5	10.8	29.4	36.9
1970	908,200	715,000	19.3	15.2	34.5	44.0

[a]Existing marriages, 1860–1949, from Jacobson (1969, Tables A6–A9, A22, number of married men); 1950–60, from U.S. Bureau of the Census, *Historical Statistics of the United States* (1975); 1961 and 1965 from *Statistical Abstract of the United States* (1971); 1970 from *U.S. Census of Population: 1970, United States Summary* (p. 311).

[b]Deaths to married persons, 1860–1955, from Jacobson (1969, p. 178); 1959–61 from U.S. National Center for Health Statistics (1970). Mortality (A) for relevant years; 1965 and 1970 estimated by present writer.

[c]Divorces, 1860–1954, from Jacobson (1969, Table 42); 1955–69 from U.S. National Center for Health Statistics, "Divorce Statistics, 1969," *Monthly Vital Statistics Report*, July 22, 1971, vol. 20, no. 4, supplement 2; 1970 from "Annual Summary for the United States, 1970," September 21, 1971, vol. 19, no. 13.

[d]Average for 1955 and 1959 only.

Source: Data from Davis (1972, Table 8, p. 256). Reprinted by permission of Professor Kingsley Davis.

life is a divorce most likely to occur? A number of studies have shown that marriages that end in divorce are generally of rather short duration. Most marriages that end in divorce do so rather quickly—within two to six years, with a separation preceding. This means that the couple probably start quarreling almost immediately and separate within a few months of the

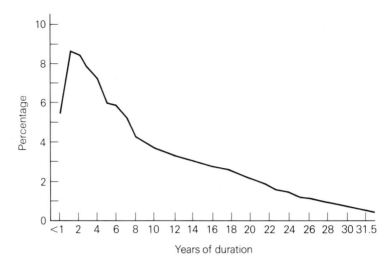

The highest incidence of divorce occurs from the third to the sixth years of marriage, peaking at the third year. After that the incidence gradually drops with each succeeding year of marriage.

FIGURE 8-2

Years between first marriage and divorce

Source: Data from U.S. National Center for Health Statistics, *Vital Statistics of the United States,* annual (1980).

marriage. The average duration of all marriages that end in divorce is about seven years; this figure includes marriages that have lasted ten, fifteen, twenty, thirty years, or longer. Figure 8-2 provides a graphic illustration of this.

Although the average marriage that ends in divorce lasts seven years between the wedding and the final divorce decree, divorces generally come sooner in the western area of this country and later in the eastern area. This is a pattern that sociologists have long noted but cannot easily explain.

Individual Probability for Divorce

In understanding and interpreting divorce figures, it is important to recognize that the individual expectation for divorce may be far re-

moved from the national rate. Thus, the statement that about half of all marriages may be expected to end in divorce rather than death says very little about the individual's expectation. Some groups have much higher rates of divorce than this, while others have much lower rates. A married couple who are characterized by several of the high-risk demographic categories have an expectation for divorce higher than a couple who are characterized by several of the low-risk categories. We shall examine the most important demographic categories that are correlated with a high or low divorce rate.

Age at First Marriage

Age at marriage is one of the most critical factors determining the probability for divorce.

"Oh, what do you two know about life? You're still on your first marriage!"

Youthful marriages (before age twenty) have a much higher divorce rate than other marriages. For example, men who marry before age twenty have twice the divorce rate of those who marry at ages twenty to twenty-four, and have *more* than twice the divorce rate of men who marry at ages twenty-five to twenty-nine. Women who marry under age seventeen have twice the divorce rate of women who marry at ages eighteen or nineteen, and *three* times the divorce rate of women who marry at ages twenty to twenty-four (Glick 1984).

Early marriages have a much higher rate of divorce than other marriages for many reasons. To begin, a person is usually less emotionally mature in the teenage years than in the twenties and is thus less able to make a sound marital choice. Moreover, teenage marriages are very highly correlated with premarital pregnancy, and premarital pregnancy is, in turn, correlated with a higher divorce rate (Carter and Glick 1976, Landis 1975).

Teenage marriages are more common in the lower class, and the relative economic instability of this class, puts financial pressure on the marriage. Early marriage curtails a person's vocational preparedness, making it very difficult to earn enough money to support a family without great economic hardship. In other words, teenage marriages usually are

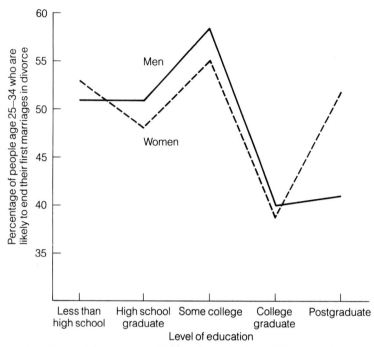

About half of the first marriages of those age twenty-five to thirty-four in 1980 may end in divorce, but the chances of divorce vary with the level of education.

FIGURE 8-3

Divorce and level of education

Source: Glick (1984). This figure, originally entitled "Young Adults and Divorce," was derived from U.S. Bureau of the Census, *Current Population Survey* (June 1980).

correlated with lower social class, lower education, lower-status occupation, and lower income—all of which correlate with a relatively high chance for divorce.

Education, Occupation, and Income

There is a complex relation between level of education and likelihood for divorce (see Figure 8-3). Women who have a high school education have a lower rate of divorce than those who do not have a high school education. For men, though, the rate of divorce is about the same for men who have not completed high school as it is for those who have graduated from high school. The likelihood for divorce rises for both men and women with some college education, but it falls sharply for college graduates. For women, the likelihood for divorce again rises sharply for those with more than five years of college; for men, though, it rises only slightly.

Age at marriage continues to influence the divorce rate, despite the educational level. For example, regardless of a woman's education, those who marry youngest are most likely to separate or divorce.

Status of *occupation* is more consistent in its

relation to the divorce rate, especially for men. The lower the occupational status of the husband, the greater is the likelihood for divorce. Foremen are more likely to have stable marriages than unskilled or semi-skilled workers, and managerial and professional men are more likely to have stable marriages than lower-level white-collar workers (Carter and Glick 1976). For women, an increase in occupational status also increases the likelihood of marital stability—*except at the top levels*, where the opposite is true. The divorce rate of top-level women executives is four times the national average.[5]

Finally, *income* appears to be a more powerful predictor of marital stability than either education or occupation. For men, the lower the income, the higher the incidence of divorce; and the higher the income, the lower the incidence of divorce. For high-income women, however, the pattern is reversed (Glick and Norton 1977, Carter and Glick 1976, Glick 1975). For example, the divorce rate of all adult women who earn $25,000 or more is more than twice the average for all women.[6]

It is not clear why the divorce rate increases for women at the upper end of the economic scale, although this pattern parallels the experience of women at the upper end of the job status scale. It may be speculated, however, that top-level women have more independence and freedom than other women, although why this should translate into a higher divorce rate remains unexplained.

The reason a relatively low income is correlated with a higher divorce rate seems obvious. Low-income families are subjected to economic pressures that can be extremely corrosive to the human spirit and the harmony of the marriage. It is, therefore, not surprising that the rate of divorce (as well as of separation and desertion) is much higher for low-income marriages (Norton 1983, Carter and Glick 1976, Rubin 1976). In fact, income is so important to marital stability that it even overrides the demographic risks of early marriage: The tendency toward marital dissolution among early marriages is moderated for the couple who have a relatively high income (Spanier and Glick 1981).

Race

The divorce rate is much higher among blacks than it is among whites (see Figure 8-4). Although income is positively correlated with marital satisfaction and negatively correlated with divorce[7]—thus the rate of marital failure declines for both races with increasing income—blacks have a much higher divorce rate than whites in all income brackets (Norton 1983, Carter and Glick 1976). In fact, the racial differential in divorce rates (the difference between the rate of divorce for blacks and the rate of divorce for whites) is actually *greater* among high-income groups than it is among low-income groups. As income increases for blacks and whites, the ratio of black divorces to white divorces increases (although the rate of divorce goes down for both groups).

Similarly, as educational level increases, divorce rates drop for both races, but the black-white differential is higher at the upper educational levels than it is at the lower levels, following the patterns of increased income (Carter and Glick 1976).

At nearly all levels of education, black persons (35–44 years of age) had a higher proportion ever divorced than did their white counterparts. Moreover, there was a definite tendency for this discrepancy to increase at the higher education levels. Evidently the mechanisms of social control that tend to inhibit divorce among better-educated whites must operate to a lesser degree among black persons with a similar amount of education (p. 436).

---

[5]U.S. Bureau of the Census, "Income and Marital Stability" (1980), and provisional data (May 11, 1981).
[6]Ibid.

[7]"Positively correlated" means they both go up (or down) together; "negatively correlated" means that as one goes up, the other goes down.

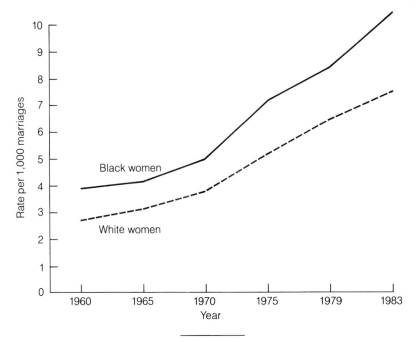

FIGURE 8-4

Black and white women—rates of divorce per 1,000 marriages of women age eighteen and older, 1960—1983

Source: Data from U.S. Bureau of the Census, "Percent Married and Divorced of the Population, 18 Years and Over: 1960 to 1983" (1985).

A similar pattern occurs with age at marriage among blacks. Although younger marriages have a much higher divorce rate for both races, Norton (1983) found that in every age-at-marriage category, the black divorce rates are significantly higher than those of whites.[8]

The reasons are not known why blacks have a higher rate of divorce at every educational, income, and occupational level as well as every age-at-marriage category. However, it may

be speculated that the factors include enormous volume of black migration, both from region to region and from country to city.

Geographic Area

Some areas have a much higher rate of divorce than other areas, with divorce rates by states generally increasing from east to west and from north to south.[9] Thus, the southern states have higher divorce rates than those in the north, and the western states have higher divorce rates than those in the east (see Figure 8-5).

---

[8]It is also presumed that the desertion rate for blacks is much higher than that for whites, although, as we have seen, the complete desertion rates are not available for either race. As an indication of the desertion rate, however, it may be noted that in 1983, fully 60 percent of all black families living at or below the poverty level had a female head with no adult man present. (U.S. Bureau at the Census, "Report on Poverty in the United States" and provisional data, 1984).

[9]U.S. National Center for Health Statistics, "Divorces and Annulments—Number and Rate, by State: 1965 to 1982" (1984).

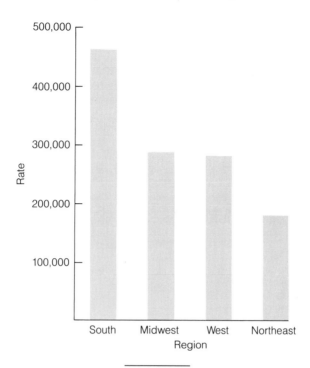

FIGURE 8-5

Divorces and annulments by region
in the United States, 1981

Source: Data from U.S. National Center for Health Statistics,
"Divorces and Annulments—Number and Rate, by State:
1965 to 1982" (1985).

Family Background

Classic studies from 1937 to 1953 have agreed that childhood background is the single most important factor determining marital success.[10] Specifically, a person most likely to have a successful marriage has the following background: (1) parents who are happy in their marriage, (2) a happy childhood, (3) lack of conflict with the mother, (4) home discipline that was firm but not harsh, (5) strong attachment to the father, (7) lack of conflict with the father, (8) parental frankness about sex, (9) in-

frequency and mildness of childhood punishment, and (10) an attitude toward sex that is anticipatory and free from disgust and aversion.

In contrast, a person whose parents were unhappily married and who was unhappy as a child is unlikely, statistically speaking, to make a successful marriage. In other words, marital happiness, as well as marital unhappiness, seems to run in families.

Influence of Children.

From a purely demographic point of view, it is interesting to note that a marriage is most likely to end in divorce if the couple have no children and least likely if they have three or

---

[10]See Burgess and Wallin (1953), Burgess and Cottrell (1939), Terman (1938), Popenoe and Wicks (1937).

TABLE 8-2

A summary of demographic factors related to divorce

Trends in divorce rates

The long-term trend in the U.S. divorce rate has been steadily upward during the past hundred years, although the rate has fluctuated in short-term intervals. By 1983, the divorce rate had reached an unprecedented high of 5.0 divorces per 1,000 total population, which was about half the marriage rate.

Family background

All Americans whose homes were broken in childhood by divorce or desertion have a higher divorce rate than those whose parents remained married.

Age at first marriage

Women who marry at ages fourteen to seventeen are twice as likely to divorce as women who marry at age eighteen or nineteen, and three times as likely to divorce as women married at ages twenty to twenty-four.

Men who marry in their teens are about twice as likely to divorce as men who marry at ages twenty to twenty-four, and more than twice as likely to divorce as men who marry at ages twenty-five to twenty-nine.

Educational level

Men and women with college degrees have an especially high rate of marital stability; those with less than a high school education have an especially low rate. However, at the highest educational levels (graduate school), the rate of marital stability drops for women but not for men.

Regardless of women's educational level, those who marry youngest are most likely to divorce; that is, women who marry before their twentieth birthday have relatively high divorce rates, even with one to three years of college education.

Income

Men and women with relatively low family income have the highest rate of marital instability, whereas those with a relatively high income have the highest rate of marital stability. However, among women who have very high incomes ($25,000 to $50,000 or more per year), the probability of divorce again increases.

Geographic location

Divorce rates increase from east to west and from north to south.

Race

Blacks have a much higher divorce rate than whites in our society at all income, educational, and occupational levels.

Influence of children

Couples with no children are most likely to end in divorce, and couples with three or more children are least likely, particularly if one child is male.

---

more children (Norton 1983, Spanier and Glick 1981). In addition, a couple who have at least one son (rather than all girls) is more likely to remain married.[11] This seems to contradict the finding discussed in Chapter 7 regarding the effect of children on a marriage. Apparently, the explanation is that it is easier for a couple to reach the decision to divorce if they do not have the responsibility for children. Even though the marriage may be unhappy, a couple may tend to resist the idea of divorce when they have children to care for.

---

[11]U.S. Bureau of the Census, "Population Profile of the United States: 1978" (1979).

For a summary of demographic factors related to divorce, see Table 8-2.

Emotional Maturity

In general, emotional maturity and incidence of divorce are negatively correlated. That is, individuals close to the emotional maturity end of the continuum may be expected to have a relatively lower incidence of divorce than those at the other end of the continuum (see Figure 8-6).

What are the characteristics of emotional maturity?

Emotionally mature persons are reality-oriented rather than defense-oriented. They

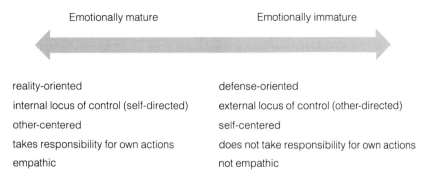

Emotionally mature · · · · · · · · · · · · · · · Emotionally immature

reality-oriented	defense-oriented
internal locus of control (self-directed)	external locus of control (other-directed)
other-centered	self-centered
takes responsibility for own actions	does not take responsibility for own actions
empathic	not empathic

The person who is near the emotional maturity end of the continuum is a much better marriage risk than one who is near the other end.

FIGURE 8-6

The continuum of emotional maturity

are more able to acknowledge the reality of marital difficulties and make appropriate efforts to resolve them than are people who are relatively immature emotionally. The emotionally mature tend to accept themselves and others as they are in reality, rather than insisting on maintaining idealized versions. They are able to sacrifice short-term goals to achieve long-term goals. They are able to make heavy emotional investments in relations that are important to them, and yet they can recover quickly from failure or disappointment (Coleman 1984).

Emotional maturity involves a twofold awareness: an awareness of one's own needs and values and of the needs and values of other people. Emotionally mature people are able to fulfill their own needs in ways that are appropriate for the needs of others. Moreover, the two-valued system of childhood (good versus bad, and so on) has been replaced, in emotionally mature people, by a recognition and acceptance of the multivalued complexities of real people in a real world, where compromise is inevitable.

The emotionally mature person is relatively independent and is self-directed, with an internal locus of control. Self-direction and independence imply a good deal more than freedom from outside authority; also implied is a willingness to make decisions and to accept the consequences. An emotionally immature person, in contrast, tends to be other-directed (to have an external locus of control) and then to blame others for failure.

Although emotionally mature persons are self-directed, they are other-centered (rather than self-centered). They are more interested in others than themselves, and they accept responsibility for the well-being of others (as well as for themselves). They are able to work toward group goals as well as individual goals (see Table 8-3).

Emotional maturity, like all other aspects of personality, exists on a continuum—from the egocentric, arbitrarily "good" and "bad" values of the child to the other-centered, self-directed wisdom of the emotionally mature adult. Most individuals, of course, fall somewhere between those two extremes. Moreover, emotional maturity is not necessarily a correlate of chronological age; emotional maturity may occur at a very early age, a very late age, or never.

Emotionally immature people are very poor marriage risks since they are scarcely able to

---
TABLE 8-3

The emotionally mature are other-centered
but self-directed

Emotionally mature	Emotionally immature
self-directed	other-directed
other-centered	self-centered

Source: Data from Coleman (1984).

provide emotionally for themselves. They are certainly unable to provide emotionally for others. They demand understanding and acceptance from others, but are able to provide neither.

This is not to say that emotionally mature people do not get divorced. The reasons for divorce are many and varied, and it is quite possible for a marriage of two emotionally mature people to be disappointing to each and end in separation and divorce. The individuals may simply be incompatible in marriage to one another—although each may be successful in other areas of life and perfectly capable of a successful marriage to someone else.

It is also possible for one person of a couple to be emotionally mature while the other is not, and for the marriage to develop irreconcilable differences for this reason.

Incompatibility

Various idiosyncratic factors may make the couple's interaction so painful that they are driven apart. Disillusionment, discouragement, and disappointment increasingly replace the joy, anticipation, and delight of their dating and courtship days for reasons that are not always clear to the couple. It is simply said that they are "incompatible"—a catchall term that means that they are no longer capable of living together with any sort of harmony or mutual satisfaction. The reasons blamed—finances, alcoholism, extramarital affairs—are only the visible symptoms of a situation that

has become intolerable (Kessler 1975). Often, effective communication has virtually collapsed, so that the two people do not really talk *to* each other, but talk at cross purposes. (For a discussion of conflict and patterns of ineffective communication in marriage, see Chapter 9.) Often, at this point, the services of a marriage counselor are sought to help put the marriage back on the track and avoid a divorce.

Marriage Counseling

The marriage counselor tries to help the couple tease out the variables associated with the disintegration of the marriage, so that a satisfactory interaction can be resumed. Professional marriage counselors may be psychologists, psychiatrists, sociologists, social workers, clergy, physicians, or lawyers. Some states regulate the use of the title "marriage counselor," but many do not, and anyone in the latter states may simply assume the title and the practice. The American Association of Marriage and Family Therapists is a national organization that rigorously screens its membership and acts to promote ethical practices in marriage counseling in all states.

By the time a couple seek out a marriage counselor, they are usually in extreme confusion and very reluctant to make any decisions. A failing marriage can be a bitter blow to their self-esteem, depriving them of an important source of emotional support and satisfaction in their lives. Disillusioned and dissatisfied with themselves, each other, and life in general, they often regard a marriage counselor as a last hope. That hope is justified if and when they are helped to take steps to deal with their problem—either to change behavior patterns significantly in the direction of increased need satisfaction or to conclude that reconciliation is not realistic and divorce is the best solution. *Successful* marriage counseling does not always lead to reconciliation.

Apparently marriage counseling is just about as effective as psychotherapy or coun-

Bohdan Hrynewych/Stock, Boston

The marriage counselor's responsibility lies in exploring the couple's problems from their own points of view and trying to help them discover for themselves what seems to be the best course of action.

seling directed at nonmarital problems. For example, a review of sixty-seven studies of marriage counseling found that when couples are seen together, the improvement rate is about 65 percent (Gurman and Kniskern 1978). This is an impressive rate of success when we consider that persons who have received marriage counseling and reconcile must learn new patterns of adjustment without making any pronounced environmental change (whereas a person with nonmarital difficulties may be able to resolve his or her problems by changing the environment—by getting a new job or moving to another neighborhood or city). Moreover, a person with marital difficulties has to consider the personality structure and adjustive responses of the other as well as his or her own personality structure and patterns of adjustive responses. Successful resolution of the difficulties depends on changes in both members of the couple.

Although professional marriage counselors vary widely in their methods, it is a rare coun-selor who would tell the client what he or she should do. In general, most psychologically oriented counselors refrain from giving specific advice, mediating differences, or providing ready-made solutions to conflicts. Instead, the counselor's responsibility and expertise lie in exploring the couple's problems from their own points of view and trying to help them discover for themselves what seems to be the best course of action. An exception to this approach usually occurs only if a marital difficulty rests on factual ignorance, such as lack of information about sexual anatomy and physiology. In this type of difficulty, the counselor may either provide such information or recommend a source.

The Relative Stability of American Marriage

One of the most interesting features of Table 8-1 is that the proportion of marriages ending each year has been virtually unchanged for the

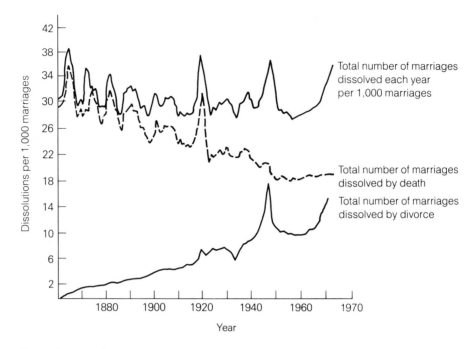

The total number of marriages dissolved each year per 1,000 existing marriages has remained remarkably stable for the past century, with the rising divorce rate almost precisely balanced by the falling death rate.

FIGURE 8-7

Total dissolutions of marriage (by death and divorce)
per 1,000 existing marriages in the United States, 1860–1970

Source: Data from Davis (1972). Reprinted by permission of
Professor Kingsley Davis.

past hundred years. In 1860, 33.2 marriages per 1,000 were ended by death or divorce, as compared with 34.5 marriages per 1,000 in 1970 (see the column headed "Combined" in the table). During this time, sweeping changes have taken place in our society—in the meaning of marriage to the individual, in social attitudes toward divorce, in divorce laws, and in family structure and function. Yet the percentage of marriages ending each year—by death or divorce—has remarkably remained the same, with the rising divorce rate almost precisely balanced by the falling death rate. This

relation between the death rate and the divorce rate is expressed graphically in Figure 8-7. Note that the line representing the total number of marital dissolutions for each 1,000 existing marriages fluctuates only within a very narrow range from year to year.

In addition, not only are about the same percentage of marriages remaining intact each year, but they remain intact much longer—since the average life expectancy has increased during the past century. Because of this increased life expectancy, today's average couple on their wedding day may expect to be

Legal Separation

A *legal separation*, which is permitted in most states, does not really terminate the marriage but merely limits the privileges of the spouses, who are still regarded as married. For example, legal separation provides for separate maintenance—the couple may not cohabit under penalty of law—but the husband is still financially responsible for the separate maintenance of his wife and family. Not surprisingly, this arrangement does not appeal to most couples, except those who, for social, religious, or professional reasons, need to retain their marital status but find it impossible to live together. Although the incidence of legal separation is no more than 3 percent of the number of divorces, Carter and Glick (1976) reported a total of over 2 million legally separated persons during the time of the 1960 census; the majority of the separated men were ages twenty-five to fifty-four, and the majority of the separated women were ages twenty-five to forty-four.

U.S. National Center for Health Statistics, "Legal Separation" (1980).

---

married forty years, about twenty-two years longer than the average marriage lasted a century ago.[12]

THE HISTORY OF DIVORCE

From the Sixteenth Century to the Present

In Western civilization, Christianity forbade divorce until the early sixteenth century. Since Christianity regarded marriage as a *sacrament*, with the couple joined together by God, a divorce, which meant dissolving the marriage by a human act, was not possible, as noted earlier (Chapter 7). In the divine concept of marriage, the couple were joined until the marriage was involuntarily dissolved by death. In extreme cases, the marriage could be *annulled*, in which case the couple were legally assumed to have never been married in the first place. (See the later section on annulment.) A *limited divorce* could also be obtained, which permitted the couple to live apart but did not permit either to remarry. A modern version of this limited divorce is *legal separation*. (See the vignette, "Legal Separation.")

With the Protestant Reformation came a repudiation of this sacramental concept of marriage, so that civil divorce legislation could be enacted. Although divorce was then theoretically available, it was still very difficult to obtain. The early reformers felt that the grounds for divorce should be very serious: adultery, cruelty, or desertion. Moreover, they felt that these grounds should be clearly demonstrable before a legislative body. Thus, from the sixteenth until the mid-nineteenth centuries in England, a divorce could be obtained—but only through a special Act of Parliament.

This necessity to introduce a private Bill of Divorcement to Parliament was a difficult and expensive procedure, which greatly limited the number of divorces applied for. Three hundred years were to pass before England, in the middle of the nineteenth century (1857),

---

[12]U.S. National Center for Health Statistics, U.S. Life Tables and Actuarial Tables (1981, 1984, 1985).

Galleria Nazionale, Rome. Photo-Alinari/Art Resource, Inc.

Prior to the Protestant Reformation, divorce was obtainable only by special Papal dispensation. When this was refused to King Henry VIII, he declared himself the head of the Church in England in order to obtain the freedom to remarry.

Hans Holbein, *Henry VIII*, 1539–40

shifted from legislative to judicial divorces (granted by court action rather than legislative action). This shift of jurisdiction to the courts paved the way for the modern concept of divorce.

The American colonies initially adopted the British pattern of granting divorce only through legislative action. In the beginning of the nineteenth century, however, the United States assigned the courts authority to grant divorce—a full half-century before Great Britain.

Divorced.

Catherine of Aragon

Beheaded.

Ann Boleyn

Died.

Jane Seymour

Divorced.

Anne of Cleaves

Beheaded.

Catherine Howard

Survived.

Catherine Parr

Until the 1970s, our divorce system was based solely on the concept of *contest*, with a "plaintiff" and a "defendant" in the divorce action, each presenting his or her own version of the case. If the divorce is granted, the plaintiff must be judged as "wronged" in the legal sense, and the defendant must be judged as "guilty." The guilt of the defendant must be established by the rules of evidence that govern any court action.[13]

The Emergence of No-Fault Divorce

In the 1970s truly revolutionary changes in divorce laws began to take place in our society as most states abandoned the concept of divorce as a legal contest and began to grant it simply because each of the couple desired it. Many states ceased to use the term *divorce* and substituted the term *dissolution of marriage*. By the 1980s almost every state had adopted some form of no-fault divorce. In this form of divorce action, the couple are permitted legally to dissolve the marriage simply by agreeing that their differences are irreconcilable. Since there is no legal contest, no plaintiff, and no defendant, the law against *collusion* no longer applies.[14]

No-fault divorce law provides that either husband or wife can be required to support the other (by alimony payments) after the marriage is dissolved; and either or both can be required to support their minor children, depending on the court's judgment.[15] With dissolution of the marriage, the property is divided, responsibility for the care and support of children is assigned, and each of the couple is freed to remarry.

Interlocutory Divorce

The *interlocutory decree* is a sort of preliminary decree and is part of a divorce action in about one-third of the states in our country. In these states, the interlocutory decree is issued first, and the divorce becomes final after a specified period of time (from one month to a year). The divorce does not become final and the parties are not free to remarry until the final decree is issued. The interlocutory decree was devised to discourage hasty divorces and encourage reconciliation.

Migratory Divorce

When the plaintiff travels out of his or her home state to obtain a divorce, it is recognized as legal in the home state (and all other states) only if (1) a *bona fide* residence has been established in the state in which the divorce is obtained, (2) a proper notice has been served on the defendant, and (3) the defendant is represented in court (either in person or through an attorney). If the defendant is not represented in court or can prove that the plaintiff was not a bona fide resident but went to the state merely

---

[13]Most contested divorces are granted on two grounds: cruelty and desertion. The most popular of these is cruelty, which is used in about 60 percent of all American divorce suits. (Cruelty may be defined in a variety of ways according to the court's judgment; it includes not only physical abuse, but psychological stress as well. In fact, several jurisdictions define cruelty specifically in terms of "mental suffering.") Desertion, the second major ground for contested divorce, is used in about 25 percent of divorce suits. Conservative estimates of the number of desertions per year is about 100,000—roughly one desertion in every four divorces (Bell 1983, Carter and Glick 1976).

[14]When a divorce suit is a contest between the plaintiff and the defendant, cooperation or agreement by the couple to obtain a divorce is regarded by the court as subverting the processes of law. If such *collusion* is suspected, the court may deny the divorce or, if the divorce is already granted, revoke it (Rheinstein 1972).

---

[15]In 1978 California passed a law designed to reduce the cost of divorce for childless couples. This bill provides for a "summary dissolution" of a marriage and requires no court appearance and no lawyers for couples married less than two years. This divorce method may be used, however, only when there are no minor children who were born or adopted during the marriage, no real property, no unpaid debts over $2,000, and total family assets of less than $5,000, excluding automobiles.

to establish residency to obtain a divorce, the divorce may be declared invalid. If the plaintiff has remarried in the meantime and has children by the second spouse, the second marriage may be declared bigamous and any children may be declared illegitimate.

The speed with which a migratory divorce can be obtained depends on the length of time it takes to become a bona fide resident. Some states require two or three years; Massachusetts has a five-year residency requirement. Two states, however—Nevada and Idaho—in an attempt to promote tourism, have established a very short residency requirement (six weeks). Undoubtedly these states have been used by couples to obtain divorces when each of the couple wished it. But if the divorce is to be contested, such "quickie" divorces must be regarded as legally risky.

In the realm of Mexican migratory divorces, the potential legal dangers multiply. Although a Mexican divorce may be considered valid even when it is obtained by proxy, if the defendant contests the divorce on technicalities, the plaintiff may be in a very uncomfortable position.[16]

ANNULMENT

Annulment, which formally and legally declares that the marriage never existed in the first place, was originally conceived to ensure that a European sovereign whose wife was barren could remarry and have an heir to the throne. (It was not yet legally possible to obtain a divorce.) English common law adopted this Roman Catholic concept, and our own statutary law developed from English common law. Therefore, nearly all American states grant annulment as well as divorce. Since annulment voids the marriage, all rights and obligations may be dissolved, and children may be declared illegitimate, although the law varies from state to state.[17]

The court usually recognizes different grounds for annulment from those for divorce, with the difference chiefly pertaining to the time the grounds occurred. The grounds for annulment generally precede the marriage, while the grounds for divorce usually follow it. For example, typical grounds for annulment include existence of a prior marriage, misrepresentation with intent to defraud, and sanguinity (too close a blood tie, such as a woman married to her half-brother). Annulment may also be granted if it can be established that one of the couple did not intend to have children at the time of the marriage. Annulment may also be granted on the ground that the marriage was not consummated.

As with divorce, in actual practice annulments have often been granted simply because the legal fiction was upheld even though the specific grounds were somewhat tenuous. Annulments have been granted, for example, because the husband had exaggerated the extent of his salary, or had reneged on his promise to have a religious ceremony following the civil proceedings, or had "certain character defects" before marriage, or because the wife had represented herself as a virgin when she was not (Kephart 1977).

For all practical purposes civil (as opposed to church) annulment is sought in our society

---

[16]For example, Rodney Stich, real estate investor, author, and aviation safety consultant, was sued for divorce by his wife, Emma, in 1982—sixteen years after he had gone to Mexico and obtained a divorce from her. She asked for $2 million (one-half the worth of his property) and spousal support, on the grounds that his Mexican divorce was not binding in California. California law holds that a divorce obtained out of state or abroad is not valid if the spouse getting the divorce was a California resident twelve months before commencing the foreign divorce and returned to California with the divorce before six more months had elapsed. If the spouse getting the divorce fails to meet these legal requirements, the divorce may be declared invalid (Viets 1984).

[17]Where there are no specific statutes to the contrary, children of an annulled marriage are generally considered illegitimate by the court.

only when divorce is not legally obtainable. Nationally, civil annulments represent about 4 percent of the total number of marital dissolutions.[18]

Because the Roman Catholic church still remains unalterably opposed to divorce, a Catholic must have the marriage annulled by the church if he or she is to be free to remarry and have the remarriage recognized by the church. Since the fourth century, Roman Catholic doctrine has held that valid, consummated marriages between baptized persons cannot be dissolved by a human agency; they may, however, be *annulled*, since an annulled marriage is regarded as never having taken place. After a church annulment, a person may then get a civil divorce, which defines legal obligations and permits remarriage in the view of the state.

According to the pronouncement by Pope Paul VI (1970), the grounds for a Catholic church annulment include incestuous marriage, impotence, nonconsummation of the marriage, intent by a spouse not to have children, marriage under duress, and marriage under age fourteen for a girl or age sixteen for a boy. In 1977, lack of love (*ex defecto amoris*) was also admitted as a ground for church annulment.

The new canonical law permits couples to get an annulment after a favorable decision by one local church court and ratification, without trial, by another. The length of time for this procedure is estimated to be about seven months, as opposed to the three to seven years of heavy expenses and even a trip to Rome that a couple were forced to bear under the old law. The new law also grants bishops of dioceses the right to annul a marriage under certain circumstances.

The number of annulments has increased in the United States since the new Catholic regulations went into effect in 1977, when psychological grounds (lack of love) were admitted as evidence that the marriage vows were improperly performed. In 1967 only 700 annulments were granted in the United States. By 1980, this figure had jumped to 40,000—a truly incredible increase (Sciolino 1984).

Since 1977, U.S. Roman Catholics who remarry after divorce are no longer excommunicated from the church, following a ruling from Pope Paul VI. (Excommunication, the most severe of church penalties, means that a person is separated from the community of the church, forbidden to receive the sacraments, and excluded from public prayers.) The lifting of the excommunication penalty in no way changes the church's traditional teaching that sacramental marriages cannot be dissolved, and remarriage after a civil divorce is still prohibited. The papal action is considered important, however, as a gesture of reconciliation to the growing number of divorced and remarried Catholics. The divorce rate for Catholics is now equal to that of non-Catholics; there are an estimated 8 million divorced Catholics in the United States (Sciolino 1984).

Although the new ruling removes the penalty of excommunication from divorced and remarried Catholics and allows them to participate in church services, it still forbids them full communion. To be eligible to participate in the full communion service, divorced and remarried Catholics must obtain a special dispensation; thus, the majority of those who have remarried have done so outside the church (Sciolino 1984).

THE MEANING OF DIVORCE FOR THE INDIVIDUAL

As Paul Bohannan (1970) points out in his classic study, divorce is a complex personal experience as well as a complex social phe-

---

[18]U.S. National Center for Health Statistics, "Annulments" (1984).

nomenon, "because at least six things are happening at once . . . six different experiences of separation." These stations or experiences are the emotional divorce, the legal divorce, the economic divorce, the coparental divorce, the community divorce, and the psychic divorce (Bohannan 1970, pp. 33–34).

Emotional Divorce

The first stage of divorce—the *emotional divorce*—occurs when serious difficulties and conflicts begin to characterize the couple's interaction, and therefore their feelings for one another begin to change. Positive feelings of love, affection, respect, and trust wear away and are replaced by negative feelings of annoyance, resentment, dislike, and distrust. Mutually provided satisfactions gradually disintegrate through a growing series of disappointments and misunderstandings; significant satisfactions that each provides for and receives from the other become less and less rewarding. In the emotional divorce, each person grows unhappier with the other and with their marriage while the disappointments and resentment that each experiences in relating to the other become more and more painful. This process of the emotional divorce begins long before either one considers the possibility of legal divorce.

One of the couple usually becomes disillusioned with the marriage before the other person does. Satisfactions may then be deliberately withheld by this spouse, perhaps because of sheer frustration or perhaps because of a desire to get even by inflicting pain on the other. As the marital interaction disintegrates, each becomes resentful and aware of the growing lack of rapport. The relationship enters a stage of accelerating decline until the couple are on the brink of an open break— separation and legal divorce (Bohannan 1985, p. 95).

As the emotional divorce enters its final phases, the pain of the marriage is perceived as greater than the potential pain of separation. Indeed, separation and divorce may even be seen as a relief from the pain of the marriage. Arriving at this perception may take years, even in a marriage that is providing little emotional satisfaction for either.

An open break, or physical separation followed by a legal divorce action, is an acknowledgment that one is no longer loved or wanted. Because this is a difficult admission to make, seemingly endless attempts may be made at reconciliation. (It is also, of course, a statement that one no longer loves and wants the other.)

Emotional divorce results in a loss of a loved one just as fully—but by quite a different route of experience—as does the death of a spouse. Divorce is difficult because it involves a purposeful and active rejection by another person, who, merely by living, is a daily symbol of the rejection. It is also made difficult because the community helps even less than it does in bereavement (Bohannan 1970, p. 42).

Legal Divorce

The step of actually seeing a lawyer institutes the second of Bohannan's six experiences of divorce. A reconciliation may be made; it is not unusual for a couple to institute a divorce action, withdraw the action, reconcile, and then start another divorce action before they are ready to enter the stage of legal divorce. Threats of divorce ("I want a divorce!") usually precede this final step—sometimes made in the hope that threat will shock the other into making a serious attempt at resolving their growing difficulties.

If there is little property involved, if the couple can agree upon its division, and if the couple have no children, legal divorce action can be relatively simple and inexpensive (in all states but South Dakota, which still does not have no-fault divorce laws). However, if there is a considerable amount of property and the couple cannot agree on how to divide it, the court must rule; if the couple has a child or children the court must rule on which parent obtains legal custody and on visitation rights for the noncustodial parent. The court must also rule on such matters as child-support payments for the noncustodial parent. Alimony payments are now rarely awarded, but spousal support payments are common and child-support payments are universal (Freed and Walker 1985, pp. 369–471). If these issues are being contested, the divorce action may be extremely bitter, drawn out, and expensive.

Economic Divorce

Bohannan's third station, or experience, of divorce is the *economic divorce,* involving all of the interacting economic ramifications that are involved in the reality of ending a marriage. An ex-wife with the custody of minor children often cannot survive without going to work. Her job skills will usually only earn a much lower pay than her ex-husband's income; moreover, she must somehow look after the children as well as work. It is not uncommon for a woman in such a position to say, perhaps a year or so after the divorce, that "being married is hard, but being divorced is even harder," because of the economic hardships and privations she and her children are now forced to undergo (Hetherington et al., 1978).

Weitzman found that although the typical ex-wife experiences a 73 percent drop in her standard of living following a no-fault divorce, the ex-husband's standard of living rises 42 percent. The husband is left with a larger proportion of his income, and therefore a higher standard of living, than he had during the marriage, because his work and income continue uninterrupted. Under the new no-fault divorce laws he is not required to contribute equally to the support of his children or to share his salary with his former wife (Weitzman 1985, p. xii).

Property Settlement

Traditionally, before the advent of no-fault divorce, the family home was usually awarded to the wife, especially if she had the custody of minor children. Under the new divorce laws, the court is instructed to divide the couple's property *equally.* (Under California no-fault law, for example, the court may make an unequal division only if the value of the property is less than $5,000 and one spouse's whereabouts are unknown, or if the debts exceed the assets.) In order to make this equal division, the court usually orders the family home sold and the proceeds divided (Weitzman 1985, p. 71).

The loss of the family home, and the subsequent residential moves it necessitates, disrupt the children's school, neighborhood, and friendship ties, and create additional dislocations for children (and mothers) at the very point at which they need continuity and stability (Weitzman 1985, p. xii).

Moreover, under the no-fault rules for dividing marital property, the courts systematically omit the assets that may be the most valuable: "the major wage earner's salary (usually the husband's), pension, medical insurance, education, license, the good-will value of a business or profession, entitlements to company goods and services, and future earning power. . . . Thus the courts allow the major wage earner, typically the husband, to keep the family's most valuable assets" (p. xiii).

Alimony

In early English common law, a man continued to be responsible for his ex-wife's economic welfare. Since he had automatically received control of his wife's property and income with marriage, it was deemed appropriate that he continue to suppport her after a divorce—while still retaining control of all property. Employment opportunities for the ex-wife were almost nonexistent, so these life-long payments, termed *alimony,* were necessary for her survival unless she and her children were to become public charges (Weitzman 1985, p. 145).

Marriage laws in the United States were based largely on English common law and followed the same principle of alimony until the advent of the no-fault divorce legislation in California in 1970. Since then, as state after state adopted variations of no-fault divorce, the concept of alimony is now usually limited to a brief period of spousal support (pp. 147, 458).

Occasionally an ex-wife receives a very large alimony settlement in a highly publicized divorce. For example, Johnny Carson's third wife asked for $220,000 a month in alimony in 1985, in addition to the other property she was to receive in the divorce settlement. Highly visible cases of this sort lead to a public perception that alimony payments are more frequent than they are (p. 181).

The Supreme Court ruled recently that men are eligible to receive spousal support payments from ex-wives, and, in a few well-publicized cases, such awards have been made. However, such cases are extremely rare (Kammeyer 1987, p. 504).

Spousal Support

Sometimes the court will award spousal support for a short time to allow the ex-wife an opportunity to acquire education or training that will make it possible for her to enter the labor market or to get a higher-paying job than she otherwise could. However, the period of spousal support awarded by the court is usually granted for only the period of time the court feels it is necessary, often no more than one to three years. If the ex-wife is an older woman with many years invested in the marriage, the court may award a higher spousal support payment than is usually awarded to a younger woman and may extend this payment for a longer period of time. Her health, age, and potential job skills may also be taken into consideration (Weitzman 1985, pp. 148–149, 165).

Child Support

In virtually all divorce actions, the custodial parent (usually the mother) is awarded child support payments to be made by the noncustodial parent (usually the father). These payments continue until the child reaches eighteen. Although the parents' marriage is legally terminated, there is no court action that divorces the child from the parents. The child's father remains the father after the divorce, and the courts hold that he is still legally responsible for his child's economic well-being.

The current legal theory guiding most divorce actions is that although the ex-husband is not responsible for his ex-wife's economic well-being for more than a short interval following the divorce, he is *partially* responsible for his children's economic care. The question the court must decide is the meaning of "partially" in precise dollars-per-month terms. If the child support award is too large, he may not be able to pay it and still provide for his own economic needs; if it is too small, the children may suffer deprivation of essential goods—food, clothes, shelter, medical–dental care.

Since the advent of no-fault divorce in 1970, courts usually stress a "father-first" rather than "child-first" principle, taking the position that if the child support award is too high the father will not be able to pay it; thus the award must leave the father sufficient funds to meet his own needs and maintain his continuing ability to earn (Weitzman 1985, p. 267). Courts rarely award more than one-third of the father's income to child support; they often award much less. Nationwide, child support averaged 13 percent of average male income in 1981 (p. 266).

On a nationwide average, the amount of support actually received is always less than the amount the court has ordered. More than half (53 percent) of women did not receive their support payments in 1981 (U.S. Bureau of the Census, 1983). In response to the widespread failure of ex-husbands to pay child-support awards, legislators are looking at various means to enforce collection of past-due accounts. For example, in 1984 legislation was approved by Congress to intercept federal and state income tax refund checks and apply them to past-due support payments. Despite such means, however, the problem of collection remains a formidable one, and is a serious problem facing many ex-wives who have custody of children.

It has been estimated that if the costs for raising a child born in 1980 to age eighteen were adjusted for inflation, they would total more than $250,000 (Tilling 1980). These costs have to be borne by someone, and if the support payments from the father do not arrive, it is the custodial parent who must, somehow or other, pay these bills.

Coparental Divorce

Bohannan calls his fourth station of divorce the *coparental divorce*. This phase deals with "custody, single-parent homes, and visitation" (Bohannan 1970, p. 52). These aspects of divorce are not only the sources of some of the most serious emotional and economic problems that a person may experience during the course of his or her lifetime, but are very persistent: they do not end with the divorce—which legally terminates the marriage—but continue as the children are growing up.

Child Custody

Although the mother is the parent most often awarded the custody of the children in our society, under English common law it was the father who obtained custody. Children were regarded as belonging to the father, and if separation occurred he automatically obtained custody. It was not until the nineteenth-century move from agriculture to industry, with fathers leaving their subsistence farms to work for wages in urban and suburban settings, that the courts began to modify the father's automatic right to custody of his children (see Chapter 2).

In 1839, the British Parliament modified the father's absolute right to custody by granting the mother the right to be awarded custody of children who were less than seven years old. Thus, the "tender years" presumption in favor of the mother—what we refer to as the traditional presumption—was itself an innovation when it was first introduced into law (Weitzman 1985, p. 219).

In the late nineteenth and early twentieth centuries in the United States, courts began to follow suit, granting custody to the mother, especially if the children were "of tender age." This new trend, which assumed that the mother, not the father, was the "natural" and "proper" caretaker of her children, was increasingly accepted by the courts, attorneys, and divorcing couples alike. By the twentieth century, it had become a well-established principle that it was in the child's best interest not to be separated from the mother unless she could be shown to be "unfit" (p. 219).

When the no-fault divorce laws were passed it was assumed that increasing numbers of husbands would sue for, and be granted, custody of their children by the divorce court. But Weitzman (1985), in her extensive research, found that there has been no increase in the percentage of fathers who have requested or have been awarded physical or legal custody of their children.

Shared or Joint Custody

In 1980, California became the first state to enact legislation favoring *joint* custody. The concept of awarding the children to both parents jointly, rather than establishing a custodial parent and a visiting parent, spread rapidly, and by 1985 thirty states had passed some form of joint custody law (Weitzman 1985, p. 245).

In 1983, the California law added the distinction between *joint legal* custody and *joint physical* custody; the court may award one of these without awarding the other. Most commonly, joint legal control may be awarded to both the father and the mother while the mother is awarded physical custody (pp. 247–249).

Researchers find, however, that despite the court order for legal joint custody the couple are no more likely to cooperate with one another in important decisions affecting the child than they were before the divorce. If a couple could not agree on many important decisions before the divorce, it may be unrealistic to expect them to bury their hostility toward one another and cooperate in such important matters as child care decisions afterward. If the parents are hostile and are forced to interact because of joint legal custody, their continuing conflict may be detrimental to the child (p. 254).

A second assumption regarding joint legal custody is that the father, who presumably is now more involved in decision making regarding his children, will be more apt to make his child support payments. However, preliminary research finds that fathers who have joint legal custody of their children are no more likely to make the support payments than fathers who do not. Having or not having joint legal custody seems to make no difference in whether the father complies with the court order for support. As we have seen, fathers are often delinquent in their support payments (p. 255).

In her careful research of California custodial awards, Weitzman (1985) finds little evidence that either joint physical or joint legal custody is necessarily beneficial either for

"It's hard. I have to be a mother and a father to them. Except on weekends when Eric has to be a father and a mother."

children or for parents. If the parents are able to cooperate without hostility, joint legal control may have some advantages; joint physical custody, on the other hand, unless it is simply a new name for liberal visitation, can be disadvantageous for the child, unless the parents are extraordinarily capable in providing security and understanding for a child who is shuttled back and forth between homes. Preliminary findings indicate that it may actually be anxiety provoking for children. They may be confused about where they belong and who is supposed to take care of them. The inevitable stress of these arrangements should not be surprising (pp. 253–255).

Nine-year-old Josh, who lives one month with his mother and one month with his father, indicated that he felt many things in his life were in disarray, that he was preoccupied with loss and anxious about his ability to keep track of things. He was not working up to his potential at school, and there was a discrepancy between his considerable abilities and his low self-concept. When Josh was contacted about our interviews, he immediately volunteered that "the big problem with joint custody is that you have to remember where the spoons are." His worry about the spoons reflected all the other worries he has, and an overall feeling of instability (Steinman 1981, p. 410).

Visitation Rights

In most divorce actions both legal and physical custody are awarded one parent (usually the mother) with visitation rights awarded the noncustodial parent (usually the father). More than 90 percent of visitation right orders are for "reasonable" visitation, leaving the couple to work out for themselves the precise details of just when visitation will occur. Only 5 percent of court orders limit the visitation rights by spelling them out precisely. Problems are more often reported by the custodial mothers regarding the father's failure to visit his children (Weitzman 1985, pp. 229–230).

Visits from the noncustodial parent are often emotionally difficult. Wallerstein and Kelly (1980) found in their extensive study of divorced families in California that 80 percent of fathers felt some sense of stress regarding the visit during the first year following the divorce; fully one-half of the part-time fathers were afraid of being rejected by their children and were uneasy about the children's hostility and disapproval of the divorce. One-third of the visiting fathers, to allay their discomfort and win the children's favor, brought expensive gifts for their children. Two-thirds of the custodial mothers experienced varying degrees of stress regarding the father's visits during the first year, and a third of the children were "consistently exposed to intense anger" regarding the visit. One-fifth of the mothers actively tried to "sabotage" the visitation by "sending the children away just before the father's arrival" or by saying that the child was ill or had homework to do and could not see the father. On the other hand, about one-half of the mothers approved of maintaining contact between the father and his children and did whatever they could to smooth the way. In between these two extremes were mothers who passively accepted the visitation with "mixed feelings," resenting the father's "excessive gift-giving" and his having "freedom from domestic responsibility" while he focused on entertaining the children, trying to win their approval (pp. 121, 124–125).

Weitzman (1985) found that 23 percent of fathers did not see their children after the divorce, 14 percent saw them less than once a month, 33 percent twice a month, and 30 percent at least once a week. It is interesting to note, however, that the parents reported different rates of visitation. The median response by the fathers was that they saw their children once a week, while the mothers' median response was that the fathers saw their children less than once a month. Weitzman also found that there is a process of "gradual disengagement" of noncustodial fathers: 70 percent of the fathers said that they would prefer to see their children less often, 30 percent said the same amount, and none said more often. Among the women with custody, 43 percent of them agreed, also wanting the father to see the children less often. Taken together, these responses show a predisposition for divorced fathers to reduce their visitation over time (pp. 258–259).

Wallerstein and Kelly (1980) found that one-quarter of the children in their study were visited "infrequently and erratically," with visits occurring less than once a month and these occasional visits erratic in their pattern (p. 130). On the other hand, they found that 40 percent of the children and adolescents in their study were seeing their fathers at least once a week, and almost half of this group were visiting two and three times weekly.

Men who could bend to the complex logistics of the visiting; who could deal with the anger of the women and the capriciousness of the children without withdrawing; who could overcome their own depression, jealousy and guilt; who could involve the children in their planning; who could walk a middle ground between totally rearranging their schedule and not changing their schedule at all; and who felt less stressed and freer to parent, were predominately among those who continued to visit regularly and frequently (Wallerstein and Kelly 1980, p. 130).

The Reaction of Family and Friends to the Divorce

Bohannan calls his fifth experience of divorce the *community divorce* phase. This phase of divorce involves the changes in one's community of friends and family—or the reaction of one's friends and family to the separation and divorce (Bohannan 1970, p. 59).

Weiss found that when a person has acknowledged the failure of the marriage and has made the decision to separate and divorce, he or she is reluctant to tell neighbors, acquaintances, friends, or family about this decision and may even put off making the final decision.

Separated individuals are generally more reluctant to report the end of their marriages to their kin than to friends, neighbors, or, indeed, anyone else, with the possible exception of their children. The anticipated discomfort of telling kin is sometimes sufficient to hold individuals in unsatisfactory marriages long after they would otherwise have abandoned them (Weiss 1975, p. 126).

In nearly all families, there is a tacit assumption that any member can seek help from another in time of need—although the expectation for help is stronger between parents and children than it is among siblings or more distant kin. Nevertheless, one's private life tends to be concealed from other members of the family unless the private matters concern important steps in one's life, such as change of job, move to a new residence, pregnancy, or separation and impending divorce. Because family members usually stay "close but not too close" and do not usually tell one another about private matters, the announcement of a separation—that a marriage is ending in a divorce—is usually received as a shock (pp. 128–129).

The woman is often the person responsible for maintaining contact with her husband's family as well as her own, and the man will sometimes push the task of telling his parents onto the wife. She, of course, tells the story of the separation from her point of view, and as a result he may find his parents more sympathetic to his wife than to him (pp. 130–131).

Reaction of the family to news of the divorce varies, of course. They may be solicitous and sympathetic, gently or severely condemning, angry, or detached—not wanting to get involved. Parents can usually understand and accept a separation caused by infidelity, drunkenness, or brutality, but are often puzzled by, and perhaps impatient with, incompatibility—a desire for change, "wanting different things out of life," or evolving into a different person. Parents may be bewildered, exasperated, and critical of a son or daughter who ends a marriage for reasons they believe to be frivolous, and they may try to urge a reconciliation (pp. 131–133).

When married friends are first told of the divorce they tend to be supportive. Soon after the separation, however, while some may continue to be sympathetic and welcoming, others may feel burdened by the heavy claims on their sympathies or feel frightened, "as though the separation were a communicable disease." Others may be envious of the person's new freedom, while still others may react to the divorce as a warning to themselves, a realization that their own marriage might also be vulnerable. The husband may see a divorced wife as sexually available, while his wife may see the divorcée as a threat and as seductive to her husband. Whatever the reaction, the friends now recognize the separated person as different from before, and inevitably adjustments must be made to their friendship (pp. 158–160).

The final phase of the friendship is often one of mutual withdrawal.

There is no explicit ending of the friendship, although once in a while the separated person or a member of a married couple may express disapproval of or disappointment in the other. Rather, the friendship is allowed to fade. Neither the separated individual or the married friends call to arrange a visit (Weiss 1975, p. 161).

The "Psychic" Divorce: The Return to Singlehood

Bohannan's sixth phase of the divorce experience is the *psychic divorce*. The psychic divorce involves the problems of regaining individual autonomy, of making the transformation from being a part of a married couple to the state of singlehood—with all its characteristics of loneliness and stress on the one hand and opportunities, hope, and promise on the other hand (see Chapter 6).

Bohannan (1970) feels that, as hard as the other five stages are, the psychic divorce is the most difficult of all. However, it may also be the most personally constructive, involving the process of becoming a "whole, complete, and autonomous individual again" (p. 60).

Most divorced persons are not able to function in their new status for about a year after the divorce. An exception, of course, is the person who has had an extramarital affair, fallen in love, and obtained the divorce in order to be free. This person will often remarry as soon as legally possible and, when single, is concerned chiefly with financial problems and custodial or visitation rights with the children (Weiss 1975).

Francke (1983), in her comprehensive study of the aftermath of divorce, found that the usual period of recovery for most divorcées is about three years, with the first twelve to eighteen months a "peak period of unavoidable stress." It is not unusual, however, for the first one to eight weeks to be a period of euphoria: the decision has been made, the die is cast, the marriage is over, and the future looks bright with promise (p. 24). However, following this eight-week euphoria, loneliness, stress, and dejection often follow.

The novelty of the first flush of single's freedom fades and loneliness begins to set in. This is not the sort of loneliness that comes with an evening's boredom, or the loneliness of having no one to share a sunset with, but loneliness that feeds on the panic that there never, ever will be anyone to share anything with again (Francke 1983, pp. 25–26).

One study found that at the end of the first year, fully 97 percent of custodial mothers and 81 percent of fathers felt that the divorce might have been a mistake; that as hard as it is to be married, it is even harder to be divorced. They wished that they had tried harder to make the marriage work instead of taking the irrevocable steps that led to legal divorce (Hetherington et al. 1978).

The second year is often experienced as a continuation of the problems that began with the divorce, and for custodial mothers it is often worse because of the economic difficulties they must face. Both men and women often plunge into a frenzy of activity at this time.

No project seems too banal for an adult who simply cannot face another evening of being alone. Suddenly, there is a burning need to learn to make jewelry, throw clay pots, take creative writing courses—anything to get out of the house. Men, adrift from family obligations, often go on a social tear and seek companionship, however temporary, in bars, at clubs, and at parties they never would have dreamed of going to while they were still married. Loneliness becomes a malignant enemy, held at bay by a schedule filled to the absurd (Francke 1983, p. 32).

However, despite the problems, the difficulties, the despair, and the depression so often associated with the post-divorce groups, most remarry within two or three years. In fact, in all age groups, the likelihood that a divorced person will marry is greater than the likelihood that a never-married person will marry, as we shall see in the later section "Remarriage following Divorce."

THE MEANING OF DIVORCE FOR CHILDREN

Each year more than 1 million children have their lives irrevocably changed when their parents become divorced. Annual vital statistics since 1960 show that in each year, more than half of the couples who obtain a divorce have at least one child under eighteen years of age.[19] Although the birth rate has declined since 1964, the total number of children involved in divorce has continued to rise—from 0.5 million in 1960 to nearly 1.2 million in 1981.[20] Although most divorced parents eventually remarry, children may live in a single-parent household for a number of years (see Chapter 10). Glick (1979) points out that if the annual increase in the proportion of children whose parents had ever obtained a divorce continues until 1990, close to one-third of the children might experience a parent's divorce before they reach the age of eighteen (p. 175).

Those children of divorce living with their father (as the custodial parent) may double by 1990, but this change would be only from 1 percent to 2 percent. Fathers are about half again as likely to have custody of school age children as they are to have custody of preschool age children (Glick 1979, p. 177).

Perhaps the most definitive study to date on the effect of divorce upon children is Wallerstein and Kelly's (1980) carefully designed research on sixty participating families in the San Francisco Bay area. In this study, several themes were found to be central in the children's response to the impact of divorce.

More than three-fourths of the children in this study were frightened, worried about what would happen to them, who would take care of them in such fundamental ways as feeding them and protecting them. After all, if the marriage of the mother and father could end and they were no longer a family living together, couldn't the parent–child relation end as well? The fragility of their situation was brought home to them with sudden and unex-

pected force. What stability was there in the world if their most fundamental basis of safety —their family—could dissolve? Fully one-half of the children in this study were intensely afraid. One-third of the very young children worried that their mothers would leave; one-half were fearful that the father, who had already left the home, would abandon them completely. Two-thirds of the young children yearned intensely for the father whose departure they found terrifying. One-half of the children were intensely concerned about their mother, aware of a feeling of precariousness, of being totally dependent upon the one remaining parent in the household. They worried about her health and well-being, about her emotional upsets and moodiness. More than half of these children suffered intense feelings of rejection, feeling that they had been deserted not only by the departing father, but also by their mother (Wallerstein and Kelly 1980, pp. 45–48).

Another pervasive theme for these children was one of profound, painful, acute loneliness; in general, the only ones not extraordinarily lonely were some of the adolescents, who were preoccupied with sports, social, or school activities and interests, who had the support of friends, and who enjoyed their father's continuing interest (p. 49).

The study also found that the problem of conflicting loyalties was a pervasive theme, with children often feeling pulled in opposite directions by their parents. Two-thirds of the parents in this study openly competed for the children's allegiance. The dilemma of being confronted by demands from each parent produced an agonizing anxiety in these children, because there was no way to resolve it to the satisfaction of both parents. If they refrained from taking either parent's side, they were left even more alone, with no place to turn for comfort, because each parent tended to react with anger at what was regarded as a betrayal by the child. The dilemma was sometimes solved by the child joining the battle with one parent and directing anger and re-

---

[19]U.S. National Center for Health Statistics. "Marriages and Divorces: 1960 to 1981" (1985).

[20]Ibid.

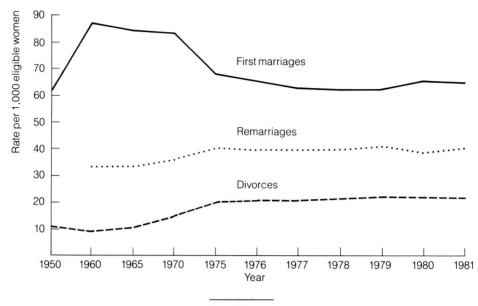

FIGURE 8-8

Rates of marriage, remarriage, and divorce per 1,000
eligible women in the United States, 1950–1981

Sources: Data from U.S. Bureau of the Census,
"Marital Status and Living Arrangements 1977–1980"
and "Households and Families by Type, March 1978" (1980);
U.S. National Center for Health Statistics,
"Marriages and Divorces: 1960 to 1981" (1985).

sentment against the other, repressing feelings of disloyalty but paying the price with rising tension and anxiety (p. 49).

Another common reaction among these children was anger, expressed in temper tantrums, in hitting, and in verbal attack. Fully one-fourth experienced explosive anger directed toward one or both parents. For another third, anger was a major aspect of the reaction to the divorce, which sometimes spilled over into other areas of their lives (p. 50).

On the other hand, the Wallerstein and Kelly study found little support for the notion that feelings of guilt, or self-blame, for the parents' separation was very common among children of divorce, except for very young children (age eight and younger). These younger children felt that they were in some measure responsible for the separation, attributing it to some "sin of omission or commission" on their part, something they had done or not done (p. 50).

Nor did the study find support for the widely held notion that divorce is better for the children than living in an unhappy marriage characterized by conflict, disagreement, and stress between the parents.

Only a few of the children in our study thought their parents were happily married, yet the overwhelming majority preferred the unhappy marriage to the divorce. As the children spoke with us, we found that although many of them had lived for years in an unhappy home, they did not experience the divorce as a solution to their unhappiness, nor did they greet it with relief at the time, or for several years thereafter (Wallerstein and Kelly 1980, p. 11).

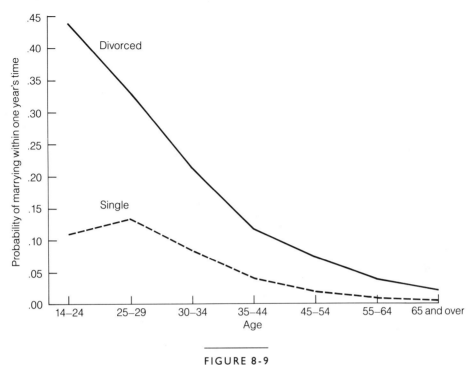

FIGURE 8-9

Probability of divorced and single women marrying, by age

Source: Carter and Glick (1976).

REMARRIAGE FOLLOWING DIVORCE

Of the almost 1 million persons who divorce each year, 90 percent remarry (see Figure 8-8). One-fourth of those who divorce in their twenties remarry within one year, and one-half remarry within three years. The time between divorce and remarriage is about twice as long for men and women in their thirties and forties than for those in their twenties (Carter and Glick 1976). The average period between the divorce and the remarriage for all age groups is 3.2 years. It is interesting that women's expectation for remarriage dwindles with each year following the divorce (Glick and Lin 1986) (see Figure 8-9).

Second marriages make up the greatest number of remarriages in the United States; only 2 percent of whites and 4 percent of blacks have married three or more times (Glick and Norton 1976).

The High Rate of Remarriage

Middle-income or affluent men have a higher rate of remarriage than those with low incomes, but for women the opposite is true. Either high-income women are choosier or it is difficult for them to find suitable prospects. The rate of remarriage for women is also influenced by their level of education. For example, a woman with five or more years of college has a lower rate of remarriage than a less-educated woman. One reason for this lower rate is the dating differential (see Chapter 5). It is speculated that other reasons are disillusionment with the realities of marriage and the difficulty of trying to combine marriage with a career (Safilios-Rothschild 1977, Carter and Glick 1976). A divorced woman with one minor child has the same statistical expectation for remarriage as a divorced woman with no children, and only a slightly lower chance of remarriage if she has two minor children. However, if she has three minor children, her chances drop somewhat (Hunt and Hunt 1977). For middle-aged and elderly women, the expectation for remarriage drops sharply because of the shorter lifespan of men and because of the dating differential (see Chapter 5). Thus there is a growing population of unmarried women in their fifties, sixties, and older.[21]

The probability that the widower will remarry within a given number of years is about half the probability that a divorced man will marry within this time. For widows, the probability for remarriage is only about one-seventh of the probability that a divorced woman will remarry.[22] Remarriages are less homogamous than first marriages, with greater variations in age, religious background, and educational level (Dean and Gurak 1978). Research data suggest that the reason is that as prospective marriage partners reach their late twenties and early thirties, they tend to affiliate more with groups from diverse backgrounds than they did in their late teens and early twenties (Bernard 1971).

Dating and engagement periods leading to second marriages are usually shorter than those leading to first marriages. The second wedding ceremony is generally much simpler,

with few guests and often no formal reception; the second honeymoon is briefer and less expensive (Bernard 1971).

The average age difference between a bride and groom in a remarriage is greater than it is in a first marriage. In the first marriage, 71 percent of the brides are younger than the grooms, 16 percent are the same age, and 12 percent are older; 49 percent of those younger brides are one to three years younger and 12 percent are five to nine years younger. When it is a remarriage for the bride but a first marriage for the groom, 50 percent of brides are younger than the grooms, 10 percent are the same age, and 40 percent are older than the grooms. In contrast, if it is a remarriage for the groom but a first marriage for the bride, nearly 90 percent of brides are younger than the grooms, 4 percent are the same age, 33 percent are five to nine years younger, and 15 percent are ten to fourteen years younger (see Figure 8-10).[23]

Social Attitudes toward Remarriage

Before about 1920, neither divorce nor remarriage had gained much public or institutional acceptance as a respectable alternative to unsuccessful marriage. Sociologists and marriage counselors discussed divorce and remarriage as "social problems" until about 1960. By the mid-1960s, however, professional views as well as those of the general public had undergone a transformation. Divorce and remarriage began to be regarded as *solutions* to problems rather than as *problems* in themselves. This change in attitude has apparently evolved from recognition of the importance of marriage in satisfying the basic affiliative needs for emotional security, understanding, acceptance, affection, and love in our mass

[21]U.S. National Center for Health Statistics, *Vital and Health Statistics,* Series 10 (1984).

[22]U.S. National Center for Health Statistics, "Marriages and Divorces: 1960 to 1981" (1985).

[23]U.S. National Center for Health Statistics, "Marriages and Divorces: 1960 to 1981" (1985).

society. Our culture has increasingly adopted the principle that if the first marriage fails in satisfying these needs, the person is justified in exchanging the marriage for another—even when children are involved (Davis 1972, Bernard 1970).

This emphasis on personal happiness in marriage is quite a departure from the earlier emphasis on marriage as an institution that chiefly protects the property and inheritance rights of the woman and offspring and provides an essential stabilizing base for society.

Remarriage following divorce is permitted by civil law in every state and is recognized and accepted by all major religions in our society except the Catholic church.[24] For a remarriage to be recognized as valid by the Catholic church, the first marriage must be annulled or a special dispensation must be obtained, as we have seen.

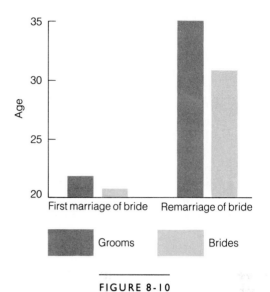

FIGURE 8-10

Median ages of brides and grooms in first marriages and remarriages, 1981

Source: Data from U.S. National Center for Health Statistics, "Marriages and Divorces: 1960 to 1981" (1985).

Motivation for Remarriage

Research studies have found that one of the chief reasons for wanting to remarry is companionship (cited by seven out of ten men and more than eight out of ten women). Satisfaction of emotional needs ranks second, and satisfaction of sexual needs ranks third. Financial security is cited by a little more than one-third of women and "the children's sake" by about one-fourth. Fewer than one man in ten gives either of these latter two reasons. To rejoin married society is the reason cited by a small minority of both men and women, as is to avoid the stigma of singleness (Hunt and Hunt 1977).

Despite the experience of an unhappy marriage and the trauma of divorce, the divorced person seeks in a remarriage precisely the same satisfactions that motivated the first marriage. Similarly, the widowed person who has experienced one successful marriage (that terminated with the death of the spouse) is motivated to remarry for the same reasons that motivated him or her to marry in the first place (Hunt and Hunt 1977).

The Divorce Rate of Remarriages

If we compare the survival rate of first marriages with the survival rate of remarriages for the same people (not remarrying the same partners, of course), the remarriages appear much stronger. After all, the survival rate of the first marriages was zero for this group, whereas the survival rate of the remarriages is about the same as that of *all* marriages (with the precise rate depending on the age of each couple and other factors).

The most recent available data show that

---

[24]The Episcopal church abolished in 1973 its centuries-old ban on the remarriage of divorced persons. Past requirements of an ecclesiastical annulment before any second marriage was also eliminated. Under the change, the church recognizes civil divorce as ending a marriage and allows those who have been divorced to remarry in the church.

for a couple in their twenties the statistical expectation that a remarriage will end in divorce is slightly higher than the expectation of divorce for a first marriage, but it is lower for a couple in their thirties or forties (Norton and Glick 1976).[25] Among blacks, the divorce rate is always lower for remarriages than for first marriages (McCarthy 1978).

If present trends continue, about 40 percent of people in their late twenties and early thirties who remarry after divorce can expect their second marriages to end in divorce also. For both men and women, twenty-five to thirty-four is the most typical age for a second divorce (Norton and Glick 1976).

The problems that a divorced person encounters in a first marriage do not necessarily carry over to a remarriage. A person in a second marriage is older, more emotionally mature, more experienced, and presumably able to make a better choice. In addition, a first marriage may serve as a learning experience, contributing to more effective communication and greater harmony and mutual satisfaction in their second marriages.

Others, of course, repeat the problems of their first marriage. They find remarriage just as unsatisfactory and divorce even more quickly than they did before: the time between the wedding and the divorce is usually about two years less than the time before the initial divorce, with a median interval of about 5.3 years compared with 7.5 years. The median age at a third marriage (following a second divorce) is about thirty-two for women and older for men (Glick and Norton 1977).

Happiness in Remarriage

When those in remarriages are asked to compare their present marriages with their first,

A controversial and widely publicized remarriage was that of Mrs. Wallis Warfield Simpson (twice divorced) to the former King Edward VIII, who abdicated the British throne in order to marry her.

United Press International

nearly 90 percent say that the second marriage is "much better." Only 3 percent find it "no different" or "worse" than the first marriage (Albrecht 1979).

However, studies comparing the self-reported marital happiness of people who are *in* first marriages with those who are remarried have found that those in first marriages are slightly happier. For example, 70 percent of wives in first marriages describe themselves as "very happy," compared to 68 percent of those in remarriages (Glenn and Weaver 1977).

---

[25]Remember, there are many complex factors involved in the divorce rate, such as age at marriage, social class, educational level, vocational preparedness, income, and race.

The widowed person who has experienced one successful marriage is motivated to remarry for the same reasons that moved him or her to marry in the first place.

A later study found that those in a remarriage are not as happy as those in a first marriage, however. This study found that black and white women and white men are less happy in a second marriage than in a first marriage. Remarried white women are moderately lower in marital happiness, whereas remarried black women are much lower and white men are slightly lower. The only group in this study who are much happier in the remarriage are black men (Glenn 1981). This research on happiness in remarriage is contradictory and puzzling. Perhaps future research will spell out the reasons for these apparent contradictions.

Researchers do agree that remarried people are happier than those who remain unmarried following a divorce. In Glenn's 1981 study, for example, those who had not remarried were lowest in their self-reported happiness than those in either a first marriage or a remarriage. These findings coincide with the report that single people (whether never-married or divorced) have a much higher incidence of physical problems, accidents, suicide, and psychological problems than married people, as we have seen (Chapter 6).

SPECIAL PROBLEMS IN REMARRIAGE

There are certain characteristics of a remarriage that make it uniquely different from a first marriage. Most significant of these differences, of course, is the presence of stepchildren. For the custodial mother, a second marriage not only means moving a new husband into the household, but also means that this new husband will have to enter the family as a stepfather to her children.

When her ex-husband remarries, he and his second wife not only face the problems, misunderstandings, and conflicts familiar to all marriages (see Chapter 9), but the new wife must, in addition, deal with the extraordinary complications and challenges of being a stepmother to his children. Studies have found that problems with stepchildren cause more difficulty than any other aspect of marriage (Duberman 1975).

Another characteristic of the remarriage that sets it apart from the first marriage are the problems relating to economics—providing the necessary goods, services, and shelter for the family in our complex mass society. Although first marriages have economic difficulties for virtually all couples (see Chapter 13), the remarriage has added economic problems that can be quite severe. Financial difficulties are among the most significant problems characteristic of remarriages (Albrecht et al. 1983, Fishman 1983).

Finally, there are the problems involving the ex-spouse. As long as the divorced couple are parents of a child they cannot completely sever their relation, but each continues to revolve around the constellation of mother–father–child, even though the marriage has formally and officially ended. (See also the section "The Blended Family" in Chapter 10.)

Stepparents and Stepchildren

The problems of stepparents and stepchildren are attracting increasing interest. Because of the rapidly rising divorce rate, 16 million children had a stepparent by 1981; there are 1 million new stepchildren each year.[26]

Problems in stepparenting seem to occur mainly from the stepparents' point of view, although Wallerstein and Kelly (1980) found that it takes some time for children to settle

down and accept the stepfather. Several studies have found that after stepchildren have made the adjustment to the new family structure, they have no more problems than children who are living with their biological parents (Marotz-Baden et al. 1979, Duberman 1975, Wilson et al. 1975). For example, a three-year study of a large sample of stepfathers and their stepchildren found that, in general, stepchildren rate themselves as being just as happy as children who live with both their biological parents; they do as well at school and get along as well with their stepfathers as other children do with their biological fathers (Bohannan and Erickson 1978).

Stepfathers

Because the mother is the custodial parent in nine out of ten divorce actions and most of these women remarry (often within two to three years), the usual stepfamily household is the mother, her children, and her second husband—who is the *stepfather* of her children.

Wallerstein and Kelly (1980) found that the custodial mother usually encouraged her second husband to take an active participatory role as a father figure in the household, and most stepfathers did take this responsibility seriously. However, entry into the role of husband and father in the household was not an easy one for these men, and it could involve uncertainty and anxiety for both the new stepfather and the children. Most stepfathers were afraid of not being accepted by the children and were particularly concerned about being compared with the children's biological father. Typically, the children did withhold their acceptance for some time, regarding the stepfather initially with caution and being rather cool in their responses to him. The expectation for "instant intimacy" for the new stepfather was disturbing for these children, who experienced it as a demand to betray their love for their biological father and replace him

---

[26]U.S. National Center for Health Statistics, "Marriages and Divorces: 1960 to 1981" (1985).

with the stepfather in their affection. "Even very young children needed to be assured that the new adult was not being presented as a substitute for the departed parent" (p. 288).

Only a few of the stepfathers in this study were sensitive to the needs of the children to go slowly after the children's recent experience of losing a father from the household. The stepfathers—because of the children's wary, tentative approval and perhaps because of their own anxiety—reacted by becoming overauthoritative, strict disciplinarians. The children typically described them as "stern" and "not affectionate" (p. 288).

Many of these stepfathers had lived in the household as the mother's lover and companion prior to the marriage, and during this period they were more likely to be casual and friendly with the children. The change in status that occurred with the marriage seemed to bring about a corresponding change in attitude toward the children (p. 288).

The age of the children was a significant factor in their acceptance of the stepfather. Younger children, especially those under eight years of age, were generally more responsive and more accepting than were older children. Little girls were especially responsive to affectionate overtures and admiration from their new stepfather (p. 289).

The expectation that children would always experience conflict between their feelings for their biological father and their feelings for their stepfather was not borne out by the Wallerstein and Kelly (1980) research. Most biological fathers continued to visit *if* they had done so before the remarriage, and the pattern of visiting seemed to be relatively unaffected. Although the stepfather's influence on the children was "enormous," the stepfather did not usually replace the departed father in most children's affection. "Most of the children in these remarried families made every effort to conceptualize the stepfather, father, and mother together, and their efforts

to make room for all of them were impressive" (p. 293).

Stepmothers

The custodial mother whose second husband was a visiting father for *his* biological children from his first marriage was quite limited in the role of stepmother to these children in the Wallerstein and Kelly (1980) study. Her importance as a stepmother was chiefly through her very significant capacity to influence her husband's relation with his biological children. Her husband's commitment to his children was very strongly related to her support or disapproval. Most of these stepmothers took a very active role in instructing their second husbands regarding the importance of fulfilling their obligations to the children of their first marriage (p. 299).

In one out of ten divorces, of course, the father is the custodial parent and his second wife plays a very active role as stepmother. Often this can be a very difficult role for her to play. Sometimes, with the best intent in the world, such families are doomed to disappointment. The children may resent their "rightful" mother's place being usurped by the stepmother, no matter what she does to try to win their acceptance.

On the other hand, stepmothers in families where the father is the custodial parent of his biological children can have very rewarding relations with their stepchildren, especially if the children are very young at the time of the remarriage. The stepmother may fill an enormous void in the children's lives, providing them with the nurture, care, love, and discipline that they have sadly lacked (p. 300).

Draughon (1975) suggests that stepmothers relate to their stepchildren with one of three possible role models. These are the "primary" mother, the "other" mother, and the "friend."

She finds that the stepmother may successfully act as the "primary" mother—essentially replacing the biological mother in the child's perception—only if the biological mother is not important to the child, or is "psychologically dead" and is not being mourned by the child. However, a physically alive biological mother is unlikely to be "psychologically dead" for the child, who may have thoughts and fantasies about her even when she is not physically available. In fact, the biological mother may be seen as his "primary source of warmth and love." He may not want a new mother, however much he might need one, and will reject any attempts to replace his mother. "Under these conditions it seems wiser for the stepmother to attempt to be a friend" (pp. 187–188).

Draughon (1975) finds that the crucial aspect of the "friend" model is that it is not structured mainly in terms of the dependency of the child, but along other dimensions, such as shared interests. The stepmother who is chiefly a "friend" does not try to replace the mother and is not seen either by the child or by herself as necessary for his survival (pp. 185–186).

The most difficult as well as the least rewarding of the three role models is that of the "other" mother. When the stepmother acts as the "other" mother, the child has two or more "mothers" at the same time. This is the model most commonly used by psychologically naive stepmothers. The child in this situation calls both the biological mother and the stepmother "mother" and is expected to turn to each for help. Moreover, each woman sees herself as having the child rely on her for all dependency needs (p. 185). With this model, the child is being pulled in different directions at the same time, creating confusion and multiplying conflicts (p. 185).

This model of the "other" mother does not appear to have any advantages over either of the other models, under any circumstances that Draughon has considered (p. 183).

Stepsiblings

About half of the stepfathers in the Wallerstein and Kelly (1980) study had children from their first marriage. Thus the incidence of stepsiblings may be presumed to be very high, involving perhaps as many as 50 percent of remarriages.

As we have seen, children are often ill-prepared for the upheaval in their lives brought about by the divorce, and may be additionally confused and bewildered by their mother's and stepfather's expectation that they form "instant" sibling relations.

It is not surprising that instant siblings may be wary of one another at first. Almost overnight, everything that has been long established is changed. A child who has always been the youngest may suddenly have a new younger stepbrother or sister. A private room is suddenly invaded by a stepsibling. Valued toys may seem threatened. One family has watched television at dinner, the other had not. One set of children were permitted soft drinks at dinner, the other set were allowed only milk and fruit juice. Suddenly they are stuck not only at the same dinner table, but presumably for life (Francke 1983).

Despite these problems and many more, most stepsibling interactions seem to work out fairly well after the initial shock. In the Wallerstein and Kelly (1980) study, after an adjustment period that usually lasted for about a year, most children came to enjoy the new situation. If the mother and stepfather did not push them too fast and were fair in arbitrating differences, some of these children even felt that the pain of the divorce had been balanced out, to some extent, by the acquisition of new stepsiblings. Rivalries were keen, as in any large family, but there were also more opportunities for valued friendships to develop (p. 297).

When the stepsiblings are teenagers, it is possible for erotic interest to develop. When an adolescent boy finds an attractive girl living in the same household it is not surprising if he finds her romantically and erotically attractive—and she might return these feelings. Because the usual taboos of blood relations do not apply, this may be a very explosive situation. Very little research has been done regarding the extent of erotic interaction between adolescent stepsiblings, however. Stepsiblings may marry in most states since they are not related by blood, although all states forbid the marriage of a brother and sister.

Financial Problems

As we shall see, financial problems are an inevitable accompaniment to marriage. For perhaps 98 percent of all families there is never enough money, and economic stress is a major source of problems in virtually all American families. Married couples have more arguments over money than any other topic, and economic stress is a major cause of marriage failure (Chapter 13).

The person who has been through a marriage, a divorce, and a remarriage is no stranger to economic problems. Such problems were probably one of the reasons the first marriage failed in the first place. Unlike problems with stepchildren, the ex-spouse, and former in-laws and friends, financial problems are certainly not unique to the remarriage.

Nevertheless, some aspects of financial problems that are characteristic of remarriage do not occur in first marriages, and some of problems are quite significant. As noted earlier, more than half (53 percent) of custodial mothers do not receive the court-ordered child support payments from the children's father (Weitzman 1985, p. 262). Apparently, when the custodial mother remarries the ex-husband often feels even *less* inclined to send his child support payments to the mother. For example, Duberman (1975) found that in nearly 70 percent of households where the custodial mother had remarried, no support payments at all were received from the children's biological father. For those who did receive some support payments, the average received was only about $2,000 a year.[27]

The noncustodial father, of course, is going to experience considerable difficulty in sending child support payments when he doesn't have enough money to support his new family. His second wife may resent money that she is helping to earn being turned over to his ex-wife. Does he pay for the braces on his biological daughter's teeth while denying his stepdaughter the opportunity to have *her* teeth straightened?

The failure to receive child support payments maintains a continuing adversary relation between the formerly married people, of course. They are forced into continuing interaction regarding the financial needs of their biological children, and this continuing conflict cannot help but bring pressure on the harmony of the remarriage (Messinger 1976).

The Ex-Spouse

One of the problems in a remarriage that does not occur in a first marriage is, of course, conflict regarding the person's continuing interaction with the former spouse. Ahrons and Wallisch (1986) found four interaction styles that characterize former spouses, ranging from very friendly to very hostile: *perfect pals, cooperative colleagues, angry associates,* and *fiery foes.* The study found that the stereotype of a divorced couple fighting over finances and their children is characteristic for about half of all ex-spouses. The other half of divorced couples remain relatively friendly, either as perfect pals or as cooperative colleagues.

---

[27]U.S. Bureau of the Census, Child Support and Alimony—Selected Characteristics of Women: 1981" (1985).

Perfect Pals

Although the smallest number of divorced couples (about 12 percent, or one in eight) are perfect pals, many of Ahrons' subjects *wished* that they were (Ahrons and Wallisch 1976). In the perfect pal group, the disappointments, discouragement, and unhappiness that are the inevitable accompaniment of divorce have not totally replaced all of the couple's positive feelings toward one another. They still like, respect, and trust one another and retain fond memories of their early closeness and intimacy. Each perceives the other as a caring and responsible parent. They both feel highly responsible for the children and regard the children's needs as having a high priority— sometimes putting the children's needs ahead of their own. Their joint parenting is very similar to the way it was during their marriage (Ahrons and Rodgers 1987, p. 122).

These ex-spouses continue to enjoy one another and their children at such family events as Christmas or Hanukkah celebrations, birthday parties, graduations, recitals, weddings, and Little League games. They are not only present at these events but they share the planning, the anticipation, and the joys of these events in a very real and intimate way (p. 122).

Cooperative Colleagues

Ahrons and Rodgers (1987) found that the cooperative colleagues are able to participate in their joint responsibilities toward the children's welfare and future and are very concerned with the need to be responsible parents. They tend to deal with the normal stresses of child rearing in ways similar to those of parents who have remained married, and they report a high degree of satisfaction with their children's development and accomplishments. They feel that it is important to minimize, for the children, the difficulties inherent in a divorce and the resultant breakup of the family (pp. 124–125).

However, unlike perfect pals, cooperative colleagues do not feel that they are good friends, and cannot depend upon their mutual feelings of friendship to act as a safety valve when problems or disagreements arise. Arrangements for visitation and other plans for the children need to be more explicitly and formally defined. However, divorce decrees do not usually state precise visiting times for these ex-spouses. The language of the decree is usually in such general terms as "suitable and reasonable." Cooperative colleagues are then able to work out mutually agreeable arrangements for themselves, which may change with circumstances. They do not typically rely on external resources and mediators such as the courts to settle their differences, but are able to resolve disagreements for themselves—with discussion, compromise and cooperation (pp. 117–118, 124–126).

Major life events are celebrated jointly with cooperative colleagues, but with less shared warmth and pleasure than is characteristic of perfect partners. For example, they may both attend an event, but not sit together (p. 125). This category is the largest—about 38 percent of divorced couples (Ahrons and Wallisch 1986).

Angry Associates

The anger that each feels for the other is an important part of post-divorce relating for angry associates—about 25 percent of divorced couples (Ahrons and Wallisch 1986). They retain bitter and resentful feelings about their past marriage and about the divorce process, which often involve long acrimonious arguments and disputes over such matters as custody, visitation rights, and support payments. Power struggles that characterized the divorce process continue. The custodial mother uses her control over the children as a weapon in this struggle, withholding visitation rights or altering visitation times. The noncustodial father controls the money and can withhold or delay support payments (Ahrons and Rodgers 1987, pp. 118, 126–127).

Thus, these divorced couples are much less capable of coparenting than are people in the two prior categories. Angry associates must have explicitly specified agreements regarding arrangements for visitation and are much less flexible in accommodating situational changes. Children are aware of the anger and discord between their parents and are troubled by the rigid limits that are set on visitation rights (p. 127).

Former in-laws and friends of the couple are typically reluctant to continue social interaction on any sort of amicable basis because if they do remain friends they are liable to find themselves caught in the middle of the couple's continuing power struggle. If they do not side with one person against the other their loyalty will be questioned. It is easier simply to withdraw gradually from the friendship (p. 127).

Major life events are not celebrated jointly as they are with perfect pals and cooperative colleagues, but instead represent major stress situations that are likely to require special negotiations. "There is a general quality of tiptoeing through a minefield for all of the participants" (p. 127).

However, as strife-torn as the angry associates are, they are not characterized by the constant violent disagreements of the fiery foes.

Fiery Foes

The fiery foes (about 24 percent of divorced couples) remain intensely angry at one another for years following the divorce (Ahrons and Wallisch 1986). Their divorce processes were often hotly contested legal battles, with fighting over the division of property and custody payments, which parent should get custody, and the specific visitation rights of the noncustodial parent. Their ability to accept each other's parenting rights is virtually lost. As with angry associates, former in-laws and friends of the couple are forced to take sides. They can't be amicable with both ex-spouses; if they try, they are accused of disloyalty. Friends of the couple are either forced to side with one person against the other or to drop them both (Ahrons and Rodgers 1987, pp. 119–126, 128–129).

The custody agreement remains a sore point with fiery foes. Access to the children (visitation rights) by the noncustodial parent is a source of continued conflict and disagreement. Support payments by the noncustodial father will either not be paid at all or will be underpaid or delayed (p. 128).

Fiery foes have no fond memories of each other or of happy times during their marriage. They focus exclusively on their perceived grievances and wrongs with destructive bitterness (p. 119).

Instead of being joyful occasions, major life events usually serve to set the scene for a power struggle that may be so acrimonious it destroys the celebratory mood for everyone (pp. 128–129).

SUMMARY

The incidence of divorce has risen steadily in the United States over the past hundred years. In 1869, the proportion of marriages ending in divorce was 3.5 percent; in 1900, it was 13.7 percent; in 1930, 23.7 percent; in 1950, 35.9 percent; in 1970, 44 percent; and in 1983, 50 percent. However, as the divorce rate rose the death rate dropped, so the total number of marriages dissolved each year (by death *and* divorce) has remained virtually unchanged. For example, in 1869, 3.3 percent of marriages were dissolved (by death and divorce) compared to 3.4 percent in 1970. Thus, the percentage of American marriages dissolved each year has remained remarkably stable in the past century.

Of course, the national rate of divorce tells us very little about any one individual's expectations for divorce at the time of marriage. Many individual factors—such as age at marriage, income, educational and occupational level of the individual, childhood background, and race—are statistically correlated with the incidence of divorce. Even geographic area is important in terms of the expectation for divorce; the rate of divorce rises, in general, from east to west and from north to south.

The meaning of divorce for the individual goes through six stages: the emotional divorce, when the couple come to grips with the fact that their marriage is failing; the legal divorce, when the divorce proceedings are actually initiated and concluded; the economic divorce, which has to do with all the money problems experienced by the ex-spouses; the coparental divorce, which has to do with child custody and visitation rights; the community divorce, which has to do with the reaction of family and friends; and the psychic divorce, which involves the problems of regaining individual autonomy.

Most people who have been divorced (about 90 percent) remarry, usually within one to three years. Middle-income or affluent men have a higher rate of remarriage than those with low incomes, whereas for women the opposite is true, with the low-income women having the higher rate.

Studies of happiness in a remarriage compared with a first marriage are inconclusive. All studies agree, however, that remarried people are happier and healthier, both physically and psychologically, than divorced people who do not remarry—or never-married singles.

Remarriages have special problems that do not occur in a first marriage. Among these, the worst are the problems of a stepparent relating to a stepchild. Financial problems in a remarriage are almost always worse than they were in a first marriage. About half of remarried people retain bitter and resentful feelings toward their ex-spouse, creating problems that can spill over into the remarriage.

QUESTIONS

1. Describe and compare three methods commonly used to estimate the divorce rate. Which method do demographers regard as the most accurate? What is the current estimate of the incidence of divorce in the United States?

2. Explain how the stability of American marriages has remained relatively unchanged for the past 100 years, despite the steadily rising divorce rate.

3. From a demographic point of view, the individual probability for divorce is related to eight factors. What are these eight factors, and what is the effect of each upon the statistical expectation for divorce?

4. Describe the emergence of divorce in England and the United States from the sixteenth century to the present.

5. What is meant by annulment? What is the difference between annulment and divorce? What is the importance of annulment in historical perspective?

6. Discuss the attitude of the Roman Catholic church toward annulment and divorce.

7. Discuss the differences between spousal support, alimony, and child support in a divorce settlement.

8. Do you think it is advisable for the father to obtain child custody? Why do you feel this way? Give an example of a case that would support your answer.

9. Discuss the problems of stepparenting.

10. Why do you think stepsiblings have less difficulty relating to one another than they do relating to a stepparent?

11. Discuss the possible meanings of divorce for children.

12. Do you think a remarriage has a greater or a less chance for success than a first marriage? Explain your reasons.

13. What are some of the special problems a couple might have in a remarriage that they did not have in the first marriage?

SUGGESTIONS FOR FURTHER READING

Burke, M., and Grant, J. B. *Games Divorced People Play*. Englewood Cliffs, N. J.: Prentice-Hall, 1982.

Cherlin, Andrew J. *Marriage, Divorce, Remarriage*. Cambridge, Mass.: Harvard University Press, 1981.

Duberman, Lucille. *The Reconstituted Family: A Study of Remarried Couples and Their Children*. Chicago: Nelson Hall, 1975.

Hunt, Bernie, and Hunt, Morton. *The Divorce Experience*. New York: McGraw-Hill, 1977.

Krantzler, M. *Creative Divorce: A New Opportunity for Personal Growth*. New York: New American Library, 1975.

Levinger, George, and Moles, Oliver C. *Divorce and Separation*. New York: Basic Books, 1979.

Matthews, Joseph. *After the Divorce: How to Modify Child Support, Child Custody, and Spousal Support*, 2nd ed. Occidental, Calif.: Nolo Press, 1985.

May, Elaine Tyler. *Great Expectations: Marriage and Divorce in Post-Victorian America*. Chicago: University of Chicago Press, 1980.

Rapoport, Rona, Rapoport, Robert N., and Strelitz, Z. *Mothers, Fathers, and Society*. New York: Random House, 1980.

Skafte, Dianne. *Child Custody Evaluation: A Practical Guide*. Beverly Hills, Calif.: Sage Publications, 1985.

Spanier, Graham B., and Thompson, Linda. *Parting: The Aftermath of Separation and Divorce*. Beverly Hills, Calif.: Sage Publications, 1984.

Wallerstein, J. S., and Kelly, J. E. *Surviving the Breakup: How Children Actually Cope with Divorce*. New York: Basic Books, 1980.

Weiss, Robert. *Going It Alone: The Family Life and Social Situation of the Single-Parent Family*. New York: Basic Books, 1981.

C H A P T E R   9

Marital Interaction: Conflict and Communication

The Nature of Conflict
Coping with Conflict Productively
Coping with Conflict Destructively
Common Patterns of Attack and Defense
Maintaining Effective Communication
The Breakdown of Effective Communication

*He who would have no trouble in this world
must not be born in it.*

Italian proverb

Marital interaction can be harmonious and provide pleasure and satisfaction for each of the couple, or it can be disruptive and bring dissatisfaction, disappointment, and pain to one or both.

About half of those marrying in this decade will find the interaction so disruptive that they will end it in divorce—usually within two or three years of the marriage. The difficulties often start immediately, then escalate during the first year, as we have seen (Chapter 8). The couple separate, reconcile, separate again, and finally end their relation irrevocably with divorce.[1]

About half of contemporary marriages are not ending in divorce, however. Moreover, the average person on the wedding day has the actuarial expectation of remaining married some twenty years longer than a couple a century ago (see Chapter 8). When long-married

---

[1] Divorce is not always irrevocable, of course; divorced couples sometimes remarry. One well-publicized example of this was the celebrated remarriage of Elizabeth Taylor to Richard Burton, which ended in a second divorce.

couples are asked, in old age, what was the happiest period of their marriages, a substantial number say, "Right now" (see Chapter 7).

What are the differences between successful marriages and those that end in divorce? Are the successful marriages free of conflict, or does conflict occur but is handled differently? Are there differences in the nature of communication? In this chapter, we shall examine the nature of conflict and the qualities of effective and ineffective communication in marriage.

THE NATURE OF CONFLICT

Even though a successful marriage is characterized by equivalence of function in all three categories of need fulfillment—material, sexual, and psychological—this does not mean that there will be no conflict. Conflict occurs when an experience that provides satisfaction for one person results in deprivation for the other. For example, if the wife wants the window open and the husband wants it closed, opening the window provides satisfaction for the wife but deprivation for the husband. Unless both persons always want the same thing at the same time, there is a conflict.

The Inevitability of Conflict in Marriage

Conflict in marriage is inevitable and unavoidable. It is simply unrealistic to expect that both persons will always want the same thing at the same time. With the amount of enforced interaction characteristic of marriage it is inevitable that one will want something that the other does not at some time. (See the vignette, "Excessive Expectations for Togetherness.")

Conflicts are much more frequent in marriage than in dating. If each of the dating couple does not want the same thing at the same time most of the time, they probably just stop seeing one another.

The Complexity of Conflict in Marriage

Conflict sometimes occurs in a very simple and obvious form (such as the open-window–closed-window controversy), but most conflicts are extraordinarily complex, involving many interrelated needs so that the initial problem spreads into other areas, becomes multidimensional, and colors almost every aspect of the couple's interaction. Before a need is acted upon or a satisfaction seized, if this action will bring deprivation to the other person, it is important that its relations to other needs and other satisfactions (both one's own and others') be seen in as clear perspective as possible.

Conflicts that occur in marriage are, ironically, more likely to escalate than conflicts that occur in business. This is because one's rights and expectations are precisely spelled out in a business agreement, together with what constitutes a violation—and the reprisal for the violation. By contrast, many of each of the couple's rights and expectations in marriage are usually left unstated, which makes the couple much more prone to misunderstanding, disagreement, and conflict.

Since the expectations in marriage (especially those related to such needs as sex, companionship, and understanding) are often not clearly spelled out, reaction to a conflict can obscure the source of the disagreement. In any conflict there must be satisfaction for one and deprivation for the other, but it is not always clear what form these take or who is experiencing which. Moreover, the reprisals that the deprived person exacts from the other are often not clearly acknowledged by either, and indeed are often unconscious.

When a conflict persists in this way—unacknowledged and displaced to other areas of the couple's interaction—it can be very damaging to each person's self-esteem and to the quality of their interaction. One reason for this is the extreme sense of frustration that often accompanies an unresolved conflict.

Excessive Expectations for Togetherness

No matter how close a couple might be, each person may be expected to have somewhat different needs, interests, and characteristics. Each is a unique individual with a unique background. Inevitable dissimilarities will be present and will invariably be a source of conflict.

The probability of such conflict is greater when one or both members of the couple are steeped in the romantic illusion of excessive togetherness. Mutual satisfaction in marriage may be very difficult to achieve if one person expects the other to give up all interests, activities, and attitudes that he or she cannot share. Further, mutual satisfaction is impossible if the couple do not structure the relation on the expectation that each must grow as an individual, maintaining the initial unshared interests and characteristics as well as developing new unshared interests and characteristics.

The vital importance and necessity of achieving and maintaining a balance between individuation and togetherness have been stated most aptly by Kahlil Gibran:

But let there be spaces in your togetherness,
And let the winds of the heavens dance between you.
Love one another, but make not a bond of love:
Let it rather be a moving sea between the shores
    of your souls.
Fill each other's cup but drink not from one cup.
Give one another of your bread but eat not from
    the same loaf.
Sing and dance together and be joyous, but let each one of
    you be alone,
Even as the strings of a lute are alone though they quiver
    with the same music.

The Results of Unresolved Conflict

Frustration

Frustration is the emotion that is experienced when an important need is being blocked. For example, suppose a husband wishes to make love to his wife, and she says she is "too tired." If his need is compelling and persistent, he will feel frustrated.[2] If, in addition, he feels that her "tiredness" represents rejection, he may experience feelings of self-devaluation as well as frustration. When these two emotions are combined, the result may be explosive.

An excellent illustration of the development of this type of situation occurs in a very perceptive passsage in John Updike's *Rabbit, Run.* The young husband wants to copulate with his wife and has been waiting to do so with increasing tension (and deprivation) throughout a long Sunday afternoon:

His wish to make love to Janice is like a small angel to which all afternoon tiny lead weights are attached. . . . He has come home from church carrying something precious for Janice and keeps being screened from giving it to her . . . they blunder about restlessly through the wreckage of the Sunday paper. . . . Rabbit, hoping to possess her eventually, hovers near her like a miser near treasure. His lust glues them together. When they are finally in bed together she refuses his advances.

"Harry, don't you know I want to go to sleep?"
"Well, why didn't you tell me before?"
"I didn't know. I didn't know."
"You didn't know what?"
"I didn't know what you were doing. I thought you were just being nice."

---

[2]Of course, this may go in the other direction as well, with the husband "too tired" and the wife frustrated (see Chapter 4).

"So this isn't nice."

"Well, it's not nice when I can't *do* anything."

"You can do *some*thing."

"No I can't. Even if I wasn't all tired and confused from Rebecca's crying all day I can't. Not for six weeks. You know that."

"Yeah, I know, but I thought. . . ." He's terribly embarrassed.

"*What* did you think?"

"I thought you might love me anyway."

After a pause she says, "I *do* love you."[3]

Her total lack of understanding and awareness, or her deliberate misinterpretation of his need (using her recent childbirth as an excuse), leaves him with so great a feeling of vulnerability and frustration that he can contain his resultant anxiety only by rising, dressing, leaving the house, and not returning.

Lowering of Self-Esteem

One reason for the young husband's feeling of rejection in this example is that his self-image was seriously devalued. Rejection from someone close to you that demeans your self-image and devalues your self-esteem can be devastating. In contrast, receiving understanding and satisfaction from someone close to you that confirms your self-image makes you feel confident, secure, relaxed, and self-assured—raising your self-esteem and enhancing your performances in all areas of your life.

Self-image is especially vulnerable in the intimacy of marriage, since each spouse usually drops the defenses normally erected in relating to others. An attack from a husband or wife on one's self-image is experienced as betrayal, and if such attacks become a persistent pattern, the marriage will disintegrate.

In any enduring paired bond—certainly in marriage, but also in friendship, dating, or

[3]From pp. 203–204, 206 of Updike's *Rabbit, Run* (1960). Reprinted by permission of the publisher, Alfred A. Knopf Inc., New York.

even business—each person usually supports and enhances the self-image and self-esteem of the other most of the time, or the relation must fail. When one person's self-image is attacked during a quarrel, the other characteristically moves to repair the damage as soon as possible. After the initial anger has worn off each person tries to put the relation back on a mutually supportive basis to maintain the harmony of the interaction.

A successful marriage is usually characterized by mutual respect and attempts to understand and adjust to the inevitable divergences of interests, values, and expectations. When a marriage has begun to disintegrate, however, one or both may sulk, bear grudges, continually attack the self-image of the other, and resist any attempt to examine the basis of conflict—returning again and again to a position of outraged morality or wounded innocence.

Displacement

When the frustration that arises because a person cannot resolve a conflict becomes very threatening to that person's self-image, he or she often unconsciously *displaces* the feelings of aggression from the source of the deprivation to a more convenient or safer target—that is, one the person feels more comfortable in handling with some possibility of success. Since such displacement minimizes the feelings of tension, frustration, and self-devaluation, it is not surprising that displacement is a universal pattern of behavior. For example, suppose an angry marital quarrel arises over a conflict about which television program to watch. The wife wants to watch a news analysis, while her husband wants to watch a baseball game. It is quite possible that the grievance that neither mentions, but that is the real source of the quarrel, is sexual frustration. If this highly complex conflict over sex is displaced to a "safer" battlefield—the conflict over which television program to view—the danger of putting the very vulnerable self-image at risk is minimized or avoided, as is the threat of significant rejection.

Displacement very often explains the surprising emotionalism that a couple exhibit in a disagreement that is itself of little consequence. When displacement occurs, the couple often cannot even remember the reason for the quarrel a day or two later because the ostensible "reason" was not important in the first place.

Defense-oriented and Reality-oriented Responses to Conflict

In general, a person may respond to deprivation or to a perceived attack on the self-image with either reality-oriented behavior or defense-oriented behavior. Behavior that is directed toward obtaining the satisfaction that one is being denied is called *reality-oriented* behavior. Behavior that is not directed toward obtaining this satisfaction but does lower the awareness of dissatisfaction by directing one's attention toward an aggressive or defensive reaction, or toward obtaining a substitute satisfaction, is called *defense-oriented* behavior. (See the vignette, "Defense-oriented and Reality-oriented Behavior.")

Reality-oriented behavior in marriage requires first trying to understand the basis of the deprivation or conflict and then attacking this problem rather than attacking the other person. Take, for example, a situation in which the wife arrives home late without a prior phone call. If her husband is angry and says that he is angry, and they both agree that coming home late creates a problem that should be resolved, they are both reacting with reality-oriented behavior. If, however, he refuses to speak (withdrawal), gets a headache (psychosomatic ailment), punishes the children (displacement), or feels no interest in a formerly enjoyable activity (apathy), or if she explains that she "couldn't reach a phone" (rationalization), this is defense-oriented behavior. These

patterns of behavior are called *defense mechanisms* and are used by all of us. However, if one or more defense mechanisms become a chronic, patterned response to conflict, replacing reality-oriented behavior to a significant extent, they obviously are counterproductive in resolving conflicts.[4]

An outsider observing someone's defense-oriented behavior often reacts with puzzled impatience. Why should anyone persistently engage in defense-oriented behavior when it is obviously failing to satisfy a basic need? Why doesn't everyone always behave in an optimal fashion, making the best possible move to resolve a perceived need?

The answer, of course, is that needs do not exist in isolation and that a person's response to a deprivation or conflict depends on which need is taking precedence at the moment. Thus a person may use a defense-oriented behavior to resolve an immediate need and reduce tension rather than fulfill a more basic, long-term need.

An unresolved conflict can be very serious if the satisfaction that is not being attained is important for the person, and if the resulting feelings of frustration and self-devaluation are serious—as illustrated in the passage from Updike's *Rabbit, Run*.

Personality Styles of Responding to Conflict

In general, each individual tends to cope with conflict with extrapunitive, intrapunitive, or impunitive behavior (Coleman 1984). *Extrapunitive* people tend to act out against the environment—striking out, blaming others, shouting—directing actions against other people or against inanimate objects. Extrapunitive people slam doors, shout, kick furniture, and break dishes.

---

[4]For a fascinating discussion of defense mechanisms, see Coleman (1984).

Defense-oriented and Reality-oriented Behavior

Defense-oriented behavior lowers the tension associated with the lack of a basic need but does nothing to obtain this need. Reality-oriented behavior, in contrast, is a persistent attempt to satisfy the need.

Defense-oriented behavior is rarely used when a physical need is involved. For example, if you are deprived of water, you become increasingly motivated to find water. If the deprivation continues, the search for water will require more and more of your attention and time, until it occupies a major part of your awareness. You might use defense-oriented behavior to temporarily alleviate the tension associated with thirst—for example, imagining cool, beaded glasses of pure spring water—but this does not usually interfere for long with the attempt to resolve the basic need.

When the need is social, however, defense-oriented behavior might be used to replace reality-oriented behavior on a relatively permanent basis. For example, when you are lonely, you might make a compromise adjustment (watching television, taking solitary walks) that lowers the immediate tension associated with loneliness; you might postpone indefinitely the attempt to resolve the basic need, to find companionship.

Since defense-oriented behavior brings the rewards of immediate satisfaction and lowered tension, it is reinforced. Since reinforced behavior tends to be repeated, a person may develop a pattern of defense-oriented behavior that temporarily resolves the tension associated with the deprivation of a social need without satisfying the need. Such a pattern of defense-oriented responses may become part of the life-style.

This is not to say that there is something wrong with watching television or taking solitary walks, of course. The point is that, although such behavior brings immediate satisfaction, it does not resolve the problem of loneliness. Reality-oriented behavior in this context might be taking a night class, joining a church group, or participating in any activity where you are likely to find companionship and make friends.

Although the marginal adjustment of defense-oriented behavior is ultimately self-defeating, it can be very difficult to change. The immediate reduction of tension is a powerful inducement to continue the behavior, and, since there are usually no other options clearly in mind, it may be very difficult to give up the immediate rewards of defense-oriented behavior.

Intrapunitive people, in contrast, tend to direct the energy aroused by the unresolved conflict inward—developing headaches, backaches, stomachaches—blaming and unconsciously punishing themselves.

Impunitive people direct the energy aroused by the failure to resolve a conflict neither outward against the environment nor inward to themselves. Instead, they use their time and energy to resolve the basic conflict. Impunitive people are thus characterized by reality-oriented behavior.

In general, a person tends to respond to a conflict in one of these three patterns. Extra-

punitive people tend to be extrapunitive and intrapunitive people tend to be intrapunitive in most situations, although they may occasionally be extrapunitive or impunitive. Even people who are characteristically impunitive may be, on occasion, extrapunitive or intrapunitive.

COPING WITH CONFLICT PRODUCTIVELY

In general, all responses to conflict can be divided into two categories: (1) productive responses that resolve the conflict in ways that

Drawing by Koren; © 1978 The New Yorker Magazine, Inc.

"Pop, you've got to be more supportive of Mom and more willing to share with her the day-to-day household tasks. Mom, you have to recognize Pop's needs and be less dependent on him for your identity."

are mutually beneficial to each of the couple and (2) destructive or counterproductive responses that establish a "winner" and a "loser," escalate the difficulties, and sow the seeds of bitterness, misunderstanding, hostility, discontent—and further conflict. We shall first examine the nature of the productive responses to conflict.

Attacking the Problem

The essence of a productive response to a conflict is that the problem is acknowledged and then attacked so that a solution is sought that is profitable, or at least acceptable, to each of the couple.

Indentifying the Basis of the Conflict

To resolve a conflict productively, those involved must first identify its basis. What are

the couple really quarreling about? What is the source of their disagreement? Conflicts are often left unidentified, while the quarrel is displaced to another topic: "And another thing, why do you always . . . ?" It is essential that each of the couple identify the true basis of the conflict, verbalize (state) it, and acknowledge it. (While doing this, the couple must deal with only one conflict at a time.)

Deciding Who Is Receiving Satisfaction or Deprivation

The conflict is not identified until it can be clearly stated who is receiving satisfaction and who is receiving deprivation in the situation. Remember the fundamental definition of a conflict: a situation in which satisfaction for one means deprivation for the other. The conflict is not identified until the precise nature of the satisfaction is clear, as well as the precise nature of the deprivation.

Looking for a Mutually Satisfactory Solution

When the conflict has been identified, and the precise nature of the satisfaction and the deprivation described (as well as who is receiving each) it becomes possible to look for a solution. The ideal solution is one that will bring satisfaction to each, but an acceptable solution is one that at least does not leave one person deprived at the expense of the other. Sometimes a compromise is possible. At other times the couple must find a completely new approach.

When compromise cannot be reached and no solution seems available, the couple must simply agree to disagree. However, if it is clear what they are disagreeing about, a certain amount of conflict can be accepted so long as there is harmony in most areas, and the discord of the conflict doesn't gradually encroach into other areas.

For example, in the open-window–closed-window conflict, once the couple openly acknowledge and talk about the problem, they may find that having the window open is far more important for the wife than having it closed is for the husband. Perhaps she simply can't sleep with the window closed, whereas he may simply *prefer* it closed. Then he could compromise by getting a warmer blanket or an electric blanket with dual controls, or by moving to the side of the bed away from the window. Or he may agree that it is worth having the window open if she provides a trade-off in some other area where satisfaction is especially important for him.

Perhaps, however, he feels very strongly about having the window closed under any circumstances, whereas she may simply *prefer* it open. Then she may be willing to compromise by using a lighter blanket, or she may trade-off having the window closed for a satisfaction in another area.

If the couple simply cannot agree to a solution—either a compromise or a trade-off—it may be necessary for them to sleep in different rooms. This is still a productive solution, if both agree to do this and know why they are doing it, and if they accept it as necessary to the well-being of each. It need not form the basis for an enduring misunderstanding that will escalate and spread into other areas of their lives.

Using Divergent Feedback

Feedback is defined as information you receive about the effects your behavior is having. *Convergent* feedback is defined as information that your behavior is bringing you the desired effect; *divergent* feedback is information that your behavior is *not* bringing you the desired effect. In order to resolve a conflict, then, it is necessary to use divergent feedback productively by making responses that will change the divergent feedback received into convergent feedback (see the vignette, "Feedback").

The important step of modifying one's behavior in order to receive convergent, instead of divergent, feedback is a step not always taken in the often emotion-laden atmosphere of a marital conflict. A couple who are not getting along well will receive increasing amounts of divergent feedback from each other that may extend to virtually every aspect of their interaction. But instead of making realistic attempts to obtain convergent feedback, each may either explode in anger or withdraw into sullen silence, which brings more divergent feedback. Each may then interpret this as further evidence that the other is being unreasonable (and aggressively unpleasant) and grow even more resentful—a descending spiral that steadily worsens their situation.

When one person does try to obtain convergent feedback by making an overture of reconciliation, the other may not accept it. Although the dynamics involved in refusing to accept such an overture are very complex—usually

Feedback

Feedback is usually received and used unconsciously and is involved in almost everything we do. For example, you cannot even sit on a chair without using feedback. Careful measurements reveal that even when you are apparently perfectly immobile in your seat, you are, in fact, constantly rebalancing. As you start to fall in one direction, this information is fed back to your central nervous system, which directs you to lean slightly in the opposite direction. Information about this corrected position is then fed back to the central nervous system, so that before you lean too far (and topple over), you may again correct the balance and lean back in the first direction. As a result of this constant feedback and constant rebalancing, you are able to remain seated upright in a chair. To cite another example, a woman learning to drive a golf ball uses feedback to correct her stroke until she can send the ball straight down the fairway.

In relating to another person the use of feedback works in precisely the same way, except that the process is more complex—principally because the other person responds differently at different times so that the feedback received is inconsistent. For example, flattery that evokes a warm response from a husband at breakfast may make him angry at dinner. (He may be in a different mood at dinner because of something that happened during the day, or he may have a low blood sugar level then, or he may be irritated by the children.) The point is that a person may react differently to the same stimulus at different times. (Or, more precisely, the "same" stimulus is perceived differently at different times because the situation has changed from one occurrence to the other, and because the person has changed.)

Feedback from another person may also be *ambiguous* or difficult to interpret. For example, a smile may have many meanings. It may be friendly, an invitation to open communication, or it may be sympathetic, pitying, or even derisive. Social feedback, therefore, is much more difficult to interpret than is physical feedback, which is usually very clear, consistent, and unambiguous.

Feedback that is open, clear, consistent, and unambiguous is called *free feedback*, whereas feedback that is ambiguous, unclear, and difficult to interpret is called *limited feedback*.

In addition, feedback may be *immediate*, with the information available within a microsecond, or *delayed*. A man who steps on the tines of a rake so that the handle flies up and hits him in the face is receiving immediate feedback. He can easily use this immediate, free, and divergent feedback simply by not stepping on the tines of a rake the next time one is lying in his path.

In the physical world of sitting on chairs and hitting golf balls, feeback is usually *immediate* and *free*, whereas in the social world of relating to other people, feedback is usually *delayed* and *limited*. Thus a husband who perceives himself as being very witty at a party may find on the way home that he has been misinterpreting his wife's smile. With the delayed and free feedback of her explosion of impatience on the drive home, he is able to accurately process the information that, in her perception, he was making a fool of himself. By the time they reach home, he may have displaced his consequent feelings of self-devaluation to an impression that she is disloyal, critical, and rejecting, and he may spend the rest of the night sleeping on the couch.

---

beyond conscious awareness or control and seldom verbalized—the person is, in effect, expressing something like the following: "I'm not ready to make up yet. I'm not through being hurt. I still feel wronged and I feel that you are not being contrite enough or haven't been punished enough for injuring me."

The person who is rebuffed in this way feels rejected. When the other person *is* ready to reconcile (or seek convergent feedback), the person initially offering the reconciliation might now be too hurt or dejected to accept it. Later, the scenario might be replayed: The first person offers an overture, the second person rejects it; then the second person offers an overture, which the first person rejects. Such alternate approach and withdrawal may continue for hours or even days; it will not stop until both persons are ready to seek convergent feedback (or reconciliation) at the same time. They are then ready to approach a solution that will resolve the conflict to their mutual satisfaction, or accept a trade-off in another area.

This alternate approach-and-withdrawal pattern is characteristic of dating, as well as of marriage, but usually doesn't last as long in dating. However, in a disintegrating relation, each person becomes progressively less willing to use divergent feedback as information and to modify his or her own behavior to elicit convergent feedback—and this is characteristic of both dating and marriage. If this pattern persists, the intimacy of the dating or the marriage is gradually eroded.

Because the interaction in dating or marriage is so intimate, and because it is expected to provide so many different essential satisfactions, failure to use divergent feedback productively is very destructive. If a person is not responsive to the meaning of divergent feedback, and doesn't modify his or her behavior so that the divergent feedback decreases and is replaced by convergent feedback, the quality of the relation will inevitably deteriorate.

Role Taking

A very effective, yet relatively simple, technique for resolving a conflict—even one that threatens to disrupt the marriage (or a seriously dating couple)—is called *role taking*. Role taking is not only extraordinarily effective in clearing up misunderstandings and resolving difficult conflicts, but it also carries the additional benefits of increasing each person's self-understanding and understanding of the other.

In role taking each person agrees to cooperate with the other in first identifying and then resolving the conflict to their mutual satisfaction, so that there is no "winner" and no "loser." The role taking itself consists of four steps:

1. The wife (for example) states her point of view as fully and completely as possible, identifying the conflict as she sees it. She must explore the emotional content (her feelings of rage, frustration, helplessness, or whatever) as well as the logical and rational aspects of the conflict. She must do this without being interrupted, but she must stick to the point of the conflict. Any topic not specifically relating to this problem must be declared out of bounds when it comes up and immediately dropped. (If it is important, it may be deferred until a later time, when *it* can be the subject of another role-taking discussion.) While she is talking and trying to explore her feelings and thoughts about the specific conflict, her husband must listen and try to understand what she is saying from her point of view. He must not interrupt, except to ask for clarification of a point he does not understand. She is allowed to continue until she is satisfied that she has stated her feelings and her position regarding the conflict as fully as possible. This ends step 1.

2. In step 2, the husband must take the wife's role (thus the term *role taking*). To do this, he must restate what she has just said, empathizing as fully as possible with her feelings. He must do this to her satisfaction. If he mistakes, misinterprets, or misses a point, she must interrupt and say, "No, that's not what I meant," and restate what she said. Step 2 continues until he is able to *identify* with the wife's point of view, stating her feelings and her concepts as *she* has stated them—to her complete satisfaction. Being able to take the other's role in this way brings about an understanding of the other person in an extraordinarily effective way. It also is not easy to do. It can be achieved, at first, only through continual trial and error. With many attempts, however, a person can become more and more skilled in listening, without interrupting, trying

to understand precisely what the situation means to the other person.

3. Step 3 consists of reversing step 1. The husband states his grievance fully and completely while the wife listens.

4. Step 4 consists of reversing step 2. She takes his role, restating the conflict from his point of view, until she is able to do so to his satisfaction.

When step 4 has been completed, not only has each person stepped into the other's shoes and visualized the conflict from the other's point of view, but each also has a better and clearer understanding of his or her *own* point of view. Moreover, relating in this way to another person is an extremely effective exercise in understanding and intimacy—the opposite of trying to "win" or to dominate the other person.

The conflict can now be examined to see what points of agreement (if any) are present. The couple now understand each other's point of view so well that they can usually find many points in common. They may now isolate and identify any remaining differences and determine whether these can be resolved to the mutual satisfaction of each. If no solution seems possible, they may agree to disagree, leaving other areas of their marriage untouched by the corrosive influence of a pervasive conflict.

Once a couple become skilled in this process of role taking, they may often relate to each other in this way informally, settling all the innumerable conflicts and disagreements as they occur, before they have a chance to escalate or be displaced.

Examining Mutual Goals

Another technique that brings mutual understanding and resolves conflict is called *examining mutual goals* (Mace and Mace 1978). This method consists of two steps.

In the first step, each of the couple takes a list of ten important areas, shown in Table 9-1. Each should sit quietly, undisturbed, and

TABLE 9-1

Examining mutual goals

The following is a list of ten important ingredients of a successful marriage. Each of the items may be rated on a scale from 0 to 10, with 0 representing a very low rating and 10 representing a very high, or ideal, rating.

If each person rates the items independently, the couple may compare their ratings and discover areas of dissatisfaction.

1. common goals and values
2. commitment to growth
3. communication skills
4. creative use of conflict
5. appreciation and affection
6. agreement on gender roles
7. cooperation and teamwork
8. sexual fulfillment
9. money management
10. parental effectiveness

think about each of the ten areas, and then enter a score (on a scale of 0 to 10) for each item on the list. This score represents the person's current subjective feelings. For example, if the person feels that his or her sexual needs and interests are not being ideally fulfilled in the marriage and feels unhappy, disappointed, or frustrated sexually, the score for this item ("sexual fulfillment") might be 1, 2, or even 0. However, if the person feels that his or her sexual needs and interests are being ideally fulfilled, the score for this item would be 9 or 10.

For "appreciation and affection," a score of 10 would mean that the other person never misses an opportunity to communicate feelings of affection, tenderness, and love, or to lavish warmth and praise. A score of 0, 1, or 2 would mean that the person feels a great lack of appreciation and is hungry for demonstrations of affection.

Each person should quickly mark down spontaneous judgments first, and then go back over the list to make a careful evaluation of each item before entering a final score. The final scores should then be totaled. Since

"'Bye and thanks for a lovely time. Your marriage looks viable."

there are ten items, a perfect total score would be 100.

In the second step, the couple exchange papers and compare their scores. If the total score is very high (80–100) for both, they have a remarkably idyllic marriage. If the total score is high for one but low for the other, the dissatisfactions of the low scorer are brought into the open, where they can be discussed and perhaps resolved (by the techniques described earlier). If the marriage score as a whole is relatively high, but one (or more) of the items is low for both, then this area can be acknowledged and explored. If one item is given a high score by one person but a low score by the other, they can discuss the discrepancy and determine why one person is satisfied while the other is dissatisfied in that specific area. A low score—either for the entire marriage or for a single item—may be seen as an unused

potential that may be drawn upon or developed with the proper techniques.

Since marriage is a dynamic, fluctuating interaction, both the total score for the entire marriage and the scores for the separate items will change over time. The procedure may thus be repeated again after an interval of time has passed, and the scores may be compared. Has a low score risen? If not, why not? Has a high score dropped? If so, this can be a useful signal, a warning that the couple should take steps to resolve the problem.

Characteristics of a Successful Marriage

Although one in every two marriages may now be expected to end in divorce, an equal number of marriages succeed. A survey of couples with successful marriages finds that men and

---

TABLE 9-2
What keeps a marriage going?

Here are the top reasons respondents gave, listed in order of frequency.

Men	Women
My spouse is my best friend.	My spouse is my best friend.
I like my spouse as a person.	I like my spouse as a person.
Marriage is a long-term commitment.	Marriage is a long-term commitment.
Marriage is sacred.	Marriage is sacred.
We agree on aims and goals.	We agree on aims and goals.
My spouse has grown more interesting.	My spouse has grown more interesting.
I want the relationship to succeed.	I want the relationship to succeed.
An enduring marriage is important to social stability.	We laugh together.
We laugh together.	We agree on a philosophy of life.
I am proud of my spouse's achievements.	We agree on how and how often to show affection.
We agree on a philosophy of life.	An enduring marriage is important to social stability.
We agree about our sex life.	We have a stimulating exchange of ideas.
We agree on how and how often to show affection.	We discuss things calmly.
I confide in my spouse.	We agree about our sex life.
We share outside hobbies and interests.	I am proud of my spouse's achievements.

Reprinted with permission from *Psychology Today*. Copyright © 1985 (American Psychological Association).

women agree on what is important in their interaction. The reason given most frequently for an enduring and happy marriage was: having a generally positive attitude toward one's spouse—viewing one's partner as one's best friend and liking him or her "as a person" (Lauer and Lauer 1985).

As one wife summed it up, "I feel that liking a person in marriage is as important as loving that person. Friends enjoy each other's company. We spend an unusually large amount of time together. We work at

the same institution, offices just a few feet apart. But we still have things to do and to say to each other on a positive note after being together through the day" (p. 24).

Most couples in the survey reported that the qualities they most liked in each other included caring, giving, integrity, and a sense of humor. Another important quality was a belief in marriage as a long-term commitment and a sacred institution. For a summary of the top reasons for marital success, see Table 9-2.

COPING WITH CONFLICT DESTRUCTIVELY

Instead of coping with conflict constructively and creatively, a person may cope with conflict destructively. This characteristically occurs when the person has a low level of self-esteem and feels threatened, overwhelmed, or inadequate in dealing with the situation. He or she may then attack the other person rather than attempting to solve the problem underlying the conflict. The couple may then move into the next stage of playing a *psychological game*, which virtually eliminates the possibility of finding a constructive or productive solution. In this section we shall examine the nature of the psychological game, and common patterns of attack and defense in a conflict.

Playing Psychological Games

When one person in a conflict seeks to inflict a loss upon the other, establishing a "winner" and a "loser," the couple have entered a pattern of interaction that may be analyzed as a psychological game (Berne 1967). A *psychological game* is defined as an interaction in which each person in a conflict tries to manipulate the other, to score a "win," instead of trying to attack the underlying conflict. It is called a psychological game because, unlike a normal game, the fact that a game is being played is not acknowledged. Unlike a normal game, a psychological game is covert (hidden) and devious. A psychological game is thus a perversion of the openness and honesty of a traditional game, in which the competition is frankly acknowledged and agreed to, as are the rules of play and the methods of scoring a win or inflicting a loss. Much of the satisfaction of a normal game lies in this open acknowledgement of hostility, which is channeled into a culturally accepted, and limited, form.

The traditional game is played consciously and deliberately, with each person agreeing that a game is being played. In contrast, the psychological game is played unconsciously. Neither player is aware that a game is being played; if the hostility is consciously or openly acknowledged, then it is simply manifested as aggressive behavior, which is characteristic of strangers competing for a limited resource. For example, if two passengers race for the sole unoccupied seat on a bus, or if one person in a boarding house spears the only remaining potato on the platter a split second before someone else does, this is simply open competition and not a psychological game.

Open aggression is very common among strangers or business competitors, who often find themselves in positions where they are competing for limited assets. Friends, companions, and others in a primary relation, however, do not usually vie for limited assets. If there is one baked potato on the platter, each would be expected either to urge the other to have it or to cut it in half and share it.

When two people who are friends, companions, or intimates find themselves in a situation in which deprivation for one means satisfaction for the other (the single potato on the platter when they are both hungry), and they are not able to resolve this conflict in a way that provides satisfaction for both (sharing the potato), they may unconsciously begin to attack each other as an expression of the frustration. This is the psychological game.

To put it another way, a psychological game occurs when one person feels resentment

toward the other that relates to a conflict, is not able to express this resentment openly, and tries to restore his or her feeling of control by making a "move" that tends to demean or "defeat" the other. The reason psychological games occur is because open hostility and aggression in vying for a limited resource are not culturally acceptable among friends, companions, or intimates. The psychological game is a disguised form of such competition.

The results of a psychological game can be very destructive. Not only do the players lose sight of the conflict that originated the psychological game and thus do not resolve it, but the possibility of *ever* resolving it is rendered virtually nonexistent. In addition, playing a psychological game tends to drive the couple apart, rather than bring them together. The ostensible "winner" in the game may obtain a sense of satisfaction by achieving victory in the exchange of charges and countercharges that constitutes the moves of the game, but he or she loses the satisfaction that was derived from the mutual caring that characterizes a harmonious, non–game-playing interaction. The loser, of course, is left with no satisfaction and so is often bitter, resentful, and vengeful; the strength of these negative emotions is in proportion to the importance of the game or the significance of the satisfaction that is in question in the underlying conflict.

An example of a psychological game might be the washing of dinner dishes by a husband who comes home exhausted after a day's work. If he washes the dishes simply to get them done, with no overtones of criticism or complaint, he is accomplishing the dual purpose of doing a necessary job and helping his wife, and no game is being played. But if he is saying, in effect, "I work hard all day at the office to support both of us and then have to come home and do your work," he is playing a game to establish his wife as lazy and selfish and himself as noble, self-sacrificing, and generous. Then, as a sort of bonus score, if she is not properly grateful for his sacrifice, she is put in a position of being ungracious and presumptuous as well. The wife quickly recognizes such an implication and the challenge (if it is a psychological game). She may respond, for example, by devaluing her husband in front of guests at a party they go to that night, but in a "teasing" way that would make him appear ungracious if he attempted a rejoinder. He responds later in a subsequent move that is apparently unrelated to her jibe at the party.

A psychological game may take the form of a direct attack but never on the issue under discussion. For example, one person might shift the focus of the discussion from the issue at hand to the personality of the other and then make a direct attack. Suppose the conflict is over whether to send a child to an expensive summer camp, and the wife shifts the discussion to a criticism of her husband's earning ability. She has instituted a psychological game. She has shifted ground to an attack on her husband rather than on the problem ostensibly under discussion. As the husband, in turn, shifts *his* ground to respond to the personal attack, he might mount an attack of his own. The couple soon lose track of the merits of whether or not to send the child to summer camp as they vigorously pursue the game. The discussion might then continue something like this:

Husband: I can't earn more without moving to a higher level of social acceptance. Yet when we were at the office party last week you drank too much and insulted an important buyer.

Wife: I drank too much because I was bored. After all, you spent the night hanging over that secretary of yours—ogling her derriere.

Husband: If you were a little more sexually responsive, it would help—it's no wonder I look at other women.

The discussion has gone from the original conflict to a personal attack on the husband's earning power; to a personal attack on the wife's insensitivity, crassness, and drinking habits; to an attack on the husband's sexual proclivities; to an attack on the wife's sexual coldness. The one who can make the most damaging remarks will "win," because the purpose of the struggle has become to defeat or demean the other person.

A move in a psychological game often takes the form of *attrition* (or withholding a satisfaction from the other) instead of an attack that demeans the other. For example, the wife in the preceding example may be friendly and supportive at the party but not understand his sexual overtures when they get home; she may develop a headache (which may be a psychosomatic response to the stress of an unresolved conflict). Or she could "accidently" burn his bacon at breakfast the next morning—not deliberately, but as an unconscious response to her repressed frustration. It is generally acknowledged that many "accidents" are really motivated by unconscious needs (Bootzin 1980). The husband may then respond with an attrition move of his own—perhaps withholding companionship when he comes home that night, simply grunting in response to her conversational overtures, "too tired" from an exhausting day at work to relate to her companionably.

Attrition, or the withholding of satisfaction in this way, is often accompanied by a plea for sympathy and understanding: "I can't talk because I am too tired"; "I can't make love because I have a headache." The other person may suspect that the other's tiredness or headache is a disguised response to a prior move in a game. Yet because all the patterns are deeply unconscious, the charge that the other is tired or sexually unresponsive because of repressed hostility renders the person vulnerable to accusations of callousness or selfishness: "You don't care how *I* feel, you just want your own way."

The deprived person is thus caught in a classic *double bind*, torn between resentment on the one hand and guilt on the other.[5] Meanwhile, the depriving person probably wears the triumph uneasily because the victory is achieved not only by cheating (although this was deeply unconscious) but also by betrayal of trust—in a relation in which trust is essential. Moreover, even though the motivation is deeply unconscious, there are some stirrings of awareness that all is not well and that the behavior was not as compassionate, generous, or empathic as one might wish.

Although withholding a satisfaction from the other is a common practice in a psychological game, it is a very dangerous move. If attrition becomes a patterned response, as a form of aggression, the erosion of intimacy is often irreversible.

A typical psychological game that Berne (1967) calls "Lunchbag" goes like this:

The husband, who can well afford to have lunch at a good restaurant, nevertheless makes himself a few sandwiches every morning, which he takes to the office in a paper bag. In this way he uses up crusts of bread, leftovers from dinner, and paper bags which his wife saves for him. This gives him complete control over the family finances, for what wife would dare buy herself a mink stole in the face of such self-sacrifice? (p. 95)

In a similar game, which Berne calls "Harried," the housewife simply attempts to do more than she can possibly accomplish and then blames the husband for her plight. Her marriage disintegrates and self-reproaches are added to her misery.

A game probably played by everyone, not only in marriage but also in many life situations, is the one Berne calls "Look How Hard I Was Trying." In this game, a person can justify failure in almost every aspect of life. How can we be blamed for failing when we have done our best?

As long as game playing remains peripheral

to the main interaction of a couple, it may not be seriously damaging; it is, perhaps, even inevitable. The danger, however, is that the couple may move further and further into a game-playing interaction, until the chief preoccupation of each becomes the struggle for dominance and the covert scoring of "points" in the unconscious game that they are playing.

In short, a psychological game almost completely disregards the goal of solving the problem underlying a conflict and instead emphasizes continuing competition—with the goal becoming the need to defeat or demean the other person. Not only is the basic conflict unacknowledged, with therefore no possibility of being resolved, but the struggle erodes trust, honesty, and intimacy. Psychological game playing is notoriously counterproductive.

It seems very clear, then, that it is extremely important to understand the pattern of game playing. If you know you are playing a game, you can stop it. When you are unconsciously playing a game, however, you are helpless to change.

How can you detect that you are playing a psychological game, since, by definition, the game is unconscious? The answer is simple in theory but may be difficult to practice. You can detect that you are playing a psychological game when you sense that something is less than candid. (See the vignette, "Eight Easy Steps to Total Misery.") You may then ask yourself, "What is it that I am trying to accomplish?" "Is my activity honestly involved with achieving a solution to a problem?" "What is the real problem?" "Am I trying to defeat the other person rather than trying to find a mutually acceptable solution to a conflict?"

If the answer to this final question is yes, you may gain sufficient insight into what you are doing so that you can simply pull up short and stop the game. You are, then, restored a measure of freedom to candidly and openly examine the problem: What really *is* the conflict

---

[5]A *double bind* is a psychological dilemma in which a person receives conflicting signals from a single source.

Eight Easy Steps to Total Misery

It is a simple matter to have a conflict-ridden, unhappy marriage, characterized by problems of communication and by the playing of psychological games. A relatively straightforward and readily resolvable conflict may easily be transformed into one of monumental proportions simply by following eight steps; they are guaranteed to produce anguish, distress, and unhappiness (Little 1977).

1. Reverse Beasley

This technique is named after Ron Beasley, who stubbornly refuses to internalize his problems. Little (1977) cites the following example: Beasley, who was stopped at a traffic signal, remained calmly unconcerned when the driver of the car behind him began to honk his horn when the signal changed to green. Little, who was riding in the car with Beasley, remarked, "That fellow is upset." Beasley, looking both ways and moving slowly forward, answered, "That is *his* problem. My problem is to make sure this intersection is safe before proceeding." Thus, Beasley simply refuses to assume problems that belong to other people.

Reversing this attitude formulates a problem-producing technique: Assume the fault is yours. Learn to say, "That is *my* problem." Internalize. Blame yourself. This reverse-Beasley approach will soon lower your self-esteem, make you helpless and inept, and probably create psychosomatic problems as well. The reverse Beasley represents the epitome of intrapunitive behavior.

2. Snowballing

A second technique for creating problems is to let them snowball. The best snowballers practice a simple rule: When it is past time to do something about a problem, wait a little longer. In marriage, for example, refuse to acknowledge a conflict and bury the resulting feelings of irritation or anger until they build up enough pressure to blow your marriage apart. After all, if you face a conflict when it first appears and take realistic steps to resolve it, these efforts are usually successful. But if you let the conflict become firmly entrenched, it can become a part of your life-style.

3. Negative Focus

To become expert in this technique, simply dwell on the times when you were treated unfairly or when someone spoke unkindly to you. Say to yourself, "I am always misunderstood and mistreated by everyone." Beware the intrusion of happy thoughts. If you should think of something good about yourself, quickly remember a corresponding weakness and focus on it. You can generate anything from anxiety to depression by the skillful use of negative thinking.

4. I-Told-Me-So Syndrome

This syndrome simply formalizes the concept that if you expect bad things to happen, they are much more likely to occur (the self-fulfilling prophecy). If you are about to join your spouse for dinner, for example, predict that it will be a terrible meal. If you are going to a party together, predict that you will have a miserable time. At the party, stand alone, aloof from others. On the way home, bemoan the fact that no one would have anything to do with you.

5. Dream the Impossible Dream

If you want to be truly frustrated, set your goals out of reach. If you live in a comfortable two-bedroom house, don't be satisfied until you have a four-bedroom house with a billiard room, a kitchen with a walk-in pantry, a living room with two fireplaces, and an indoor-outdoor Olympic-sized swimming pool—all set on three acres of wooded land overlooking a beach.

Never be satisfied, and blame yourself for your failure to achieve impossible goals. Be an "underaccepting overachiever." Then, no matter what successes may come your way, they will be tinged with sadness and overtones of frustration.

6. Fool's Golden Rule

Simply reverse the Golden Rule of doing unto others as you would have them do unto you. Take advantage of others whenever possible, treating them as contemptible, craven incompetents. Now, take the important step of applying this rule to yourself. Say, "I'm no good. I have no value." Once you have lowered your self-esteem to a suitable level, rejection, loneliness, and misery will soon follow.

7. Barrier Building

If you discover that your marital interaction has been yielding increased harmony, satisfaction, and growth, several general principles, consistently applied, will soon restore barriers to effective communication. First, avoid all encouraging remarks and never compliment. Second, increase the criticism: Nag, complain, and fuss. If you have children, tell them, "As long as you drive my car, eat my food, and live under my roof, you'll do as I say." Their resentment will soon build into a satisfying generation gap.

8. Martyrdom

No program of problem production would be complete without the capping triumph of martyrdom. This puts the final touch on a towering structure of a strife-ridden, conflictful, unhappy marriage, with everyone working at cross purposes. Say, "No one really cares about me. As far as my family is concerned, I'm just a slave." Or point out, "I work my fingers to the bone without any appreciation. I never have any time for myself. Everyone uses me." Chronic, progressive martyrdom is not only useful in generating bad feelings about yourself, but it also disgusts the people around you, which enables you to feel even worse.

These eight steps, especially when used together, will lower your self-image, drive away your friends, and quickly achieve a total collapse of your marriage (Little 1977).

---

underlying the problem? Who is being deprived? What is the nature of the deprivation? Who is being satisfied? What is the nature of the satisfaction? How can the conflict be resolved to the mutual benefit of each, without creating a winner and a loser?

Berne's (1967) point is that we all play psychological games much of the time in almost every aspect of our lives. However, if we can become aware of this, it increases the likelihood that we can be free to play fewer games—relating to others openly, honestly, and candidly more of the time and attacking problems rather than other persons. The more often our behavior is characterized by attacking problems and achieving goals rather than playing psychological games, the richer and the more rewarding all our interactions will become—in friendship and business interactions as well as in marriage. A marriage or any other relation cannot be happy and rewarding if the couple characteristically play psychological games with each other.

COMMON PATTERNS OF ATTACK AND DEFENSE

People who attack the other person, instead of attacking the source of a conflict, tend to follow certain patterns, depending upon the personality structure of the individual. Some people are quite authoritarian, while others are more passive, or evasive. Thus, patterns of attack and defense tend to fall into categories that can be recognized and described as authoritarian resolution, permissive acceptance, passive aggression, or evasion.

Authoritarian Resolution

Probably the most obvious and certainly the most common method of resolving a conflict is *authoritarian resolution*—"I win, you lose." With this method, one person simply dictates the solution and insists that the other yield to the decision.

Lynne Jaeger Weinstein/Woodfin Camp & Associates

In a familiar pattern of ineffective communication, one person attempts to reconcile while the other withdraws into silence, effectively blocking any chance for resolving the conflict.

This method can be very effective when used with insubordinates, or in a situation where power is assigned to recognized authority figures, such as in the police ranks or the judiciary, or when the other person is smaller and weaker or much younger, or with animals. However, it is not usually an effective way to resolve a conflict with a colleague, a companion, a friend, or a husband or wife. This is because the method of authoritarian resolution creates a "winner" and a "loser" in the conflict, and if the person who loses is a colleague, companion, friend, husband, or wife, he or she is likely to feel deprived and resent this deprivation. Moreover, if the relation is based on friendship, trust, respect, intimacy, or love, the winner may feel ashamed or guilty. The tension created by the establishment of a "winner" and a "loser" often leads to further conflict over the issue in question, and to other conflicts over other issues unrelated to the original conflict, as we have seen.

Permissive Acceptance

Resolving a conflict by *permissive acceptance* means simply to give in and accept the needs of the other as dominant over one's own. If a person genuinely feels this way and yields to the other because it brings pleasure to do so, then there is no conflict. A conflict occurs only if satisfaction for one brings deprivation to the other, and there is no deprivation if the person yielding finds satisfaction in doing so.

However, if a conflict is resolved by simply accepting the domination of the other, even though this brings deprivation, a "winner" and a "loser" are just as surely created as they are with the method of authoritarian resolution. For this reason, permissive acceptance must be judged to be nearly as destructive as authoritarian resolution in resolving a conflict, although it may appear, at the time, to be a creative solution. A person who continuously accepts deprivation in this way, so that the other may experience satisfaction, will very likely feel a sense of growing resentment. This feeling will result in lowering such positive feelings as admiration, respect, and trust, and it will eventually drive a wedge between the couple, forcing them further and further apart.

Passive Aggression

A method of resolving a conflict that appears to be permissive acceptance, but is actually very aggressive, is *passive aggression*. In this type of conflict resolution, the person apparently gives in—but ultimately has his or her way. Since the aggression is indirect (covert rather than overt), it can be very difficult to handle.

Passive-aggressive persons find ways not to do what the other expects when a conflict occurs, but never openly take a stand or state a refusal. Rather, passive aggressors covertly sabotage the expectation of the other by pointedly ignoring a request, making careless (or intentional) errors, putting something important off, or simply dawdling. For example, a husband who is unwillingly left to care for a toddler while his wife is out may spill baby powder all over the floor, pin the diapers on inside out, and even "forget" to feed the child.

Passive-aggressive persons often appear to be easy-going, pliant, and good-natured. However, passive aggressors tend to have troubled marriages, characterized by an undercurrent of resentment, hostility, and frustration.

Evasion

A pattern of coping with a conflict that is similar to passive aggression is *evasion*. Evasion often amounts to passive aggression but lacks the underlying hostility. Evaders simply avoid confrontation, putting off a resolution of the conflict. Like passive aggression, evasion has the appearance of permissive acceptance. The difference is that permissive accepters provide apparent solutions; evaders avoid doing this by simply withdrawing into silence, reading a newspaper, watching television, or refusing to address the issue of the conflict. They may avoid a confrontation by physically removing themselves—getting up and walking out of the room, or even out of the house.

This absence of effective communication is, of course, a type of communication in itself, since it is sending a message. The conflict remains, however, and can be very oppressive, creating pressure for the other to yield.

MAINTAINING EFFECTIVE COMMUNICATION

Avoiding psychological game playing and destructive patterns of conflict resolution cannot be accomplished without maintaining effective communication. Effective communication minimizes unresolved conflicts and increases feelings of self-esteem in a couple. If a conflict occurs, attempts to acknowledge and identify the precise nature of the conflict, and then to strive for a mutually acceptable solution, rely upon communication. Communication is an essential element of all marital interaction, and effective communication is characterized by relating honestly and candidly, avoiding patterns of confrontation, and avoiding psychological game playing.

In a paired bond, good communication also involves physical touching. When a couple are dating, they demonstrate the open and intimate communication they have established in dozens of physical gestures: stroking, caressing, holding, brushing, pressing, hugging, and squeezing, as well as kissing. When a marriage

San Francisco Museum of Modern Art, purchased with a gift from W. W. Crocker.

Effective communication is characterized by attempts to relate honestly and candidly, avoiding patterns of confrontation, and avoiding psychological game playing.

Rufino Tamayo, *The Lovers*, 1943

becomes characterized by conflicts, the couple touch each other usually only in rage or in sex.

Since good communication is essentially a blend of active listening and leveling, we shall explore these concepts in some detail.

Active Listening

One of the most important aspects of effective communication is to listen actively to what the other is saying. Active listening consists of trying to understand what is being said—not only the factual content but the emotional content, and not only the verbal content but the body-language, or nonverbal, content as well.

While listening, active listeners do not think about what they are going to say in rebuttal, or impatiently wait for a chance to present their own views and arguments, or interrupt the other. They listen—wholly, completely, and fully. Active listeners respond sympathetically, empathically, nondefensively, and nonaggressively to the total message the other is sending.

If the message is complex, obscure, or puzzling, active listeners check on the accuracy of their comprehension every so often, saying, for example, "As I understand it, you mean . . ." or "What I hear you saying is . . ." and then trying to iterate what has been said.

Listen with hungry earnest attention to every word. In the intensity of your attention, make little nods of agreement, little sounds of approval. You can't fake it. You have to really listen . . . a good listener is far more rare than an adequate lover (MacDonald 1964, p. 25).

Active listeners are closely attentive to the nonverbal communication that is being sent, since this is a very important aspect of the message. In fact, when emotional material is communicated, researchers have found that more than 90 percent of the message is carried by tone of voice, facial expression, eye contact, gestures, body attitudes, and other nonverbal factors (Mehrabian 1971). Good listeners not only respond to the body language of the other but also communicate to the speaker by their own body language that an active attempt to understand is taking place.

Being actively listened to can be an enormously rewarding experience and builds bridges between conflicting people. Being listened to in this way—with the listener intent on every word, wholly absorbed in what is being said—opens wide the conduits to effective communication, smooths out differences, and makes it possible to deal with the underlying source of a conflict.

Moreover, people who are actively listened to are more likely to become active listeners themselves. A good conversation consists of two active listeners alternately responding to each other and trying to understand what each is conveying. When this happens, the conversation builds; each person alternately contributes and is drawn along by the other person. Ideas that were only dimly perceived emerge into a full clarity of expression during such conversational interplay; it becomes an enormously rewarding experience for both persons.

Leveling

Active *listening* is only one aspect of effective communication, of course; the other part consists of *sending* a clear, unequivocal message. An active listener receives a message from the other and reflects it back to ensure that understanding has occurred. But for full communication to take place, the person must also *send* a message that conveys precisely what he or she thinks and feels at that moment. Attempting to communicate what you think and feel—openly, honestly, directly, and candidly, to the best of your abilities—is called *leveling* (Satir 1972).

Levelers are self-assertive but temper self-assertion with empathy. Thus, the perceptive self-assertion of leveling does not ride roughshod over the sensibilities of the other. On the contrary, levelers recognize and acknowledge the feelings and needs of the other, as well as frankly, openly, candidly, and nondefensively expressing their own feelings and needs. When leveling is combined with active listening, the two together embody the ideal of good communication.

When leveling, the person unifies the verbal message with the body language so that the total communication is one of directness, honesty, and candor. The tone of voice, facial expression, gestures, and body stance all convey the same message as the words. For example, if a leveler says, "I like you," the voice is warm. If the words are, "I am angry with you," the voice is harsh and tight. In either case, the message is straightforward, unambiguous, and clear.

The self-esteem of each person is enhanced in a relation that is characterized by leveling. Each member of the couple is able to function optimally from a firm base of self-esteem, optimism, and feelings of integrity. This maximizes the chances for success, contentment, satisfaction, and happiness not only within the marriage but in all outside interactions as well.

Satir (1972) defines a leveler as a person who is

. . . honest to and about himself and others; a person who is willing to take risks, to be creative, to manifest competence, to change when the situation calls for it, and to find ways to accommodate to what is new and different, keeping that part of the old that is still useful, and discarding what is not . . . a productive human being . . . who can love deeply and fight fairly and effectively, who can be on equal terms with both his tenderness and his toughness, know the difference between them, and therefore struggle effectively to achieve his goals (pp. 2–3).

People who are both levelers and active listeners not only are comfortable to be with, but also engender deep feelings of loyalty, affection, and love in others. They are relatively free of unresolved conflicts because when the inevitable conflict occurs, levelers try to be aware of it and communicate this awareness to the other in an open, nondefensive, and nonhostile way. Leveling and active listening enable the couple to work through conflicts and resolve them, so that the marriage may be a mutually harmonious interaction.

Leveling is a type of communication that makes it possible for two people to live in harmony and mutual self-enhancement in marriage. Leveling heals ruptures, breaks impasses, and builds bridges between the couple. Being a leveler allows the individual to live as a whole person, in touch with his or her head, heart, feelings, and body.

Being a leveler enables you to have integrity, commitment, honesty, intimacy, competence, creativity, and the ability to work with real problems in a real way. The other forms of communication result in doubtful integrity . . . dishonesty, loneliness, and shoddy competence (Satir 1972, p. 77).

Increasing Self-Esteem

Effective communication is closely related to self-esteem. Communication that is disruptive, belittling, or argumentative tends to lower the self-esteem of the other, whereas communication that is open, honest, clear, and nondefensive tends to increase it. A person who has relatively high feelings of self-esteem is characteristically responsive, sympathetic, empathic, and has the ability to express affection and love freely. Such people act from a firm base of appreciating their own worth and can accept and appreciate the worth, and the points of view, of others. People with relatively high feelings of self-esteem tend to attack the basis of the conflict, rather than the other person in the conflict.

This tendency leads to a relatively high ratio of success experiences (as opposed to failure experiences) in resolving conflicts. High self-esteem people are characteristically optimistic and cheerful; they expect things to go well. When things do not go well, the problems are assumed to be temporary difficulties that will yield to sustained effort. Maintaining a high level of self-esteem is facilitated by receiving recognition and praise from others whose opinion one respects. (See the vignette, "Acknowledging the Need to Seek Praise.")

In contrast, people who characteristically have a relatively low level of self-esteem are not only not surprised by persistent failure but usually expect it, with each failure then confirming this expectation. People with low self-esteem, who anticipate failure, rarely put forth their best efforts, but instead erect walls of isolation and distrust that protect them from expected slights, depreciation, and attacks. They withdraw into apathy and loneliness.

In any primary relation—certainly in marriage—almost everything a person says or does has some effect on the self-esteem of the other, either raising it or lowering it. Thus, the quality of communication in marriage is directly related to the level of self-esteem of both the husband and the wife. In communicating with each other, responses that are understanding, accepting, sympathetic, and perceptive enhance self-esteem; but responses that miss the point, reject the statement, introduce a *non sequitur*,[6] or contradict the other person lower self-esteem.

In effective communication, questions are

---

[6]A *non sequitur* is a statement that does not follow logically from anything previously said.

Acknowledging the Need to Seek Praise

Because the braggart is both tiresome and boring, we have been conditioned from childhood to believe that seeking praise from others is unworthy and unseemly.

Richard C. Robertiello, psychiatrist and author, points out, however, that the need to have others recognize our accomplishments is both normal and healthy. Indeed, the importance of enhancing self-esteem is just as great as any other basic need. He gives an interesting example from his own experience of recognizing and acknowledging the importance of this need and then acting to fulfill it.

Robertiello had been invited to speak at a psychiatric meeting on "The Psychology of the Self," a subject in which he is much interested and to which he has given much thought and made some contributions. However, the conference was to be held in a distant city. His first impulse was to turn down the invitation since it would involve a considerable expenditure of time and money.

When I reconsidered my decision, I realized that I wanted and needed the admiration and professional recognition that my address would bring me. It would raise my level of self-esteem, would make me feel important. I had the expertise to present the paper, and my audience would consist of professionals likely to appreciate my contribution. I would certainly receive applause, admiration, and recognition for my efforts. Having gone through this process, despite my initial impulse to refuse, there was no way now that I could possibly turn down . . . this opportunity for an experience that would certainly add to my self-esteem and help buttress me against future failures, mistakes, and misfortunes (Robertiello 1978, pp. 180–81).

---

designed to clarify meaning, not attack it. Debate is sometimes necessary, but only to explore the issue, not to attack the other.

The timing of a response is an aspect of communication that is very significant in its effect on self-esteem. Does the response interrupt the other or serve as a way of ignoring something the other has said? In addition, a nonresponse, such as walking away or starting a noisy task (running the dishwasher, vacuum cleaner, or power drill), is a direct attack on the self-esteem of the other. In general, sentences that begin with "But . . ." or "Yes, but . . ." are disruptive and counterproductive; if persistent, they will lower the self-esteem of the other.

Being listened to actively, however—with the listener intent on every word, wholly absorbed in what is being said—is enormously enhancing to the speaker's self-image. A good listener has the capacity for making the other person feel that he or she is especially valued and is saying something of significance and concern.

The listener can accomplish this enhancement of the self-esteem of the other even under very difficult conditions. For example, a good listener can pay uninterrupted attention to the speaker during a crowded cocktail party, despite the noise and turmoil, acting totally fascinated and absorbed by what is being said and focusing (for the moment) exclusively on a very important interaction. A good listener can make the other person feel that the two of them are enclosed in a bubble of intimate understanding, shutting out the confusion and interruption of the most distracting environment. In contrast, a listener whose eyes are darting about the room, or who is distracted by other conversations while paying only partial attention to the one at hand, can make the speaker feel devalued and insignificant.

THE BREAKDOWN OF EFFECTIVE COMMUNICATION

If a person characteristically uses either extra-punitive or intrapunitive behavior when confronted with a conflict, or tries to resolve a conflict by authoritarian resolution, permissive acceptance, passive aggression, or evasion, the relation with the other person in the conflict will probably degenerate into a psychological game. This is usually accompanied by a breakdown in the couple's communication.

The purpose of communication is to achieve mutual understanding of each other's point of view, so that a creative solution to a conflict may be found. When communication begins to break down, however, it furthers *mis*understanding rather than understanding. As the attempts at communicating become increasingly counterproductive, the conflict is worsened rather than resolved. Ineffective communication not only fails to improve understanding, it extends misunderstanding.

Virginia Satir (1972), who specializes in the study of patterns of communication in troubled families, describes the atmosphere in these families as follows:

The atmosphere in a troubled family is easy to feel. Whenever I am with such a family, I quickly sense that I am uncomfortable. Sometimes it feels cold, as if everyone is obviously bored . . . or, it may have an air of foreboding, like the lull before a storm, when thunder may crash and lightning strike at any moment. Sometimes the air is full of secrecy, as in a spy headquarters.

When I am in any of these kinds of troubled atmospheres, my body reacts violently. My stomach feels queasy; my back and shoulders soon ache, and so does my head. I used to wonder if the bodies of the people who lived in that family responded as mine did. Later, when I knew them better and they became free enough to tell me what life was like in their family, I learned that they did indeed feel the same way . . . their bodies were simply reacting humanly to a very inhuman atmosphere.

In troubled families the bodies and faces tell of their plight. Bodies are either stiff and tight, or slouchy. Faces look sullen, or sad, of blank-like masks. Eyes look down and past people. Ears obviously don't hear. Voices are either harsh and strident, or barely audible (pp. 9–10).

Analyzing the major patterns of communication in a troubled marriage can be very helpful. If an ineffective pattern can be identified, the probability of replacing it with a combination of active listening and leveling is improved.

Patterns of Ineffective Communication

As we have seen, effective communication is a combination of active listening and leveling. Ineffective communication is the opposite; when communication breaks down between a couple, neither listen actively to the other, and instead of leveling, they become hostile and aggressive, or defensive and withdrawn.

Automatic Disagreement

Automatic disagreement, or stating an opposite point of view to whatever is said, is a chronic form of ineffective communication. The automatic disagreer takes an opposite point of view on almost every topic that comes up—never agreeing with, but constantly contradicting the other person. This pattern continually creates blocks to a smooth interaction, defeating the goal of effective communication.

Even when the issue is trivial, automatic disagreers always contradict the statement.

"It's a beautiful day, isn't it?"
"Yes, but it looks like it might rain later."
"In that case, shall we take the dog for a walk now?"
"That would be nice, but we probably won't have time."

Chronic disagreers also take an opposite point of view when the other person makes a negative statement. For example, if a wife says, "I am worried about the physiology mid-term tomorrow," the husband who is a chronic disagreer might reply, "You have nothing to worry about; you are very well prepared." Ostensibly this is a supportive statement, but he completely misses the point by failing to empathize and identify with the wife's concern. He is disagreeing with what she is saying, and denying her right to be worried. "You feel you're not prepared?" would be a much better reply. Even an attentive silence would be better since this would encourage her to verbalize her fears and anxieties further and then come to her own conclusion.

Chronic Advice Giving

Automatic disagreers usually follow up the disagreement with suggestions or *advice*. For example, suppose the wife in the preceding example persists, saying "I can't help worrying. I've read the assignment but I don't understand it." Her husband might reply, "Don't worry. I'm sure you understand more than you think. Just get a good night's sleep and I'm sure you'll do fine on the exam in the morning." Although this sounds supportive, in reality it extends the ineffective communication. The wife is not only blocked in her attempts to express her fears and tension, but she is then blandly directed to engage in an action contrary to what she is doing. Even if the advice is ostensibly good, it completely misses the point of effective communication.

An active listener would acknowledge the other's worry, try to understand it, and accept it without providing a prescription for solving it: "I can see you are worried. What seems to be giving you the most trouble?" Thus prompted, the wife might be encouraged to give full vent to her anxieties: "What's really troubling me is. . . ." She is then much more likely and able to attack the problem realistically, finding her own solution: "Well, thanks for listening. I always feel better after talking to you." Her right to have her own feelings is recognized, and she is accorded the dignity of being treated as one who is capable of solving her own problems: "If

you don't mind, I think I'll just go over Chapter 3 once more; I'll come to bed in about an hour." "OK, honey. Would you like me to fix you a cup of hot chocolate?"

It is important to recognize that effective communication consists of providing ample attention, affection, nurture, respect, and support when the other is tense, uneasy, insecure, or worried. Contradicting, giving opposite points of view, and pointing out a logical solution to a problem (even if the solution is a good one) are all examples of ineffective communication and are counterproductive unless advice is being sought or directions are asked for—for example, "How many teaspoons *are* there in a tablespoon?"

Although there is certainly a time when exploring logical solutions to a problem is both productive and creative, imposing them on another ("Why don't you . . .") when the other is trying to express frustration is not only counterproductive, but frustrates further efforts at effective communication and drives a wedge between the couple.

"Mind Reading"

"Mind readers" assume they know what the other person is thinking and feeling, and they respond only to *these* assumptions rather than to what the other person really thinks and feels. Mind reading makes it impossible for a couple to come to grips with a conflict; the two are always talking at cross purposes.

We all act on our own assumptions in this way, but most of us check these assumptions for accuracy from time to time—asking the other person how he or she feels, and then trying to deal with the reality.

Mind reading is an especially maddening form of ineffective communication since it renders an open discussion of the conflict totally impossible. A husband who is an inveterate mind reader feels that he knows more about his wife's innermost feelings, thoughts, and intentions than she does. Chronic mind readers are

Gilles Peress/Magnum Photos, Inc.

Effective communication consists of each person providing the other
with ample attention, affection, nurture, respect, and support.
When this does not happen, communication breaks down.

so implacable and unshakable in their convictions that it is not unusual for them to contradict another's statement ("I know you don't really feel that way") and then tell the other how he or she "really" feels.

As long as a person continues mind reading in this way, rather than actively listening and trying to respond to what the other person is saying, it is virtually impossible to establish good communication.

Sending Double Messages

When a couple have lost the ability to communicate openly and directly with each other, a pattern of ineffective communication that often emerges is the double message. A *double message* is one that is contradictory or has two meanings, one of which contradicts the other, and thus puts the receiver in a "double bind."

The person who is receiving a double message does not know which aspect to respond to and thus feels confused, uncomfortable, and irritated, and is likely to respond defensively or aggressively.

Sarcasm, for example, attacks the other (sending a critical message) yet ostensibly in a friendly way (sending a supportive message). For example, when the wife says in a sarcastic tone, "You were really the life of the party tonight," she is sending a double message. If the husband responds with resentment, "Why do you say that?" the wife might reply, "What did I say?" The stage is then set for a series of charges and countercharges, with the communication becoming progressively ineffective.

Another way of sending a double message is to contradict a verbal statement with body language—for example, saying "That's very interesting" while yawning.

Gunnysacking

Gunnysacking is a widely used term for nursing past grievances and wrongs and bringing them all up for review while trying to resolve a current conflict (Bach and Wyden 1970). Gunnysacking is, of course, notoriously counterproductive to good communication. It not only fails to focus on the specific issue underlying the current conflict and thus prevents it from being resolved, but it also tends to feed upon itself by creating new grievances that enter the gunnysack. In consequence, the gunnysack bulges with so many past grievances and smoldering grudges that the couple are immersed in a morass of ancient resentments along with the current conflicts. As each new confrontation is crammed into the gunnysack, to be retrieved and reviewed along with all its predecessors, the satisfactions that each person provides for the other are increasingly diminished, while the pleasures they initially enjoyed become faded memories, occasionally recalled nostalgically.

Stereotyping

Stereotyping places the other in a category, or assigns a label, and avoids the issue that underlies the conflict. Stereotypers deal with the category or the label, never with the real person. This not only avoids the basic issue of the conflict, but also is dehumanizing to the other. Stereotyping focuses on preconceived ideas instead of on the reality of the current interaction, especially when it is combined—as it often is—with mind reading. Thus the basic issue of present feelings and emotions is shunted aside.

For example, the statement "You're a very cruel person" is simply applying a label. The person so categorized is liable to either retaliate aggressively or withdraw—thus enlarging the area of conflict while the issue that was the basis of the initial conflict becomes blurred, obscured, and may be completely lost sight of.

Interrupting

One very common type of ineffective communication is simply the *interruption,* breaking into the middle of whatever the other is saying. When this is a persistent pattern, it virtually paralyzes all efforts at effective communication.

Everyone interrupts another occasionally, and this can simply indicate an eagerness to communicate. However, chronic interrupting rarely lets the other person finish a sentence (or a thought) and is often combined with mind reading.

"I think I would like to go to—"
"The beach?"
"No, what I was trying to say was—I think I'd like to take a run down to the—"
"Corner store?"
"No. I thought I'd just go over to the —"

Even if the interrupter is not being hostile or aggressive, the pattern obviously disrupts good communication. In effective communication each person finishes a sentence (which presumably contains some information of interest) while the other listens.

Monologuing

While *monologuing* is an obvious form of ineffective communication, it may be very difficult to handle since monologuers are notoriously resistant to change (or to criticism). A chronic monologuer can proceed from one topic to another, brooking no interruption, for interminable periods of time. In social situations, monologuers can be either fascinating or dreadful bores, depending on how interesting the topic is. In a conflict situation in which the couple are trying to resolve a problem, monologuing is always counterproductive.

Although good monologuers may give the impression that they are working for the resolution of a conflict, they will not listen to another point of view. Instead they simply continue to present their own positions as forcefully and reasonably as possible, citing innumerable examples and endless illustrations.

It is impossible to interrupt skilled monologuers even by jumping in at a natural pause—such as the end of a sentence—when a speaker usually draws a breath. Skilled monologuers run their sentences together, breathing in the middle of a sentence, so that interruption becomes virtually impossible.

In a conflict, monologuing is characteristically used by a person who is working toward an authoritarian resolution.

Using "You" Sentences

Sentences that start with *you* are perfectly acceptable, of course, in most situations ("You look very beautiful tonight"). However, when a couple are in a discussion involving a conflict, a "you" sentence is almost always analytic, critical, or hostile, and may be counted upon to provoke a hostile or defensive response. "You always want to have your own way" and "You never listen to what I have to say" are examples of sentences often heard in an argument. They are not only "you" sentences, but are also examples of stereotyping and gunnysacking. They are virtually guaranteed to bring about either a defensive response or an attack, while the basic conflict is left unresolved and the couple expand the area of misunderstanding and hostility.

A statement that focuses on the issue at hand, rather than on the personality characteristics of the other person, is much more likely to lead to a mutual attack on the problem.

Using "Why" Sentences

In a nonconflict situation sentences that begin with why are also perfectly acceptable. They may lead to intriguing speculation and creative thought. However, like "you" sentences, "why" sentences are almost invariably counterproductive when the discussion involves a conflict.

"Why" sentences not only challenge the other person—and so are likely to provoke either a defensive or a hostile response—but are counterproductive in another way: They move the discussion into a synthetic area of analytic thought, rather than dealing with the immediacy of present feelings. For example, "Why do you always act like I'm the one to blame?" calls for a depth analysis of the couple's characteristic interactions. It is an invitation for gunnysacking and mind reading, and lays the groundwork for an endless round of charges and countercharges.

"Why did you burn the toast?" is much more likely to elicit a defensive response and start a psychological game than the simple statement "This toast is burned" or the question "May I please have another piece of toast?" The response to the latter is very likely to be "Oh, I'm sorry. I didn't notice it was burned." After all, you wouldn't ask a waitress in a restaurant why she burned your toast; you would simply ask for another piece.

Openly expressing one's feelings, wants, and desires enables the other person to deal with them directly and concretely, rather than moving the exchange into the covert interaction of a psychological game. Self-assertive, empathic, leveling people use "I" statements in a marital conflict rather than "you" or "why" statements. They try to say precisely and openly what they think and how they feel. The other person will, in turn, usually recognize an "I" statement when it is used in a conflict as an attempt to openly communicate a feeling or conviction. It is then possible to deal with these feelings and convictions nondefensively on a candid, specific basis.

Using "Yes, but" Sentences

Finally, in a conflict situation, any sentence that begins with "Yes, but" is going to be argumentative and produce either a defensive or an attacking response from the other. Like "You" and "Why" sentences "Yes, but" sentences are a tip-off that the confrontation is disintegrating—moving from the active listening that is characteristic of good communication to a pattern of defense, attack, and counterattack.

Since no one consciously or deliberately wishes to engage in counterproductive, ineffective communication, being aware of the effects of such a conversational ploy can be very helpful. If you hear yourself saying "Yes, but" and know what it means, you can remind yourself to question your own motives and intentions. Is what you are about to say going to be a productive step in confronting the problem underlying the conflict? Or will it move the discussion further in the direction of attacking the other while justifying yourself?

Personality Styles of Ineffective Communicators

Virginia Satir (1972) suggests that ineffective communicators tend to fall into one of four different types of personalities: the blamer, the placater, the distracter, and the computer. These four personality types utilize many of the patterns of ineffective communication described above.

The Blamer

Blamers act like petty dictators. Their voices are often hard, tight, shrill, or loud. Blamers have in internal feeling of tightness in the muscles and chest, their eyes may bulge, tendons in their necks may stand out, and nostrils may flare. Blamers not only fail to listen and fail to try to understand what the other is trying to express, but they also ride roughshod over the feelings of others. Their attitude is that the best defense is an attack.

The Placater

Placaters are the opposite of blamers. They try to ingratiate, please, or apologize, and they never disagree no matter how great the provocation. Placaters' voices tend to be whiny or squeaky. Placaters never achieve what they really want; despite their true thoughts or feelings they say "yes" to every proposal. As a result, there is little possibility of a satisfying mutual interaction between a couple when one is a consistent placater. Failure to achieve this mutually satisfying interaction lowers the self-esteem of each.

The Distracter

Distracters never make simple, straightforward responses but either say something irrelevant to what the other person is saying (a *non sequitur*) or ignore what is being said by failing to reply, walking away, starting a noisy task, or turning to speak to a pet. (Being totally ignored by a person who is talking to a parakeet lowers one's self-esteem very effectively.)

Distracters often win an argument by simply shifting the ground to a new topic. A typical example of this is the classic reply of Lucy in the comic strip "Peanuts." When Charlie Brown was demolishing her statement that "the number of stars in the sky is the same as the number of leaves on a tree," Lucy looked at Charlie very intently and said, "You sure have a funny-shaped head."

The Computer

People who are computers are very reasonable, logical, and rational, with completely controlled emotions and correct demeanor. Computers' voices are often dry monotones as they coolly analyze a situation and express their convictions in abstract terms and concepts. Computers think it is important to say the right words, to show no feelings, and to avoid any emotional reaction. They fail to come to grips with a conflict by ignoring the feelings of the other and not listening to the total meaning of what is being communicated. They reduce any discussion to an abstract analysis, leaving the other person frustrated and angry, defeated and helpless—but with the sense that somehow or other the real point has been missed.

All of these personality types characteristically use one or more of the patterns of ineffective communication described in this chapter.

SUMMARY

A conflict occurs when something that means satisfaction for one person means deprivation for another. Since it would be unrealistic to expect a married couple to always want the same things at the same time, conflict is inevitable. When conflict occurs, it often leads to a sense of frustration and self-devaluation for the person experiencing the deprivation. This person will then respond with either defense-oriented or reality-oriented behavior. Reality-oriented behavior examines the nature of the conflict and attempts to resolve it in a way that does not mean deprivation for either person. Defense-oriented behavior does not resolve the conflict but attacks the other person (establishing a "winner" and a "loser") or accepts the deprivation, breeding resentment and encouraging for further conflict. Impunitive people tend to be reality-oriented and seek a solution that will be mutually beneficial; extrapunitive people tend to blame and attack the other; intrapunitive people tend to punish themselves.

Conflict may be coped with productively by focusing on the problem: identifying the basis of the conflict, deciding who is receiving satisfaction or deprivation in the conflict, and then looking for mutually satisfying solutions that do not mean a "win" for the one and a "loss" for the other. To do this, it is important to utilize divergent feedback as information rather than resenting it or becoming defensive. A technique that is often successful in resolving a conflict is *role taking*, wherein each person takes the other's role to the satisfaction of that person, stating the problem from the other person's point of view. Another effective technique is for each person to rate a number of mutually valuable goals in terms of how successful the other is in fulfilling the goal (such as "providing sexual fulfillment"). If one person's rating is high and the other's is low, or if both persons' ratings are low, a significant problem has been identified. Identifying a problem in this way makes it much more likely to be resolved.

Resolving a conflict depends upon maintaining effective communication, which is a combination of active listening and leveling. Listening attentively and trying to understand what the other is saying while leveling—being frank, open, and nondefensive—not only maintains effective communication but increases self-esteem in each of the couple.

When effective communication begins to break down, the conflict may turn into a psychological game, in which each person attacks and attempts to defeat the other rather than attacking the underlying conflict. A psychological game may take the form of attrition, with satisfaction being withheld from the other, or aggression, in which the other is directly attacked. Whatever form it takes it almost always fails to achieve the goal of solving the underlying problem; instead, it emphasizes continuing competition. Psychological game playing is thus counterproductive since it not only leaves the underlying conflict resolved, but also erodes trust and intimacy. It is difficult, but possible, to stop psychological game playing if each of the couple can gain insight into the fact that the game is occurring.

The breakdown of effective communication is signaled by such patterns as automatically disagreeing, chronic advice giving, "mind reading," sending double messages, "gunnysacking," stereotyping, interrupting, monologuing, or using "You" sentences, "Why" sentences, and "Yes, but" sentences in a conflict. A person who characteristically uses one or more of these patterns in ineffective communication usually falls into the personality type of the Blamer, Placater, Distracter, or Computer.

QUESTIONS

1. What is the definition of a conflict? Give an example of a conflict in a marital interaction.

2. Why is conflict inevitable in marriage?

3. What is meant by defense-oriented behavior? Give an example of defense-oriented behavior in a marital conflict.

4. What is meant by reality-oriented behavior? Give an example of reality-oriented behavior in a marital conflict.

5. The text describes eight easy steps to total misery. What are these steps? Give a brief description, or example, of each.

6. There are three personality styles of responding to conflict. Name each of these three and give an example.

7. What is meant by divergent feedback? Give an example.

8. What is meant by convergent feedback? Give an example.

9. When may divergent feedback be used productively in a conflict? Give an example.

10. Describe how the technique known as role taking may be used to resolve a conflict.

11. Describe how the technique known as comparing mutual goals can be used to resolve a conflict.

12. Briefly describe the characteristics of a successful marriage.

13. Define the term "psychological game." What are its chief characteristics? Give an example of a psychological game.

14. Name and briefly describe four common patterns of attack and defense in a conflict.

15. What is meant by *active listening?*

16. What is meant by *leveling?* Give an example of leveling as a response to a marital conflict.

17. What is meant by using "I" statements? Give an example of using an "I" statement in trying to resolve a marital conflict.

18. What is meant by "mind reading" in a conflict? Give an example.

19. What is meant by sending double messages in a conflict? Give an example.

20. What is meant by gunnysacking in a conflict? Give an example.

21. What is meant by stereotyping? Give an example.

22. Why are "You," "Why," and "Yes, but" sentences usually counterproductive in a conflict? Give examples.

23. Name four personality styles of ineffective communicators, and describe each.

SUGGESTIONS FOR FURTHER READING

Berne, Eric. *Games People Play*. New York: Grove, 1964.

Broderick, Carlfred B. *The Therapeutic Triangle: A Sourcebook on Marital Therapy*. Beverly Hills, Calif.: Sage Publications, 1983.

Coleman, James C. *Abnormal Psychology and Modern Life*, 7th ed. Glenview, Ill.: Scott, Foresman, 1984.

Coulson, Robert. *Fighting Fair*. New York: The Free Press, 1983.

Filsinger, Erik E., and Lewis, Robert A. *Assessing Marriage: New Behavioral Approaches*. Beverly Hills, Calif.: Sage Publications, 1981.

Kelley, Harold H., et al. *Close Relationships*. New York: W. H. Freeman, 1983.

Kleinke, Chris L. *Self Perception: The Psychology of Personal Awareness*. New York: W. H. Freeman, 1978.

Knapp, Mark L. *Interpersonal Communication and Human Relationships*. Boston: Allyn & Bacon, 1984.

Lederer, William J. *Marital Choices*. New York: Norton, 1981.

Rubin, Lillian Breslow. *Intimate Strangers: Men and Women Together*. New York: Harper & Row, 1983.

Sager, Clifford J., and Hunt, Bernice. *Intimate Partners: Hidden Patterns in Love Relationships*. New York: McGraw-Hill, 1979.

Satir, Virginia. *Peoplemaking*. Palo Alto, Calif.: Science and Behavior Books, 1972.

Sherlock, Basil J., and Moller, Ingrid K.S. *After the Honeymoon: The First Years of Marriage*. Lexington, Mass.: Ginn, 1984.

Stewart, J. *Bridges not Walls*, 3rd ed. Reading, Mass.: Addison-Wesley, 1982.

P A R T   F O U R

The Family

The Nature of the Family

The Importance of the Family
The Meaning of Family
The Family in Transition
Family Violence

*It is easier to rule a kingdom than to
regulate a family.*

Chinese proverb

The family is the oldest and toughest of all human institutions and has outlasted much that seemed eternal—gods, empires, and systems of political economy.

The family is the third component of the family system—preceded by the first component, courtship, and the second component, marriage. As we have seen, the family system is one of the few universals of societal organization: It has been found in all societies ever discovered on our planet. Courtship leads to

marriage, and marriage forms the basis for the family.

The family is essential in all known societies because it provides the social structure through which the society and its culture endure. The family brings new members into the society[1] and then plays a chief role in nur-

---

[1] Because aging and death are inevitable, new members must be added to the society to balance the loss of the older members. Otherwise the society would cease to exist in one generation, unless it could depend upon perpetual immigration, which has never occurred in any known group. Although there have been small societies (usually religious cults) that have banned marriage, copulation, and family groups, and so have had to depend on continual recruitment of new members for their continuing existence, these societies have never lasted very long, usually disintegrating with the death of the leader.

turing and socializing these new members, indoctrinating them into the culture norms for expectations, values, knowledge, skills, and behavior during the critical initial years of their lives (see Chapter 12).

THE IMPORTANCE OF THE FAMILY

The importance of the family is demonstrated very clearly by the statistics of the number of people living within families. In 1982, 99 percent of the children in America were living within families, as were 86 percent of all adults between the ages of eighteen and sixty-four. (After age sixty-five the number of adults living within families decreases to about 68 percent, chiefly because either the husband or the wife has died and left the other alone.)[2]

Most children are not only born within families and get their food and shelter from their families, but also fill essential emotional needs (vital to the development of the child's potential as a human being) through their families (see Chapter 12). Certainly, although many specialized functions of the family have been replaced by other institutions in our post industrial society, the family remains the chief socializing agency for children.

As the chief agency of socialization, the family reproduces culture patterns in the individual. It provides the child with the initial experiences in relating to others, imparts social rules and conventions, and shapes the child's personality by instilling modes of thought and action, systems of values, and ethical standards that become habitual (see Chapter 12).

These child-production and child-socialization functions of the family are so universal that we take them for granted, and their arbitrariness becomes apparent only when we imagine other possibilities. For example, there is no necessary reason why the biological parents should rear the child. We can easily imagine a society in which children are produced by professional childbearers (chosen for that function) and then brought up by a different set of persons (professional child rearers) chosen for their proficiency in *that* activity. Obviously, a child can be reared by someone other than the biological parent. What is essential is that *someone* fulfill the role of parent. In their rearing, children could also be associated with age mates (perhaps on the basis of talent or personality) rather than with siblings. Although these and other ways of raising children are possible, and have been used in small segments of a society,[3] they have never occurred as a society-wide norm (Lorber 1975).

The average person is concerned not with statistics, of course, nor with a theoretical analysis of social structure—but rather with his or her own personal experience in day-to-day life. From this point of view the family is central in the consciousness of virtually everyone (see Figure 10-1). As we have seen, most Americans are born within a family and raised within a family (the *family of origin*) and each person's initial experiences—which form the basis for the person's self-image and view of the surrounding world—are chiefly derived in a family setting. It is within the family that one first experiences the myriad of interpersonal interactions and functions that make up the fabric of life.

The family then continues to remain an important aspect of experience and consciousness after childhood and into adulthood. Most people not only continue to interact with their families of origin, but also establish new families

---

[2] U.S. Bureau of the Census, "Households, Families, Subfamilies, Married Couples, and Individuals: 1950–1982" and earlier reports (1984).

[3] For example, upper class children in England are raised by professionals. Their origin is within the nuclear family, however, and the sense of family membership is very strong.

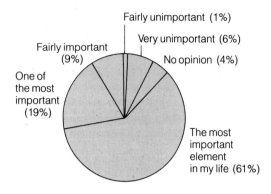

Fairly unimportant (1%)

Very unimportant (6%)

Fairly important (9%)

No opinion (4%)

One of the most important (19%)

The most important element in my life (61%)

How important is family life to you?

FIGURE 10-1

How Americans look at family life

Source: White House Conference on Families (1980).

with marriage (the *family of procreation*), starting a new generation and continuing the cycle. The interaction between the family of origin and the family of procreation is usually quite extensive, occupying a significant amount of one's time and awareness (Troll et al. 1979).

THE MEANING OF FAMILY

Although family is a very simple concept to understand and *family* is a frequently used word in our language—readily comprehensible even to small children—it is virtually impossible to define *family* precisely because of the many forms the family may take.

Anthropologists and historians have identified between two and three thousand distinct cultures—groups of people with ways of life so different form one another that they are regarded as separate cultures. Each of these thousands of cultures has evolved a different version of the family (Gordon 1978).

Despite the thousands of books and articles that have been written on the family, not to mention the multitude of courses in college catalogues, there is

still no agreement on what is meant by the term "family" (p. 25).

The Wide Range of Meanings of Family

The classic explanation of the term *family,* and the one most often cited as definitive, is the straightforward statement of Murdock (1949):

The family is a social group characterized by common residence, economic cooperation, and reproduction. It includes adults of both sexes, at least two of whom maintain a socially approved sexual relation, and one or more children, own or adopted, of the sexually cohabiting adults (p. 1).

Murdock further classifies the family into three types: (1) the *nuclear* family, consisting of a married couple, man and woman, with their offspring; (2) the *polygamous* family, consisting of two or more nuclear families joined by multiple marriage; and (3) the *extended* family, consisting of two or more nuclear families living together (with various additional relatives) in one household.

The problem with this definition and classification, however, is that a family as it commonly occurs in our society may take other forms. For example, the U.S. Bureau of the Census defines a family as "any two or more related people living in one household," and according to this definition, one of the most frequently occurring forms of the family in our society *is* simply two persons. For example, in 1982, 32 percent of all family households in the United States consisted of two persons.[4] Moreover, the two persons comprising a family according to the U.S. Bureau of the Census definition are not necessarily of different genders. They may be two brothers, two sisters, mother and daughter, father and son, and so on. Or the two persons may be adults of oppo-

---

[4]U.S. Bureau of the Census, "Households, Families, Subfamilies, Married Couples, and Individuals: 1950–1982" and earlier reports (1984).

site genders who are *not* maintaining a "socially approved sexual relation," such as father and grown daughter, mother and grown son, or brother and sister. Even if a family does consist of a man and a woman, married, maintaining a "socially approved sexual relation," the couple may not necessarily have children. Or a family may consist of all adults of the same gender, such as a father and his grown sons. In this type of family, there are no married couple, no sexual relations, and no children. This family form is exemplified by the Cartwright family of "Bonanza," one of the most popular television series ever produced. Furthermore, all the members of a family do not necessarily live in one household. After all, a brother or sister who has moved away from home to go to college (for example) is still regarded as a functional part of the family.

Moreover, the concept of family may extend into the past to include members who are not alive. Often a person's ancestors or "roots" are a significant part of his or her consciousness. The concept of family may also extend into the future, with its continuity including anticipated members. For example, children who have not even been conceived may be registered in restricted schools, or have trust funds set up for them, or be provided for in wills.

Finally, in its broadest meaning, the term *family* may even mean a group of people who are *not* related by blood *or* by law, but who are bound by ties that are generally regarded as family characteristics, who feel themselves to be members of a family, and who are referred to as a family in the press.[5] This type of voluntary family is characterized by shared residence, shared income, common interests, emotional attachments, interdependence, and loyalty—characteristics that are not usually available

in the "outside world" of industry, commerce, and business. In all likelihood, such features are the appeal of communal religious cults such as the widely publicized People's Temple of San Francisco.[6] The need to belong to some form of a "family" is exceedingly strong.

The Nuclear Family

Although many different groupings may be regarded as a family, the nuclear family, as described by Murdock (1949), is certainly one of the most important and fundamental in our society. The chief importance of the nuclear family, of course, is that it is the source of children and so provides the basis of continuing generations.[7]

In addition to being the source of children, the nuclear family nurtures and socializes these children. This function of the nuclear family is so essential that it occurs in some form in all known societies (Stephens 1982). It also occurs among all birds and mammals—in short, among any species in which the young must be cared for after birth. (See the vignette, "The Importance of Nurture.")

The society usually assigns responsibility for the care and socialization of children to the married couple that produce them. The couple are, in a sense, "licensed" to produce children (the marriage license), and these children are then placed and identified with the couple. The married couple's rights and obligations are defined not only with regard to each other but also with regard to their children, and the parents are expected to remain together and provide a stable background for the children. (After a divorce, the children remain within an abbreviated version of the nuclear family: the

---

[5]For example, the well-publicized "Manson family" of the 1960s and early 1970s was a group of people held together by their acceptance of the domination of Charles Manson (Bugliosi and Gentry 1974).

[6]The People's Temple was the cult that participated in the large-scale (913) murder-suicides in Guyana in 1978.

[7]It should be noted that the nuclear family may be established in all societies by the *adoption* of children. Although it is commonly assumed that the family is based on a hereditary bond between parents and the children they bear, the biological tie is not an essential family ingredient.

The Importance of Nurture

In all species of animals in which the young are not immediately independent, the mother devotes her attention to the care, training, and upbringing of her helpless offspring. In many of these species, the father protects and cares for his mate during this period; in many species he assists the mother in protecting, caring for, and socializing the young as well (Lorenz 1966).

Primates are especially slow in maturing, and the care and socialization of the young must be quite extensive, sometimes continuing for several years. The baboon baby, for example, remains in physical contact with its mother for a full two years following birth and then ventures only a few feet away for another year. During this time, its needs are provided for by both the mother and the father, and it is taught (mainly by the mother) the physical and social skills and knowledge necessary for survival—what food to eat and where to find it, what dangers to avoid, how to respond and make the calls and gestures that constitute communication among his species, and how to relate properly and effectively to the other members of the group. When the baboon baby is about three years of age (and until about the age of five), older peers take over this socialization process.

Recent research on the behavior of birds and mammals (particularly the primates) has confirmed that in most animal societies, functionally discrete family units occur. (The major exception to this pattern is the ungulate species—the hooved animals—that relate chiefly as herds. (See Ardrey 1966, Altman 1965, Devore 1965, Schaller 1964, Schaller and Selsam 1969, and Schrier et al. 1965.)

single-parent family.) Despite the many family forms and variations, there has never been any widespread departure from some form of the nuclear family based on some form of marriage. Other systems have been tried but with little success.[8] (See the vignette, "The Monogamous Nuclear Family in Primitive Societies.")

The Extended Family

The extended family, as defined by Murdock (1949), consists of two or more nuclear families living in one household with shared obligations and responsibilities. Other versions of the extended family involve a single nuclear family with additional relatives, such as a grandparent, a brother-in-law, or a sister-in-law, and are more common in our society.

Very elaborate versions of the extended family have emerged in some societies. For example, the *corporate* family—which reached its greatest development during the Ch'ing Dynasty in China, A.D. 1644–1911—often contained as many as seventy or eighty people living together in a walled-in compound of several buildings. The oldest man exercised patriarchal domination over his wife and concubines, their unmarried sons and daughters, their married sons and their wives and children, and even married grandsons and *their* wives and children. The ideal was to have six generations of the family living under one roof, and for the family to go through nine generations without a division of property. However, the most frequently occurring family form in societies that idealize the extended family, such as the

---

[8]The closest any society has come to using an institution other than the family as a basic socializing force is the *kibbutz* of Israel. However, less than 4 percent of the Israeli society have been raised in a kibbutz, and as an experiment, it seems to have been only marginally successful (Davis 1985). Experiments with state care of children and very restricted parental contact were carried out in the early years of the Soviet Union, but these experiments were stopped after a few years, apparently because the results were not satisfactory (Clayton 1979).

The Monogamous Nuclear Family in Primitive Societies

It was thought at one time that early in human history group marriage was the norm—with several adult men relating sexually to several adult women, forming an interdependent and relatively permanent group that was a basis for a family structure. It is now doubted, however, that group marriage ever occurred as a dominant form. The monogamous nuclear family was probably the basis for a family structure from earliest human history—existing in even the most primitive societies. For example, in every contemporary primitive society that has been discovered, the social structure is based on the monogamous nuclear family.

An interesting development in this regard was the 1971 discovery of a surviving Stone Age tribe in the mountains of the Philippine island of Mindanao. This tribe (the Tassidy) have no permanent dwellings, no crops, and only the crudest tools of stone and bamboo; they make fire by the friction of wood against wood and feed no domestic animals. Nevertheless, the Tassidy live in basic nuclear family units, each consisting of a husband, a wife, and unmarried children.

An even more primitive society is the Pygmies of the Andaman Island forests, who were discovered by European explorers two centuries ago. The Andaman Island Pygmies were so primitive that they did not even know how to make fire. Yet, the basis of their social structure was the nuclear family based on a monogamous marriage.

Ch'ing Dynasty in China, has always been the nuclear family; the average household in these societies has never been more than three to five people (Reiss 1980, Gordon 1978, Shorter 1975).

A rather unusual version of the extended family occurs among the Mentawei of western Sumatra. Here, couples are committed to each other but do not marry until middle age. Meanwhile, the woman continues to live in her father's household, while the man lives apart in *his* father's household. Children are adopted at birth by their mother's father and are supported by her brothers. When the couple reach middle age, they marry, and the husband then formally adopts his children. A typical household among the Mentawei, then, consists of a set of grandparents, their sons and daughters, and their daughters' children. (In other words, adult sons live with their parents and sisters and support their sisters' children rather than their own children, who live in other households with their mothers, aunts, uncles, and grandparents.)

Another interesting version of the extended family is the *stem* family of rural Ireland. (This version of the family also occurs in other societies). In the stem family, a son inherits the farm (which is usually too small to be subdivided) from his father. However, instead of the eldest son automatically inheriting, the father can designate any son he wishes as his heir.[9] This gives the father enormous power, since he does not usually indicate his choice until late in life; sons who do not move to jobs in cities, or emigrate, must work on the farm in virtually total subordination to their father, each hoping to be the one chosen to inherit the property. Even after the sons are in their thirties and forties, any wages from extra jobs that they may have (such as working on another farm) traditionally go to the father. Since marriage involves a property settlement, and the sons

---

[9]When the eldest son automatically inherits property from his father, the system is called *primogeniture*. This system is found in many societies.

Coping with Problems of Polygyny

One example of an existing polygynous culture is the Bogand tribe in central Africa. To minimize wifely jealousy in this society, husbands and wives live apart. The husband provides each wife with a house and a garden of her own, and he invites the women, one at a time, to come to his own house for visits. Conflict is further reduced by a system of clearly defined responsibilities. The first wife, outranking all her successors, looks after the family's religious fetishes—objects such as buffalo horns filled with herbs and clay and presumably inhabited by powerful spirits. The second wife is charged with shaving her husband's head, cutting his nails, and then protecting the trimmings from enemies who might use them in death-dealing magic ceremonies. Additional duties are assigned to other wives (Wernick 1974, p. 38).

---

have no property until an heir is named, they may not marry until the father is ready to reveal his choice and retire. The son and heir then marries and moves his wife into the household, turning over one of the rooms to the old couple, his parents, and providing them with food, fuel, and other provisions. The household in a stem family thus consists of the parents and their children until the father retires, after which it consists of the old couple, the son and heir, his wife and children, and the other unmarried sons or daughters who remain.

The Polygamous Family

Another version of the family that is quite common in other societies, although it is illegal in the United States, is the form based on multiple or *polygamous* marriage. The most common form of polygamy is *polygyny,* in which the nuclear family consists of one husband, two or more wives, and their children. An alternate form of polygamy is *polyandry,* in which the nuclear family consists of one wife, two or more husbands, and their children.

Polygyny

Most societies (about 85 percent) permit polygyny, which indicates that it must have certain advantages not available in monogamy. One advantage, of course, is that the system relieves the first wife from performing arduous or boring household tasks, which she may assign to younger wives. (The first wife always has the highest status in the household in a polygynous society, and she supervises the other wives). If the ratio of men to women in a society is uneven (usually because of periodic wars), polygyny makes it possible for more women to marry. In some societies, the motive for polygyny is to provide additional status to wealthy or powerful men.

Even in societies in which polygyny is legal (and admired), the dominant family form is monogamous. One reason for this is simply demographic. Most societies have about equal numbers of men and women. Thus, only a minority of men can have more than one wife, since one man must remain a bachelor for every man who has two wives. A second reason is economic determinism. Extra wives in families can be acquired only by rich and powerful men, since a household containing multiple wives and their children is very expensive to maintain.

Finally, the chances of conflict, strife, and disharmony are multiplied in a polygynous marriage. As we have seen (Chapter 9), problems of conflict inevitably emerge even in the

Collection of the Artist

When two previously married people, each with custody of children, marry one another, the result is a blended family.
Gary van der Steur, *Step Family Lives,* © 1979

ditions. For example, among the Nayar of the Malibar coast in southern India, a girl is married at puberty to a young man, preferably of higher social position than herself (who is chosen by an astrologer). The bridegroom might or might not consummate the marriage, but he is subsequently expected to have nothing more to do with his wife. She then takes a succession of several husbands who visit her at night, but each has no legal commitment except to bring a suitable gift of cloth if the union results in a baby whose paternity he chooses to recognize. All the children by this succession of fathers are brought up by the mother and her sisters in a large house that is ruled by the mother's eldest brother. The children address all the husbands by the same title: *Acchan* (Lord).

The Nayar polyandrous family startled early anthropologists and sociologists, who debated whether the arrangemant even fitted into the concept of marriage and family. The Nayor, however, certainly thought so, and they took their rules very seriously, strangling any girl who broke the rules (if, for example, she copulated with a man of a lower caste).

Viewed in the context of the Nayar society, the rules make sense. The Nayars are a caste of professional soldiers, and all the young men are away from the community for most of the year—fighting or training. The family arrangements allow them to have women when they return on leave, and at the same time provide a stable home for the children (Reiss 1980).

The Blended Family

Although polygamy is illegal in our society, American law does permit multiple marriages so long as they are separated by divorce. Thus, although it is illegal to be married to more than one person at a time, a man may have a series of wives and a woman may have a series of husbands. This form of marriage, which has been called *serial polygamy,* results in *blended* families.

most harmonious marriage between *two* people, and such difficulties are multiplied in a polygynous marriage. For these reasons, the incidence of polygyny is relatively low even in societies in which it is the preferred form. (See the vignette, "Coping with Problems of Polygyny.")

Polyandry

Polyandry has been permitted by only a tiny percentage of the world's societies at any time, and it has nearly vanished today. Nevertheless, it was perfectly logical under certain con-

When two previously married people, each with custody of children, marry each other, the resultant family consists of children from different families of origin blended into a new family. If the couple have their own offspring, for these children the husband and the wife are biological parents. For other children the mother or father is stepparent. Since the stepchildren maintain membership in their original families of origin—with emotional ties, loyalties, and visiting rights—the structure and interactions of a blended family can be extraordinarily complex. If there is another divorce and remarriage, the structure of the blended family becomes even more convoluted. Nevertheless, the blended family, in all its possible forms, is very common in our society. (See the section, "The Rising Number of Blended Families" later in this chapter.)

The Single-Parent Family

Another form of the family is the single-parent family. Unlike the blended family, the single-parent family has a relatively simple structure. In fact, it is the simplest possible version of a nuclear family.

Although the single-parent family does not fit into Murdock's classic definition, it is very common in our society (especially among blacks). In fact, the single-parent family is our fastest growing family form. The incidence, causes, importance, and complexities of the single-parent family are discussed in the section, "The Rising Number of Single-Parent Families" later in this chapter.

THE FAMILY IN TRANSITION

As we have seen (Chapter 2), until the eighteenth century, the family in England and Western Europe was a self-sufficient economic unit with the members consuming what they produced. The family also served the basic function of "placement"—fitting a person into the social structure as a family member. The family name was important, and a person was less an individual than a member of a family. The family also provided protection and support for its members from infancy through old age—physically and psychologically. The family exercised religious functions, saying prayers and grace at meals and reading together from the Bible.[10] Recreation usually occurred within a family setting instead of at a commercial center outside the home.

When the change from agriculture to industry began in the eighteenth century in England, the family entered a transitional period. Factories, mills, offices, and government agencies increasingly came to provide the economic goods and services that were formerly provided within the family. Status and prestige became related more to individual accomplishment than to family name. As Western culture proceeded from the nineteenth into the twentieth century and as we approach the twenty-first, teachers have become responsible for the education of children after about age five. Unemployment compensation, welfare, social security, Medicare, reform schools, and police have largely assumed functions formerly fulfilled by the family. Professional clergy—priests, Protestant ministers, rabbis, and others—have virtually taken over the family's religious functions. (In the average family in our society, the only religious observances remaining are such vestigial rites as celebrating Christmas and saying grace before meals, although the family often regard themselves as a religious unit and attend church together.) Recreational activities still occur within the

----

[10]It is interesting to note that in the early Roman family, which was the precursor of both canon (church) and secular (civil) law regarding the family in England (and most of Western Europe), the husband and father possessed all religious rights as priest of the family. In ancient Rome, the father was regarded as a priest and was responsible for perpetuating the worship of the household gods. In some parts of the Orient, family life still revolves around the worshiping of distant ancestors.

home but have also moved to playgrounds, tennis courts, golf courses, bowling alleys, and other hangouts away from the home.

In short, except for producing and nurturing children, and providing a sense of belonging, emotional security, and support for each member, all traditional functions of the family that have endured for ages have become much less important or have disappeared from the family altogether as they have been assumed by other agencies of the society.

The Impact of Industrialization on the Family

As noted in Chapter 2, these changes in family function came about in response to the sweeping social, economic, and political developments that initially took place in England during the eighteenth century. The mechanization of the textile industry, technical advance and expansion in the iron industry, the harnessing of steam power, the establishment of the factory system, and other related developments of that period revolutionized the English economy. What was essentially an agrarian system in the middle of the eighteenth century became an industrial system by the middle of the nineteenth.[11]

As the society of England shifted to industrialization, the impact on the family was enormous. The agrarian family that had endured for some 5,000 years was changed to an urban family in a relatively short time.[12] Instead of 90 percent of the population living in rural areas and 10 percent in the cities, 90 percent moved to live in (or near) cities. Farmers, craftsmen, and artisans were transformed into factory workers and miners who worked apart from the family household. Then, because women were cheaper to hire than men, more and more women moved into the world of work outside the household. Children were even cheaper to hire than women and began working outside the household as well, laboring in factories beginning at age five, sometimes for twelve hours per day, six and a half days per week. This forced the state to recognize that a completely *laissez-faire* policy was working great hardship on the working class.[13] As cities and towns became more crowded, open space disappeared, and people accustomed to fields and woodlands found themselves living in filthy, crowded streets and tenements, breathing polluted air, and working long days, rarely relieved by experiences of either hope or beauty.

The misery of the new urban dwellers was compounded by the harshness of the factory system, which often operated along quasi-penal lines. Regardless of how hard life had been before, country folk had at least had some control over their own hour-to-hour movements; but now, work was . . . longer, more arduous, more confining. Women and children, though they had always worked extremely hard in their homes and fields, now worked in factories with dangerous, noisy machinery or in dark and dangerous mines. Minor infractions of complex rules, such as whistling on the job or leaving a lamp lit a few minutes too long after sunrise, led to fines, more serious infractions to floggings. One observer of the period wrote poignantly of hearing children, whose families could not, of course, afford clocks, running through the streets in the dark, long before time for the mills to open, so fearful were they of being late (Lenski and Lenski 1974, pp. 298–99).

[11]England (and northwestern Europe) had always been one of the most technologically underdeveloped areas of Eurasia—a remote and underdeveloped cultural backwater—until the mid-eighteenth century. All other crucial technological breakthroughs of the prior ten thousand years had occurred in the Middle East; plant cultivation, animal domestication, metallurgy, the plow, and the sailing ship.

[12]Agrarian societies emerged (with the invention of the *plow*) from earlier horticultural societies about 3000 B.C. in the Middle East. (The plow was invented in the Middle East about 4000 B.C. but was not widely adopted for about a thousand years.) Horticultural societies practiced planning, harvesting, and animal husbandry, and emerged about 7000 B.C. from earlier hunting and gathering societies (Lenski and Lenski 1974).

[13]*Laissez-faire* means literally to "let alone" and is the doctrine in economics and politics that an economic system functions best when there is no interference (or regulation) by government.

The father was usually the dominant figure in nineteenth-century families.
Frances B. Johnston: *A Hampton Graduate at Home*, plate from an album of Hampton Institute, 1899–1900.

Interaction between parents and children is much more informal today than it was in the families of the nineteenth century.

Farming families often have three or more generations in one
household, with everyone participating in family oriented activities.
Nina Leen, *Four Generations of Ozark Farmers and Families*, 1948.

Many families adopt children of ethnic backgrounds different from their own.

Children and the Factory System

The following testimony was given to a Parliamentary committee investigating working conditions in 1832 by Peter Smart. Similar testimony was provided by numerous others.

Q. Where do you reside?
A. At Dundee.

Q. Have you worked in a mill from your youth?
A. Yes, since I was 5 years of age.

Q. Had you a father and mother in the country at the time?
A. My mother stopped in Perth, about eleven miles from the mill, and my father was in the army.

Q. Were you hired for any length of time when you went?
A. Yes, my mother got 15 shillings for six years, I having my meat and clothes.

Q. What were your hours of labor, as you recollect, in the mill?
A. We began at 4 o'clock in the morning and worked till 10 or 11 at night; as long as could stand on our feet.

Q. Were you kept on the premises constantly?
A. Constantly.

Q. Locked up?
A. Yes, locked up.

Q. Night and day?
A. Night and day; I never went home while I was at the mill.

Q. Do the children ever attempt to run away?
A. Very often.

Q. Were they pursued and brought back again?
A. Yes; the overseer pursued them and brought them back.

Q. Did you ever attempt to run away?
A. Yes; I ran away twice.

Q. And you were brought back?
A. Yes; and I was sent up to the master's loft and thrashed with a whip for running away.

Q. Do you know whether the children were, in point of fact, compelled to stop during the whole time for which they were engaged?
A. Yes, they were.

Q. By law?
A. I cannot say by law; but they were compelled by the master; I never say any law was used there but the law of their own hands.

Source: Parliamentary Papers, 1831–32, Vol. XV. Quoted in Lenski and Lenski 1974, p. 299.

By the late eighteenth century, legislators were passing laws designed to impose regulations on factory owners. One of these was the requirement that children receive some education, and gradually this function was moved from the family to schools. Thus, a basic function of the family that had endured for centuries of agrarian life was transferred as England became industrialized.

Other political changes took place as the power base shifted from the landed aristocracy to the factory owners, merchants, and bank-ers. During the nineteenth century, English women were granted equal rights with men, although not without a struggle. These changes had an effect on the family. By the end of the nineteenth century, the old Roman-based laws regarding the sovereignty of the husband-father in the family were reformed.[14]

---

[14]The husband-father was the only person recognized as an independent individual under roman law. He possessed all economic rights as sole owner of the family property, real and personal, and he had literal power of life and death over other mem-

Women (including wives) were granted the rights to be recognized as independent individuals, to own and control property, to exercise control over children, to take court action, and even to sue for divorce.

America was still largely an agrarian society in the eighteenth century and well into the nineteenth. Large families had become economical, since children were a valuable source of labor on large farms. (Families in Western Europe were smaller.)[15] However, as the nineteenth century progressed, American families also were transformed by the twin forces of industrialization and urbanization. By the late nineteenth and early twentieth centuries, more and more wives and mothers had followed men to employment outside the home, as they had in England a century earlier (see Chapter 2)

Although few types of jobs were open to women initially, a great surge of employment for women in business and industry occurred as part of the social upheaval at the time of World War I.[16] Another great surge occurred during World War II, when women moved into an even wider range of occupations and activities. Meanwhile, women were granted increasing legal rights, although in the United States as well as in England they did not win the right to vote until the early twentieth century.

Thus a period of rapid transition occurred in the United States from the mid-nineteenth to the mid-twentieth century. These changes were chiefly due to the wholesale societal movement from an agrarian economy to one based upon industry and all the related factors that accompanied this change, especially such technological developments as the telephone, the typewriter, the electric light, the internal combustion engine, the automobile, and the moving assembly line. These and other changes led to the entry of women into the work world outside the home as part of the social upheaval, especially with the impact of World War I and then World War II on our society (see Chapters 2 and 5).

Patterns that were current a generation or two ago are no longer the norm. So many mothers with small children work outside the home that only 5 percent of households fit the American stereotype of a working father, a stay-at-home mother, and minor children.[17] More than half of all married women with school-aged children now hold some kind of job, nearly one married couple in two have no children under age eighteen, and fully 30 percent have no children at all. Married couples who do have children, have far fewer children. A substantial number of children live in single-parent families. And in most families, both the husband and the wife work, providing a dual income (see Chapter 2).

The Contemporary Family

The changes in family life are still continuing.[18] The most rapid changes are the continuing entry of women into the work world outside the family, leading to a rising number of double-income families; the high divorce

---

bers of the family, exercising the functions of a monarch. At his death, his name, property, and authority descended to his male heirs. The Roman system was transferred in many of its details into both canon and secular law of Western Europe and was little modified (except for the power of life and death) until the nineteenth century.

[15]For example, in the mid-nineteenth century in England, there were 6.4 persons in the average farmer's household and 4.9 in the average laborer's—3.5 resident children for the farmer and 2.8 for the laborer (Shorter 1975).

[16]In the nineteenth and early twentieth centuries in the United States, women were usually employed only as seamstresses, laundresses, scrubbing and cleaning women, maids, cooks, housekeepers, governesses, teachers, and nurses. Only very unusual women were able to work at other employment. (See Chapter 2 for further discussion.)

---

[17]U.S. Bureau of Labor Statistics, *Special Labor Force Bulletin* 191, 83–160 (1984).

[18]The family as a social unit is in a transitional period in many other societies throughout the world as well. The African chief sees his sons go off to work in a city and marry women from other tribes who do not speak the ancestral tongue and who will bring up their children unaware of ancestral gods and customs. The elderly Japanese gentleman is dismayed at the breakdown of the family norms when he sees women sitting down at the same table as the men.

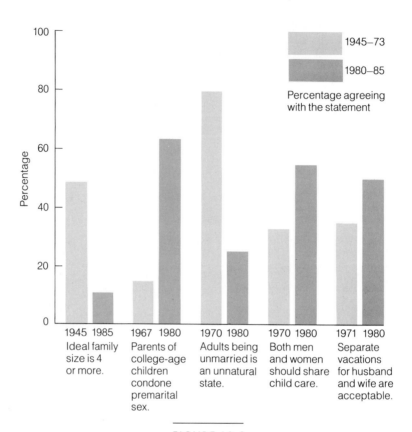

FIGURE 10-2

Changing attitudes toward family life-styles

Sources: Data from Yankevich (1981), Gallop (1985).

rate and high rate of illegitimacy (especially among blacks), leading to a rising number of single-parent families and a rising number of blended families; and the combination of factors that are leading to a drop in the birth rate and a corresponding rise in the number of smaller families (see Figure 10-2).

The Rising Number of Double-Income Families

The rise in the incidence of working wives (that is, working outside the home in gainful employment) is one of the most significant changes in the contemporary family. As we have seen, most women with children under age eighteen now work outside the home.

Couples in dual-income marriages face the problem of providing for child care, of course, but the problem can be solved in so many different ways that it is difficult to evaluate the effect of the dual-career marriage on children. The number of variables in child care is very large, and the mother's outside employment is only one of them. What is important is the *quality* of child care, however it is provided. Moreover, different children react differently to the same situation, depending on their own characteristics.

Martha Stewart/The Picture Cube

The number of child care centers is rapidly increasing in response to the growing number of double-income families.

There are few data regarding the effect of a wife's working on the harmony of marital interaction or on the success of the marriage. But the existing data indicate that dual-income marriages are probably happier than single-income marriages because of the lowered economic pressures (Rapoport and Rapoport 1978). However, the wife's working does have a significant effect on the power structure of the marriage; the wife who provides a share of the income has relatively more power than a wife who does not.

There are also strains that are unique to a dual-income marriage. Obviously, some provision must be made for the care and well-being of the children, and someone has to do the marketing, prepare the meals, clean the house, take out the garbage, and so on. Studies have found that working wives bear the chief responsibility for housekeeping and child care—husbands do about 20 percent of such tasks while working wives do about 80 percent. Further studies have found that only about one-third of working mothers hire domestic help (Townsend 1985).

It is interesting to note, however, that a survey of dual-career Canadian couples found that the more money the wife made, the more housework was done by the husband, although men who described themselves as "liberated" were more likely to help around the house, whereas "traditional" husbands were more likely to be uneasy about wives who earned high salaries. Apparently, the Canadian husbands were perfectly willing to help around the house—as long as their working wives' contributions to the family income were significant. This attitude held constant for husbands of all social classes, religions, and levels of education (Harrell 1985).

There is little free time for family activities in dual-income marriages.

One of the most striking things about dual career couples is how incredibly busy they are. With both partners following demanding occupations, there just doesn't seem to be enough time to get everything done . . . mornings, before work, are frantic. Everyone has to get ready for work or school. Breakfast must be prepared and eaten and the dishes cleared away . . . when they finally do get home from work, both partners need time to relax and unwind. But there is still dinner to be prepared and cleaned away, shopping and laundry to be done, and at least occasional cleaning of the home. There is, in short, more work to be done than time in which to do it (Leslie and Leslie 1977, p. 284).

Dual-Professional couples are a special category of dual-income families, with at least one additional strain: It may be difficult, and perhaps impossible, to find two professional positions within practicable commuting distances of the same house. The career opportunities of one person must then yield to those of the other. If one person is already employed in a satisfactory position, the other is limited to opportunities in the same geographic area.

Advancement for executives or professionals often requires a change in geographical location. If one spouse is required by the employer to move to another location, the other must then resign and start job hunting in a new area—a change that disrupts his or her career. Although there are very little data in this regard, wives probably more often follow husbands than husbands follow wives.

Impressionistic evidence suggests couples more often follow the demands of the husband's career, and that it is the wife's career that usually suffers. She packs up and moves with him, hoping that she can find an equally good job in the new location (Leslie and Leslie 1977, p. 282).

Perhaps the most famous dual-professional family of all time was that of Pierre and Marie Curie in the late nineteenth and early twentieth centuries. They reputedly had an idyllically happy marriage as well as great professional success, sharing a Nobel Prize in physics in 1903.[19] In addition, their family life was so successful that one of their daughters, Irene, not only followed her mother's example in having an idyllic dual-career marriage herself, but was also extraordinarily successful in her work as a scientist, sharing a Nobel Prize in chemistry with her husband, Frederick Jolliot, in 1935. The Curie's other daughter, Eve, became a successful writer.

Both Marie Curie and her daughter Irene Curie Jolliot were, of course, trailblazers who entered fields normally restricted to men during a time when it was virtually impossible to do so. They not only exemplified the dual-professional marriage, but they did so in the oppressive atmosphere (in this regard) of the nineteenth and early twentieth centuries.

It is anticipated that more and more women will move into the world of work outside the family, and that the incidence of dual-income marriages will increase among both professionals and nonprofessionals.

The Rising Number of Single-Parent Families

The single-parent family is the fastest growing family type in the United States. The percentage of single-parent families has increased among both whites and blacks in recent years, but the increase has been much greater among blacks. In 1984, nearly three out of five (59 percent) of black families were single-parent families (up from 52 percent in 1980 and 36 percent in 1970). By contrast, the 1984 figure for whites was 20 percent (up from 17 percent in 1980 and 10 percent in 1970).[20]

Mothers continue to dominate in caring for children in one-parent households, however; in 1984, 11 percent of single-parent families

---

[19]After Pierre Curie's death in a street accident in 1906, Marie Curie went on to win a *second* Nobel Prize in 1911, this time in chemistry.
[20]U.S. Bureau of the Census, "Report on Household and Family Characteristics, 1970 to 1984" (1985).

were headed by the father (up from about 2 percent in 1980 and about 1 percent in 1970).[21] This is quite a significant increase in father-headed single-parent families in a very short period of time.

A single-parent family is usually created by divorce, desertion, or the death of one parent, so that the household consists of a single parent or stepparent with children and perhaps stepchildren. However, a single-parent family may also consist of an unwed mother who elects to keep her child. (If she lives with her parents, the household becomes a version of the extended family, but if she establishes a household of her own, it is a single-parent family.) A single-parent family is also created when an unmarried person—man or woman—adopts a child. Until recently, courts usually permitted adoption only by couples or single women, but they are now increasingly permitting single men to adopt children as well.

The single-parent family may endure for the entire time that the children are growing up, or it may be only a temporary form lasting a few months or a few years until a remarriage transforms it back into a nuclear family with a stepparent. If the parent in a single-parent family *is* a stepparent, remarriage creates a family with *two* stepparents and their stepchildren, with no blood ties at all. (The married couple may then produce their own children, of course, or adopt children, creating further complications of family memberships.)

Among whites, the greatest number of single-parent families are caused by death of the husband, with divorce being the second most common cause, and desertion third. The incidence of unmarried mothers heading families is relatively low.

Among blacks, the greatest number of single-parent families are caused by desertion of the husband, with death being the second most

common cause. The incidence of single-parent families headed by an unmarried mother is almost as high as the incidence of those caused by the death of the husband. Divorce is the fourth most common cause of the single-parent black family.[22]

Most single-parent families are in much worse financial straits than are two-parent families. For example, nearly half of all female-headed single-parent families are below the poverty line.[23] Since black children are three times as likely to live in such families, it is consistent with demographic patterns that they are three times as likely to be poor and five times as likely to be on welfare, as white children.[24]

The average woman who works full-time does not earn as much as the average man, and a woman with no husband can expect to have only about one dollar for every two dollars available to two-parent families.[25] Despite the hardships encountered by a single-parent family headed by the mother, the incidence of this family type has been increasing sharply (see Figure 10-3).

In the single-parent family, one parent must fulfill the responsibilities that are normally shared by two—responsibilities for socializing the child as well as for providing appropriate nurture, affection, and love. However, there are so many variables involved in child care—the presence or absence of a second parent is only one of them—that it is difficult to separate the effect of an absent parent from other factors. In consequence, little research evidence

---

[21]Ibid.

[22]U.S. Bureau of the Census, "Report on Household and Family Characteristics" (December 1980) and provisional data (October 1981).

[23]U.S. Bureau of the Census, "Persons below Poverty Level and below 125 Percent of Poverty Level, by Race of Householder, and Family Status: 1959 to 1982" (1985).

[24]U.S. Children's Defense Fund, "Widening Schism Between Black and White Children in America" (1985).

[25]U.S. Bureau of the Census, "Report on Household and Family Characteristics" (December 1980) and provisional data (October 1981).

is available regarding the effect of having a single parent on children.

It is important, of course, that children receive adequate care and socialization, but it is the *quality* of the care that is important, not the source. Some children receive better care in single-parent families than other children do in two-parent families. Just as a two-parent family does not guarantee happy, well-adjusted, adequately socialized, fully functioning, creative, productive children, neither does a one-parent family automatically signify the opposite.

The limited research data available indicate that the father's absence from home does not necessarily cause severe distress and conflict or leave the mother unable to supervise the children adequately. Moreover, available evidence indicates that boys who grow up in fatherless homes are no more likely than other boys to suffer inadequate masculine identity. Thus, while fathers are important in the family and contribute to the development of children, it is apparently quite possible for mothers alone to nurture and socialize children adequately in single-parent families (Bould 1977, Pedersen 1976, Brandwein et al. 1974).[26]

Contrary to many of our prejudices, one-parent families need not be a deviant or distorted family form, for in many settings it may be the one viable and appropriate one. Defects in the functioning of one-parent families may stem more from adverse social judgements than from intrinsic feelings. Where some sense of stability and continuity is achieved, it can provide a "humane setting" for its members despite certain deficiencies in resources (Eshleman 1978, p. 667).

Fathers usually feel capable and successful in their abilities to function as single parents, and there is little evidence that they experience severe problems of role strain or adjust-

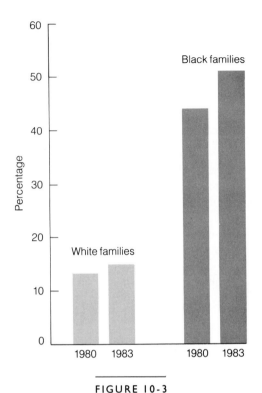

FIGURE 10-3

Increase in incidence of single-parent families headed by women with children under age eighteen, by race, 1980–1983

Source: Data from U.S. Bureau of the Census, "Percent Married and Divorced of the Population, 18 Years and Over: 1960 to 1983" (1985, p. 46).

ment. While they express concern over their abilities to provide appropriate nurture and socialization for their children, these concerns appear similar to those of most parents in two-parent families (Orthner et al. 1976). The chief difficulty of home management for single fathers seems to be chiefly the feeling of being overburdened with multifarious demands (Gasser and Taylor 1976).

Although delinquency rates have been found to be higher for children from single-parent families than those from intact families, they are higher still in chronically disturbed families. Conflict-ridden homes apparently create more problems for children than does

---

[26]Data also from U.S. Department of Health and Human Services, *Adolescent Abuse and Neglect: Intervention Strategies* (1980).

Bruce Kliewe/Jeroboam, Inc.

In a single parent family, one parent must fulfill the responsibilities that are normally shared by two—responsibility for socializing the child as well as for providing appropriate nurture, affection, and love.

living in a single-parent family (Brandwein et al. 1974).[27]

When a single-parent family is created by death, children experience greater strain than when it is caused by divorce. After all, a divorced parent may still be available to some extent; death, however, is an irrevocable and frightening loss.

The Rising Number of Blended Families

As we have seen, when a previously married person with custody of the children remarries and the couple produce offspring of their own

so that there are two sets of children, the family is known as a *blended* family. If the marriage is a remarriage for both persons and both have custody of children from prior marriages, each is a stepparent to the other's children. The couple may then, of course, conceive additional offspring of their own, so that the blended family may contain children of three different parentages. Or the couple may adopt a child, so that they are at once "natural" parents, stepparents, and adoptive parents, with each parent having a different relation to each child in the family. If a parent divorces and remarries more than once, retaining custody of the children from each marriage, the blended family may have children with three or even more sets of parents.

[27]Ibid.

Drawing by Weber; © 1982 The New Yorker Magazine, Inc.

"Good evening. I am Martha's son by a previous marriage."

Although only one set of parents is in residence in a blended family as part of the household, absent parents may still maintain visiting rights, have custody of a child for part of the year, and be legally liable for child support. A child may be considered very much a part of the absent parent's family, and attachment to the absent parent may persist. Ties to the absent parent may include frequent visits to grandparents and other relatives, observances of family birthdays, and participation in other ritualistic family events, such as Christmas and Bar Mitzvahs—all of which foster a strong sense of membership in the family of the absent parent. A child in a blended family, then, may be an active, functioning member of two (or even more) families, maintaining ties with the absent parent's family as well as with his or her own parent in residence, with siblings, and with half-siblings.

As the child grows into adulthood, active membership in various aspects of these diverse family patterns remains, even after a new family (of procreation) is established with marriage. If divorce and remarriage then occur, the complexity of family membership may be extraordinary.

The rising rate of divorce followed by a rising rate of remarriage, and the rising rate of illegitimacy (with some unwed mothers electing to keep their children and marry men other than the fathers), have acted in concert to increase the incidence of the blended family. In 1980 there were more than 18 million stepchildren in blended families, and the number is growing.[28] Divorces, and the number of children involved, have nearly tripled from 1958 to 1980 (see Figure 10-4).

[28]U.S. National Center for Health Statistics, "Divorces and Children Involved in the U.S. 1958–1980" (1984).

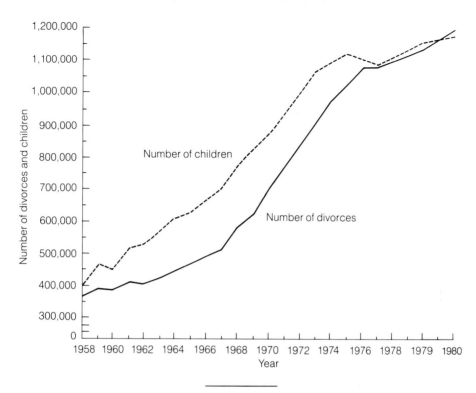

FIGURE 10-4

Divorces and children involved, in the United States,
1958–1980

Source: Data from U.S. National Center for Health Statistics,
Vital Statistics of the United States annual (1984, p. 84).

The Rising Number of Smaller Families

At the beginning of the nineteenth century the average wife had seven children, and at the beginning of the twentieth century, she had five children, as we have seen (Chapter 2). The birth rate has continued to decline to the present, with the exception of the sustained "baby boom" following World War II (see Figure 10-5). Even during the baby boom, however, there was little increase in the proportion of women having three or more children; the baby boom was caused by the large increase in the numbers of women having at least *two* children. There was no return to the large families of the past (Westoff 1978). Between 1970 and 1979, the proportion of large families (four or more children) declined from 9.8 percent to 4.5 percent—cutting the number of these families in half.[29]

The average size of American families began to diminish steadily, declining to 3.7 persons in the mid-1960s and 3.3 persons by the late 1970s. Demographers expect it to decline even further, to reach 3.0 persons by 1990.[30]

---

[29]U.S. Bureau of the Census, "Changes in Family Size" (December 1980).
[30]Ibid.

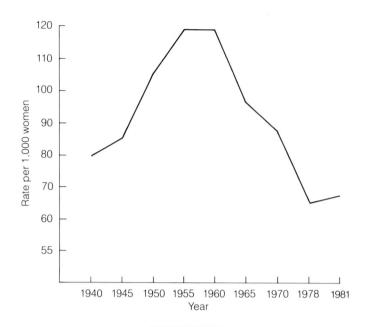

FIGURE 10-5

Birth rate per 1,000 women, ages fifteen to forty-four,
1940–1981

Sources: Data from U.S. Department of Health, Education,
and Welfare, *Public Service Annual* (1970); U.S. National
Center for Health Statistics,
Vital Statistics of the United States
(1985, p. 58).

There is also a rising incidence of couples who have *no* children. Fully 47 percent of all married couples now have no children under age eighteen,[31] and, as we have seen, demographers predict that 25 to 30 percent of young married women will elect to have no children, opting for child-free marriages (see Chapter 7).

A return to higher fertility rates may occur, of course, as couples who have postponed having children begin to have them. However, most demographers predict that the trend toward smaller families (and child-free families) will continue because it is related to a broad array of fundamental social changes, chief among which is the move from agriculture to industry with the resultant changes in the economic function of women and children.

The trend toward greater economic independence and social freedom for women, with a decreasing emphasis on childbearing and housekeeping, will undoubtedly persist, while children become an ever-increasing economic liability. The trend of increasing numbers of women (mothers included) working outside the home will probably continue, and there seems little doubt that working outside the home and fertility are negatively correlated (as the incidence of one goes up, the incidence of the other goes down). The autocratic husband and father of earlier times who provided the only source of financial support for the entire

[31] Ibid.

family shows no sign of returning. Westoff (1978) sums this up as follows:

The important thing about this catalogue of social changes is that the changes all seem to be irreversible, and that some of them, particularly those linked with the status of women, have not yet run their full course. In spite of some signs of net migration to rural areas, no return to an agrarian economy is likely . . . not withstanding some recent disenchantment with the economic rewards of higher education, a prolonged period of education and training has become the norm. It does not take a professional economist to discern that the hunger for consumer goods has not abated in spite of the antimaterialist sentiments of the environmentalist movement. Birth-control technology, although it is still far short of ideal, is more widely used and more effective than ever before. . . . In short, nothing on the horizon suggests that fertility will not remain low (pp. 54–55).

The Stability of the Family

Although it is undeniable that the family is undergoing a period of transition, and recent changes in family patterns and functions are significant (as well as related changes in patterns of dating, courtship, and life-styles), it is important to emphasize that there is nevertheless an underlying stability in family life. Although the incidence of living together without being married has increased sharply, and the average age at first marriage is about two years higher than a decade ago, only about 4 percent of couples who share a household are not married, and about 95 percent of singles ultimately marry, as we have seen (Chapter 6).

Moreover, not only has the annual rate of marital dissolution (marriages dissolved by either divorce or death) remained remarkably constant for more than a century, but the length of time the average couple may expect to remain married has increased twenty-two years (from eighteen years to about forty years) because of improved life expectancy (see Chapter 8).

Despite the long-term progressive rise in the divorce rate, the average married couple today may expect to live together more than twice as long as their grandparents did, before the marriage is ultimately dissolved by death.

In short, the family is a very stable and sound institution in demographic perspective, despite the high divorce rate, the rising number of singles, the rising incidence of cohabitation, and the rising number of single-parent families, blended families, and child-free families. The family forms have changed and diversified, as have family functions, but the family itself—in one form or another—is stubbornly persistent.

FAMILY VIOLENCE

A curious paradox is that the family is often a source of turmoil, conflict, and strife for the individual even though one of the essential functions of the family is to provide emotional satisfaction. One-third of all police calls involve family fights. Yet police officers are as cautious in answering these calls as they are in answering calls involving armed robberies because families typically close ranks quickly at the first hint of outside intervention and cease attacking one another to attack the police (Dunnigan 1985). This polarity—loyalty and emotional dependence on the one hand, coupled with strife, dissent, and violence on the other—is characteristic of no other human institution.

Violence in the family is an ancient custom. The Roman husband was by law allowed to kill any member of his family. The early records of the settlers in America indicate no lack of violence between all possible combinations of family members. Infanticide in history is common—with mothers being the usual persons to carry out the act. There is widespread acceptance of "minor" forms of "violence" in the family, e.g., spanking of children. But much of the violence that happens is of a more severe sort (Reiss 1980).

This paradox of the family as a source of both conflict and emotional security is illustrated in the prototype of the family: Adam and Eve and their children. At the very core of our religious heritage is a dualistic view of the family that acknowledges it as a cradle of violence as well as stability. Adam and Eve are portrayed as heading a loving and interdependent family, yet they experience the ultimate discord and strife when the eldest son (Cain) commits fratricide, murdering his brother (Abel). This portrayal of the prototypical family of Adam and Eve is generally regarded as symbolizing deeply unconscious wellsprings of human nature.

Wife Battering

Although no one knows the full extent of wife battering since most cases are not reported, it is estimated that nearly 6 million women are battered by their husbands, ex-husbands, or lovers in any one year in the United States, and two to four thousand women are' beaten to death (O'Reilly 1983).

Any wife can be routinely battered, regardless of social class. Wife battering occurs in affluent, in middle class, and in working class families alike. For example, a woman in Stamford, Connecticut, married to an executive of a *Fortune 500* company,[32] routinely locked herself into their Lincoln Continental to escape her husband's kicks and punches. She did not leave him because she mistakenly feared he could sue for divorce on the ground of desertion and that she, otherwise penniless, would get no alimony (O'Reilly 1983).

A middle class housewife in South Hadley,

Massachusetts, was first beaten by her husband when she was pregnant. Five years later (in 1982) he hurled a dinner plate across the kitchen at her. His aim was off. The plate shattered against the wall, and a piece of it struck their four-year-old daughter in the face, blinding the child in one eye (O'Reilly 1983).

In Atlanta, Georgia, a lower class housewife was giving a birthday party including neighborhood children when her husband, a hospital worker, asked her to come into the bedroom (O'Reilly 1983).

He slapped me blind. He pulled the shotgun from the wall and dared me to move. I cried and asked him why he was bothering me. He just tore my clothes off. He said I was a bitch and used other ugly words. I asked him not to do that because the children and their parents were here but he just left the room and told everyone to leave. Then he told me to get back in bed and that we were going to make love. I said no. But he had the .38 and a knife and hit me. I got in and we did it. My nose was still bleeding (p. 26).

Often a battered woman has grown up with violence and accepts it as a form of caring, or at least as something inevitable. She may feel desperately that the world is a dangerous place and that she needs a protector—even a man who beats her. Ashamed, terrified that any resistance will provoke greater violence, isolated from her family and friends, and often without any means of support other than her husband, she may sink into a morass of despairing submission—from which the only escape may be death—her own murder (or, perhaps in a flash of retaliatory rage, her husband's), or suicide. Twenty-five percent of all women suicide attempts are preceded by prior histories of battering (O'Reilly 1983).

Before the 1960s, wife battering was regarded as essentially a private matter and received little formal attention from social agencies, the judicial system, the clergy, family, or friends. When a battered wife complained to her family, friends, or the clergy she was often not believed, or she was told that it was her

---

[32]*Fortune* magazine annually lists the top 500 companies (in terms of gross receipts) in the United States; They are known as the *Fortune 500*.

fault for provoking her husband or that a good wife could reform a husband. If she reported the abuse to the police or to a social agency, little help could be expected. It wasn't until 1964 that the first shelter for battered wives was established (in Pasadena, California). The demand for such shelters proved to be staggering, and in 1983 there were about 800. The YWCA alone has 210 shelters in thirty states; these accommodate only about 20 percent of those who need help. All shelters have long waiting lists (O'Reilly 1983).

With the change in societal attitude toward wife battering—society now regards it as a serious concern to be acknowledged and remedied rather than a private matter to be hidden and endured—states and municipalities are enacting legislation that gives battered women a realistic chance of getting protection from the police and the judiciary. A brush with the law may have a significant effect on the husband, driving the message home that battering is inappropriate and unacceptable (O'Reilly 1983).

What kind of man would not only hit a woman but blacken her eyes, break the bones in her face, beat her breasts, kick her abdomen, and threaten her with a knife or gun? The typical wife beater is unable to cope effectively with the traditional male role in our society, which expects the man to be in control and, when there is a problem, to use force. Instead of using appropriate measures of control— effective communication, compromise, cooperation, and mutual understanding of the problem—a wife beater adopts the role of the childhood bully, using oppression and violence to obtain his ends (O'Reilly 1983).

Battering, then, is the ultimate breakdown in effective communication. When an impasse has been reached the batterer uses body language to prevail. It is the last stage of the authoritarian resolution of a conflict: "I win; you lose" (see Chapter 9).

When a persistent conflict occurs, the bat-

Mark Antman/The Image Works

The first shelter for battered wives was established in the mid-1960s. Since then the demand for such havens has steadily increased, and all shelters have long waiting lists.

terer shouts, screams, and explodes into violence as a demonstration of his male role as he understands it. He demands not only acquiescence, but love and affection, since this is the man's right as he perceives it. He believes that his wife is at fault, that she is betraying him by not returning his love, that he has not done anything wrong, and that he is simply (and reasonably) punishing her for outrageous and intolerable behavior. This "love me or I'll kill you" syndrome is then manifested as battering (see Chapter 3).

Specialists in the problem of wife battering find that the batterer is typically afflicted with severe problems of insecurity. Despite his displays of violence, he is desperately afraid of losing the woman he is punishing. This curious contradiction between feelings and behavior is exemplified by the Atlanta birthday-party-batterer, who said, "She liked to play the song 'Slip Away' and I knew she was going to do it"

(O'Reilly 1983, p. 26). The last time he saw his wife he beat her until he tired.

When it was over, I picked her up off the floor and kissed her and told her I was sorry. I wanted to feel the pain that she felt. So I kissed her. Her nose was running and she was crying, and I loved her very much (O'Reilly 1983, p. 26).

Such displays of tenderness are not unusual. This aspect of battering ("I hit you because I love you") may explain the persistent attachment that is so puzzling to the outsider. ("Why do you put up with it?")

The batterer who hits because he loves may even beat his victim to death. In his perception, she has betrayed him by failing to return his love. This is the ultimate betrayal, and violence may seem to be the only answer. He may beat her even as she proclaims her innocence—and her love—if he cannot believe her.

This aspect of battery is exemplified in Dicken's classic novel *Oliver Twist* (1846) when Bill Sikes has come to believe that Nancy has informed upon him (she has not).[33]

Without one pause, or moment's consideration; without once turning his head to the right or left, or raising his eyes to the sky, or lowering them to the ground, but looking straight before him with savage resolution; his teeth so tightly compressed that the strained jaws seemed starting through his skin; [he] held on headlong course, nor muttered a word, nor relaxed a muscle, until he reached his own door. He opened it, softly, with a key; strode lightly up the stairs; and entering his own room, double-locked the door, and lifting the heavy table against it, drew back the curtain of the bed.

The girl was lying, half dressed upon it. He had roused her from her sleep, for she raised herself with a hurried and startled look.

"Get up!" said the man.

"It is you, Bill!" said the girl, with an expression of pleasure at his return.

"It is," was the reply. "Get up."

There was a candle burning, but the man hastily drew it from the candlestick, and hurled it under the grate. Seeing the faint light of early day, without, the girl rose to undraw the curtain.

"Let it be," said Sykes, thrusting his hand before her. "There's light enough for what I've got to do."

"Bill," said the girl, in the low voice of alarm, "Why do you look like that at me!"

[He] sat regarding her, for a few seconds . . . then, grasping her by the head and throat, dragged her into the middle of the room, and looking once towards the door, placed his heavy hand upon her mouth.

"Bill, Bill!" gasped the girl, wrestling with the strength of mortal fear, "I—I won't scream or cry—not once—hear me—speak to me—tell me what I have done! . . . I have been true to you, upon my guilty soul I have!"

[He] freed one arm, and grasped his pistol. The certainty of immediate detection if he fired, flashed across his mind even in the midst of his fury; and he beat it twice with all the force he could summon, upon the upturned face that almost touched his own (pp. 353–354).

There is, of course, wife battering that is simply brutality, with the batterer beating his wife in the same way that a nineteenth-century farmer might beat his horse—with no overtones of punishment for betrayal, or of love or remorse, or of fear of being deprived of her love, simply because he is annoyed or to secure obedience. With this type of battery, the wife is much more likely to leave the husband when the first episodes of violence occur.

Unemployment does not, in itself, cause battering, but does increase pressure and exacerbate conflicts, so the incidence of battering increases when the unemployment rate rises. Similarly, alcohol does not cause battering, but in most incidents of battering, alcohol is involved (O'Reilly 1983).

Husband Battering

The proportion of husbands physically beaten by their wives is hard to estimate since men are

---

[33]*Oliver Twist*, by Charles Dickens, was first published in 1837. The text quoted is from the "New Edition, revised and corrected," which was published in 1846 by Bradbury and Evans in London, England. Many editions have since been published.

Spouse abuse can take the form of verbal attack—being sarcastic, belittling, demeaning, and undermining the other's self image—as illustrated in this scene from "Who's Afraid of Virginia Woolf" (Elizabeth Taylor and Richard Burton).
Scene from "Who's Afraid of Virginia Woolf" with Elizabeth Taylor and Richard Burton.

much less likely to report such an attack. Husband battering is still regarded as essentially a private or family matter. Resort to violence in an attempt to resolve a conflict is traditionally seen as essentially a male, not a female, characteristic. If a woman is abusive, she is expected to engage not in physical violence, but in a verbal attack—being sarcastic, belittling and demeaning the husband, and undermining his self-image. The attempt to wield power may also take the form of attrition—withholding emotional support and perhaps blatantly (and tauntingly) shifting it to another (rival) person. (The husband also may use attrition as a weapon in a conflict—see Chapter 9).

Causes of husband battering may only be speculated upon since little attention has been paid to the phenomenon and there are little research data. Presumably the causes are much the same as those of wife battering: breakdown of effective communication, feelings of injustice and outrage, frustration, and simple brutality.

Some observers have suggested that the incidence of husband battering might be indicated by the husband-wife homicide figures, which are unevenly divided between husbands and wives as the victims.[34] This could be interpreted to mean that the incidence of husband battering (which stops short of homicide) may be close to that of wife battering (O'Reilly 1983, Steinmetz 1978). It seems more likely, however that husband-as-victim homicides are the last-ditch defense of battered wives in *response* to battery.

---

[34]Husband-wife homicides (which are the single most likely type of homicide in the United States) account for more than 15 percent of all murders committed in a year.

Since husbands are rarely inclined to report wife battering, and since men are traditionally regarded as being more able to look after themselves than women are—both physically and economically—and since professional agencies in the United States show little interest in husband battering, research is still lacking in this area, and no one really knows the extent of the problem. As yet, there is no community-provided shelter for battered husbands in the United States.

Child Abuse

There are two categories of child abuse: battering and sexual molestation. In the literature, the two terms are often used interchangably, so that the term *child abuse* may mean either battering or sexual molestation.

Battering of Children

The number of reported cases of child battering in the United States is rising sharply. In 1976 the American Humane Association recorded 413,000 cases that had been reported to state and local authorities. By 1981 this figure had doubled to 851,000; in 1982 it reached 953,000. Experts on the problem estimate that only about 10–25 percent of cases are reported. If this is true, the number of child abuse cases in 1982 would be between 3,800,000 and 9,530,000 (Magnuson 1983).

Studies have found that women are more apt to be child batterers than are men; that the unwanted, the unusually brilliant or retarded, and the physically handicapped tend to be battered; and that mothers who were themselves battered as children tend to batter their own children (Anderson 1983, Magnuson 1983).

For example, a thirty-four-year-old mother who severely abused her child, remembers this about her own childhood.

What I remember most about my mother was that she was always beating me. She'd beat me with her high-heeled shoes, with my father's belt, with a pota-

to masher. When I was eight, she black-and-blued my legs so badly I told her I'd go to the police. She said, "Go, they'll just put you into the darkest prison." So I stayed. When my breasts started growing at thirteen, she beat me across the chest until I fainted. Then she'd hug me and ask for forgiveness. When I turned sixteen, a day didn't pass without my mother calling me a whore, and saying that I'd end up in Potter's Field, dead, forgotten, and damned for all eternity (Magnuson 1983, p. 20).

Another mother who was herself a battered child states:

I started abusing my boy because he was an accident and a screamer. When he was four months old, I hit him so hard my engagement ring carved a bloody furrow. . . . His screams shattered my heart . . . Deep down, I knew he couldn't understand. But I also thought he was doing it on purpose. He'd start crying again and I'd hit him again, and I felt so helpless when this happened (Magnuson 1983, p. 20).

Whether poor people and the disadvantaged tend to batter their children more than middle-class parents do is unclear because there is a social class bias against the poor in reporting child abuse. Physicians, teachers, and police are less likely to accuse middle class families of abusing their children even when the evidence is clear. Moreover, clinics and social welfare agencies deal more frequently with the poor.

Father Ritter, a Roman Catholic priest who runs a shelter for teenage runaways and cast-offs in Manhattan's Times Square, observes:

The girls who walk in off the streets with babies abuse them. If a two-week-old baby is crying, the mother will slap the baby. We try to teach her not to do that (Andersen 1983, p. 19).

Just as increases in unemployment rates are accompanied by a rise in the incidence of wife battery, rises in child-battery reports suggest that stress over money matters tends to make parents lose their tempers more readily when a child cries too long or is unruly (Magnuson 1983).

As with wife battering, public attention is

now being directed toward the problem of child abuse. Not only are more cases being reported, but attempts are being made to help protect the children of battering parents and to help parents control their impulses. As yet, however, U.S. legislation still stops short of that enacted in Sweden, where it is against the law for parents to strike their children (Reiss 1980).

Sexual Molestation of Children

Sexual molestation of children is in a different category from battering but can be just as damaging. Cultural and social taboos against incest and sexual abuse have fostered the belief that these are extremely rare problems. However, recent increases in reporting, as a result of improved public awareness and professional training, reveal that sexual molestation of children is a widespread and serious form of child maltreatment. Moreover, it is not limited by racial, ethnic, or economic boundaries—sexual molestation of children exists in all strata of society.[35]

Experts on the problem of child abuse estimate that there are 4 million child molesters in the United States, about 95 percent of whom are men. The majority make no distinction between natural and stepchildren, and 20 percent molest both boys and girls. A disproportionate number of child molesters are outwardly religious and manage to hide their deviant behavior from their spouses, colleagues, and closest friends. Most *pedophiles* began as teenagers to molest children (McCall 1984).[36]

It began for me when I was nine years old. My brothers and sisters had been sent to bed; I was getting a special treat by being allowed to stay up and watch TV with my stepfather. I was reading our small-town newspaper and was puzzled about a word. "Daddy, what does assault mean? Is it like when the *Three Strooges* say 'I've never been so *assaulted* in my life?'" He had a strange expression on his face. "I'll show you what it means," he said. He took me into my parent's bedroom—when mother was waitressing the evening shift. He removed my yellow pajamas and took off his clothes. Nothing was ever the same for me again (McCall 1984, p. 35).

Experts on the problem of child abuse contend that it is just as common in urban areas as in rural communities, and among middle class families as among the poor. Nor are victims only girls. Homosexual abuse of boys by adult males in the family is more common than is generally recognized, as is incest between mother and son. There are simply no reliable statistics. For example, incest between mother and son is hardly ever reported (Magnuson 1983).

Experts in the field of child abuse find that, behind the mask of normalcy, the pedophile is emotionally retarded and feels inadequate and threatened in the adult world (McCall 1984). Some psychiatrists find that the incestuous father (natural or stepfather) who sexually molests his own children or stepchildren falls into one of four different categories, depending upon the age of the children:

There are four very distinctive kinds of incestuous fathers. The natural father who is incestuous with pre-pubescent kids (0–12) is likely to be psychotic; the one with post-pubescent kids (13–17) is likely to be disabled or unemployed, and his son or daughter takes the wife's role. The incestuous step-father who molests the younger kids is a pedophile who is likely to have abused other kids . . . and married the woman because of her children. The step-father who is sexual with teen-age kids usually has some criminal history and other anti-social behavior (Seeley 1984, p. 49).[37]

---

[35]U.S. Department of Health and Human Services, *Child Abuse: Incest, Assault, and Sexual Exploitation* (1981).

[36]A *pedophile* is a person who derives satisfaction from sexual contact with a child. Pedophilia is universally regarded as a perversion (see Chapter 4).

---

[37]Richard Seeley is Director of the Program for Sexual Aggressives at the Minnesota Security Hospital.

The most common form of sexual molestation is father-daughter (either natural or stepfather). This usually starts when the daughter is in the preschool years, often at age two or younger. The most common pattern involves an escalation (over the years) from genital fondling to fellatio, to copulation. Physical coercion may occur, but it is not as common as psychological persuasion. This pattern escalates until the daughter reaches adolescence, which is usually the point at which the abuse is discovered. During adolescence the girl begins to understand more about sex, and she begins to question and resent sexual maltreatment. She has also developed a network of resources outside the family by this time, and therefore, can usually find someone to confide in. Report to an outside agency then follows.[38]

However, it is extremely common for girls to feel intense guilt and fear after they reveal sexual abuse and they then often withdraw their accusations. It is not easy for the adolescent to break out of a family pattern such as a secret conspiracy.[39]

A second pattern of sexual molestation (not as common) begins in adolescence. It is normal for daughters to "practice" awareness of their emerging sexuality with their fathers, and in most instances fathers respond appropriately, with affection but no overt sexual contact. However, in some cases the fathers respond inappropriately. Generally the father in such a case is experiencing midlife concerns about sexual confidence or attractiveness. which are often reinforced by conflicts with his wife and doubts about competency in other areas of his life, such as his work, his social network, or his physical abilities. He may therefore not respond appropriately to his daughter's normal adolescent sexual testing.

Instead he may turn to her for a sexual relation that he perceives as less emotionally demanding, one in which he can feel "in charge." The adolescent girl's reaction may be one of fascination that her sexual provocativeness has elicited a response, coupled with a sense of guilt.

Whether the pattern of sexual abuse is initiated in adolescence or follows the more typical pattern of developing gradually from early childhood, it is equally difficult for the girl to stop it, unless she can get help.[40]

Child abuse—battering, incest and sexual exploitation—is a serious problem in the United States that is just beginning to receive the attention necessary to make significant progress toward prevention and treatment.

SUMMARY

Despite its imperfections, the family is the oldest and toughest of all human institutions; it is essential to a continued existence of a society. Since death is inevitable, new members must be added to balance the loss or the society would cease to exist in the one generation. The family fulfills this function in all societies that have been investigated by cultural anthropologists. A family also plays other key roles in the society: It provides "social placement" for its members, provides for a kinship structure, and in many ways acts as a fundamental unit of social organization.

The term *family* may be used to describe many different kinship groupings. The grouping that consists of two parents living together in a household with one or more minor offspring is called the *nuclear* family. The *polygamous* family consists of two or more nuclear

---

[38]U.S. Department of Health and Human Services, *Adolescent Abuse and Neglect: Intervention Strategies* (1980).
[39]Ibid.

[40]Ibid.

families joined by a multiple marriage. The *extended* family consists of a nuclear family together with various additional relatives living together in one household. The U.S. Bureau of the Census defines a family as "any two or more related people living in one household."

Throughout the world's societies, the most preferred form of the family is the one based on polygynous marriage, consisting of one husband and two or more wives and their children (a form of marriage that is illegal in the United States). The family form based on the polyandrous marriage, consisting of one wife and two or more husbands and their children, is rare in world societies. The most frequently occurring form of the family in world societies is the nuclear family based on a monogamous marriage.

A rapidly growing form of the family in our society is the *blended* family, which is based on a form of marriage that has been called *serial polygamy*. If a married couple with children divorces and then each remarries another person with children, the two new nuclear families blend the children from the earlier marriages. A blended family may have any number of combinations, with the children still retaining ties of allegiance and loyalty to divorced parents in other blended families, so that the structure and interaction may become extraordinarily complex.

The fastest-growing family form in our society is the single-parent family. These are usually headed by women, but an increasing number of single-parent families are headed by men. Among blacks, the single-parent family is the dominant type (59 percent). Most single-parent families are in much worse financial straits than are two-parent families, and there may be additional problems with child care—although the father's absence from home does not necessarily cause severe distress and conflict or leave the mother unable to supervise the children adequately.

Another form of the family that is rapidly increasing in our society is the double-income family, with both parents working outside the home in gainful employment. Only about five families in one hundred now fill the family pattern of the husband-father working outside the household, supporting the family, while the wife-mother looks after the children.

Beginning in the eighteenth century in Great Britain, family form and function began to change significantly because of the move from agriculture to industry. Until this time, the family was a unit of production as well as a unit of consumption. The family educated its children, providing an occupation and an income for its members from childhood to old age, and provided protection for its members. It was also the center of religious life. Even recreation was usually a family function, occurring within the home rather than at a commercial center.

With the advent of industrialization, factories, mills, offices and government agencies began to provide the economic goods and services that were normally provided by the family. Status and prestige stemmed more from individual ability or achievement than from family name. Teachers became responsible for the education of children, a function of protection began to be fulfilled by the police, and unemployment compensation, medicare, welfare, and social security have replaced the functions formerly provided by the family. Professional religious figures have virtually replaced the family's religious functions. All of these changes in family function came about as a result of industrialization, which led to sweeping changes in the individual's way of life. As families moved from farm to urban areas so that the father could go to work in a factory or a mill, family structure and function changed. Women soon followed men into the world of work outside the household, and family size began to drop.

Our contemporary family is still in a period of transition, and patterns that were current a generation ago are no longer the norm. More than half of all married women with school-aged children work; nearly one married couple in two has no children under age eighteen; the incidence of child-free couples is rising; the long-term trend of the birth rate is down, which means that those married couples that do have children have fewer children; the divorce rate is rising, as is the illegitimacy rate and the desertion rate, resulting in the single-parent family becoming the most rapidly growing family form in the United States; the incidence of blended families, single-parent families, and double-income families is rising. All these factors are resulting in a change in the structure and function of American families, leading to a wide diversification of family types.

Despite these changes, the contemporary family remains a basically stable institution, with the rate of family dissolution (by death or divorce) almost precisely the same today as it was a century ago. In fact, the family is even more stable than it was then because of increasing life expectancy.

A curious paradox of family life is that it is often the source of strife as well as of emotional satisfaction. No one knows the full extent of wife battering, husband battering, and child abuse, since most cases are not reported. However, it is estimated that nearly 6 million women are battered by their husbands, ex-husbands, or lovers in any one year and 2 to 4 thousand are beaten to death. The incidence of husband battering is thought to be much lower. The incidence of child abuse is estimated to be as high as 9 million cases per year. The batterers are usually women who themselves were usually battered as children. Sexual molestation, or pedophilia, is usually a male pattern, with the father or step-father molesting female children and teenagers. It is estimated that there are 4 million child molestors in the United States, about 95 percent of whom are men (20 percent molest both boys and girls). A disproportionate number of child molestors

are outwardly religious and manage to hide their deviant behavior successfully.

QUESTIONS

1. About what percentage of our population live in a family setting? About what percentage of American children are born and raised within a family?

2. Give an example of the paradoxical nature of the family.

3. The term *family* is very difficult to define since it can have so many meanings and take so many forms. Discuss the wide range of meanings of the term *family*. Give examples. What does the term *family* mean to you?

4. Define the following: *nuclear* family, *extended* family, *monogamous* family, *polygamous* family, *polygynous* family, *polyandrous* family.

5. What important changes took place in the family as a result of industrialization?

6. The contemporary family in the United States is undergoing a period of change. What are some of the changes that characterize the contemporary family? Give examples.

7. What are some of the special difficulties of the blended family, single-parent family, and double income family?

8. Despite the rising divorce rate and the recent changes in family patterns and functions, the family is still a stable institution in the United States. Discuss the reasons for this stability.

9. Discuss the problem of wife battering in the United States.

10. Discuss the differences between wife battering that is simple brutality, and wife battering that the perpetrator "hitting because he lost."

11. Discuss the problem of husband battering in the United States. Why is so little known

about husband battering? Discuss the differences between these two categories.

SUGGESTIONS FOR FURTHER READINGS

Albin, Mel, and Cavallo, Dominic, eds. *Family Life in America, 1620–2000.* St. James N.Y.: Revisionary Press, 1981.

Aldous, J. *Two Paychecks: Life in Dual-earner Families.* Beverly Hills, Calif.: Sage Publications, 1982.

Becker, G.S. *A Treastise on the Family.* Cambridge, Mass.: Harvard University Press, 1981.

Degler, C.N. *At Odds: Women and Family in America from the Revolution to the Present.* New York: Oxford University Press, 1980.

Geerken, Michael, and Gove, Walter R. *At Home and at Work: The Family's Allocation of Labor.* Beverly Hills, Calif.: Sage Publications 1983.

Gelles, Richard J., and Cornell, Claire Pedrick. *Intimate Violence in Families.* Beverly Hills, Calif.: Sage Publications 1985.

Gelner, C.J.R., and Zigler, E., eds. *Child Abuse: An Agenda for Action.* New York: Oxford University Press, 1980.

Kessler-Harris, Alice. *Out-to-Work: A History of Wage-Earning Women in the United States.* New York: Oxford University Press, 1982.

Nason, Ellen Mara, and Poloma, Margaret M. *Voluntary Childless Couples: The Emergence of a Variant Life Style.* Beverly Hills, Calif.: Sage Publications 1977.

Olson, David H., et al. *Families.* Beverly Hills, Calif.: Sage Publications 1983.

Pepitone-Rockwell, Fran, ed. *Dual-Career Couples.* Beverly Hills, Calif.: Sage Publications 1980.

Reiss, Ira L. *Family Systems in America,* 3rd ed. New York: Holt, Rinehart & Winston, 1980.

Scanzoni, John. *Shaping Tomorrow's Family: Theory and Policy for the 21st Century.* Beverly Hills, Calif.: Sage Publications 1983.

Scott, Donald M., and Wishy, Bernard, eds. *America's Families: A Documentary History.* New York: L Harper & Row, 1982.

Shorter, Edward. *The Making of a Modern Family.* New York: Basic Books, 1975.

Skolnick, Arlene, and Skolnick, Jerome H., eds. *Family in Transition,* 4th ed. Boston: Little, Brown, 1983.

Straus, Murray A., and Hotaling, G.T. *The Social Causes of Husband-Wife Violence.* Minneapolis: University of Minneapolis Press, 1980.

Sussman, Marvin B., and Hess, Beth B., eds. *Women & the Family: Two Decades of Change.* New York: Haworth Press, 1984.

Thorman, G. *Family Violence.* Springfield, Ill.: Thomas, 1980.

Turnbull, Colin. *The Mountain People.* New York: Simon & Schuster, 1973.

CHAPTER 11

Reproduction: The Biological Basis of the Family

Pregnancy
Childbirth
Infertility and Its Treatment
Methods of Birth Control
Abortion

Therefore choose life . . .

Deuteronomy 30:9

A new individual comes into existence when the *gametes* or germ cells—the *sperm* and the *egg*—combine to form a *fertilized egg*. The fertilized egg is a single-celled organism that carries all the genetic characteristics of the sperm and the egg. These genetic characteristics are contained in the DNA molecules that make up the genes,[1] which in turn make up the chromosomes in each cell of the human body.

DNA is composed of building blocks called *nucleotides* (which are a combination of atoms). The DNA in each human chromosome is built from about 5 billion pairs of nucleotides. These 5 billion pairs of nucleotides carry 20 billion "bits" of information. Each bit carries a single unit of information coded in the sequence of atoms and molecules. How much information

---

[1]Deoxyribonucleic acid (DNA) is the chemical basis of life. The information that directs the formation and function of living matter is encoded in long, extremely complex, chainlike molecules that together have a ladderlike structure. The structure and function of DNA were discovered by James Watson and Francis Crick, for which they were awarded the Nobel Prize in medicine and physiology in 1962.

is this? If it were put into printed form, the amount of information contained in one human chromosome would fill 4,000 volumes.[2]

Since there are forty-six chromosomes (and 100,000 genes) in each human cell, the amount of information carried in *each cell*, if it were printed out—for example how to build an eyeball, how to build a brain, and how these two organs interact to provide vision—would fill 184,000 volumes of text.[3] This information is astonishingly miniaturized. The 184,000 volumes of textual information is condensed (in molecular form) into a space about the size of the dot above this *i*.

Once the fertilized egg is created—from the union of the sperm cell and the egg cell, each of which contains twenty-three chromosomes— no new information about its construction is fed into it from the outside. The cell takes in material (such as food, minerals, oxygen), which it then uses to construct further cells (following the "blueprint" in its DNA). The cells become more and more complex and then begin to form *tissue* (groups of cells with a specialized function). The tissue forms the highly complex organs, all of which are separate structures but are integrated to interact with one another to form the entire organism or person.

The early form of the individual constructed in this way (following the instructions in the DNA of each cell) is called a *germinal disc*. The germinal disc continues to grow as the cells divide and subsequent cells become more specialized for about two weeks, at which time the developing individual is called an *embryo*.

Growth by cell division and development of specialized tissue and organs continue until, at about six weeks following conception, the individual is called a *fetus*. After nine months, the original cell has multiplied into billions of cells organized into the countless highly specialized functions of the human body. By adulthood, the original cell has multiplied into 100 trillion cells—each a separate living entity in contact with other cells and relating and interacting with them. It is the totality of these 100 trillion cells that makes up the conscious, functioning creature called the human being. This astonishingly complex structure—conscious, self-directing, questioning the nature of the universe and the meaning of its own existence— stems from the 20 billion bits of information contained in the 5 billion pairs of nucleotides in each of the forty-six chromosomes of the fertilized egg.

In this chapter, we shall trace this development of the individual from the instant of conception to the moment of birth. We shall also look at some of the factors that might prevent or interfere in this development.

PREGNANCY

Conception

At ovulation a mature egg is released from one of the thousands of egg sacs (follicles) that line the exterior walls of the ovaries. The egg then moves from the ovary to the mouth of a fallopian tube. The fallopian tubes are between two and four inches long and are extremely narrow. At their ovarian ends, the diameter is about that of a whisker. The fallopian tube serves a number of functions in reproduction: It is responsible for taking the egg from the rupturing follicle; for providing a hospitable environment for the egg and the sperm in which fertilization is likely to occur, and also for the fertilized egg, which begins a series of cell divisions

---

[2]Twenty billion bits is the equivalent of about 500 million words. This corresponds to about 2 million printed pages, assuming 300 words per page. Assuming about 500 pages per book, this corresponds to 4,000 volumes (Sagan 1977).

[3]If each chromosome contains information that would require 4,000 volumes of print, and there are forty-six chromosomes in the fertilized egg—twenty-three from the sperm cell and twenty-three from the egg cell—this amount of information would fill 184,000 (46 × 4,000) volumes of text if it were printed out.

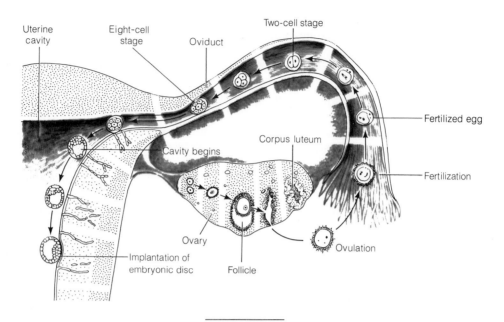

FIGURE 11-1
Ovulation, fertilization, and the germinal
period of pregnancy

here during the early stages of human life; and for transporting the fertilized egg to the uterus, which takes about seven or eight days. Fertilization or conception usually takes place when the egg is about one-third of the distance from the ovary to the uterus. (If conception does not take place, the egg usually disintegrates before reaching the uterus.) The outer walls of the fallopian tube contain muscles that contract and relax rhythmically, creating a wavelike motion, called *peristalsis*, that helps move the fertilized egg along. Aiding this peristaltic movement are the cilia, hairlike structures that line the inner walls of the tube. Their constant undulation creates a current that moves the fertilized egg in the direction of the uterus.

Development of the Germinal Disc

The first two weeks of pregnancy—from the fertilization of an egg until it is firmly embed-

ded in the uterine wall—are called the *germinal period* (see Figure 11-1). During this period, the woman discerns no sign that she is pregnant, and pregnancy can be reliably detected only by a pregnancy test.

By the time the fertilized egg reaches the uterus—about seven or eight days after conception—it has become a multicellular hollow sphere, with an outer layer of cells (the *trophoblast*) and, growing inward from this layer, an inner cluster of cells containing the germinal disc together with other tissue that provides a protective nutrient environment for the developing disc. (It is the germinal disc that will develop into a human being.)

Meanwhile, the uterine wall has thickened and become enriched with blood and a supply of nutrients, in response to hormones triggered by ovulation. The trophoblast embeds itself in this wall by secreting enzymes that erode a cavity in the wall. Tiny tendrils (*chorionic villi*) begin to extend from the trophoblast into the uterine wall—marking the end of the germinal period and the beginning of the *embryonic period* of pregnancy, about two weeks after conception.

Development of the Embryo

About two weeks after conception, the germinal disc begins to assume an animal shape, although its length is still no more than one-twelfth of an inch. It is now called an *embryo*. A *neural plate* forms in what will become the head of the embryo, and *somites*, the spinal segments that will develop into vertebrae, have begun to appear. The heart, at first a single tube, begins to develop by a process of looping and infolding and will soon begin to beat, even before there is any blood to be circulated. A primitive digestive tract also begins to develop.

The chorionic villi burrow into the blood-filled uterine tissue, absorbing nutrients, oxygen, and immunizing agents, and passing back, into the bloodstream of the woman, carbon dioxide and other waste products. However, no blood is mixed between the developing embryo (or later fetus) and the woman. All embryonic (or fetal) blood originates within the embryo (or fetus) itself.

The villi are connected to the embryo by a *body stalk*, which develops from the inner cluster of cells containing the germinal disc. The cluster of cells that develops into the body stalk also develops into the *amnion*, a sac filled with amniotic fluid in which the embryo (and later the fetus) floats—separated from the uterine wall, cushioned against injury and temperature change, and free to move and shift about.[4]

By three weeks, the embryo's tissues have become specialized—differentiating into the *mesoderm*, which will become bone, muscle, and supportive tissue; the *endoderm*, from which the alimentary tract and digestive organs develop; and the *ectoderm*, which becomes skin and neural tissue. Circulation of blood also begins in the embryo and in the body stalk by the third week following conception.

By the end of the third week, the embryo has grown to about one-seventh of an inch in length and has a clearly distinguishable head and spinal cord and buds of arms and legs. Lenses are forming in the eye areas, the location of ears has been marked off, a few isolated nerves have appeared, and various other glands and organs are taking rudimentary shape.

About the fourth week, the woman becomes aware of the possibility that she is pregnant. (Figure 11-2 illustrates the development of the embryo to the fourth week.) The woman's menstrual period is now about two weeks overdue, and she may have noticed a heaviness and fullness in her breasts and an enlargement and darkening of her areolae and nipples (which may exude a secretion when pressed). She may also have to urinate more often than usual because of the pressure on the bladder from the expanding uterus. In the early weeks of pregnancy, she may experience nausea and vomiting.[5]

By the fifth week, the body stalk has developed into the *umbilical cord*. The umbilical cord, which contains blood vessels that link the circulatory system of the embryo (and later the fetus) to the uterine wall, is a rubbery, transparent tube containing two arteries and one vein. The rush of blood (about four miles per hour) through the cord keeps it relatively

---

[4]This cluster of cells also develops into the yolk sac, an organ that is largely vestigial among mammals. (Among birds and amphibians, whose fertilized eggs are separate from the mother, the yolk sac serves as the source of nutrition for the developing organism.) At first, the yolk sac is a large protrusion from the midsection of the embryo, but it grows gradually smaller and is eventually integrated into the umbilical cord. For a

brief period, it appears that the yolk sac aids in the manufacture of blood cells, a process that is gradually taken over by the developing liver and bone marrow.

[5]All these symptoms can also occur in "false pregnancy," a psychosomatic response to various psychological stimuli (including fear of pregnancy). False pregnancy may even counterfeit the gradual swelling of the abdomen for a full nine months.

1. About 15 days after fertilization.

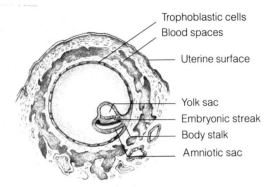

Trophoblastic cells
Blood spaces

Uterine surface

Yolk sac
Embryonic streak
Body stalk
Amniotic sac

2. Buildup of placental villi, about
two and a half weeks after
fertilization.

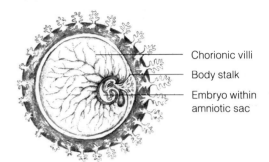

Chorionic villi
Body stalk
Embryo within
amniotic sac

3. Dwindling of yolk sac;
embryo about three weeks old.
Umbilical vessels are forming.

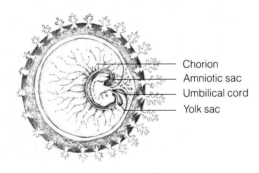

Chorion
Amniotic sac
Umbilical cord
Yolk sac

4. Embryo at about four weeks.
Embryo and placenta well formed.

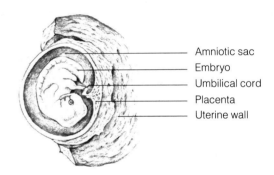

Amniotic sac
Embryo
Umbilical cord
Placenta
Uterine wall

FIGURE 11-2
The development of the embryo

stiff and prevents it from entangling (or strangling) the embryo or fetus.[6]

Several early signs of pregnancy that a physician can detect at this time are changes in the shape of the abdomen, darkened color of the vaginal area, softening of the cervix and the area between the cervix and the uterus, and enlargement of the uterus.

Pregnancy Tests

In the early (germinal disc and embryonic) stages of pregnancy, which last for about five weeks, only laboratory tests can determine without doubt whether a woman is pregnant. All of these tests are designed to discover

---

[6]At full term, the umbilical cord is about twenty inches long and about three-fourths of an inch in diameter.

whether the gonadotrophic hormone hCG is present in the urine or the blood of the woman.[7] If this hormone is detected in sufficient amounts in the urine or the blood, the woman is pregnant. The tests are based on the fact that the early chorionic villi of the implanted ovum secrete hCG, which is then excreted in the woman's urine and blood (Krupp et al. 1985).[8]

Pregnancy tests are most accurate when performed in a certified laboratory. However, the do-it-yourself pregnancy tests now on the market are fairly reliable. They are also inexpensive and can be picked up, without prescription, in any drugstore. They are intended for use as early as nine days after a missed period and are about 80 percent accurate.

Early diagnosis makes it possible to end the pregnancy—if desired—by a process that takes just a few minutes in a physician's office and requires no anesthesia. Since the patient has been pregnant for only a few days, it is usually regarded not as abortion but as "menstrual regulation," or "menstrual extraction" (see the section, "Preventing Implantation after Conception" later in this chapter).

Development of the Fetus

About the sixth week after conception, the *fetal period* begins. During the fetal period, the organs and structural systems that budded during the embryonic period are further developed and refined. Moreover, the primitive gonadal tissue now begins to secrete hormones

---

[7]hCG is an abbreviation for the full name of the gonadotrophic hormone: human chorionic gonadotrophic hormone.

[8]*Urine slide tests* are the fastest, easiest, and least expensive pregnancy tests and are accurate for most women at about twenty-seven days after conception or when a menstrual period is about thirteen days late. Because hCG appears earlier in the blood than in the urine, blood tests are more sensitive than urine tests; they can detect low levels of hCG even before the first missed period and are accurate beginning seven to seventeen days following conception. Pregnancy test results can be positive, negative, or inconclusive, and must sometimes be repeated (Pincus and Wolhandler 1984, Reeder and Mastroianni 1983).

that direct the differentiation of tissue into male (if there is an XY chromosomal structure) or female (if the chromosomal structure is XX), as we have seen in Chapter 2. At this time it is possible to discover the sex of the fetus using the technique of *amniocentesis* (see the section, "Prenatal Testing of the Fetus" later in this chapter).

By the tenth week following conception, the fetus begins to make breathing movements and reflex movements of the lips resembling sucking. The external genitalia are now differentiated into male or female forms if development is proceeding normally (see Chapter 2).

During the third month following conception, the fetus reaches a length of about three inches. The features of the face become more differentiated: The lips take shape, the nose begins to stand out, and the eyelids are formed, although they remain fused. The fingers and the toes are well developed, and the fingernails and toenails are forming. The primitive kidneys begin to secrete small amounts of urine. The fetal heart can be heard by the twelfth week with an ultrasonic stethoscope.

By the fourteenth week, spontaneous movements of the fetus can be detected by a stethoscope. The first fetal movements of which the woman herself is aware do not occur until about the seventeenth week, however. The fetal movements that are detected by the mother are called *quickening* and have great historical and theological significance, since they were thought by St. Augustine to indicate the entrance of the soul into the unborn child and the moment when the fetus may be considered a human being.

By the fourth month, the chorionic villi have disappeared, except for those that are functioning in direct contact with the uterine wall and the umbilical cord. These villi, together with the portion of uterine tissue in which they are embedded, become the *placenta*. The placenta holds the fetus in place in the uterus while continuing and increasing the nurturing

Alan Carey/The Image Works

A 15-month-old tries to feel her soon-to-be-born sibling kick.

functions that the villi served. On the side connected to the uterine lining, the placenta is a spongy mass of blood vessels; on the other side, to which the fetus is connected by the umbilical cord, the placenta is smooth. At full term the placenta weighs about a pound and is about eight inches in diameter and one inch thick.

As the villi that are not connected to the uterine tissue disappear, the trophoblast, now called the *chorion*, remains as a sac around the amniotic sac and gradually fuses with the amnion as the fetus and the amniotic sac grow larger.

In the fourth month, the fetus grows to about six inches and weighs about four ounces. Most of its bones have been formed, although they are still cartilage and will not be completely hardened into a bone (a process called *ossification*) until many years after birth. The fetus begins to develop increasingly complex func-

tions during the fourth month. Hormonal secretion becomes greater, the liver begins to secrete bile, and digestion starts to take place.

In the fifth month quickening becomes quite apparent to the woman, first as a mild fluttering and later as solid kicks against the inside of her abdomen. Any nausea she may have had is probably gone, and she is now in the most comfortable period of pregnancy.

During the sixth month, the fetus grows to about a foot in length and about twenty ounces in weight. The eyelids are now separated and may be opened and closed. Eyelashes and eyebrows begin to appear. The fetus now makes slight, but regular, breathing movements. A fetus of this age is not just a smaller version of a full-term infant, however. If the baby is born at this time, the chances of survival are very slim (Newland 1981).

By seven months, the fetus is about fifteen inches long and weighs about two and a half

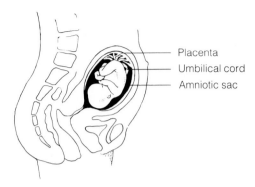

Placenta
Umbilical cord
Amniotic sac

Fifth month

Fetus measures about 10 to 12 inches
and weighs ½ to 1 pound.

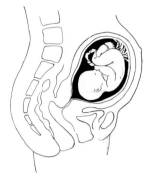

Sixth month

Fetus measures 11 to 14 inches
and weighs 1¼ to 1½ pounds.

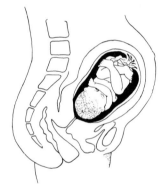

Seventh month

Fetus measures 14 to 17 inches
and weighs 2½ to 8 pounds.

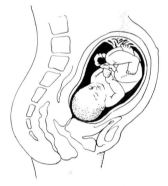

Eighth month

Fetus is 16½ to 18 inches long
and weighs 5 to 8 pounds.

FIGURE 11-3
The development of the fetus

pounds or more. If the baby is born now there is a *good* chance for survival with the aid of specialized attention and equipment.[9]

A baby born in the eighth month of pregnancy has a *very good* chance of survival, since development is virtually complete. In the eighth and ninth months, changes consist mainly of a very rapid gain in weight (an average of nearly half a pound a week). (Figure 11-3 illustrates the development of the fetus from the fifth to the eighth month.)

During the final three months of pregnancy, the woman probably feels generally healthy,

---

[9]Up until a few years ago the mortality rate for premature neonates weighing under thiry-five ounces at birth was 80–85 percent. Because of advances in their care, the mortality rate has dropped to 15–20 percent (Sunshine 1984).

Collection of the Artist

Pregnancy is often a time of happiness, contentment, and feelings of fulfillment.
Joanne Leonard: *Sonia 1966*

but she is likely to be uncomfortable because of the crowding of her organs caused by her expanding uterus and because the increasing weight of the fetus causes some problems in moving and maintaining equilibrium. Many women feel awkward and cumbersome in these months and look forward to childbirth as liberation. Many others, however, report that the later stages of pregnancy are a time of unparalleled physical and mental well-being (Kitzinger 1978).

Prenatal Influences

It has long been known that biological and psychological factors affecting the woman's body also have an effect on the development of the fetus. The most obvious of these factors, of course, is nutrition. The pregnant woman's diet must enable her body to pass on to the fetus an adequate supply of building materials necessary for its development. (If her diet contains, for example, too little calcium or vitamin A, the teeth of the baby will develop improperly and no amount of postnatal care will repair the damage.) Nutrition in pregnancy significantly affects maternal health and infant size and well-being (Krupp et al. 1985).

Since the placenta (the organ that attaches the umbilical cord to the uterine wall) allows the passage of drugs and many viruses and bacteria (as well as food and oxygen), any drug taken or illness contracted by the woman during pregnancy is potentially harmful to the fetus. For example, pregnant women who smoke cigarettes have a significantly greater incidence of still births and neonatal deaths (*U. S. Surgeon General's Report* 1985). Smoking is also significantly correlated to low birth weight; moderate smokers have twice the incidence of small babies as compared with nonsmokers. Mothers who smoke more than twenty cigarettes a day give birth to babies weighing less than 5½ pounds two to three times more often than mothers who do not smoke. Some 900,000 infants are born each year to American women who smoke.[10]

A pregnant woman who drinks alcohol is also liable to damage the fetus. The condition known as *fetal alcoholic syndrome* may begin as early as the third week after conception (Sulik et al. 1981). Fetal alcoholic syndrome is now the leading cause of birth defects (including mental retardation) in the United States.[11] The effects of alcohol are intensified if the woman smokes, although the effects of alcohol occur independently of other variables such as poor eating habits and smoking (*U.S. Surgeon General's Report* 1985, Fried and Oxorn 1980). (In addition, alcohol is known to enter breast milk readily and thus be transmitted to a nursing infant, so it is not advisable for nursing mothers to drink alcohol.)

There is evidence that aspirin may cause birth defects if taken during the first three months of pregnancy. It can also accumulate in the fetal bloodstream after this time, causing bleeding problems in the newborn infant. The incidence of infant deaths and stillbirths has been found to be nearly three times as high among babies whose mothers took aspirin as little as once a week during pregnancy (Turner and Collins 1975).[12]

Research has found that even caffeine (contained in coffee, cocoa, tea, and cola drinks) has been linked to birth defects (King et al. 1980). It is also suspected, but not definitely established, that other drugs (even such commonly used substances as diuretics) may damage the fetus (King et al. 1980). Apparently, for a pregnant woman who wants to make sure her child will be healthy, the only really safe course is to avoid all drugs except those prescribed by a physician in case of absolute necessity.

Among infections that the pregnant woman may pass on to the fetus are typhoid, influenza, diphtheria, syphilis, and German measles. German measles (rubella) is particularly dangerous, especially if contracted during the first three months of pregnancy, since this almost invariably causes brain damage, deafness, or blindness in the embryo or fetus.[13] Indeed, a woman should consult a physician about any illness she contracts at any stage of pregnancy, no matter how mild the effects seem to her.

Similarly, x-rays and other forms of radiation are damaging to the embryo or fetus and must be avoided if possible.[14] A study conducted at Johns Hopkins Hospital showed that the incidence of children with Down's syndrome[15] born to older women was closely related to the numbers of diagnostic and therapeutic

---

[10]U.S. Public Health Service, "Fetal Tobacco Syndrome" (1985). Cigarette smoking by the father will also contribute to fetal damage. An increased rate of perinatal deaths and birth defects has been found among the progeny of men who smoke tobacco. The explanation apparently lies in the fact that cigarette smokers are more likely than nonsmokers to produce abnormal sperm (*Science News*, April 18, 1981, p. 247).

[11]U.S. Public Health Service, "Fetal Alcohol Syndrome" (January 13, 1984).

---

[12]U.S. National Center for Health Statistics, "Advance Report of Final Natality Statistics, 1979" (1981).

[13]Fortunately, the use of rubella vaccine has greatly reduced the number of victims born with serious defects because their mothers had contracted German measles (U.S. Public Health Service, "Congenital Malformations" 1984).

[14]It has become routine in many hospitals to administer a pregnancy test before taking x-rays of a nubile woman.

[15]The incidence of Down's syndrome, which once accounted for a third of all birth defects, dropped by 25 percent in the early 1980s, apparently because of prenatal detection (using amniocentesis) and abortion (U.S. Public Health Service, "Congenital Malformations" 1984).

medical and dental x-rays to which the women had been exposed during their lifetimes (Reeder and Mastroianni 1983). There is no safe range of exposure, although x-rays must sometimes be taken for diagnostic purposes.

Modern science is also learning more and more about psychological factors that affect the relation of the woman and the fetus. Research has revealed that emotional stress in a pregnant woman can alter her body chemistry in ways that may be transmitted to the embryo or fetus and affect its development.

Prenatal Testing of the Fetus

The past decade has seen a revolution in the prenatal diagnosis of chromosomal and genetic diseases. Prospective parents can now learn through the technique of *amniocentesis* whether their unborn child has any of a wide variety of chromosomal or genetic disorders. The nearly 6 percent of women whose fetuses are found to be defective thus can either have a therapeutic abortion or prepare for the birth of a defective child.[16] The 94 percent of women whose fetuses are found normal are spared months of anxiety over whether their infants will be normal.

Amniocentesis, which is usually done in about the fifteenth week of pregnancy on an outpatient basis in a hospital or a physician's office, is a remarkably safe as well as effective procedure.[17] A slender, hollow needle is inserted through the woman's abdomen into the uterus, and a small amount of amniotic fluid is drawn off. This amniotic fluid contains cells from the fetus's skin, eyes, and digestive tract.[18] The cells are cultured for three to four weeks in a nutrient broth made from fetal calf serum, antibiotics, protein, and salt. When they have multiplied to about a thousand cells, the chromosomes are examined for abnormality.

Amniocentesis is especially important in detecting such serious abnormalities as Down's syndrome, sickle cell anemia,[19] and Tay-Sachs disease.[20]

Determining the sex of a fetus is a key step in prenatal diagnosis of genetic disorders. For example, if the fetus is female it is extremely unlikely to develop muscular dystrophy. Fetal sex is found by analyzing a sample of cells obtained by amniocentesis.

Determining the Rh factor in a pregnant woman's blood is another important diagnostic procedure. About one woman in seven has Rh-negative antibodies,[21] which cross the placenta into the fetus's bloodstream and destroy the Rh-positive blood cells. Testing for the Rh factor is now a simple process, and since 1969 a medical treatment (RHOGAM) has been available that prevents the mother's immunity

---

[16]As yet, physicians remain largely powerless to cure even minor genetic defects, even though specialists have learned to diagnose many such problems long before birth (Enkin and Chalmers 1982).

[17]In large city hospitals specializing in prenatal testing, about one fetus in 400 dies as a result of amniocentesis—a risk factor of 0.25 percent (Pincus et al. 1984).

[18]Before the three-inch needle is inserted, the physician obtains a picture of the fetus and the placenta using ultrasound waves, inaudible sound pulses in the frequency range of 20,000 to 10 million cycles per second. The sound pulses are sent through the body, and their echoes are viewed electronically. Ultrasound provides the most direct observation of the human fetus and is in widespread obstetrical use, although some researchers are concerned that it might have subtle detrimental effects (*Science News*, February 18, 1984, p. 102). In the technique, acoustic pulses are sent into the pregnant woman's body from a probe applied to her abdominal skin. A computer analyzes the pulses that are reflected back to the skin and can reveal structures as small as the pupil of an eye of a second-trimester fetus (Miller 1985). Recent research has found that ultrasound scans of pregnant women should only be performed when medically warranted and not on a routine basis (U.S. National Institutes of Health Consensus Development Conference, "Antenatal Diagnosis" (1979).

[19]Sickle cell anemia is an inherited, incurable disorder that causes the body to produce abnormal hemoglobin; it primarily affects blacks, but it is also found in whites, especially those of Mediterranean origin.

[20]The victims of Tay-Sachs disease appear normal until about six months of age, but they invariably die before age five. There is no known cure. Tay-Sachs disease is thought to have originated in a Jewish community in Europe in the Middle Ages and is therefore more prevalent among Jews of Eastern European origin than among the general population.

[21]Thirteen percent of white Americans, 7 percent of blacks, and 1 percent of Asians have Rh-negative blood (Young 1982).

Multiple Births

Normally only one egg is released by the ovary, but occasionally two or more are released and the result may be a multiple birth. More rarely, a fertilized egg divides into two separate structures before proceeding in its development, and two individuals develop from the single egg. Twins occur approximately every ninety-three white births and every seventy-three nonwhite births. Triplets occur approximately once in every 9,400 births, while quadruplets occur only once in every 620,000 births.

Twins produced by the fertilization of two separate eggs are called *fraternal twins*. Since they are the product of separate eggs, separate sperm, and separate sets of genes, fraternal twins are no more closely related genetically than any other siblings, except that they happen to be born at the same time. The incidence of fraternal twins varies with unknown environmental factors, racial group, genotype (family heredity) of the mother, and age of the mother. The incidence of fraternal twins increases with maternal age up to a maximum of thirty-seven years and then falls sharply. Certain families have a higher incidence of fraternal twins than the average.

Twins produced by the splitting of a single fertilized egg are called *identical twins*. Since they are the products of a single egg, a single sperm, and the same set of genes, identical twins are indistinguishable biologically—although environmental factors may cause differences in their physical and psychological development. In the United States (and elsewhere) about 33 percent of twins are identical (Reeder and Mastroianni 1983).

---

system from producing antibodies that attack the red blood cells of the fetus (Reeder and Mastroianni 1983).[22]

CHILDBIRTH

Toward the end of pregnancy, the fetus usually changes position so that the head is in the lower part of the uterus. This may occur as early as four weeks before birth, or it may not occur until the onset of *labor*, which is the process by which the baby is propelled from the woman's body. Labor consists of involuntary contractions of the longitudinal uterine muscles, voluntary contractions of the abdominal muscles, and relaxation of the sphincter muscles

---

[22]It is estimated that before the introduction of this treatment at least 10,000 infants died from Rh complications every year in the United States, with another 20,000 suffering major birth defects (Reeder and Mastroianni 1983).

of the cervix. By these means, the baby is gradually squeezed out of the uterus and through the cervix and vagina.

Human births are usually single, but multiple births do occur, the most common of which is fraternal twins. (See the vignette, "Multiple Births.")

The beginning of labor is signaled by recurrent contractions of the uterine muscles. Initially these occur at regular intervals of about fifteen to twenty minutes and are rather mild. As labor progresses, the contractions become more intense and the time between them shortens, eventually to about two or three minutes.

During the last weeks of pregnancy, the woman may experience frequent uterine contractions that do *not* signal the beginning of labor. She may mistake these "false labor" contractions for true labor and check in to the hospital prematurely. Several signs help distinguish true from false labor. One sign is an increase in the intensity and frequency of the contractions as well as a continuing regularity. By itself, however, this sign does not necessarily indicate that true labor has begun. A second sign (called the "show") is the discharge of a small plug of mucus, often spotted with blood, from the cervix. This mucous plug helps prevent infection from entering the uterus through the cervix during pregnancy; it is released in the early hours of labor as the cervix begins to relax and dilate. The release of the plug is followed by varying amounts of bloody discharge—the nearer the onset of labor, the greater the amount of discharge. A third sign is the release of amniotic fluid when the amniotic sac ruptures. When this occurs, the onset of labor is usually imminent. However, the only certain indication that true labor is actually commencing is the dilatation of the cervix.

Obstetricians recognize three stages of childbirth. The first and longest begins with the onset of uterine contractions and involves dilatation of the cervix to permit passage of the baby's head. This stage usually lasts about six to eighteen hours for first births, and about three to ten hours for subsequent births. In our society, when uterine contractions become very regular and are five to ten minutes apart, the woman is usually taken to a hospital. There the cervix is examined often by the obstetrician or obstetrical nurses until it reaches a diameter of about ten centimeters and the baby's head starts to press through. At this point the woman is usually moved to the delivery room, and the first stage of childbirth merges into the second.[23]

The second stage of labor—the stage of expulsion—begins with the complete dilatation of the cervix and ends with the delivery of the baby. Many hospitals now routinely monitor the fetal heart rate and the uterine contractions with internal and external electronic pickups during the second stage of labor. In high-risk labor, such as prematurity, the simultaneous recording of uterine contractions and fetal heart rate is an enormous aid in recognizing and managing difficulties before they become critical (Reeder and Mastroianni 1983, Haverkamp 1981). Another useful instrument is the fetal heart detector, portable ultrasound equipment that enables one to hear signals from the fetal heart beginning about the twelfth week. When used during labor, the fetal heart detector can be a valuable aid in monitoring the condition of the fetus, although its safety in routine use has yet to be proven.[24]

The woman can speed the birth process during the second stage of labor by tightening her diaphragm and her abdominal and back muscles to aid the uterine muscles in pushing the baby through the cervix. The woman's active participation at this point also seems to help reduce her discomfort. It has been found that sitting up during the delivery, using gravity to help expel the baby, makes the birth process easier for both the mother and the child. (For centuries women in preliterate societies have used the squatting position to give birth to babies.)

It is also being recognized that fewer drugs are needed to control pain when the woman is sitting up during the delivery process (Haire 1981). This discovery is very important, since there is apparently a strong relation between the use of pain-killing drugs administered immediately preceding or during labor, and neurological problems in the infant (King et al. 1980). These harmful effects to the infant may persist throughout the first year of life and in many cases are evident years later. For example, these children are often retarded in

---

[23]If the woman has elected to deliver in an *alternative birth center*, she remains in the same room throughout her labor and delivery and postpartum care.

[24]Because routine use of the fetal heart detector has not significantly decreased the newborn death rate or the incidence of brain-damaged children, some authorities now feel that its use should be limited to specific high-risk groups (U.S. National Institutes of Health Consensus Development Conference, "Antenatal Diagnosis" (1979); Haverkamp and Orleans 1982).

cognitive development and use of language, as compared with children whose mothers did not receive drugs (Henig 1978).

When the baby appears at the vaginal opening, the head turns so that the back of the skull emerges first. If it seems likely that the size of the emerging head will tear the vaginal tissues, the obstetrician makes an incision (*episiotomy*) at the top of the perineum to enlarge the opening (an incision heals more quickly than a tear).[25] Once the back of the skull has been squeezed out, the rest of the head quickly follows, face down and draining. While supporting the head with one hand and drawing gently as the shoulders slip out, the obstetrician uses a finger on the other hand to remove mucus from the baby's mouth so that it will not be aspirated (inhaled) with the baby's first breath.

Because the head and shoulders of the baby are the largest part of the body, once they have passed through the vagina the torso and legs slip out quickly and easily, followed by the umbilical cord, which is still attached to the placenta. The obstetrician suctions the remaining mucus out of the baby's mouth and throat with a small syringe and then usually places the baby on the mother's abdomen, where the weight helps in the later expulsion of the afterbirth.

As the baby lies on the mother's abdomen, the obstetrician holds the umbilical cord, feeling for the pulsations of its blood vessels to stop. When they do, the cord is clamped off an inch or two from the baby's abdomen, and a second clamp is placed about four inches from the first. The cord is then cut midway between the two clamps. (The stump later dries and drops off.)

Nearly 95 percent of births involve the normal *vertex presentation*, just described, in which the baby's head emerges first (Reeder and Mastroianni 1983). The remaining 5 percent are more difficult deliveries because the baby's buttocks (*breech presentation*), shoulders (*shoulder presentation*), foot (*incomplete breach*), or face (*brow presentation*) emerges first.

Oversized babies can cause difficulty since the head must pass between the bones of the mother's pelvic arch. If the baby is too large or if the mother's or baby's physical condition makes the stress of childbirth dangerous, the baby is delivered by *cesarean section* (so-called because of the legend that Julius Caesar was born in this fashion), an operation in which delivery is made by cutting through the mother's abdominal and uterine walls.

The average male baby weighs about seven and a half pounds, and the average female baby weighs about seven pounds (Reeder and Mastroianni 1983).

If uterine contractions weaken or stop during labor, the baby may have to be delivered by forceps, tongs that fit around the baby's head and enable the obstetrician to assist in the baby's emergence. In the vast majority of cases, forceps are used only when the baby's head is visible or almost so (*low forceps*). If the head is not yet through the cervix, the procedure is known as *high forceps*. The use of high forceps is never indicated unless the cervix is completely dilated, and even then the procedure is extremely dangerous for both mother (possibly causing hemorrhage and infection) and baby (possibly causing disfiguration and brain damage) (Reeder and Mastroianni 1983).

As soon as the cord is cut, antibiotic ophthalmic ointment or one drop of silver nitrate solution is applied to each of the neonate's eyes to prevent *ophthalmia neonatorum*, a severe eye disease that can occur in a newborn baby if an infection is picked up while passing through the birth canal. (The infection is frequently gonococcal.) This treatment is so important that it is mandatory by law in all fifty states. Identifying bands are then fastened around the baby's wrists and ankles. Usually the baby's

---

[25]It should be noted, however, that some authorities now feel that there is no justification for routine episiotomy—that there will be little tearing if the woman is squatting, or if her perineum is carefully massaged and relaxed with warm oil and wet compresses (Banta and Thacker 1982).

footprint is placed on the same identifying card as the mother's thumbprint.

One minute after delivery and again five minutes after delivery, the baby is rated on an evaluation scale called the *Apgar* scoring system, a useful and precise way of assessing the newborn's condition at birth. In this assessment, the newborn is given a rating of 0, 1, or 2 in each of the following five indexes: heart rate, respiratory effort, muscle tone, reflex irritability, and skin color. The optimum Apgar score is, thus, 10.

In 1981, about half of all American infants, white and black, received high one-minute Apgar scores, and almost nine in ten received high five-minute scores. However, black infants were twice as likely to receive low Apgar scores at one and five minutes after delivery according to natality statistics.[26] Apgar scores are useful to the pediatrician in observing the child's development and diagnosing any health problems that may emerge (Young 1982).

The third and final stage of childbirth occurs two to twenty minutes after delivery and consists of the expulsion of the afterbirth—that is, the placenta, the amniotic sac, the chorionic membranes, and the remainder of the umbilical cord. (See Figure 11-4.) The obstetrician carefully examines the afterbirth for signs of abnormality and to make certain that all of it has been expelled. While this is going on, the mother is usually given hormone injections to hasten the shrinkage of her uterus and to stimulate her milk production.[27] If she does not

wish to breast-feed the baby, she is given medication that will help dry up her milk. Her abdomen may also be kneaded to help restore tone to the uterine muscles. Meanwhile the baby is washed, wrapped in a warming blanket, placed in a crib, and taken to the nursery to be observed carefully. Or the baby may be kept in a crib at the mother's side until she leaves the delivery room. The mother is then transferred to a postpartum unit to rest and be observed. If she has elected to have "rooming-in" (a private room where her baby may also stay with her), her baby is transferred with her and cared for by both nursery and postpartum staff, as well as by the mother.

If the woman chooses to deliver in an *alternative birth center* (a special area of the maternity unit in the hospital), her labor and delivery, postpartum care, and nursery care take place in the same room, which is large and comfortable and designed to allow the husband to stay with her. This involvement of the husband is the preferred choice of many women who apply early in pregnancy for acceptance into the alternative birth center. Prior to acceptance the woman must be examined by her physician to make sure that she is not in a high-risk category,[28] and that she understands what is involved in this type of childbirth. In the alternative birth center the newborn receives more attention and care from the family than are provided in the communal nursery. The mother becomes actively involved with

---

[26]Mothers of black babies were less likely than those of white babies to have received prenatal care during pregnancy, and this shows up clearly in the birth weights of black and white babies. Of babies born to black women, 12.5 percent were of low birth weight, compared to 5.7 percent of those born to white women in 1981. (U.S. National Center for Health Statistics, "Live Births, by Attendant and Place of Delivery, and Median and Low Birth Weight, by Race: 1950 to 1981" 1985).

[27]The incidence of breast-feeding more than doubled from 1970 to 1981, from less than one in four mothers to more than one in two mothers—following discoveries that breast-fed babies have a higher resistance to infections with a much lower risk of contracting almost all common childhood diseases. It is also thought to encourage better development of the dental

arch, preventing the need for future orthodonture. In addition, breast-feeding is more satisfying psychologically for both the mother and the neonate (Hatcher et al. 1984, Coleman 1984, La Leche League International 1981).

[28]A woman is put in a high-risk category if prenatal screening identifies such hazards as prematurity, a breech or transverse position of the baby, multiple births, an Rh problem, a too small pelvis, diabetes, high blood pressure, or an active herpes infection. One-third of the newborns afflicted with either herpes I or herpes II virus die from the illness, and one-fourth of the survivors suffer brain damage. It is important to note, however, that most women with herpes deliver healthy babies through vaginal delivery; only an *active* herpes episode within a few days preceding delivery could be dangerous for the infant (*Science News*, December 24, 1983, p. 413).

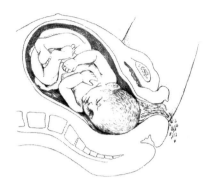

Contractions and breaking
of the amniotic sac

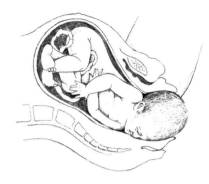

Dilation of the cervix

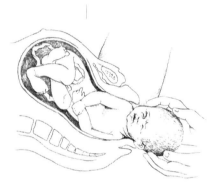

Delivery of the head

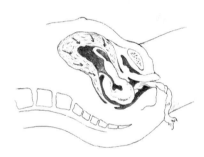

Uterine contractions

FIGURE 11-4
Childbirth

the baby almost immediately after birth, and the father and the siblings can share the experience.

There is apparently a particularly important period immediately following delivery during which *bonding* will occur if mother and baby have sufficient close tactile (skin-to-skin) contact. Mothers who have early and extended contact during the first hours after birth demonstrate a higher quality of child care, a greater capacity for mothering, and a stronger commitment to the child than mothers who do not have this early contact (Marano 1981, Spezzano and Waterman 1977, Klaus and Ken-

nell 1976).[29] (For a further discussion of bonding, see Chapter 12.)

The woman may also elect to enter a *free-standing birth center* instead of a hospital. Free-standing birth centers were developed to help offset the rising cost of maternity care in hospitals, where even a routine delivery with the

---

[29]A disproportionate number of premature babies are battered by their parents, and one of the contributing factors for this seems to be the prolonged separation of mothers and babies that is often routine following premature births. Such separation can interfere with the bonding that usually occurs between the mother and the newborn (Marano 1981).

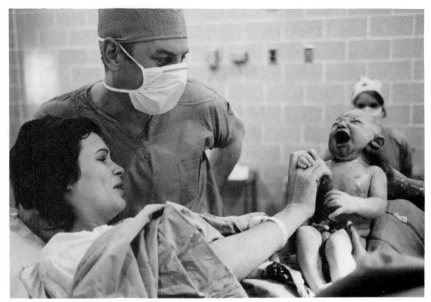

Mary Ellen Mark/Archive Pictures Inc.

Many hospitals allow and even encourage the father to share in the birth experience.

mother staying just twenty-four hours is very costly. There were more than a hundred of these centers in the United States in 1982, and their popularity is increasing (Lubic 1983). They are staffed by physicians, skilled nurse practitioners, and midwives, and are usually situated near a major hospital.

Finally, the mother may deliver the baby at home. This, however, is unusual in the United States, and may be dangerous, since emergency facilities and procedures are not available if the birth does not go smoothly.

High-risk women may require cesarean sections in order to deliver safely—an operation that is generally performed in the hospital operating room. About 19 percent of the 3.6 million babies born in the United States in 1983 were delivered by cesarean section (Klein 1985).

According to a recent report (Sachs et al. 1982), the incidence of American women who die in pregnancy or childbirth has decreased dramatically in recent decades. Health experts cite many reasons for this: advances in prenatal and obstetrical care, improvements in the general health of pregnant women, the increasing tendency for women to have smaller families and to complete their childbearing at relatively young ages, and the legalization of abortion (Sachs et al. 1982).

INFERTILITY AND ITS TREATMENT

The ability to produce offspring falls on a normal curve of variability, as do most human traits. Every human being occupies a position on the scale from total sterility, which is fairly rare, to high fertility. Moreover, each person's position on the scale varies from day to day with such factor's as illness, fatigue, nutrition, drug consumption, and emotional stress. Infertility is higher among blacks than among whites (Mosher 1982).

The term *infertility* is usually reserved to describe those who have tried to conceive for a year or more without success. According to this definition, one in six American couples are infertile, and the incidence is rising. For example, among married women age twenty to twenty-four the incidence of infertility nearly doubled from 1965 to 1982.[30] Contributing factors to the rise in infertility are the widespread use of the contraceptive pill (which causes ovulatory problems), use of IUDs (which often leads to pelvic inflammatory diseases, causing scarring and subsequent infertility), women's decision to delay childbearing into their thirties (when fertility decreases), and an increase in environmental and industrial toxic products that can affect both the male and the female reproductive systems (Clapp and Swenson 1984).

Relative infertility may be traced to the husband, to the wife, or to a combination of factors relating to both. It is estimated that in 40 percent of involuntarily childless marriages the cause is primarily the husband's infertility, in another 40 percent it is the wife's, and in 20 percent it is impaired fertility in both. About one in six of all married couples of childbearing age do not conceive after one year of trying, or the pregnancy is not carried to a live birth.[31]

Before selecting a method of treatment for infertility, the couple and their physician should try to identify the cause, evaluating seminal, cervical, ovarian, tubal, peritoneal, and uterine factors. In addition, the frequency and techniques of copulation should be considered.

Treatment of male infertility includes various nutritional, hormonal, of surgical procedures, depending on the nature of the problem. However, the most common physical symptoms of male infertility are a relatively low number of sperm cells in the ejaculate, a high proportion of low-mobility sperm,[32] and blocked sperm ducts. There is evidence that smoking may produce lower sperm counts or abnormal sperm, lowering the likelihood of pregnancy (Evans et al. 1981). It is estimated that for conception to be probable, the man must ejaculate at least 2–3 million active sperm.

If a sperm count reveals a deficiency in either the quantity or the quality of sperm, and if the man does not respond to hormonal, surgical, or nutritional treatment, conception is sometimes effected by artificial insemination. A physician accumulates several of the husband's ejaculations (which can be preserved through refrigeration) and, using a syringe, injects this semen into the vagina of the wife when she is ovulating. The sheer quantity of the ejaculate introduced into the vagina may overcome the effect of sperm deficiencies.

If, however, diagnostic procedures reveal total sterility of the husband, or if repeated artificial inseminations using his sperm fail to result in pregnancy, sperm from a donor other than the husband is sometimes obtained and mixed with that of the husband. When a donor's sperm is used, the physician usually attempts to match the donor's physical traits, blood type, and general characteristics with those of the husband, so that fertilization by the husband's sperm will still seem a possibility. This possibility that a child produced by such artificial insemination may still be the natural offspring of the husband carries great psychological weight for the couples who choose this procedure.

Infertility is far more complicated when it occurs in the wife as compared to that in the husband. While he must simply produce a sufficient quantity of viable sperm and deposit

---

[30]U.S. National Center for Health Statistics, *Vital Statistics of the United States*, annual (1984).
[31]Ibid.

[32]Such low-mobility sperm are often malformed when viewed under a microscope.

them in the vagina, fertility in the wife involves such complex factors as proper ovulation;[33] passage of the egg through the fallopian tube; maintenance of a chemically hospitable medium for the sperm in the vagina, uterus, and fallopian tubes; and successful implantation of the germinal disc in the endometrium (lining) of the uterus.

In examining for female infertility, a physician first tries to determine whether ovulation occurs, since without ovulation conception is impossible. Ovulation is usually (though not always) indicated by the regularity of the menstrual cycle and by the slight temperature rise (0.5 degrees F) at the midpoint of the cycle. If ovulation is presumed to take place (there is no way to know for sure), the next queston is whether the egg can penetrate the fallopian tube. It is possible to discover whether the fallopian tubes are open by gently forcing a small amount of carbon dioxide through them, or by filling them with an opaque liquid that shows up on an x-ray. Sometimes either of these procedures is sufficient in itself to open a blocked tube.

If the tubes are not blocked and an examination of sperm in the vagina immediately after copulation indicates that the sperm are not surviving their passage, the chemistry of the female genital fluid may be tested to determine whether it is a hospitable medium for sperm. If the degree of acidity in the reproductive tract is found to be excessive, for example, chemical treatment is often possible.

Various structural problems of the uterus, fallopian tubes, or cervix can often be corrected by surgical procedures (Clapp and Swenson 1984).

Fertility drugs have been developed for the treatment of female infertility. However, these drugs are helpful for only certain types of infertility, and they may increase the possibility of multiple birth (Johnson 1981).

Infertile couples who go to a specialist for treatment have about a 50 percent chance of conceiving a child (Clapp and Swenson 1984). When an artificial insemination procedure is used with a donor other than the husband, the success rate is 90 percent (Corson 1983).

A couple whose infertility problems cannot be solved can still become voluntary parents by adopting a child. In this way they fulfill all the normal responsibilities of parenthood, with the exception of actual conception and birth. In addition, they help solve the human and social problems of unwanted children. The rising rate of infertility, the increasing use of abortion, and the growing societal acceptance of single mothers have greatly reduced the number of babies available for adoption, however. The waiting period to adopt a child may be as long as seven to ten years after the couple have been deemed acceptable by the adoption agency (Clapp and Swenson 1984, Kennedy 1982). To avoid such a long wait many couples adopt babies through private channels, arranging for the adoption through the mother, her physician, or an attorney. In this "gray market" the adopting parents usually agree to pay the medical and legal costs of the mother and the baby. There is also an illegal baby "black market" where a healthy white infant may be obtained for as much as $50,000 (Kennedy 1982).

BIRTH CONTROL

In most of the world's societies, it has been important to control the size of the population. Studies of surviving Stone Age cultures, such as the Bushmen of the Kalahari Desert of South Africa, show that even primitive people have rigorously limited their numbers to assure that there would be enough food for all during sparse years. Various methods of birth control have been practiced for at least as far

---

[33]The average fertile woman has three or four nonovulatory menstrual cycles per year, and some women have many more (Corson 1983).

back as humans have recorded history. The ancient cultures of Greece, Rome, India, China, and Japan and those of medieval Islam, the Christian world during the Middle Ages, and preindustrial Europe have all left records of birth control methods. The ancient Egyptians, for example, devised techniques of blocking the cervix with cloth or plant leaves and used condoms of animal membranes. The ancient Greeks encouraged homosexual relations and through discriminative taxes discouraged heterosexual marriage. Many societies legitimized abortion. (For an interesting discussion of the history of contraceptive practices, see Finch and Green 1963.) In addition, infanticide has been used to a surprising extent to control population, not only in Asian and African cultures but also in our own Western civilization as recently as the nineteenth century. (For a discussion of the surprising extent of infanticide in nineteenth-century England and Western Europe, see Skolnick 1983, Shorter 1975, Trexler 1973, and Langer 1972. For a discussion of infanticide in the Solomon Islands of Melanesia, Tahiti, and Hawaii see Davies 1984.)

The Increasing Population of the World

From a very broad perspective, birth control is becoming mandatory since the world's population of about 4.7 billion is increasing at the rate of about 1.7 percent per year, adding 76 million persons each year—the equivalent of the entire nations of Denmark, Finland, Norway, Sweden, Ireland, Austria, Belgium, The Netherlands, Switzerland, and Bulgaria. At the current pace of births and deaths, 1 million persons are added to the world's population every five days. This rate will double the world's population in forty-one years (see Figure 11-5). The undeveloped countries of the world have an even higher current rate of growth, which will double their population in only twenty to twenty-eight years (Hartley 1982).

Given the limited resources of our planet, it is clear that this rate of increase simply cannot continue. Two-thirds to three-fourths of the people of the world are currently deprived of many of the aspects of life that are considered bare necessities in the more advanced nations of the world. Pure and uncontaminated drinking water, for instance, is unavailable to a majority of the people of the world. In spite of the fact that world food production has increased faster in the last twenty years than ever before in recorded history, food production in the countries of rapid population increase has often not kept pace with the increasing numbers of human beings (Hartley 1982).

Every day the malnutrition in the poorer countries kills and damages more children than all other catastrophies—both man-made and natural—combined. . . . One out of every three babies in the developing countries dies before he or she reaches the age of five (UNICEF 1981, p. 1).

There is only one way a human being can arrive on this planet, and that is to be born; similarly, there is only one way a human can permanently leave this planet, and that is by dying. Since the growth rate of the planet's population equals the birth rate minus the death rate (there are no other factors involved), there is no way to change the growth rate except by manipulating one of these two variables. If the birth rate is not lowered, the death rate must rise to maintain a population that can be supported by planetary resources. Since it is unthinkable to deliberately raise the death rate to control population, the only other possibility is to deliberately lower the birth rate (see Figure 11-6).

The Increasing Number of Illegitimate Births

Curiously enough, despite the recent innovations in birth control techniques, the incidence of out-of-wedlock births increased 50 percent

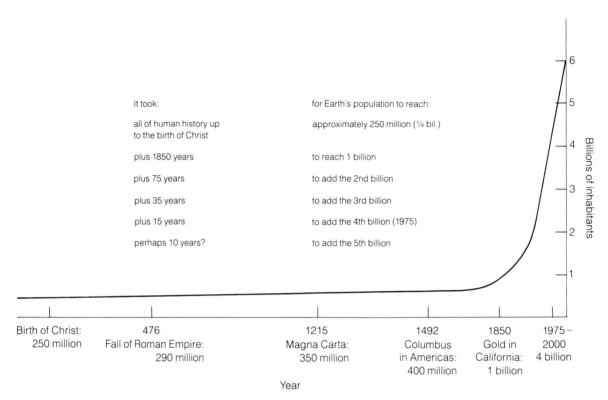

It took:	for Earth's population to reach:
all of human history up to the birth of Christ	approximately 250 million (¼ bil.)
plus 1850 years	to reach 1 billion
plus 75 years	to add the 2nd billion
plus 35 years	to add the 3rd billion
plus 15 years	to add the 4th billion (1975)
perhaps 10 years?	to add the 5th billion

Billions of inhabitants

Birth of Christ: 250 million	476 Fall of Roman Empire: 290 million	1215 Magna Carta: 350 million	1492 Columbus in Americas: 400 million	1850 Gold in California: 1 billion	1975— 2000 4 billion

Year

No one knows exactly how many human beings are alive on earth. The number reported from individual countries and for the world as a whole are always the best available estimates, taking into account the census enumeration, birth registration, death records, and adjustments of these for supposed errors. There is a good deal of agreement, however, that the population of the world passed the 4 billion mark in 1976, reached 4.5 billion by 1980 (Hartley 1982), and was at 4.7 billion by 1984 (U.S. Bureau of Census, "World Population Characteristics, 1975 to 1984, and Projections to 2000." 1985).

The most interesting feature in this figure about the growth of the world's population is that it has taken place relatively recently. At the time of the birth of Christ, the best available estimates fixed world population at 250 million people. By 1850, this population had quadrupled to 1 billion. Since then, it has quadrupled again. In other words, it took all of human history up to the year 1850 to reach a world population of 1 billion, and yet only 15 years to add the latest billion.

FIGURE 11-5

The world's population is exploding

Sources: Data from Hartley (1982, p. 5); U.S. National Center
for Health Statistics, "Birth and Birth Rates: 1950 to 1981"
(1985, p. 838).

---

in the last decade. In 1981, nearly one of every five American babies was born to an unwed mother—about 12 percent of white babies and 56 percent of black babies. This represents nearly a fivefold increase since 1950. In 1950, 4 percent of all births in the United States were illegitimate; by 1981, this figure had risen to 19 percent (see Figure 11-7).[34] Among

teenagers, the rate of illegitimate births is even higher (see Figure 11-8). American teenagers become pregnant, give birth, and have abortions at significantly higher rates

---

[34]U.S. National Center for Health Statistics, "Births to Unmarried Women, by Race and Age of Mother: 1950 to 1981" (1985).

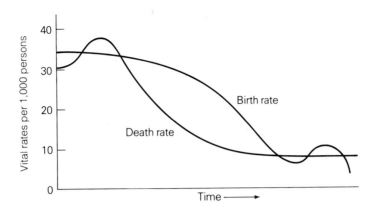

The demographic transition is divided roughly into three stages. In the first stage there is high growth potential because both birth and death rates are high. The second stage is the transition from high to low birth and death rates. During this stage the growth potential is realized, as the death rate drops before the birth rate drops, resulting in rapid population growth. Finally, the last stage is a time when death rates are as low as they are likely to go, while fertility may continue to decline to the point that the population might eventually decline in numbers. In the developed countries, the full transition took place roughly as schematized. However, the less developed nations have not yet followed the full pattern of change.

FIGURE 11-6

Relation between the birth rate and the death rate

Source: From *Population, An Introduction to Concepts and Issues,* 2d ed., by John R. Weeks. © 1981 by Wadsworth Publishing Company, Inc., Belmont, California 94002. Reprinted by permission of the publisher.

than do adolescents in other industrialized nations according to an Alan Guttmacher Institute report in 1985. The report concluded that the lowest rates of teenage pregnancy were in countries that had liberal attitudes toward sex, and easily accessible contraceptive services for young people, with contraceptives being offered free or at low cost and without parental notification, and had comprehensive programs in sex education. The report concluded that:

In the United States, teenage birth rates are much higher than each of other industrialized countries at every age (15 through 19) by a considerable margin. The contrast is particularly striking for younger teenagers.

The tragic circumstances related to these unwanted births are indicated by the high suicide rate among unmarried mothers—a rate that is ten times that of the general population. Moreover, more babies of unmarried teenage mothers are born with birth defects than those of other women. Many of these young girls are poor or ignorant of medical needs, and they do not receive adequate prenatal care or nutrition.[35] Others are not fully grown and are physically unprepared to bear the strains of having a baby. According to government figures, teenage mothers have more hemorrhages, anemia, toxemia, and lower-weight

---

[35]Seventy percent of deaths of newborn babies in the United States are due to low birth weight (U.S. National Center for Health Statistics, "Advance Report of Final Natality Statistics, 1979," 1981; U.S. Children's Defense Fund, "Widening Schism Between Black and White Children in America," 1985).

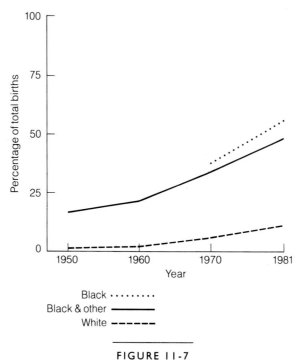

FIGURE 11-7

Percentage of illegitimate births by race, 1950–1981

Source: Data from U.S. National Center for Health Statistics,
"Births to Unmarried Women, by Race and Age of Mother:
1950 to 1981" (1985, p. 64).

babies, and higher death rates than women in their twenties. Also, infants of teenage mothers are three times more likely to die in the first year of life than children born to older women; and when they do survive, they have a higher incidence of mental and emotional handicaps.[36] In addition, studies have found that more than half of all pregnancies in America each year are *unintended,* occurring either because the couple do not use any contraceptive method or because a contraceptive is misused (Klein 1984).

A large number of pregnancies among married couples also are unwanted.[37] The precise figure cannot be obtained, of course, since it is impossible to define what is meant by *unwanted* in this context. Many couples who are dismayed upon discovering the wife is pregnant later welcome the baby to the best of their ability. In 1981, about 300,000 abortions were performed on married women—a graphic illustration of the widespread lack of knowledge regarding contraception in our society (Henshaw 1985).

[36]U.S. National Center for Health Statistics, "Advance Report of Final Natality Statistics" (1981).

[37]Census data in 1985 indicated that 7.8 percent of currently married mothers did not want the child at the time of conception (U.S. National Center for Health Statistics, "Unwanted Birth of All Mothers, 15–44 Years Old: 1973 and 1982" (1985).

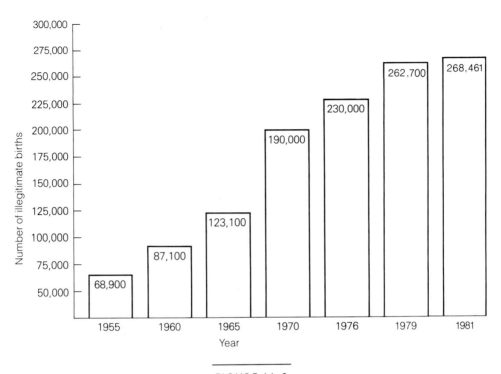

FIGURE 11-8

Incidence of illegitimate births to teenage mothers,
1955–1981

Source: Data from U.S. National Center for Health Statistics,
"Births to Unmarried Women, by Race and Age of Mother:
1950 to 1981" (1985, p. 64).

METHODS OF BIRTH CONTROL

Contraception literally means "against conception" or preventing the sperm from reaching the egg. If the sperm cannot reach the egg, conception, of course, cannot occur. There are many methods of contraception, ranging from "organic" methods to surgical sterilization.

Some methods of contraception are more effective than others (see Figure 11-9). No matter how effective a method is, however, if it is not *always* used, conception may occur. Using a contraceptive most of the time and "taking a chance" occasionally is an excellent way to become pregnant. It is estimated that about one-third of couples who are using some form of contraception, and who do not want a child, nevertheless conceive within five years. This relatively high incidence of failure is thought to be largely attributable to occasional carelessness (Hatcher et al. 1984).

Organic Methods of Contraception

The simplest and most obvious method of keeping the sperm from encountering the egg is for the man to ejaculate outside the vagina. There are many techniques of petting that culminate in extravaginal ejaculation (see Chapter 4). An extension of this petting-to-orgasm

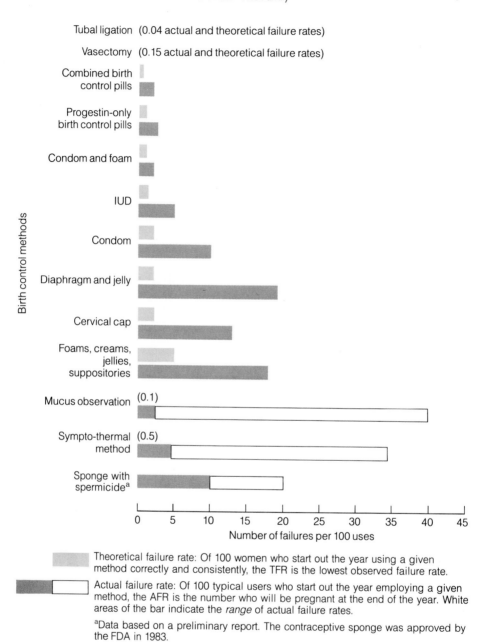

Tubal ligation (0.04 actual and theoretical failure rates)

Vasectomy (0.15 actual and theoretical failure rates)

Combined birth control pills

Progestin-only birth control pills

Condom and foam

IUD

Condom

Diaphragm and jelly

Cervical cap

Foams, creams, jellies, suppositories

Mucus observation (0.1)

Sympto-thermal method (0.5)

Sponge with spermicide[a]

Birth control methods

Number of failures per 100 uses

Theoretical failure rate: Of 100 women who start out the year using a given method correctly and consistently, the TFR is the lowest observed failure rate.

Actual failure rate: Of 100 typical users who start out the year employing a given method, the AFR is the number who will be pregnant at the end of the year. White areas of the bar indicate the *range* of actual failure rates.

[a]Data based on a preliminary report. The contraceptive sponge was approved by the FDA in 1983.

FIGURE 11-9

Theoretical and actual failure rates of birth control methods

Sources: Data from Hatcher et al. (1984); Bell (1984); Tatum and Connell-Tatum (1982); "Periodic Abstinence: How Well Do the New Approaches Work?" *Population Reports*, Series I, No. 3 (September 1981).

There is no one "best" method of birth control. The choice of contraceptive depends on many individual factors.

realistic to always expect the man to withdraw just as the intensely pleasurable moment of ejaculation is approaching. In view of these shortcomings, it is not surprising that withdrawal is one of the least popular methods of contraception in our society. As a chief method of birth control it is used by only one couple in fifty (Westoff 1976b). Couples who use withdrawal as their sole method of birth control report a failure rate of 20–25 percent (Hatcher et al. 1984).

It is also possible to copulate indefinitely without ejaculating—a method of contraception known as *coitus reservatus*. The ability to copulate without ejaculating has been an important part of other cultures (such as in India), but it is so rare in the United States that there are no figures regarding its use.[38]

Another organic method that is often used in preindustrial societies is prolonged breast-feeding. Breast-feeding delays the onset of the ovulation cycle after childbirth for five to six weeks (Young 1982). When used as a contraceptive measure for longer periods, however, prolonged breast-feeding is notoriously ineffective. For example, prolonging breast-feeding for twelve months following childbirth (as a birth control technique) has a reported failure rate of 40 percent (Hatcher et al. 1984).

Another organic method makes use of the natural rhythmic cycles of ovulation in a woman's body, and so is called the *rhythm method*. A woman can conceive only during approximately twenty-four hours of each menstrual cycle—the time the egg is in the fallopian tube. If she does not copulate during this period, or for the seventy-two hours (three days) preceding ovulation (since the sperm can live in her genital tract for that long), she will

technique is for the couple to copulate, but without ejaculation taking place inside the vagina. When the man feels ejaculation is imminent, he withdraws the penis to ejaculate extravaginally. This technique of contraception is called *coitus interruptus* or simply *withdrawal*.

There are two problems with withdrawal. The first is that the preejaculatory fluid may contain sperm, which may reach the fallopian tube so that conception may occur even without ejaculation. The second is that using withdrawal consistently prevents the physical and psychological satisfactions of ejaculating inside the vagina, which are a significant part of the pleasure of copulation. Indeed, it is un-

---

[38]Coitus reservatus in our society is well known in relation to the *Oneida Perfectionists*, the community led by John Humphrey Noyes in the nineteenth century. Young adolescent males were taught sexual skills by women of the community, including the art of coitus reservatus.

not conceive. In calculating the rhythm method, the couple usually add another day to be on the safe side (since sperm may live longer than seventy-two hours), ruling out copulation during five days of each menstrual cycle.

The rhythm method would be a perfect contraceptive technique if the precise time of ovulation could always be determined. Since this is not possible, however, the rhythm method has a high failure rate—estimated to be about 19 percent (Hatcher et al. 1984).

Because of the high failure rate of the rhythm method, two methods of natural birth control have been developed to augment the rhythm method: the ovulation method and the sympto-thermal method.

Using the *ovulation method* (sometimes called mucus observation) the woman observes her fertility on a daily basis by keeping track of her vaginal sensations of wetness or dryness. When there is a feeling of vaginal dryness and no mucus is present at the vaginal opening, sperm will not be able to survive in the acid environment of the vagina—such days are considered infertile. As ovulation approaches, the cervix produces enough mucus to coat the vagina with a protective covering that promotes sperm survival—this is the fertile period. Since each woman is unique in her cycle, the number of fertile days varies from cycle to cycle and from woman to woman. Learning to recognize her own cycle usually takes the woman from two to three cycles.[39]

In the *sympto-thermal method* (STM), observation of cervical mucus is combined with observation of the basal body temperature, which is taken each morning just before rising. Usually, the basal body temperature rises slightly following ovulation and stays high until menstruation begins (it falls as the menses start and stays low until the next ovulation). The temperature method does not pre-

dict ovulation in advance, of course. If an unexpected ovulation should occur and the woman has copulated within the preceding three days, she may conceive. A further difficulty is that her temperature does not rise during a cycle when ovulation fails to occur. Thus, when no increase is recorded, the woman cannot be sure whether she is having delayed ovulation or a cycle with *no* ovulation. Also a fever due to infection may lead her to think she has ovulated when she has not (Bell 1984).

Because of the "naturalness" of these methods they are approved by the Roman Catholic church. They are the *only* methods of birth control currently approved by the church because Catholic doctrine considers reproduction the primary function of marriage and forbids the use of any "artificial" contraceptive device.

The ovulation method has a theoretical failure rate of 0.01–5.7 percent and an actual failure rate of 2.3–39.7 percent. The sympto-thermal method (STM) has a theoretical failure rate of 0.5–13.1 percent and an actual failure rate of 4.5–34.4 percent.[40]

Douche

Douching consists of flushing the vagina with water or other liquid and is one of the oldest methods of attempting contraception.[41] In the United States, a douche is usually administered with a syringe or nozzle connected to a douche bag.[42] In most European hotels and private homes, the *bidet*, a low basin especially

---

[39] If spermicidal foam, jelly, or cream is in the vagina, it is not possible to observe cervical mucus.

---

[40] "Periodic Abstinence: How Well Do the New Approaches Work?" *Population Reports* (1981).

[41] A folk method related to the douche is the woman's practice of urinating immediately after copulation. This method is based on a faulty knowledge of anatomy. While the penis conducts both sperm and urine, the vagina is a separate structure from the urethra, so urination can serve no flushing function whatsoever.

[42] Another method of douching is to shake up the contents of a soft-drink bottle and use it to flush the vagina after copulation. This, however, is notoriously ineffective.

designed for douching, is standard equipment (see Chapter 4).

The douche is not really a method of contraception, since it has very little contraceptive effect. No matter how soon after ejaculation a woman douches, it is not soon enough. Within one minute after ejaculation, millions of sperm have found their way through the cervix.

It should also be noted that internal douching is inadvisable since it washes away protective levels of residual acidity in the vagina, thus making it more vulnerable to infection. Internal areas need no cleansing. External areas should, of course, be washed with soap and water simply in the interests of cleanliness. It is important, however, to distinguish between the hygienic and prophylactic effects of douching and the contraceptive effect, which has a reported failure rate of 40 percent (Hatcher et al. 1984).

Spermicides: Chemical Control of Conception

Chemical contraceptives that have a spermicidal (sperm-killing) function are *spermicides*. Formulas for vaginal spermicides appear in early writings as far back as the nineteenth century B.C., and modern chemists think they must have been fairly effective. Probably through trial and error, the ancients discovered that environments that were either strongly acid or strongly alkaline were hostile to sperm. In the fourth century B.C., Aristotle suggested oil of cedar and frankincense in olive oil to block the cervix. Cleopatra and other prosperous Egyptians used a vaginal paste of honey, sodium carbonate, and dried crocodile dung. In Europe, a sponge moistened with diluted lemon juice has been a popular contraceptive device since biblical times.

Salt in an 8 percent solution is deadly to sperm, and eighth-century Indian writers describe the use of rock salt dipped in oil or honey. By the twelfth century, the Moslems also

had developed suppositories or tampons based on these ingredients. The English feminist Annie Bessant (a late nineteenth-century Margaret Sanger) advocated the use of a sponge soaked in quinine solution.

Contemporary spermicides in the form of aerosol foams, creams, and jellies have a high failure rate when used alone, but they are effective when used for extra protection with a condom. A vaginal suppository should also be used only in combination with a condom and must be inserted into the vagina ten to thirty *minutes* before copulation. The use of spermicides also provides protection against gonorrhea and trichomoniasis (Hatcher et al. 1984).

Aerosol vaginal foam spermicide has a theoretical failure rate of 3–5 percent but an actual failure rate of 18 percent. When used in combination with a condom, however, it is virtually 100 percent effective (Hatcher et al. 1984).

Physical Barriers

The four most commonly used contraceptive devices that act as physical barriers to prevent the sperm from reaching the egg are the condom, the diaphragm, the cervical cap, and the contraceptive sponge.

The Condom

The *condom* is a thin sheath of rubber or animal tissue that is rolled over the erect penis before copulation to contain the ejaculate. The modern condom was devised in 1564 by an Italian anatomist; by the eighteenth century it was usually made of lamb membranes, and its use had become widespread. With the development of the vulcanization of rubber in 1849, rubber condoms became available and popularly know as "rubbers."

The condom—in both the rubber and the animal membrane versions—is the most widely used barrier method of contraception in the

United States today. The condom provides virtually 100 percent effectiveness when combined with spermicidal foam, cream, or jelly.[43] However, like all contraceptive devices, the condom has a failure rate because of carelessness. The condom may fail, of course, if it has even a microscopic hole in it, but the quality control in the manufacture of condoms is so high that imperfections are rare. The condom may also fail if it slips off the penis after ejaculation, so care must be taken in withdrawal. Moreover, if a couple copulate for a long time before rolling the condom over the penis, the preejaculatory fluid may contain sufficient sperm for conception to take place. Most failures of the condom probably occur because of carelessness or occasionally "taking a chance" (Hatcher et al. 1984).

A good-quality condom—used as directed but not with spermicidal foam, cream, or jelly—has a theoretical failure rate of about 2 percent. About 10 percent of those who use condoms report unwanted pregnancies (Hatcher et al. 1984).

The Diaphragm

The *diaphragm* is a circular piece of thin rubber with a stiffened but flexible rim. It is designed to lie along the roof of the vagina, between the back wall and the pubic bone, so that it covers the cervix. It must be carefully fitted by a physician, nurse, or paramedic, and the diaphragm should be the most comfortable choice from the various models available. A woman may need a larger size after childbirth, abortion, or pelvic surgery, and she should have the device checked about once a year (Hatcher et al. 1984).

The diaphragm by itself is not a contraceptive device; it works by holding spermicidal jelly in the position most likely to encounter sperm. Ideally, the jelly in the diaphragm will kill whatever sperm swim near the cervical opening. Since the shape of the vagina varies during copulation and orgasm, and only a minute amount of ejaculate is necessary to effect conception, there is a margin of error built into the concept of the diaphragm (Berkowitz 1981).

Vaginal diaphragms in combination with spermicidal pastes or jellies were invented in the early 1880s. Prior to this, various devices were used to block the entrance to the cervix in conjunction with various spermicides. For example, a small sponge saturated with soapy water was a popular device and is still used in many parts of the world. Casanova, for his many conquests, devised the use of a half lemon as a kind of diaphragm, with the citric acid acting as a spermicide (Finch and Green 1963).

Some researchers regard the diaphragm, when fitted and used properly, as extremely reliable. For example, the Margaret Sanger Research Bureau found that only 2 percent of diaphragm users experienced accidental pregnancies, and among these, two-thirds admit that they had not used the diaphragm consistently (Seaman 1980, Lane et al. 1976). Other researchers, however, have found the failure rate of the diaphragm to be as high as 19 percent (Hatcher et al. 1984). The reason for this discrepancy is probably failure in consistent use. Researchers have found that many women think they are infertile for a few days just before, during, and after their menstrual periods, and they may forgo use of the diaphragm on these days. However, women who copulate without the diaphragm during these presumably "safe" days have more accidental pregnancies than women who practice the rhythm method alone (Berkowitz 1981, Seaman 1980). Also, the diaphragm must be left in place for at least six hours after copulation to allow the spermicide to kill all the sperm. If a woman

---

[43]"Update on Condoms—Products, Protection, Promotion," *Population Reports* (1982). As noted in Chapter 4, the condom not only is an extremely effective contraceptive device when properly used but also provides significant protection against STDs (sexually transmissible diseases).

copulates again during this time she must insert more aerosol, cream, or jelly into her vagina, leaving the diaphragm in place (Bell 1984).[44]

The Cervical Cap

The cervical cap is similar in construction to the diaphragm, but it is designed to cover only the cervix, which is about one inch in diameter and projects into the vagina about one inch. The cervical cap is easy to use and more secure than the diaphragm, fitting tightly over the woman's cervix and held in place by suction. Unlike the diaphragm, which is fitted only approximately to the diameter of the vagina near the cervical opening, the cervical cap is fitted exactly to the cervix (Berkowitz 1981). Because of this, the cervical cap acts as an effective contraceptive without the use of a spermicide, although usually a small amount of spermicide is used on the inside of the cap to kill any sperm that might break through the suction seal (Bell 1984).

The cervical cap is thousands of years old. It was used in ancient Sumatra, where women molded opium into caplike devices to cover their cervixes (Seaman and Seaman 1978). The modern cervical cap was perfected in 1838 and became popular in Europe. It is still widely used in Europe (and other countries) but has never become very popular in the United States. Most American women who use cervical caps have obtained them from foreign physicians, although a scattering of U.S. physicians stock and prescribe them. The reason for the cervical cap's unpopularity is twofold. First, physicians dislike it because more time is required to fit the cap and to teach a woman how to use it than to fit and give instructions in the use of the diaphragm. Second, pharmaceutical companies dislike the cap because it cuts into the sales of spermicides. The profit is not in the sale of the initial item—diaphragm or cervical cap—but in the continuing sales of spermicides that must be used with the diaphragm (Seaman 1980).

The theoretical failure rate of the cervical cap is about 2 percent, but the actual failure rate is 13 percent (Hatcher et al. 1984).

The Contraceptive Sponge

The *contraceptive sponge* was approved by the FDA in 1983 for general over-the-counter marketing, and by 1984 it had been used by 400,000 women in the United States. It is made of polyurethane and comes in one size—two and one-fourth inches in diameter and three-fourths of an inch thick. It contains a spermicide that is released slowly to kill the sperm.

The contraceptive sponge has a loop of tape attached to facilitate removal and a dimple in the center. It should be inserted into the vagina so that the dimple covers the cervix, blocking the opening, so it is not necessary to have an exact fit (as it is with the diaphragm and the cervical cap). To avoid the risk of toxic shock the contraceptive sponge should not be used during menstruation.[45] After the sponge is inserted, copulation may occur any number of times without having to add more spermicide. It must be left in place, however, for at least six hours after copulation and can be left in the

---

[44]Although Toxic Shock Syndrome (TSS) is usually associated with the use of tampons, several cases have been reported with use of the diaphragm. For this reason, it may be advisable to avoid leaving the diaphragm in place for more than twenty-four hours, and to avoid using it during a menstrual period. Although only a small number of menstruating women have developed TSS, a few of them have died. TSS is probably caused by a new strain of *Staphlococcus aureus*, which infects some part of the body, often the vagina, and produces toxins that go into the bloodstream (Radetsky 1985). Early symptoms of toxic shock syndrome include fever (101 degrees Fahrenheit or more), diarrhea, vomiting, muscle aches, and sunburnlike rash (Hatcher et al. 1984).

---

[45]Although Toxic Shock Syndrome (TSS) has usually been associated with the use of tampons, as noted earlier it has also occurred with the use of diaphragms and contraceptive sponges (Radetsky 1985).

vagina for up to twenty-four hours. It is removed by pulling on the tape and then thrown away.

No long-term studies have been conducted on the safety of the spermicide used with the contraceptive sponge (nonoxynol-9) or on the effects of the polyurethane. About 2 percent of women using the sponge have reported allergic reactions, and some sponges have shredded while in place. Preliminary reports show an actual failure rate of about 16 percent (Hatcher et al. 1984).

The Pill: Hormonal Control of Conception

The oral contraceptive pill that is most commonly used controls a woman's reproductive physiology by introducing hormones that feign pregnancy and thus fool the body into stopping ovulation. This combination pill is composed of the female sex hormone (*estrogen*) and a synthetic substance (*progestin*), which is chemically similar to *progesterone*, a hormone produced in the ovaries, Progestin-only pills do not inhibit ovulation but cause the cervical mucus to become thicker and impede the development of the uterine lining, so that the germinal disc does not implant itself. Progestin-only pills are not quite as effective in preventing pregnancy as the combination pills (Hatcher et al. 1984).

As recently as 1976, the pill was the contraceptive preferred by more than one-third of all American married women and two-thirds of young unmarried women (Westoff 1976b). However, about half the women who start on the pill stop taking it within two years because they are afraid of unwanted side effects (Seaman 1980). For example, researchers have found that the longer a woman takes the pill, the greater is her risk of heart attack; the risk increases two to three times in women who have used the pill for more than ten years (Slone et al. 1981). Researchers have also

found that some women experienced other undesirable side effects—many of them quite severe. For example, 5 percent of pill users experience a rise in blood pressure, 13 percent have some manifestations of chemical diabetes, and 30 percent suffer mild to severe depression. Women over age forty who take birth control pills face nearly four times the risk of heart attack or stroke as those under age forty.[46] Other complications involve blood clots, liver disease, neurologic and eye disturbances, and increased risk of cervical cancer. Five percent of women are infertile for a time after they stop taking the pill, and sometimes this infertility is permanent. (Seaman 1980, Royal College of General Practitioners' Oral Contraceptive Study 1978, Tietze et al. 1976).

In addition, contrary to original expectations, the contraceptive pill can lower a woman's sexual interest and responsiveness. Studies carried out in the United States, England, and Sweden have found that a decrease in sex drive is prevalent among pill users (Bragonier 1976, Gambrell et al. 1976).

If a woman has other health risk factors—such as high blood pressure, diabetes, obesity, or a high level of blood cholesterol—the use of the pill is not advised. Problems with the pill are also markedly increased for cigarette smokers, so a woman may either use the pill or smoke cigarettes but definitely should not do both (Layde et al. 1982, Tietze et al. 1976, Stern et al. 1976).

It is commonly thought that, although pregnancy may be dangerous for some women, the pill is even more dangerous. This is simply not true, however. Studies have shown the risk of death from pregnancy itself is greater than the risk from contraceptives (Klein 1984). (See Table 11-1.)

---

[46]The risk of circulatory disease is relatively low for nonsmokers who are health and under age thirty-five (Hatcher et al. 1984).

TABLE 11-1

Risk of death associated with different birth control
methods, pregnancy, and abortion, 1982–1983

	Chance of Death within a Year
Birth control pills (nonsmoker)	1 in 63,000
Birth control pills (smoker)	1 in 16,000
IUDs	1 in 100,000
Barrier methods	none
Organic methods	none
Sterilization:	
laparoscopic tubal ligation	1 in 10,000
hysterotomy	1 in 1,600
vasectomy	none
Pregnancy:	
continuing pregnancy	1 in 10,000
terminating pregnancy:	
illegal abortion	1 in 3,000
legal abortion:	
before 9 weeks	1 in 400,000
between 9 and 12 weeks	1 in 100,000
between 13 and 16 weeks	1 in 25,000
after 16 weeks	1 in 10,000

Source: Adapted from data in Hatcher and Stewart (1982),
which lists the following references: Cates (1980); Dinman
(1980); Tietze (1977); U.S. National Center for Health
Statistics, "Final Mortality Statistics, United States,
1976–78" (1980); and U.S. Public Health Service,
"Abortion-Related Mortality, United States, 1976–78" (1982).

TABLE 11-2

Popularity of different methods of birth control, American
women ages fifteen to forty-four in 1982

Method	Percentage of women who use the method
Sterilization	33.0
female	22.0
male partner	11.0
Pill	28.6
Condom	12.2
Diaphragm	8.3
IUD	7.3
Rhythm	4.0
Other	5.7

Source: Data from U.S. National Center for Health Statistics,
"Contraceptive Use by American Women, 15–44 Years Old by
Age, Race, and Method of Contraception, 1982" and
provisional data from the National Survey of Family Growth
(1984).

It should be noted that, whereas spermicidal foam lowers the likelihood of contracting sexually transmissible disease and other vaginal infections, the contraceptive pill neutralizes normal vaginal acids, making the user more susceptible to gonorrhea. Pill takers also develop an increase in vaginal carbohydrates, which encourage bacterial growth. Sexually transmissible diseases (STDs) and other infections, such as common vaginitis, are twice as common among pill users compared with other women (Hatcher et al. 1984, Seaman 1980).

Since it is a very effective method of contraception the pill is very popular. Moreover, it is very simple to use (the woman just remembers to take one pill every day), requires no special preparation, and causes no interruption between foreplay and copulation.

Some 10 million women in the United States now use birth control pills. It is the method of choice for nearly 29 percent of American women who use contraception (Klein 1984).[47]

A new birth control pill more closely geared to the female hormone cycle was approved by the FDA in 1984. This "triphasic" pill is an alternative for women who cannot use the lowest-dose combination pill and is about 99 percent effective in preventing pregnancy (Pasquale 1984).

The actual failure rate of the combination pill is 0.14 percent according to a long-term study of contraception in England (Vessey et al. 1976). In the United States, the failure rate is reported to be 0.5–2 percent, probably due to carelessness or inconsistent use (Hatcher et al. 1984).

Next to sterilization, the pill is the most popular method of birth control in the United States (see Table 11-2).

[47]Data also from U.S. National Center for Health Statistics "Methods of Birth Control" (1984).

Sterilization: Surgical Control of Conception

The most dramatic change in contraceptive practices in the United States since 1970 has been the accelerated use of surgical sterilization, which is now more popular than the pill for American couples past age thirty. From 1973 to 1982, sterilization rose from 23 percent to 41 percent among married couples who practice birth control, while pill use dropped from 36 percent to 29 percent. Little difference was found in the incidence of birth control methods used by Catholic as compared with Protestant women.[48]

The number of Planned Parenthood clients choosing surgical sterilization is about the same for the middle and the lower classes, but which of the couple is sterilized usually differs. Among middle class couples who choose sterilization it is usually the man who is sterilized, while among lower class couples, particularly blacks, it is usually the woman.[49] More than 500,000 American women are surgically sterilized each year (Johnson 1982). (See Figure 11-10.)

Female Sterilization Operations

Sterilization operations on women consist of treating a section of each fallopian tube surgically so that an egg cannot pass through. Blocking the tubes can be accomplished by ligation, coagulation, or mechanical occlusion with clips, bands, or rings. The female pelvic structures can be approached in two ways: through the abdomen or through the vagina. Tubal sterilization is a relatively safe procedure—posing far less threat to the life and health of women than do oral contraceptives or term pregnancy (Hatcher et al. 1984).

The surgical procedures for accomplishing tubal blocking are: *salpingectomy, laparoscopy, minilaparotomy,* and *culpotomy.*

Salpingectomy requires the surgeon to open the abdominal wall—a major procedure with the usual attendant risks and therefore not generally recommended unless the abdomen is already open for a cesarean section (or other operation). The surgeon locates the fallopian tubes, cuts out a short section of each tube, and ties off the incision with surgical thread (tubal ligation). All sexual functions are left intact except that fertilization cannot occur; with a section of the fallopian tubes removed, it is impossible for the sperm to reach the egg. The operation may be successfully reversed in about 60 percent of cases (Hatcher et al. 1984).

Laparoscopy is a much simpler and shorter procedure that does not require major abdominal surgery, and the patient is seldom in the hospital for more than a few hours. In this procedure, an instrument called *laparoscope* is inserted through a tiny incision in the navel, while a teflon-coated forceps is inserted through a one-inch incision further down the abdomen; the forceps carries high-intensity radio waves that cauterize and destroy small sections of the fallopian tubes. The laparoscope contains a lens surrounded by microscopic glass rods that are capable of transferring light but not heat; it enables the physician to look into the depths of the woman's abdomen without opening it up.[50]

Through the laparoscope the physician can clearly see the white ovaries and the pink fallopian tubes. When the tube has been located, it is held with forceps and burned in two places until it pales and tissues are destroyed. The uterus is then rotated, and the other tube is similarly burned in two places. The instruments are then rapidly removed, and the two

---

[48]Ibid.
[49]U.S. National Center for Health Statistics, *Vital Statistics of the United States* annual (1980).

---

[50]Two and a half liters of carbon dioxide are pumped through a needle into the abdomen until its walls are raised away from the intestines and other organs; after the operation, the carbon dioxide is simply allowed to escape.

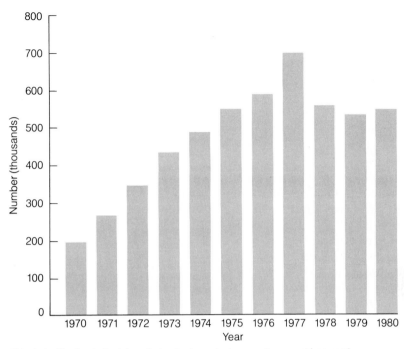

Tubal sterilization is the intra-abdominal surgical procedure most frequently performed on reproductive-age women. The number of tubal sterilizations performed in the United States hospitals increased from 201,000 in 1970 to 702,000 in 1977 and decreased to 650,000 in 1980. According to data from the National Hospital Discharge Survey, in the two-year period of 1979–1980, an estimated 1.3 million women ages 15 to 44 years had tubal sterilizations in U.S. short-stay hospitals. It is possible that this decrease reflects, at least in part, an increased performance of outpatient tubal sterilizations.

FIGURE 11-10

Surgical sterilization; number of tubal sterilizations performed in hospitals,[a] on women ages fifteen to forty-four, United States, 1970–1980

[a]Nonfederal, short-stay hospitals

Source: Data from U.S. Public Health Service, "Surgical Sterilization of Women" (December 1983).

small incisions are each closed with a few stitches and a band-aid. (Laparoscopy is sometimes called "band-aid" surgery.) The operation may be successfully reversed in about seventy percent of cases (Hatcher et al. 1984).

A *minilaparoptomy* is a method of abdominal tubal ligation that is gaining popularity in the United States as well as in many other countries. In this procedure, an instrument is inserted through the cervix and into the uterine cavity to push the uterus up against the lower abdominal wall. A one-inch incision is then made directly over the top of the elevated uterus. The tube is brought up into the operative field and is either cut or tied. A great advantage to this procedure is that it may be performed under local anesthesia on an outpatient basis; the woman is able to go home four to six hours later. The procedure may be successfully reversed in fifty to seventy percent of cases (Hatcher et al. 1984).

Culpotomy is a hospital procedure that allows direct visualization of the fallopian tubes, ovaries, and exterior of the uterus through a tube and optical system. A small incision is made in the back wall of the vagina to perform the tubal ligation. The procedure is done under general, spinal, or local anesthesia and is brief (ten to twenty minutes) and there is no visible scar. However, complication rates are double those of laparoscopy and minilaparotomy. (Hatcher et al. 1984).

It is important to emphasize that these sterilization procedures have no effect on a woman's sex life, except for the psychological benefit of no longer having to worry about the possibility of conception. She continues to ovulate, her hormone system remains undisturbed, and the menstrual cycle goes on. The only change is that sperm cannot travel up the fallopian tubes to reach an egg.

Reversal of these operations is difficult because of the minuteness of the structures involved and the technical difficulty of realignment. Success has been achieved in reversal operations in about 50 percent of cases (Hatcher et al. 1984).

A method of female sterilization still in clinical trials involves blocking the fallopian tubes by injecting into them a small amount of liquid silicone rubber that forms a plug. Tubal blockage occurs about five minutes after the injection, when the substance solidifies. The procedure is extremely simple, requires only a mild local anesthetic, takes less than forty minutes in the physician's office, and requires no recovery period. Its cost is about half that of surgical methods. The reversal rate has not yet been proven in humans, but in experiments with animals, the plugs were removed after 200 days, and some of the animals became pregnant (Kresch 1981).

Female sterilization is legal in all states, although Utah and Connecticut restrict it (along with male sterilization) to cases of "medical necessity."

Inasmuch as there is no difficulty for the physician in identifying the fallopian tubes, and since spontaneous regeneration and realignment are unlikely, the probability of conception after a sterilization is virtually zero.

Vasectomy: The Male Sterilization Operation

Vasectomy is the surest and safest surgical or medical procedure known to prevent unwanted pregnancy (Shapiro 1977). It is a simple and inexpensive procedure in which the *vas deferens,* the tubes through which the sperm pass from the testicles to the seminal vesicles, are cut and tied off, or cauterized. It can be performed in a physician's office under local anesthesia in fifteen to twenty minutes. The vas deferens lie close to the surface and can be reached through a small incision in the scrotum that is then closed with a suture or two. After the operation, the hormone system is undisturbed, erection and ejaculation occur exactly as before, and sperm cells continue to form—but they never complete their journey up the *vas.* Instead, they are attacked by the antibodies that defend the body against foreign intruders and are carried away by white blood cells.

During copulation, the same amount of fluid is released, the sensations and pulsations are the same, the ejaculate looks and feels as it did before. But examination of the semen under the microscope reveals that the sperm are missing. Thus, vasectomy does not interfere with the man's sex life in any way—except to make him sterile.

The man may copulate immediately after the operation—but some other birth control measure must be taken, since sperm may remain in the male genital system for several weeks and pregnancy may occur if they are ejaculated. It takes about twelve ejaculations to empty a man's reservoirs and bring his sperm count to zero (Westoff 1976a). To be absolutely certain that no sperm are present, a postoperative microscopic examination of the ejaculate is necessary.

The vasectomy can be reversed only an estimated 50 percent of the time. Therefore it should be used as a contraceptive measure only when the man is quite sure that he does not want further children (Johnson 1981). Vasectomy is legal in all states, although as noted above, it is restricted in Utah and Connecticut to cases of "medical necessity."

The incidence of failure with vasectomy is virtually zero, since conception can occur only if the vasectomized male copulates too soon after the operation. The operation may also fail, of course, if the physician severs the wrong tube, if a severed tube spontaneously regenerates and realigns, or if the man has an undiscovered extra vas deferens that continues to function—all of which are exceedingly unlikely.

Preventing Implantation after Conception

After the sperm has fertilized the egg, it is too late for any contraceptive measures to be effective—conception has already occurred. Nevertheless, preventing the successful implantation of the germinal disc in the uterine wall is usually called *contraception*. (After a few days have gone by, the expulsion of the embryo from the uterine wall is called *abortion*.)

There are currently three methods of preventing successful implantation of the germinal disc in the uterine wall, or expelling it within a few days of implantation: the intrauterine device (IUD), the "morning-after" pill, and menstrual extraction (menstrual regulation).

The Intrauterine Device (IUD)

The *intrauterine device (IUD)* is a small, inert plastic object (which may have a copper component) that is inserted through the vagina into the uterus where it may be left for months or even up to three years, depending on the type (Gotwald and Golden 1981). IUD's are used by a little more than 7 percent of American women.[51]

IUDs come in a variety of shapes. Each one has its own advantages and disadvantages. The most commonly used devices are the Lippes loop, the Progestasert, the Copper-7, and the Copper-T.

The IUD usually has a nylon string attached that serves two purposes: (1) It aids in removal, and (2) it allows the woman to check for the presence of the IUD by feeling the string at the cervix. A woman using an IUD should check for its presence before each copulation because of the possibility of spontaneous expulsion.

Because of the possible side effects of the IUD—which include discomfort, bleeding, and infection—an IUD should not be used except under close medical supervision. During the fifteen days after insertion, one user in twelve develops an infection, after which the rate declines. In the fourth through sixth years of use, serious IUD-associated infections continue to afflict at least one of every 100 women per year. IUD users are cautioned to be alert for such symptoms as fever, abdominal or cervical tenderness, and a foul discharge. It is estimated that women using IUDs are nine times more likely to contract pelvic inflammatory disease than are women using other forms of birth control (*Science News,* August 1983). Antibiotics usually control pelvic inflammatory disease, but many young women in their twenties and especially in their teens fail to seek help soon enough, and damage often results in sterility. Since 1979, the FDA has required physicians to give every IUD patient a long, printed warning, so that she is informed

---

[51]U.S. National Center for Health Statistics, "Methods of Birth Control" (1984).

of the contraindications. It is not known, however, how many of these patients heed the warning or even read it. No IUD user should ever ignore a pain in her abdomen. If she cannot find the device, she should go to a physician for x-rays.

The IUD has a theoretical failure rate of 1.5 percent and an actual failure rate of 5 percent (Hatcher et al. 1984).

The Morning-After Pill

As long as condoms break, inclination and opportunity unexpectedly converge, men rape women, diaphragms and cervical caps get dislodged, IUDs fall out, people are "swept away" with romantic or passionate urges, or optimistically or cynically "take a chance" we will need morning-after birth control. *Ovral,* a combination of synthetic estrogen and progesterone will usually cause menstruation to commence, and if conception has occurred, the germinal disc is swept away in the menstrual flow. Two Ovral tablets must be taken within seventy-two hours of copulation, and two more tablets must be taken twelve hours later. Failure rates are about 0.16 percent to 1.6 percent. There is as yet no clear evidence whether Ovral is harmful to the woman—or to her offspring should the pregnancy not be terminated (Hatcher et al. 1984).[52]

Menstrual Extraction

Menstrual extraction—also known as menstrual regulation—terminates a pregnancy if used within a few days following conception. Menstrual extraction can be done in a minute or two in a physician's office.

Remember that during the first week after conception the germinal disc is being propelled down a fallopian tube. In the second week it is embedding itself in the uterine wall, and at the end of this week the embryonic stage begins. (This is the time of the menstrual cycle when the woman usually begins to menstruate.) Two weeks after the first missed period, the embryo is a month old.

At any time during these stages, the endometrium (lining of the uterus) may be aspirated with no dilatation of the cervix and no medication. The procedure brings about menstruation, and the germinal disc or embryo (depending on the state of development) is discharged with the menstrual flow.[53]

In short, a woman who fears she is pregnant may simply visit her physician within two weeks after her missed period to have her menstruation "regulated." Without medication, the physician inserts through her undilated cervix a flexible plastic tube attached to a special syringe. The syringe then quickly sucks out the uterine lining, and with it (if present), the germinal disc or embryo. Since no determination of pregnancy is made, menstrual regulation is less likely to provoke the guilt that may be caused by a later abortion, and it is, of course, much cheaper. Menstrual regulation is simple and safe if it is performed within a few days of a missed period. The optimal time is ten to eighteen days after the implanting of the germinal disc. Before this, the disc may be missed (and pregnancy may continue), whereas after eighteen days the embryo is growing quite

---

[52]The morning-after pill DES, used until recently, produced severe side effects and the drug is no longer recommended for postcoital contraception in the United States (Hatcher et al. 1984).

---

[53]After the embryo is more than four weeks old (or more than two weeks past the first missed period), it is well embedded in the uterine wall, and the technique to remove it is called *vacuum curettage,* which can be done in the doctor's office. The essential difference, then, between menstrual extraction and vacuum curettage is that the first procedure is done within two weeks of the first missed period to "regulate the menses," while the second procedure removes a month-old (or older) embryo that is well embedded in the uterine wall and so is considered an abortion. (See the section, "Methods of Inducing Abortion during the First Trimester," later in this chapter.)

rapidly. After twenty-two days the procedure may not be effective (Goldthorp 1977).

Possible Future Methods of Birth Control

Except for sterilization, oral contraceptives are undoubtedly the most reliable birth control method available. Since they have been linked to an increasing number of complications, however, scientists are trying to find other methods that will be just as effective as the pill but with fewer side effects. Many new methods have been developed to the testing stage, but they are not yet commercially available. For example, recent developments with *prostaglandins* may prove to be the basis for the long-sought, routine, "after-the-fact" pill that will cause an implanted embryo to be sloughed off with menstruation up to a month after conception.[54] Another possibility being investigated is the use of an intravaginal disc that contains synthetic prostaglandin. This would provide a steady release of the drug.

A totally new birth control concept—one that could have profound cultural implications because of its simplicity and permanence—is a method that would render a woman indefinitely sterile with a single injection. This method, now under active investigation, involves the discovery, isolation, and synthesis of an active agent in sperm cells that, researchers believe, will cause an allergic reaction to sperm in virtually any woman. The injection of this agent would cause the woman's body chemistry to form antibodies that would either inactivate the sperm before fertilization of the egg or make the fertilized egg incapable of implantation.

Still awaiting development are a once-a-month pill that will either control ovulation or prevent the sperm from reaching the egg, a once-a-year pill that is implanted under the skin to release small measured doses of the drug throughout the year,[55] and a male pill that will render the male temporarily infertile.

ABORTION

If the germinal disc, embryo, or fetus is expelled from the uterus, whether through the natural process of the woman's body or by deliberate medical or surgical intervention, it is called an *abortion*. There are two types of abortion: spontaneous abortion (commonly called a *miscarriage*) and induced abortion (commonly called simply *abortion*).

Spontaneous Abortion

Spontaneous abortion is the body's way of eliminating a malformed or malfunctioning germinal disc, embryo, or fetus, and it is much more common than generally realized. In fact, it occurs in an estimated three-fourths of all pregnancies—with the woman never realizing that she was pregnant (Lowe and Roberts 1975).

If something goes wrong with the development of the germinal disc or embryo, the uterine wall disintegrates and the menses are sloughed off, making way for the possibility of a new conception and a new implantation at the next ovulatory cycle.

Spontaneous abortion may also occur in the fetal stage of development, serving the same

---

[54] *Prostaglandins* are fatlike chemicals found in their natural state in the bodies of all men and women. They may be synthesized in the laboratory and have been successfully used to induce abortion.

[55] A five-year contraceptive, that is injected just beneath the skin of a woman's upper arm, has been found safe and effective by the World Health Organization. Because of the small doses of progestin released over five years, potential side effects are minimal. Ovulation is inhibited, and the cervical mucus becomes thickened and so impedes the sperm penetration (*Bulletin of the World Health Organization* 1985).

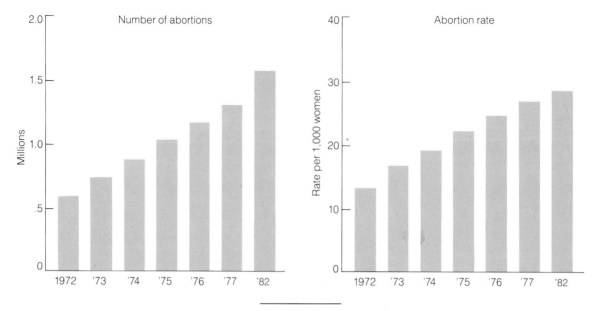

FIGURE 11-11

Legal abortions: number and rate per 1,000 American women age fifteen to forty-four, 1972–1982

Source: Data from U.S. Bureau of the Census, "Legal Abortions—Estimated Number, Rate, and Ratio, by Race: 1972 to 1982" (1985, p. 67).

purpose as a spontaneous abortion of the germinal disc or embryo. Sixty percent of spontaneously aborted fetuses are grossly abnormal, and most of the others have serious problems (Brotherton and Craft 1972).

Women who are older than thirty-five, who require six months or longer to conceive (with regular copulation), and who have had prior abortions have a higher rate of spontaneous abortion than women under twenty-five who conceive within three months of regular copulation and who have never aborted before. In the first group the chances of spontaneous abortion are 40 in 100, whereas in the second group the chances are only 4 in 100 (Young 1982). (These figures, of course, are for those pregnancies that come to the attention of the obstetrician; they do not include the earlier spontaneous abortions that occur simply as "late menstruation.")

Induced Abortion

Induced abortion is deliberately causing the expulsion of the embryo or fetus by medical or surgical intervention. (When the germinal disc is deliberately expelled in this way, the process is called menstrual regulation or menstrual extraction as explained earlier.) Since induced abortion is usually simply called *abortion,* this is the term that will be used for the remainder of this section.

Prior to 1973, abortion was illegal in the United States. In 1973 the U.S. Supreme Court handed down the decision that a woman can choose to have an abortion for any reason in the first trimester of pregnancy. (Certain restrictions apply in the second trimester, and even more restrictions apply in the third trimester.) Since 1973 the number of legal abortions in the United States each year has

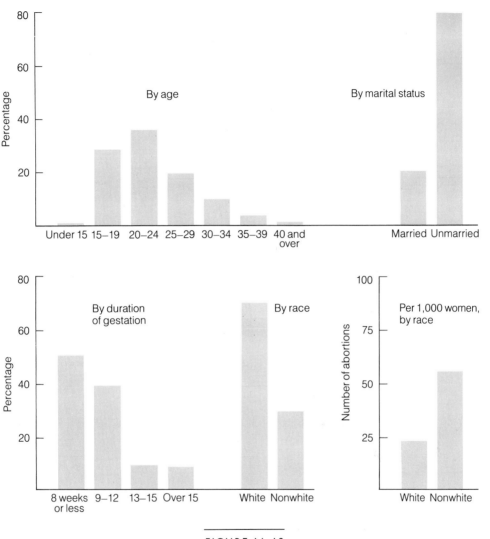

FIGURE 11-12

Who has abortions

Source: Data from Henshaw, S. K., ed. "Abortion in the United States, 1981–82." Copyright © 1985 The Alan Guttmacher Institute. Reprinted by permission.

been rising steadily, reaching more than 1.5 million in 1982 (see Figure 11-11).

Henshaw (1985) of the Alan Guttmacher Institute reported that about one in eight women of reproductive age in the United States has had a legal abortion; a little less than one-third of legal abortions were performed on teen-agers, and more than three-fourths were obtained by unmarried women (see Figure 11-12). Among the world communities, the United States ranks about midway in its annual rate of legal abortion (see Figure 11-13).

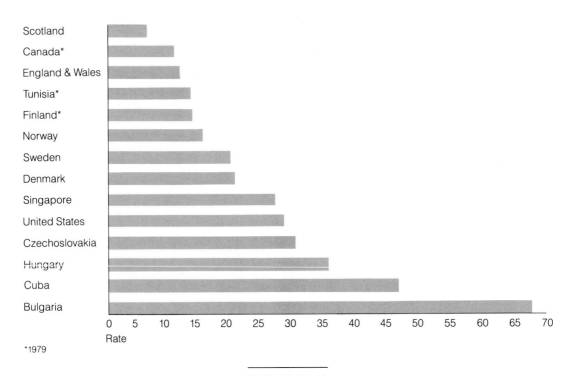

FIGURE 11-13

Rates of legal abortion per 1,000 women age fifteen to
forty-four, various countries, 1980

Source: Data from C. Tietze, *Induced Abortion: A World
Review*, The Population Council, New York (1981), and data
collected by C. Tietze from various sources.

It is interesting to note that more than one-third (36 percent) of abortion patients had never used any method of birth control. Almost another third (31 percent) had used contraception "sometimes," while nearly one-fifth (18 percent) were "thinking about using it" (Francome 1981).

Despite the very strong position of the Catholic church opposing abortion, a surprising number of abortion patients are Catholics. An estimated 25 percent of the 1.5 million American women who have abortions in any given year are Catholic.[56] Thus, Catholic women are overrepresented among those having abortions, since only 22 percent of American women are Catholic (National Council of the Churches of Christ 1984). In a study of a Boston abortion clinic in 1980, 66 percent of the patients were Catholic (in the overall Boston population 35 percent are Catholic). The study also found that 70 percent of those who had second abortions were Catholic. Of these Catholic women who had abortions, 82 percent never, or only occasionally, used contraception. According to the director of the clinic, Catholic patients believe that it is a sin every time they use contraception, so they would rather sin occasionally with an abortion than sin repeatedly by using birth control.

[56]U.S. National Opinion Research Center (1984).

"Catholic youngsters tell me that if they used the pill for 21 days that's 21 sins. But if they have an abortion, that's only one sin" (Francome 1981).

Surveys by the National Opinion Research Center (affiliated with the University of Chicago) between 1982 and 1984 found that 72 percent of Catholic women would consider abortion under certain circumstances, and only 10 percent believe abortion should be illegal under all circumstances. Some Catholic women who had had abortions say they based their decisions on "an informed conscience" and do not believe they have sinned even though they may have found the decisions odious. The National Conference of Catholics Prolife Committee considers this view to be "religious drifting" and has countered with an all-out antiabortion campaign (Sciolino 1984).

Abortion is one of seven grave sins still punishable by automatic excommunication under the new code of Canon Law completed in 1983. According to Catholic church doctrine, both the woman who has the abortion and the person who performs it incur automatic excommunication. However, they may be absolved by a priest after admitting the seriousness of their sins, recognizing their guilt, and seeking forgiveness in confession. The automatic excommunication ruling does not apply to anyone under eighteen years of age (Sciolino 1984).

More then 90 percent of sexually active Catholic women have used methods of birth control other than the church-approved rhythm or organic methods.[57]

Methods of Inducing Abortion during the First Trimester

Vacuum Curettage

The most common method of inducing an abortion during the first trimester (three months) of pregnancy is *vacuum curettage*. It take little time, is done without cervical dilatation, requires no anesthesia, and can be done in the physician's office with no hospital stay.

Vacuum curettage is very similar to menstrual extraction discussed earlier as a birth control measure involving the prevention of a successful implantation after conception. However, vacuum curettage is done after the pregnancy has been diagnosed and is in the first trimester, whereas menstrual extraction involves the suction of the endometrium to induce menstruation, without knowing whether a germinal disc or embryo is present.

Of all the methods of abortion, vacuum curettage carries the least chance of complications and considerably less risk than pregnancy, labor, and delivery (Wolhandler and Weber 1984).

Dilatation and Curettage (D & C)

Another method commonly used to induce an abortion during the first trimester of pregnancy is dilatation and curettage (D & C). The D & C method involves dilating (stretching) the cervix and scraping away the lining of the uterus, together with the embryo or fetus, with a sharp instrument (curette). D & C usually requires hospitalization, since it must be done under anesthesia. D & C used to be the most common method for first-trimester abortions, but it has virtually been replaced by vacuum curettage (Wolhandler and Weber 1984).

Methods of Inducing Abortion after the First Trimester

Dilatation and Evacuation (D & E)

After the first trimester of pregnancy a combined procedure of dilatation and evacuation (D & E) is required to remove the fetus. D & E is a procedure that is an extension of both the

---

[57]Ibid.

traditional D & C and vacuum curettage. It may be used from the beginning of the second trimester to about the twentieth week of gestation. The cervix requires more dilatation than with the traditional D & C, and since the products of conception are much larger, the surgeon may require the help of crushing instruments followed by a large bore vacuum curette. Although D & E is more complicated, is more dangerous, and requires a higher level of skill to perform than dilatation and curettage, it is safer than inducing labor in the woman so that she delivers the fetus (see the next section). It is also much quicker than inducing labor—ten to forty-five minutes compared with many hours and an overnight stay in a hospital. D & E can be done in a properly equipped physician's office or in a clinic under local anesthesia, although most are done in hospitals using general anesthesia (Hatcher et al. 1984, Wolhandler and Weber 1984).

Inducing Labor

After pregnancy has passed its sixteenth week (or one month after the first trimester), the physician can induce abortion by injecting a solution through the woman's abdominal wall and into the amniotic sac, under local anesthesia. A small amount of amniotic fluid is then withdrawn and replaced by a 20 percent salt (saline) solution. This usually causes fetal death followed by uterine contractions and the onset of labor. Instead of the saline solution the physician can inject a prostaglandin solution, which also causes uterine contractions and a much speedier labor.

The saline solution abortion method has a lower complication rate, a lower rate of incomplete abortion (necessitating a D & C), and a lower chance of having to repeat the injection than the prostaglandin method has. However, the disadvantages of the saline solution method include a longer wait before labor begins (the woman generally goes into labor with-

in forty-eight to seventy-two hours) and a slight risk of serious emergency (such as shock). Liver or kidney problems, heart failure, high blood pressure, and sickle cell anemia are medical reasons not to have a saline-induced abortion (Wolhandler and Weber 1984, Shapiro 1977). Following delivery of the fetus and the placenta, the woman may usually leave the hospital within a few hours.

Prostaglandin is a powerful drug that stimulates the smooth muscles of the uterus to contract and expel the fetus. The prostaglandin solution injected through the woman's abdominal wall works more quickly than the saline solution and does not have the same risk of serious emergency. However, prostaglandin has side effects—nausea, vomiting, diarrhea, a higher rate of failure of the first injection, and a high rate of excessive bleeding and retained placenta. Uterine contractions during labor are usually faster, stronger, and more painful than with the saline solution (Bell 1984).

Another method of inducing abortion that is often used during the second trimester (and sometimes during the first trimester) is the intramuscular injection of prostaglandin. (As we have seen, prostaglandin may also be administered as early as a few days following the first missed menstrual period, causing any implanted germinal disc to be discharged along with the menses two or three hours later) (Shapiro 1977).

Hysterotomy

Hysterotomy consists of making an incision in the abdominal wall through which the fetus is removed. A hysterotomy is a major surgical procedure that is usually used only when a woman wants to combine a sterilizing operation (salpingectomy) with the abortion.[58]

---

[58]This is not to be confused with a *hysterectomy*, which is the surgical removal of the uterus.

The Emotion-Laden Arguments Regarding Abortion

The Roman Catholic church has remained a consistent opponent of induced abortion despite the 1973 U.S. Supreme Court decision legalizing abortion. The Roman Catholic church currently maintains that abortion at any stage of pregnancy is a denial of the human right to life. Nevertheless, many Catholic women get abortions. A clinic in Omaha, for example, reports that Catholics account for 35 percent of all abortion patients, while in New York a clinic reports the figure is 40 percent (Fraker et al. 1978). These statistics are interesting, since formal Catholic dogma so vehemently prohibits abortion. Apparently, Catholics are as likely as Protestants or Jews to get abortions, despite the prohibition of their church.

In addition to the Roman Catholic church, other "right-to-life" groups are very actively opposed to legalized abortion. For both sides, abortion is an emotional issue that does not lend itself to compromise or cool debate. At its simplest, it is an argument between those who regard abortion as murder and those who believe women must have the right to choose whether to bear a child or not. The issue is fraught with inconclusive medical and theological arguments about the precise point when the organism must be regarded as a human being—at conception, at birth, or at some hard-to-define point in between. Although it is clear that a new life form begins at the instant of conception, does the organism become a "person" as a fertilized egg? As a germinal disc? As an embryo?

Roman law, from which a large part of our own law is derived, considered the fetus a part or possession of the mother, and abortion was punishable as "property damage." With Christianity came the idea that the fetus is a human being, but the precise stage at which it becomes human remained a matter of speculation. St. Augustine distinguished between a "formed" and an "unformed" fetus and believed the soul does not enter the fetus until it is "formed." Thomas Aquinas felt that life occurs only at the moment of "quickening," the first perceptible movement of the fetus, and this concept became part of the common law of England.

The debate still continues and has been revitalized as part of the controversy over the 1973 U.S. Supreme Court decision, which made abortion the right of every woman in the United States. Strictly speaking, no one is *for* abortion. Those who advocate abortion are *prochoice*. They emphasize that what matters is that a pregnant woman have the option to choose abortion if she wishes.

Social, Economic, Political, and Moral Aspects of Abortion

Abortion is a very controversial topic. Prior to 1973 it was illegal in the United States, and since the U.S. Supreme Court decision of that year made it possible for a woman to choose to have an abortion if she wishes, many well-publicized individuals, both within and outside the U.S. government, and many powerful lobbying groups have been attempting to have the ruling overturned. (One of these proposals is that a constitutional amendment be passed to prohibit abortion in the United States.)

It is estimated that until the change in the abortion law, more than 1 million criminal abortions were performed in the United States each year by unqualified personnel using improper techniques. Three-fourths of these illegal operations were performed on married women who felt that financially, physically, or emotionally they could not afford more children. These illegal abortions caused an enormous toll of uncounted tragedies—death, serious injury, and sterility. Poor women and black women ran the greatest risks with illegal abortions. In 1969, 75 percent of the women who died from abortions (most of them illegal) were black women (International Family Digest, Alan Guttmacher Institute 1979).

In addition to these illegal abortions, many women have seriously and sometimes fatally injured themselves while trying to terminate their pregnancies themselves. A common method involves inserting a long sharp instrument (such as a knitting needle) through the cervix and into the uterus. Severe infection, often combined with shock and kidney failure, is a common consequence of such crude efforts (Reeder and Mastroianni 1983). Other methods of self-induced abortion consist of taking drugs such as quinine or castor oil, which usually do nothing or, if taken in sufficient quantities to produce an abortion, are extremely dangerous for the woman.

Since 1973, when abortion became legal in the United States, abortion-related deaths have decreased by 73 percent (Sachs et al. 1982). Abortion-related deaths decreased dramatically, reaching a low of just sixteen reported deaths in 1980.[59]

It should be noted, however, that the right to have an abortion is chiefly the privilege of urban, upper and middle class women. The U.S. Supreme Court ruled in 1977 that although every woman has a legal right to abortion, the government is not obliged to pay for it. Since then, Congress has eliminated federal Medicaid funds for most abortions for the poor, and few states continue to fund them on their own. According to guidelines established by Congress and the Department of Health and Human Services federal funds may be used to pay for abortion only if the woman's life is endangered, if the pregnancy will cause severe and long-lasting health damage, or if the pregnancy resulted from rape or incest.

Poor women, who cannot afford the fee for a legal abortion, continue to have illegal or self-induced abortions or out-of-wedlock births. At least one-third of American women who wanted abortions in 1975 were unable to get them—mainly the poor, the young, and those outside the biggest cities (International Family Digest, Alan Guttmacher Institute 1979, Tietze and Lewit 1977).

The prolife (or antiabortion) forces point out that the life of the new individual begins at conception, with the fertilized egg. This is, of course, the beginning of the new life form, and, indisputedly, it does contain the forty-six chromosomes that have the capacity to direct the building of a human being. The controversy revolves around this point. Is it a human being when it is a single cell? Or is it a human being in the germinal disc stage? The embryo stage? The fetal stage? Does it become a human being when the heart starts to beat—at the stage of "quickening"? Or is it a human being only after birth?

These questions have not yet been resolved to the satisfaction of biologists or theologians. However, although opinions vary, conviction may be deep and the issue may be extremely important to the individual or the group. Prolife groups lobby for legislative action that will overturn the U.S. Supreme Court decision of 1973. Their members feel strongly that the new life form represents a human being beginning with conception, and that induced abortion is, therefore, murder. (See the vignette, "The Emotion-Laden Arguments Regarding Abortion" on the previous page.)

SUMMARY

A new individual is created with the fertilization of the ovum by a sperm and with the fusion of these two gametes (the sperm and egg) into a single-celled organism, the fertilized egg. The fertilized egg then multiplies and differenti-

[59]Centers for Disease Control, "Abortion," *Morbidity and Mortality Weekly Report*, 32 (54) December 1983, p. 103.

ates into the trillions of cells that make up the human being. The direction of the reproductive process is governed by DNA molecules within the genes, which contain the coded information that determines the development and characteristics of the organism.

Conception (the fertilization of the egg by the sperm) is the beginning of the pregnancy. Although there are many natural signs of pregnancy (cessation of menstruation, swollen breasts, darkening areolae, frequent urination, liquid exuding from the nipples, nausea), all these may be counterfeited by false pregnancy. The only way to determine for certain that conception has occurred is through an examination by a physician and a laboratory test. There are three stages of pregnancy: the germinal, the embryonic, and the fetal.

At full term, labor begins, consisting of regular uterine muscular contractions that force the baby through the birth canal. Labor consists of three distinct stages. The first stage, or the dilatation stage, begins with the first true labor contractions and ends with the complete dilatation of the cervix. The second stage, or the stage of expulsion, begins with the complete dilatation of the cervix and ends with the delivery of the baby. The third stage, or placental stage, begins with the delivery of the baby and ends with the passage of the placenta.

concern but is now a growing social concern as well because of our rapidly expanding population. Birth control may be achieved by preventing conception in the first place, preventing implantation of the germinal disc after conception, or aborting the embryo or fetus.

In accordance with the 1973 Supreme Court decision, abortion by demand is now legally available to all women in the United States during the first six months of pregnancy, although it is often still out of reach for the poor and disadvantaged. (During the final three months of pregnancy, the court's decision found that the state's interest in "potential life" outweighs the woman's individual right, and the state may prohibit abortion except when necessary to protect the health and preserve the life of the woman.) This Supreme Court ruling legalizing abortion in the United States is a landmark decision recognizing the rights of women and may be expected to have many far-reaching sociological implications.

QUESTIONS

1. Describe the *germinal period* of pregnancy. How long does this period last?

2. Describe the *embryonic period* of pregnancy. How long does this period last?

3. Describe the *fetal period* of pregnancy. How long does this period last?

4. Describe the technique of amniocentesis. Why is this procedure performed?

5. Describe the three stages of childbirth.

6. What are some of the procedures that might help the woman to conceive with an infertile couple?

7. What are the various methods of birth control? Discuss the advantages and disadvantages of each method.

8. What are some of the future possibilities of contraception?

9. The issue of abortion is still very controversial in our society. Discuss the pros and cons of abortion.

SUGGESTIONS FOR FURTHER READING

Bennet, Neil. *Sex Selection of Children.* New York: Academic Press, 1983.

Bogue, Donald J. *The Population of the United States: Historical Trends and Future Projection.* New York: The Free Press, 1985.

Choderow, Nancy. *The Reproduction of Mothering.* Berkeley, Calif.: University of California Press, 1978.

Fox, Greer Litton, ed. *The Childbearing Decision: Fertility Attitudes and Behavior*. Beverly Hills, Calif.: Sage Publications, 1982.

Goldsmith, Judith. *Childbirth Wisdom from the World's Oldest Societies*. New York: Congdon & Weed, 1984.

Howe, Louise Kapp. *Moments on Maple Avenue: The New Reality of Abortion*. New York: Macmillan, 1984.

Klinman, D., and Kohl, R. *Fatherhood U.S.A.: The First Guide to Programs, Services, and Resources for and About Fathers*. New York: Garland, 1984.

Macfarlane, Aidan. *The Psychology of Childbirth*. Cambridge, Mass.: Harvard University Press, 1977.

Verny, T., and Kelly, J. *The Secret Life of the Unborn Child*. New York: Simon & Schuster, 1981.

Zelnick, M., Kantner, J., and Ford, K. *Sex and Pregnancy in Adolescence*, Beverly Hills, Calif.: Sage Publications, 1981.

CHAPTER 12

The Family with Small Children

The Developmental Sequence
Components of Healthy Development
The Nature of Discipline
A Child's Personality: Its Effect on the Family

*Children have more need of models
than of critics.*

    Joseph Joubert (Pensée)

After the birth of a child, a new and irrevocable life phase begins for the married couple. With parenthood, they assume responsibility for a new human being. The couple are no longer a *dyad*, relating only to each other within the household. Now there is a third person to consider as well—an individual with his or her own wants, needs, and characteristics.

  One aspect of this new life-style is the helplessness of the *neonate*[1]—a helplessness and dependency that will continue for several years. In light of the great importance of these early years, this chapter will present a close look at the developmental process and the needs of the infant and the young child.

THE DEVELOPMENTAL SEQUENCE

Relatively few specific elements that the child acquires during the socialization process are the same in different societies, but the developmental sequence of children *is* the same

---

[1] A newborn baby is called a *neonate* for the first month of life. With the second month, babies begin *infancy*, which ends when they are walking and beginning to talk (usually at about twelve to fifteen months).

in all societies. Children everywhere proceed from dependency to independency, from self-centeredness to an awareness of and responsiveness to others, and from responding only to immediate satisfaction to an ability to delay gratification in order to obtain long-term goals. This developmental process starts at birth, with the neonate.

The Neonate

The neonatal period occupies approximately the first month of extrauterine life. During this time a complete transition must take place from fetal to postnatal ways of living. Before birth, the fetus is a waterborne, water-breathing parasite, completely secluded in a dark, warm environment with its needs automatically cared for. Oxygen, nutrients, immunizing agents, and hormones are fed directly into the bloodstream through the umbilical cord, which also receives the waste products of metabolism.

With birth, the newborn is suddenly expelled into a completely different environment. Life within the mother, floating in a warm fluid, pitch-black, with all needs automatically cared for—is abruptly, and irrevocably, ended. Neonates must adapt to a new medium quickly—or die. Once the umbilical cord is cut a few moments after birth, neonates must immediately begin to independently oxygenate their own bodies—they must breathe air. Their systems are programmed to make the shift from fluid to air with the first breath. The task of aerating the blood, which has previously been provided by the oxygen in the pools of maternal blood in the placenta, is taken over by the neonate's breathing mechanism. With the first breath, the shift from fetal to postnatal blood circulation begins. The muscle groups coordinated in breathing must acquire a complex, subtly balanced interaction, and for some weeks after birth the neonate's respiration tends to be irregular, shallow, and noisy.

In coordination with this shift to becoming an air-breathing creature, the abdominal muscles surrounding the umbilical cord contract, and circulation through the umbilical arteries and vein stops. The shutting off of the umbilical arteries forces blood into the lungs, and the oxygen level of the blood (which drops when the umbilical cord is cut) reaches 90 percent of the normal level within about three hours. The alkaline balance of the blood is normal after about a week, and the blood pressure normalizes in about ten days.

Mechanisms for internal temperature control must also develop once the neonate is exposed to the external world. Until this happens, the neonate is at the mercy of changes in temperature and may easily become overheated or chilled. The sweat glands don't begin operating for about a month, and the inability to sweat makes it hard for neonates to adjust to heat. Parents often err by keeping neonates too warm, which not only makes them uncomfortable, but also may interfere with the normal development of temperature-regulating mechanisms.

All neonates' first attempts at eating (which consist, of course, of sucking) are very unskilled, and they lose weight for the first few days. When they are hungry, the engage in complex *rooting* (pressing nose and mouth into the breast), which stops only when the nipple is placed in their mouths. When they have found the nipple, they clasp and pump the breast with their hands, even though at all other times they usually keep their hands closed into fists and are unable to grasp things that are put into their hands.

The intestinal bacteria necessary for digestion must be taken in from the environment, so the digestive system is rather delicate for the first few days. These intestinal bacteria also produce vitamin K, which is important for blood clotting; until these bacteria are present, any cut or scratch that the neonate suffers holds the grave threat of serious hemorrhage.

Neonates are very susceptible to infections since the immunity systems that they have been receiving from their mothers' bloodstreams are no longer available to them. The skin, the gastrointestinal tract, and the respiratory system are especially prone to infection. Although precautions should be taken to avoid infection, overprotecting neonates may have the paradoxical result of retarding the necessary formation of their own immunities, making them even more vulnerable to infection.

Neonates are also relatively insensitive to pain during the first few days. For example, circumcision can be performed a few days after birth with no anethesia. However, newborns do feel internal pain (such as cramps from hunger or colic), and this can be quite severe. After the first few days, sensitivity to pain develops rapidly.

Neonates spend about twenty hours a day sleeping. During the first few weeks, in fact, waking and sleeping are really only a matter of degree; neonates are rarely fully awake except when hungry, startled, or likewise distressed. Asleep or awake, they are subject to fits and starts and tremors reflecting the spread of stimulation in their still immature nervous systems. When "awake," they are likely to stare fixedly and blankly at a face or spot of light that happens to fall within their field of vision.

Sleeping neonates show the same brain wave patterns and rapid eye movement (REM) that accompany dreaming in adults. In fact, neonates have a higher proportion of REM in their sleep than is characteristic of adult sleep. The purpose that such REM serves has still not been discovered.

For the most part, neonates are blankly unemotional, whether awake or asleep, although they may smile when contented. There is no indication that neonates feel affection toward anybody or anything, although such affection develops quickly in the first few months of infancy.

Individual differences are important from the very moment of birth. Neonates differ from one to another not only in their anatomical and physiological features (such as blood chemistry, hormonal balance, and size and shape of body organs), but also in their muscle tone, the vigor with which they root and suck, and the forcefulness or sluggishness with which they act and move, whether crying or waving their arms and legs. Some neonates are lively, active, and squirming, whereas others lie limp—so passive and unresponsive that they may seem disjointed.

Neonates also differ greatly from one to another in such psychological factors as alertness, irritability, and sensitivity and responsiveness to the environment (such as light and noise).

Whether these differences are genetic, or are acquired during the first nine months of life in the uterus, or are a combination of both of these factors is not known—although the latter seems most likely. Whatever the cause, the differences that are obvious and important from one person to another are very noticeable from birth on.

Because childbirth usually occurs in seclusion in our society, many people have never seen a neonate until they see their own, and they are frequently startled by the newborn's appearance. Neonates are surprisingly small—the average weight is about seven and a half pounds—and because they keep their legs drawn up, they look even smaller. Their heads make up a quarter of their length and seem to rest almost directly on their tiny shoulders. Their features are still largely undifferentiated: Neonates seem almost chinless, their noses are nearly flat, and their heads may be slightly misshapen as a result of the passage through the cervix and vagina (this *molding* of the head usually disappears within a week or two). Neither eye nor skin pigmentation is developed at birth, so virtually all neonates (even blacks) have smoky blue eyes and pinkish skins. Their skulls have six soft spots (*fontanels*), where certain structural bones have not yet grown together, and the most conspicuous of these (at the very top of the head) may not close over until the child is a year or more old.

The genitals of the neonate are quite prominent, and both boys and girls have prominent breasts, which may temporarily secrete a milky substance ("witch's milk"). Girls may have a brief discharge that resembles a menstrual flow just after they are born. Both the breast secretions and the bleeding are caused by hormones absorbed from the mother's bloodstream and will subside rapidly a few hours after birth.

The Infant

Infancy begins with the second month after birth and ends when the baby is walking and beginning to talk, at about twelve to fifteen months. During infancy, babies begin to look like persons. They gain weight and develop the natural layer of fat that fills out their scrawniness. Their hands and feet are now chubby, and their abdomens are round. Their skin loses its redness, and their heads and noses fill out to normal shapes. They now have large foreheads, small noses, small chins, plump cheeks, and large eyes. The irises of their eyes have now changed to their adult color.

During the second month, infants are more awake than they were as neonates and show more sustained responses to an increasing variety of sights and sounds, such as vacuum cleaners, television programs, and ringing telephones. They can usually raise their heads slightly to look at something, and, although they still cannot really change position, they can usually arch their backs. Also during the second month, their crying stops at the sight of their mothers, and most infants respond with a smile to a human face. At this age, they still awaken for two or more night feedings.

Early in the third month, infants may reach out and bat at dangling objects, but they are not yet able to open their fingers to grasp them. (An institutionalized baby may not reach out to grasp until almost five months of age.) By the age of three months, the infant's eyes are able to focus on near and far objects and can converge on an object as it approaches the nose. Infants are quite social at three months, gurgling and cooing in response to adult overtures and even to music. They recognize members of the family and smile and wriggle and gurgle at them, and they meet strangers with a solemn, reserved, watchful stare. They are now usually sleeping through the night.

Infants first laugh when they are about four months old. They can now be propped in a sitting position for short periods of time, and they can half recline indefinitely in a baby carrier. They begin to eat semisolid, strained foods, although it will be months before they eat without spluttering, choking, coughing, and spitting. They become able to grasp things that they first notice visually (until now they could just bat at them), but they still cannot release anything. If they want to get rid of something they have grasped, they will rub it against the body until it is loosened from their grip.

By age five months, infants can study their fingers, pick up something to examine or taste, show preference when given different colored patches, and remain in a sitting position for some time before their heads begin to loll and their bodies to slump.

By the time they are six months of age, they are able not only to grasp but also to manipulate and release something they are gripping. Between the ages of six and nine months, infants are usually able to roll completely over. They are now on our culture's three-meal-a-day eating schedule, and they sleep through the night. (They still have occasional snacks throughout the day and take naps.) During this stage, they begin to hold out their arms to be picked up, and they become highly responsive to the moods of those around them. Their vocalization becomes more differentiated, with consonants emerging to break up the vowel sounds, and babbling replacing the gurgling and cooing.

Infants can usually sit up without support when they are six months old. They can now amuse themselves with noises, toys, and the movement of objects. They are fascinated with repetition, discovery, experimentation, and imitation. Social games (and learning) evolve from the infants imitating what parents do and the parents, in turn, imitating the infants. Usually by about seven months, infants begin *creeping* for short distances, and by eight months they can *crawl*.[2] They also begin to feed themselves with spoons at about this age—developing the essential feedback necessary for coordinating the muscle control used for contacting an object (the mouth) that they can feel but not see. The first two teeth appear by about the seventh month (though some babies are *born* with teeth).

By about eleven months, infants can creep or crawl up and down stairs. They have also learned by this time that it is possible to detour around obstacles to get something they want. (In contrast, a chicken separated from food by a short length of wire fence may starve to death without ever discovering that it can walk around the fence to get the food.)

Infants are quite active by the time they are eleven months old, and they no longer lie quietly while being dressed. They can now cooperate—holding their hands out for sleeves, raising their head and shoulders to allow the shirt to pass behind their backs. They can now play pat-a-cake, work simple cupboard latches, turn electric lights off and on, regulate the volume on a television set, distinguish pictures of objects in books, and recognize themselves in a mirror.

By the time they are twelve to fifteen months

old, infants are actively relating to others, making eye contact, smiling, and laughing. Not only can they pull themselves up and stand alone, but they are well on the way to becoming highly active, self-directed, willful pedestrians. They can now not only imitate sound and words, but also understand much of the language of their culture, both verbal and nonverbal. They can engage in verbal, as well as nonverbal, social interaction—especially with their mothers.

During the transition period from neonate to early childhood, one of the most important elements of socialization is established: the all-important sense of basic *trust*. Without this sense of trust, the sense of *autonomy*, which is fundamental to much future development, cannot be established (more on this later).

The Young Child

By the age of two years, children are walking, running, climbing stairs, taking off their shoes and socks, and eating with a spoon. They now have a speaking vocabulary of about twenty-five words.

By three years of age, they can play for short periods without supervision, color with crayons, dress dolls, and build with blocks. They can now get a glass of water from the kitchen faucet. They can eat safely with a fork. They are relatively toilet trained, with only occasional daytime "accidents."

Most four-year-olds can wash their hands and button their clothes. They show some sense of rhythm in running, skipping, and marching, and they can participate in simple group activities, such as kindergarten games. They can perform short errands and pick up after themselves if they are asked to.

At five years of age, most children can dress themselves completely except for tying and lacing, wash both face and hands, play in the immediate neighborhood unattended, and maintain unsupervised group games with their age-mates and with older children. They also

---

[2]*Creeping* is defined as achieving a forward locomotion when prone by pulling oneself forward with the arms and legs. When *crawling*, the person is up on hands and knees. Soldiers in combat under enemy fire must creep rather than crawl, or they will present too obvious targets.

can draw recognizable objects such as a house, a person, a tree. By age five they are usually completely toilet trained.

From age six to age twelve, children are extremely busy acquiring information and mastery skills. In the highly structured organization of the classroom, they learn to read, write, and solve arithmetic problems. They absorb a very wide range of knowledge—geographic, historical, grammatical, and scientific. They also develop physical skills, such as roller skating, bicycle riding, throwing and catching a ball, and jumping rope. And they acquire the skills of social behavior—the skills of group participation and of interpersonal relating— that are as important to functioning in our mass society as harness mending and wool spinning were in the past.

With more and more experience, children of this age range achieve an increasingly realistic—that is, accurate—frame of reference in regard to their own natures and the nature of their environment. They develop physical, intellectual, and social competence in dealing with their culture. And finally, they learn, through facing specific problems, what kinds of problems they are likely to confront in the future, and how they should prepare for and resolve such problems (see Coleman 1979).

As individuals develop from early childhood into adults, their perception and discriminative abilities become successively more differentiated and precise. They first learn to differentiate between mother and father, to select one toy and not another, to recognize a song, or to hear the difference between the sounds of a clarinet and a trumpet. When they reach adulthood, they will have refined these early differentiations to an astonishing degree. They may be able to distinguish the voices of two sopranos singing the same aria, or tell a genuine Van Gogh from a skillfully rendered copy.

Similarly, the behavioral skills and abilities are also progressively improved and refined— from putting one block on another to building a tower of blocks, from rolling a ball back and forth to playing catch, from riding a tricycle to riding a bicycle, from driving a car to flying a jet aircraft; from solving a simple mechanical puzzle to building a radio, from putting a bandaid on a doll to performing a delicate surgical operation, from learning the names of animals pictured in a book to arguing a case before the Supreme Court.

This differential development takes place as part of the socialization process, for which the family is chiefly responsible in the early stages. This process of early socialization within the family lays the foundation for the continuing development of perceptual and manipulatory skills throughout childhood, adolescence, and adulthood—as well as for the continuing acquisition of information, knowledge, and, ideally, wisdom. If the initial stage of socialization lays an optimal foundation in childhood, the probability for the development of the child's full potential will be maximized.

COMPONENTS OF HEALTHY DEVELOPMENT

There are many components of healthy development that are genetically programmed. However, given the genetic programming that is present at birth, how far the individual's potential is developed is largely in the hands of the parents. It is they who must provide the necessary ingredients for the individual's development. This process begins before birth (and even, to some extent, before conception) with the important component of *nutrition*, which provides the essential building blocks for the physical and intellectual development of the human being.

Behavioral Effects of Nutrition

Nutrition has an extraordinarily important influence from conception on because it provides the basic elements that are necessary for the development of all the organs of the body, including the brain. Whether individuals reach their optimal potential depends initially on having these building blocks available from the time each begins life as a fertilized egg.

It has taken humankind millions of years to realize that the center of all thought, emotion, sensation, and bodily control lies somewhere in the skull. The adult human brain is a moist, pulsing, jellylike tissue weighing about three pounds. It contains more than 10 billion nerve cells. It is the most complex electrochemical entity in the known universe. It performs miracles with dazzling speed: sight, sound, memory, coordination, anger, love, sensuality, creativity, hunger, thirst. Yet the brain is virtually completed in size and mass at birth, when about 90 percent of all the brain cells that a person will ever have are in place.[3]

The second stage of brain development, during which time the brain cells grow in size, occurs during infancy. By about twelve months after birth virtually all the brain cells that a person will have are present, and cell division stops. The final stage of brain development consists of forming connections (*synapses*) between the brain cells (*neurons*). This connection of neurons is thought to be virtually complete by the time a child is about two years old (although some connections may continue to form indefinitely).[4] The connections between the neurons are extraordinarily complex, with each neuron being connected to as many as ten thousand others.

The physical stages of brain development are thus complete at a surprisingly early age. Since the brain develops its full physical potential by age two, the importance of adequate nutrition during this period cannot be overemphasized.

If the fetus is undernourished, the neonate will have about 20 percent fewer brain cells than normal at birth. If the newborn is undernourished during the first six months, cell division is again slowed by about 20 percent. If the individual is malnourished both as a fetus and during the first six months as a newborn, the brain will have only about 60 percent of the number of neurons (brain cells) that a normal brain has (Jastrow 1981). And the brain never gets a second chance to grow.

To cite one example of the effect of nutrition on brain development, Chilean babies under six months of age, who had been malnourished since birth, were brought to a hospital where they were put on a carefully balanced, nutritious diet. Two years later, these children were evaluated and found to be severely retarded. Fifty-one percent were "educable" but needed special teaching; 36 percent were not educable but only "trainable" to do simple tasks; 3 percent could not even be trained and required custodial care (Wyden 1971).

The extent of childhood malnutrition in the United States is not known, but some studies suggest that it may be shockingly high. For example, a fifteen-state study of 15,444 preschoolers—ranging from lower to upper class—found that a significant number in all social classes lacked certain proteins, vitamins, and minerals in their diets. Another survey found that nearly half of all preschoolers suffer from iron deficiencies. Evidence indicates that affluent as well as low-income mothers often provide their children with less than optimal diets (Wyden 1971). To ensure that the individual develops the intellectual potential that was genetically programmed, it is necessary to balance the diet with a variety of foods from the four basic food groups: (1) fish,

---

[3]The number of working parts in the brain is extraordinary. To put the number of neurons in perspective (10 billion), imagine all these nerve cells dissected out of the brain and laid end to end. If this could be done, they would reach from the earth to the moon—and back again! Since each of these 10 billion neurons is connected to perhaps 10,000 others, the circuitry is unbelievably complex: There are perhaps 1,000 trillion circuit connections in the average human brain. It is the complexity of interaction between these neurons that gives rise to our awareness, our sense of self, and even the ability to examine the nature of our own brains (Jastrow 1981).

[4]It is not known, for example, whether memories and new patterns of behavior occur as a function of new connections being formed among brain cells or by some other means.

meat, or poultry, (2) dairy products, (3) fruits, nuts, and vegetables, and (4) breads and cereals. Vegetarians who exclude fish, meat, and poultry from their diet must make sure they include enough high-quality protein in other foods.

The Importance of Early Bonding

Optimal (or at least adequate) nutrition is the first component of healthy development. A second key component, which comes into play immediately after birth, is bonding. *Bonding* is defined as a close, intimate, mutual regard and attachment that is established between the mother and the neonate.

The first few hours after birth are apparently a critically sensitive period for bonding to take place. This is illustrated by a research study on skin-to-skin contact. One group of mothers were given their naked babies to hold for one hour immediately after birth and for five more hours during each of the next three days. Meanwhile, a second group of mothers were limited to holding their neonates for about a half-hour each day, a few minutes every four hours (during feeding). A month later, compared with the other mothers, the "early-contact" mothers fondled their babies more, spent more time soothing them when they cried during the pediatric examination, and maintained more eye-to-eye contact during feedings; they were also more reluctant to leave their babies with someone else. A year later, their babies had been breast-fed longer than the other mothers' babies, and had gained more weight; these babies also smiled and laughed more and cried less. At five years of age, the children of the early-contact mothers had significantly higher IQs and more advanced scores on language tests than the children of the other mothers (Klaus and Kennell 1976).

In a study that was designed to ascertain the limits of the critical bonding period, one group of mothers had forty-five minutes of skin-to-skin contact with their babies immediately following delivery, while a second group had the same contact twelve hours after delivery. The study found that when the babies were thirty-six hours old, the early-contact mothers were significantly more attached to them than were the mothers who had contact twelve hours later. The early-contact mothers held their babies face to face more often, fondled, kissed, caressed, talked to them, and smiled at them more. This and other studies indicate that the critical bonding period apparently occurs immediately after birth (Henig 1978, Newton and Modahl 1978, Klaus and Kennell 1976).

Another study compared a group of mothers who spent eight hours a day with their babies in the hospital for the four days after delivery, with a group of mothers who were with their babies only to feed them during the four days (which was standard hospital procedure at that time).[5] When the babies of these two groups of mothers were compared two years later, significantly fewer instances of neglect, abuse, abandonment, or inadequate care were found with the early-contact mothers (Spezzano and Waterman 1977).[6]

It is interesting to note that the distance at which newborns see best is nine to twelve inches—which just happens to be the distance between the mother's and the neonate's eyes when the mother is breast-feeding or just holding the baby in her arms. In addition to the importance of eye contact and being held in the mother's arms, an interaction between the neonate and the mother occurs through *sound*. Neonates appear to move in rhythm with their mothers' voices and pay more attention to high-pitched female voices than to male voices (Macfarlane 1977, Klaus and Kennell 1976).

---

[5]Mothers and newborns are now often kept in the hospital for only one day if no complications occur.

[6]See the discussion of alternative birth centers in Chapter 11 for more on how early contact is facilitated between mother and baby.

Providing Emotional Security

All neonates, infants, and young children need to feel *emotionally secure* for optimal development of their genetic potential. Babies and children feel emotionally secure in an atmosphere that is characterized by parental affection, acceptance, understanding, and respect. The critical period for meeting this need for emotional security seems to be from birth to about five years of age. If this need is met during the first five years, the child will likely regard the world as a relatively good, stable, pleasant, and, ultimately, *manageable* place. Conversely, if the need for emotional security is *not* met during this critical period, the child will likely perceive the world as relatively unpleasant, unstable, dangerous, and threatening and will feel inadequate to cope with the exigencies and demands of a hostile environment (Coleman 1979).

A child whose needs for emotional security are met becomes increasingly easy to love, whereas a child whose emotional needs are not met becomes increasingly hard to love—irritable, demanding, and petulant. Thus, there is either an ascending or descending spiral: The child who is provided with ample demonstrations of love responds by becoming more lovable and receives even more love—an ascending spiral. Conversely, a child who is insufficiently loved becomes less lovable and receives even less love—a descending spiral.

As noted earlier, a child whose need for emotional security is fulfilled develops a sense of *basic trust*. Acquiring this sense of basic trust is a very important developmental step for children because without it, they experience the world as quicksand—unstable, undependable, and liable to shift unpredictably. Without a sense of basic trust children cannot establish the all-important *autonomy* (self-reliance) that is necessary if they are to develop, through successive stages, their full potential as individuals (Erikson 1963).

Evidence for the importance of emotional

Oil on canvas, 63 X 43 in. The Corcoran Gallery of Art.

Breast-feeding the baby can be a source of deep satisfaction to both the mother and child.
Gari Melchers, *Maternity*, c. 1913.

security and the establishment of basic trust has come from several sources. One source is the research studies that have compared children reared in institutions with those reared within their families. All of these studies have found that long separation from the mother (or other supportive figure) and from a secure home environment leads to intellectual, emotional, and social retardation. The consequences of early emotional deprivation are inconsolable distress, blunted responsiveness, incommunicability, impaired learning ability, ritualistic (and even bizarre) mannerisms, generalized apathy, and susceptibility to infection.[7] The more isolated and deprived the

---

[7]For more detail on such studies, see Coleman (1984), Bowlby (1973), Pines (1971) and Wyden (1971).

The Harlow Studies

The Harlow studies regarding the importance of emotional security in the Rhesus monkey demonstrated several far-reaching and significant relations between early tactile, companionate, and nurturant experiences and later adult personality manifestations in these animals. In the first phase of his study (1959), Harlow found that animals who were reared with two "mother" figures, one made of wire and one covered with a soft terry cloth, preferred the soft cloth figure, whether they were fed by it or by the wire "mother." This finding contradicts the theory that the need for tactile comfort is learned (as a result of receiving it together with food, protection, and other material support) and suggests that it is *innate*—a basic rather than a conditioned need.

Harlow also found that the baby monkeys would seek out the cloth mother and derive comfort and security from it in times of stress, whether they had been fed by her or by the wire mother. He put into a monkey's cage an unfamiliar and frightening object, such as a mechanical toy bear that would move forward beating a drum. The terrified baby monkey would run screaming to the cloth mother. After a few moments of clinging and rubbing the cloth, he would be calm and relaxed and would examine the toy bear.

In the absence of the cloth mother, the terror and anxiety would persist, and the baby monkey would continue to scream in distress. The presence of the wire mother made no difference to this behavior, even though the baby monkey had been fed by it.

The monkeys who from birth had known only the wire mother would run to the wall, clasp their heads, and rock convulsively. "Such activities clearly resemble the . . . behavior seen frequently among neglected children" (Harlow, 1959).

The second phase of Harlow's research (1962) had to do with the importance of peer contact. Harlow established that monkeys who were reared with no peer contact became severely psychologically disturbed; they sat in their cages and stared fixedly into space, occasionally chewing and tearing at their bodies until they bled. As adults, these monkeys never did engage in affectional or sexual behavior. When the females were artificially impregnated, they rejected their offspring, failing to provide even minimal maternal care and affection.

The critical period of emotional deprivation was found to be up to the age of six months; beyond this time personality damage was both severe and irreversible. (This is the equivalent of two to three years in the human child.) Thus, Harlow concluded that normal personality development requires both (1) sufficient early bodily contact (warmth and cuddling) and (2) early companionate contact with peers. If both these experiences do *not* occur in infancy, the adult will be antisocial, asexual, aloof, and self-destructive.

---

child, the greater is the deterioration. Moreover, adults who have experienced such deprivation in childhood are less able than others to care for their own children properly (Sroufe and Waters 1977).

One of the earliest research studies on child care was conducted by a Prussian king in the thirteenth century. He instigated an experiment in which babies were deliberately subjected to institutional deprivation to determine what languages children would develop if they grew up speaking to no one. Such an experiment could not be conducted today, of course, since it would be considered highly unethical. What the experiment revealed had nothing to do with language—all the babies died. Salimbene (a contemporary of the king) described the experiment as follows:

So he bade foster mothers and nurses to suckle the children, to bathe and wash them, but in no way to prattle with them, or to speak to them, for he wanted to learn whether they would speak the Hebrew language, which was the oldest, or Greek, or Latin, or Arabic, or perhaps the language of their parents, of whom they had been born. But he labored in vain because the children all died. For they could not live without the petting and joyful faces and loving words of their foster mothers. And so the songs are called "swaddling songs" which a woman sings while she is rocking the cradle, to put a child to sleep, and without them a child sleeps badly and has no rest (Salimbene, quoted in Ross and McLaughlin 1949).

Since experiments of this sort cannot be conducted on children in our society, researchers use monkeys as subjects and extrapolate the findings to human behavior. (Monkeys are closest to human beings in terms of their developmental characteristics.) The prototype of these studies is the trailblazing work of Harry F. Harlow (1962, 1959) with the Rhesus monkey—a course of experimentation that demonstrated several far-reaching and significant relations between early tactile, companionate, and nurturant experiences and later adult personality manifestations in these animals. (See the vignette, "The Harlow Studies".)

It is true, of course, that parents are individuals and have different ways of expressing their affection. Some parents are lavish with physical demonstrations of their feelings; others are not but still manage to convey them. Some parents are soft and tender; some are bluff and hearty.

Moreover, nobody can love a baby equally at all times and under all circumstances. Each mother has her own life with its inevitable disappointments, discouragements, and conflicts, and she is not always in the same mood. In addition, the baby's mood varies from time to time. Babies are sometimes cranky and sometimes exasperating. They can destroy a favorite treasure; they often destroy parents' sleep.

What is important in terms of the baby's developing basic trust is the *reliability* of the parents' love—and the *clarity* with which it is felt—despite the inevitable mood swings, strains, problems, difficulties, and conflicts that are inherent in the human condition.

The Problem of "Spoiling" a Child

Parents sometimes feel that too much affection or attention will "spoil" a child, and with the best of intentions they may deprive children of appropriate affection for this reason. There is a strong historic tradition in our society (but rarely in others) that babies are born with "original sin," and that this must be tempered by rigorous control. (See the vignette, "Changes in Philosophies of Child Rearing.")

It is undeniable that some children demonstrate the patterns of behavior that are usually labeled "spoiled"—children who frequently sulk, pout, or have temper tantrums. It is also undeniable that such children often develop into adults who also have unrealistic expectations and are unprepared to cope effectively with reality.

The crucial question, however, is: What causes the pattern of behavior that is commonly regarded as "spoiled"? Current psychological thought, based on very solid evidence, suggests that "spoiled" behavior occurs as a result not of lavish affection and a relatively permissive and creative family environment, but of a relative *lack* of emotional support and affection (Coleman 1979). Children who characteristically experience this lack of emotional support have relatively low self-esteem compared with other children, perceive themselves as relatively inadequate in dealing with the world, and are then likely to manifest the behavior patterns that are called "spoiled."

Of course, "spoiled" behavior may also develop in children who are *overprotected* or smothered with attention. That is, children who are not given the independence that they

Changes in Philosophies of Child Rearing

In the nineteenth century, child-rearing philosophies emphasized sternness, work, and "denial of the flesh." The following admonition from American colonial times is typical:

Never sit at the table until asked, and after the blessing. Ask for nothing; tarry til it be offered thee. Speak not . . . sing not, hum not, wriggle not . . . when any speak to thee, stand up. Say not I have heard it before . . . . snigger not; never question the truth of it (quoted in Calhoun, 1945).

As recently as 1928, John B. Watson, one of the most distinguished psychologists of the period and often regarded as the father of American psychology, offered the following advice for parents:

There is a sensible way of treating children. Treat them as though they were young adults . . . never hug and kiss them, never let them sit on your lap. If you must, kiss them once on the forehead when they say good-night. Shake hands with them in the morning. Give them a pat on head if they have made an extraordinarily good job of a difficult task. Won't you remember when you are tempted to pet your child that mother love is a dangerous instrument? An instrument that may inflict a never-healing wound, a wound that may make infancy unhappy, adolescence a nightmare; an instrument that may wreck your adult son or daughter's vocational future and their chances for marital happiness (Watson, 1928, p. 87).

Watson saw as the ideal result of his child-rearing philosophy:

. . . . a child as free as possible of sensitivities to people and one who, almost from birth, is relatively independent of the family situation. (p. 186).

It is interesting to note that, in a relatively short time, philosophies of child rearing have reversed themselves.

---

need (in accordance with their developmental readiness)[8] and who are inappropriately sheltered from experience (or from "reality testing") are just as likely to manifest low self-esteem, lack a sense of basic trust, and demonstrate "spoiled" behavior as are children who are denied sufficient emotional support and affection (Coleman 1979).

Apparently, the rearing of the well-adjusted, happy, and competent "unspoiled" child requires that parents find a balance between acceptance and loving regard on the one hand, and overprotective, inappropriate indulgence on the other. Finding this middle ground of appropriate.affection and attention is not as difficult as it may sound, however, for children usually do not ask for more emotional support and affection than they need for the moment. When infants cry, they may be seeking comfort *or* attention. When babies lift their arms, they are showing that they need emotional support and cuddling. When children follow their parents about, asking endless questions, or cry over some frustration, they are usually seeking reassurance that they are valued and regarded with affection and love.

Conversely, when children struggle to get free or want to go out to play, they have had all the parental nurture they need and want for the moment. When they want more, they return for it. In short, if parents are sensitive and responsive to their child's behavior—which usually indicates the need that is currently paramount—there is a very good chance that the child will get a proper balance of love and freedom.

---

[8]The concept of *developmental readiness* is explored in the section, "Teaching Mastery Skills," later in this chapter.

The Importance of Early Childhood Experiences

A significant finding of behavioral scientists is that the critical period for the intellectual developmental of the child is not the fifth grade, not the first grade, not the preschool years from three to six—it is the eight-month period from ten to eighteen months of age. In this brief span of time, it appears, the mother's actions do more to determine her child's future competence than at any time before or after. The discovery that this eight-month period is so significant came from the Harvard Pre-school Project.[9]

It has been observed that a child's intelligence is highly flexible before age four, and after this, more and more powerful forces are required to produce a given amount of change. The Harvard Pre-school Project set out to find a procedure for raising the intellectual competence of children before this critical age of four.

To raise intellectual competence, of course, it was necessary to define what is meant by *competence* in small children. The researchers defined *competence* in terms of the child's readiness for first grade, the ability to deal with problems that came up in the schoolyard, and the ability to deal with problems that came up in the classroom. Judgments were made by eighteen experienced observers, teachers and psychologists, who agreed very closely in their evaluations. On the basis of these judgments, the researchers were able to distinguish two quite different groups of children: the *A* group, which rated exceptionally high, and the *C* group, which rated exceptionally low.

In sensory perception and in motor skills, the two groups of children were virtually identical, but differences were clearly noted in seventeen specific intellectual and social skills. The children in the *A* group had these skills; the children in the *C* group did not. For example, children in the *A* group were clearly superior in *anticipating consequences, planning and carrying out complicated projects,* and *understanding complex sentences.* In addition, the *A* children knew how to get the attention of adults for information or help when they needed it; the children in the *C* group did not, but instead were generally either unnoticed or disruptive in the classroom.

The researchers then directed their attention to discover the youngest age at which the two categories of *A* and *C* children could be differentiated. They found that the youngest members of the *A* group, who were barely three years old, had exactly the same cluster of abilities as the six-year old *A*'s. Moreover, the three-year-old *A*'s were already well ahead of the six-year-old *C*'s in both social and intellectual skills. Whatever produced the differences between the *A* and *C* children, it must have occurred before the age of three.

The project then deployed to the homes of the toddlers between the ages of one and three, and the researchers found that the differences between the *A*'s and the *C*'s were already clear by age eighteen months. The researchers were unable to find enough differences in children ten months old or younger, however, to divide them into *A* and *C* groups. Apparently, then, something very important must have happened between the ages of *ten months* and *eighteen months* that resulted in the highly significant differences between the two groups of children.

Since the children had been equated in terms of race, income, education, and residence, it was hypothesized that the difference in the children's behavior stemmed from their *interaction with their mothers.* Attention was then directed toward determining what differences, if any, occurred in the behavior of the mothers of the *A* and the *C* children.

After two years of painstaking work, the differences in the mothers were tracked down.

---

[9]Material in this section is drawn from White (1976, 1975) and Pines (1971).

The *A* mothers provided a rich variety of toys and household objects to play with and allowed their children to roam all over the living area, placing dangerous objects beyond the toddler's reach. If a wandering one-year-old ran into something particularly exciting or encountered an insurmountable obstacle, the *A* mother would pause for a few seconds, interrupting whatever she was doing, to deal with the problem—encouraging the child's curiosity or suggesting a related idea—thus transmitting (perhaps unwittingly) the important skill of how to use adults as a resource. The *A* mothers did this in as short as ten- or twenty-second episodes, many times during the day. The initiative came from the children, but the *A* mothers encouraged the children to master the tasks they gave themselves.

The *A* mothers managed to turn even the dullest everyday situation—diaper changing—into an occasion for a game such as peek-a-boo (which teaches the baby that things exist even when they are hidden from sight). The *A* mother did not spend a good deal of *time* interacting with their children, however, nor did they do much *deliberate* teaching. It was estimated than an *A* mother seldom gave her undivided attention to a child for more than 10 percent of the child's waking time. For a baby who is awake 12 hours a day that's only 1.2 hours.

The *C* mothers, in contrast, protected their possessions and their children by ruling a large number of places out-of-bounds and restricting the children's tendency to explore. *C* mothers also made themselves much less available. They might be patient, loving, and well-meaning, but they talked to their babies much less. *C* mothers seldom encouraged their babies' attempts at making sense of the world, failed to stimulate them intellectually, and did not share their babies' excitement at making new discoveries and solving problems.

To become an *A* mother, then, it is important to fill the world of the ten- to eighteen-month-old child with small, manipulable, visually detailed objects (either toys or household articles) and things to climb on, and to make them all freely available. This freedom may conflict with a spotless home, but *A* mothers are not meticulous housekeepers. It is important to pack the most interaction into the brief snatches of consulting "on the fly"—to try first to understand what the child's activity means to the child, and what he or she might be learning from it, and then provide something new and interesting to think about or to do along the same lines.

Though a mother need not always drop whatever she is doing to attend to her child's requests, she should respond with shared enthusiasm *most* of the time, stimulating the child's desire to do things well and perhaps suggesting a related occupation or game that the child could try next. In every case the mother should talk to the child a great deal, even before the mother is certain the child can understand—for evidence indicates that this will nourish the child's intellectual development.

Teaching Mastery Skills

While emphasizing the importance of fulfilling emotional needs and providing emotional security for children, we must not lose sight of the equal importance of providing the opportunities for acquiring mastery skills or the abilities to manipulate objects, play games, solve puzzles, and construct things.

Autonomy (independence and self-reliance) is initially founded on basic trust, as we have seen. As neonates become infants, and infants grow into young children, their early experiences with manipulating objects result either in increasing autonomy and the eager pursuit of further skills or in self-doubt, the perseverance of dependency needs, and the disinclination (or inability) to acquire skills and competency. The parents' failure to provide for the maturational needs related to mastery skills is just as stultifying to the child's development as failure to fulfill emotional needs.

Children who are familiar beforehand with everything they will be expected to manipulate in nursery school have an advantage that will raise their self-images and increase their abilities to gain manipulative skills. Conversely, children who are unfamiliar and ill at ease with nursery school materials are at a disadvantage. Although there are great individual differences in abilities and attitudes, some of which are genetically programmed, children who are not prepared for nursery school will be at a disadvantage—poor performance, anxiety, and lowering of the self-image is likely to result. Children who find themselves at a disadvantage in nursery school, and then in the first grade, tend to find their school experiences increasingly difficult from grade to grade, since the skills and information acquired in later grades are usually based upon skills and information acquired in earlier grades.

Developmental Readiness

Developmental readiness is a complex of the child's maturing muscular and neurological capacities to do something. For example, children do not have the necessary sphincter muscle control to be toilet trained until they are between two and three years old. An attempt to teach this or any other ability or skill before the child has the necessary developmental readiness will not only end in failure, but will cause the child to have feelings of defeat. The child who has too many failure experiences will come to expect failure, and the groundwork is thus laid for feelings of self-devaluation, frustration, and a sense of inadequacy in coping with the reality of the environment.

However, teaching a child a skill just as the child reaches the critical period of developmental readiness not only avoids the emotional problems associated with failure, but maximizes the possibility that the skill will be readily acquired. This is a happy experience for both the parent and the child. Repeated

From infancy on, children are extremely busy from acquiring information and mastery skills as well as the skills of social behavior.
Mary Cassatt, *Playing on the Beach*, 1884

National Gallery of Art, Washington. Ailsa Mellon Bruce Collection.

failures in trying to teach a child a skill engender frustration in the parent as well as in the child—and it is a rare parent who does not become discouraged and angry. If such failure occurs too often and becomes characteristic of the household, the atmosphere becomes one of tension and fear for the child, disappointment for the parent, and frustration for both.

The period of developmental readiness is critical for a second reason. Not only is it fruitless to try to teach a mastery skill before the necessary muscular and neural control has been established, but introducing the challenge too late (after the critical period of developmental readiness) may also result in failure—because the child may be inattentive and bored. If the challenge is too simple and easy, it does not stimulate interest, and success is not rewarding.

The ideal is to provide the child with the challenge just as the child reaches the developmental readiness for that activity. Then it is neither so difficult that the child is doomed to fail, nor so simple and easy that it is not interesting.

Providing Success Experiences

Success experiences, as opposed to failure experiences, breed confidence, optimism, and a sense of the world as being ultimately manageable.

Obviously, not all the child's experiences can be successful, but, as a general rule, if initial experiences are successful, occasional subsequent failures will act as stimuli to further effort. Moreover, when success experiences are characteristic, the child perceives the family as being warm, accepting, respectful, loving, and affectionate. Conversely, too many failure experiences will lead the child to expect failure, to regard the world as unmanageable, unfriendly, cold, and rejecting.

It is important that parents maximize the probability for success experiences to occur and minimize the probability for failure experiences.

Providing Tools and Information

To acquire mastery skills, children must have available the *tools* and the *information* necessary for challenging their abilities and stimulating their interest at their level of developmental readiness.

For infants, the appropriate tools for acquiring mastery skills are such objects as a rattle (for manipulative skills) and a rag doll (for relational skills). Small children can play with building blocks, pull toys, coloring books, dolls, and other toys (a large ball, a tea set, miniature tools) that allow the participation of others (parents, brothers, or sisters, play-

mates). As they grow older, children can use dull, round-nosed scissors, colored paper, paste, soft balls, puzzles, and the thousand and one items of play that reflect our cultural preoccupations. Picture books lead to reading; building sets, balls and bats, and tricycles lead to manipulative skills and interests, to neuromotor coordination, and to a knowledge of spatial relations. And all these skills lead to a self-image of adequacy in control of the environment and effectiveness in relating to others.

Information is just as important as tools in providing for the development of appropriate mastery skills. In fact, information and mastery skills often go hand in hand. Children who have their questions answered promptly and candidly, and as thoroughly as they are able to understand, will not only acquire information, but will also be self-assured intellectually. Children want to learn; they are as eager to acquire information as they are to acquire skills and abilities.

Instilling Values

A child not only acquires information and skills, but also acquires a sense of *values* in interaction with the family. Things that have *value* are wanted or prized. The information and skills transmitted through initial socialization within the family are those that are valued by the society. In other words, societal (and parental) values determine what information is learned and what skills are acquired by the child.

For example, information or an activity that is valued in a contemporary metropolitan area in our society is quite different from information or activities that are valued in an agricultural village. Riding a tricycle and dialing a telephone are valued activities in our society, but they would have no value in an African Pygmy society, which would value the abilities to read tracks and to throw a spear accurately. Youthful Masai are taught herding techniques.

Children who grow up in a house where reading is valued usually learn to read faster and to read more than children who grow up in households where reading is not valued.

Young Norwegians often master skiing before age five. Manu children in New Guinea learn to swim almost as soon as they can toddle. American children learn how to ride tricycles, throw and catch balls, change stations on a television set, shop in grocery stores, and manipulate all the other various tools and artifacts of our society because these activities are *valued* by our society.

Values are standards by which people measure the relative worth of everything from material objects to philosophical ideals. Initially, through socialization within the family, a child acquires a pattern of values—what is respected or disdained, what is loved or hated, what is idealized or scorned. The values held by the family, and transmitted to the child, direct both the type and the extent of the information and the skills that the child acquires. For example, children who grow up in a

house where reading is valued, a house that is filled with books and magazines, usually learn to read earlier and to read more than children who grow up in a household that is "culturally deprived" in this regard.

An interesting example of the pervasive influence of implicit value is revealed by how a child answers the question, "Which do you think is more important in determining success—*ability* or *luck*?" Most middle-class children (who have been raised to believe that effort should be valued, because it can be counted upon to bring a reward) reply *ability*. Most lower class children (whose economically deprived parents have little reason to regard effort as a value or to anticipate success through their own efforts) reply *luck* (Wernick 1974). The subtle values related to social class position are inadvertently handed down from parent to child, profoundly affecting the child's

"*You've been a very, very bad sibling.*"

attitudes, self-image expectations, and social behavior.

Children of poverty usually do not perform as well in school as more affluent children for many complex interrelated reasons. But one reason is that they apparently expect to gain little (or nothing) from hard work. Middle class children, however, are more likely to be more attentive and to work harder, because they have been indoctrinated with the value that "work pays off" (Wernick 1974).

THE NATURE OF DISCIPLINE

Discipline is defined as setting limits on behavior and inducing wanted behavior that eventually becomes self-perpetuating. Sociologists and psychologists agree that discipline not only is advisable, but is essential for happiness, security, accomplishment, and contentment. The undisciplined person, whether adult or child, is not only unsocialized, but unfulfilled.

It is important to note that discipline is *not* defined as punishment, however. The definition of *punishment* is the deliberate infliction of deprivation, discomfort, pain, or suffering.

The concepts of discipline and punishment are often confused and may even be equated or regarded as identical.[10] Those who equate discipline with punishment, however, completely miss the point of what discipline is all about.

Punishment

Discipline and punishment are related, of course, since punishment, if applied judiciously, may bring about discipline in certain selected cases. That is, when punishment is effective and achieves the desired results, it will stop an unwanted behavior. If a behavior is followed by a punishment the behavior may be discontinued. Examples of this principle are very clear in the physical world. For example, we do not eat rocks, or jump from very high places, or drink liquids that are too hot, because the results of such behaviors are immediately and automatically punishing—as the function of physical reality. We might en-

---

[10]Discipline and punishment were equated in most Western societies until late in the nineteenth century. Corporal (physical) punishment was maintained in the U.S. Navy, for example, under the impression that men who were not flogged for disobedience would be unruly and unmanageable, especially under enemy fire. The few officers and administrators who objected to flogging were ridiculed as "bleeding hearts." Flogging is no longer permitted in the Navy, nor is any form of corporal punishment, and discipline has, of course, not suffered as a result of this more enlightened and logical view.

gage in such behavior once, but because the punishment is immediate and inevitable—pain—it effectively stops the behavior. There are people who persist in behaviors that are automatically followed by punishment, but such people are regarded as abnormal and are usually institutionalized where they can be protected from the effects of their own actions.

Punishment that is applied deliberately by a social agency (such as a parent) does not necessarily have the same effect as punishment received automatically from the environment. Paradoxically, when punishment is deliberately applied it may even have the opposite effect—*prolonging* the behavior it is designed to stop.

There are many reasons for this paradoxical effect. The punishment may be resented, and the person may continue the behavior as a way of showing this resentment. The person may feel the punishment is unjustified or misapplied and may continue the behavior as a gesture of independence and integrity. The motivation for the behavior may be so strong that the person continues despite the punishment. The behavior may be caused by anxiety or tension, and it may simply increase if the punishment intensifies the anxiety.[11] If the behavior is genetically programmed, of course, punishment is futile.[12]

Since punishment deliberately applied by a social agent is sometimes the most effective and economical way to stop an unwanted be-

havior, an intriguing and practical question is: When or under what circumstances will punishment work, and when will it be ineffective or damaging? Psychologists have been very interested in investigating this question. They have found that punishment is effective in stopping an unwanted behavior when four conditions are present.

First, *there must be no significant emotional involvement with the behavior or with the punishment.* If there is, punishment may cause resentment, which may then cause the punished behavior to continue and even increase. Moreover, if the punishment is resented, it may cause a breach in the essential bond of closeness between the parent and the child, and it may engender self-devaluation in the child. It is, of course, very difficult to avoid emotional involvement with punishment when it is deliberately applied by a social agent. (When punishment occurs naturally as a function of physical reality, it is not usually resented).[13]

Second, *there must be no strong motivation for the behavior.* If motivation is strong and persistent, punishment will usually not stop the behavior (when it is applied by a social agent). Thus, a person will park next to a red curb despite the anticipated punishment of the parking ticket, if the need to park is strong enough. Or, to use a more complex example, Christian martyrs would go to their deaths in the Roman Colosseum rather than stop proclaiming the divinity of Jesus Christ. In the face of strong motivation, punishment is ineffective.

Third, *an alternate course of action must be available.* The person must be able to avoid the

---

[11]For example, a child who is punished for stuttering is likely to stutter more. Although there are many different causes of stuttering, it is usually accompanied by tension and anxiety, both of which augment the pattern of stuttering. Punishment increases tension and anxiety, which in turn increase the incidence of stuttering.

[12]An interesting example is the case of the small puppy who urinates on the rug and is slapped with a folded newspaper by his master, who is under the impression that the urinating on the rug will stop because of the punishment. However, the puppy is genetically programmed to demonstrate his acceptance of the dominance of the alpha member of the pack by urinating. Thus, the show of dominance by the puppy's owner simply elicits further urination.

---

[13]It is possible, of course, for the punished person to feel resentment even when the punishment occurs as a result of physical reality. For example, a tennis player who flubs a shot may throw his racket over the fence. A golfer who misses a four-foot putt may throw his entire bag of clubs into the water hazard. A disgruntled farmer in North Carolina whose car refused to start on a cold morning went into the house, got a shotgun, and fired both barrels at the engine. However, the person who resents the failure of a tennis ball to fall within the court, the failure of a golf ball to drop in the hole, or the failure of a car to start is obviously being illogical.

punishment by engaging in an alternate course of action or behaving in another way. It is important, in other words, to provide an "out"—an alternate behavior that is equally satisfying (for example, disapprove coloring on the wallpaper and provide a coloring book).

Fourth, *the punishment must be informative.* The child must be able to relate the punishment to the behavior. This usually means that punishment must immediately follow the behavior. Punishing a child for an unwanted behavior long after it occurred will probably be ineffective in stopping future occurrences, unless the punishment is clearly informative.[14]

It is clear that, although punishment can be very effective in bringing about discipline (by stopping an unwanted behavior), it is a very "iffy" procedure since it rarely satisfies all four of these conditions when it is deliberately applied.

Although our society tends to use punishment to instill discipline in children, there are significant differences between lower and middle classes in this regard. For example, corporal (physical) punishment is common in the lower class but relatively rare in the middle class. As might be predicted from the foregoing discussion, lower class children tend to be relatively poorly disciplined yet frequently punished. Middle class children tend to be relatively better disciplined yet not punished as often or as severely as children in the lower class. The more severe child-training practices in the lower class may be related to this class's relatively high frustration level, crowded living conditions, and economic pressures (Reiss 1980).

---

[14]This principle of relating the punishment to the unwanted behavior can be seen very clearly with animals. For example, if a cat that is clawing a piece of furniture is punished a few moments later, this punishment will have no effect on the behavior because there is no way the cat can connect the two events (scratching the furniture and the punishment). If a cat is punished at the instant of clawing, however—by a loud noise, for example—this will effectively stop the behavior.

Reinforcement

Reinforcement is defined as something that causes a behavior to happen more frequently when it follows the behavior. For example, we eat because we are hungry, because eating brings a sense of satisfaction and alleviates the hunger pangs. Food, then, is very reinforcing when we are hungry. We turn on a televison program and watch it because we find this provides a sense of pleasure or satisfaction, which reinforces the action of turning on the set. Similarly, we work to receive paychecks because paychecks act as reinforcers.

The term *reward* is often used to mean a reinforcement, but what is thought of as a reward by one person may not be rewarding to another. By definition, a reinforcement is *always* rewarding.

The relation between reinforcement and discipline is very clear. If a behavior is followed by a reinforcer, the incidence of this behavior will increase. In other words, the behavior will occur more often if it picks up a reinforcer. Behavior, then, is both *established* and *maintained* by reinforcement.

Initially, it may be necessary for a reinforcer to follow every example of the behavior. After a time, however, a pattern of behavior is established, and the reinforcement need only occur intermittently.

Reinforcers may vary in effectiveness from one occasion to another. Something that acts as a reinforcer at one time may not act this way at another time. Something that a parent may think of as a reinforcer may not be perceived as a reinforcer by the child. Some behaviors may be established by a single reinforcement, whereas other behaviors may require a long pattern of reinforcement. Despite these complications, any mistake made in using reinforcement can be easily corrected or modified. Parents will not damage or destroy the parent-child bond by using reinforcement, nor will its use threaten the important aspect of *trust*. Providing the positive reinforcement of *acceptance* and *approval* following desired behavior in a child is a very effective socializing device.

This procedure is often combined with *modeling*—that is, the parent acting as a model, an example to be imitated, for the child. When the child bases his or her behavior on that of the parent, the parent responds with approval, which is a powerful reinforcer. Thus, modeling is often combined with reinforcement in bringing about a desired behavior.

Finally, it should be emphasized that, as noted earlier, reinforcement, by definition, *establishes* and *maintains* a behavior, whereas punishment may stop a behavior. In order, thus, to establish or maintain a behavior, it is necessary to use reinforcement.

Discipline and Love

Experience has shown that depriving children of love is a very poor way to bring about discipline. Perhaps worst of all is making love conditional upon good behavior or using love as a bargaining chip. Such conduct is liable to injure the parent-child bond. When love is withheld unless wanted behavior occurs, a descending spiral often follows. The unwanted behavior continues, which leads to increased withholding of love, which is followed by an increased incidence of unwanted behavior. This unhappy pattern leads to frustration and unhappiness for both parent and child. Once established, the descending spiral is very difficult to reverse. It is much simpler to avoid the pattern in the first place.

Another basic principle regarding the relation between discipline and love is that a child should never be allowed to feel that parental discipline is a *rejection*. A parent should criticize or correct the *action*, not the child, by saying in effect, "I love you, but that was a naughty thing to do." A parent should not say, "You are a naughty child; I do not love you when you do that." In short, instilling disciplined behavior should never be accompanied by a withdrawal of nurture, love, or affection;

A child should never be allowed to feel that parental discipline is rejection; discipline should always be based on a foundation of love and respect.

Ken Robert Buck/The Picture Cube.

these should be considered a child's right, to be freely and warmly provided.

At the base of all socialization there must be a foundation of love and respect. A child whose needs for affection, attention, and creative and intellectual stimulation are adequately fulfilled is generally a happy, good-natured, cooperative, productive, and well-disciplined child.

Setting Limits

One aspect of discipline is setting limits on behavior. The question that often occurs, however, is: Precisely where should these limits be set?

Obviously, children cannot be permitted to behave in ways that are dangerous. They cannot be allowed to ride their tricycles on the freeway. Children should also be stopped from behaving in ways that infringe on the rights or the freedom of others.

A good rule of thumb is to ask oneself whether the limit being set is really necessary. If it seems so at the moment, set it, but be sure the child is diverted with another activity equally attractive and that the diversion does not cause feelings of rejection or resentment. When behavioral limits set by the parent are realistic and consistently enforced, children usually accept them—although they will occasionally "test the limits."

Limits set in this way should be as few as possible, and children should be permitted as much freedom as is practical within these limits. Allowing children to experience reality for themselves is a very effective method of socialization, wherever practicable. (For example, a child who is allowed to eat a piece of soap is not likely to repeat the experience, but a child cannot be allowed to eat poison.)

The more freedom children are allowed within the limits that must be set, the greater will be their potential for development as competent, creative, and emotionally secure individuals. Since community organizations (such as schools) that handle children in large groups often tend to enforce uniformity, it is important for parents to permit as much freedom as possible.

Children understand and accept occasional unreasonableness in their parents and are not harmed by it if they feel generally wanted, accepted, and respected; if they have enough activities to perform; and if they feel that most of the limits imposed on them are realistic and reasonable. They know they may write on paper but not on the wall, may cut out patterns but not curtains, and may kick a ball but not the baby.

In summary, there are four principles regarding the setting of limits on children's behavior:

1. Children should not be allowed behavior that is dangerous to themselves.

2. Children should not be allowed behavior that infringes on the rights of other people.

3. The limits set on behavior should be realistic, and they should be as few as possible. Within these limits, children should be allowed as much freedom as is practicable.

4. The limits should be extended as quickly as possible; that is, children should be allowed increased freedom of movement and access to possibly dangerous objects as soon as their developmental level is appropriate.

A CHILD'S PERSONALITY: ITS EFFECT ON THE FAMILY

Although providing the components for healthy development gives maximum opportunity for a child's full potential to emerge, children have quite different potentials, temperaments, and personalities at birth, as noted earlier. And a child's innate disposition inevitably affects the parent-child interaction: The parent's attitude and behavior are influenced by the child's attitude and behavior.

The parent-child interaction should not be looked on as proceeding in one direction only—from the parent to the child. For example, the cooing and smiling of an easily contented baby can soothe the most harassed parent, whereas the howls of the cranky and irritable baby are likely to cause the most patient parent to become angry and self-pitying.

Children tend to fall into three categories in terms of inborn temperament: the "easy" child, the "difficult" child, and the "slow-to-warm-up" child. The "easy" child is a pleasure to have around most of the time and is least likely to develop psychological, social, or intellectual problems. These children respond with interest to new situations, enjoy strange new foods, have no eating problems, and are, in general, happy, cheerful, and responsive.

At the other extreme is the "difficult" child, whose troublesome behavior can drain a generous supply of patience, disturb the emotional equilibrium, and irritate the calmest parent. These children either protest vigorously or withdraw when exposed to new situations. They reject new foods and people, are reluctant to learn new games or take part in new activities, and often display temper tantrums, violence, and hostility.

Between these two extremes are the "slow-to-warm-up" children who do not actively withdraw or protest new situations, new foods, or new people, but are very passive in their responses. As babies, when they are given a new food they may simply let it dribble out of their mouths. They may remain on the sidelines for several weeks in nursery school or kindergarten, and struggle quietly to escape when urged to take part in some activity. Throughout childhood they tend to passively withdraw from new situations, and they adapt to new experiences slowly (Thomas and Chess 1977).

Each of these three types of children can have a great deal of influence on parental behavior and therefore on their own subsequent development. If the child is easy and rewarding to relate to, the mother is more likely to provide the child with affection, warmth, security, and love. Mothers of "easy" children tend to stay closer to them, look at them more, and play with them more. As a result, the social and intellectual development of the "easy" child is enhanced. For example, such children tend to score significantly higher than other children on IQ tests at age thirty months (Sameroff 1974).

In contrast, mothers of "difficult" children tend to leave them alone more, look at them less, and socialize and play with them less. They do not provide the stimulation and care that lead to optimal socialization and intellec-

tual development. Children rated as having "difficult" temperaments at the age of four months are most likely to score lowest of the three categories of children on an intelligence test at age thirty months (Sameroff 1974). Apparently the child's temperament at four months of age influences how the mother is going to relate to the child, and this in turn influences the child's intellectual development.[15]

Researchers have found that one key difference among babies that provokes different reaction patterns among parents is the babies' sleep patterns.

Some babies slip into solid and predictable patterns of sleep, lifting a tired mother's spirits. Others never seem to be able to drop off easily or to stay asleep when they do, and such a child can readily cause the very same mother to feel bitter and resentful. . . . [A mother may view] her child's erratic sleep habits as a sign of failure in child-rearing. . . . Tears and runaway anger are understandable responses to a child whose fractured sleep spells for the mother fatigue, frustration, and guilt (Segal and Yahraes 1978, p. 93).

Another key difference is in babies' capacities to make eye-to-eye contact. This capacity has been found to be an important factor in bonding and the development of parental attachment (Segal and Yahraes 1978).

Another key difference is in the babies' predispositions for gurgling, smiling, and other expressions of contentment. An alert, contented, and responsive baby has a very positive effect on the parent's self-concept and, in consequence, on the parent's development of skills in relating to the baby. A baby who has the temperamental characteristics of the "easy" child helps get the parent-infant relation on the right track quickly and makes the

---

[15]It is also possible, of course, that the "difficult" children are genetically programmed to develop lower intelligence. There is no evidence to support this hypothesis, however (Sameroff 1974).

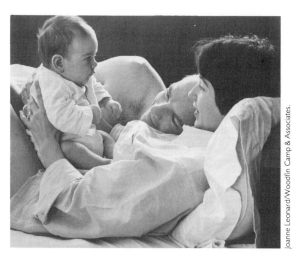

Joanne Leonard/Woodfin Camp & Associates.

Eye contact is an important factor in bonding and in the development of parental attachment.

parents feel optimistic and confident about their abilities to relate effectively to the baby (Thomas and Chess 1977).

Babies have the capacity not only to discourage warmly nurturant behavior, but even to evoke outright abuse. Such children violate the common parental expectations that babies will be attractive and lovable; they are neither. Such babies make almost impossible demands for patients, time, and nurture. They sleep less, cry more, are more irritable, and feeding disturbances are common. Progress in muscular development, speech, and social interaction is much slower than expected during the first two years, and periods of developmental readiness are delayed. In consequence, parents of such a child often develop feelings of guilt, inadequacy, and anger toward the child (Sameroff 1974).

It is instructive to note, in this regard, that it is often only one child in a family who is a target of abuse, and some abused children continue to be victimized in a succession of foster homes in which no other child has met a similar fate.

Child battering is an unspeakable act that can never be justified, leaving unerasable scars on the child's

mind as well as body. Still, to help deal with the problem, researchers must ask whether the victims play a role in evoking parental violence. The evidence increasingly indicates that, in fact, they do . . . clinical interviews with abusive parents suggest that certain characteristics of the newborn can help push parents beyond their threshold of violence. Newborns who fret a great deal appear to run a greater risk of harm than those who are placid and easily soothed. The abused child is typically the one who is irritable, colicky, fretful, and difficult to feed, satisfy, or diaper. Parents of such children develop feelings of inadequacy, guilt, and anger; nothing about the baby's behavior makes them feel good about being parents. For adults with a low flash point, such an infant can soon precipitate vicious attacks (Segal and Yahraes 1978, p. 96).

A most interesting finding of researchers is that babies in different ethnic groups have predictably different characteristics of temperaments at birth. This finding suggests that ethnic differences may play a more important role than was hitherto suspected. This does not necessarily mean, of course, that any such differences necessarily result from genetic factors; since ethnic groups have different cultures, such differences could very well be based on cultural factors. Whatever the basis, however, the differences among infants of different cultures are present from birth on. (See the vignette, "Ethnic Differences in Babies.")

In summary, the child-parent relation is an interaction between the parent and the child, with each affecting the other. The parent not only shapes the child's behavior, but also the parent's behavior is shaped *by* the child. Everything the child does affects the parent, and this is reflected back to the child. Thus, two possible spirals may occur—ascending or descending. Babies who, at birth, have responsive, lovable characteristics, are loved more, become increasingly lovable, consequently receive even more love, and in consequence become more lovable. Babies who at birth are cranky, colicky, passive, or unresponsive to a parent's overtures are, in general, less lovable,

Ethnic Differences in Babies

Research has found not only that babies have significantly different temperaments at birth, but also that there are characteristic *ethnic* differences that show up only a few hours, days, or weeks after birth. For example, white babies cry more easily and are harder to console than Chinese babies. When being undressed for an examination, Chinese and white babies start to cry at about the same time, but Chinese babies stop sooner. When picked up and cuddled, Chinese babies usually stop crying immediately, whereas the crying of white babies only gradually subsides. White babies turn their faces to one side when they are placed face down in their cribs, whereas Chinese babies tend to keep their faces buried in the sheets (Freedman 1979).

Navajo babies are very similar to Chinese babies, even outdoing them in calmness and adaptability. Japanese babies, in contrast, are more sensitive and irritable than either the Chinese or the Navajo, though not as irritable as the typical white baby. Studies indicate that such differences in temperament among these and other ethnic groups maybe have a biological or genetic basis, although the evidence is as yet far from conclusive (Freedman 1979).

These studies open up intriguing new areas of speculation about characteristic differences in ethnic temperaments, as well as the importance of different personality traits in infants.

---

receive less love, become less lovable, and in consequence receive even less love.

It is easy to love a lovable baby. It is more difficult to relate effectively to a baby who is not initially lovable. Consequently, it is the child who most needs attention, affection, and love who, ironically, is most often deprived of them.

By acknowledging both sides of the parent-child equation, mothers and fathers will more easily accomplish a key task of parenthood: listening for, comprehending, and dealing wisely and compassionately with the unique characteristics of each child (Segal and Yahraes 1978, p. 96).

SUMMARY

During the first month of extrauterine life, a period of extraordinarily rapid change and development, the baby is called a neonate. From the moment of birth, individual differences are evident. Some neonates are lively and active, whereas others are passive and relatively un-responsive. It is not known if these differences are genetic, if they are acquired during the first nine months of life in the uterus, or—more probably—if they are a combination of both these factors.

The first few hours after birth are a critical period in which bonding takes place. Bonding is defined as a close, intimate, regard and attachment that is established between the mother and the neonate. "Early-contact" mothers fondle their babies more, spend more time soothing them when they cry, and maintain more eye contact during feedings. Their babies smile and laugh more, cry less, and gain weight faster. At five years of age, children of early-contact mothers have significantly higher IQs and higher scores on language tests than children of other mothers.

Infancy begins with the second month after birth and ends when the baby is walking and beginning to talk—usually at about twelve to fifteen months. Infants first laugh when they are about four months old and can usually sit up without support when they are about six months old. By seven months, infants usually begin to creep for short distances, and by eight months they can crawl. One of the most important elements of socialization that is established during infancy is a sense of basic trust.

The brain is virtually completed in size and mass at birth, when about 90 percent of all the brain cells that a person will ever have are in place. The second stage of brain development, during which time the brain cells grow in size, occurs during infancy. By about twelve months after birth, virtually all the brain cells that a person will have are present, and cell division stops. The final stage of brain development, when connections are formed between the brain cells, is thought to be virtually complete by the time a child is about two years old. Since the brain develops its full physical potential by this age, the importance of adequate nutrition, from conception to age two, cannot be overemphasized. If the fetus is undernourished, the neonate will have about 20 percent fewer brain cells than are normal at birth. If the neonate is undernourished during the first six months, cell division is slowed down by about 20 percent. If the individual is malnourished both as a fetus and during the first six months after birth, the brain will have only about 60 percent of the number of neurons that a normal brain has.

Children are usually walking, running, climbing stairs, eating with a spoon, speaking with a vocabulary of about twenty-five words by the time they are two years old. By the time they are five years old, most children can dress themselves completely except for tying and lacing, and can play in the immediate neighborhood unattended, maintaining unsupervised group games with their age-mates and with older children.

The critical period for meeting the need for emotional security seems to be from birth to about five years of age. A child whose need for emotional security is fulfilled during this period develops a sense of basic trust and will establish a sense of autonomy, or self-reliance, that makes it possible to develop his or her full potential. The development of mastery skills also occurs during this time, and it is important to provide the child with implements and information in accordance with his or her developmental readiness. Success experiences, as opposed to failure experiences, breed confidence, optimism, and a sense of the world as being ultimately manageable. It is important that parents maximize the probability for success experiences to occur and minimize the probability for failure experiences.

It is also in the first five years that a child will also acquire a sense of value. Values are standards by which people measure the relative worth of everything from material objects to philosophical ideals. The values held by the family and transmitted to the child direct both the type and the extent of the information and skills that the child acquires.

Discipline is essential for happiness, security, accomplishment, and contentment, but it should not be confused with punishment. Discipline is defined as the setting of limits on behavior, and inducing wanted behavior, whereas punishment is defined as the deliberate infliction of deprivation, discomfort, or pain. The most reliable way to bring about discipline is to reinforce wanted behavior. Punishment may stop an unwanted behavior, but only if there is no significant emotional involvement with the behavior or the punishment, and no strong motivation for the behavior. Moreover, an alternate course of action must also be available, and the punishment must be informative. Behavior is only established and maintained by reinforcement; punishment may only be effective in stopping behavior.

The family is the social institution that produces children and provides them with a sense of stability, emotional support, affection, and love. The family is also the chief socializing agency, especially for the first five years, giving the child a sense of identity, a value system, a language, and important mastery skills and information that serve as the basis for all future development.

Socialization—which has as its ideal the development of a person who is able to make full use of his or her potential—is accomplished best by positive guidance, encouragement, stimulation, example, and the provision of success experiences. However, the socialization of children must rest upon a foundation of love and emotional support, which provides children with a sense of themselves as competent and significant persons. When children have this self-assurance, and when they are provided with discipline as well as with a permissive and creative environment, the possibility is maximized that they will develop into competent, loving, emotionally mature, and resourceful persons.

The parent-child interaction does not proceed in one direction only—from the parent to the child—but is an interaction. Children have different temperaments at birth. Some children are much easier to relate to and love than others, and the parent is inevitably affected by the child's disposition and temperament. Thus, children affect parents just as parents affect children. Indeed, a child can have a significant effect on a parent's personality. Children who have temperaments that provide immediate rewards for parents facilitate "good parenting." Other children have temperaments that do not provide these rewards, even for conscientious parents, and thus they are more liable to be relatively neglected. Children tend to fall into three categories in term of inborn temperament: the "easy child," the "slow-to-warm-up" child, and the "difficult" child.

QUESTIONS

1. Discuss the importance of nutrition for the maximal development of intellectual capac-

ity during the intrauterine period and during infancy and childhood.

2. What is the importance of early bonding for the mother and for the child?

3. What is the importance of emotional security for children?

4. Discuss the importance of early experience in the first few months of life.

5. What is meant by a *success experience*? What is the importance of success experiences in infancy and childhood?

6. Define the concepts of *discipline, reinforcement (reward),* and *punishment*?

7. Punishment will be effective in stopping behavior if four circumstances are present. What are they?

8. It is obvious that parents have a significant effect on the development of a child, but it is also true that the child's personality has a significant effect on the parents. Discuss this parent-child interaction and its effect on family life.

9. Babies have different personality characteristics and temperaments at birth. What characteristics may a baby have? What effects may these characteristics have on the parents?

SUGGESTIONS FOR FURTHER READING

Ariès, Philippe, *Centuries of Childhood: A Social History of Family Life.* New York: Vintage, 1962.

Cable, Mary. *The Little Darlings: A History of Child Rearing in America.* New York: Charles Scribner's Sons, 1975.

Children's Bureau. *Infant Care,* 13th rev. ed. U.S. Department of Health and Human Services Publication (OHDS) 80-30015. Washington, D. C.: Government Printing Office, 1980.

Clarke-Stewart, A. *Daycare.* Cambridge, Mass.: Harvard University Press, 1982.

Coleman, James C. *Contemporary Psychology and Effective Behavior*, 4th ed. Glenview, Ill.: Scott, Foresman, 1979.

Davis, Glenn. *Childhood and History in America*. New York: Psychohistory Press, 1976.

Fisher, Seymour, and Fisher, Rhoda L. *What We Really Know About Child Rearing: Science in Support of Effective Parenting*. New York: Basic Books, 1976.

Hanson, Shirley, M. H., and Bozett, Frederick W., eds. *Dimensions of Fatherhood*. Beverly Hills, Calif.: Sage Publications, 1985.

Kamerman, S. B., and Hayes, C. D., eds. *Families that Work: Children in a Changing World*. Washington, D. C.: National Academy Press, 1982.

Kliman, Gilbert W., and Rosenfeld, Albert. *Responsible Parenthood*. New York: Holt, Rinehart and Winston, 1980.

Kramer, R. *In Defense of the Family: Raising Children in America Today*. New York: Basic Books, 1983.

Lamb, M. E., ed. *The Role of the Father In Child Development*, 2d ed. New York: Wiley, 1981.

LaRossa, Ralph, and LaRossa, Maureen Mulligan. *Transition to Parenthood: How Infants Change Families*. Beverly Hills, Calif.: Sage Publications, 1981.

Margolis, Maxine L. *Mothers and Such Views of American Women and Why They Changed*. Berkeley, Calif.: University of California Press, 1984.

Rubin, Zick. *Children's Friendships*. Cambridge, Mass.: Harvard University Press, 1980.

Saunders, Antoinette, and Remsberg, Bonnie. *The Stress-Proof Child*. New York: Holt, Rinehart, & Winston, 1984.

Sommerville, John. *The Rise and Fall of Childhood*. Beverly Hills, Calif.: Sage Publications, 1982.

CHAPTER 13

The Family and Economic Reality

Money and Marital Conflict
The Meaning of Money Management
Directing Cash Flow
The Meaning of Credit
Getting Your Money's Worth
Paying Taxes
The Importance of Regular Investments

Getting money is like digging with a needle;
spending it is like water soaking in the sand.

Japanese proverb

Money is a vital force in nearly every facet of life. More waking hours are engaged in earning money than in anything else, and the typical American life-style is tied to patterns of spending money. Most of us are concerned more or less continually—both consciously and unconsciously—with our economic problems, and all ramifications of money have a powerful effect on our feelings of satisfaction or tension. The psychological effect of money is such that spending it is often necessary for feelings of security and self-confidence.

All of this is not to imply, of course, that a fixation on the possession of money for its own sake, or for the objects that it can buy, is essential to the pursuit of a meaningful, productive, rewarding life. The point is, rather, that a lack of sufficient money, or its improper use, can mean deprivations, indignities, anxieties, and conflict for the person as well as loss of opportunities for his or her children. Sufficient

Drawing by Koren; © 1982 The New Yorker Magazine, Inc.

"My darling, I want to share my money worries, my tensions, and my unhappiness with you for the rest of my life."

money, properly used, brings much good for the person—adequate medical and dental care; easy access to the material necessities and comforts of life; the benefits and pleasures of education, travel, and the arts; and, finally, the ability to launch children successfully.

Despite the extreme importance of money—and, most important, the management of that money, or personal finance—the subject is often cloaked in virtually impenetrable silence. Most people are as secretive and ignorant about their financial situations as Victorian women were about their sexuality.

Together, the areas of money and sex form a twin dimension of ignorance and ineptness in American life and particularly in American marriage. In fact, the average person knows even less about personal finance than he or she knows about sex, for the onus of dullness that surrounds the subject of economics makes it even more forbidding to most people. Economics *per se* is regarded as a boring subject and is often called "the dismal science."

It is curious that the study of money and how to handle it effectively is so often considered dull. Money is certainly one of the most important aspects of our experience. (See the vignette, "The Importance of Money.")

Since money is involved in almost everything we do, it should be one of the most fascinating subjects imaginable. Moreover, the study of how to handle it effectively pays immediate and rich dividends not only in directing cash flow in such a way as to enhance the person's life-style, but also in greatly lessening the tension and anxiety of financial uncertainty. Mishandled money, however, results in a depressed and deprived life-style and, far too often, an unhappy or ruined marriage.

MONEY AND MARITAL CONFLICT

One of the most obvious and basic facts about marriage in the United States is that for perhaps 98 percent of the families, there will

The Importance of Money

The importance of money is reflected in an enormous number of aphorisms on the subject.

A heavy purse makes a light heart (sixteenth-century English proverb).

It's a kind of spiritual snobbery that makes people think they can be happy without money (Albert Camus).

Money is like a sixth sense without which you cannot make the most of the other five (Somerset Maugham).

Lack of money is the root of all evil (George Bernard Shaw).

Wine maketh merry but money answereth all things (Ecclesiastes 10:19).

There are three faithful friends—an old wife, an old dog, and ready money (Benjamin Franklin).

Certainly there are lots of things in life that money won't buy, but it's very funny—Have you ever tried to buy them without money? (Ogden Nash)

---

never be enough money. For families in the lower-lower class, money problems revolve around simply getting enough food to stay alive and reasonably healthy and enough clothing to keep covered and reasonably warm.[1] These families feel that if they had an annual income of $20,000, they would be affluent.[2] However, most families in the United States do have this income and still do without many things they want while struggling to meet the monthly bills. They feel that if they earned only $5,000 a year more, their financial needs would be satisfied. However, families with incomes of $25,000 feel just as economically oppressed as those earning $20,000; they are convinced that if they were earning $30,000, they would be satisfied. Incomes of $30,000, $50,000, and even $70,000 do not seem to provide enough

money for the family to do *everything* they want. As income increases, the family's perceived needs and its spending increase even faster. Specialists in family finance find that high-income families are often deeper in debt than medium-income families, who are deeper in debt than low-income families (Feldman 1977).

In short, whatever the family's income, sound money management is an essential ingredient of marital harmony. Marriage counselors and family service agencies agree that economic stress is a major cause of conflict in American families. Married couples quarrel over money more than any other topic, and economic stress is a major cause of marital failure (Feldman 1977, Landis and Landis 1977, Rubin 1976).

THE MEANING OF MONEY MANAGEMENT

Sound money management consists simply of allocating available funds in ways that maximize need fulfillment and minimize deprivation. Few people, however—even knowledgeable, well-educated, middle-income people—are able to do this. In fact, experts in personal

---

[1] One in five families in the United States had an income of less than $12,000 in 1983 (U.S. Bureau of the Census, "Money Income of Families—Income and Percent of Aggregate Income at Selected Positions received by Each Fifth and Top 5 Percent of Families: 1983," 1985); one out of every four children under age six lives in poverty (U.S. Congressional Research Service, "Report on American Children Living in Poverty," 1985).

[2] Median income for families in the United States was $20,885 in 1983—for whites the figure was $21,902; for blacks it was $12,429; and for Hispanics it was $15,906 (U.S. Bureau of the Census, "Money Income of Households—Median Household Income in Current and Constant 1983 Dollars, By Race and Spanish Origin of Householder: 1967 to 1983," 1985).

Erika Stone/Peter Arnold, Inc.

Married couples quarrel over money more than any other topic, and economic stress is a major cause of marital failure.

finance agree that, as difficult as it is to make money, it is easier to make money than it is to handle money wisely. Unless the person is a professional in one of the fields of money management, his or her economic affairs are likely to be pretty much of a jumble. Few people know with any accuracy, for example, even how much money they have to spend; and they are only vaguely aware of how they spend it. They regard a *budget* as anathema, buy what advertising and convenience impel them to, pay what they can of their bills, and have little clear notion of what the flow of money (cash flow) means in their lives.

Virtually overnight, the average newly married couple become buyers not only of the day-to-day necessities of running a household and maintaining a family but also of the "big-ticket" items such as furniture and appliances. Yet they have little or no training in the basic principles and skills of successful money management and personal finance.

In addition to this lack of training and skill,

the young American couple live in a society in which it is very difficult to avoid overspending, for ours is a culture that emphasizes consumption and the flow of easy credit. Advertising appeals confront us constantly—demonstrating the affluence that others presumably have and that we should attain, and urging us to buy. The young family that responds to these appeals, making use of credit, can find themselves hopelessly in debt in a very short time. The dangers of mismatching income and outgo and making careless choices in discretionary spending can be very insidious, and an enormous number of young families are trapped in needless, lifelong peonage.

As difficult as sound money management may be, however, the basic principles of good personal finance may be stated quite simply:

— *Direct the cash flow.* You must direct your money where you most want it to go. This involves (1) knowing what your spendable income is and not exceeding it, (2) acknowledging that you cannot buy everything you would like and making an attempt to define what you most want, (3) putting some money each month into a temporary reserve (savings), and (4) putting some money each month into a long-term investment. These accomplishments are usually made possible only through the use of a budget.

— *Use credit properly.* You must know the proper use of credit—how to let it work for you for your financial or personal gain. There are three good uses of credit, which will be explained in this chapter. You should know them and use them.

— *Buy wisely.* You must work at getting the proper value for your money—a dollar's worth out of a dollar—whether you pay cash or use credit.

The rest of this chapter will examine these three basic principles of personal finance—budgeting cash flow, using credit properly, and getting your money's worth.

DIRECTING CASH FLOW

Cash flow means the movement of money through a couple's hands; that is, money flows into the family through various sources (such as wages) and then flows out, channeled into various expenditures, for such things as groceries, clothes, electricity, telephone service. Directing this cash flow is something that everyone does whether the person realizes it or not. However, few people know what their cash flow consists of. They simply spend money when they have it and use credit when they don't, with little awareness of what is really happening to them financially.

The Importance of a Budget

A budget lays out the cash flow very simply and precisely in a brief page or two, making it possible for you to see exactly what your financial options are, so that you can manage your financial destiny. It is not a financial straitjacket—designed to force you to keep track of every penny you spend—although this is a common misconception and probably explains why many people dislike the idea of a budget and refuse to keep one. A budget makes it possible for you to direct your cash flow into channels that will bring the most satisfaction. The alternative to keeping a budget is for you to let your money seep away in such a fashion that you know only that you are continually broke, in debt, and without the things you want, wondering where all the money went.

The Principle of Forced Alternate Choice

A brutal fact of life is that everything a person does involves a choice (often unconscious) between available alternatives, and that choosing one often eliminates the possibility of choosing the other. If you choose A, you may not have B. In the realm of personal finance, this means that as long as your available income is limited, you cannot buy everything you would like. Diverting funds to one channel (buying A) automatically diverts them away

from another (buying B). A budget makes it possible to see these options, or alternatives, very clearly, so that you can make the choice you most want to make—the one that will bring you the greatest satisfaction with the least cost.

Developing a Budget

The first step in setting up a budget is to list all monthly *assets*—that is, spendable or "take-home" income per month from whatever source.

The second step is to list all the *fixed* or *nondiscretionary expenses*. These are the expenditures over which you have little or no control—rent, transportation costs, utility payments, insurance premiums.

The third step is to list all the *variable* or *discretionary expenses*. These are items whose cost is not fixed but varies from time to time. For example, although food is an essential, you have the choice of eating a steak or a hamburger. (See Table 13-1 for a sample budget form.)

It is important that the total monthly expenses (fixed and discretionary) not exceed the total income. If it does, you are in trouble. Since you can't lower the fixed expenses, you must lower the discretionary expenses (or increase the income). If you are tempted to make up the difference between the amount spent and the income by borrowing (or buying on credit), the following month you must add the repayment of the debt to the fixed expenses total. You will then have that much less for discretionary expenses. If you cannot manage now, you will then have even greater difficulty, for you will have less to manage with.

Eventually, of course, this kind of creeping indebtedness can so swell the fixed expenses column with debt repayments that there is not enough money available in the discretionary column to cover anything that is not absolutely essential—which is listed in the "fixed" column. At this point, you are face to face with financial disaster—collection agencies, repos-

TABLE 13-1
Sample budget form

Monthly Income

Source	Amount
_____	_____
_____	_____
_____	_____
_____	_____
_____	_____
_____	_____

T. _____

Monthly Fixed Expenses

Source	Amount
_____	_____
_____	_____
_____	_____
_____	_____
_____	_____
_____	_____
_____	_____
_____	_____

T. _____

Available for Discretionary Expenses
(difference between total income
and total fixed expenses)

_____

Monthly Discretionary Expenses

Source	Amount
_____	_____
_____	_____
_____	_____
_____	_____
_____	_____
_____	_____
_____	_____

T. _____

The amount spent for discretionary expenses must not exceed the amount available for discretionary expenses. If it does, you are going into debt, and the interest on the debt as well as part of the principal must be added to next month's fixed expenses, leaving you even less for discretionary expenses and pushing you further into debt. This descending spiral can lead to financial ruin.

sessions, evictions, lawsuits—the whole, miserable, dehumanizing lot. Moreover, long before this crisis is reached, the marriage is usually seriously undermined, if not destroyed, by tensions, anxieties, and frustrations of insoluble financial pressure.

Involving the Whole Family in the Budget

Money and the goods money can buy have different meanings for different people; each of us has our own values and goals. For some, the acquisition of material things is important. For others, humanistic values and experiences—travel, education, the arts, recreation, and entertainment—are more important. A family budget should acknowledge and attempt to harmonize these differences, so that each person in the family can feel that he or she has appropriate rights in the allocation of the family's spendable income. Any other policy of allocating available funds breeds dissension and resentment.

This does not mean, of course, that the children should have a determining voice in where the family lives or what car the family owns. But children should be included in budgetary discussions (when they are old enough to understand and express their consumer needs) so that they are aware of where the money is going and the various ways that they benefit from this cash flow. Certainly, for all matters that directly concern them (such as clothing, allowance, recreation, toys), children should be included in these discussions, and the family should seek a consensus regarding the distribution and direction of cash flow.

Discussions about the budget should bring the family closer together as they share in money problems and solutions. All spendable income should be treated as the *family's*, and all decisions should be made as a matter of consensus, directing cash flow where it provides the greatest satisfaction for all concerned. Being secretive about money breeds resentment and bad spending habits, which create

tension for everyone in the family—children and parents alike. If the attitude with which the family members discuss the subject of money is one of reasonable optimism, practicality, and openness—a frank acknowledgment of the principle of forced alternate choice in the allocation of limited funds—the children will gradually develop a healthy awareness of the dollars-and-cents world of economic reality.

Budgeting for a Child's Allowance

A child's ability to understand the uses of money does not suddenly emerge full-blown at any particular age. It depends upon the experiences the child has regarding the uses of money. Average children can learn the principle of exchanging a quarter for a candy bar by the time they are five years old. For the next two or three years, they should be given money in appropriate amounts when they can use it—50 cents for the ice cream vendor, 75 cents for popcorn at the movies, and so on, until they are in the third or fourth grade and can grasp the concept of deferred spending and planning ahead. (Many people never do grasp this concept.) At the age of eight or nine, children should be ready for a regular fixed weekly allowance so that they can begin to understand such concepts as cash flow, budgeting, and forced alternate choice.

The size of the allowance should be determined by consultation. Decide with the child how much he or she needs for personal expenditures, allowing an appropriate amount for "pocket money." Experience has shown that when their counsel is sought, children are very reasonable, even modest, in their demands.

Children should learn at the outset, however, that the allowance is a fixed amount. If they spend it before the end of the week and ask for more, they should be told that the amount given was the allowance agreed upon in the budgetary discussion. (They should *not* be told that there is no more money, for they will know that this is not the truth; a budget, by its very nature, is a series of *choices*.) If they can establish that they need more, then the allowance should be raised. They should not be given "advances" or extra amounts. It is obviously a serious mistake to make children feel like burdens or drains on the family's finances. It is *equally* wrong, however, to provide for all their wants as though the family's funds were inexhaustible.

If their allowances are scaled properly, children will learn for themselves, through their own experience and through the family's budgetary counsels, sound principles of money management—not spending more than they have, making choices wisely, and saving for things they want and cannot afford right now.

Children's allowances should be theirs to spend with no need for an accounting. Their initial purchases may seem outrageous; it is important, however, that they be allowed to make, and learn from, their own mistakes. After all, these mistakes cannot be too serious if they are kept within the bounds of a fixed allowance.

It is important that the children's allowances are openly acknowledged as their fair share of the family's resources. They should not be expected to earn their allowance by doing household chores; these should be assigned and performed as the children's roles in fulfilling family functions. If they do some work that an outsider would have had to be paid for, then by all means they deserve to be paid as well. But this work-for-pay arrangement should be in addition to their allowance.

Similarly, withholding children's allowances as a disciplinary measure is never advisable. They will then perceive their allowance as payment to be good—a very poor idea with which to indoctrinate a child. Children should be good because they want to be good and enjoy pleasing adults, and their allowances should be theirs by right. Remember, reinforcement establishes and maintains wanted behavior; punishment may stop an unwanted

behavior (under certain circumstances). Withholding an allowance is a punishment (and a poor one); it will not establish or maintain a wanted behavior. In principle, behavior that you want the child to do should be reinforced. Punishment is sometimes useful (to stop a behavior), but the child's allowance is a poor bargaining chip, as is love (see Chapter 12).

Budgeting for a Personal Allowance

One important item in the budget should be a personal allowance for the husband and the wife—a fixed sum of money that does not have to be accounted for. This personal allowance in the budget gives each of the couple a sense of economic freedom. The size of the allowance should be scaled to the overall budget, of course, but it should be generous enough so that it doesn't give the feeling of being in some sort of financial straitjacket. Experience has shown that a tight, overly detailed budget that demands accounting for every penny spent does not work. If the person is forced to feel like a cheat or a miser every time he or she contemplates buying something, the budget will soon be abandoned—with more relief than guilt.

Budgeting for Savings

There is a good deal of confusion regarding the concept of saving. Actually, money that is saved is not removed from spendable income; rather, it is temporarily held for *deferred* spending. If you think of saving as an act of self-denial, you probably will not save. However, you *are* likely to save if you understand that saving is simply a means for buying wanted items in the relatively near future without incurring costly finance charges, or that saving provides funds for unexpected family emergencies. In addition, saving can actually increase a family's discretionary funds by the amount of interest the savings earn (which go into the income column) and by the bargains the family can take advantage of because they have cash at hand. The penalty for not having such reserved cash to use for deferred purchases or emergencies can be substantial.

Savings is a very important item of discretionary expenses and should always be included as an item in the discretionary expenses column. Most experts on personal finance emphasize that about 10 percent of a person's spendable income should be reserved as savings.

Budgeting for Investment

Putting away a portion of your income for a long-term program of growth is called *investing* (as distinguished from *saving*). Invested money is not meant to be spent; the investor's anticipation is that the money will be left undisturbed, so that it will eventually provide income, without touching the principal. Experts in personal finance all agree that it is very important for a married couple to budget a regular sum for investment—*from the first year of their marriage*. The goal of investing is not deferred spending (which is defined as *savings*), but rather removing money from spendable resources and allowing it to grow.

Major Budgetary Problems

As a family goes through the life cycle—from the newlywed and childless years, to rearing growing children, to putting them through college, and finally to preparing for retirement—the financial pattern changes significantly. The first stage—from the wedding until the first child is born—is the most financially carefree stage, although it rarely seems so at the time. Even though the young couple face much financial uncertainty and have limited resources and few belongings, they have no one to look after but themselves and they usually have a double income with which to do that.

Most couples feel financially oppressed when they are first married because there are so many things they want—a house (or at least a better apartment), furniture, appliances, sports and hobby equipment, travel. However, it is during this period that a couple spend more money on personal items, on pleasure, and on leisure activities than they ever will again—unless they become relatively affluent by middle age. In fact, the double income and the relatively low household and family expenses during this period often give the couple a false sense of financial security. The fixed expenses seem comparatively easy to meet until they enter the second stage of their marriage—when they have responsibility for children as well as for themselves just as the wife's earnings cease (at least for a while).

With the addition of children, the costs of maintaining a family begin to soar; medical care, food, clothing, babysitters, the need for larger living quarters, and more furniture and appliances contribute to continually swelling expenditures. Not surprisingly, during this period, when the couple plunge from relative prosperity into financial difficulties, money becomes a leading cause of disagreement.

The wise newlywed couple have the foresight to live in a modestly furnished apartment during the childfree period and avoid spending money beyond their means for entertainment, eating out, recreation, clothes, and vacations. Thus, they will be able to save a substantial amount for this second stage and continue their comfortable life-style without becoming embroiled in debt and financial recriminations. Entering the second stage with no savings and a backlog of debts is not only foolish but potentially disastrous.

Estimates regarding the cost of rearing a child to age eighteen vary, of course, and depend on social class. *Parents* magazine has found that, for a middle class family, the cost of raising a child to age eighteen is a shocking $254,000, if the earnings lost to the mother from the time of the child's birth to enrollment in kindergarten are figured in (assuming

Drawing by F. B. Modell; © 1968 The New Yorker Magazine, Inc.

"Oh, for pity's sake! Put it on your American Express card and blow your top when you get the bill."

$10,000 a year as her salary) and a reasonable allowance for inflation is taken into account (Tilling 1980).

College costs vary widely, of course; private institutions cost more than public institutions, and high-prestige colleges cost more than those with a lower ranking. The cost at one of this country's prestigious private colleges could exceed $16,000 for the year, while public colleges average close to $6,000. These charges include tuition, room and board, fees, and books. If the student is able to go to a nearby college and live at home, the room and board costs might be shaved somewhat (American Council on Education 1984).

There are ways for college students to obtain financial help, and all avenues should be explored.[3] Information regarding grants,

work-study programs, and scholarships can be obtained from the college's financial aid officer, the school guidance counselor, or the state department of education. The expenses of students who commute from home and attend two-year community colleges average about $3,500 annually when all expenses related to living and eating at home are included. Average annual tuition for such students would be about $600, lower than any other type of institution of higher education (American Council on Education 1984).

A third period of potential financial difficulty for the family occurs during the middle years, when the couple must prepare for retirement and old age. At this time, the couple are in the middle and late forties; they have discharged their obligations to their children; their home, furniture, and appliances are largely paid for; and the middle class husband and wife are reaching their peak earning years. This should be a second period of relative affluence and comfort for them. However, during this period, substantial sums must be budgeted for investment, since retirement is

[3]Surveys have found that 59 percent of students in private colleges and 31 percent of those at public institutions received some financial aid. Students at independent colleges who were financially dependent on their parents borrowed an average of $1,965 and those at public schools an average of $976. Government sources provided most of the loans (American Council on Education 1984).

now only fifteen or twenty years away. If the couple can invest sufficiently during this time, they may have a graceful, dignified old age. If not, they may experience old age as another period of financial crisis—this time without the advantages of youthful resilience and promise.

THE MEANING OF CREDIT

Properly used, credit (buying now and paying later) can make a person's life richer and fuller; improperly used, it can bring ruin. To take advantage of the good uses of credit (and to avoid pitfalls) it is essential to know its various forms, to understand how each works, and then to handle credit—as one would any useful but potentially dangerous tool—with caution and respect.

Three Sound Uses of Credit

There are three sound uses of credit. Two— *open credit* and *profit-making credit*—are sensible and fairly safe if they are properly used. The third—*non-profit-making credit*—is only marginally safe or sensible and requires especially careful consideration. Let us examine these categories of credit in detail (see Table 13-2).

Open Credit

Open credit is the term used for credit advanced with no finance charges.[4] The grocer years ago who kept an account of the items a person bought during the month and then set-tled the bill on payday was extending open credit. Today, open-credit opportunities are offered by dairy and bread delivery companies, diaper services, telephone companies, utility providers, newspaper subscription departments, cable television services, doctors and dentists, and many other businesses, stores, and professions that have the facilities for sending monthly statements to their customers and are willing to provide their products or services in advance of payment.

Department stores and gasoline companies also extend open credit if the credit cardholder pays the bill in full at the end of the billing cycle (usually thirty days). Multipurpose bank credit cards (MasterCard, Visa, and so on) usually have a small annual charge for the use of the card, but they also extend open credit if the bill is paid in full at the end of the billing cycle.[5] However, if the user does not pay in full, the account is financed, or charged with interest—usually a minimum of 1½ percent per month on the unpaid balance, which is 18 percent in true annual interest.

Some merchants with charge account systems compute their interest charges from a different base than the monthly unpaid balance so that the actual true interest rate is higher than 18 percent. For example, many department stores charge 1½ percent interest on the previous month's balance rather than on the current unpaid balance (which may work out to a true annual interest rate of more than 18 percent, depending on the size of the current payment in relation to the unpaid balance). Other stores charge interest on the original purchase price rather than on the unpaid balance; applied this way, the 1½ percent per month is a true annual rate of 36 percent. Interest is often computed this way by car dealers.

---

[4]Open credit is not really free, of course, since the costs are included in the purchase price. But because these costs are buried in the price regardless of whether a person pays cash or defers the payment, he or she may as well have the advantage of the open credit. If pressed, some merchants make a 5 or 6 percent discount if a customer uses cash instead of a credit card.

[5]The Truth in Lending Law now provides that a cardholder is not liable for charges on a stolen or lost card if he or she has informed the issuer that the card has been lost or stolen. The maximum liability for charges on an unreported card is now $50.

TABLE 13-2

The effective use of credit

Type	Cost	Risk	Use or purpose	Advisability	Sources
Open	Free (that is, cost buried in the purchase price, whether or not the credit is used).	Safe—if monthly bills are paid in full.	Any purchase that a person wants, can use, and can afford.	Good—if the item satisfies the test of "forced alternate choice."	Revolving charge accounts, credit cards, medical and dental bills, etc.
Profit-making	Financed, but cost is temporary (that is, cost is free in the long run, since cost of the credit is repaid by the use to which the credit is put).	Safe—if the income realized from the use of the credit will ultimately repay the cost of the credit.	Any purchase that can increase a person's income or reduce living costs—for example, education, car, clothing, or tools for work, investments, etc.	Good—if the item satisfies the test of "forced alternate choice."	Any of the above, plus cash loans. If cash loans, finance charges should be kept low by shopping for money as one would for any other commodity.
Non-profit-making	Full finance charges.	Risky. Is the cost of the credit worth the need satisfaction? Costs can lead to reduced standard of living, continual financial difficulties and tensions, and repossession if payments are not kept up.	Anything a person would like to have but cannot immediately afford—for example, hobby or sports equipment, recreation and pleasure, travel, new furniture, clothes, car, etc.	Questionable— even if the item satisfies the test of "forced alternate choice." May be good, however, if used with exceptional caution and with available alternates and all possible consequences clearly in mind.	Same as above.

It should be clear that a couple can use open credit wisely and properly only to the extent that they are certain of being able to settle the account in full at the end of the billing cycle, and are aware of the merchant's method of computing interest charges.

Used properly, however, open credit is not only a great convenience, but a real bargain. It also provides a cost-free way to build credit references that are essential if you need to borrow money for major purchases. People often have the mistaken idea that they will be regarded as good credit risks if they have always paid cash for everything. This is not true. You are regarded as a good credit risk only if you have borrowed money (used credit) and demonstrated your ability to repay it. Always paying cash for everything can actually create unnecessary hardships when you need to make a major purchase that requires credit financing (such as buying major appliances, a car, or a house).

Profit-Making Credit

Profit-making credit—financed loans or credit purchases that promise a financial return—is a sound use of credit if the consumers will eventually profit more from the use of the borrowed money or credit purchase than they will pay in finance charges. An example of a good use of profit-making credit is borrowing for an education or for vocational training, thereby acquiring the knowledge or skills that will enable the borrower to earn more. Similarly, good uses of profit-making credit might include borrowing to buy tools that are needed to produce income or to save money (a sewing machine, for example), to buy or maintain a car that is needed to get to work or school, to buy work clothes or office space, and to make an investment that will bring more income than the costs of the credit. This use of financed credit is the basis of all commerce.

Non-Profit-Making Credit

Non-profit-making credit—the third category for the sound use of credit—is that shadowy region of potential financial difficulty in which you borrow money or make a financed-credit purchase to satisfy an immediate need, the satisfaction of which you value more than the cost of the finance charges. This use of credit requires the greatest exercise of judgment; the borrower must weigh the subjective value of the satisfaction against the costs of the finance charges and the decrease of subsequent monthly discretionary funds as a result of these charges. This is not only a "buy now and pay later" plan but also a "buy now and buy *less* later" plan. If you make too many purchases in this way, with each purchase reducing your future spendable income by the amount that you will be paying for credit, you may eventually reduce your standard of living severely and find yourself in financial distress. It is generally far wiser to follow a deferred spending (*savings*) plan.

An example of the sound use of non-profit-making credit, however, might be buying a refrigerator that provides more convenience in storing larger amounts of food, thus making it possible to shop less often. This form of credit might also be used wisely in buying a vacuum cleaner that shortens housecleaning time, or in buying a piano so that you can start piano lessons at once instead of waiting until you have the purchase price, or in buying a camera that will provide a great amount of pleasure and capture moments that will never return, or in providing for a vacation or travel opportunity that may not recur in just the same way. Countless examples could be given. The important point is that the couples know what the costs of the credit are and weigh the relative values carefully. Routine use of non-profit-making financed credit can be a serious drain on even a solvent family's spendable income. For example, the family that carries a continuous average of $1,500 of financed debts (not including a mortgage)—a rather modest amount by today's standards—pays about $225 a year in finance charges, or $7,000 over the family's major buying years.

Pitfalls of Installment Buying

The use of installment contracts (rather than revolving charge accounts or credit cards) is often required by stores and dealers when they sell what they call "big-ticket" items, such as major appliances, large pieces of furniture, carpeting, and automobiles. An *installment contract* is a legal agreement between the consumer and the dealer for the financed purchase of a specific item. It provides for delayed payment for the item on a weekly or monthly basis for a specified period, at the end of which the contract is fulfilled.

Credit installment contracts usually involve higher interest rates than almost any other source of financing. Dealers often charge rates as high as 4 percent per month on the unpaid balance of installment contracts, which amounts to a true annual interest rate of 48 percent. In addition to interest cost, service charges (credit investigation, accounting expenses, and so on), and insurance payments are often tacked on, so that the actual cost for the installment contract may range as high as 80 percent in true annual interest. The most costly way to make a purchase is to get credit from the dealer who is selling the time. The rule is simple: When buying a big-ticket item, borrow the money elsewhere and then pay cash for the purchase. (Be wary of the store that boasts, "We carry our own credit.")

In addition to the high cost of the installment purchase, another pitfall is that the contract usually specifies that the item purchased may be repossessed by the seller if the customer fails to keep up the payments. If repossession occurs, the item may then be resold by the merchant, with the proceeds from the second sale used to cover the expenses of repossession, the resale, and the remaining indebtedness on the item. If the proceeds from the resale fail to pay everything off, the original customer owes the remainder even though he or she no longer has the item. Thus, a credit installment plan is not only costly, but may be risky—especially if the item purchased this way depreciates rapidly, as do furniture, any major appliance, and cars.

In addition to the repossession clause in installment plan contracts, many of these contracts have an *add-on clause*—a device by which all the items purchased by a customer from one dealer over a long period of time are written on the *same* installment contract, with payments and charges prorated, divided among *all* debts outstanding, and the repossession clause applicable to all items. For example, suppose you buy a stereo-television console on an installment plan, make regular payments, and then, when the console is within one month of being paid off, you buy a re-

frigerator from the same dealer. When this is within a month of being paid off, suppose you buy an electric range. Now, when you have made all but the final payment on the electric range, suppose you buy a vacuum cleaner. Two months later you are laid off and cannot make the installment payments. You must now return the vacuum cleaner—and the electric range, the refrigerator, and the stereo-television console as well. For according to the add-on clause that was a part of the contract you signed, all payments that you had been making were prorated among all items, so that none was paid off, and all are subject to repossession.

Still another device found in installment contracts is the *balloon payment clause*, which requires a very large final installment payment on the contract. Such a clause is often added to a contract to make the monthly payments for an expensive item small enough to be within the present means of the buyer. Then, with the final balloon payment, the buyer must make up the difference between the sum of the small monthly payments he or she has been making and the total cost (principal and finance charges) of the time. A customer who is careless about preparing for this final balloon payment must either refinance the loan (at still further cost) or have the item repossessed—losing both the item and *all* the money already paid for it.

Another pitfall of an installment contract is the *default judgment*. This might occur when a merchant prepares a legal notice that the buyer is being sued for nonpayment of debt. However, an unscrupulous process server hired to deliver the notice may file a false affidavit saying that the notice has been delivered or that the buyer was never at home (the so-called "sewer service"). Not knowing that he or she is being sued, the buyer fails to show up in court and automatically loses by default. Default judgments are among the most serious traps facing installment buyers, particularly

Signing a Contract

There are a few basic rules to observe when you sign a contract. Remember, a contract once signed is legally binding—whether you have read it and whether or not you understand it. Once you have signed an installment contract, you are legally obligated to pay for the item in full, even if the item is repossessed. You should also keep in mind that any agreement that is *not* in writing is *not* legally binding. You will avoid a good deal of difficulty in following these rules:

— Never sign a contract without reading and understanding it.

— Never sign a contract involving a substantial sum of money without having a lawyer check it.

— Never sign a contract unless all the spaces are filled in. If

a space is to be left blank, draw a line through the space.

— Always know precisely what the finance charges are in true annual interest.

— Always get a copy of the signed contract.

---

those in lower-income brackets or in neighborhoods where this is an everyday technique used by creditors to force payments (Porter 1979). The goods and services involved may range from dancing lessons to vocational courses by mail to burglar alarm systems. But any default judgment automatically leaves the buyer vulnerable to repossession of the property, on which he or she is *still* required to make installment payments.

Home improvement contracts often are written so that if the purchaser fails to make a payment, the contractor may take over the house, with no foreclosing procedure necessary. Suppose, for example, you live in a $130,000 house, and sign a contract to have a $5,000 air conditioning unit installed. The contract may have a clause (often in fine print) stipulating that if you miss a single monthly payment of $300 on the air conditioning unit, your house is automatically forfeited without even a court judgment. The contractor then sells your house to recover the balance of the contract. Although this may seem unscrupulous, it is a perfectly legal procedure, as many unwary buyers have found to their sur-

prise and regret. (See the vignette, "Signing a Contract.")

Sources of Loans

You should shop for money as carefully as you would for any other commodity. The charge for money is called *interest*, and interest rates vary considerably from one lender to another. (Moreover, other charges are often tacked on.) For example, a pawnbroker is usually a very poor source of money, since his charge for using money generally ranges from 36 to 50 percent in true annual interest. A small-loan company is a poor source of money, since charges usually range from 30 to 36 percent in true annual interest, and often even higher. For example, in the procedure known as *flipping*, the loan company charges interest on the total amount of the principal borrowed as new loans are granted. Porter (1979) cites an example of a customer who borrowed $1,150 from a small-loan company and signed a note for $1,632 that included the interest. During the following two years, while this loan was being repaid, the loan company granted the customer several small additional loans, bringing the total amount borrowed to $1,805. At the end of the two-year period, the customer had paid off $1,405 but discovered that his outstanding balance was now $3,040! Following the practice of flipping, the loan company had simply added on his later loans to the initial loan and continued to charge interest on the total sum of *all* the loans.

Bank credit cards, such as Visa and Master-Card, usually charge about 24 percent in true annual interest for cash. A better source for convenient credit from a bank is a "balance plus" type of account, which is automatically credited to your checking account and usually costs 15 to 18 percent in true annual interest. If you have collateral—such as equity in a home, stocks, bonds, or a life insurance policy with a cash surrender value—you may borrow from a bank with relatively low cost.

Credit unions are a good source of loans for those who are eligible to become members. Personal loans are available on the member's signature with no collateral, up to a minimum amount fixed by the policies of the union. Interest rates vary but are usually somewhat lower than comparable bank rates.

Questioning a Credit Rating

Anyone who is refused credit, a loan, insurance, or a job and has reason to believe that the refusal stems from a bad credit rating may do something about it under the Federal Fair Credit Reporting Act, which took effect in 1971. Whoever turns down the request for credit (or whatever) must give the person the name of the credit agency that made the negative report. This agency must, in turn, let the person see exactly what its files contain under his or her name. If the information is inaccurate or includes data that cannot be verified, the credit agency must promptly delete such data from the file. Moreover, any information that is disputed must be checked again for accuracy. Finally, the person has a right to enter an explanatory statement in the file about any entries that might be misleading. (For example, the file might record late payment of a bill that the person deliberately delayed because merchandise was unsatisfactory).

Even if the unflattering information is accurate, it cannot stay in the file forever under the 1971 act. Most adverse information, even criminal records, must be deleted after seven years; information on bankruptcy must be deleted after fourteen years. If the agency's negligence in this regard causes a person financial loss or embarrassment, he or she may sue the credit agency.

Women's Fight for Credit Rights

Before the passage of the 1975 Equal Credit Opportunity Act, it was not possible for a married woman to obtain credit in her own name (for example, Mrs. Mary Smith). She could get credit only in the name of an employed husband (Mrs. John Smith), and she would thus be left without a credit rating if she became separated, divorced, or widowed. It is now illegal, however, for a bank or other lender to deny a woman personal or commercial credit on the basis of gender or marital status. This legislation was, of course, a significant step in establishing equal opportunity and equal rights for women in this regard.

It is important to note that a woman will have a credit rating, should she be separated, divorced, or widowed, only if she established credit in her own name (Mrs. Mary Smith) during the marriage. Given the high incidence of separation and divorce, and the statistical expectation that those women who remain married will outlive their husbands (by an average of eleven years), the value of a married woman obtaining credit in her own name is considerable. (For further discussion, see Porter 1979, Nelson 1977, and Chesley and Goodman 1976).

GETTING YOUR MONEY'S WORTH

The decisions on whether to make a purchase and then whether to make it with credit or cash are only the first steps to sound personal finance. A third step consists of getting the greatest return for each dollar spent. Wise consumers get more for their money by not wasting it on things that will not last or work or that simply do not give full value in relation to their cost.[6] They must know not only value and comparative prices but also how to distinguish quality merchandise from the cheap and shoddy.

The prices for the same or equivalent items often vary widely, depending on the store, the neighborhood, the season, or even the type of reduced-price sale in which the item is offered. Wise consumers must recognize misrepresented merchandise, inflated prices, phony markdowns, and fictitious discounts. Guarantees and warranties are always limited in some way, and wise consumers read the fine print and know precisely what they are entitled to if something should go wrong with the product.

Wise consumers rarely pay cash for an item. Whenever possible, they get the item, try it out, and *then* pay for it before it is subject to an interest charge. The use of open credit in this way puts the consumer at an enormous advantage. If something is wrong with the item, the consumer is in a much stronger position regarding exchanges or returns if he or she has not yet paid for it (unless, of course, an installment contract has been signed).

Fredrik D. Bodin/Stock, Boston

Although rising prices have kept most young couples from entering the housing market, for those who are able to make the down payment, a house is probably the best investment they can make.

---

[6]An immensely valuable source of consumer information is *Consumer Reports* magazine. The professional shoppers and evaluators of the staff carefully compare and evaluate packaged food, clothing, cameras, automobiles, all types of appliances, and many other consumer goods for durability, safety, effectiveness, and price value. *Consumer Reports* is published monthly by Consumers Union, a nonprofit organization, at 256 Washington Street, Mount Vernon, New York, and may be obtained by subscription, on newsstands, or in the public library. Consumers Union also publishes an annual digest, *Buying Guide*, which covers the most popular consumer items.

Such businesslike attention to getting a dollar's worth out of a dollar is more difficult than one might think. The fact is that for a great number of young families especially, the money that is not drained off in excessive credit charges is lost through bad shopping.

Buying a House

A house is the single most expensive item a couple will ever buy unless they are in that very small minority that has enormous sums available for luxury items such as yachts, jewelry, and art.

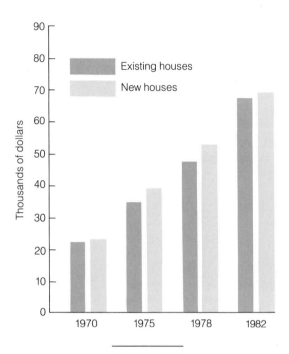

Existing houses

New houses

FIGURE 13-1

Median salesprice of existing and new one-family houses
in the United States, 1970–1982

Source: Data from *U.S. Department of Housing and Urban
Development Construction Reports* (1984, pp. 745–46)

Housing costs increased drastically during the 1970s (see Figure 13-1). Interest rates also began rising during the late 1970s and fluctuated around 14-15 percent in the mid-1980s. Even at these rates, the thirty-year mortgage was not always possible to obtain.

The Federal Home Loan Bank Board approved regulations in 1981 that allowed federally chartered savings and loan associations to write loans with *variable* interest rates. With such loans, the interest rate could be raised without limit and adjusted as often as the lender desired. In signing this type of mortgage, the buyers might find themselves, some years later, obligated to make a much higher mortgage payment each month than they had originally planned for. If their income did not rise by an equivalent amount they would not be able to make the monthly payments and would lose their home. These four factors—high housing prices, high interest rates, the difficulty of obtaining a thirty-year fixed-rate mortgage, and variable interest rates—have frozen most young couples out of the home-buying market.

The first rule in buying a home is that the price of your home should not exceed 2½ times your gross annual income. For example, if you earn $30,000 per year you can theoretically afford a $75,000 home (Connolly 1985).

Couples who have the necessary down payment and are earning enough to afford a house should carefully check out the many pitfalls of home buying. An excellent source of such information is *Sylvia Porter's New Money Book for the Eighties.*

Buying a Car

The average price of a car has been rising so that a new car today often costs what a house did thirty years ago. Since most cars depreciate very rapidly, it is much more economical to buy a used car than a new car. Typical used car purchase prices range from 20 to 80 percent below the prices of comparable new cars. The older the car, of course, the greater the savings. Also, your taxes, insurance and interest are much less on the lower priced used car. It is, therefore, not surprising that the average age of American cars is now 7.4 years, which is older than at any time since World War II (Federal Highway Administration 1984).

Although it is cheaper to buy a used car than a new car, upkeep costs climb as a car ages. So the most economical way to buy a car is to buy one that is a few years old and keep it until the maintenance costs are higher than the costs of buying another car. The precise point when this occurs varies from one person to another (depending on the amount and type of driving done) and from one car to another.

The cost of owning and operating a medium-sized car reached $34,000 in 1984, for an average twelve-year life. Buying a smaller model can trim the tab by $9,500 or more.[7] Compact cars are the cheapest to own and operate, but even these cost the owner an average of about fifty cents a mile. This figure includes purchase price, tax, loan interest, depreciation, insurance, license fees, average repairs and maintenance, gasoline and other service charges, but does not include parking fees and tolls (Hertz 1985).

Cars have great psychological meaning for many people, in addition to their function in simply providing transportation. Again, in making such a purchase it is important to understand and have a clear view of your options—applying the principle of forced alternate choice. If you choose to buy an uneconomical car for the psychological satisfaction it will provide, be sure that you are thoroughly aware of the other things you will *not* be able to buy in consequence. If the car, in your perception, is worth it, then it is a good buy—for *you*.

If you are seriously interested in a car, you should haggle with the dealer over the price. The sticker price on the window of a car is there because the law says it must be, but only a naive buyer accepts the sticker price as anything but a starting point for negotiations. Shop around, shop carefully, and never pay the asking price. A good time to close a deal is often late Sunday night (or the last night of the week the dealer is open) or at the end of the month. Many dealerships offer bonuses to the person who has the best sales record at the end of the week or the month. It is good to deal directly with the sales manager or the assistant manager, because this person is authorized to agree on a price.

When you have decided which car you want

and have agreed with the salesperson on a price, you should have the dealer put the agreement in writing *before* you make a deposit. The order form for this agreement should include a statement of the precise car being bought, the accessories agreed on (if any), the sales tax, registration fee, and the value of the trade-in (if any). In addition, an officer of the firm must sign the order form or it has no legal value. The salesperson's signature means nothing; you may find, when it is time to close the deal, you have been "low-balled" (promised a better deal than you are actually able to get) or "high-balled" (offered more on your trade-in than you will actually get). A person might be both high-balled and low-balled during the course of the negotiations. Both practices are very common among car dealers.

In arranging for money to buy a car, it is usually better (as with all big-ticket items) to shop for the money elsewhere and pay cash to the dealer. Similarly, the insurance for a car should be shopped for as carefully as for the car itself. Insurance is one of the most costly items of automobile operations; without some comparison shopping, a car owner can spend a lot of money unnecessarily.

A good source of information on car buying is the year-end issue of *Consumer Reports*, which contains invaluable and detailed information on the precise steps to take in buying a new or used car. Another useful source of information for the used-car buyer is an electronic diagnostic center, which for about $30 will analyze the faults in the car and itemize the costs of repair.

Buying Big-Ticket Items

Big-ticket items are such items as the heavy pieces of furniture and the expensive appliances that a young couple need to furnish their apartment or house. Furniture is one item for which buying top quality is the most economical as well as the most aesthetically

---

[7]U.S. General Services Administration, *Cost of Owning and Operating Automobiles and Vans* (1984).

satisfying. Poor-quality furniture very quickly loses its appeal and is a constant source of irritation and expense as it breaks down or wears out and needs repairs or replacement. Good-quality furniture, in contrast, remains a continuing pleasure and will, with proper care, last a lifetime. If well chosen, its value may even increase.

There is generally no particular urgency in selecting furniture, so shoppers can take their time, choose carefully, and watch for bargains. It is possible, for example, to save 15 to 30 percent on quality furniture sales, usually in June or September.

Unless they are usually knowledgeable about furniture standards and prices, it is risky for consumers to shop for furniture in cut-rate stores, "discount" houses, and stores featuring distress sales. There are legitimate discount houses and distress sales that offer bargains or furniture, but it is important to be very sure that the furniture (or the appliance) is a standard item and that the price is genuinely a bargain. Again, comparison shopping is important.

Do not overlook bargains in unfinished furniture and do-it-yourself kits. These are good ways to acquire simple chairs, desks, bookcases, and tables. Do-it-yourself labor saves up to 40 percent of the total cost—and it provides the reward of having had a creative hand in the finished project.

Used furniture can also be a very good bargain. Quality pieces can sometimes be picked up for next to nothing in thrift shops or at auctions or through the classified ads in the newspaper. But again, the shopper must be wary, especially with the latter. There are people who make quite a good living by filling their houses or apartments with junk from second-hand stores during the week and disposing of it through the Sunday want ads. Be skeptical and compare values carefully.

One furniture merchandising swindle that every consumer should be aware of is the type of store known in the trade as a *borax store.* Such stores specialize in selling furniture by the room. An ad typically reads something like "three rooms of furniture for $198." The couple who responds to such an ad is shown the advertised furniture stacked in a dark, dusty corner. Then the salesperson leads them to a different area with better lighting and display—and higher prices. (This is called "bait and switch.") The store management counts on the fact that many people are unable to resist the need to show the salesperson that they can afford the better merchandise, which is either standard-quality merchandise that is outrageously overpriced or highly priced junk.[8] (The store profits, of course, even if the couple insist on buying the low-quality merchandise for the advertised price.)

The electronics, jewelry, and appliance businesses, stores with frozen-food and freezer "bargain" plans, and carpet dealers also have their share of "borax" stores and swindles.[9] Carpet selling seems to lend itself particularly well to the "borax" store racket, and the Sunday paper and late-night television programs are filled with ads for bargain carpeting "for your whole house." Area rugs are actually

---

[8]"Borax" stores charge two to five times the usual price for ordinary household furniture and appliances. One investigation, for example, cited a case where a customer was sold a Philco washer for $479, including finance charges. The same washer would have cost $250 with standard price and legitimate financing (Florence Rice, Consumer Education Director of the League of Autonomous Bronx Organizations). Rice cites another typical example of a customer who was sold a double mattress and box spring in a "borax" store for $500; the same item was available in reputable stores in the same area for less then $100! Comparison shoppers in the government-sponsored "Project Money-Wise" found that people paid $170 to $280 in a "borax" store for a standard-brand television set that could be bought in any legitimate store in the same area for $105 to $140 (Miller 1983).

[9]For example, an inspector for the Virginia Department of Agriculture and Commerce visited a bulk-meat retail plant that had advertised a side of beef at less than half the price being quoted in the supermarkets. By making the test purchase, the inspector was told that the bargain-priced beef was old, tough, and would not be satisfactory for general cooking. He was also advised that the cutting and trimming loss on the meat would be high, as much as 70 percent of the gross weight. He was then

much more economical than carpeting, but if you do decide on carpeting, you must be wary of misrepresentation and outright rackets. There is an enormous range of carpeting grades, and the unwary consumer can easily be sold an overpriced and inferior grade that stretches, fades, and wears quickly. Some retailers will also advertise "free" installation, when actually the cost of installation is made up by the profit in foisting an inferior grade of carpet on the gullible buyer. It is especially important when buying carpets to deal only with reputable, conservative stores. The buyer should also take advantage of legitimate sales (usually in January and February) but should expect to save no more than about 20 percent. (With a discontinued mill-end, the savings could go as high as 50 percent.)

Consumer Reports magazine is a reliable source for the quality rating of carpeting, as well as for major appliances, bedding, radio and television and stereo equipment, household tools, typewriters, and just about every other consumer item from swimming pools to shower stalls.

There is no reason a consumer should be swindled with cheap or faulty merchandise or inflated prices. Unfortunately, however, most consumers willingly cooperate in their own exploitation. They are victimized not so much because they are gullible—although that certainly helps—but because they try to impress the hustler with their worth and shrewdness in realizing that the once-in-a-lifetime bargain being offered is only for the daring (and only the daring succeed in this world).

---

guided to a more expensive meat—USDA Choice—and told that this beef would be much better and the cutting loss would be less than 20 percent. The inspector bought 188 pounds of this choice beef at a "reduced" price. Back at the lab, the inspector weighed the beef and found that he had received a little over 120 pounds—a 36 percent cutting loss against a guarantee of less than 20 percent. Thus the 120 pounds of meat actually cost *much more* than the supermarket prices; on top of this, more than half the 120 pounds was delivered as hamburger! (Porter 1979).

Consumers also get taken because everybody loves a bargain. Legitimate stores know this and offer bargains hoping that customers will pick up something else along the way or return often for other items. Swindlers know this and play to greed with glib promises and an airtight procedure for taking money without giving just value in return.

Here are some general principles for any kind of buying:

— Don't be misled by the dealer who lures you into his or her place of business with an attractive ad and then tries to talk you into a higher-priced article.

— Don't be blinded by "bargains" offered at impossible-to-believe prices.

— Don't be fooled by phony markdowns of overpriced items or the substitution of poorer-quality merchandise during special sales.

— Don't be rushed into making a decision by the salesperson who talks about "the last chance to get in on a good thing" or the "golden opportunity" you might miss by not signing immediately.

— Don't permit door-to-door salespersons to leave merchandise with you "on approval." You may find that you are obligated to pay, whether you keep the merchandise or not.

— Never, never sign a contract that you do not understand or that has not been completely filled in.

Buying Life Insurance

The basic purpose of life insurance should be to provide income protection for the family of the deceased. For a relatively modest sum, term insurance will provide precisely this. The survivors are left with an "instant estate"; and this may be the only substantial amount of money most people are able to leave their survivors. There is no question about the value and the importance of insurance coverage. Both husband and wife should be insured for as substantial a sum as appropriate to the family's income and budget.

There are, however, two different kinds of life insurance policies: *term* insurance and various types of *insurance-plus-investment.* The insurance-plus-investment policy goes by various names, such as "ordinary life," "straight life," "mortgage insurance," "twenty-pay life," and so on.[10]

Insurance agents can make a very good case for the insurance-plus-investment type of policy, and most insurance policies sold are of this type. In fact, most agents will not even discuss term insurance with a prospect because it pays such a small commission. If you want term insurance you must usually go directly to the company to get it, unless it is part of a group insurance plan (which are usually term insurance policies).

The arguments that an insurance agent can make for the insurance-plus-investment type of policy may seem very convincing. Unlike a term insurance policy, an insurance-plus-investment type of policy has a cash surrender value (which increases during the life of the policy); the policy holder may borrow on this cash value at a relatively low interest rate; the premiums (payments per month) do not increase periodically but are fixed for the duration of the policy; the face value of the policy (the amount paid out in the event of the policy holder's death) does not drop periodically; and the policy will not be canceled when the insured reaches age sixty-five (when it is, presumably, most needed).

Let us see precisely why—despite these arguments—the insurance-plus-investment policy is, nevertheless, a very poor buy compared with a term insurance policy.

The monthly premiums that you pay for the insurance-plus-investment type of policy are

divided into two parts. One part goes to buy a term insurance policy for you (you could buy it for yourself at a much lower premium). The other part of the premium is simply an investment, for which the insurance company pays you a very modest rate of return (usually 2½ percent compounded annually). This part of your premium, accumulated with interest added, comprises the "cash surrender" value of your policy. However, if you withdraw this money the insurance company cancels the term insurance part of your policy and the face value is now worthless. In other words, you have now lost all the premiums that went into the term insurance part of your policy. Suppose, instead of withdrawing the cash surrender value of your policy, you borrow it (borrowing money from the insurance company using the cash surrender value of your policy as collateral). This avoids canceling out your policy, and lets you get your hands on your money, but you will have to pay interest on the loan (usually 5-6 percent) until the money is repaid. (This is ironic, since you are paying to borrow your own money.) Moreover, if you die before the money is repaid, the face value of your policy is reduced by the amount of the loan, and your beneficiaries will get that much less. What if you neither cash in your policy nor borrow on it but keep the face value intact, making the premium payments regularly until you die or reach age sixty-five? Your benificiary then collects the term insurance part of your policy (the face value), but the insurance company keeps the cash surrender value—the total of all the premiums that have gone into the investment part of your policy (plus accumulated interest). In other words, if your beneficiaries collect the face value of the policy, they have lost the cash surrender value; if you withdraw the cash surrender value, you lose the premium payments that have gone into the term insurance part of your policy when your policy is canceled. Whatever you do, you are going to lose one or the other—the premium payments you have made for the term insurance part or

[10]Twenty-pay life is an example of a *limited-payment* insurance-plus-investment policy, with the insurance paid up after a specified time (or sometimes at a specified age). With this type of policy the insurance company calculates the premiums the insured would pay if he (or she)lived to age 100 and then collects them over a shorter period of time (such as twenty years). The annual premium payment for this type of policy is accordingly much higher than the premium for other types of policies, and it is an especially bad buy.

those you have made for the investment part of your policy.

The solution is obvious: Buy a term life insurance policy and invest the difference between the premium of this policy and the premium of the insurance-plus-investment type of policy—or "buy term and invest the difference." With the amount of the premium you save invested at even 5 percent interest (which is the absolute minimum guaranteed by any bank), you will have saved (by age sixty-five) more than the face value of the insurance-plus-investment type of policy. The "cash surrender" money is available to you at any time without canceling out the entire policy, you can borrow it (from yourself) without paying interest, and the money you have saved continues to grow (at compound interest) after you reach age sixty-five.

To illustrate: Suppose you are thirty years old and decide that you want $50,000 worth of life insurance income protection for your family. The premium for *renewable term insurance* at this age comes to about $3.85 per $1,000, so your total premium will be about $192 per year for the $50,000 coverage.[11]

Ordinary life (the most common insurance-plus-investment plan) at this age would carry a premium of about $15 per $1,000, or $750 per year for the same coverage. If you invest the $558 (the difference between the $750 and the $192) at 5 percent interest, after five years you will have accumulated $3,083. At this time your renewable term policy must be renewed.[12] However, you will need only $47,000 of life insurance coverage (to match the insurance-plus-investment policy, for example, ordinary life) since you now have over $3,000 in investments. The premium would be about

$202, since you are five years older. During the second five-year period you will accumulate another $3,028 which, when added to the prior savings (which has been growing at 5 percent per year compounded), brings your total savings to $6,962. At the end of the second five-year period, then, your total worth to your beneficiaries would be $53,962 ($47,000 of insurance coverage plus $6,962 in savings). For each succeeding five-year term, you simply continue to invest the difference between the cost of the two premiums and add the results to the prior accumulated savings.

The figures are easier to see and understand if we put them in the form of a table (see Table 13-3, "The 'Buy Term and Invest the Difference' Plan").

It should be clear that the "buy term and invest the difference" plan, even at the modest return of 5 percent, provides substantially greater protection for your survivors from the outset until age sixty-five, and a much higher protection if you live beyond this age. For example, at age seventy-five you will have $70,840 in your savings account, and this sum will continue to grow substantially. (Actually you could safely get much more than 5 percent, so that these estimates are very conservative. For example, five-year, $10,000 Certificates of Deposit were paying up to 16.5 percent in 1984.)

In summary, a married couple should purchase life insurance because it provides them with an "instant estate" if one of them should die. Term insurance should be considered essential and should be budgeted for. They should, however, buy just that—*term insurance*—and they should invest the difference between the premium for this policy and the

---

[11]Premiums vary from one company to another, and with various demographic factors of the insured in addition to age, such as sex, gender, smoking habits, and so on. The example given is about average for a white, non-smoking male.

[12]Term insurance guarantees the payment of the face value of the policy at death for a prescribed period of time (a "term") from the signing of the policy contract. That period is generally

five years, after which the policy must be renewed at a higher premium (that reflects the advancing age and higher death risk of the insured). When the insured reaches age sixty-five, the term insurance policy is usually canceled and nonrenewable. It is important, therefore, when buying a term insurance policy, to make sure that it is a "renewable" policy that can be renewed each time it expires, until the insured reaches age sixty-five.

TABLE 13-3
The "Buy Term and Invest the Difference" Plan

Age	Annual premium for ordinary life policy with $50,000 face value	Annual premium for renewable term policy (5-year period)	Amount saved per year	Accumulated saving at end of 5-year period at 5% interest compounded	Face value of renewable term policy at end of 5-year period	Total face value of renewable term insurance policy plus accumulated savings at end of each 5-year period
30–35	$750	$192	$558	$ 3,083	$50,000	$53,083
35–40	750	202	548	6,962	47,000	53,962
40–45	750	240	510	11,703	43,000	54,703
45–50	750	298	452	17,434	38,000	55,434
50–55	750	359	391	24,410	31,000	55,410
55–60	750	421	329	32,972	24,000	56,972
60–65	750	495	255	43,490	15,000	58,490
65–70	—	—	—	55,505	—	55,505
70–75	—	—	—	70,840	—	70,840

premium for an insurance-plus-investment type of policy and let this investment accumulate at the highest rate of interest consistent with safety.

Buying the Daily Essentials

In addition to the major items of expense, there are daily expenditures for food, frequent expenditures for clothing, and expenditures for all the small items that make up the fabric of day-to-day existence. Getting your money's worth for these items is also important, and a good rule to remember is the principle of forced alternate choice. If you have limited funds available, every time you buy one item, you are making it impossible to buy another item.

Buying Food

Food has many meanings, of course, and its pleasures and amenities may be of such im-

portance to the couple that it is worth budgeting a relatively high proportion of their discretionary funds for it. This is perfectly sensible, as long as they have weighed the relative values and options and know what they are doing. To use their shopping dollars wisely, then, they should buy food that meets their psychological as well as nutritional needs at the best possible price. In short, buying food should rest on a threefold knowledge: (1) the personal factor of the psychological meaning of food for the individual, (2) the nutrition factors, and (3) the purely monetary factor of getting full value for each dollar spent.

Consumer experts agree that when buying a large amount of groceries, it is important to shop from a list that has been based in part on preplanned menus. Supermarkets make a science of inducing shoppers to buy more than they want or need. Packaging, lighting, displays, and other psychological lures are carefully designed by specialists in consumer practices to encourage shoppers to fill their carts.

Jane Scherr/Jeroboam, Inc.

Wise shoppers buy food that meets their psychological as well as nutritional needs at the best possible price.

buying prepackaged meat, for example, wise consumers read the price-per-pound figure on the label as well as the net price. (A large steak with a lower price may actually cost more per pound of meat because of the bone, which must be paid for but cannot be eaten.) Wise consumers also know that foodstuffs that carry the private label of the market or chain are usually of the same quality as the nationally known brands but significantly cheaper, that most fresh fruits and vegetables are in plentiful supply and therefore relatively cheap during certain seasons, and that buying at the small corner store or late-night market is justified only in terms of convenience, for prices are inevitably higher than in large chain markets or co-ops.

Convenience foods are becoming increasingly popular, but some are very uneconomical. For example, frozen beef patties sometimes sell for as much as two and a half times more than fresh ground beef, which must be shaped for cooking. Yet other convenience foods are not only time-saving but also relatively economical. For example, frozen, fresh-cut string beans provide a reasonably fresh vegetable out of season with the time-consuming jobs of cutting and cleaning already done. Convenience foods cannot be written off as either "good" or "bad" in themselves. So long as you know what you are paying for and what you are getting, you can make the choice.

Buying Clothing

As with food, clothing fulfills psychological as well as practical needs. Again, wise shoppers must know values, weigh alternatives, and then try to get the most for their money. As with shopping for food, they should decide what they want before they shop, so that they can resist subtle pressures of skilled salespersons, clever displays, and phony (or even legitimate) sales on items that they do not really want. They should comparison shop, know values, and be certain that what they are

People who just wander about the market picking up anything that looks good—and especially those who do this when they are hungry—wind up with things that may be overpriced or that they do not really want. Wise shoppers first plan menus that ideally provide a week's meals and are arranged to take advantage of leftovers—as well as advertised sales and specials. They then prepare a shopping list from these menus. Shoppers should be flexible enough, however, to take advantage of on-the-spot bargains and to buy in quantity when they find these bargains.

It is also important for shoppers to compare prices and to know and read labels, so that they are aware of what and how much they are getting and how much they are paying for it. In

paying for an item is what the item is really worth both on the market and to them. One important point to consider in choosing clothes is how many times they can be properly laundered before they need to be mended or thrown out. Another thing to remember is that price is not a dependable guide; low prices do not necessarily mean lower quality in terms of such important factors as durable fabric, good seams and thread, and washability. At the same time, a high price does not guarantee high quality and long life.

Clothing expenses can be cut substantially by planning ahead and taking advantage of seasonal reductions. Winter coats usually go on sale the day before Christmas, with reductions of as much as one-third or one-half. All varieties of clothing go on sale in January before the stores make their inventories.

Children's clothes usually go on sale in September, just after school starts. Women's coats, woolen dresses, and men's suits are often marked down in November, which is also the month for manufacturers' closeout sales of men's shirts. Men's and boy's suits and women's dresses and hats also go on sale after Easter, in late April. Ski sweaters and bathing suits sell for half their preseason price after the season.

Even during these seasonal sales, shoppers must always beware of phony markdowns and closeouts and the substitution by the stores of lower-quality and shoddy sale merchandise for the store's regular fare. Most important, shoppers should buy only what they would buy anyway, even if it were not on sale. Buying something that will not be used or is not needed at a sale price is certainly no bargain, no matter how cheap it is.

PAYING TAXES

The U.S. Internal Revenue Service does not expect you to pay any more in income tax than you are legally liable for. Taxpayers are encouraged to take advantages of all the opportunities for lowering their personal taxes that the tax laws make available. Yet the IRS expects that as many as three out of four people who figure their own tax returns will overpay their taxes (U. S. Office of Management and Budget, "Personal Taxes," 1984).

The biggest mistake that people make is using the *short form*, which allows only fixed deductions from a person's total income for all his or her legally deductible expenses. Most taxpayers use the short form every year because it is simpler and faster to use than the long form. They should be aware, however, that it can also be very expensive. The average student who works only part-time probably saves on the short form because he or she has very few deductions and a limited income. For all others, relying on the short form is likely to be an expensive luxury.

Tax laws are not only very complicated, but they change from year to year. It is therefore difficult for the average couple to figure their own income tax and take advantage of all the legal deductions to which they are entitled. They will probably pay lower tax if they pay for professional help. A tax expert is likely to find enough deductions to more than pay for the fee—another deductible item, by the way. The tax expert must have something to work with, however, and a wise consumer makes a practice of saving and then sorting into categories all sales receipts, canceled checks, and records of unreceipted deductible expenditures for the year. The tax expert will make good use of these data.

Before taking their form and records to the professional, a couple should first try to compute the long form themselves. They will then be much more knowledgeable in discussing the deductions and problems with the tax expert; they also will be aware of just how much the expert has saved them. In making this initial and informational attempt, the couple will need a tax guide. A good manual, which is available for about a dollar, is the government's own *Your Federal Income Tax*, which can be ordered from the U. S. Superintendent of Documents, Washington, D. C. 20402. J. K. Lasser's annual *Income Tax Guide* is another good source of information available at libraries and book stores.

A curious provision of the tax law is the "marriage penalty," which provides that if two fully employed people are married and file a joint return, they will pay a higher tax than if they are simply living together (without being married) and file individual returns. (They cannot legally file individual returns if they are married.) This discriminatory tax law can be quite substantial for couples in the higher tax brackets. Many couples who are living together have decided not to marry in order not to pay the higher tax. Still others who have been living together and filing individual returns have received profound shocks when, ignorant of the tax law, they marry and file a joint return. Other couples have decided to divorce, while maintaining a common residence and telling no one but their tax accountant. Although the income tax law is a labyrinth of confusion and contradiction in many respects, none is more puzzling than this government tax penalty on marriage.

Every couple should take advantage of the opportunity to shelter taxable income through IRA accounts. An IRA (Individual Retirement Account) is the most valuable tax shelter ever devised for individual tax payers. You may deposit up to $2,000 into an account of your choice (for example a Certificate of Deposit in a bank). The $2,000 may then be deducted from your income that year, so that you do not pay taxes on this amount (thus the term *tax shelter*). Moreover, the interest earned on the investment is also free from income tax while it accumulates. After you reach age 59½ you may withdraw all your funds in a lump sum at very low tax rates via a ten-year averaging tax computation; or, if you prefer, you may let the funds build, tax free, until you reach age 70½. (You may continue to contribute to the IRA

during this time.) At that age, you may either use the lump-sum, ten-year averaging plan, or you can withdraw the amount as a pension over your life expectancy or the joint lives of yourself and your spouse.

The contribution may be up to $2,250 for a married couple filing a joint return, with only one spouse employed. If both are employed, the contribution may be $4,000 ($2,000 each). A contribution of $4,000 per year from age twenty-five to sixty-five would not only provide a significant savings in taxes each year, but if compounded at 10 percent (available in many money market funds) it would reach $181,037. At that time, it would continue to appreciate $18,103 per year with no further contributions.

The Keogh plan is similar to the IRA but is available only to the self-employed. If you are self-employed, you may contribute 20 percent of your net income, up to $30,000.[13] You may also have both an IRA and a Keogh plan.

THE IMPORTANCE OF REGULAR INVESTMENTS

As we have seen, the goal of investing is not deferred spending (which is properly called *saving*) but rather removing the invested money from spendable resources and allowing it to grow. Eventually, withdrawals may be made, but only from dividends or interest, and never (at least ideally) from the principal; the principal should always be left undisturbed.

There are three criteria for a good investment: *safety*, *yield*, and *growth*. A good investment balances these three factors. If an investment is safe but provides a yield less than the rate of inflation and no growth at all, it is obviously a poor investment. If the investment is safe but provides safety and a relatively high yield but fails to grow with the economy, it is

---

[13]This is a 1985 ruling, subject to change.

TABLE 13-4

One dollar compounded at different interest rates, from one to fifty years, showing the doubling time

Year	3%	4%	5%	6%	8%	10%	20%
1	1.03	1.04	1.05	1.06	1.08	1.10	1.20
2	1.06	1.08	1.10	1.12	1.17	1.21	1.44
3	1.09	1.12	1.16	1.19	1.26	1.33	1.73
4	1.13	1.17	1.22	1.26	1.36	1.46	2.07
5	1.16	1.22	1.28	1.34	1.47	1.61	2.49
6	1.19	1.27	1.34	1.41	1.59	1.77	2.99
7	1.23	1.32	1.41	1.50	1.71	1.94	3.58
8	1.27	1.37	1.48	1.59	1.85	2.14	4.30
9	1.30	1.42	1.55	1.68	2.00	2.35	5.16
10	1.34	1.48	1.63	1.79	2.16	2.59	6.19
11	1.38	1.54	1.71	1.89	2.33	2.85	7.43
12	1.43	1.60	1.80	2.01	2.52	3.13	8.92
13	1.47	1.67	1.89	2.13	2.72	3.45	10.70
14	1.51	1.73	1.98	2.26	2.94	3.79	12.80
15	1.56	1.80	2.08	2.39	3.17	4.17	15.40
16	1.60	1.87	2.18	2.54	3.43	4.59	18.50
17	1.65	1.95	2.29	2.69	3.70	5.05	22.20
18	1.70	2.03	2.41	2.85	4.00	5.55	26.60
19	1.75	2.11	2.53	3.02	4.32	6.11	31.90
20	1.81	2.19	2.65	3.20	4.66	6.72	38.30
25	2.09	2.67	3.39	4.29	6.85	10.80	95.40
30	2.43	3.24	4.32	5.74	10.00	17.40	237.00
40	3.26	4.80	7.04	10.30	21.70	45.30	1,470.00
50	4.38	7.11	11.50	18.40	46.90	117.00	9,100.00

also a poor investment. Finally, if the growth is phenomenal and the yield outstanding, but the potential is too risky, it is a poor investment (buying this type of security is called *speculating* rather than investing).

One important concept that should be understood is *compound interest*. This refers to interest *upon* interest; that is, if the interest that is earned on an investment is itself reinvested each month, this reinvestment (of the interest) will *itself* earn interest. At compound rates, money will double in this way, with the *doubling time* depending upon the rate of interest. For example, money will double (reproduce itself) in twenty-five years at 3 percent interest or in twelve years at 6 percent in-

terest. At 20 percent interest, it will double in just four years (Table 13-4).

Suppose you could invest $100 per month at 10 percent interest, compounded. Then, after eight years, suppose you began to withdraw $100 per month (making no further deposits). How long could you continue such withdrawals before exhausting the principal? Eight years? Sixteen years? Twenty-four years? Forever? The answer is *forever*. This is because the doubling time at 10 percent interest is eight years. Therefore, for every $100 you put in the first month, you would have $200 eight years later. You could continue to withdraw this $100 month after month forever, leaving the principal untouched.

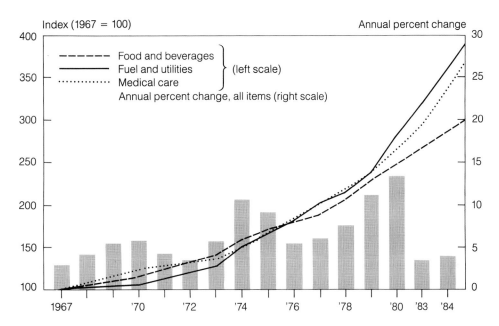

The Consumer Price Indexes are a measure of the costs of goods and services and are based on approximately 3,000 items. The three lines in the graph represent changes in the prices of food and beverages, fuel and utilities, and medical care. The vertical bars at the bottom of the figure represent the percentage change each year of all these items combined.

FIGURE 13-2

Consumer price indexes: the steadily rising costs of goods and services in the United States, 1967–1984

[a]1984 figures are annual rate for four months, ending April 1984.

Source: Data from U.S. Bureau of Labor Statistics, "Annual Percent Change in Selected Price Indexes: 1960 to 1984" (1985) and "Consumer Price Indexes for Selected Items and Groups: 1970 to 1984" (1985).

A point that is especially important to consider in making an investment is the long-range trend of inflation. If your investment does not keep pace with inflation, your funds will lose value in terms of purchasing power, or what they will buy, when they are withdrawn. For example, an annual rate of inflation of about 6 percent would double prices in about twelve years, and then double them again twelve years later. An investment, therefore, would have to earn at least 6 percent (after

taxes) just to keep pace with inflation. If you were in the 33 percent tax bracket, your investment would have to earn 9 percent just for your money to be worth as much when withdrawn as when invested.

All societies have experienced steady, long-term inflation (interrupted by short periods of deflation) from earliest recorded history. In the United States, for example, the rate of inflation for the past 200 years (until the 1970s) was about 2 percent annually. Thus, what George

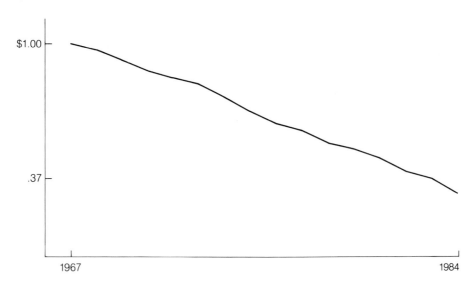

The purchasing power of the dollar has been dropping steadily. In the period from 1967 to 1983, the dollar lost about two thirds of its purchasing power. In other words, a 1967 dollar could buy three times as much as a 1984 dollar.

FIGURE 13-3

Purchasing power of the dollar, 1967–1984

Source: Data from U.S. Bureau of Labor Statistics, Monthly Data in U.S. Bureau of Economic Analysis. (1985, p. 466).

Washington would sell for $1 would sell for $60 in 1970, and what Abraham Lincoln could sell for $1 would sell for $80 (see Figure 13-2). It is impossible, of course, to predict the rate of future inflation, but whatever it is, an investment must keep up with it or the value of the capital will *depreciate* rather than *appreciate*.

For example, putting $100 in a sugar bowl and hiding it on the top shelf would be a very poor investment since there would be no yield and no growth (and only moderate safety). If inflation were, say 6 percent per year, the value of the $100 would depreciate by 6 percent each year, compounded. After twelve years, it would be worth only $50 in purchasing power. If you put the $100 into a savings and loan account that paid 6 percent annually, compounded, this would keep up with the inflation,

so that the $100 would still be worth $100 in purchasing power twelve years later. However, this still does not allow for taxes. If your tax bracket is, say, 33 percent, 2 percent (one-third) of the 6 percent should go for taxes, leaving only 4 percent appreciation. Thus, the $100 would, after taxes, actually depreciate by 2 percent each year in purchasing power (see Figure 13-3).

A classic investment is bonds, which pay a fixed rate for their lifetime. The drawback to bonds, however, is that this fixed rate may look good at the time of purchase but may not be adequate in a time of rapid inflation. During a period of very rapid inflation, such as in Germany in 1923, fixed-value instruments such as bonds or cash (either in the bank or in something like a money market fund) become virtually worthless. (See Shapiro's *The Penniless Billionaires* [1980] for a fascinating discussion of the impact of inflation.)

Common stocks are another traditional investment vehicle. Investment experts agree that, no matter how good a stock looks, it is impossible to predict its movement with certainty. Therefore, they advise that no more that 5 percent of one's investment should be put into any single stock. However, it is difficult for the nonprofessional to keep track of a great number of stocks. One answer to this problem is to let a professional money manager make the decisions for you regarding the type of stock and the timing of its purchase and sale. This can be done by buying a mutual fund (rather than an individual stock). A mutual fund is an investment company. It pays a professional money manager to buy a stock in anticipation of its rising value, sell it when it appears to be near its peak value, and withdraw from the market (holding assets in cash) when this seems to be indicated. When you buy a share in a mutual fund, you buy a share in the entire portfolio of stocks that the fund owns. Some funds are much better than others, of course; some funds manage to lose money in a rising market, while others make money in a falling market. How do you select a fund that will appreciate? The best answer to this seems to be to rely on the "track record" or past performance of the fund over at least ten years. If it has a record of steady appreciation during both up (*bull*) and down (*bear*) markets, the presumption would be that the investment man-magazine puts out an annual rating in their sions of buying, holding, and selling. *Forbes* magazine puts out an annual rating, in their August issue, showing the performance records of all the mutual funds in the United States. Other publications also analyze the performance of mutual funds. For example, both *Barrons* and *Money* magazines publish mutual fund ratings on a periodic basis. The *Weisenberger Report*, published annually, tracks the record of each existing fund for periods up to twenty years. (It is expensive but is available in libraries.) The *Wall Street Journal* often has articles on mutual funds, and its back issues may be consulted in the library.

Mutual funds are either *no-load* or *load*. The no-load fund charges no investment fee; the load fund charges about 8 percent. There are also low-load funds, which usually charge about 3 percent. The charge is a "front-end" load, charged when shares in the fund are purchased. There is not charge for selling shares.

Shares in mutual funds are usually purchased by mail. A phone call or a letter to a mutual fund asking for their *prospectus* will bring a description of the fund, its track record, and an application form.

Other traditional investments are various commodities such as gold, silver, diamonds, oriental carpets, coins, stamps, and rare books. Whether any of these commodities appreciates or depreciates depends on many variables. (See Table 13-5 for a summary of the compounded annual rates of growth of various investments from 1971 to 1981.)

What then, is a good investment? This question has no single answer; the answer varies from time to time and situation to situation. It depends on the rate of inflation and the nature of the national economy, as well as on the individual item chosen. Deal with a trusted firm, beware of get-rich schemes, and remember the three cardinal principles of investing—safety, yield, and growth—with safety of paramount importance. Finally, you should begin your investment program early to take advantage of the growth-upon-growth aspect of compound interest. Even a 6 percent annual return will double your investment, and then redouble it, every twelve years.

SUMMARY

One of the most difficult things a young couple face when they strike out on their own is the hard economic reality of making a living and

TABLE 13-5

How investments have played in ten-year, five-year, and one-year periods,
June 1971 to June 1981

	Compounded annual rates of growth					
	1971–81	R[a]	1976–81	R[a]	1980–81	R[a]
Oil	30.8%	1	20.9%	5	14.3%	6
Gold	28.0	2	30.7	3	−13.9	14
Oriental carpets	27.3	3	20.9	6	−0.2	11
U.S. coins	27.1	4	29.7	4	−8.0	12
U.S. stamps	23.5	5	32.9	1	18.0	4
Chinese ceramics	22.9	6	30.7	2	36.5	1
Silver	21.5	7	20.1	7	−26.6	16
Rare books	16.8	8	13.8	11	18.0	5
Old masters	15.4	9	16.8	9	22.9	3
Farmland	14.6	10	14.8	10	9.7	8
Diamonds	14.5	11	16.9	8	0.0	10
Housing	10.3	12	11.6	12	8.1	9
Inflation rate (CPI)	8.3	13	9.7	14	10.0	7
Stocks	5.8	14	9.8	13	25.3	2
Foreign exchange	5.3	15	3.1	15	−17.3	14
Bonds	3.8	16	1.1	16	−9.6	13

[a]R = rank from best investment (1) to worst within the group (16). Notice how ranking changes from the 10-year investment column to the 1-year investment column.
Source: Salomon Bros., *San Francisco Chronicle,* July 19, 1981, p. D1.

meeting expenses. Research indicates that couples quarrel more about money than any other topic and that the various economic pressures on a family are among the major sources of marriage failure. In the complex world of our mass society, wresting a living means, in essence, directing one's cash flow for few of us can provide our own goods or services directly.

Keeping a budget can help a couple to maximize their need satisfactions with available funds, that is, to maintain a cash flow that directs spendable income where they most want it to go. Since there is never enough money for everything a couple needs or wants, they are always forced to choose between available alternatives, whether or not they realize it at the time. It is impossible to make such choices wisely if the alternatives are not

clear. The budget is an indispensable tool that clarifies these choices and puts them into perspective.

Credit is a potentially dangerous tool; it is a fundamental element of economic life in our society, though, and the wise use of it can provide significant enhancement of a couple's lifestyle. There are three major forms of credit: open credit (which is not financed and is therefore "free" and a great bargain and convenience); profit-making credit (which is financed but potentially profitable); and non-profit-making credit (which is financed and costly). The wise consumer is aware of the ways that each of these forms of credit can be used effectively, as well as the risks inherent in each form. Credit installment buying of a big-ticket item is expensive, risky, and usually an unwise use of credit. Instead, the couple should borrow the money and pay cash for the item. They should shop for the money as carefully as for any other commodity, looking for the best "buy"—that is, the lowest interest rate.

Wise consumers understand not only the principles of budgeting (especially the concept of forced alternate choice) and the effective uses of credit, but also the principle of *value return*—getting a dollar's worth out of a dollar. They know what they want and why they want it; they learn to comparison shop, to recognize overpriced or shoddy merchandise and faulty contracts; to distinguish the legitimate from the phony sale; to handle the smooth or bullying salesperson who uses high-pressure techniques; and to recognize and avoid completely the "borax" stores. They know that they cannot get something for nothing and are especially wary of offers of "free services" or unbelievable bargains.

Finally, sound personal finance requires the breadwinners of the family to have an income-protecting, renewable, term life insurance policy and a regular program of saving and investing. *Saving* is the term used for the accumulation of money for deferred spending and for an emergency reserve. *Investing* is the term used for a long-range program in which the money is left undisturbed to use the "growth on growth" principle of capital funds, doubling and redoubling over the years.

Personal finance is one of the least understood and most neglected areas of family life, although it is at the heart and core of most familial interaction. Acquiring financial expertise will pay rich dividends far beyond the amount of time and attention it demands.

QUESTIONS

1. Why is the problem of money a main source of conflict in marriage?

2. What are the benefits of keeping a budget?

3. What are the basic principles of sound personal finance?

4. What is meant by the principle of *forced alternate choice*? Why it is so important to sound money management?

5. What are nondiscretionary expenses? Discretionary expenses?

6. Discuss the importance of the personal allowance (a) for adults; (b) for children.

7. How does the advent of children into the family affect the family's expenditures?

8. What are the three sound uses of credit? Discuss.

9. Discuss the pitfalls of credit installment buying.

10. Explain the "balloon payment" clause in installment contracts.

11. What are some good and bad sources of loans?

12. What is a "borax" store?

13. How do most consumers cooperate in their own exploitation?

14. Discuss the economics of buying a car, whether new or used.

15. Discuss the economics involved in owning and driving a car.

16. What is the basic purpose of life insurance?

17. What is meant by *term insurance*? What is meant by *insurance plus investment*? Which is the better buy? Why?

18. If two persons are living together without being married and pay taxes as single persons, will they pay more or less taxes than a similar married couple that files a joint return? Explain your answer. Do you think this differential in tax liability is justified? What is its rationale?

19. What is compound interest? Explain the "growth on growth" principle of capital funds.

20. Discuss the difference between *saving* and *investing*.

21. What three factors must be considered in any long-term investment?

22. How does *investment* differ from *speculation*?

SUGGESTIONS FOR FURTHER READING

Barret, Nancy S. "Women in the Job Market: Occupations, Earnings, and Career Opportunities." In *The Subtle Revolution*, edited by Ralph E. Smith, pp. 31–61. Washington, D.C.: The Urban Institute, 1979.

Casey, Douglas R. *Strategic Investing*. New York: Simon & Schuster, 1982.

Erdman, Paul. *Paul Erdman's Money Book: An Investor's Guide to Economics and Finance*. New York: Random House, 1984.

How to Prepare Your Personal Income Tax Return. Englewood Cliffs, N. J.: Prentice-Hall, published annually.

Lingren, Henry Clay. *Great Expectations: The Psychology of Money*. Los Altos, Calif.: William Kaufman, 1980.

Mott, F. *The Employment Revolution: Young Women in the 1970s*. Cambridge, Mass.: The MIT Press, 1982.

Shapiro, Max. *The Penniless Billionaires*. New York: Truman Tally, 1980.

Smith, Adam. *Paper Money*. New York: Summit, 1981.

Stein, Benjamin J. *Financial Passages*. New York: Doubleday, 1985.

Tobias, Andrew. *Money Angles*. New York: Simon & Schuster, 1984.

U. S. Department of Transportation, National Highway Traffic Safety Administration. *The Car Book: A Consumer's Guide to Car Buying*. Washington, D. C.: published annually.

Westfall, David. *Every Woman's Guide to Financial Planning*. New York: Basic Books, 1984.

G L O S S A R Y

abortifacients Substances or objects that interfere with the implantation or development of the germinal disc or embryo in the wall of the uterus. The "morning after" pill and IUDs (intrauterine devices) are examples.

Acquired Immune Deficiency Syndrome (AIDS) A fatal disease affecting the body's immune system—thus subjecting the victim to a host of serious infections and diseases. The incidence of AIDS—whose virus is thought to be transmitted by semen and blood—is rising rapidly among homosexuals.

active listening Involves listening fully, completely, and intently—attempting to understand what the other person is saying without interrupting, arguing, or changing the subject.

amniocentesis An important prenatal diagnostic tool. A long hollow needle is inserted through the mother's abdomen and into the amniotic sac, where a sample of the amniotic fluid is drawn off. This fluid contains sloughed-off cells from the fetus that may be examined microscopically for signs of disease or birth defects, enabling early treatment to be instituted. These cells also indicate the baby's gender.

androgen Often called the "male sex hormone," it is active in many ways, such as directing the differentiation of embryonic tissue into male genitalia, directing the differentiation of prenatal brain tissue that governs various male physiological functions, and directing the development of secondary gender characteristics at puberty. It is produced in the testicles and adrenal cortex of the male and, to a lesser extent, in the ovaries and adrenal cortex of the female.

Apgar scoring system A system of evaluating the general condition of the newborn infant. The newborn's score later serves as an aid to the pediatrician in following the development and health of the child.

attachment A component of love characterized by an intense bonding. Attachment may persist long after the other aspects of love have vanished.

bride price Goods paid to a bride's family by the groom's family in recognition of the economic value of the bride. This is the opposite of *dowry*.

cash flow The relation between expenditures and income—how much a person makes and spends and how he or she spends it. A budget is the best means for directing cash flow wisely.

cerebral erection Penile erection caused by psychological stimuli.

chlamydia A bacterial infection of the uterine lining and fallopian tubes, causing pelvic inflammatory disease (PID) in women. It is usually less serious in men, causing difficult or painful urination, although the intensity of the symptoms varies and if the infection goes deeper it can affect the male sperm ducts and cause sterility.

clitoris The small organ situated just under the upper portion of the labia minora of the female genitalia. It is the homologue of the male penis, consists of a shaft and a glans, and extends with erotic arousal. It is the chief organ for erotic response in most women.

coitus Copulation.

coitus reservatus Copulating without ejaculation.

compound interest Interest that itself earns interest.

conflict The occurrence of two opposing needs in a situation in which only one of them can be fulfilled. Marital conflict occurs when satisfaction of a need for one of the couple means deprivation for the other.

congenital A condition existing at birth or before birth that is not caused by heredity.

congruence of role perception An interaction in which each person perceives his or her own role about the same as the other person does; the basis for reciprocity of role performance and equivalence of role function.

contraception An action or device designed to prevent conception.

convergent feedback Information that one's behavior is bringing a desired result.

copulation Insertion of the erect penis into the vagina. The basis for reproduction, as well as a source of sexual pleasure, intimacy, and communication.

culture The way that persons in a society or subsociety behave and the implements, artifacts, institutions, and concepts that they characteristically use in their behavior.

cunnilingus Oral stimulation of the vulva, especially the clitoris.

dating The basis for marital choice in our society, but rare in other societies. Dating also serves other functions, such as providing adventure, excitement, romance, and other sociosexual satisfactions. It came into existence in our society early in the present century as a result of the economic and social changes brought about by the Industrial Revolution.

dating differential The tendency of the man in our society to prefer women who are smaller, younger, somewhat less intelligent and less educated, and of somewhat lower status than he is, and the tendency of women to prefer men who have the converse of these qualities. This cultural phenomenon results in a residue of relatively high-status women and low-status men who do not date and often do not marry.

defense-oriented Behavior directed toward alleviation of the stress and self-devaluation associated with the failure to achieve a basic need rather than toward the resolution of the basic need itself.

demography The statistical study of the characteristics of human populations.

developmental readiness A concept that describes the optimal periods in an infant's and

child's development when he or she has reached the neuromotor maturity necessary for learning a particular skill. If the child is not developmentally ready, the skill cannot be learned, and if the period of developmental readiness has passed, the learning of the skill is not economical.

developmental sequence The highly predictable sequence of growth and development in infancy and childhood.

displacement As an ego-defense mechanism; refusing to recognize or acknowledge the basic cause of a frustration and regarding another event as the cause.

divergent feedback Information that one's behavior is not bringing the desired result.

DNA molecules (deoxyribonucleic acid) Contained within each gene, these complex chain-like structures encode the information of heredity and direct all activities of the cell.

ejaculate Semen.

ejaculation The rhythmic discharge of seminal fluid from the penis during orgasm.

embryo The developing organism from the second to the eighth week of pregnancy. During the embryonic period—the second stage of pregnancy—all the organs and tissues are differentiated into their human form.

endogamy The inclination or the necessity to marry within a particular group.

episiotomy A surgical incision made in the mother's perineum during childbirth to prevent tearing of the vaginal tissues.

equivalence of role function Receiving as much satisfaction *from* the other as one is providing *for* the other, in an interaction.

erogenous zones Areas of the human body—for example, the genitalia, the mouth, the breasts—that are sensitive to tactile stimuli and respond with erotic pleasure and arousal.

erotic Pertaining to sexual stimulation and gratification.

erotic response The inevitable result of appropriate and sustained erotic stimuli. The sequence of erotic response is divided into four phases—excitement, plateau, orgasm, and resolution—each of which has predictable physiological characteristics.

erotophile A person who enjoys erotica in all its forms.

erotophobe A person who dislikes or is bored by erotica and to whom sexual expression is not very important.

estrogen Often called the "female hormone," it is active in many important ways, such as directing the differentiation of embryonic tissue into female genitalia, governing various female physiological functions, and directing the development of female secondary gender characteristics at puberty. It is produced chiefly in the ovaries and adrenal cortex of the female and, to a lesser extent, in the testicles and adrenal cortex of the male.

estrus The period of maximum sexual receptivity in the infrahuman female. It is also called *heat* or *rut*.

ethnic group A subsociety that shares the same cuisine, language, dress, religious observance, and recreational interests and that is embedded in a larger and ethnically different society.

exogamy The inclination or the necessity to marry outside a particular group.

feedback Information received by a person about the effects of his or her behavior.

fellatio Oral stimulation of the penis.

fetus A developing human being, from eight weeks after conception to birth—a time termed the *fetal period*.

forced alternate choice The concept that using money to buy A eliminates the possibility of using it to buy B. An extremely important principle in the management of personal finance and the basis for making a budget.

frigid A woman who is nonorgasmic and usually erotophobic. The term frigid is being replaced by the term preorgasmic.

frustration The feeling of depression or anger that occurs with significant deprivation. It is often combined with feelings of self-devaluation.

gamete The germ cell. In the male, it is called the *sperm*; in the female, it is called the *ovum* or *egg*.

genes The subcellular structures within the chromosomes in the cell nucleus that contain DNA molecules and determine the traits of the differentiating cells of the organism.

germinal disc The stage of the developing organism during the first two weeks following conception.

germinal period The first two weeks of pregnancy from the formation of the zygote in the fallopian tube to the embedding of the germinal disc in the uterine wall. During this period, pregnancy may be reliably detected by laboratory pregnancy tests.

gonadotropic hormone (hCG—human chorionic gonadotropic hormone) The hormone that stimulates the ovarian follicles for the development of the ovum. Presence of this hormone in large quantities indicates pregnancy; it can be detected in the blood as early as seven days after conception.

gonads The organs that produce the *gametes* or reproductive cells. In the male, the gonads are called *testicles* and produce sperm cells; in the female, the gonads are called *ovaries* and produce *egg cells* or *ova*.

gonococcus The microorganism causing gonorrhea. It is found in the mucous discharge from membranes affected by the disease. This discharge is highly infectious.

gonorrhea A sexually transmissible disease caused by gonococci. Unlike syphilis, which typically involves the entire body, gonorrhea usually remains localized in the genitalia and is self-limiting, although it may persist and cause serious and permanent damage, including sterility. Symptoms are common in men, but the disease is often asymptomatic (without symptoms) in women and difficult to detect.

hermaphrodite A person who has both male and female organs, or organs that are indeterminate (such as a clitoris that resembles a penis).

Herpes II Genital herpes is a sexually transmissible virus infection that has been spreading rapidly throughout the world. When the virus leaves the nerve cell nucleus (where it may have been dormant for years) it produces a fluid-filled blister that is highly contagious. If the victim of genital herpes is pregnant, the baby may be infected during birth, with serious, even fatal, results.

heterogamy The mutual attraction and compatibility of persons with opposite and complementary personality traits—for example, dominance-submission, nurturance-dependence, achievement-vicarious.

homogamy Similar or shared demographic characteristics in a dating or married couple, such as race, religion, ethnic group, educational level, social class, and age.

homologue Developed from the same prenatal tissue. For example, the same tissue will develop into a penis or a clitoris depending upon the prenatal hormone mix present, which in turn depends upon the presence (or absence) of sex chromosomes (XX in the female, XY in the male).

impotence The inability of a man to experience erection. It may be caused by either physical or psychological factors and is usually temporary.

incest Copulation (or marriage) between closely related persons, either blood relatives or in-laws; the degree of relatedness considered incestuous varies from state to state and from society to society.

infancy The period from the second month after birth to the time when a baby is walking and beginning to talk (usually about fifteen months).

intermarriage The marriage of persons of different races, ethnic groups, religions, or social classes. Also called *mixed marriage.*

intimacy The experiencing of the essence of one's self in intense physical, intellectual, and emotional communion with another. With some intimates the physical aspect is most important; with others, the intellectual or emotional factor may be most important.

laparoscopy A short, simple female sterilization procedure that does not require major abdominal surgery.

lesbianism Female homosexuality.

leveling A way of communicating that is open, honest, direct, and does not lower the self-worth of the other; the only category of communication that makes it possible to live in harmony and mutual self-enhancement in marriage.

limerence An aspect of love that is characterized by a compulsive attachment to another person, with thoughts of the other occupying up to 90 percent of one's consciousness. It is accompanied by feelings of extreme joy when it is reciprocated, or extreme pain when it is not.

mass society An industrialized and urbanized society that functions according to mass production, mass consumption, mass manipulation of taste, and highly specialized institutional and individual roles. In a mass society, with its relative decline of primary institutions and intrinsic satisfactions, the person is often disoriented, devalued, and desperately in need of the intrinsic love, nurture, and emotional support that are provided by the paired relation.

menarche The beginning of ovulation and the menstrual cycle in the pubescent woman.

menopause The cessation of ovulation, menstruation, and fertility in the woman. It usually occurs between age forty-five and fifty.

menstrual cycle The twenty-eight-day cycle of the postpubescent woman in which ovulation, engorgement of the uterine wall with blood and nutrients, and expulsion of this material through the vagina (when the ovum is not fertilized) occur. The cycle ceases with menopause. The final stage of this cycle, *menstruation*, lasts for about four days.

miscegenation Interracial marriage.

neonate The newborn during the first month of extrauterine life. During this neonatal period, the baby must make the extremely complex transition from fetal to postnatal ways of living.

ovulation The regular monthly process in the fertile woman whereby an ovarian follicle ruptures and releases a mature ovum, or egg.

pair bonding The process of forming a paired bond. Pair bonding has been the subject of speculation by poets, philosophers, and theologians since earliest recorded history.

paired bond A very strong reciprocal attraction or attachment between two people; an expression of shared communion, intimacy, affection, respect, admiration, emotional dependency, and love. (A paired bond may also form between a person and an animal.)

perineum The erotically sensitive area between the anus and the genitalia.

pedophile A person who sexually abuses a child, or one who can only obtain erotic or sexual gratification through intimate contact with a child.

petting Any deliberately erotic contact except copulation. It may be either heterosexual or homosexual.

photoplethysmograph A device placed just inside the entrance of the vagina to measure erotic response in the woman.

placenta The organ, developing from the chorionic villi, that joins the fetus to the uterine tissue. The placenta serves as the medium for the metabolic exchange between the mother and the fetus.

polyandry A form of marriage in which one woman has more than one husband.

polygamy Marriage with multiple spouses (as opposed to *monogamy*, with one spouse).

polygymy A form of marriage in which one man has more than one wife.

preejaculatory fluid A clear, viscous fluid secreted by the erect penis when the man becomes erotically aroused.

prepubertal orgasm The experiencing of orgasm before puberty or sexual maturity. Prepubertal orgasm in the male is not accompanied by ejaculation.

prenatal Before birth.

primary relation A relation characterized by affection, respect, informality, immediacy, spontaneity, intimacy, and intrinsic satisfaction of needs.

primary gender characteristics The biological characteristics of men and women directly related to reproduction, such as the production of sperm in the man and ovulation, menstruation, and lactation in the woman.

progesterone The female hormone (known as the pregnancy hormone) that is produced in the corpus luteum, and whose function is to prepare the uterus for the reception and development of a fertilized ovum.

progestin A synthetic hormone related in chemical structure to the male hormone androgen.

propinquity Nearness in place, or time, or both.

psychoendocrine The effect of hormones from the endocrine glands upon physiological responses, emotions, and behavior.

quickening The first fetal movements that the mother can feel, usually at about the seventeenth week of pregnancy.

reciprocity of role performance An interaction in which each person performs the expected role behavior anticipated by the other.

reflex erection Penile erection caused by tactile stimulation.

refractory period A characteristic of the resolution phase of male erotic response during which the man is physiologically incapable of responding to erotic stimulation; its duration may be anywhere from a few minutes to several hours, or even a day or more.

salpingectomy Major abdominal surgery in which the fallopian tubes are surgically cut and tied off to prevent conception.

secondary relation A relation or interaction that is formal, impersonal, highly structured, and functional, with rewards symbolic and delayed rather than intrinsic and immediate. In such a relation each person is important to the other chiefly for the function he or she performs.

secondary gender characteristics The physical characteristics that emerge at puberty as a function of the sex hormones—for example, body contour, muscular strength, distribution of body and facial hair, depth of voice, and breast development.

sex hormones Hormones secreted by the gonads and responsible for the development of the secondary gender characteristics.

socialization The process of a person's learning—from parents, peers, social institutions, and other sources—the skills, knowledge, and roles necessary for competent and socially acceptable behavior in the society.

society An aggregate of persons in an associational group that has some measure of permanence.

spermicides The chemical substances that destroy or immobilize sperm and are used as contraceptives.

spirochete A spiral-shaped microorganism that causes syphilis. Transmission of the spirochete from one host to another is invariably from an infectious lesion of a person in the first or second stages of syphilis through the mucous membrane or broken skin of the person contracting the disease.

syphilis A venereal disease caused by a microorganism called a *spirochete*. Syphilis goes through four stages, each with separate and distinct characteristics, and can involve every part of the body. It is transmitted by contact of mucous membrane or broken skin with an infectious syphilitic lesion.

tactile Pertaining to the sensation of touch.

testosterone An important component of the male sex hormone androgen. It is responsible for inducing and maintaining the male secondary gender characteristics.

trimester A period of three months; one of the three time divisions of pregnancy.

uterus The thick-walled, expandable female organ that contains, protects, and nurtures the developing embryo and fetus and, at full term, has regular muscular contractions to force the fetus through the cervix and vagina.

vacuum curettage A suction procedure used to induce labor after the embryo is more than four weeks old in order to terminate the pregnancy. It requires no anesthesia and can be done in a physician's office.

vagina The elastic sex organ of the woman that extends from the lips of the erotically sensitive external genitalia to the cervix, the opening to the uterus.

vasocongestion The flow of blood into veins and capillaries causing the area to become engorged, and, in the case of genital tissue, erotically sensitive and responsive.

vulva The external genitalia of the female, consisting of the labia majora, labia minora, clitoris, and opening of the vagina.

womb The uterus.

X chromosome The chromosome that determines female traits. All ova and half of all sperm carry an X chromosome.

Y chromosome The chromosome that determines male traits. Half of all sperm carry a Y chromosome.

zygote The fertilized egg after it has begun to divide.

BIBLIOGRAPHY

Abortions and the Poor: Private Morality, Public Responsibility. New York: Alan Guttmacher Institute, 1979.

Abramson, P. R. "The Relationship of the Frequency of Masturbation to Several Personality Dimensions and Behavior." *Journal of Sex Research* 9 (1973): 139.

"Active Herpes in Childbirth." *Science News* 124 (December 24, 1983): 413.

Adams, M. *Single Blessedness.* New York: Basic Books, 1976.

Ahrons, C. R., and Rodgers, R. *Divorced Families.* New York: Norton, 1987.

———, and Wallisch, L. "The Close Relationship between Former Spouses." In S. Duck and D. Perlman (Eds.). *Close Relationships: Development, Dynamics, and Deterioration,* pp. 269–96. Beverly Hills, Calif.: Sage, 1986.

Albin, Mel, and Cavallo, Dominic, eds. *Family Life in America, 1620–2000.* St. James, N.Y.: Revisionary Press, 1981.

Albrecht, Stan L. "Correlates of Marital Happiness among the Remarried." *Journal of Marriage and the Family* 41 (November 1979): 857–67.

Albrecht, Stan L., Bahr, H. M., and Goodman, K. L. *Divorce and Remarriage: Problems, Adaptations, and Adjustments.* Westport, Conn.: Greenwood, 1983.

Allport, F. H. *Social Psychology.* Boston: Houghton Mifflin, 1924.

Altman, S. A. "Primate Behavior in Review." *Science* 150 (1965): 1440–42.

American Council on Education. "Financial Burden for College Student." *San Francisco Chronicle,* August 21, 1984, p. 18.

Amundsen, Kristen. *The Silenced Majority.* Englewood Cliffs, N.J.: Prentice-Hall, 1971.

Andersen, Kurt. "Private Violence." *Time,* September 5, 1983, pp. 18–19.

Andreas, Carol. *Sex and Caste in America.* Englewood Cliffs, N.J.: Prentice-Hall, 1971.

Angyal, A. *Neurosis and Treatment: A Holistic Theory.* New York: John Wiley, 1965.

Anonymous. *My Secret Life,* volume I–XI. Introduction by G. Legman. New York: Grove Press, 1966.

Arafat, I., and Yorburg, B. "On Living Together without Marriage." *Journal of Sex Research* 9 (1973): 97–106.

Ardrey, Robert. *The Territorial Imperative.* New York: Atheneum, 1966.

Argyle, M. *The Psychology of Interpersonal Behavior.* Baltimore, Md.: Penguin Books, 1967.

Argyle, M.; Lallijee, M.; and Cook, M. "The Effects of Visibility on Interaction in a Dyad." *Human Relations* 21 (1968): 3–17.

Ariès, Philippe. *Centuries of Childhood.* New York: Vintage, 1965.

Aronoff, Joel, and Krano, William D. "A Reexamination of the Cross-Cultural Principles of Task Segregation and Sex-Role Differentiation in the Family." *American Sociological Review* 40 (February 1975): 12–20.

Athanasiou, Robert; Shaver, Phillip; and Tavris, Carol. "Sex." *Psychology Today* 4 (1970): 37–52.

Atwater, Lynn. "Getting Involved: Women's Transition to First Extramarital Sex." *Alternate Lifestyles* 2 (February 1979): 33–68.

Auchincloss, Douglas. "The Gay Crowd." In *Sex and the Sixties,* edited by Joe David Brown, pp. 65–75. New York: Time-Life Books, 1968.

Bach, George R., and Wyden, Peter. *The Intimate Enemy: How to Fight Fair in Love and Marriage.* New York: Avon, 1970.

Bachrach, Leona L. "Marital Status and Mental Disorder: An Analytical Review." Department of Health, Education, and Welfare Publication No. (ADM) 75-217. Washington, D.C.: Government Printing Office, 1975.

Badwinter, Elisabeth. *Mother Love Myth and Reality: Motherhood in Modern History.* New York: Macmillan, 1981.

Baldwin, Wendy, and Nord, Christine. "Delayed Childbearing in the U.S.: Facts and Fictions." *Population Bulletin,* Population Reference Bureau, Inc., Vol. 39, No. 4. Washington, D.C.: Government Printing Office, November 1984.

Banta, D., and Thacker, S. "The Risks and Benefits of Episiotomy: A Review." *Birth* 9 (Spring 1982): 25–30.

Barlow, Brent A. "Notes on Mormon Interfaith Marriages." *The Family Coordinator* 26 (April 1977): 143–50.

Bartell, G. "Group Sex among Mid-Americans." *Journal of Sex Research* 6 (1970): 113–30.

Baumrind, Diana. "From Each According to Her Ability." *School Review* (February 1972): 161–95.

Beecher, Catherine E. *A Treatise on Domestic Economy.* 1841. New York: Schocken, 1977.

Bell, Alan P., and Weinberg, Martin S. *Homosexuality: A Study of Diversity among Men and Women.* New York: Simon & Schuster, 1978.

Bell, Alan P.; Weinberg, Martin S.; and Kiefer Hammersmith, Sue. *Sexual Preference: Its Development in Men and Women.* Bloomingdale, Indiana: Indiana University Press, 1981.

Bell, Robert R. *Marriage and Family Interaction.* 6th ed. Homewood, Ill.: Dorsey, 1983.

Bell, Robert R., and Coughey, Kathleen. "Premarital Sexual Experience among College Females, 1958, 1968, and 1978." *Family Relations* 29 (July 1980): 353–56.

Bell, Robert, R., and Silvan, L. "Swinging—The Sexual Exchange of Marriage Partners." Paper presented at the meeting of the Society of Social Problems, August 1970, Washington, D.C.

Bell, Sanford. "A Preliminary Study of the Emotion of Love between the Sexes." *American Journal of Psychology* 13 (1902): 325–54.

Bell, Susan. "Birth Control." In *The New Our Bodies, Ourselves,* by The Boston Women's Health Collective, pp. 220–62. New York: Simon & Schuster, 1984.

Bem, Sandra L., and Bem, Daryl. "Training the Woman to Know Her Place: The Power of Non-Conscious Ideology." In *Beliefs, Attitudes, and Human Affairs,* by Daryl Bem, pp. 89–99. Monterey, Calif.: Brooks/Cole, 1970.

Berg, S. W., and Harrison, W. O. "Spectinomycin as Primary Treatment of Gonorrhea in Areas of High Prevalence of Penicillinase-producing *Neisseria gonorrhoeae." Sexually Transmitted Diseases: Journal of the American Venereal Disease Association* 8 (1981): 38–39.

Berger, P., and Kellner, H. "Marriage and the Construction of Reality." In *Recent Sociology, no. 2,* edited by H. P. Dreitzel. New York: Macmillan, 1970.

Berkowitz, Gila. "Why the Diaphragm Doesn't Work." *San Francisco Magazine* 25 (December 1981): 72–75.

Bernard, Jessie, *Remarriage: A Study of Marriage.* New York: Russell, 1971.

Berne, Eric. *Games People Play.* New York: Grove Press, 1967.

Berscheid, Ellen; Walster, Elaine; and Bohrnstedt, G. "Body Image." *Psychology Today* 6 (1972): 57–66.

Bieber, Irving, et al. *Homosexuality: A Psychoanalytic Study.* New York: Basic Books, 1962.

Biegel, H. G. "Romantic Love." *American Sociological Review* 16 (1951): 326–34.

Blake, Judith. "Coercive Pronatalism and American Population Policy." In *Aspects of Population Growth Policy,* edited by Robert Park, Jr., and Charles F. Westoff. Washington, D.C.: Commission on Population Growth and the American Future, 1973.

Blood, Robert O., Jr., and Wolfe, Donald W. *Husbands and Wives: The Dynamics of Married Living.* New York: Free Press, 1960.

Bohannan, Paul. *Divorce and After.* New York: Doubleday, 1970.

———. *All The Happy Families.* New York: McGraw-Hill, 1985.

Bohannan, Paul, and Erickson, Rosemary. "Stepping In." *Psychology Today* 11 (January 1978): 53–54, 59.

Bootzin, Richard R., et al. *Abnormal Psychology: Current Perspectives.* 3rd ed. New York: Random House, 1980.

Boston Women's Health Book Collective. *Ourselves and Our Children: A Book By and*

For Women. New York: Random House, 1978.

———. *The New Our Bodies, Ourselves.* New York: Simon & Schuster, 1984.

Bould, Sally. "Female-Headed Families: Personal Fate Control and the Provider Role." *Journal of Marriage and the Family* 39 (May 1977): 339–49.

Bower, Donald W., and Chrisopherson, Victor A. "University Student Cohabitation: A Regional Comparison of Selected Attitudes and Behavior." *Journal of Marriage and the Family* 39 (August 1977): 447–53.

Bowlby, John. *Attachment and Loss.* Vols. 1–2. New York: Basic Books, 1969, 1973.

Bragonier, J. R. "Influence of Oral Contraception on Sexual Response." *Medical Aspects of Human Sexuality* 143 (October 1976): 130–43.

Bram, Susan. "Through the Looking Glass: Voluntary Childlessness as a Mirror of Contemporary Changes in the Meaning of Parenthood." In *The First Child and Family Formation,* edited by Warren B. Miller and Lucille F. Newman, pp. 368–91. Chapel Hill, N.C.: Population Center, 1978.

Brandwein, Ruth A.; Brown, Carol A.; and Fox, Elizabeth Maury. "Women and Children Last: The Social Situation of Divorced Mothers and Their Families." *Journal of Marriage and the Family* 36 (August 1974): 498–514.

Brauer, Alan, and Brauer, Donna. "ESO (Extended Sexual Orgasm)." *Playboy,* July 1984, p. 40.

Brecher, Edward M. "Women: Victims of the V.D. Rip-off." *Viva* I (October and November 1973).

———. "Prevention of the Sexually Transmitted Diseases." In *Handbook of Sexology,* edited by John Money and Herman Musaph, pp. 1037–44. Amsterdam: Elsevier-North Holland Biomedical Press, 1977.

———. (and the Editors of Consumer Reports Books). *Love, Sex, and Aging: A Consumers Union Report.* Boston: Little, Brown, 1984.

Brecher, Edward M., and Brecher, Jeremy. "Sex Is Good for Your Health." *Playboy,* June 1976, p. 125.

Brecher, Edward M., and Brecher, Ruth, eds. *An Analysis of Human Sexual Response.* Boston: Little, Brown, 1966.

Brock, Connie. "Menopause." *Human Behavior* 8 (April 1979): 38–46.

Brotherton, Janet, and Craft, I. L. "A Clinical and Pathological Study of 91 Cases of Spontaneous Abortion." *Fertility and Sterility* 23 (1972): 289–94.

Brown, Judith K. "A Note on the Division of Labor by Sex." *American Anthropologist* 72 (1970): 1073–78.

Brown, Stuart T., et al. "Treatment of Uncomplicated Gonococcal Infection with Trimethoprim-Sulfamethoxazole." *Sexually Transmitted Diseases: Journal of the American Venereal Disease Association* 9 (January–February 1982): 9–14.

Bugliosi, Vincent, and Gentry, Curt. *Helter Skelter.* New York: W. W. Norton, 1974.

Bumpass, Larry, and Sweet, James A. "Differentials in Marital Instability, 1970." *American Sociological Review* 37 (1972): 754–66.

Burgess, E. W., and Cottrell, L. S. *Predicting Success or Failure in Marriage.* Englewood Cliffs, N.J.: Prentice-Hall, 1939.

Burgess, E. W., and Wallin, Paul. *Engagement and Marriage.* Philadelphia: J. B. Lippincott, 1953.

Burns, Mark, et al. "A Preliminary Evaluation of the Gonozyme Test." *Sexually Transmitted Diseases: Journal of the American Venereal Disease Association* 10 (October–December 1983): 180–83.

Busselen, Harry J., and Busselen, Carol Kincaid. "Adjustment Differences Between Married and Single Undergraduate University Students: An Historical Perspective." *The Family Coordinator* 24 (1975): 281–87.

Byrne, Donn. "A Pregnant Pause in the Sexual Revolution." *Psychology Today* 11 (July 1977): 67–68.

Calhoun, A. W. *A Social History of the American Family.* New York: Barnes & Noble, 1945.

Campbell, Angus. "The American Way of Mating: Marriage, Si; Children, Maybe." *Psychology Today* 8 (May 1975): 37–43.

Carter, Hugh, and Glick, Paul C. *Marriage and Divorce: A Social and Economic Study.* Rev. ed. Cambridge, Mass.: Harvard University Press, 1976.

Cash, Thomas F., and Janda, Louis H. "The Eye of the Beholder." *Psychology Today* 18 (December 1984): 46–52.

Cates, W. "Putting the Risks in Perspective." In *Contraceptive Technology* 1 (November 1980): 111.

Cavan, Ruth Shonle. *The American Family.* 4th ed. New York: Crowell, 1969.

Chesley, Phyllis, and Goodman, J. *Women, Money and Power.* New York: Morrow, 1976.

Clanton, Gordon, and Smith, Lynn G., eds. *Jealousy.* Englewood Cliffs, N.J.: Prentice-Hall, 1977.

Clapp, Diane, and Swenson, Norma. "Infertility and Pregnancy Loss." In *The New Our Bodies, Ourselves*, by The Boston Women's Health Collective, pp. 419–31. New York: Simon & Schuster, 1984.

Clayton, Richard R. *The Family, Marriage, and Social Change.* 2nd ed. Lexington, Mass.: D. C. Heath, 1979.

Clayton, Richard R., and Voss, Harwin L. "Shacking Up: Cohabitation in the 1970s." *Journal of Marriage and the Family* 39 (May 1977): 273–83.

Cohen, Alan I.; Rein, Michael F.; and Noble, Robert C. "A Comparison of Rosoxacin with Ampicillin and Probenecid in the Treatment of Uncomplicated Gonorrhea." *Sexually Transmitted Diseases: Journal of the American Venereal Disease Association* 11 (January–March 1984): 24–27.

Coleman, James C. *Abnormal Psychology and Modern Life.* 7th ed. Glenview, Ill.: Scott, Foresman, 1984.

———. *Contemporary Psychology and Effective Behavior.* 4th ed. Glenview, Ill.: Scott, Foresman, 1979.

Conant, Marcus A.; Spicer, Delano W.; and Smith, Creed D. "Herpes Simplex Virus Transmission: Condom Studies." *Sexually Transmitted Diseases: Journal of the American Venereal Disease Association* 11 (April–June 1984): 94–95.

Connolly, William G. *The New York Times Guide to Buying or Building a Home.* New York: Times Books, 1985.

Cooper, Pamela E.; Cumber, Barbara; and Hartner, Robin. "Decision-making Patterns and Post-decision Adjustment of Childfree Husbands and Wives." *Alternative Lifestyles* 1 (February 1978): 71–94.

Cordes, Colleen. "Black Males Face High Odds." *American Psychological Association Monitor* 16 (January 1985): 9–11, 27.

Corson, Stephen L. *Conquering Infertility.* Norwalk, Conn.: Appleton-Century-Crofts, 1983.

Corzine, William L. "The Phenomenon of Jealousy: A Theoretical and Empirical Analysis." Ph.D. dissertation, United States International University, San Diego, 1974.

Coulton, G. G. *Life in the Middle Ages.* London: Cambridge University Press, 1930.

Cowan, Phillip; Cowan, Caroline; Coie, Lynne; and Coie, John. "The Impact of Children upon Their Parents." In *The First Child and Family Formation.* Chapel Hill: University of North Carolina Press, 1978.

Crawley, Lawrence; Malfetti, James L.; Stewart, Ernest I., Jr.; and Vas Dias, Nini. *Reproduction, Sex and Preparation for Marriage.* 2nd ed. Englewood Cliffs, N.J.: Prentice-Hall, 1973.

Cromie, William J. "Everyone's Private Bubble." *Enterprise Science News*, January 8, 1978.

Cuber, John F., and Harroff, Peggy B. *The Significant Americans: A Study of Sexual Behavior among the Affluent.* New York: Appleton-Century-Crofts, 1965.

Curran, James. U.S. Centers for Disease Control, AIDS Task Force Report from International AIDS Conference, April 15, 1985, Atlanta, Ga. (cosponsored by the World Health Organization and the U.S. Public Health Service).

Cutright, Phillips. "Income and Family Events: Marital Stability." *Journal of Marriage and the Family* 33 (1971): 291–306.

Cutright, Phillips, and Polanto, Karen. "Areal Structure and Rates of Childlessness among American Wives in 1970." *Social Biology* 24 (Summer 1977): 52–61.

Danielsson, Bengt. "Sex Life in Polynesia." In *The Encyclopedia of Sexual Behavior*, edited by Albert Ellis and Albert Abarbanel. New

York: J. Aronson, 1973.

Danziger, C. "Unmarried Heterosexual Cohabitation." Ph.D dissertation, Rutgers University, 1976.

Darnley, Fred. "Adjustment to Retirement: Integrity or Despair." *The Family Coordinator* (April 1975).

Darrow, R. Morton. *Report on State of Families Today*. New York: Family Service Association of America, October 1984.

Davies, Nigel. *The Rampant God*. New York: William Morrow, 1984.

Davis, David, rabbi and chairman, Judaic Studies, University of San Francisco. Interview, March 15, 1985.

Davis, Keith E. "Near and Dear: Friendship and Love Compared." *Psychology Today* 19 (February 1985): 22–30.

Davis, Kingsley. "The American Family in Relation to Demographic Change." In *Demographic and Social Aspects of Population Growth*, edited by Charles F. Westoff and Robert Parke, Jr., pp. 235–65. U.S. Commission on Population Growth and the American Future. Washington, D.C.: Government Printing Office, 1972.

———. "The Future of Marriage." *Bulletin of the American Academy of Arts and Sciences* 36 (May 1983): 33.

Dean, Gillian, and Gurak, Douglas T. "Marital Homogamy the Second Time Around." *Journal of Marriage and the Family* 40 (August 1978): 559–70.

Dearborn, Lester W. "Autoeroticism." In *The Encyclopedia of Sexual Behavior*, edited by Albert Ellis and Albert Abarbanel, pp. 204–15. New York: J. Aronson, 1973.

DeCrow, Karen. *Sexist Justice*. New York: Random House, 1974.

DeJong, Gordon F., and Sell, Ralph R. "Changes in Childlessness in the United States: A Demographic Path Analysis." *Population Studies* 31 (March 1977): 129–41.

Dell, Floyd. *Love in Greenwich Village*. New York: George H. Doran, 1926.

DeMartino, Manfred F. *Sex and the Intelligent Woman*. New York: Springer, 1974.

DeRougement, Denis. *Love in the Western World*. New York: Pantheon, 1956. Reprint. New York: Harper & Row, 1974.

Desai, Kalani, and Robson, Hugh G. "Comparison of the Gram-stained Urethral Smear and First-Voided Urine Sediment in the Diagnosis of Nongonococcal Urethritis." *Sexually Transmitted Diseases: Journal of the American Venereal Disease Association* 9 (January–March 1982): 21–25.

Devore, Irven, ed. *Primate Behavior*. New York: Holt, 1965.

Dickens, Charles. *Oliver Twist*. New ed., revised and corrected. London: 1846.

———. *A Tale of Two Cities*. New York: Oxford University Press, 1926.

Dickerson, R. E. *So Youth May Know*. New York: Association Press, 1930.

Dinman, B. D. "The Reality and Acceptance of Risk." *Journal of the American Medical Association* 244 (1980): 1226–28.

Dion, K.; Berscheid, Ellen; and Walster, Elaine. "What Is Beautiful Is Good." *Journal of Personality and Social Psychology* 24 (1972): 285–90.

Doress, Paula Brown, et al. "Women Growing Older." In *The New Our Bodies, Ourselves*, by The Boston Women's Health Collective, pp. 435–72. New York: Simon & Schuster, 1984.

Doress, Paula Brown, and Wegman, Peggy Nelson. "Working Toward Mutuality: Our Relationships with Men." In *The New Our Bodies, Ourselves*, by The Boston Women's Health Collective, pp. 123–40. New York: Simon & Schuster, 1984.

Douglas, John H., and Miller, Julie Ann. "Record Breaking Women." *Science News* 112 (September 10, 1977): 172–74.

Draughon, M. "Stepmother's Model of Identification in Relation to Mourning in the Child." *Psychological Reports* 36 (1975): 183–89.

Duberman, Lucille. *The Reconstituted Family: A Study of Remarried Couples and Their Children*. Chicago: Nelson Hall, 1975.

———. *Marriage and Other Alternatives*. New York: Praeger, 1977.

Dundes, Alan. "Here I Sit—a Study of American Latrinialia." In *The Kroeber Anthropological Society Papers*, pp. 93–103. Berkeley: University of California Press, 1966.

Dunkle, Margaret, co-director of the Equality Center in Washington, D.C. "How Sexism 'Encourages' Pregnancies." *San Francisco Chronicle*, December 18, 1984, p. 2.

Dunnigan, Phillip, sergeant of police, San Francisco. Private discussion, March 1, 1985.

Durant, Will. *The Age of Faith. The Renaissance. The Reformation.* The Story of Civilization, vols. 4–6. New York: Simon & Schuster, 1950, 1953, 1957.

Durbin, Karen. "On Sexual Jealousy." In *Jealousy*, edited by Gordon Clanton and Lynn G. Smith, pp. 36–45. Englewood Cliffs, N.J.: Prentice-Hall, 1977.

Elder, G. H., Jr. "Appearance and Education in Marriage Mobility." *American Sociological Review* 34 (1969): 519–33.

Ellis, Albert. "A Study of Human Love Relationships." *Journal of Genetic Psychology* 75 (1949): 61–71.

English, O. Spurgeon, and Pearson, Gerald H. J. *Emotional Problems of Living.* New York: W. W. Norton, 1945.

Enkin, Murray, and Chalmers, Iain, eds. *Effectiveness and Satisfaction in Antenatal Care.* Philadelphia: J. B. Lippincott, 1982.

Erikson, Erik H. *Childhood and Society.* 2nd ed. New York: W. W. Norton, 1963.

Eshleman, J. Ross. *The Family: An Introduction.* 2nd ed. Boston: Allyn & Bacon, 1978.

Evans, H. L., et al. "Sperm Abnormalities and Cigarette Smoking." *The Lancet* 1 (March 21, 1981): 627–29.

"Existing One-Family Houses Sold and Price, by Region: 1970–1982." *Existing Home Sales*, monthly. Washington, D.C.: National Association of Realtors, 1984.

Federal Highway Administration. *Cost of Owning and Operating Automobiles and Vans.* Washington, D.C.: Government Printing Office, 1984.

Feldman, Frances Lomas. *The Family in Today's Money World.* 2nd ed. New York: Family Service Association of America, 1977.

Feldman, Philip. "Extramarital Sex as a Substitute for Communication." *Medical Aspects of Human Sexuality* (April 1981): 52J–52X.

Feldman, Y. M., and Nikitas, J. A. "Nongonococcal Urethritis: A Clinical Review." *Journal of the American Medical Association* 245 (1981): 381–86.

Feshback, Seymour, and Feshback, Norma. "The Young Aggressors." *Psychology Today* 6 (April 1973): 90–95.

Festinger, Leon, "Architecture and Group Membership." *Journal of Social Issues* 1 (1951): 152–63.

Finch, B. F., and Green, Hugh. *Contraception Through the Ages.* Springfield, Ill.: Charles C Thomas, 1963.

Fisher, Seymour. *The Female Orgasm.* New York: Basic Books, 1973.

Fishman, K. B. "The Economic Behavior of Stepfamilies." *Family Relations* 32 (1983): 359–66.

"Five-Year Birth Control Device." *Bulletin of the World Health Organization*, Vol. 63, No. 3, June 1985.

Flaubert, Gustav. *November.* New York: Serendipity Press, 1966.

Flax, Carol. "Columbia University Survey on Sex, Eroticism, and Sensuality." *San Francisco Chronicle*, October 25, 1984, p. 10.

Ford, C. S., and Beach, F. A. *Patterns of Sexual Behavior.* New York: Harper, 1970.

Fowles, John. *The Collector.* Boston: Little, Brown, 1963.

Fraker, Susan. "Why Women Aren't Getting to the Top." *Fortune*, April 16, 1984, pp. 40–45.

Fraker, Susan, et al. "Abortion Under Attack." *Newsweek*, June 5, 1978, pp. 36–47.

Francis, D. P.; Curran, J. W.; and Essex, M. "Epidemic Acquired Immune Deficiency Syndrome: Epidemiologic Evidence for a Transmissible Agent." *Journal of the National Cancer Institute* 71 (1983): 1–4.

Francke, Linda Bird. *Growing Up Divorced.* New York: Fawcett Crest, 1983.

Francome, Colin. "Survey of Abortion Patients at Bill Baird Centers, Boston." *San Francisco Chronicle*, January 9, 1981, p. 7.

Frank, Ellen; Anderson, Carol; and Rubinstein, Debra. "Frequency of Sexual Dysfunction in 'Normal' Couples." *New England Journal of Medicine* 299 (July 20, 1978): 111–15.

Freed, Doris Jonas, and Walker, Timothy B. *Family Law Quarterly* 18 (Winter 1985): 369–471.

Freedman, Daniel G. "Ethnic Differences in Babies." *Human Nature* 2 (January 1979): 36–43.

Freeman, Ruth, and Klaus, Patricia. "Blessed or Not? The New Spinster in England and the United States in the Late Nineteenth and Early Twentieth Centuries." *Journal of Family History* 9 (Winter 1984): 394–414.

Freud, Sigmund. *The Basic Writings of Sigmund Freud*, edited by A. A. Brill. New York: Modern Library, 1938.

Fried, Peter A., and Oxorn, Harry. *Smoking for Two: Cigarettes and Pregnancy*. New York: Macmillan, 1980.

Fromm, Erich. *The Art of Loving*. New York: Bantam, 1970.

Fromm-Reichmann, Frieda. "Loneliness." *Psychiatry* 22 (January 1959): 1.

Frumkin, Robert M. "Sexual Freedom." In *The Encyclopedia of Sexual Behavior*, edited by Albert Ellis and Albert Abarbanel. New York: J. Aronson, 1973.

Fuller, Margaret. *Woman in the Nineteenth Century*. New York: W. W. Norton, 1971.

Gagnon, John H. *Human Sexualities*. Glenview, Ill.: Scott, Foresman, 1977.

Gagnon, J. H., and Greenblat, C. S. *Life Designs: Individuals, Marriages, and Families*. Glenview, Ill.: Scott, Foresman, 1978.

Galenson, Marjorie. *Women and Work: An International Comparison*. Ithaca, N.Y.: Cornell University Press, 1973.

Gallo, Robert C. National Cancer Institute. Paper presented at the International Conference on Recombinant DNA, February 5, 1985, San Francisco.

Gallop, George, Jr. "Preference Widens for Small Families." Gallop Poll. *San Francisco Chronicle*, March 21, 1985, p. 5.

Gambrell, D. R., et al. "Changes in Sexual Drives of Patients on Oral Contraceptives." *The Journal of Reproductive Medicine* 17 (1976): 165–71.

Gasser, Rita D., and Taylor, Claribel M. "Role Adjustment of Single-Parent Fathers with Dependent Children." *The Family Coordinator* 25 (October 1976): 397–401.

Gaylin, Jody. "Those Sexy Victorians." *Psychology Today* 10 (December 1976): 137–39, 143.

Gerson, Marvin; Portnoy, Joseph; and Hamelin, Claude. "Reliable Identification of Herpes Simplex Viruses by DNA Restriction Endonuclease Analysis with ECORI." *Sexually Transmitted Diseases: Journal of the American Venereal Disease Association* 11 (April–June 1984): 85–90.

Gibran, Kahlil. *The Prophet*. New York: Alfred A. Knopf, 1923.

Gladue, Brian A. "Hormone Markers for Homosexuality?" *Science News* 126 (September 29, 1984): 198.

Glass, Shirley P., and Wright, Thomas L. "The Relationship of Extramarital Sex, Length of Marriage, and Sex Differences on Marital Satisfaction and Romanticism: Athanasiou's Data Reanalyzed." *Journal of Marriage and the Family* 39 (November 1977): 692.

Glenn, Norval D. "Psychological Well-Being in the Post-parental Stage." *Journal of Marriage and the Family* 37 (1975): 105–10.

————. "The Well-Being of Persons Remarried after Divorce." *Journal of Family Issues* 2 (1981): 61–75.

————. "Interreligious Marriage in the United States: Patterns and Recent Trends." *Journal of Marriage and the Family* 44 (August 1982): 555–66.

————. "A Note on Estimating the Strength of Influences for Religious Endogamy." *Journal of Marriage and the Family* 46 (August 1984): 725–27.

Glenn, Norval D., and Weaver, Charles N. "The Marital Happiness of Remarried, Divorced Persons." *Journal of Marriage and the Family* 39 (May 1977): 331–37.

Glick, Ira O.; Weiss, Robert S.; and Parkes, C. Murray. *The First Year of Bereavement*. New York: Wiley-Interscience, 1974.

Glick, Paul C. "Some Recent Changes in American Families." In *Current Population Reports: Population Characteristics*, Series P-23, No. 52, by U.S. Bureau of the Census. Washington, D.C.: Government Printing Office, 1975.

————. "Children of Divorced Parents in Demographic Perspective." *Journal of Social Issues* 35 (1979): 170–82.

———. "American Household Structure in Transition." *Family Planning Perspectives* 16 (September–October 1984): 204–11.

———. "How American Families Are Changing." *American Demographics*, January 1984b, pp. 21–25.

Glick, Paul C., and Lin, Sung-Ling. "Recent Changes in Divorce and Remarriage." *Journal of Marriage and the Family* 48 (November 1986): 737–47.

Glick, Paul C., and Norton, Arthur J. "Frequency, Duration, and Probability of Marriage and Divorce." *Journal of Marriage and the Family* 33 (1971): 301–17.

———. "Marrying, Divorcing, and Living Together in the United States Today." *Population Bulletin* vol. 32, no. 5. Washington, D.C.: Population Reference Bureau, 1977.

Goldthorp, W. O. "Ten-Minute Abortions." *British Medical Journal* 2 (1977): 562–64.

Goleman, Daniel. "Special Abilities of the Sexes: Do They Begin in the Brain?" *Psychology Today* 12 (November 1978): 48–59, 120.

Goode, William J. "The Theoretical Importance of Love." *American Sociological Review* 24 (1959): 38–47.

Gordon, Linda. *Woman's Body, Woman's Right: Birth Control in America.* New York: Penguin Books, 1977.

Gordon, Michael. *The American Family: Past, Present, and Future.* New York: Random House, 1978.

Gordon, Michael, ed. *The American Family in Social-Historical Perspective.* New York: St. Martin's Press, 1983.

Gordon, Suzanne. *Lonely in America.* New York: Simon & Schuster, 1976.

Gottschalk, Helmuth. *Problems of Jealousy.* Copenhagen: Fremad, 1936.

Gotwald, William H., and Golden, Gale Holtz. *Sexuality: The Human Experience.* New York: Macmillan, 1981.

Gough, Kathleen E. "The Origins of the Family." *Journal of Marriage and the Family* 33 (1971): 760–71.

Goy, R. W. "Experimental Control of Psychosexuality." In *A Discussion on the Determination of Sex*, edited by G. W. Harris and R. G. Edwards, pp. 149–62. Philosophical Transactions of the Royal Society, Series B, vol. 259. London: 1970.

Gravell, M.; London, W. T.; and Houff, S. A.; et al. "Transmission of Simian Acquired Immunodeficiency Syndrome (SAIDS) with Blood or Filtered Plasma." *Science* 223 (1984): 74–76.

Gray, Madeline. *Margaret Sanger.* New York: Marek, 1979.

Graziano, William, et al. "Eye to Eye Appeal: Taller Isn't Better." *Human Behavior* 7 (October 1978): 41.

Green, Richard. "Children of Homosexuals Seem Headed Straight." *Psychology Today* 12 (November 1978): 44, 46.

Greenberg, Dan, and Jacobs, Marsha. *How To Make Yourself Miserable.* New York: Random House, 1966.

Griffitt, W. "Environmental Effects on Interpersonal Affective Behavior: Ambient Effective Temperature and Attraction." *Journal of Personality and Social Psychology* 15 (1970): 240–44.

Groenman, Sjoerd. Interview by Nino Lo Bello at the University of Groningen (Sociology Dept.) in Staphorst, Holland. Published as "The Bride Must Be Pregnant." *San Francisco Examiner and Chronicle*, September 17, 1978, p. 21.

Guittar, E. C., and Lewis, R. A. "Self-Concepts among Some Unmarried Cohabitants." Paper presented at the annual meeting of the National Council of Family Relations, October 1974, St. Louis.

Gurman, Alan S., and Kniskern, D. P. "Research on Marital and Family Therapy: Progress, Perspective, and Prospect." In *Handbook of Psychotherapy and Behavior Change: An Empirical Analysis.* 2nd ed., edited by S. L. Garfield and A. E. Bergin. New York: John Wiley, 1978.

Haire, Doris. "Research on Drugs Used in Pregnancy and Obstetrics." Paper presented to the Subcommittee on Investigations and Oversights of the House Committee on Science and Technology, July 30, 1981, Washington, D. C.

Hales, Dianne. "Psycho-Immunity." *Science Digest* 89 (November 1981): 12.

Hall, Edward T. *The Silent Language.* New York: Anchor Press, 1973.

——. *Beyond Culture.* New York: Anchor Press, 1976.

Hall, W. J. *From Youth into Manhood.* New York: Association Press, 1909.

Haller, John S., and Haller, Robin M. *The Physician and Sexuality in Victorian America.* New York: W. W. Norton, 1974.

Hamilton, R. *The Herpes Book.* Los Angeles: J. P. Tarcher, 1980.

Hammond, Dorothy, and Jablow, Alta. "Women: Their Familial Roles in Traditional Societies." A Module of Benjamin/Cummings Publishing Company. Menlo Park, Calif.: Benjamin/Cummings, 1975.

Harlow, Harry F. "Love in Infant Monkeys." *Scientific American* 200 (1959): 68–74.

Harlow, Harry F., and Harlow, Margaret Kuenne. "Social Deprivation in Monkeys." *Scientific American* 207 (1962): 136–46.

Harrell, W. Andrew. "Survey of Dual-career Canadian Couples." Paper read at the meeting of the California State Psychological Association in San Franciso, January 9, 1985.

Harris, J. R. W. "Sexually Transmitted Diseases." In *Handbook of Sexology,* edited by John Money and Herman Musaph, pp. 1023–34. Amsterdam: Elsevier-North Holland Biomedical Press, 1977.

Harris, Marvin. "Why It's Not the Same Old America." *Psychology Today* 15 (August 1981): 23–51 *passim.*

Hartley, Shirley Foster. *Comparing Populations.* Belmont, Calif.: Wadsworth, 1982.

Hastings, Donald W. *Impotence and Frigidity.* Boston: Little, Brown, 1963.

Hatcher, Robert A., and Stewart, Gary. *Contraceptive Technology, 1982–83.* 11th rev. ed. New York: Irvington, 1982.

Hatcher, Robert A., et al. *Contraceptive Technology, 1984–85.* 12th rev. ed. New York: Irvington, 1984.

Haverkamp, Albert, Department of Obstetrics and Gynecology, Denver General Hospital. Address to the American Foundation for Maternal and Child Health, October 19, 1981, New York.

Haverkamp, Albert, and Orleans, Mirium. "An Assessment of Electronic Fetal Monitoring." *Women and Health* 7 (1982): 132.

Heaton, Tim B. "Religious Homogamy and Marital Satisfaction Reconsidered." *Journal of Marriage and the Family* 46 (August 1984): 729–33.

Heer, David M. "The Prevalence of Black-White Marriage in the United States, 1960 and 1970." *Journal of Marriage and the Family* 36 (May 1974): 247.

Heiman, Julia R. "The Physiology of Erotica: Women's Sexual Arousal." *Psychology Today* 8 (1975): 91–94.

Heiss, J. S., and Gordon, M. "Need Patterns and the Mutual Satisfaction of Dating and Engaged Couples." *Journal of Marriage and the Family* 26 (1964): 337–39.

Henig, Robin Marantz. "Perils of Painless Childbirth." *Human Behavior* 7 (October 1978): 50–51.

Henshaw, S. K., ed. "Abortion in the United States, 1981–82." *Family Planning Perspectives* 16 (May–June 1984): 119–27.

——. "Legal Abortions—Estimated Number, Rate, and Ratio, By Race: 1972 to 1982." The Alan Guttmacher Institute, New York. In *Statistical Abstract of the United States,* 105th ed., p. 67. Washington, D.C.: Government Printing Office, 1985.

Henze, L. F., and Hudson, J. W. "Personal and Family Characteristics of Non-Cohabiting and Cohabiting College Students." *Journal of Marriage and the Family* 36 (1974): 722–26.

"Herpes Pill Gets OK." *Science News* 127 (February 2, 1985): 71.

Hertz Corporation. "Compact Car's Yearly Cost." *San Francisco Chronicle,* March 26, 1985, p. 2.

Hess, E. H. "The Role of Pupil Size in Communication." *Scientific American* 233 (1975): 110–19.

Hetherington, E. Mavis; Cox, Martha; and Cox, Roger. "The Aftermath of Divorce." In *Mother/Child, Father/Child Relationships,* edited by Joseph H. Stephens, Jr., and Marilyn Matthews, pp. 149–75. Washington, D.C.: NAEYC, 1978.

Hill, Charles T.; Rubin, Zick.; and Peplau, Letitia. "Breakups before Marriage: The End of 103 Affairs." *Journal of Social Issues* 32 (1976): 147–68.

Hite, Shere. *The Hite Report.* New York: Macmillan, 1976.

Hong, Lawrence K. "Race to the Swiftest." *Playboy,* December 1984, p. 51.

Hooker, E. "The Adjustment of the Male Overt Homosexual." *Journal of Projective Techniques* 21 (1957): 18–31.

Horn, Jack C. "Vasectomy—the Unpopular Choice." *Psychology Today* 18 (June 1984): 17.

Horn, Jack C., and Meer, Jeff. "The Pleasure of Their Company." *Psychology Today* 18 (August 1984): 52–58.

Hosken, Fran. *The Hosken Report: Genital and Sexual Mutilation of Females.* Lexington, Mass.: Women's International Network News, 1979.

Houseknecht, S., and Spanier, G. B. "Marital Disruption and Higher Education among Women in the United States."*Sociological Quarterly* 21 (1980): 375–89.

Howard, George E. *A History of Matrimonial Institutions.* Chicago: University of Chicago Press, 1904.

Howe, Florence. "Sexual Stereotypes Start Early." *Saturday Review,* October 16, 1971, pp. 76–82, 92–94.

Hsia, Shyuan, et al. "Unregulated Production of Virus and/or Sperm Specific Anti-idiotypic Antibodies as a Cause of AIDS." *The Lancet* 1 (June 2, 1984): 1212–14.

Humphrey, Michael. "Sex Differences in Attitude to Parenthood." *Human Relations* 30 (August 1977): 737–50.

Hunt, Morton. *The Natural History of Love.* New York: Alfred A. Knopf, 1959. Reprint. New York: Funk and Wagnalls, 1967.

———. *Sexual Behavior in the 1970s.* Chicago: Playboy Press, 1974.

Hunt, Morton, and Hunt, Bernice. *The Divorce Experience: A New Look at the Formerly Married.* New York: McGraw-Hill, 1977.

International Family Digest (Fall Quarterly 1978). New York: Alan Guttmacher Institute, Research and Development Division, 1979.

"IUD's and Pelvic Inflammatory Disease." *Science News* 124 (August 20, 1983): 127.

Jacoby, Susan. "Forty-Nine Million Singles Can't Be All Right." In *Life Styles: Diversity in American Society.* 2nd ed., edited by Sol D. Feldman and Gerald W. Thielbar, pp. 115–23. Boston: Little, Brown, 1975.

Jacobson, Paul H. *American Marriage and Divorce.* New York: Rinehart, 1959.

Jaffe, Harold W., associate director of Centers for Disease Control AIDS Task Force. Address at the Conference sponsored by the Scientists' Institute for Public Information and the AIDS Medical Foundation, February 8, 1985, New York.

Jaffe, Harold W.; Choi, K.; and Thomas, P. A.; et al. National Case-control Study of Kaposi's Sarcoma and *Pneumocystis carinii* Pneumonia in Homosexual Men: Part I, Epidemiologic Results. *Ann. Intern. Med.* 99 (1983): 145–51.

James, P. D. *Unnatural Causes.* New York: Charles Scribner's, 1967.

Jastrow, Robert. *The Enchanted Mind in the Universe.* New York: Simon & Schuster, 1981.

Jensen, Gordon D. "Human Sexual Behavior in Primate Perspective." In *Contemporary Sexual Behavior: Critical Issues in the 1970s,* edited by Joseph Zubin and John Money, pp. 17–31. Baltimore, Md.: Johns Hopkins University Press, 1973.

Johnson, Jeanette H. "Tubal Sterilization and Hysterectomy." *Family Planning Perspectives* 14 (January–February 1982): 28–30.

Johnson, R. "A Study of Extramarital Sex." In *Beyond Monogamy,* edited by Lynn G. Smith and James R. Smith. Baltimore, Md.: Johns Hopkins University Press, 1974.

Johnson, Timothy, director of Lay Health Information at Harvard Medical School. Interview, *The New York Times,* February 21, 1981.

Judson, Franklyn N. "Epidemiology and Control of Nongonococcal Urethritis and Genital Chlamydial Infections: A Review." *Sexually Transmitted Diseases: Journal of the American Venereal Disease Association* 8 (April–June 1981): 117–26.

Kagan, Jerome, and Haveman, Ernest. *Psychology: An Introduction.* 4th ed. New York: Harcourt Brace Jovanovich, 1980.

Kalish, Richard A. *Death, Grief, and Caring Relationships.* Monterey, Calif.: Brooks/Cole, 1981.

Kammeyer, Kenneth C. W. *Marriage and Family.* Boston: Allyn and Bacon, 1987.

Kanin, E. J.; Davidson, K. D.; and Scheck, S. R. "A Research Note on Male-Female Differentials in the Experience of Heterosexual Love." *Journal of Sex Research* 6 (1970):64–72.

Karlen, Arno. *Sexuality and Homosexuality.* New York: W. W. Norton, 1971.

Katchadourian, Herant A., and Lunde, Donald T. *Fundamentals of Human Sexuality.* 3rd ed. New York: Holt, 1980.

Kaufman, Raymond H., et al. "Herpes Virus— Induced Antigens in Squamous-cell Carcinoma in Situ of the Vulva." *New England Journal of Medicine* 305 (August 27, 1981): 483–88.

Kaye, Donald. "Gonococcal Disease." In *Textbook of Medicine.* 15th ed., edited by Paul B. Beeson, Walsh McDermott, and James B. Wyngaarden, pp. 405–10. Philadelphia: W. B. Saunders, 1979.

Kellogg, J. H. *Plain Facts for Young and Old.* Burlington, Ia: Segner & Condit, 1879.

Kelly, G. Lombard. "Impotence." In *The Encyclopedia of Sexual Behavior*, edited by Albert Ellis and Albert Abarbanel. New York: J. Aronson, 1973.

Kennedy, Donald. "Why Adoptions Get Harder Every Year." *U.S. World and News Report,* September 20, 1982, p. 54.

Kephart, William M. *The Family, Society, and the Individual.* 4th ed. Boston: Houghton Mifflin, 1977.

Kessler, S. *The American Way of Divorce: Prescriptions for Change.* Chicago: Nelson Hall, 1975.

Kiefer, Otto. *Sexual Life in Ancient Rome.* 1934. London: Abbey Library, 1976.

Kieffer, Carolynne. "New Depths in Intimacy." In *Marriage and Alternatives: Exploring Intimate Relationships*, edited by Roger W. Libby and Robert N. Whitehurst, pp. 267–93. Glenview, Ill.: Scott, Foresman, 1977.

King, Theodore; Morelli, Irene; and Acevedo, Zoila Ortega. "Childbirth Seminars for Health Professionals." *Washington Post,* November 5, 1980.

Kinsey, Alfred C.; Pomeroy, Wardell B.; and Martin, Clyde E. *Sexual Behavior in the Human Male.* Philadelphia: W. B. Saunders, 1948.

Kinsey, Alfred C.; Pomeroy, Wardell B.; Martin, Clyde E.; and Gebhard, Paul H. *Sexual Behavior in the Human Female.* Philadelphia: W. B. Saunders, 1953.

Kitzinger, Sheila. *The Experience of Childbirth.* New York: Penguin Books, 1978.

Klaus, Marshall H., and Kennell, John H. *Maternal-Infant Bonding.* St. Louis, Mo.: Mosby, 1976.

Klein, Luella, president of the American College of Obstetrics and Gynecology. Press releases. *San Francisco Chronicle,* June 9, 1984, p. 42, and January 26, 1985, p. 6.

Knox, Samuel R.; Corey, Lawrence; Blough, Herbert; and Lerner, Martin A. "Historical Findings in Subjects from a High Socioeconomic Group Who Have Genital Infections with Herpes Simplex Virus." *Sexually Transmitted Diseases: Journal of the American Venereal Disease Association* 9 (January–March 1982): 15–20.

Kolata, Gina Bari. "Strategies for the Control of Gonorrhea." *Science* 192 (April 1976): 245.

Komarovsky, M. *Dilemma of Masculinity.* New York: W. W. Norton, 1976.

Kresch, Arnold J., Stanford University Medical Center. Interview, *San Francisco Chronicle,* October 30, 1981, p. 28.

Kronhausen, Phyllis, and Kronhausen, Eberhard. *Erotic Fantasies: A Study of the Sexual Imagination.* New York: Grove Press, 1969.

Krupp, Marcus A.; Chatton, Milton J.; and Werdegar, David, eds. *Current Medical Diagnosis & Treatment.* Los Altos, Calif.: Lange Medical Publications, 1985.

Ladas, A. K.; Whipple, B.; and Perry, J. D. *The G Spot and Other Recent Discoveries about Human Sexuality.* New York: Holt, Rinehart & Winston, 1982.

La Leche League International. "The Womanly Art of Breast Feeding." Publication No. 315, 3rd. ed. July 1981.

Lambert, Wallace E.; Hammers, Josiane F.; and Frasure-Smith, Nancy. *Child-rearing Values: A Cross-National Study.* New York: Praeger, 1979.

Landis, Judson T., and Landis, Mary G. *Building a Successful Marriage*. 7th ed. Englewood Cliffs, N.J.: Prentice-Hall, 1977.

Landis, Paul H. *Making the Most of Marriage*. 5th ed. Englewood Cliffs, N.J.: Prentice-Hall, 1975.

Lane, Mary E., et al. "Successful Use of the Diaphragm and Jelly by a Young Population: Report of a Clinical Study." *Family Planning Perspectives* 8 (March–April 1976): 81–86.

Langer, W. L. "Check on Population Growth: 1750–1850." *Scientific American* 27 (1972): 93–100.

Lasagna, L. *The V.D. Epidemic*. Philadelphia: Temple University Press, 1975.

Lauer, Robert, and Lauer, Jeanette. "Marriages Made to Last." *Psychology Today* 19 (June 1985): 22–26.

Layde, Peter M.; Ory, Howard W.; and Schlesselman, James J. "The Risk of Myocardial Infarction in Former Users of Oral Contraceptives." *Family Planning Perspectives* 14 (March–April 1982): 78–80.

Lee, G. A. "Marriage and Anomie: A Causal Argument." *Journal of Marriage and the Family* 36 (1974): 523–32.

Lee, John Alan. *The Colours of Love*. Toronto, Canada: New Press, 1973.

———. "Styles of Loving." *Psychology Today* 8 (1974): 44–51.

Lenski, Gehard, and Lenski, Jean. *Human Societies: An Introduction to Macrosociology*. 2nd ed. New York: McGraw-Hill, 1974.

Leslie, Gerald R. *The Family in Social Context*, 4th ed. New York: Oxford University Press, 1979.

Leslie, Gerald R., and Leslie, Elizabeth M. *Marriage in a Changing World*. New York: John Wiley, 1977.

Letter, *Playboy*, May 1985, p. 51.

Levine, M. I., and Bell, J. I. "Psychological Aspects of Pediatric Practice: Masturbation." *Pediatrics* 18 (1956): 803.

Lewis, Michael. "Culture and Gender Roles: There's No Unisex in the Nursery." *Psychology Today* 5 (May 1972): 54–57.

Lews, Judith Long, and Schwartz, Pepper. *The Sexual Scripts*. New York: Holt, Rinehart & Winston, 1977.

Liberatore, Paul. "AIDS." *San Francisco Chronicle*, December 7, 1984, p. 2.

Linden, Fabian. "Working Women: A Progress Report." *Consumer Research Center*. Washington, D.C.: October 3, 1984.

Lindenmayer, Jean Pierre; Steinberg, Maurice D.; Bjork, Darla A.; and Pardes, Herbert. "Psychiatric Aspects of Voluntary Sterilization in Young, Childless Women." *The Journal of Reproductive Medicine* 19 (August 1977): 87–91.

Little, Bill L. *This Will Drive You Sane*. Minneapolis, Minn.: Compcare, 1977.

Lobsenz, Norman M. "Taming the Green-Eyed Monster." In *Jealousy*, edited by Gordon Clanton and Lynn G. Smith, pp. 26–34. Englewood Cliffs, N.J.: Prentice-Hall, 1977.

Lopata, Helena Z. *Women as Widows: Support Systems*. New York: Elsevier Press, 1979.

Lorber, Judith. "Beyond Equality of the Sexes: The Question of the Children." *The Family Coordinator* 24 (1975): 465–72.

Lorenz, Konrad. *On Aggression*. Translated by Marjorie K. Wilson. New York: Harcourt, Brace, 1966. Reprint. New York: Bantam Books, 1970.

Lowe, Charles, and Roberts, Colin. "Where Have All the Conceptions Gone?" *The Lancet* 1 (March 1, 1975): 498–99.

Lowenthal, Marjorie; Thurnher, Majde; and Chiriboga, David. *Four Stages of Life*. San Francisco: Jossey-Bass, 1975.

Lubic, Ruth Watson. "Childbirthing Center Service and Costs for 1980." *American Journal of Nursing* 83 (July 1983): 1054–56.

Lynch, James J. *The Broken Heart: The Medical Consequences of Loneliness*. New York: Basic Books, 1977.

Maccoby, Eleanor Emmons, and Jacklin, Carol Nagy. *The Psychology of Sex Differences*. Palo Alto, Calif.: Stanford University Press, 1974.

MacDonald, John D. *Nightmare in Pink*. Greenwich, Conn.: Fawcett, 1964.

———. "The Random Noise of Love." *Seven*. Greenwich, Conn.: Fawcett, 1971.

Mace, David, and Mace, Vera. *We Can Have Better Marriages*. Nashville, Tenn.: Abingdon Press, 1974.

———. "Measure Your Marriage Potential: A Simple Test Tells Couples Where They Are." *The Family Coordinator* 27 (January 1978): 63–67.

Macfarlane, Aidan. *The Psychology of Childbirth.* Cambridge, Mass.: Harvard University Press, 1977.

Macklin, Eleanor D. "Comparison of Parent and Student Attitudes toward Non-Marital Cohabitation." Paper presented at the annual meeting of the National Council of Non-Family Relations, October 1974, St. Louis.

———. "Unmarried Heterosexual Cohabitation on the University Campus." In *The Social Psychology of Sex,* edited by J. P. Wiseman. New York: Harper & Row, 1976.

———. "Non-Marital Heterosexual Cohabitation." *Marriage and Family Review* 1 (March–April 1978): 1–12.

Magnuson, Ed. "Child Abuse: The Ultimate Betrayal." *Time,* September 5, 1983, pp. 20–23.

Maisel, Richard. "Report on the Continuing Audit of Public Attitudes and Concerns." Mimeographed. Boston: Harvard Medical School, Laboratory of Community Psychiatry, 1969.

Makepeace, James Michael. "The Birth Control Revolution: Consequences for College Student Life Styles." Ph.D. dissertation, Washington State University, 1975.

Malinowski, Bronislaw. *The Sexual Life of the Savages in Northwest Melanesia.* New York: Eugenics Publishing, 1929.

Mancini, Jay A., and Orth er, Dennis K. "Recreational Sexual Preferences among Middle-Class Husbands and Wives." *Journal of Sex Research* 14 (May 1578): 96–105.

Marano, Hara Estroff. "The Bonding of Mothers and Their Babies." *Smithsonian* 2 (February 1981).

Marcus, Steven. *The Other Victorians.* New York: Basic Books, 1966.

Margolis, Maxine. *Mothers and Such: Views of American Women and Why They Changed.* Berkeley: University of California Press, 1984.

Marotz-Baden, Ramona, et al. "Family Form or Family Process? Reconsidering the Deficit Family Model Approach." *Family Coordinator* 28 (January 1979): 5–13.

Marshall, Donald S. "Too Much in Mangaia." *Psychology Today* 4 (1971): 43–44, 70–79.

Martindale, Don. *Institutions, Organization, and Mass Society.* Boston: Houghton Mifflin, 1966.

Marvin v. *Marvin,* 18 Cal. 3d. 660, 134 California Reporter 815, 557 P.2d106 (1976).

Maslow, Abraham H. *The Farther Reaches of Human Nature.* New York: Viking, 1971.

Maslow, Abraham H., and Mintz, N. L. "Effects of Aesthetic Surroundings: Initial Effects of Three Aesthetic Conditions Upon Perceiving 'Energy' and 'Well-Being' in Faces." *Journal of Psychology* 41 (1956): 247–54.

Massarik, Fred, and Chenkin, Alvin. "United States' National Jewish Population Study: A First Report." In *American Jewish Yearbook,* Vol. 74. Philadelphia: Jewish Publication Society of America, 1973.

Massie, Robert K. *Nicholas and Alexandra.* New York: International Collector's Library, 1967.

Masters, William H., and Johnson, Virginia E. *Human Sexual Response.* Boston: Little, Brown, 1966.

———. *Human Sexual Inadequacy.* Boston: Little, Brown, 1970.

———. *Homosexuality in Perspective.* Boston: Little, Brown, 1979.

McCall, Cheryl. "The Cruelest Crime." *Life,* December 1984, 35.

McCarthy, J. F. "A Comparison of Disillusion of First and Second Marriages." In "Remarriage as an Incomplete Institution," by A. Cherlin, *American Journal of Sociology* 84 (1978): 634–50.

McCary, James Leslie, and McCary, Stephen P. *McCary's Human Sexuality.* 4th ed. Belmont, Calif.: Wadsworth, 1982.

McCauley, B. "Self-Esteem in the Cohabiting Relation." Master's thesis, University of Delaware, 1977.

McGuinness, Diane. "How Schools Discriminate against Boys." *Human Nature* 2 (February 1979): 82–88.

McGuinness, Diane, and Pribram, Karl H. "The Origins of Sensory Bias in the Development of Gender Differences in Perception and Cognition." In *Cognitive Growth and Development—Essays in Honor of Herbert G. Birth*, edited by Morton Bortner. New York: Brunner/Mazel, 1979.

Mead, Margaret. Introduction to *Premarital Dating Behavior*, by Winston Ehrman. New York: Holt, 1959.

———. "A New Look at Early Marriages." *U.S. News and World Report*, June 6, 1960, pp. 80–86.

Meer, Jeff. "Pet Theories." *Psychology Today* 18 (August 1984): 60.

Mehrabian, Albert. *Silent Messages*. Belmont, Calif.: Wadsworth, 1971.

Meredith, Nikki. "The Gay Dilemma." *Psychology Today* 18 (January 1984): 52–62.

Messinger, L. "Remarriages between Divorced People with Children from Previous Marriages: A Proposal for Preparation for Remarriage." *Journal of Marriage and Family Counseling* 3 (1976): 193–200.

Meyers, Robert. *The Bitter Pill*. New York: G. P. Putnam's, 1983.

Miller, Julie Ann. "Window on the Womb." *Science News* 127 (February 2, 1985): 75, 77.

Miller, Roger LeRoy. *Economic Issues for Consumers*. 4th ed. St. Paul, Minn.: West, 1983.

Miller, Warren B. "Psychological Antecedents to Conception among Abortion Seekers." *Western Journal of Medicine* 122 (1975): 12–19.

Minge-Klevana, Wanda. "Does Labor Time Increase with Industrialization? A Survey of Time Allocation Studies." *Current Anthropology* 21 (June 1980): 279–98.

Mohr, James C. *Abortion in America: The Origins and Evolution of National Policy, 1800–1900*. New York: Oxford University Press, 1978.

Moll, Albert. *The Sexual Life of the Child*. New York: Macmillan, 1925.

Monahan, Thomas P. "Are Interracial Marriages Really Less Stable?" *Social Forces* 48 (1970): 461–73.

Money, John. *Love and Love Sickness: The Science of Sex, Gender Difference, and Pair Bonding*. Baltimore, Md.: Johns Hopkins University Press, 1980.

Money, John, and Ehrhardt, Anke. *Man and Woman, Boy and Girl*. Baltimore, Md.: Johns Hopkins University Press, 1972.

Money, John, and Tucker, Patricia. *Sexual Signatures: On Being a Man or a Woman*. Boston: Little, Brown, 1975.

Morris, Desmond. *Intimate Behavior*. New York: Bantam, 1973.

Mosher, William D. "Infertility Trends among U.S. Couples: 1965–1976." *Family Planning Perspectives* 14 (January–February 1982): 22–27.

Mowat, Ronald Rae. *Morbid Jealousy and Murder: A Psychiatric Study of Morbidly Jealous Murderers at Broadmoor*. London: Tavistock, 1966.

Mullahy, Patrick. *Oedipus, Myth and Complex*. New York: Grove Press, 1955.

Murdock, George. *Social Structure*. New York: Macmillan, 1949.

———. "World Ethnographic Sample." *American Anthropologist* 59 (August 1957): 664–87.

Murstein, Bernard I. "The Complementary Needs Hypothesis in Newlyweds and Middleaged Married Couples." *Journal of Abnormal and Social Psychology* 63 (1961): 194–97.

———. "Self-Ideal–Self-Discrepancy and the Choice of Marital Partner." *Journal of Consulting and Clinical Psychology* 35 (1971): 231–36.

———. *My Secret Life*. Vols. I–XI. Introduction by G. Legman. New York: Grove Press, 1966.

National Council of the Churches of Christ in the United States of America. "Religious Bodies—Church Membership, 1960 to 1981, and Number of Churches, 1981." *Yearbook of American and Canadian Churches*, annual. New York: 1984.

National Opinion Research Center. *General Surveys, 1972–1982: Cumulative Codebook*. Chicago: University of Chicago Press, 1984.

Nelson, Paula. *The Joy of Money: The Guide to Women's Financial Freedom*. New York: Bantam, 1977.

Newland, Kathleen. *Worldwatch Paper 47, Infant Mortality and the Health of Societies*. Worldwatch Institute, 1776 Massachusetts Avenue N.W., Washington, D.C. 20036, December 1981.

Newton, Niles, and Modahl, Charlotte. "Pregnancy: The Closest Human Relationship." *Human Nature* 1 (March 1978): 40–49.

Norton, Arthur J. "Family Life Cycle: 1980." *Journal of Marriage and the Family* 45 (May 1983): 267–75.

Norton, Arthur J., and Glick, Paul C. "Marital Instability: Past, Present, and Future." *Journal of Social Issues* 32 (1976): 5–20.

Norton, R. "Measuring Marital Quality: A Critical Look at the Dependent Variable." *Journal of Marriage and the Family* 45 (February 1983): 141–51.

"Nutritional Services in Prenatal Care." National Research Council. Washington, D.C.: National Academy Press, 1981.

O'Herlihy, Colm. "Jogging and Suppression of Ovulation." Letter to *The New England Journal of Medicine* 306 (January 7, 1982): 50.

O'Neill, Nena. *The Marriage Premise*. New York: Evans, 1977.

O'Neill, Nena, and O'Neill, George. *Open Marriage: A New Life-Style for Couples*. New York: Evans, 1972.

O'Reilly, Jane. "Wife Beating: The Silent Crime." *Time*, September 5, 1983, pp. 23–26.

Orthner, Dennis K.; Brown, Terry; and Ferguson, Dennis. "Single-Parent Fatherhood: An Emerging Family Life Style." *The Family Coordinator* 25 (October 1976): 429–37.

Paige, Karen Erickson. "The Ritual of Circumcision." *Human Nature* 1 (May 1978): 40–48.

Parlee, Mary Brown. "The Sexes Under Scrutiny: From Old Biases to New Theories." *Psychology Today* 12 (November 1978): 62–69.

Pasquale, Samuel. "The Triphasic Pill." *San Francisco Chronicle*, April 11, 1984, p. 54.

Paul VI, Pope. "An Apostolic Letter Determining Norms for Mixed Marriages." April 29, 1970.

Paul, William, Harvard University. *San Francisco Chronicle*, August 29, 1981, p. 7.

Pearlin, Leonard I., and Johnson, Joyce S. "Marital Status, Life Strains, and Depression." In *Single Life: Unmarried Adults in Social Context*, edited by Peter J. Stein, pp. 165–78. New York: St. Martin's Press, 1981.

Pedersen, Frank A. "Does Research on Children Reared in Father-Absent Families Yield Information on Father Influences?" *The Family Coordinator* 25 (October 1976): 459–64.

"Periodic Abstinence: How Well Do New Approaches Work?" *Population Reports*, Series I, No. 3 (September 1981). (Available from Population Information Programs, Johns Hopkins University, 624 N. Broadway, Baltimore, Md. 21205.)

Perlman, David. "AIDS Deaths." *San Francisco Chronicle*, September 7, 1984, p. 22.

Petersdorf, Robert G., and Adams, Raymond D. *Harrison's Principles of Internal Medicine*. 10th ed. New York: McGraw-Hill, 1983.

Petersen, James R. "The Extended Male Orgasm." *Playboy*, May 1977, pp. 90–92, 232–36.

Petersen, James R., et al. "The *Playboy* Readers' Sex Survey, Part I." *Playboy*, January 1983, pp. 108, 241–50.

Petros, John W. *Sex Male, Gender Masculine*. Port Washington, N.Y.: Alfred, 1975.

"Pharaonic Circumcision." *San Francisco Chronicle*, May 7, 1977, p. 14. © World Health Organization.

Pickett, Mirium. "A Story of Three Promises— the Deflation of Ideals in Everyday Life." *San Francisco Chronicle*, November 22, 1980, p. 34. © The New York Times Company, 1980.

Pietropinto, Anthony, and Simenauer, Jacqueline. *Beyond the Male Myth*. New York: Times Books, 1977.

Pincus, Jane, and Wolhandler, Jill. "If You Think You Are Pregnant: Finding Out and Deciding What to Do." In *The New Our Bodies, Ourselves*, by The Boston Women's Health Collective, pp. 284–85. New York: Simon & Schuster, 1984.

Pincus, Jane; Swenson, Norma; and Poor, Bebe. "Pregnancy." In *The New Our Bodies, Ourselves*, by The Boston Women's Health Collective, p. 356. New York: Simon & Schuster, 1984.

Pines, Maya. "A Child's Mind Is Shaped before Age 2." *Life*, 1971, pp. 63, 67–68.

Planned Parenthood Press Release, "Age at Puberty." United Press, November 4, 1878.

Plato. *Symposium*. In *The Dialogues of Plato*, Vol. I. Jowett translation. New York: Random House, 1937.

Popenoe, Paul, and Wicks, Donna. "Marital Happiness in Two Generations." *Mental Hygiene* 21 (1937): 218–23.

Porter, Sylvia. *Sylvia Porter's New Money Book for the Eighties*. New York: Doubleday, 1979.

Poston, Dudley L., Jr., and Gotard, Erin. "Trends in Childlessness in the United States, 1910–1975." *Social Biology* 24 (Fall 1977): 212–44.

Proctor, E. B.; Wagner, N. N.; and Butler, Julius C. "The Differences of Male and Female Orgasm: An Experimental Study." In *Perspectives on Human Sexuality*, edited by Nathaniel N. Wagner, pp. 115–32. New York: Behavioral Publications, 1974.

Radetsky, Peter. "The Rise and (Maybe Not The) Fall of Toxic Shock Syndrome." *Science 85* 6 (January–February 1985): 73–78.

Rapoport, Robert N., and Rapoport, Rhona. "Dual-Career Families, Progress and Prospects." *Marriage and Family Review* 1 (September–October 1978): 1, 3–12.

Reeder, Sharon R., and Mastroianni, Luigi, Jr. *Maternity Nursing*. 15th ed. Philadelphia: J. B. Lippincott, 1983.

Reid, John. *The Best Little Boy in the World*. New York: Random House, 1973.

Reik, Theodore. *Of Love and Lust*. New York: Farrar, Straus, 1949.

Rein, Michael F. "Therapeutic Decisions in the Treatment of Sexually Transmitted Diseases: An Overview." In *Sexually Transmitted Diseases: Journal of the American Venereal Disease Association* 8 (January–March 1981): 93–99.

Reiss, Ira L. *Family Systems in America*. 3rd ed. New York: Holt, Rinehart & Winston, 1980.

Reiss, Ira L., and Miller, Brend. "A Theoretical Analysis of Heterosexual Permissiveness." Technical Report No. 2. Minneapolis: University of Minnesota, Family Study Center, 1974.

Reiss, Ira, L., et al. "A Multivariate Needed in the Determinants of Extramarital Sexual Permissiveness." *Journal of Marriage and the Family* 42 (May 1980): 395–411.

Renne, Karen S. "Correlates of Dissatisfaction in Marriage." *Journal of Marriage and the Family* 32 (1970): 54–67.

———. "Childlessness, Health, and Marital Satisfaction." *Social Biology* 23 (Fall 1976): 183–97.

Report on Why United States had High Rate of Teenage Pregnancy. New York: Alan Guttmacher Institute, March 12, 1985.

Rheinstein, Max. *Marriage Stability, Divorce, and the Law*. Chicago: University of Chicago Press, 1972.

Robertiello, Richard C. *Your Own True Love*. New York: Richard Marek, 1978.

Robinson, Ira E., and Jedlicka, Davor. "Change in Sexual Attitudes and Behavior of College Students from 1965 to 1980: A Research Note." *Journal of Marriage and the Family* (February 1982): 237–240.

Rollins, Boyd C., and Feldman, Harold. "Marital Satisfaction over the Life Cycle." *Journal of Marriage and the Family* 32 (1970): 20–28.

Rosen, David H. *Lesbianism: A Study of Female Homosexuality*. Springfield, Ill.: Charles C Thomas, 1974.

Rosen, Raymond, and Hall, Elizabeth. *Sexuality*. New York: Random House, 1984.

Rosenblatt, Paul C. "Behavior in Public Places: Comparisons of Couples Accompanied and Unaccompanied by Children." *Journal of Marriage and the Family* 36 (November 1974): 750–55.

Ross, J. B., and McLaughlin, M. M., eds. *Portable Medieval Reader*. New York: Viking, 1949.

Rossi, Alice S. "The Biosocial Side of Parenthood." *Human Nature* 1 (June 1978): 72–79.

"Routine Fetal Scans Nixed." *Science News* 125 (February 18, 1984): 102.

Royal College of General Practitioners' Oral Contraceptive Study. "Oral Contraceptives, Venous Thrombosis, and Varicose Veins." *Journal of the Royal College of General Practitioners* 28 (July 1978): 893–99.

Rubin, Lillian Breslow. *Worlds of Pain.* New York: Basic Books, 1976.

Rubin, Zick. *Liking and Loving: An Invitation to Social Psychology.* New York: Holt, Rinehart & Winston, 1973.

———. "Dating Project Research Report." Unpublished manuscript. Harvard University Department of Psychology and Social Relations, April 1975.

Russell, Bertrand. In "Jealousy" by Ewald Bohm. In *The Encyclopedia of Sexual Behavior*, edited by Albert Ellis and Albert Abarbanel, pp. 567–78. New York: J. Aronson, 1967.

Rutledge, Aaron. "Can an IUD Make Me Sterile?" *San Francisco Chronicle*, October 3, 1978, p. 22.

Ryan, Bruce. *Singhalese Village.* Miami, Fla.: University of Miami, 1958.

Sachs, Benjamin P.; Layde, Peter M.; Rubin, George L.; and Rochat, Roger W. "Reproductive Mortality in the United States." *Journal of the American Medical Association* 247 (May 28, 1982): 2789–92.

Sadker, Myra, and Sadker, David. "Sexism in the Schoolroom of the '80s." *Psychology Today* 19 (March 1985): 54–57.

Safilios-Rothschild, Constantina. *Love, Sex, and Sex Roles.* Englewood Cliffs, N.J.: Prentice-Hall, 1977.

Sagan, Carl. *The Dragons of Eden: Speculations on the Evolution of Human Intelligence.* New York: Random House, 1977.

———. *Cosmos.* New York: Random House, 1980.

Salomon Bros. "How Investments Have Played in 10-Year, 5-Year, and 1-Year Periods (June 1971–June 1981)." *San Francisco Chronicle*, July 19, 1981, p. D1.

Sameroff, A. J. "Early Influences on Development: Fact or Fancy?" *Merrill-Palmer Quarterly* 21 (1974): 267–94.

Sanger, Margaret. *An Autobiography.* New York: W. W. Norton, 1937.

Satir, Virginia. *Peoplemaking.* Palo Alto, Calif.: Science and Behavior, 1972.

Schaller, George B. *The Year of the Gorilla.* Chicago: University of Chicago Press, 1964.

Schaller, George B., and Selsam, Millicent. *Tiger: Its Life in the Wild.* New York: Harper, 1969.

Schellenberg, J. S., and Bee, L. S. "A Re-Examination of the Theory of Complementary Needs in Mate Selection." *Marriage and Family Living* 22 (1960): 227–32.

Schlegel, Alice, ed. *Sexual Stratification: A Cross-Cultural View.* New York: Columbia University Press, 1977.

Schmidt, Gunter, and Sigusch, Volkman. "Sex Differences in Responses to Psychosexual Stimulation by Films and Slides." *Journal of Sex Research* 6 (1970): 268–83.

———. "Women's Sexual Arousal." In *Contemporary Sexual Behavior: Critical Issues in the 1970s*, edited by Joseph Zubin and John Money. Baltimore, Md.: Johns Hopkins University Press, 1973.

Schrier, Allan M.; Harlow, Harry F.; and Stollnitz, Fred, eds. *Behavior of Nonhuman Primates.* New York: Academic, 1965.

Schupp, C. "An Analysis of Some Socio-Psychological Factors Which Operate in the Functioning Relationship of Married Couples to Exchange Mates for the Purpose of Sexual Experience." Ph.D. dissertation, U.S. International University, 1970.

Schwartz, M. A. "Career Strategies of the Never-Married." Paper presented at the annual meeting of the American Sociological Association, August 1976, New York.

Schoolnik, Gary K. "Gonorrhea Vaccine." Reported to the proceedings of the National Academy of Sciences, February 1985.

Sciolino, Elaine. "Sex and the Church." *San Francisco Chronicle, This World*, December 16, 1984, pp. 7–8.

Seaman, Barbara. *The Doctor's Case against the Pill.* Garden City, N.Y.: Doubleday, 1980.

Seaman, Barbara, and Seaman, Gideon. *Women and the Crisis in Sex Hormones.* New York: Bantam Books, 1978.

Sears, Robert R. *Survey of Objective Studies of Psychoanalytic Concepts.* New York: Social Science Research Council, 1943.

Secondi, J. J. *For People Who Make Love: A Doctor's Guide to Sexual Health.* New York: Taplinger, 1975.

Seeley, Richard. *Life,* December 1984, p. 49.

Segal, Julius, and Yahraes, Herbert. *A Child's Journey: Forces that Shape the Lives of Our Young.* New York: McGraw-Hill, 1978.

Seligman, Jean; Hager, Mary; and Seward, Debbie. "Tracing the Origin of AIDS." *Newsweek,* May 7, 1984, pp. 101–2.

Shapiro, Howard I. *The Birth Control Book.* New York: St. Martin's Press, 1977.

Shapiro, Max. *The Penniless Billionaires.* New York: Times Books, 1980.

Shorter, Edward. *The Making of the Modern Family.* New York: Basic Books, 1975.

Silverman, I. "Physical Attractiveness and Courtship." *Sexual Behavior* (September 1971): 22–25.

Simenauer, Jacqueline, and Carroll, David. *Singles: The New Americans.* New York: New American Library, 1982.

Singh, B., et al. "In Vitro Effect of Vaginal Contraceptives and Selected Preparations." *Candida Albacans and Trichomonas Vaginalis Contraception* 5 (1972): 401–11.

Skolnick, Arlene. *The Intimate Environment: Exploring Marriage and the Family.* 2nd and 3rd eds. Boston: Little, Brown, 1978, 1983.

Skolnick, Arlene, and Skolnick, Jerome H., eds. *Family in Transition.* 4th ed. Boston: Little, Brown, 1983.

Slone, Dennis, et al. "Risk of Myocardial Infarction in Relation to Current and Discontinued Use of Oral Contraceptives." *New England Journal of Medicine* 305 (August 20, 1981): 420–24.

Smith, Daniel Scott. "Family Limitation, Sexual Control, and Domestic Feminism in Victorian America." In *Clio's Consciousness Raised,* edited by Mary Hartmann and Lois W. Banner, pp. 119–36. New York: Harper & Row, 1974.

Smith, James P. "Women's Salaries Will Gain on Men's." Rand Corporation. Address to Population Association of America. April 1, 1985, Boston.

Smith, James P., and Ward, Michael P. *Report on Wage Gap between Men and Women.* Santa Monica, Calif.: Rand Corporation, October 31, 1984.

Smith, J. R., and Smith, L. G. "Comarital Sex and the Sexual Freedom Movement." *Journal of Sexual Research* 6 (1970): 131–42.

"Smoking and Sperm." *Science News* 119 (April 18, 1981): 247.

Soiffer, Bill. "Doctors Examine Role of Emotion in Sickness, Health." *San Francisco Chronicle,* February 15, 1982, p. 13.

Sorokin, P. "Altruistic Love." In *The Encyclopedia of Sexual Behavior,* edited by Albert Ellis and Albert Abarbanel. New York: J. Aronson, 1973.

Spanier, Graham B. "Married and Unmarried Cohabitation in the United States: 1980." *Journal of Marriage and the Family* 45 (May 1983): 277–88.

Spanier, Graham B., and Glick, Paul C. "Marital Stability in the United States: Some Correlates and Recent Changes." *Family Relations* 30 (July 1981): 329–38.

Spanier, Graham B.; Lewis, Robert A.; and Cole, Charles L. "Marital Adjustment over the Family Life Cycle: The Issue of Curvilinearity." *Journal of Marriage and the Family* 37 (May 1975): 263–77.

Sparling, P. Frederick. "Syphilis." In *Textbook of Medicine.* 15th ed., edited by Paul B. Beeson, Walsh McDermott, and James B. Wyngaarden, pp. 505–18. Philadelphia: W. B. Saunders, 1979.

Spence, Janet T., and Helmreich, Robert L. *The Psychological Dimensions of Masculinity and Femininity: Their Correlates and Antecedents.* Austin: University of Texas Press, 1978.

Spezzano, Charles, and Waterman, Jill. "The First Day of Life." *Psychology Today* 11 (December 1977): 110–16.

Spicer, J., and Hampe, G. "Kinship Interaction after Divorce." *Journal of Marriage and the Family* (February 1975): 113–19.

Stafford, R.; Backman, E.; and diBona, P. "The Division of Labor among Cohabiting and Married Couples." *Journal of Marriage and the Family* 39 (1977): 43–57.

Starr, Bernard D., and Weiner, Marcella Bakur. *Sex and Sexuality in the Mature Years.* New York: Stein & Day, 1981.

Starr, J., and Carns, D. "Singles in the City." *Society* 9 (1972): 43–48.

Stein, Marsha L. *Friends, Lovers, Slaves.* New York: G. P. Putnam's, 1974.

Stein, Peter J. "Singlehood: An Alternative to Marriage." *The Family Coordinator* 34 (1975): 489–503.

———. *Single.* Englewood Cliffs, N.J.: Prentice-Hall, 1976.

Stein, Peter J., ed. *Single Life: Unmarried Adults in Social Context.* New York: St. Martin's Press, 1981.

Steinman, Susan. "The Experience of Children in a Joint-Custody Arrangement: A Report of a Study." *American Journal of Orthopsychiatry* 51 (July 1981): 403–14.

Steinmetz, Susanne K. "Violence between Family Members." *Marriage and Family Review* 1 (May 1978): 1–16.

Stendahl. [Marie Henri Beyle.] *Love.* Translated by Gilbert and Suzanne Sale. New York: Penguin Classics, 1975.

Stephens, William N. *The Family in Cross-Cultural Perspective.* Lanham, Md.: University Press of America, 1982.

Stern, Michael P., et al. "Cardiovascular Risk in Use of Estrogens or Estrogen-Progestagen Combinations." *Journal of the American Medical Association* 186 (1976): 811–15.

Stern, P. "Stepfather Families: Integration around Child Discipline." *Issues in Mental Health Nursing* 1 (1978): 50–56.

Sternberg, Robert J. "The Measure of Love." *Science Digest* 93 (April 1985): 60, 78–79.

Stinnett, N.; Carter, L.; and Montgomery, J. "Older Persons' Perception of Their Marriages." *Journal of Marriage and the Family* 34 (1972): 665–70.

"Stolen Children." *Los Angeles Times*, August 8, 1980, p. 7.

Stratton, Joanna L. *Pioneer Women: Voices from the Kansas Frontier.* New York: Simon & Schuster, 1982.

Straus, Stephen E., et al. "Suppression of Frequently Recurring Genital Herpes: A Placebo-Controlled Double Blind Trial of Oral Acyclovir." *The New England Journal of Medicine* 310 (June 14, 1984): 1545–56.

Strong, Bryan; DeVault, Christine; Suid, Murray; and Reynolds, Rebecca. *The Marriage and Family Experience.* 2nd ed. New York: West, 1983.

Stroufe, L. Alan, and Waters, Everett. "Attachment as an Organizational Construct." *Child Development* 48 (1977): 1184–99.

Styron, William. *The Confessions of Nat Turner.* New York: Random House, 1967.

———. *Sophie's Choice.* New York: Random House, 1979.

Sulik, Kathleen K.; Johnston, Malcolm C.; and Webb, M. A. "Fetal Alcohol Syndrome: Ambriogenesis in a Mouse Model." *Science* 214 (November 20, 1981): 936–38.

Sullivan, Harry Stack. *The Interpersonal Theory of Psychiatry.* New York: W. W. Norton, 1953.

Sunshine, Phil, director of nurseries at Stanford University Hospital. Interview, *San Francisco Examiner, Scene Arts*, March 4, 1984, pp. 1–2.

"Survey of Herpes Visits to U.S. Physicians in Private Practice." *National Disease and Therapeutic Index Review,* January 1985, p. 72.

Symons, D. *The Evolution of Human Sexuality.* New York: Oxford University Press, 1979.

Tannahil, Reay. *Sex in History.* New York: Stein & Day, 1980.

Tatum, Howard J., and Connell-Tatum, Elizabeth B. "Barrier Contraception: A Comprehensive Review." *Fertility and Sterility* 36 (July 1981): 1–2.

Tavris, Carol, and Sadd, Susan. *The Redbook Report on Female Sexuality.* New York: Redbook, 1977.

Tennov, Dorothy. *Love and Limerence.* New York: Stein & Day, 1979.

Terman, Lewis M. *Psychological Factors in Marriage Happiness.* New York: McGraw-Hill, 1938.

Thomas, Alexander, and Chess, Stella. *Temperament and Development.* New York: Brunner/Mazel, 1977.

Thomas, Clayton L. *Taber's Cyclopedic Medical Dictionary.* 14th ed. Philadelphia: Davis, 1981.

Thompson, Clara. *Psychoanalysis: Evolution and Development.* New York: Hermitage, 1951.

Tietze, Christopher. *Induced Abortion: A World Review.* New York: The Population Council, 1981.

———. "New Estimates of Mortality Associated with Fertility Control." *Family Planning Perspectives* 9 (1977): 74–76.

Tietze, Christopher, and Lewit, Sarah. "Legal Abortion." *Scientific American* 236 (January 1977): 21–27.

Tietze, Christopher; Bongaarts, John; and Schearer, Bruce. "Mortality Associated with the Control of Fertility." *Family Planning Perspectives* 8 (1976): 6–14.

Tilling, Thomas. "Your $250,000 Baby." *Parent's Magazine,* November 1980, 83–87.

Tissot, S. A. *Onanism: A Treatise on the Disease Produced by Onanism.* Lausanne: Marc Chapius et Cie, 1764.

Tolstoy, Leo. *War and Peace.* Translated by Constance Garnett. New York: Crowell, 1976.

Townsend, Bickley. "Profile on Working Women." *American Demographics Magazine* 7 (January 1985): 4–7.

Trexler, R. C. "Infanticide in Florence, New Sources and First Results." *History of Childhood Quarterly* 1 (1973): 98–116.

Troll, Lillian E.; Miller, Sheila J.; and Atchley, Robert C. *Families in Later Life.* Belmont, Calif.: Wadsworth, 1979.

Tuchman, Barbara W. *A Distant Mirror.* New York: Alfred A. Knopf, 1978.

Turner, Gillian, and Collins, Edith. "Infant Deaths and Aspirin Usage." *The Lancet* (August 23, 1975).

Twitchell, J. "Sexual Liberty and Personality: A Pilot Study." In *Beyond Monogamy,* edited by James R. Smith and Lynne G. Smith. Baltimore, Md.: Johns Hopkins University Press, 1974.

Udry, Richard J. "Sex and Family Life." *Annals of the American Academy of Political and Social Science* 376 (March 1968): 25–35.

———. *The Social Context of Marriage.* 3rd ed. Philadelphia: J. B. Lippincott, 1974.

UNESCO, *Statement on the Nature of Race and Race Differences.* Paris: UNESCO House, Place de Fontenoy 7e, 1952.

UNICEF, United States Committee. 1978–1979, Nutrition. *UNICEF's World,* p. 1. New York: U. S. Committee for UNICEF, 1981.

"Update on Condoms—Products, Protection, Promotion." *Population Reports,* Series H, No. 6 (September–October 1982). (Available from Population Information Programs, Johns Hopkins University, 624 N. Broadway, Baltimore, Md. 21205.)

Updike, John. *Rabbit, Run.* New York: Alfred A. Knopf, 1960.

———. *Too Far to Go.* New York: Ballantine, 1979.

———. *Rabbit Is Rich.* New York: Alfred A. Knopf, 1981.

U.S. Bureau of the Census. "Birth Rates, by Race, 1860–1975." *Current Population Reports,* Series P-23, No. 70. Washington, D.C.: Government Printing Office, 1978.

———. Census of Population: 1980. *Marital Status,* Final Report PC (Z)-4C. Washington, D.C.: Government Printing Office, December 1982.

———. "Changes in Family Size." *Current Population Reports,* Series P-20, Nos. 326, 340, and 352. Washington, D.C.: Government Printing Office, December 1980.

———. "Childless Women and Children Ever Born, by Age of Women: 1950 to 1983." *Current Population Reports,* Series P-20, No. 387, and earlier reports. Washington, D.C.: Government Printing Office, 1984.

———. "Children Ever Born to Single Women, by Age and Race of Women: 1970 to 1982." *Current Population Reports,* Series P-20, No. 375. Washington, D.C.: Government Printing Office, 1984.

———. "Children under 18 Years Old, by Presence of Parents and Whether Living with Mother Only, by Marital Status of Mother: 1970 to 1982." *Current Population Reports,* Series P-20, No. 380. In *Statistical Abstract of the United States,* 104th ed., p. 53.

Washington, D.C.: Government Printing
Office, 1984.

———. "Child Support and Alimony—Selected
Characteristics of Women: 1981." *Current
Population Reports*, Series P-23, No. 124.
Washington, D.C.: Government Printing
Office, 1985.

———. "College Enrollment by Major Field of
Study and Sex: 1966 and 1982." *Current
Population Reports*, Series P-20, No. 183. In
Statistical Abstract of the United States, 104th
ed., p. 162. Washington, D.C.: Government
Printing Office, 1984.

———. "College Enrollment of Persons 18–24
Years Old, and Percent of High School
Graduates Enrolled in College by Sex and
Race: 1960–1982." *Current Population Re-
ports*, Series P-20, No. 373. Washington,
D.C.: Government Printing Office, 1984.

———. *Current Population Survey.* Department
of Commerce. Washington, D.C.: Government Printing Office, March 1957.

———. *Historical Statistics of the United States,
Colonial Times to 1970*, Parts I and II.
Bicentennial Edition. Department of Com-
merce. Washington, D.C.: Government
Printing Office, 1975.

———. *House Select Committee Report on Children, Youth and Families.* Washington, D.C.:
Government Printing Office, 1984.

———. "Households, Families, Subfamilies,
Married Couples, and Unrelated In-
dividuals: 1950–1982." *Current Population
Reports*, Series P-20, No. 381, and earlier
issues. Washington, D.C.: Government
Printing Office, 1984.

———. "Income and Marital Stability." *Current
Population Reports*, Series P-60, Nos. 118
and 123. Washington, D.C.: Government
Printing Office, 1980, and provisional data,
May 11, 1981.

———. "Interracial Married Couples: 1970 to
1983." *Current Population Reports*, Series
P-23, No. 77, and Series P-20, No. 388. In
Statistical Abstract of the United States, 105th
ed., p. 38. Washington, D.C.: Government
Printing Office, 1985.

———. "Labor Force Participation of Married
Women with Husband Present." *Current

Population Reports*, Series P-20, No. 336.
Washington, D.C.: Government Printing
Office, 1979.

———. "Marital Status and Living Arrangements." *Current Population Reports*,
Series P-20, No. 380, and earlier reports. In
Statistical Abstract of the United States, 104th
ed., pp. 44–46. Washington, D.C.: Government Printing Office, 1984.

———. "Marital Status and Living Arrange-
ments 1977–1980" and "Households and
Families by Type, March 1978." *Current
Population Reports*, Series P-20, No. 349.
Washington, D.C.: Government Printing
Office, 1980.

———. "Money Income of Families—Income
and Percent of Aggregate Income at
Selected Positions Received by Each Fifth
and Top 5 Percent of Families: 1983." *Current Population Reports*, Series P-60, No.
145. In *Statistical Abstract of the United
States*, 105th ed., p. 448. Washington, D.C.:
Government Printing Office, 1985.

———. "Money Income of Households—Median Household Income in Current and Constant (1983) Dollars, By Race and Spanish
Origin of Householder: 1967 to 1983." *Current Population Reports*, Series P-60, No.
145. In *Statistical Abstract of the United
States*, 105th ed., p. 442. Washington, D.C.:
Government Printing Office, 1985.

———. "Number of Workers with Earnings
and Median Earnings, by Occupation of
Longest Job Held and Sex, 1981." *Current
Population Reports*, Series P-60, Nos. 137,
138, and 140. Washington, D.C.: Government Printing Office, 1984.

———. "Orphans, by Type: 1960–1982." Social
Security Administration Report. In *Statistical Abstract of the United States*, 104th ed.,
p. 396. Washington, D.C.: Government
Printing Office, 1984.

———. "Percentage of Women with a Premari-
tally Conceived First Birth Who Married
Before the Birth by Age and Race: 1982."
Current Population Reports, Series P-20,
No. 387. In *Statistical Abstract of the United
States*, 105th ed., p. 387. Washington, D.C.:
Government Printing Office, 1985.

———. "Percent Married and Divorced of the Population, 18 Years and Over: 1960 to 1983." *Current Population Reports*, Series P-20, No. 389. In *Statistical Abstract of the United States*, 105th ed., p. 39. Washington, D.C.: Government Printing Office, 1985.

———. "Persons in Families by Age, Sex, and Type of Family: 1970–1982." *Current Population Reports*, Series P-20, No. 381, and earlier issues. Washington, D.C.: Government Printing Office, 1984.

———. "Persons 65 Years Old and Over—Characteristics, by Sex: 1960 to 1983." *Current Population Reports*, Series P-20, No. 389; Series P-23, Nos. 57, 59, 917, and 949; and Series P-60, Nos. 142 and 144. In *Statistical Abstract of the United States*, 105th ed., p. 30. Washington, D.C.: Government Printing Office, 1985.

———. "Population Profile of the United States: 1978 and 1981." *Current Population Reports*, Series P-20, No. 336 (1979), and No. 374 (1982). Washington, D.C.: Government Printing Office, 1979 and 1982.

———. "Ratio of Males to Females, by Age Group, 1910 to 1983." *Current Population Reports*, Series P-25, No. 949. In *Statistical Abstract of the United States*, 105th ed., p. 30. Washington, D.C.: Government Printing Office, 1985.

———. "Report on Household and Family Characteristics." *Current Population Reports*, Series P-20, No. 345. Washington, D.C.: Government Printing Office, December 1980, and provisional data, October 20, 1981.

———. "Report on Household and Family Characteristics, 1970 to 1984." *Current Population Reports*, Series P-20, No. 388, and forthcoming reports. Washington, D.C.: Government Printing Office, 1985.

———. *Report on Population Projections*. Washington, D.C.: Government Printing Office, June 20, 1984.

———. "Retirement Benefits Based on Wages Earned." *Current Population Reports*, Series P-60, No. 133 (1983), and Nos. 519 and 929 (1984). Washington, D.C.: Government Printing Office, 1983 and 1984.

———. "Single (Never-Married) Persons 18 Years Old and Over as Percent of Total Population, by Age and Sex: 1960 to 1983." *Current Population Reports*, Series P-20, No. 389. In *Statistical Abstract of the United States*, 105th ed., p. 39. Washington, D.C.: Government Printing Office, 1985.

———. *Social Indicators III*, Table 1/14, p. 50. Department of Commerce. Washington, D.C.: Government Printing Office, 1980.

———. Special Demographic Analyses, CDS-80-8, *American Women: Three Decades of Change*. Washington, D.C.: Government Printing Office, August 1983.

———. *Statistical Abstract of the United States*, 92nd, 104th, and 105th eds. Washington, D.C.: Government Printing Office, 1971, 1984, and 1985.

———. "Unmarried Couples, by Selected Characteristics, 1970 to 1984." *Current Population Reports*, Series P-20, No. 391. In *Statistical Abstract of the United States*, 105th ed., p. 40. Washington, D.C.: Government Printing Office, 1985.

———. *U.S. Census of Population: 1930*, Vol. II; *1940*, Vol. II, part 1, and Vol. IV, part 1; *1950*, Vol. II, part 1; *1960*, Vol. I, part 1; *1970*, Vol. I, part B; and *Current Population Reports*, Series P-25, No. 929. Washington, D.C.: Government Printing Office, 1984.

———. "World Population Characteristics, 1975 to 1984, and Projections to 2000." *World Population 1984*, forthcoming and unpublished data. In *Statistical Abstract of the United States*, 105th ed., p. 838. Washington, D.C.: Government Printing Office, 1985.

———. "Young Adults and Divorce." *Current Population Reports*. Washington, D.C.: Government Printing Office, June 1980.

U.S. Bureau of Labor Statistics. "Annual Percent Change in Selected Price Indexes: 1960 to 1984." *Monthly Labor Review*. Washington, D.C.: Government Printing Office, 1985.

———. "Consumer Price Indexes for Selected Items and Groups: 1970 to 1984." *Consumer Price Indexes, Detailed Report*. Washington, D.C.: Government Printing Office, June 1985.

———. "Employed Persons by Selected Characteristics: 1970 to 1983." *Employment and Earnings,* monthly. In *Statistical Abstract of the United States,* 105th ed., p. 394. Washington, D.C.: Government Printing Office, 1985.

———. "Employed Persons, by Sex, Race, and Occupation: 1972 to 1982." *Employment and Earnings,* monthly. In *Statistical Abstract of the United States,* 104th ed., pp. 419–20. Washington, D.C.: Government Printing Office, 1984.

———. "Employment Status of the Noninstitutional Population 16 Years and Over by Sex: 1950 to 1984." *Employment and Earnings,* monthly. In *Statistical Abstract of the United States,* 105th ed., p. 390. Washington, D.C.: Government Printing Office, 1985.

———. "Labor Force Participation Rates of Married Women." *Current Population Reports,* Series P-20, No. 336. Washington, D.C.: Government Printing Office, 1979.

———. "Labor Force Participation Rates of Married Women, Husband Present, by Presence and Age of Own Children, 1950 to 1976." *Special Labor Force Reports.* Washington, D.C.: Government Printing Office, 1977.

———. Monthly Data in U.S. Bureau of Economic Analysis. *Survey of Current Business,* June 1984. In *Statistical Abstract of the United States,* 105th ed., p. 466. Washington, D.C.: Government Printing Office, 1985.

———. "Occupation of Employed Workers, by Sex and Race: 1960 to 1982." *Employment and Earnings,* monthly. In *Statistical Abstract of the United States,* 104th ed., p. 417. Washington, D.C.: Government Printing Office, 1984.

———. "Purchasing Power of the Dollar, 1940 to 1983." U.S. Bureau of Economic Analysis, *Survey of Current Business.* In *Statistical Abstract of the United States,* 104th ed., p. 484. Washington, D.C.: Government Printing Office, 1984.

———. *Special Labor Force Bulletin* 191, 83–160. Washington, D.C.: Government Printing Office, 1984.

———. *Special Labor Force Bulletin* 2096, *Employment and Earnings,* monthly. In *Statistical Abstract of the United States,* 104th ed., pp. 413, 417, 419–20. Washington, D.C.: Government Printing Office, 1984.

———. *Special Labor Force Reports,* Nos. 13, 130, and 134 (1984), and *Monthly Labor Review* (January 1985). Washington, D.C.: Government Printing Office, 1984 and 1985.

———. "Women in the Work Force, 1983." *National Commission on Working Women Report.* Washington, D.C.: Government Printing Office, October 1984.

U.S. Commission on Civil Rights. *Child Care and Equal Opportunity for Women.* Clearinghouse Publication No. 67. Washington, D.C.: Government Printing Office, June 1981.

U.S. Congressional Research Service. "Report on American Children Living in Poverty." Washington, D.C.: Government Printing Office, May 1985.

U.S. Department of Agriculture. Economic Research Service, *Farm Population Estimates,* annual. In *Statistical Abstract of the United States,* 104th ed., p. 649. Washington, D.C.: Government Printing Office, 1984.

U.S. Department of Health, Education, and Welfare. *Public Service Annual.* Washington, D.C.: Government Printing Office, December 1970.

U.S. Department of Health and Human Services. *Adolescent Abuse and Neglect: Intervention Strategies.* DHHS Publication No. (OHDS) 80–30266. Washington, D.C.: Government Printing Office, July 1980.

———. *Child Abuse: Incest, Assault, and Sexual Exploitation.* DHHS Publication No. (OHDS) 81–30166. Washington, D.C.: Government Printing Office, April 1981.

U.S. Department of Housing and Urban Development. *Construction Reports,* Series C-25, *Characteristics of New Housing,* annual. In *Statistical Abstract of the United States,* 104th ed., p. 745. Washington, D.C.: Government Printing Office, 1984.

U.S. General Services Administration. *Cost of Owning and Operating Automobiles and Vans.* Pueblo, Colo.: Consumer Information Center, Department 422M, 1984.

U.S. Internal Revenue Service, *Statistics of Income, 1962 and 1972*; Supplemental Report, *Personal Wealth and Statistics of Income.* Washington, D.C.: Government Printing Office, Summer 1983.

U.S. National Center for Educational Statistics. *Digest of Education Statistics*, annual, and *Financial Statistics of Institutions of Higher Education*, annual. Washington, D.C.: Government Printing Office, 1984.

U.S. National Center for Health Statistics. "Annulments." *Monthly Vital Statistics Report.* Washington, D.C.: Government Printing Office, January 1984.

——. "Birth and Birth Rates: 1950 to 1981." *Vital Statistics of the United States*, annual. In *Statistical Abstract of the United States*, 105th ed., p. 58. Washington, D.C.: Government Printing Office, 1985.

——. "Births to Unmarried Women, by Race and Age of Mother: 1950–1981." *Vital Statistics of the United States*, annual. In *Statistical Abstract of the United States*, 105th ed., p. 64. Washington, D.C.: Government Printing Office, 1985.

——. "Contraceptive Use by American Women, 15–44 Years Old, by Age, Race, and Method of Contraception, 1982." Advance data from Vital and Health Statistics, No. 9, and provisional data from the National Survey of Family Growth. Washington, D.C.: Government Printing Office, December 1984.

——. "Deaths to Married Persons." *Vital Statistics of the United States*, 1956–1969, Vol. III, pp. 3–14. Washington, D.C.: Government Printing Office, 1970.

——. "Divorces and Annulments—Number and Rate, by State: 1965 to 1982." *Vital Statistics of the United States*, annual. Washington, D.C.: Government Printing Office, 1985.

——. "Divorces and Children Involved in the United States, 1958–1980." *Vital Statistics of the United States*, annual. Washington, D.C.: Government Printing Office, 1984.

——. "Final Mortality Statistics, United States, 1976–1978." *Monthly Vital Statistics Report.* Washington, D.C.: Government Printing Office, 1980.

——. "How Families Have Changed, 1970–1980." *Monthly Vital Statistics Report.* Washington, D.C.: Government Printing Office, December 1982.

——. "Legal Separation." *Monthly Vital Statistics Report.* Washington, D.C.: Government Printing Office, December 1980.

——. "Live Births, By Attendant and Place of Delivery, and Median and Low-Weight Births, by Race: 1950 to 1981." *Vital Statistics of the United States*, annual. In *Statistical Abstract of the United States*, 105th ed., p. 60. Washington, D.C.: Government Printing Office, 1985.

——. "Marriages and Divorces: 1950 to 1980." *Monthly Vital Statistics Report.* In *Statistical Abstract of the United States*, 104th ed., p. 84. Washington, D.C.: Government Printing Office, 1984.

——. "Marriages and Divorces: 1960 to 1981." *Vital Statistics of the United States*, annual; *Monthly Vital Statistics Report.* In *Statistical Abstract of the United States*, 105th ed., p. 80. Washington, D.C.: Government Printing Office, 1985.

——. "Methods of Birth Control." *National Survey of Family Growth.* Washington, D.C.: Government Printing Office, December 1984.

——. *Monthly Vital Statistics Report*, Vol. 15, No. 3 (May 31, 1966). In *Marriage and Divorce: A Social and Economic Study*, rev. ed., edited by Hugh Carter and Paul C. Glick. Cambridge, Mass.: Harvard University Press, 1976, p. 47.

——. *Special Report on Common Infectious Diseases—Including STDs*, Vol. 37, No. 9. Washington, D.C.: Government Printing Office, 1984.

——. "Total Fertility Rate and Intrinsic Rate of Natural Increase: 1940 to 1984." *Vital Statistics of the United States*, annual and unpublished data. Washington, D.C.: Government Printing Office, 1985.

——. "Unwanted Birth of All Mothers, 15–44 Years Old: 1973 and 1982." *Vital and Health Statistics*, No. 9. In *Statistical Abstract of the United States*, 105th ed., p. 66. Washington, D.C.: Government Printing Office, 1985.

——. U.S. Life Tables and Actuarial Tables,

1949–1951, 1959–1961, 1974–1984. *Monthly Vital Statistics Report*, Washington, D.C.: Government Printing Office, March 6, 1981; July 8, 1984; and February 8, 1985.

———. *Vital and Health Statistics*, Series 10, and *Monthly Vital Statistics Reports*. Washington, D.C.: Government Printing Office, December 1984 and January 1985.

———. *Vital Statistics of the United States*, annual. Department of Health, Education, and Welfare Pub. No. PHS 81-1223. Washington, D.C.: Government Printing Office, 1980, 1983, and 1984.

U.S. National Commission for UNESCO. *Report on Women in America*. Department of State Publication 8923. Washington, D.C.: Government Printing Office, November 1977.

U.S. National Institutes of Health. Consensus Development Conference. *Antenatal Diagnosis*. NIH Publication No. 79-1973. Bethesda, Md., 1979.

U.S. Office of Management and Budget. "Personal Taxes." *The Budget of the United States Government*, annual. Washington, D.C.: Government Printing Office, 1984.

U.S. Public Health Service. "Abortion." *Morbidity and Mortality Weekly Report*. Atlanta, Ga.: Centers for Disease Control, December 1983.

———. "Abortion-Related Mortality, United States, 1976–78." *Morbidity and Mortality Weekly Report,* Atlanta, Ga.: Centers for Disease Control, December 1980.

———. Acquired Immune Deficiency Syndrome (AIDS): Precautions for Clinical and Laboratory Staffs." *Morbidity and Mortality Weekly Report*, Vol. 31, No. 54. Atlanta, Ga.: Centers for Disease Control, 1982.

———. "AIDS Update." *Morbidity and Mortality Weekly Report*. Atlanta, Ga.: Centers for Disease Control, AIDS Task Force, December 10, 1983; November 30, 1984; January 28, 1985; February 8, 1985; April 10, 1985; and May 10, 1985.

———. "Congenital Malformations." *Morbidity and Mortality Weekly Report*, Vol. 31. Atlanta, Ga.: Centers for Disease Control, 1984.

———. *Criteria and Techniques for the Diagnosis of Gonorrhea*, Publication No. 96–552.

Atlanta, Ga.: Centers for Disease Control, 1979.

———. "Fetal Alcohol Syndrome." *Morbidity and Mortality Weekly Report*, Vol. 33, No. 1. Atlanta, Ga.: Centers for Disease Control, January 13, 1984.

———. "Fetal Tobacco Syndrome." *Morbidity and Mortality Weekly Report*. Atlanta, Ga.: Centers for Disease Control, May 23, 1985.

———. "Genital Herpes Infection—United States, 1966–1979." *Morbidity and Mortality Weekly Report*. Atlanta, Ga.: Centers for Disease Control, March 1982.

———. *Morbidity and Mortality Weekly Report*, annual supplement. Atlanta, Ga.: Centers for Disease Control, December 1984.

———. *STD Fact Sheet*, editions 35 and 40. HHS Publication No. (CDC) 8-8195. Atlanta, Ga.: Centers for Disease Control, March 1980 and March 1985.

———. "STDs." *Morbidity and Mortality Weekly Report*, Vol. 33, No. 24. Atlanta, Ga.: Centers for Disease Control, December 1984.

———. "Surgical Sterilization of Women." *Morbidity and Mortality Weekly Report*. Atlanta, Ga.: Centers for Disease Control, December 1983.

———. "Update on Acquired Immune Deficiency Syndrome (AIDS)—United States." *Morbidity and Mortality Weekly Report*, Vol. 31, No. 54. Atlanta, Ga.: Centers for Disease Control, December 1982.

U.S. Social Security Administration, "Aid to Families with Dependent Children (AFDC)—Percent Distribution of Recipient Families and Children, by Characteristics: 1975 to 1982." In *Statistical Abstract of the United States*, 105th ed., p. 382.

———. "Orphans, by Type: 1960 to 1982." In *Statistical Abstract of the United States*, 104th ed., p. 396. Washington, D.C.: Government Printing Office, 1984.

U.S. Surgeon General's Report on Health Risks of Smoking. Washington, D.C.: Government Printing Office, January 1985.

Van Buren, Abigail. "Dear Abby." *San Francisco Chronicle*, October 19, 1978, p. 53.

Van Deusen, Edmond L. *Contract Cohabitation: An Alternative to Marriage*. New York: Avon, 1975.

Van Keep, P. A., and Schmidt-Elmendorff, H. "Involuntary Childlessness." *Journal of Biosocial Science* 7 (1975): 37–48.

Varni, Charles. "An Exploratory Study of Spouse Swapping." *Pacific Sociological Review* 15 (1972): 507–22.

Veevers, J. E. "Voluntary Childless Wives: An Exploratory Study." *Sociology and Social Research* 57 (April 1973): 356–66.

———. "The Life-Style of Voluntary Childless Couples." In *The Canadian Family in Comparative Perspectives*, edited by Lyle Larson, pp. 395–411. Toronto: Prentice-Hall, 1975.

———. "Voluntary Childlessness: A Review of Issues and Evidence." *Marriage and Family Review* 2 (1979): 1, 3–20.

Vessey, Martin P., et al. "A Long-Term Follow-up Study of Women Using Different Methods of Contraception—an Interim Report." *Journal of Biosocial Science* 8 (October 1976): 373–427.

Viets, Jack. "A Californian's Mexican Divorce—in Doubt 16 Years Later." *San Francisco Chronicle*, November 16, 1984, p. 2.

Viorst, Judith. "Confessions of a Jealous Wife." *Redbook*, March 1970, pp. 92, 166–68.

Wallechinsky, David; Wallace, Amy; and Wallace, Irving. *The People's Almanac Presents the Book of Predictions*. New York: William Morrow, 1981.

Wallerstein, Judith S., and Kelly, Joan Berlin. *Surviving the Breakup: How Children and Parents Cope with Divorce*. New York: Basic Books, 1980.

Walster, Elaine, and Walster, G. William. *A New Look at Love*. Reading, Mass.: Addison-Wesley, 1978.

Walster, Elaine; Walster, G. William; Piliavin, J.; and Schmidt, L. "Playing Hard to Get: Understanding an Elusive Phenomenon." *Journal of Personality and Social Psychology* 26 (1973): 113–21.

Washington, A. Eugene; Grove, Sandra; Schachter, Julius; and Sweet, Richard. "Oral Contraception, Chlamydia Trachomatis Infection, in Pelvic Inflammatory Disease." *Journal of the American Medical Association* 253 (April 19, 1985): 2246–50.

Watson, John B. *Psychological Care of Infant and Child*. New York: W. W. Norton, 1928.

Weeks, John R. *Population*. Belmont, Calif.: Wadsworth, 1978.

Weisenberger Investment Companies. *Mutual Funds and Other Types*. 5th ed. New York: Weisenberger Services, 1985.

Weismer, Paul. *Venereal Diseases Division, Special Report*. Atlanta, Ga.: Centers for Disease Control, November 11, 1978.

Weisner, Thomas, and Gallimore, Ronald. "My Brother's Keeper: Child and Sibling Care Taking." *Current Anthropology* 18 (1977): 169–90.

Weiss, Robert S. *Marital Separation*. New York: Basic Books, 1975.

———. *Unmarried Adults in Social Context*, edited by Peter J. Stein, pp. 152–64. New York: St. Martin's Press, 1981.

Weitzman, Lenore J. *The Divorce Revolution*. New York: Free Press, 1985.

Wernick, Robert. *The Family*. New York: Time-Life Books, 1974.

Wertheimer, Wendy. "American Social Health Report on PID and Chlamydia." *Newsweek*, February 4, 1985, p. 72.

Westoff, Charles F. "Coital Frequency and Contraception." *Family Planning Perspectives* 6 (1976a): 136–41.

———. "Trends in Contraceptive Practice: 1965–1973." *Family Planning Perspectives* 8 (1976b): 54.

———. "Marriage and Fertility in the Developed Countries." *Scientific American* 229 (December 1978): 51–57.

Westoff, Charles F., and Parke, Robert Jr., eds. *Demographic and Social Aspects of Population Growth*. Vol. I, p. 39 and 593. U.S. Commission on Population Growth and the American Future. Washington, D.C.: Government Printing Office, 1972.

White, Burton. *The First Three Years of Life*. Englewood Cliffs, N.J.: Prentice-Hall, 1975.

———. "Blueprint for Rearing Happy Children." Paper presented at the annual meeting of the American Association for the Advancement of Science, February 19, 1976, Boston.

White House Conference on Families. *Families and Economic Well-Being*. Washington, D.C.: Government Printing Office, 1980.

Wilson, Barbara Foley. "Marriage Melting

Pot." *American Demographics Magazine* 6 (July 1984): 4–7.

Wilson, Kenneth L.; Zurcher, Louise A.; McAdams, Dianna Claire; and Curtis, Russell L. "Stepfathers and Stepchildren: An Explanatory Analysis from Two National Surveys." *Journal of Marriage and the Family* 37 (August 1975): 526–36.

Wilson, Margaret Gibbons. *The American Woman in Transition: The Urban Influence, 1870–1920.* Westport, Conn.: Greenwood, 1979.

Wilson, Marilyn L., and Green, Roger L. "Personality Characteristics of Female Homosexuals." *Psychological Reports* 28 (1971): 407–12.

Winch, Robert F. *Mate Selection: A Study of Complementary Needs.* New York: Harper & Row, 1958.

Winokur, Scott. "Fearing AIDS." *San Francisco Examiner*, August 26, 1984, p. A2.

Wirth, Eileen. "Loans Made Easier: Singles Becoming Homeowners, Too." *Omaha World Herald*, December 10, 1979, p. 1-B.

Wolhandler, Jill, and Weber, Ruth. "Abortion." In *The New Our Bodies, Ourselves*, by The Boston Women's Health Collective, pp. 291–316. New York: Simon & Schuster, 1984.

Women's Center of the Democratic National Committee. "Political Power of Women in America." *San Francisco Chronicle*, September 2, 1984, p. A-5.

Wood, Vivian, and Robertson, Joan F. "The Significance of Grandparenthood." In *Time, Roles, and Self in Old Age.* New York: Human Sciences Press, 1976.

———. "Friendship and Kinship Interaction: Differential Effects on the Morale of the Elderly." *Journal of Marriage and the Family* 40 (May 1978): 367–75.

Wyden, Barbara. "Growth: 45 Crucial Months." *Life* 25 (1971): 93, 95.

Wynne-Edwards, V. C. "Population Control in Animals." *Scientific American* 230 (1964): 94–100.

Yankelovich, Daniel A. *The Changing Values on Campus.* New York: Washington Square Press, 1972.

Yankevich, Daniel. *New Roles.* New York: Random House, 1981.

Yeager, Anne. "Infections and Pregnancy." *The Helper* 1 (October 1979): 1–2.

Young, Diony. *Changing Childbirth: Family Birth in the Hospital.* New York: Childbirth Graphics, 1982.

Young, P. T. *Emotions in Animals and Man.* New York: John Wiley, 1943.

Zajonc, R. B. "Attitudinal Effects of Mere Experience." *Journal of Personality and Social Psychology* 9 (1968): 129.

Zerfoss, Nancy. "School Marm to School Ms." *Changing Education* 6 (1974): 23, 48.

Zilbergeld, B. "Pursuit of the Grafenberg Spot." *Psychology Today* 16 (1982): 82–84.

Zimbardo, Philip G. *Shyness.* Reading, Mass.: Addison-Wesley, 1977.

NAME INDEX

Abramson, P. R., 133 n. 27
Adams, Raymond D., 221
Adenauer, Konrad, 277
Ahrons, C. R., 325–327
Albin, Mel, 71, 397
Albrecht, Stan L., 320, 322
Aldous, J., 397
Alexandra, Czarina of Russia, 76
Allport, F. H., 85
Altman, S. A., 368
Amundsen, Kristen, 66
Andersen, Kurt, 392
Angyal, A., 5
Aquinas, Thomas, 441
Arafat, I., 227
Ardrey, Robert, 6, 368
Argyle, M., 37, 189
Ariès, Philippe, 53 n. 29, 471
Aristotle, 425
Aronoff, Joel, 63
Arthur, King of England, 85
Athanasiou, Robert, 256 (also n. 17)
Atwater, Lynn, 254
Auchincloss, Douglas, 48

Bach, George R., 327
Bachrach, Leona L., 219
Badwinter, Elizabeth, 71
Baldwin, Wendy, 259–261, 273
Banta, D., 411 n. 25
Barlow, Brent A., 262
Barret, Nancy S., 506
Bartell, G., 256 n. 17
Baumrind, Diana, 32
Beach, Frank A., 118, 131 n. 26, 165
Becker, G. S., 397
Bee, L. S., 185
Beecher, Catherine, 53 n. 29
Beer, W., 284
Bell, Alan P., 45–46, 48–49, 162, 166
Bell, Alexander Graham, 178 n. 8
Bell, J. I., 115
Bell, Robert R., 200–202, 231, 254, 256
    n. 17, 304 n. 13
Bell, Sanford, 85
Bell, Susan, 422, 424, 427, 440
Bem, Daryl, 68
Bem, Sandra, 68

Bennet, Neil, 443
Berg, S. W., 155 n. 48
Berger, P., 5
Berkowitz, Gila, 426–427
Bernard, Jessie, 318–319
Berne, Eric, 342, 345, 347, 361
Berscheid, Ellen, 194
Bessant, Annie, 425
Bieber, Irving, 44 (also n. 22)
Biegel, H. G., 87–89 (also n. 20)
Blake, Eubie, 277
Blake, Judith, 260
Blood, Robert O. Jr., 272
Blumstein, Philip, 284
Bogue, Donald J., 443
Bohannan, Paul, 306–308, 310, 313–314,
    322
Bond, James, 89 n. 20
Bould, Sally, 382
Bower, Donald W., 225–228
Bowlby, John, 453 n. 7
Bozett, Frederick W., 472
Bragonier, J. R., 428
Bram, Susan, 260
Brandwein, Ruth A., 382–383
Brauer, Alan, 127
Brauer, Donna, 127
Brecher, Edward M., 108, 124, 147–149,
    162, 251–252, 254–255
Brecher, Jeremy, 124
Brecher, Ruth, 251
Brock, Connie, 139
Broderick, Carlfred B., 361
Brotherton, Janet, 436
Brown, Judith K., 53 n. 27
Brown, Stuart T., 155
Browning, Elizabeth Barrett, 84
Browning, Robert, 84
Brubaker, Timothy H., 287
Bugliosi, Vincent, 367 n. 5
Bumpass, Larry L., 264, 315
Burgess, E. W., 295 n. 10
Burgwyn, Diana, 284
Burke, M., 328
Burnett, Carol, 196
Burns, Mark, 155 (also n. 46)
Burton, Richard, 330 n. 3, 391
Busselen, Carol Kincaid, 269
Busselen, Harry J., 269

Byrne, Donn, 140

Cable, Mary, 71, 471
Caesar, Julius, 411
Calhoun, A. W., 456
Camara, K., 312
Campbell, Angus A., 274
Camus, Albert, 82, 475
Cargan, Leonard, 231
Carns, D., 215, 221
Carroll, David, 213, 216
Carson, Johnny, 309
Carter, Hugh, 182–183, 197, 212, 214,
    240, 267, 291, 293, 301, 304 n. 13,
    317–318
Carter, L. A., 284
Cartland, Barbara, 91 (also n. 24)
Casals, Pablo, 277
Casanova, 426
Casey, Douglas R., 506
Cash, Thomas F., 186
Cavallo, Dominic, 71, 397
Cavan, Ruth Shonle, 69, 88, 90
Cease, L., 311
Chalmers, Iain, 408 n. 16
Chenkin, Alvin, 262–263
Cherlin, Andrew J., 328
Chesley, Phyllis, 488
Chess, Stella, 467–468
Chichester, Francis, 277
Child, Julia, 188
Choderow, Nancy, 443
Chopin, Frederic, 68 n. 55
Christ, Jesus, 463
Christopherson, Victor A., 225–228
Churchill, Winston, 277
Clanton, Gordon, 100, 103, 108
Clapp, Diane, 415–416
Clarke-Stewart, A., 471
Clayton, Richard R., 368 n. 8
Cleopatra, 425
Coe, Jo-Anne, 63
Cohen, Alan I., 155
Coleman, James C., 100, 102, 192, 197,
    220, 297–298, 334 (also n. 4), 361,
    412 n. 27, 450, 453 (also n. 7),
    455–456, 472
Collins, Edith, 407

Collins, Martha Layne, 63
Conant, Marcus A., 148 n. 38
Connell-Tatum, Elizabeth, B., 422
Connolly, William G., 490
Cooper, Pamela E., 260
Cordes, Colleen, 17
Cornell, Claire Pedrick, 397
Corson, Stephen L., 416 (also n. 33)
Corzine, William L., 101
Cottrell, L. S., 295 n. 10
Coughey, Kathleen, 200–202
Coulson, Robert, 361
Coulton, G. G., 87
Coutts, Robert L., 108
Cowan, Philip, 274
Cox, Martha, 314
Cox, R., 314
Craft, I. L., 436
Crawley, Lawrence, 105 n. 33
Crick, Francis, 398
Cromie, William J., 190–191
Cuber, John F., 94, 250–252
Curie, Marie, 62 n. 42, 380 (also n. 19)
Curie, Pierre, 62 n. 42, 380 (also n. 19)
Curran, James, 160, 162
Cutright, Phillips, 258, 267

Danielsson, Bengt, 111
Danzinger, C., 226
Darnley, Fred, 278
Darrow, R. Morton, 224
Davies, Nigel, 110 (also n. 2), 417
Davis, David, 368 n. 8
Davis, Glenn, 472
Davis, Keith E., 73–75
Davis, Kingsley, 288–289, 300, 319
Dean, Gillian, 318
Dearborn, Lester W., 114–115
DeCrow, Karen, 309–310
Degler, C. N., 397
DeJong, Gordon F., 261
DeKaplany, Geza, 101 n. 28
Dell, Floyd, 99
DeMartino, Manfred F., 133 n. 27
Deneuve, Catherine, 225
Dennis, Walter, D., 48
Derek, Bo, 89 n. 20
DeRougemont, Denis, 87
Devore, Irven, 368
Dickens, Charles, 82, 390 (also n. 33)
Dickerson, R. E., 113
Dinman, B. D., 429
Diocles, 113
Dion, K., 186
Doress, Paula Brown, 226, 275

Douglas, John H., 39
Draughon, M., 323–324
Duberman, Lucille, 212, 322, 325
Dundes, Alan, 113
Dunkle, Margaret, 62
Dunnigan, Phillip, 387
Durant, Will, 87
Durbin, Karen, 101

Edward VIII, 76, 320
Edwin, L., 285
Ehrenreich, B., 71
Ehrhardt, Anke A., 34, 36 n. 16, 79
Elder, G. H., Jr., 194
Elizabeth I, Queen of Great Britain, 63 n. 43
Ellis, Albert, 85, 3
Empedocles, 115
English, O. Spurgeon, 105 n. 33
Enkin, Murray, 408 n. 16
Erdman, Paul, 506
Erickson, Rosemary, 322
Erikson, Erik H., 453
Eshleman, J. Ross, 382
Evans, H. L., 415

Father Ritter, 392
Feldman, Frances Lomas, 475
Feldman, Harold, 166, 272 n. 39
Feldman, Philip, 259
Felman, Yehudi M., 166
Feshbeck, Norma, 36 n. 18
Feshbeck, Seymour, 36 n. 18
Festinger, Leon, 187
Filsinger, Erik E., 361
Finch, B. F., 58, 417, 426
Fisher, Mary Pat, 166
Fisher, Rhoda L., 472
Fisher, Seymour, 133 n. 27, 472
Fishman, K. B., 322
Flaubert, Gustav, 98
Flax, Carol, 141
Fleming, Ian, 89 n. 20
Ford, C. S., 118, 131 n. 26, 187
Ford, Henry, 179
Ford, K., 443
Ford, Susan, 188
Fowles, John, 196
Fox, Greer Litton, 443
Fraker, Susan, 63–64, 441
Francis, D. P., 160
Francome, Colin, 438–439
Francke, Linda Bird, 314, 324
Frank, Ellen, 142, 143 n. 32

Franklin, Benjamin, 277, 475
Freed, Doris Jonas, 308
Freedman, Daniel G., 469
Freeman, Ruth, 212 n. 4
Freud, Sigmund, 117, 105 (also n. 33), 106
Fried, Peter A., 407
Fromm, Erich, 5, 104–105, 108
Fromm-Reichmann, Freida, 217
Frumkin, Robert M., 110 (also n. 1)

Gagnon, John H., 212, 255
Galenson, Marjorie, 67
Gallimore, Ronald, 53 n. 26
Gallo, Robert C., 160
Gallop, George Jr., 378
Gambrell, D. R., 428
Gandhi, Indira, 63 n. 43
Gasser, Rita D., 382
Gaylin, Jody, 88
Geerken, Michael, 397
Gelles, Richard J., 397
Gelner, C. J. R., 397
Gentry, Curt, 367 n. 5
Gerson, Marvin, 149
Gibran, Kahlil, 332
Gibran, Mary G., 332
Gladue, Brian A., 48
Glass, Shirley P., 254
Glenn, Norval D., 262 n. 28, 264, 275, 320–321
Glick, Ira, 81
Glick, Paul C., 182–183, 197, 212, 214, 240, 267, 291–293, 296, 301, 304 n. 13, 315, 317–318, 320
Golden, Gale Holtz, 146, 166, 433
Goldsmith, Judith, 443
Goldthorp, W. O., 435
Goleman, Daniel, 38
Goode, William J., 79, 87
Goodman, J., 488
Gordon, Michael, 57, 60, 71, 185, 366, 369
Gordon, Suzanne, 162, 216, 231
Gotard, Erin, 261
Gottschalk, Helmuth, 101
Gotwald, William H., 146, 166, 433
Gough, Kathleen E., 53 (also n. 29), 54, 71
Gove, Walter R., 397
Goy, R. W., 33
Graham, Katherine, 63
Grandma Moses (Anna Mary Robertson), 277
Grant, J. B., 328
Gravell, M., 160
Gray, Madeline, 57, 59–60, 62, 71

Graziano, William, 187
Green, Hugh, 58, 417, 426
Green, Richard, 48
Green, Roger L., 49
Greenberg, Dan, 197
Greenblat, C. S., 212
Greenwood, Sadja, 166
Grier, Rosey, 196
Griffitt, W., 191
Groenman, Sjoerd, 174
Grumbach, Doris, 166
Guinevere, 85
Guittar, E. C., 227
Gurak, Douglas T., 318
Gurman, Alan S., 299
Guttmacher, Alan, 419, 437, 442

Haire, Doris, 410
Hales, Dianne, 281
Hall, Edward T., 188–189, 190–191
Hall, Elizabeth, 115, 123, 148 n. 38, 152, 166
Hall, W. J., 115
Haller, John S., 71
Haller, Robin M., 71
Hamilton, R., 150
Hammond, Dorothy, 63
Hanson, Shirley M. H., 472
Harlow, Harry F., 83, 104 n. 30, 454–455
Harrell, W. Andrew, 379
Harris, J. R. W., 77
Harris, Marvin, 53 (also n. 30), 56 n. 34, 62
Harrison, W. O., 155 n. 48
Harroff, Peggy B., 94, 250–252
Hartley, Shirley Foster, 417–418
Hastings, Donald W., 121 n. 12
Hatcher, Robert A., 412 n. 27, 421–426, 427 (also n. 44), 428 (also n. 40), 429–432, 434 (also n. 52), 440
Haveman, Earnest, 281
Haverkamp, Albert, 410 (also n. 24)
Hayes, C. D., 472
Heaton, Jim B., 264
Heer, David M., 266
Heiman, Julia R., 144
Heiss, J. S., 185
Helmreich, Robert L., 42
Henshaw, S. K., 420, 437
Hendrick, Clyde, 19, 207
Hendrick, Susan, 19, 207
Henig, Robin Marantz, 411, 452
Henry VIII, 302
Henze, L. F., 225, 227
Hess, Beth B., 397

Hess, E. H., 190, 312
Hetherington, E. Mavis, 308, 314
Hill, Charles T., 91
Hinde, R. A., 19
Hite, Shere, 130, 133 n. 27, 134
Hitler, Adolph, 277
Hong, Lawrence K., 84
Hooker, E., 48
Horn, Jack C., 5
Hosken, Fran, 110
Hotaling, G. T., 397
Howard, George E., 87
Howe, Florence, 32
Howe, Louise Kapp, 443
Hsia, Shyuan, 160
Hudson, J. W., 225, 227
Humphrey, Michael, 260
Hunt, Bernice, 314, 318, 319
Hunt, Morton M., 43 (also n. 19), 44 (also n. 22, 23), 48, 84, 87–88, 112, 133, 142, 143 n. 32, 162 (also n. 62), 216, 218, 253, 318–319
Hyde, Janet Shibley, 71, 166

Jablow, Alta, 63
Jacklin, Carol Nagy, 38
Jacobs, Marsha, 197
Jacobson, Paul H., 289
Jacoby, Susan, 215, 222
Jaffe, Harold W., 16–162 (also n. 62)
James, P. D., 193
Janda, Louise H., 186
Jastrow, Robert, 451 (also n. 3)
Jay, Karla, 166
Jedlicka, Davor, 162 n. 61, 200–201, 204
Jensen, Gordon D., 33
Johnson, Jeannette H., 430
Johnson, Joyce S., 219–220, 307
Johnson, Miriam M., 71
Johnson, R., 256
Johnson, Timothy, 417, 433
Johnson, Virginia E., 48, 115–117, 121–123, 127, 130, 132–133, 135–136, 139, 142, 143 n. 32, 144, 158–159, 166
Johnston, Malcolm C., 407
Jolliot, Frederik, 380
Joubert, Joseph, 445

Kagan, Jerome, 281
Kalish, Richard A., 281
Kamerman, S. B., 472
Kanin, E. J., 91
Kanmeyer, Kenneth C. W., 19, 207

Kantner, J., 443
Karlen, Arno, 43–44
Katchadourian, Herant A., 120
Kaufman, Raymond H., 146
Kaye, Donald, 155
Kelley, Harold H., 19, 207, 361
Kellner, H., 5
Kellogg, J. H., 114–115
Kelly, G. Lombard, 122, 129
Kelly, Joan Berlin, 312, 315–316, 322–324
Kennedy, Donald, 416
Kennell, John H., 413, 452
Kephart, William M., 83, 305
Keshet, H., 311
Kessler, S., 298, 307
Kessler-Harris, Alice, 397
Kett, Joseph F., 207
Kieffer, Carolynne, 5–7
King, Theodore, 407, 410
Kinsey, Alfred C., 42–43 (also n. 19), 44 (also n. 22, 23), 115–117, 122 (also n. 13), 123–124, 128–129, 131, 137, 143 (also n. 32), 158–159, 164, 183, 199–200, 252–253, 280
Kitzinger, Sheila, 406
Klaus, Marshall H., 413, 452
Klaus, Patricia, 212 n. 4
Klein, Luella, 414, 420, 428–429
Kleinke, Chris L., 361
Kliman, Gilbert W., 472
Klinman, D., 443
Knapp, Mark L., 19, 231, 361
Kniskern, D. P., 299
Knox, Samuel R., 150
Kohl, R., 443
Kolata, Gina Bari, 148
Komarovsky, M., 68
Kramer, R., 472
Krano, William D., 63
Krantzler, M., 329
Kresch, Arnold J., 432
Kronhausen, Eberhard, 130 n. 22
Kronhausen, Phyllis, 130 n. 22
Krupp, Marcus A., 403

Ladas, A. K., 133
Lamb, M. E., 472
Lambert, Wallace E., 53 n. 26
Landis, Judson T., 182, 197, 237 n. 5, 261 n. 25, 475
Landis, Mary G., 182, 197, 237 n. 5, 261 n. 25, 475
Landis, Paul H., 291
Lane, Mary E., 426
Langer, W. L., 58, 60, 417

LaRossa, Maureen Mulligan, 472
LaRossa, Ralph, 472
Lasser, J. K., 499
Lauer, Jeanette, 247, 342
Lauer, Robert, 247, 342
Launcelot, 85
Layde, Peter M., 428
LeClair, Lydia, 223
Lederer, William J., 361
Lee, G. A., 219
Lee, John Alan, 92–93, 95–97, 107–108
Lenski, Gerhard, 373 n. 12, 376
Lenski, Jean, 373 n. 12, 376
Leslie, Elizabeth M., 380
Levine, M. I., 115
Levinger, George, 329
Lewis, Robert A., 227, 324, 361
Lewit, Sarah, 442
Lews, Judith Long, 162, 216
Libby, Roger W., 166, 213
Liberatore, Paul, 148
Lin, Sung-Ling, 317
Lincoln, Abraham, 502
Linden, Fabian, 66
Lindenmayer, Jean Pierre, 258
Lingren, Henry Clay, 506
Little, Bill L., 346–347
Lobsenz, Norman M., 103
Lopata, Helena Z., 218
Lorber, Judith, 365
Lorenz, Konrad, 6, 368
Lowe, Charles, 435
Lowenthal, Leo, 275
Loy, Myrna, 89 n. 20
Lubic, Ruth Watson, 414
Lunde, Donald T., 120
Lynch, James J., 14, 19, 81, 220, 281

Maccoby, Eleanor Emmons, 38
MacDonald, John D., 93, 350
Mace, David, 168, 170, 340
Mace, Vera, 168, 170, 340
Macfarlane, Aidan, 443, 452
Macklin, Eleanor D., 223 (also n. 10), 224, 226–228, 231
Magnuson, Ed, 392–393
Maisel, Richard, 218
Makepeace, James Michael, 225–227
Malinowsky, Bronislaw, 85
Mancini, Jay A., 141, 143 n. 32
Manson, Charles, 367 n. 5
Marano, Hara Estroff, 413 (also n. 29)
Marcus, Steven, 88, 108

Margolis, Maxine, 52–53 (also n. 26, 29), 60, 62, 71, 472
Markson, E. W., 285
Marlowe, Christopher, 208
Marotz-Baden, Romana, 322
Marshall, Donald S., 111, 141
Marshall, Megan, 108
Martindale, Don, 12
Marx, Groucho, 22
Maslow, Abraham H., 5–6, 191, 251
Massarik, Fred, 262–263
Massie, Robert K., 76
Masters, William H., 48, 115–117, 121–123, 127, 130, 132–133, 135–136, 139, 142, 143 n. 32, 144, 158–159, 166
Mastroianni, Luigi, Jr., 157 n. 50, 403 n. 8, 408, 409 (also n. 22), 410–411, 442
Matthews, Joseph, 329
Maugham, Somerset, 475
May, Elaine Tyler, 329
McCall, Cheryl, 393
McCarthy, Eugene, 271
McCarthy, J. F., 320
McCary, James Leslie, 100
McCary, Stephen P., 100
McCauley, B., 227
McGuinness, Diane, 36
McLaughlin, M. M., 455
Mead, Margaret, 177, 179, 269
Meer, Jeff, 5
Mehrabian, Albert, 188–189, 351
Meir, Golda, 63 n. 43, 277
Melko, Matthew, 231
Meredith, Nikki, 162
Millar, Dan P., 207
Millar, Frank E., 207
Miller, Julie Ann, 39, 408 n. 18
Miller, Roger LeRoy, 492 n. 8
Miller, Rrend, 48
Miller, Warren B., 268
Minge-Klevana, Wanda, 53 n. 27
Mintz, N. L., 191
Moch, Leslie Page, 207
Modahl, Charlotte, 452
Modell, John, 207
Mohr, James C., 57, 60
Moles, Oliver C., 329
Moll, Albert, 85
Moller, Ingrid K. S., 361
Monahan, Thomas P., 266
Money, John, 19, 25–27, 30, 33 (also n. 12), 34–36, 44–45, 50–52, 71, 76, 78–79, 108, 129, 158, 173, 176

Moore, Mary Tyler, 89 n. 20, 180, 222
Morris, Desmond, 79
Mosher, William D., 257, 414
Mowat, Ronald Rae, 101
Mullahy, Patrick, 105 n. 33
Murdock, George Peter, 236, 252, 366–367
Murstein, Bernard I., 108, 185, 191, 207, 231

Narcissus, 105
Nash, Ogden, 475
Nason, Ellen Mara, 397
Nass, Gilbert O., 166
Nelson, Paula, 488
Newland, Kathleen, 404
Newton, Niles, 452
Nicholas II, Czar of Russia, 76
Nord, Christine, 259–261, 273
Norton, Arthur J., 293–296, 320
Norton, R., 275
Noyes, John Humphrey, 423 n. 38
Nyad, Diana, 39

O'Herlihy, Colm, 24 n. 3
O'Neill, George, 100, 257
O'Neill, Nena, 100, 257
O'Reilley, Jane, 388–391
Oedipus, 105
Olson, David H., 397
Orleans, Mirium P., 410 n. 24
Orthner, Dennis K., 141, 143 n. 32, 382
Ostrow, David G., 166
Ovid, 167
Oxorn, Harry, 407

Paige, Karen Erickson, 120 n. 9
Parke, Robert, 57
Parrot, Andrea, 166
Pasquale, Samuel, 429
Paul, William, 48
Pearlin, Leonard I., 219–220, 307
Pedersen, Frank A., 382
Pepitone-Rockwell, Fran, 397
Perlman, David, 146, 160
Perry, J. D., 133
Petersdorf, Robert G., 156
Petersen, James R., 127, 253–254
Petros, John W., 67
Pickett, Mirium, 271–272
Pietropinto, Anthony, 43 n. 19, 44 n. 22
Pincus, Jane, 403 n. 8, 408 n. 17

Pines, Maya, 453 n. 7, 457 n. 92
Plato, 3, 7–8, 113
Poloma, Margaret M., 397, 11
Polonto, Karen, 258
Pope John XXIII (Cardinal Angelo Roncalli), 277
Pope Paul VI, 263, 306
Pope Pius XII, 113
Popenoe, Paul, 295 n. 10
Porter, Sylvia, 487–488, 490, 493 n. 9
Poston, Dudley L. Jr., 261
Pribram, Karl, H., 36
Proctor, E. B., 123, 135–136

Radetsky, Peter, 427 n. 44, 45
Rapoport, Rhona, 329, 379
Rapoport, Robert N., 329, 379
Reeder, Sharon R., 157 n. 50, 403 n. 8, 408–409 (also n. 22), 410–411, 442
Reid, John, 50
Rein, Michael F., 152, 159
Reiss, Ira L., 48, 67 (also n. 53), 175 n. 5, 235, 240 n. 8, 254–255, 263, 266, 369, 371, 393, 397, 464
Remsberg, Bonnie, 472
Renne, Karen, 260, 272
Retton, Mary Lou, 38–39
Rheinstein, Max, 304 n. 14
Rice, Florence, 492 n. 8
Rivers, Joan, 187
Robertiello, Richard C., 353
Roberts, Colon, 435
Robertson, Joan F., 279
Robinson, Ira E., 200–201, 204
Robinson, Joan F., 162 n. 61
Rodgers, R., 326–327
Rogers, Carl, 231
Rollins, Boyd C., 272 n. 39
Rosen, Raymond, 115, 123, 148 n. 38, 152, 166
Rosenblatt, Paul C., 260
Rosenfeld, Albert, 472
Ross, J. B., 455
Rubenstein, Carin, 19
Rubin, Lillian Breslow, 3, 16, 19, 143 (also n. 32), 183, 207, 231, 274–275, 285, 293, 361, 475
Rubin, Roger H., 231
Rubin, Zick, 189, 207, 226, 472
Ryan, Bruce, 170–171
Ryan, Mary P., 207

Sachs, Benjamin P., 414, 442

Sadd, Susan, 44 (also n. 23), 201–205, 216, 252–254
Sadker, David, 32
Sadker, Myra, 32
Safilios-Rothschild, Constantina, 318
Sagan, Carl, 23 n. 1, 399 n. 3
Sager, Clifford J., 361
St. Augustine, 112–113, 403, 441
Salimbene, 454–455
Sameroff, A. J., 467 (also n. 15), 468
Sand, George, 68
Sandholzer, Terry Alan, 166
Sanger, Margaret, 57, 59, 61, 425–426
Satir, Virginia, 351–352, 354, 359, 361
Saunders, Antoinette, 472
Scanzoni, John, 397
Schaffer, Kay F., 71
Schaller, George B., 368
Schellenberg, J. S., 185
Schlegel, Alice, 63
Schmidt, Gunter, 144
Schmidt-Elmendorff, H., 260
Schoolnik, Gary K., 155 n. 46
Schrier, Allan M., 368
Schupp, C., 256 n. 17
Schwartz, M. A., 221
Schwartz, Pepper, 162, 216, 284
Sciolino, Elaine, 48, 306, 439
Scott, A. F., 284
Scott, Donald M., 397
Seaman, Barbara, 147–149, 153, 426–427, 429
Seaman, Gideon, 427
Secondi, J. J., 148 n. 38
Seeley, Richard, 393 (also n. 37)
Segal, Julius, 467–469
Seligmann, Jean, 160 n. 53
Sell, Ralph R., 261
Selsam, Millicent, 368
Seward, Rudy R., 71
Shakespeare, William, 109, 194–195, 270
Shapiro, Howard I., 150, 153, 432, 440
Shapiro, Max, 503, 506
Shaver, Phillip, 19
Shaw, George Bernard, 475
Sherlock, Basil J., 361
Shorter, Edward, 58, 369, 377 n. 15, 397, 417
Sigusch, Volkman, 144
Silverman, I., 192
Simenauer, Jacqueline, 43 n. 19, 44 n. 22, 216, 231
Simon, William, 43 (also n. 19)

Simpson, Wallis Warfield, 320
Singh, B., 148
Skafte, Dianne, 329
Skolnick, Arlene, 58, 71, 275, 397, 417
Skolnick, Jerome H., 71, 397
Slone, Denis, 428
Smith, Adam, 506
Smith, Daniel Scott, 57
Smith, James P., 54, 67
Smith, James R., 256 (also n. 17), 257
Smith, Lynn G., 256 (also n. 17), 257
Soiffer, Bill, 281
Sommerville, John, 472
Spanier, Graham B., 224, 272 n. 39, 273, 293, 314, 329, 396
Sparling, P. Frederick, 158
Spence, Janet T., 42
Spezzano, Charles, 413, 415, 452
Spicer, J., 326
Sroufe, L. Alan, 454
Stafford, R., 227
Stark, Gary D., 207
Starr, Bernard D., 122, 128–129, 276, 279 (also n. 46), 280, 285
Starr, J., 215, 221
Stein, Benjamin J., 506
Stein, Marsha L., 148
Stein, Peter J., 212–213, 215, 217–218, 221, 231, 243
Steinberg, Lawrence D., 285
Steinman, Susan, 311
Steinmetz, Suzanne K., 391
Stephens, William N., 236, 367
Stern, Michael P., 323, 428
Stewart, Gary, 429
Stewart, J., 361
Stich, Rodney, 305 n. 36
Stinnet, N., 278
Stockard, Jean, 71
Stratton, Joanna L., 71
Straus, Murray A., 397
Straus, Stephen E., 146, 151
Strelitz, Z., 329
Strong, Bryan, 256
Stuart, I. R., 285
Styron, William, 175
Sulik, Kathleen K., 407
Sullivan, Harry Stack, 217
Sunshine, Phil, 405 n. 9
Sussman, Marvin B., 397
Sweet, Richard, 264
Swenson, Norma, 415–416
Symons, Donald, 145, 166

Tannahill, Reay, 118 n. 8, 166
Tatum, Howard J., 422
Tavris, Carol, 44 (also n. 23), 201–205, 216, 252–254
Taylor, Claribel M., 382
Taylor, Elizabeth, 330 n. 1, 391
Terman, Lewis M., 295 n. 10
Thacker, S., 411 n. 25
Thatcher, Margaret, 63 n. 43
Thomas, Alexander, 467–468
Thomas, Clayton L., 155
Thompson, Linda, 329
Thorman, G., 397
Tiberius, 149–150
Tietze, Christopher, 428–429, 438
Tilling, Thomas, 310, 482
Tissott, S. A., 114
Tobias, Andrew, 506
Tolstoy, Leo, 196
Townsend, Bickley, 379
Trexler, R. C., 58, 417
Troll, Lillian E., 276, 366
Tuchman, Barbara W., 173
Tucker, Patricia, 25–27, 30, 34–36, 44–45, 50–52, 71
Turnbull, Colin, 397
Turner, Gillian, 407
Twitchell, J., 256

Udrey, Richard J., 219, 248
Updike, John, 113 n. 6, 139 (also n. 31), 332–333 (also n. 3), 334

Van Deusen, Edmond L., 229 (also n. 13)
Van Keep, P. A., 260
Varni, Charles, 256 n. 17
Veevers, J. E., 258–260

Verny, T., 443
Vessey, Martin P., 429
Victor, Jeffrey S., 166
Victoria, Queen of Great Britain, 62 n. 42, 63 n. 43
Viets, Jack, 305 n. 36

Walker, Timothy B., 308
Wallechinsky, David, 270
Wallerstein, J. S., 312, 315–316, 322–324
Wallin, Paul, 295 n. 10
Wallisch, L., 325–327
Walster, Elaine, 192–193, 195, 249
Walters, G. William, 192–193, 195, 249
Ward, Michael P., 54, 67
Warner, Ralph, 231
Washington, A. Eugene, 146, 152
Washington, George, 501–502
Waterman, Jill, 413, 452
Waters, Everett, 454
Watson, James, 398 n. 1
Watson, John B., 456
Weaver, Charles N., 320
Weber, Ruth, 403 n. 8, 439–440
Weeks, John R., 419
Wegman, Peggy Nelson, 226
Weinberg, Martin, S., 45–46, 48, 162, 166
Weiner, Marcella Bakur, 122, 128–129, 276, 279 (also n. 46), 280, 285
Weismer, Paul, 153
Weisner, Thomas, 53 n. 26
Weiss, Robert S., 19, 217–219, 231, 313–314
Weitzman, Lenore J., 308–312, 325
Welk, Lawrence, 196
Wells, J. Gipson, 285

Wernick, Robert, 370, 461–462
Wertheimer, Wendy, 152
Westfall, David, 506
Westoff, Charles F., 57, 385, 387, 423, 428
Whipple, B., 133
White, Burton, 457 n. 9
Whitehurst, Robert N., 231
Wicks, Donna, 295 n. 10
Wilson, Kenneth L., 322
Wilson, Marilyn L., 48, 57
Winch, Robert F., 185
Winokur, Scott, 163
Wirth, Eileen, 215
Wishy, Bernard, 397
Wolfe, Donald W., 272
Wolhandler, Jill, 403 n. 8, 439–440
Wood, Vivian, 279
Wright, Thomas L., 254
Wyden, Barbara, 451, 453 n. 7
Wyden, Peter, 357

Yahraes, Herbert, 467–469
Yankelovich, Daniel L., 212
Yankevich, Daniel, 378
Yeager, Anne, 150–152
Yorburg, B., 227
Young, Allen, 166
Young, Diony, 408 n. 21, 412, 423, 436

Zajonc, R. B., 187
Zelnick, M., 443
Zerfoss, Nancy, 68
Zigler, E., 397
Zilbergeld, B., 133
Zimbardo, Philip G., 19, 196, 207, 231

SUBJECT INDEX

Abortion, 433
  availability of, 441–443
  controversy over, 441–443
  illegal, 59–60, 441–442
  incidence of, 436–438
  induced, 436–440
  laws, 60, 112 n. 5, 203, 225, 436, 441–443
  motives for, 59–60
  self-induced, 442
  spontaneous, 435–436
  teenagers and, 418–419, 437
Active listening, 350–351, 353, 360
Adolescence, 30
  attachment and, 81
Adolescent sterility, 139
Adoption, 367 n. 7, 381, 383, 416
  kinship rights and, 240 n. 8
Adultery (see Comarital sexuality; Extramarital copulation)
Adult period, personality development of, 106
Agape, 82, 107
Aggression:
  chromosomal anomalies and, 50
  gender trait of, 25 n. 6, 31–32, 36–37, 40–41
  infrahumans and, 30
Aggressiveness sexual, 254
Agrarian family, 373 (also n. 12), 377, 395
Agricultural Period, 53 n. 29
AIDS (acquired immune deficiency syndrome), 146, 160 (also n. 53, 57) 161–163
Alcohol, fetal damage and, 407
Alternate birth centers, 410 n. 23, 412 (also n. 28)
Amerafrican legacy of courtship, 172, 175 (also n. 4), 176, 205
American Psychiatric Association, 42, 46–47
American Psychological Association, 42, 46–47
Amniocentesis, 408 (also n. 17)
Amnion, fetal cells contained in, 408 (also n. 18, 19)
  function of, 404, 408
Amniotic sac, rupture of, 410

Anatomy, female, 28–30, 129 (also n. 20, 21), 130–132
Anatomy, male, 28–29, 118–119, 126
Androgen, 28–29, 33, 34 n. 14
  chromosomal anomalies and, 50
  infrahumans and, 30
  prenatally androgenized females and, 33–34
Androgyny, 42
Annulment, 236, 286 (also n. 1), 301, 305–306
Antisexual societies:
  courtly love and, 87 (also n. 16), 88–89
  marriage and, 88 (also n. 18)
Apgar rating, of neonate, 412
Artificial insemination, 415–416
Art of Love (Ovid), 86
Athletic ability and gender, 38–41
Athletics, copulation before, 117
Attachment, 79–80, 81 (also n. 5 and 6), 92, 106, 390
Attraction, 185–195
Attraction quotient, 195
Automobile, costs of, 490–491

"Baby boom," 60–61, 212–213, 385
Big-ticket items, buying 491–493
Bigamy (polygamy), 236 (also n. 2), 305
Birth (see Birth rate, Childbirth)
Birth control, 258, 416–417
  attitudes toward, 57 (also n. 37), 58–61, 70
  failure rate of methods of, 422–434
  future methods of, 429, 435 (also n. 55)
  history of, 58, 60
  ignorance of, 57–59, 419–420
  laws against, 57–60
  methods of, 58, 60, 421–440, 429
Birth, gender assignment at, 31, 34–36, 51, 69
Birth, illegitimate, 62, 175 (also n. 5), 205, 305 (also n. 17), 378, 384, 396
Birth rate, 60–62, 67, 70, 385–386, 417, 419
Bisexuality, 44

Blended family, 312, 321–325, 328, 371–372, 381, 383–384, 395
Body language, eye contact and, 93, 189–190
Borax stores, 492 (also n. 8), 505
Brain:
  complexity of, 451 (also n. 3, n. 4), 470
  gender differences in, 24
  prenatal influences on, 29, 32–34
Breast feeding, 412 n. 27, 423
Bride price, 169–170, 237
Budget, 476–481, 504
Budget, principle of forced alternate choice in, 477, 479, 484, 505
Buying, principles of, 493, 496–498

Campus marriage, 267–269, 283
Castration, 24 n. 4
  of infrahumans, 30
Cell, human, 23, 27, 120, 388 (also n. 1), 399 (also n. 2, 3)
Cervical cap, 427
Cervix:
  cancer of, 146, 150
  dilatation in labor, 410, 443
  fitting cervical cap, diaphragm, and sponge, 426–427
  sperm survival in, 424, 428
Cesarian section, 411, 414
  genital herpes and, 150
Chaperones, 171–172, 177, 180
Child abuse, 80–81, 413 n. 29
  battering, 392–393, 396
  sexual molestation, 393–394, 396
Childbearing:
  change in women's function of, 57–62
  postponement of, 258, 260–261, 273
Childbirth, 409–414 (see also Labor; Paired bond; Neonate)
  drugs used during, 410
  facilities for, 412–414
  high-risk category of, 412 (also n. 28)
  mortality rate of mother during, 414, 420, 428–429
  stages of, 410–412, 443
Child care, responsibility for, 268–284, 311, 377–379, 380, 382

Child custody, 310–312, 314–316, 328, 384

Childfree marriage, 60, 377, 386

Childless marriage, infertility and, 415–416

Childrearing (*see also* Children; Gender-role socialization; Infancy; Neonate)
philosophies of, 456
responsibility for, 25, 52 (also n. 26), 54–57, 67, 69, 91, 173, 175–176, 205

Children:
abuse of, 80–81
affected by STDs, 146, 150, 152, 153 n. 39, 155
basic trust and, 453–455
in blended families, 321–325, 328, 371–372, 381–384
care of, 52 (also n. 26), 54–57
dependency needs of, 103–104
developmental readiness and, 459–460
developmental sequence of, 445–450
discipline of, 323–324, 462 (also n. 10), 465–466, 470
economic liability of, 57, 60, 258–259, 261, 273, 386, 481–482
effect of on marriage, 272–275
importance of nutrition for, 450–452, 470
importance of peer contact for, 454
independency needs of, 104
instilling values for, 460–461, 470
intellectual development of, 457–458
of interracial marriages, 266
"latch-key," 55–56
legitimization of, 235, 257
love and affection for, 103, 453–456, 471
mastery skills and, 458–460, 471
meaning of divorce for, 310–312, 314–316, 328
number in family, 57
number involved in divorce, 384–385
personal allowance for, 479–480
postponement of, 386
poverty and, 475 n. 1
punishment of, 462–463 (also n. 11, 13), 464 (also n. 14), 470
reinforcement for, 464–465
self-esteem and, 455
in single-parent families, 224, 372–373, 380–383
socialization of, 365, 367, 382,
449–450, 453–466, 470–471
"spoiling", 455
stepfamilies and, 321–325, 328
temperaments of, 466–469, 471
wanted, 260–272, 283

Child support, 175 (also n. 5), 176, 304, 309–312, 325, 328, 384

Chlamydia, 146, 151–152

Choice points, in life, 242 (also n. 11), 243

Chromosomes:
anomalies of, 49–51
contained in human cell, 27, 388–399 (also n. 3)
patterns of, 27 n. 8, 35
sex, 23, 26–27, 35, 69

Circumcision, 36, 120 n. 9

Clitoris, 28–29
anomaly of, 35, 51
erotic sensitivity of, 130 (also n. 22), 131–133, 164

Cohabitation, 174, 180, 182, 198, 203, 213–214, 216, 221, 223–230, 387
children and, 224
college students and, 223 (also n. 10), 225–226, 267, 283
increase in, 259
legal problems of, 228
marriage vs., 241–243

Coitus interruptus (withdrawal), 423

Coitus reservatus, 423 (also n. 38)

Common-law marriage, 236, 240

Communication, effective, 349–353

Communication, ineffective, 342–349, 354–361, 389

Community property laws, 308

Companionate love, 82, 85, 107

Conception (*see* Fertilization)

Condom, 148 (also n. 38), 225 n. 11, 425–426 (also n. 43)

Confessions of Nat Turner (William Styron), 175

Contemporary romantic love, 85, 90–92

Contraception (*see* Birth control)

Contraceptive creams and jellies, 149

Contraceptive sponge, 427–428

Contract cohabitation, 228–229 (also n. 12, 13), 230

Copulation, 130–133, 137, 139
aging and, 128–129
euphemisms for, 88 (also n. 19)
extramarital, 202, 253 (also n. 14, 15), 254–256
following vasectomy, 432–433

nineteenth-century view of, 88 (also n. 18), 89
premarital, 199–105
regulation of female, 171–172
societal attitudes toward, 173–174, 199–206

Courtly love, 84, 86–87 (also n. 14 and 16), 88–89 (also n. 24)

Courtship, family system and, 235
infrahumans and, 167 (also n. 1), 168
patterns of, 168, 172 (also n. 3), 173–176, 205

Credit:
installment contracts and, 485–487, 489, 504
sound uses of, 483 (also n. 4), 484–485, 489, 504

Credit rating, 488

Crimes of passion, 101 (also n. 28), 102

Crystallization (*see* Limerance)

Culpotomy, 432

Cultural conditioning, 103, 171

Culture:
social class and, 14–16, 18
subcultures and, 14–18

Cunnilingus, 111, 118, 130 n. 22, 144, 200, 203

Dating (*see also* Courtship; Dating differential; Marital choice)
attraction and, 185–187, 189–191, 194–195
automobile and, 178–179
body language and, 188–191
coeducation and, 177
differences from prior sociosexual behavior in, 178–180, 206
differential, 197–199, 318
double, 181
functions of, 180–182, 205
"going steady," 181, 200
mass media impact on, 179
premarital copulation and, 199–205
propinquity and, 187–188
qualities valued in, 192–194, 206
romantic love and, 91
self-esteem in, 197, 206
shyness and, 196–197
social-class patterns in, 182–183, 206

D & C (dilatation and curettage), 439–440

D & E (dilatation and evacuation), 439–440

Defense-oriented behavior, 334–335, 360

Dependency needs, 103–104

Depersonalization, 13–14

Desertion, 268 (also n. 1), 294 n. 8, 304 n. 13, 396

Diaphragm, 426–427

Displacement, in marital conflict, 333–334

Division of labor, 25, 67, 69–70

Divorce:
acceptance of, 244, 282
arranged marriages and, 171
causes of, 237
child custody and, 310–312, 314–316, 328
child support and, 304, 309–312, 328
duration of marriages ending in, 288–290
grounds for, 304 (also n. 13)
history of, 236 (also n. 4), 301–305
influence of children on, 295–296
in-laws and, 313
interracial marriage and, 267
laws concerning, 252
loneliness and, 218, 220
meaning of, for children, 310–312, 314–316, 328
phases of, 306–314, 327–328
physical ailments and, 220
premarital copulation and, 203, 206
probability for, 287–298, 327
race and, 293–294, 296
rate, 213, 237, 287–288, 316, 327–328
reaction of family and friends to, 313, 326–327
relation of education, occupation, and income to, 292–293, 296
relation of family background to, 295–296, 328
relation of geographic area to, 294–296, 328
remarriage and, 213
singles and, 214
societal acceptance of, 318–319
spousal support and, 309

DNA (deoxyribonucleic acid) molecule, 23–24, 27 n. 7, 119, 398 (also n. 1), 399

Dominance:
men and, 62–64, 66–67
submission and, 37–38, 40

Double standard, 173

Douche, 424 (also n. 41, 42), 425
precoital and postcoital, 148

Down's syndrome (mongolism), 407 (also n. 15), 408

Dowry, 169, 237

Dual career marriage, 62 n. 42, 380 (also n. 19)

Dual income marriage, 53–55, 56 (also n. 34), 57, 60, 62, 380

Economic determinism, 60 (also n. 40), 61

Education, cost of, 482 (also n. 3)

Egg:
fertilization and, 137–139, 164, 398–399 (also n. 3), 400, 409, 442
production of, 129

Ejaculation, 124–125, 127–128, 130

Embryo, 399, 401 (see also Pregnancy, embryonic period of)

Emotional deprivation, critical period of, 454

Emotional immaturity, 103, 106, 192, 297–298

Emotional maturity, 92, 105–106, 192, 296–298

Emotional security, critical period of, 453–455

Employment, women and, 53–55, 56 (also n. 34), 57, 60, 62, 380

Engagement, 172 n. 3, 177

Equal Credit Opportunity Act, 488

Equal pay for equal work, 64 (also n. 51), 70

Equal Rights Amendment (ERA), 67

Erogenous zones, 122, 131, 133

Eros, 82, 93, 97–98, 107

Erotic response:
aging and, 128–129, 139
complexities of, 139–145, 164
cultural influences on, 143–145, 164
female, 132–137, 139, 142–143, 159, 163–164
male, 122–129, 164
physiological correlates of, 116
prepubertal, 123–124, 127, 137, 164

Erotophiles, 139–140, 142, 164

Erotophobes, 140, 142, 164

Estrogen, 24, 35, 28–29, 35

Excitement phase, of erotic response, 122–123, 132–137

Extended family, 3, 366, 368

External genitalia, 29, 31 (see also Anatomy)
ambiguous, 35, 51
surgical repair of, 36, 51–52

Extramarital copulation, 202, 225, 252 (also n. 13), 253 (also n. 14, n. 15), 254–256, 283

Fallopian tube:
fertilized egg in, 152, 399–400
infertility and, 415
PID and, 152–153
sterilization and, 430–432

False labor, 409–410

Family:
female headed, 175–176, 205
impact of industrialization on, 373 (also n. 11, 12)
meaning of, 366–372
size of, 57, 59–60, 366–377 (also n. 15), 385–386
stability of, 176, 387, 394, 396
transition phase of, 372–373 (also n. 11, 12), 374–387

Family of origin, 365–366

Family of procreation, 366

Family system, 364
and courtship, 235

Family violence, 387–394

Feedback, in marital conflict, 337–339, 360

Fellatio, 88 n. 19, 144, 200, 203

Fertility, 62
maximizing time of, 424

Fertilization (conception), 27–28, 31, 49–50, 137–139, 164, 398–400, 409, 433, 442–443
by artificial insemination, 415–416
infrahumans and, 167 (also n. 1), 168

Fetal alcohol syndrome, 407

Fetus (see Pregnancy, fetal period of development)

Fixation, 106 (also n. 34)

Fraternal twins, 409

Freestanding birth centers, 413–414

Gay Rights Movement, 47

Gender:
anomalies, 26, 49–52, 69
assignment at birth, 31, 34–36, 51, 69
biological factors of, 22–32, 35, 69
historical perspective of, 52–69
pychological factors of, 34–36
reassignment of, 31, 34–36
social factors of (behavior), 23, 25–26, 30–34
social visibility of, 31, 36

Gender identity, 34–37, 49, 51–52, 69

Gender identity/role, 22–27, 30–32, 36, 67, 69

Gender inequities, 53–54, 57, 62, 64

Gender role, 51

Gender-role socialization, 23, 26, 31, 34–36, 49, 51–52, 69
Gender-role stereotypes, 31, 67, 68 (also n. 55)
Genes, 23, 27 n. 7, 399
Genital herpes, 146–147, 149–151
Genitalia:
  female, 126, 130–131
  male, 126, 130–131
  precoital and postcoital disinfection of, 148
Germinal disc, 399–401, 428
  deliberate expulsion of, 433–436, 440
  spontaneous expulsion of, 436
Gestation (see Pregnancy)
Gonorrhea, 146–148, 153–155, 159, 164
Group marriage, 235–236
"G" spot, 131, 133

HCG (human gonadotropic hormone), 403 (also n. 7, n. 8)
Hermaphroditism, 34 (also n. 34, n. 14), 35, 49, 51, 69
Herpes infection, during childbirth, 412 n. 28
Heterosexual-homosexual rating scale, 42–43
Heterosexuality, 43, 49
Heterosexual period of personality development, 105–106
Homosexual-heterosexual continuum, 158
Homosexuality, 42–49, 69, 417
  attitudes toward, 46–48
  causes of, 48–49
  episodic, 44–45, 49
  incidence of, 43, 44 (also n. 23)
  obligatory, 44–45, 49–50
  religious affiliation and, 43–44
  stereotyping, 45 (also n. 24)
  transvestism and, 52
Homosexual period of personality development, 105–106
Hormones (see Sex hormones)
House, buying a, 215, 489–490
Housework, responsibility for, 379
Human Sexual Response (Masters and Johnson), 116
Hunting and Gathering Period, 53 n. 29
Husband battering, 390–392, 396
Hymen, 130 (also n. 23, 24)

Identical twins, 33–36, 409
Illegitimate births, 62, 305 (also n. 17),

378, 384, 396, 417–418, 442
  legal aspects of, 228, 230
Impotence, 122 n. 13
Incest, 240–241, 325, 393–394
Income:
  education and, 62
  inequities of, 53–54, 57, 62, 64
  marital power structure and, 379
  median, 65, 475 n. 2
  old age and, 278–279
  race and, 65
  retirement and, 64
  single-parent family and, 381, 395
  spendable, 480–482
  teenage mothers and, 62
  of traditional nuclear family, 54
Industrialization, impact on family, 373 (n. 11, 12), 374–377, 395
Infancy, 448–449, 469
Infanticide, 58, 60, 417
Infantile love, 103, 105, 107–108
Infatuation, 96–99, 107
Infertility, 414–416, 428, 435
  oral contraceptive pill and, 260 n. 22
  STDs and, 152–153
Inflation, purchasing power and, 501–502
Infrahumans, 30, 32–35, 83, 104 n. 30
  aggression and, 30
  courtship and, 167 (also n. 1), 168
  fertilization and, 167 (also n. 1), 168
  nurture and, 368, 454–455
Interclass marriage, 267, 283
Interest, compound, 500, 503, 505
Interethnic marriage, 266–277, 283
Interfaith marriage, 184, 261 (also n. 26), 262–264, 283
Interlocutory divorce, 304
Intermarriage, 16, 184 (also n. 11), 261 (also n. 25, 26), 262–267, 283
Internal genitalia, 28, 31 (see also Anatomy)
Interracial marriage, 64 (also n. 29), 184 (also n. 11), 265–266, 283
Intimacy, 5–8, 75, 81–82, 85, 90, 204–206, 242–244, 246, 251–252
  loss of, 99–100, 102
  search for, 214–216
Intrinsic marriage, 250–252, 283
Investments, budgeting for, 480, 505
IRA accounts, 499
IUD (intrauterine device), 149, 433–434

Jealousy, love and, 99–101 (also n. 28), 102–103

Judaism, interfaith marriage and, 262–263
Julius Caesar (William Shakespeare), 270

Kinsey report, 42, 43 (also n. 19)

Labia, 28–29, 35
  erotic sensitivity of, 130–132
Labor (in childbirth), 409–411, 443
Lactation, 23–24
Laparoscopy, 430
"Latch-key" children, 55–56
Legal separation, 286 (also n. 1), 301
Lesbians, 44–46, 48
Leveling, 351–352, 360
Life cycle, 234–235, 269–284, 208, 481
Life expectancy, 27, 213 (also n. 8), 270, 399
Life insurance, buying, 493–494 (also n. 10), 495–496
Life-styles, changes in, 211–216, 221, 223, 230
Limerance, 75–80, 82–83, 92–93, 96–97, 106–107, 186
  crystallization and, 76–88, 95, 98, 106
  negative, 95, 98, 106
Loans, sources of, 482 n. 3, 487–488, 505
Loneliness, 13–14, 81, 106, 217–220, 230, 279–281, 313
Love:
  72–79, 81–83 (see also Paired bond)
  agape, 82
  altruistic, 82, 107
  attachment and, 79, 81, 106
  children and, 453–456
  classical Greece and, 82, 86, 92, 107
  coefficient of correlation and, 73 (also n. 1)
  companionate, 82, 107
  courtly, 84, 86–89
  eros, 82, 97
  heartbreak and, 78, 81, 95–96
  idealization and, 77, 79
  infantile, 103, 105, 107–108
  infatuation and, 96–99
  jealousy and, 99–101 (also n. 28), 102–103
  learning to, 103–106
  limerance and, 75–79, 82–83
  ludus, 93–94, 97
  manic, 93, 95–97, 107
  meaning of, 72–74
  paired bond and, 72, 75

Love (continued)
    passionate, 74–75, 82–84, 109
    philos, 82
    platonic, 84 n. 8
    romantic, 82, 84–94, 96, 98, 107, 244
    sexual, 82–85, 88–92
    storge, 93–95, 97
Love (Stendhal), 76
Love and Limerance (Dorothy Tennov), 76
Loving and liking, 73–75
Ludus love, 93–94, 96–97

Male, dominance and power of, 372 n. 10, 376 (also n. 14)
Manic love, 93, 95–97, 107
Marital choice (see also Cohabitation; Courtship; Love)
    compromises (trade-offs) in, 193–194
    dating and, 168, 172, 176–177, 180–183, 205
    endogamous and exogamous factors in, 184–185
    field of eligibles in, 183
    heterogamous factors in, 185 (also n. 13)
    homogamous factors in, 184, 197
    parental arrangement and, 168–171, 173, 205
Marital conflict, 331–349, 354–361
    coping with constructively, 335–341, 350–353
    coping with destructively, 342–349, 360–361
    defense-oriented behavior in, 334–335, 360
    displacement in, 333–334
    examining mutual goals in, 340–341, 360
    feedback in, 337–339, 360
    frustration in, 331–332 (also n. 2), 333
    money and, 475–475, 504
    reality-oriented behavior in, 334, 360
    role taking in, 339–340, 360
Marital success, 244–252, 260, 272, 341–342, 351–353
    cohabitation and, 227–228
Marriage:
    age at, 211–212, 241, 290–291, 296, 387
    average duration of, 300–301, 330
    companionate love and, 82
    childlessness in, 257–261, 266, 270, 283

childrearing years of, 272–275
children's rights and, 240
division of labor in, 247, 260
dual career, 62 n. 42, 380 (also n. 19)
dual income, 53–55, 56 (also n. 34), 57, 60, 62, 380
interfaith, 184
duration of ending in divorce, 288–299, 387
duration of, 387
expectations in, 234, 236–239, 331–332
forms of, 235–236
functions of, 235, 247–250, 257
in-laws and, 240
incompatibility in, 298
institution of, 235, 282, 320
interracial, 184 (also n. 11)
love and, 244, 249
median age of bride and groom, 319
middle age, 275–276
monogamy and, 253, 256–257
motivation for, 241–243
need fulfillment in, 92, 247–250
parental arrangement, 92
personal happiness in, 241, 243–244, 267, 272, 282, 320, 322
popularity of, 187, 211–212, 230, 234, 387
pregnancy at, 272–273
pregnancy leading to, 172 (also n. 2)
premarital copulation and, 202–203
property rights and, 236–237 (also n. 7)
quid pro quo in, 246–247 (also n. 12)
role performance in, 171, 244–247, 282–283
romantic love and, 85, 87–92
sacred aspect of, 237, 243, 301
sexual compatibility in, 110
sexual love and, 88 (also n. 17, 18), 89–92
stability of, 299–300, 327, 330
trade-offs in, 246, 248, 261
types of interaction in, 250–252, 283
Marriage broker, 170
Marriage contract, 168, 236–239 (also n. 7), 240, 282
Marriage counseling, 298–299
Marriage laws, 236
Marriage license, 241
Marriage rate, 316–317
"Marriage squeeze," 213 (see also Dating differential)
Masculinity and femininity, 40–42, 45, 69

Mass media, impact of, 88, 89 (also n. 20, 21, 22), 91, 179, 203
Mass societies, 12–14
Masturbation, 132–133 (also n. 27), 134, 158, 164
Mattachine Society, 44 n. 22, 48
Men:
    macho qualities of, 40
    power and dominance of, 62–64, 66–67, 173
Menarche, 139
Menopause, 129–139
Menstrual cycle, 138–139, 423–425, 434
Menstrual extraction (regulation), 434–435
Menstruation, 23 n. 2, 24 (also n. 3), 129, 138, 434–435
Migratory divorce, 304–305 (also n. 16)
Minilaparotomy, 431
"Miniorgasms," 127
Money (see also Credit; Life insurance; Loans; Personal finance; Saving; Investing)
    budgeting of, 477–483
    importance of, 473–475
Monogamy, 216, 235–236, 369, 395
Morning-after pill, 434 (also n. 52)
Mortality rate:
    birth ratio and, 27–28
    infant, 58, 60, 146, 150, 419 n. 35
    illegal abortions, 59, 441–442
    pregnancy vs. birth control methods, 428–430
    pregnancy and childbirth, 407, 414, 420, 428–429
    relation to marriage, 289, 327
    singles and, 220, 230
    teenage mothers and, 420
Multiple births, 409, 416
Mutual funds, 503
Mutual goals, examining in marital conflict, 340–341, 360

National Conference of Catholics Prolife Committee, 439
Neonate, 445 (also n. 1), 469
    developmental sequence of, 446–448
    genetic programming of, 450
    providing emotional security for, 453–455, 471
    STDs and, 146, 150, 152, 153 n. 39, 155, 157 n. 50
    weight of, 411, 412 n. 26, 419 n. 35
No-fault divorce, 304

Nuclear family, 52 n. 25, 54, 366–367
  (also n. 7), 368–369, 394–396
Nurture, 368, 454–455
Nutrition, importance of, 406–407, 419,
  450–452, 470

Old age:
  living arrangements in, 279–280, 282
  loneliness and, 279–281
  poverty and, 279
  sexual activity and, 280–281
Oral contraceptive pill, 203, 415,
  428–429
  popularity of, 149, 225
  STDs and, 152–153
Organic methods of birth control,
  423–424
Orgasm:
  female, 132–137
  male, 127–129, 137
  similarities and differences of
    male–female, 132–137, 141–143,
    164
Ovaries, 28, 30, 69, 399
Ovulation, 129–130, 138, 416, 435
  failure of (nonovulation), 416 n. 33
  fertilization and, 399
  probable time of, 416, 423
Ovum (see egg)

Paired bond, 3–6, 8–12, 17, 23, 333,
  349
  animals and, 5–6
  neonate, 412–413, 452, 469
Parenthood, joys of, 272, 283
Parenthood, transition to, 272–274
Passionate love, 109
The Passionate Shepherd to His Love
  (Christopher Marlowe), 208
Pedophilia, 393 (also n. 36), 396
Penis:
  cerebral erection of, 120–121, 123
  erotic sensitivity of, 120–125
  prolonged erection of, 127
  reflex erection of, 121–123 (also n.
    15), 281
Personal finance:
  directing cash flow and, 476–483,
    504
  getting your money's worth,
    489–498, 505
  importance of budget in, 477–481,
    504

PID (pelvic inflammatory disease), 152,
  415, 433
Polyandry, 235–236, 371, 395
Polygamy, 366, 370, 394–395
Polygyny, 235–236, 370–371, 395
Population control, 416–417, 443 (see
  also Birth control)
Poverty, 279, 294 n. 8, 475 n. 1
Predicting baby's sex, 408
Pregnancy (see also Abortion; Childbirth;
  Labor)
  artificial insemination and, 415–416
  birth defects and, 407 (also n. 10, 13,
    15), 408
  embryonic period of, 433–434 (also
    n. 53)
  false, 401 n. 5
  fetal circulation in, 401, 408
  gender determination in, 408
germinal period of development,
  400–401, 434–436
  multiple births in, 409
  placenta's role in, 401, 404, 408, 443
  prenatal influences in, 406–407 (also
    n. 10), 408
  tests, 402–403 (also n. 7, n. 8), 443
  tests for abnormality in, 408 (also n.
    16–22)
Preindustrial societies, 12
Premarital copulation, acceptance of,
  235
Premarital pregnancy, divorce and, 291
Premature birth, 404–405 (also n. 9)
Premature ejaculation, 127–128
Prenatal androgenization, 33–35
Prenatal sex differentiation, 28–29, 129
  (also n. 20)
Primary gender characteristics, 23–24,
  36
Primary relations, 9–14, 17–18,
  243–244, 267
Prochoice groups (abortion), 441
Prolife groups (abortion), 441–442
The Prophet (Kahlil Gibran), 332
Propinquity, 4 n. 1
Prostaglandins, 435 (also n. 54), 440
Protestants:
  homosexuality and, 43
  interfaith marriage and, 260–262,
    264
Psychological games, 342–345, 347
Puberty, 24–25, 51
  age at, 139
  erotic response at, 123–124, 127, 137,
    164

sex hormones at, 30

Rabbit Is Rich (John Updike), 113 n. 6
Rabbit, Run (John Updike), 332–334
Race, U.S. Census survey of, 265 n. 30
Reality-oriented behavior, 297–298, 334,
  368
Refractory period of erotic response,
  126–128
Religion:
  childlessness and, 259
  extramarital sexual behavior and,
    252, 256–257
Remarriage:
  child support and, 309–310
  civil divorce and, 306
  divorce and, 213
  divorce rate in, 320 (also n. 25),
    328
  ex-spouse and, 325–327
  financial problems in, 325
  interval between divorce and, 314,
    317–318, 320, 328
  median age of bride and groom, 319,
    320
  motivation for, 319
  older women and, 318
  rate of, 316–319, 384
  societal acceptance of, 318–319
  special problems in, 321–328
  widowed person's chances of, 281
    (also n. 50), 282
Reproduction, human (see Fertilization)
Resolution phase, of erotic response,
  125–127, 136
Retirement:
  budgeting for, 482–483
  income in, 64
Rh factor, 408 (also n. 21)
Rhythm method, of birth control,
  423–424
Role behavior, 8–9, 17–18, 244–247,
  282–283
Role taking, in marital conflict, 339–340,
  360
Roman Catholicism:
  abortion and, 438–439, 441
  annulment and, 306
  birth control and, 424, 438–439
  divorce and, 236
  homosexuality and, 43
  interfaith marriage and, 262–263
  remarriage and, 319
Romantic love, 82, 84–94, 96, 98, 107,
  144

Romeo and Juliet (William Shakespeare), 109

Savings, budgeting for, 480–481, 505
Scrotum, 30, 51
Secondary gender characteristics, 24, 49, 51–52
Secondary relations, 9–14, 17–18
Self-esteem, 23, 42, 69, 455
  increasing, 351–353
  marital conflict and, 333
Semen (ejaculate), 124–125, 164
Sex (see Copulation; Erotic response; Gender; Homosexuality; Intimacy; Love; Masturbation)
  cultural attitudes toward, 110–118
  procreational, 110, 112
  range of interest in, 139–144, 164
Sex-change surgery, 36, 51–52
Sex chromosomes, 23, 25–26, 27 (also n. 7), 28, 69, 119, 129 n. 21
Sex drive:
  and chromosomal anomaly, 51
  contraceptive pill and, 428
  effect of sterilization on, 432
Sex education, lack of, 419–420
Sex hormones, 23–25, 27–29, 30, 33–36, 49, 69, 129
Sex hormone therapy, 51–52
Sex myths, 158–159
Sexual anomalies, 26, 49–52, 69
Sexual Behavior in the Human Female (Alfred C. Kinsey), 116
Sexual Behavior in the Human Male (Alfred C. Kinsey), 42, 116
Sexual compatibility, 248–249
Sexual dysfunction, 122 n. 13, 127–128, 144 (also n. 33)
Sexual energy, sublimation of, 158, 164
Sexual incompatibility, 109–110
Sexual love, 109, 139 (also n. 30), 216, 223–225
Sickle cell anemia, 408 (also n. 19)
Single fathers, 310–312, 314, 380–382
Single mothers, 294 n. 8, 310–312, 314, 380–382
Single-parent family, 294 n. 8, 310–312, 314–316, 372–373, 380–383, 395
Single parents, 214, 220
Single-person households, rise of, 224
Singles:
  categories of, 213–214, 230
  cohabitation and, 216, 223 (also n. 10), 225–226
  depression and, 219–220

divorced, 314
housebuying and, 215
incidence of, 208–211, 213, 229–230
life-styles of, 211–212, 214–216, 221, 223, 230
loneliness and, 217–220, 223, 230
reevaluation of goals and, 221
sexual intimacy and, 216, 223–226, 230
stereotyping of, 222–223
stress and, 214, 217–221
trade-offs for, 247
voluntary, 213–214, 226, 230
Smoking:
  infant mortality and, 407
  oral contraceptive use and, 428
Society, 14, 18
  subcultures in, 14–18
Sperm, 27, 119, 407 n. 10
  allergic reaction to, 435
  fertilized egg and, 398–399
  life of, 424–425
  mobility and amount of, 415
  production of after vasectomy, 432
  sex determination factor of, 27, 399
Spermatogenesis, 23–24, 119, 129, 432
Spermicides, 425–427, 429
Spousal support, 308–309, 325
STDs (sexually transmitted diseases), 146–163
  children affected by, 146, 150, 152, 153 n. 39, 155
  incidence of, 146–148, 149, 152–154, 159–161, 165
  number of sex partners, 257
  prevention of, 147–148 (also n. 36, 38), 149
  transmission of, 146–147, 149, 154–157, 160 (also n. 57), 161–163
  treatment of, 146, 151–162, 155 (also n. 47), 156, 159, 163
Stepfamilies, 322–325, 328, 371–372, 381, 383–384, 395
Sterility:
  chromosomal anomalies and, 50
  following vasectomy, 432
  oral contraceptives and, 428
  PID and, 433
  STDs and, 152–153
Sterilization, female, 430–432
Sterilization, male, 432–433
Stillbirths, 407
Sublimation, Doctrine of, 158, 164
Subsistence farms, 53 (also n. 28), 69
Suicide:
  battered wives and, 388

divorce and, 220
unmarried mothers and, 419
Syphilis, 146, 155–159

Tale of Two Cities (Dickens), 82
Taxes, paying, 498–499
Tay-Sachs disease, 408 (also n. 20)
Teenage marriage, economic pressures of, 291–292
Teenage mothers, 418–419
Testicles, 28, 30, 69, 119
  undescended, 51
Testosterone, 25 n. 6, 30
  psychoendocrine aging and, 129
  well-being and, 123–124
Tomboyism, 34–35
Too Far to Go (John Updike), 139
Traits and abilities, genetic differences in, 36–41
Transsexualism, 49, 51–52, 69
Transvestism, 49, 52
Trichomoniasis, 152
TSS (toxic shock syndrome), 427 n. 44, 45

Umbilical cord, 401–402 (also n. 6), 412
Unwanted births, 268 (also n. 35), 272, 283
Uterus, 28–29
  contractions during labor, 409–411
  IUD and, 433–434
  removal of, 440 n. 58
  role in pregnancy, 400–402
Utilitarian marriage, 250–252, 283

Vacuum curettage, 434 n. 53, 439
Vagina, 28–29
  lack of erotic sensitivity in, 132
  lubrication of, 125, 132, 144, 164
Vas deferens, 28–29, 432
Vasectomy, 432–433
Venereal diseases (see Sexually Transmitted Diseases [STDs])
Venereal warts, 155–156
Virginity, pregnancy and, 125 n. 17

Widows, 213
Wife battering, 388–390, 396
Women:
  career vs. marriage and, 64

Women *(continued)*
    changing role of, 57–62, 69
    college enrollment and, 66, 212,
      259
    economic productivity of, 53 (also n.
      29), 61, 69

economic and social independence of,
    212 (also n. 4)
employment and, 53 (also n. 30),
    54–57, 60–62, 70, 244, 259, 377
    (also n. 16), 395–396
legal rights of, 377

movement toward equality for, 67,
    70
pay inequities of, 53–54, 57, 62, 64,
    70
right to vote for, 68 n. 54